SPORTS

IN

NORTH

AMERICA

FOR

NATHAN S. KIRSCH

SPORTS
IN
NORTH AMERICA

A DOCUMENTARY HISTORY

EDITED BY
GEORGE B. KIRSCH

VOLUME 3

THE RISE OF MODERN SPORTS

1840–1860

Academic International Press

1992

**SPORTS IN NORTH AMERICA. A DOCUMENTARY HISTORY
VOLUME 3. THE RISE OF MODERN SPORTS, 1840–1860.**
Edited by George B. Kirsch

ISBN: 0-87569-156-0

Composition by Mary Lucas

Printed in the United States of America

By direct subscription with the publisher

*A list of Academic International Press publications
is found at the end of this volume*

ACADEMIC INTERNATIONAL PRESS
POB 1111 • GULF BREEZE • FL • 32562 • USA

CONTENTS

13   RACKETS

14   TRACK AND FIELD

SELECTED BIBLIOGRAPHY

PREFACE

The purpose of this volume is to present a comprehensive collection of the most important primary source documents pertaining to the development of sports in North America between 1841 and 1860. These materials include rules and regulations, constitutions, and by-laws for clubs and associations, personal accounts of significant developments and events, newspaper reports of contests, and other contemporary descriptions of athletics during this period. The selections are reprinted here as they originally appeared, without any changes in form or spelling except for deleted sections. Illegible words and misspellings are indicated in the annotation in the text.

The Introduction and Chapter 1 provide background explanations and articles on the dramatic rise of organized sports in North America during this era. The Introduction begins with a brief definition of the characteristics of premodern and modern sports. It then surveys the main factors that contributed to the early development of Canadian and American athletics. In particular, it reviews the influence of British sportsmen and traditions, industrialization and the changing patterns of work and leisure, transportation and communication trends, and urbanization. The subject of Chapter 1 is the ideological shift that brought a more positive attitude toward athletics to Canadian and American society. It includes five essays that explain the religious, moral, and physiological arguments that provided the foundation for the North American sporting revolution.

The remaining chapters reprint a variety of documents that chronicle the diversity of the North American sporting experience during this era. My decisions concerning which pastimes to include in this anthology have been governed by my definition of a sport as a competitive game that involves some significant degree of physical activity by the participants. I have given most of the space to the major sports of the period, which include aquatics, baseball, boxing, cricket, equestrianism, and track and field. I cover equestrianism because of the strength and skill required of the riders of the horses. The animal blood sports of dog and cock fighting and the work sports of fire engine playing and steamboat racing are borderline cases. I have included the canine and game fowl battles because of the efforts of the trainers and their importance for the sporting fraternity of the times. The fire engine and steamboat contests merit attention because they provide early examples of the adaptation of machines to sport. I exclude all recreational activities that were non-competitive, including fishing, hunting, horseback riding, swimming, sleigh-riding, and other such activities. Although gymnastics was not an organized competitive sport during this period I have decided to include it because of its growing importance and the participation of both men and women. Chapter 1 begins with a document on calisthenics for women and children, while Chapter 10 presents a description of a gymnastics exhibition.

The gathering of these sources presented many difficulties. First, during this period there were very few formally organized sporting clubs or associations that published records of their proceedings. Secondly, much of the original material either was never published or was printed in pamphlets or brochures that no longer exist. Fortunately, a great many of these documents were printed in sporting periodicals or local newspapers. That explains my heavy reliance on the Spirit of the Times, the New York Clipper, and the daily press of New York City.

I have made every effort to find sources that describe the athletic experience of peoples from all regions of North America and from all social classes, racial and ethnic groups, and both sexes. Yet these documents must reflect the athletic dominance of the time of white upper and middle class males from certain Canadian and United States cities, especially Montreal, Toronto, Boston, New York, and Philadelphia. This volume does include several pieces that describe the sporting experience of people from the American South and West, native North American Indians, immigrants, and women. Because of the scarcity of sources there are only very minor references to blacks.

Finally, I would like to thank the wonderful librarians at the following institutions who helped me track down these sources: the New York Public Library, the New York Historical Society, the Columbia University Library, the Cardinal Hayes Library at Manhattan College, the Municipal Library of the City of Montreal, the National Library and the National Archives of Canada, the Historical Society of Pennsylvania, and the Racquet and Tennis Club of New York City. For their patience and diligence I owe a great deal to my student assistants, Ann-Margaret Paturzo, John Cavanagh, and Angela Sweeny.

Once again I express my love and appreciation to my wife, Susan Lavitt Kirsch, and my son Adam for their understanding and support over the past few years. This book is dedicated to my father, Nathan S. Kirsch. He was my first coach when I fell in love with baseball at the age of five. Now, more than four decades later, he continues to teach me invaluable lessons about the game of life.

George B. Kirsch

Manhattan College

INTRODUCTION

The period from 1841 to 1860 witnessed a major transformation in the nature of North American sports. At the beginning of this era premodern patterns of recreation predominated in both Canada and the United States. But on the eve of the American Civil War more modern forms of competitive play were developing in both countries. Many factors contributed to this athletic revolution, including the influence of British pastimes and the impact of new trends in industrialization, transportation, communication, and urbanization. These years also ushered in a major religious and ideological shift that produced more positive attitudes towards sports in both nations. (See Chapter 1)

Canadians and Americans enjoyed a wide variety of amusements and games during the seventeenth, eighteenth, and early nineteenth centuries. These recreations were an important part of the cultural lives of the various groups that constituted early Canadian and American society. Their traditional pastimes often lacked clear-cut distinctions between work and leisure, as men and women mixed labor and play in hunting, fishing, barn raisings and corn huskings. Individual competitions were more common than team sports. Contests were either spontaneous or required only the most rudimentary organization. Participants used readily available materials and natural playgrounds. Rough frontier contests such as wrestling, boxing, and feats of strength were popular, as were such animal and blood sports as horse racing, cockfighting, and dog fighting. While the rural gentry entertained themselves with field sports, country folk enjoyed shooting, fighting, and simple ball games. Urban artisans and immigrants had their favorite town and ethnic festivals, volunteer fire company activities, and tavern amusements.

The great variety of ball games in North America during this period shared some common characteristics that place them in the category of folk recreations. These simple pastimes lacked formal club organization and uniform rules, with participants mediating disputes. Natural factors determined the shape and size of the field, and there were no limits on the number of players. Equipment was homemade, and there was very little specialization by position. Players were unskilled, and brute force counted more than finesse. Individualism took precedence over teamwork. Spectators were few, and media coverage was nonexistent. While someone always tallied runs or goals scored, there was no interest in keeping statistics or permanent records.

By the middle of the nineteenth century more modern forms of sport were appearing in North America. Democratization, rationalization, bureaucratization, specialization, regional, national, and international competition, extensive media coverage, and fascination with numbers all characterized the new style of athletics. Whereas distinctions based on wealth and social status were still apparent in the pastimes of the elite, middle, and working classes, there was also a clear trend toward greater participatory equality. Players also were inventing new codes of rules and were experimenting with new techniques to raise their level of skill. Sporting clubs and associations of organizations scheduled matches and legislated regulations to govern play on and off the field. Professionalism and commercialism inevitably followed as the mania for sports spread throughout society. Specialization of skills fed an obsession with statistics that in turn stimulated a fascination with record performance.

In the new versions of individual and team sports that appeared before 1860, men competed according to a detailed code formulated by a sport association. Standardized regulations fixed the dimensions of the playing space, the size and weight of the equipment, and the number of contestants on each side. Factories manufactured sporting goods. Managers trained athletes for specific roles and taught them the latest techniques. Finesse and crafty strategy replaced brute force as the keys to victory. Players traveled hundreds (even thousands) of miles by railroad and steamboat to challenge their rivals. Spectators paid to see their heroes in action; the telegraph and printing press kept millions abreast of the latest results. Journals and yearbooks recorded statistics and compiled records.

The preceding comparison of premodern and modern pastimes illustrates the dimensions of change that marked the development of athletics in mid-nineteenth century North America, but it does not explain that transformation. The modernization model is helpful in defining the precise nature of the two types of recreation. But a more complete understanding of the subject requires a careful investigation of the influence of specific transformations in many dimensions of life. These years witnessed a series of revolutions in industry, transportation, communication, urban life, and values. These innovations provided the preconditions that made modern sports possible in Canada and the United States. People who lived through these developments at first tried to maintain their traditional patterns of play and leisure. Yet the changes in most areas of their lives forced them to abandon their older practices or adapt them to new circumstances. They transformed traditional recreation or invented new forms to suit their new needs. Their desire to play remained strong, but it was expressed in new contexts and in new ways.

Whereas sport historians have recognized the broad impact of industrialization on the growth of athletics in North America, they have not been precise about how it shaped the leisure experiences of all classes. Scholars once argued that the coming of the machines increased the free time available for the average person, but it now appears that this is a gross oversimplification. In fact, industrialization undermined premodern patterns of work and play. In the kind of traditional society that characterized Canada and the United States until the early 1800s farmers and townsmen alternated long hours of hard labor with periods of sociability and relaxation. Much work was cyclical and seasonal in nature, and its tempo was irregular. Intense preoccupation with crops, crafts, or cargoes gave way to days or weeks of relative inactivity. A typical year also included religious and political holidays, family celebrations, and other diversions. In traditional society an individual had very little choice in selecting leisure activities that did not involve some kind of group obligation. If one defines true leisure as a free activity some one chooses without regard to work, family, religion, or social responsibilities, there was precious little of it in early North America.

The advent of new technology did not revolutionize agricultural life patterns in Canada and the United States prior to 1860, but it did transform drastically the culture of cities and towns. The logic of capitalism and the increasing use of machines eliminated the traditional casual workday of sporadic labor. As the tyranny of the clock gripped factories and countinghouses, work and free time became more distinct. Recreation must come before or after work on weekdays or on weekends. Since most people worked six days a week, and since Sunday amusements either were prohibited or discouraged in many localities, free time was in very short supply. Thus one of the major effects of industrialization was to deprive people of traditional rest periods and compel them to schedule special time for leisure acitivities.

The industrial revolution transformed the lives of all city dwellers and town populations, but its effects varied considerably according to occupation. For the sake of clarity, it is convenient to discuss the impact of industrialization on leisure by referring to five groups: high white collar (industrial capitalists, managers, professionals), low white collar (petty proprietors and clerks), skilled artisans, semi-skilled workers, and unskilled workers. It is obvious that the coming of machines enriched a few captains of industry and enabled them to enjoy more leisure time as well as spend a great deal of money on recreation. Many of these men patronized the elite sports of thoroughbred horse racing and yachting, but a few either played or supported such middle class recreations as baseball and cricket. Many prosperous lawyers and merchants followed their example.

City dwellers were more directly involved in commercial than industrial pursuits, but they also felt the increased pressures of the new work discipline of industrial capitalism. Low white collar merchants, grocers, small shopkeepers, clerks, and bookkeepers labored through long hours in stores, offices, banks, and countinghouses, trying to keep pace with the paperwork generated by expanding business. These sedentary workers naturally sought relief from their toil, many flocking to ball fields during early morning hours, after work, or on summer Saturday afternoons when many employers closed their shops, stores, and businesses.

Artisans experienced the cruelest effects of the industrial revolution, which dramatically altered their premodern habits of work and play. Yet the impact of metropolitan industrialization varied enormously on the different crafts and their workers. Some trades, such as carpentry, blacksmithing, food preparation, and shipbuilding, retained their traditional structures throughout the mid-1800s. Skilled craftsmen employed in these fields possessed sufficient income and time for leisure. Other less fortunate artisans found themselves in shops where new systems of production divided traditional skills into a series of more specialized and simpler tasks.

Workers who labored under the direction of master craftsmen to produce clothing, shoes, hats, furniture, and other items found that the advent of the first machines and the new organization of manufacturing standardized and often sped up the pace of work. They experienced deteriorating conditions as they performed repetitive tasks in tight quarters with little or no break before lunch or the end of the day. Hatters, shoemakers, trunk makers, and others in such trades sought relief through recreation. Heavy manufacturing and large-scale factories were not yet dominant in North American cities, but some crafts (such as printing) were advanced in the use of technological innovations. Given the nature of the work of compositors and pressmen and their relatively high wages, it is not surprising that many of them took up baseball or cricket.

Factory laborers and outworkers who sweated at home doing piecework suffered much more than the shop artisans and independent mechanics from the changes of this period. Most of them were too preoccupied with the struggle for survival and too poor to participate in the athletic boom of the times. Semiskilled and unskilled immigrants and natives in manufacturing, as well as carmen, laborers, waiters, coachmen, and others on the lowest rungs of society found an escape in taverns and burlesque halls, but very few participated in modern sport.

As industrial technology and the expansion of commerce forced city people to adjust their work and play habits, mass production and new inventions in transportation and communication facilitated modern forms of athletics. Factories manufactured large quantities of bats, balls, bases, uniforms, and other sporting goods at a range of prices, thus providing a reasonable quality and selection of supplies that most players could afford. The railroad and steamboat made intercity and interstate competition possible, permitting traditional urban, state, and regional groups to play out their rivalries on ball grounds. The telegraph and high-speed printing presses allowed daily and weekly newspapers to recount the excitement of major matches while they were still fresh in people's minds.

If the industrial, transportation, and communications revolutions profoundly shaped the early development of modern American sport, urbanization was a more critical factor. The nineteenth-century city influenced new forms of athletics in many complex ways. City dwellers could not enjoy many traditional rural recreations and suffered from an increasingly oppressive, congested, and unhealthy environment. The new types of amusements they created were not merely a reaction to the negative features of city life; rather, they were also a positive product of many dynamic forces. The city may be viewed as a physical structure, social organization, or state of mind. Each of these three aspects of urbanization affected the growth of modern sport in North America. Furthermore it is essential to emphasize the interdependence of cities during the mid-1800s. There was extensive athletic interactions among many large and lesser cities, towns, and villages.

The physical development of North American cities had two major implications for the modernization of sport. First, the deteriorating environment bred sickness and psychological stress that endangered the people's corporal and mental health. Huge population increases, higher density, and inadequate housing created staggering disease problems, as municipalities struggled to supply better water, sewerage, and sanitation services. The public health crisis led many to lobby for more healthful recreation for the masses. Second, as expanding cities encroached upon traditional recreational areas, residents had to organize formal associations to acquire and maintain playing grounds. New York, Boston, and other cities established parks for public recreation; sportsmen joined together to rent or purchase space for cricket, baseball, yachting, rowing, and other athletic clubs. The modern city thus threatened the physical well-being of its inhabitants as well as their premodern patterns of informal and spontaneous play.

The social organization of these cities also contributed a great deal to the rise of modern sports. The metropolitan centers of the United States grew more diverse in race, religion, and ethnicity as native and European migrants arrived in record numbers. In Canada tensions between the English and French communities appeared in Montreal and other cities. Communities grew fragmented as social and class relations were strained. Many urbanites sought a sense of identity and fellowship in voluntary associations for political, religious, cultural, or sporting purposes. Since North Americans enjoyed a long heritage of grouping themselves into private organizations, it is not surprising that cricketers and baseball players followed this practice. Because of the complex social structure of these cities, men could group themselves by neighborhood, vocation, wealth, or membership in some common social or religious association. Sportsmen who banded together to acquire some playing space for themselves were also trying to preserve and strengthen their social identities in an increasingly impersonal environment.

The population explosion and the accompanying trend toward pluralism in American cities of this era also contributed to the expansion of modern forms of leisure and especially to their commercialization. Since the urban masses were now cut off from most of their former modes of recreation, they sought diversion through whatever activities the new urban life could provide. Their sizeable numbers not only filled the rosters of hundreds (even thousands) of clubs but also supplied the audiences for all types of entertainment. Entrepreneurs satisfied the growing demand for entertainment by creating the modern business of leisure. Whereas only the privileged few enjoyed such choices in premodern society, now all classes had some freedom over how to spend their time and money after work.

Cities exist not only in their streets, blocks, buildings, and avenues, or in the social, political, economic, and cultural relations among their residents. They live also in the minds of their inhabitants. Urban symbolism was a powerful force in North America as communities searched for identities that would distinguish them from their neighboring and distant rivals. Upstart towns competed for political and economic supremacy; Local boosters puffed up their settlements and denigrated competitors. Modern sport both reflected and intensified boosterism and intercity rivalry.

The twin trends of urban imperialism and interdependence are linked intimately to the rise of modern sport in North America. Cities tried to extend their political, economic, and cultural influence over as wide an area as possible. Through this process of urban imperialism each sought to retain and expand its hinterland. But while each metropolis and town vied with its rivals, each also depended on them as well. The cities were part of a dynamic, complex system that exchanged people, produce, and finished products and shared information, expertise, and political power.

This system of cities helped to promote modern sport in many ways. In both Canada and the United States it fostered standardized rules as well as the formation of regional and national associations and leagues. Urban interdependence facilitated player and club mobility as well as communication about sport. Thus, in both the internal development of cities and their mutual interdependence, urbanization and the modernization of athletics were closely related.

Economic, social, technological, and urban forces shaped the development of North American sports during the middle of the nineteenth century. Yet it should be emphasized that the growth of athletics in Canada and the United States depended not only on these external factors, but also (and, perhaps, more important) on the institutional requirements and peculiar nature of each sport. Social forces combined with the unique qualities of each to determine their respective fates. The following chapters present a brief narrative and a selection of the most significant documents for each pastime during this era.

Chapter 1

THE RISE OF MODERN SPORTS

A critical prerequisite for the development of modern North American sport was the appearance of an ideological justification of athletics that would supercede the traditional religious and social objections to sport. The British enthusiasm for wholesome physical activity moderated this hostility in Canada; in the United States resistance to athletics was stronger. Until the middle of the nineteenth century most Protestant clergymen, educators, newspaper and magazine editors, and business leaders discouraged physical exercise and sport on grounds that they were immoral, useless, and socially improper. Although Puritan ministers usually had tolerated moderate amusements to refresh one for work and study, they were always deeply syspicious of idle play and were especially hostile toward the gambling that frequently accompanied such premodern pastimes as horse racing and cockfighting. As late as the 1850s some churches disciplined their members for participating in ball games. In 1859 a Maryland congregation expelled several young men for playing cricket and warned a few others not to follow their example.

School and college teachers and administrators, journalists, and businessmen also frowned upon sport. In 1859 Harper's Weekly noted: "Men of thirty can remember well that when they were at school, proficiency in the athletic games of the play-ground was regarded rather as a drawback than a merit." Most schoolteachers still discouraged games "as tending to interfere with 'legitimate studies,'" it added. "As with our boys, so with our men. Bank clerks, young merchants, mercantile aspirants, all seem to think time devoted to any exercise wasted, and the model clerk him who drudges six days of every week at his desk without an hour of physical labor." The magazine questioned whether, during the late 1830s, "any leading family journal would have dared to intimate that it is perhaps as important for boys to learn baseball as prosody or conic sections."

Whereas these attitudes persisted during the mid-1800s, a new viewpoint toward physical fitness and athletics came into being during this period and eventually replaced the older ideas. The damaging effects of industrialization and urbanization on health, coupled with changes in philosophical and religious thought, contributed to this ideological shift. The negative economic and social consequences of modernization certainly moved many to reconsider earlier notions about exercise and play. Within this changing social context, physicians, physical educators, Romantics, Transcendentalists, Unitarians, and reformers propounded a positive philosophy of sport. These theorists believed that American citizens required athletics to meet the challenges of an uncertain future. While most were optimistic, many were deeply worried about the latest developments in poliiics, industry, urban growth, and social structure. In their view, physical training, recreation, and sport would help people cope successfully with these changes.

Propagandists for the new philosophy of athletics aimed their message at children and women as well as men. Frank Queen's New York Clipper praised those colleges that were encouraging physical fitness because they gave their students a better hope of a long life as they reaped their academic honors. The journal maintained that "the physical...should be studied before the mental" and that from the age of five bodily training should accompany schooling. It concluded that the results for the grownup men and women would be "the excellencies of mind and body in union." The sporting weekly also applied traditional ideas of women's roles to argue for female fitness, praising young ladies who rowed and skated. Those girls who glided gracefully on the ice "would be much better fitted to become mothers of American children....If the children are born of puny mothers, the race degenerates, mentally and physically...whatever will tend to render the mothers of future generations robust and hearty, will conduce immensely to the well being of the race." One of the first crusaders for fitness for women and youngsters was Catherine E. Beecher. Below is an excerpt from a book she wrote to urge families and educational institutions to adopt a thorough system of physical training for both sexes and all age groups.

To win over the dominant Protestant middle class to the new attitudes, the approval of the clergy was critical. If some pastors remained skeptical, many used their pens and pulpits to preach the new gospel of "muscular Christianity." Perhaps the most famous was Thomas W. Higginson. In 1858 he published the influential article "Saints and their Bodies" in the Atlantic Monthly, which is included below. More important, many less prominent ministers delivered sermons to their congregations in which they praised ball games and other sports. Clergymen began to appear on baseball diamonds and cricket pitches, and there were even a few clubs whose rosters were exclusively pastors.

Other influential champions of the new ideology of sport were journalists and public officials. It is not surprising that the editors of the national sporting weeklies published in New York City and Philadelphia were ardent advocates of the new gospel of sport. William T. Porter, Frank Queen, George Wilkes, Henry Chadwick, William Meeser, and others had a vested interest in amusements and athletics, for the more the masses believed in the message, the more their publications would prosper. It is significant that weekly and monthly family periodicals and daily newspapers also actively promoted physical fitness and sport. Harper's Weekly printed several articles and editorials praising the new trends. Just a few months after presenting its readers with Higginson's piece the Atlantic Monthly published an essay reprinted here by Oliver Wendell Holmes on the value of physical training. When the visit of the All-England cricket team stirred a sporting mania in New York City in the fall of 1859, the New York Times endorsed the craze for physical fitness. "National Gymnastics" is an editorial from that newspaper.

Municipal officials in New York, Boston, and other cities endorsed the new thinking by planning and building the first public parks in the United States. The town fathers finally recognized that modem urban conditions were threatening the health of the citizens. The people's physical and mental well being required space for a retreat from the oppressive conditions of their cities. One of the first and most extensive of these projects was Manhattan's Central Park. In 1860 the Spirit of the Times printed an early positive endorsement of the beneficial effects of the new facility for the population of New York City. Its editorial on the city's new playground is included here.

The writers and preachers who championed the cause of athletics attacked the American obsession with work and money-making and the poor physical condition of the populace and urged all citizens to find escape and relief in sport. The Brooklyn Eagle stated: "We pay far too much attention to our desks, counters, and offices than the laws of Dame Nature will admit of without the accompanying penalty of ill health." The Clipper claimed that sport (not the frontier) was "the great safety valve of society," especially when periodic depressions caused public disorders. It explained: "Work! work! work! grates harshly on the ear of those who seldom if ever get time to devote to anything else, the consequence of which is, that a general moroseness pervades those classes of society so situated, and no sooner does 'hard times' put in an appearance, than we are treated to such scenes as have of late been witnessed in our parks and public squares, instead of which it were just even more easy that the contrary should be the case, by...*a proper encouragement* of sport."

The enthusiasts for fitness and sport stressed that exercise promoted good physical, mental, and spiritual health, fostered proper moral and social conduct, and drew young men away from more sordid amusements. Frank Queen repeatedly argued that "sports and amusements are not incompatible with gentlemanly deportment and a high state of learning, or even antagonistic to the proper fulfillment of the duties of the pulpit." He also, wrote that the old Puritan suppression of sport "led to sensual indulgences and solitary vices, far worse...than any supposed evils which might possibly arise from attending out-door games or athletic sports." Porter's Spirit of the Times noted that the baseball fever would "work no harm to the church interests of pious Brooklyn" because the ball clubs furnished "both innocent amusement and healthful exercise" and were "valuable adjuncts to the church, inasmuch as a healthy bodily condition is undoubtedly essential to the enjoyment of a peaceful and religious state of mind."

Finally, those who propounded the new philosophy of sport maintained that physical activity instilled character traits and strengthened the bonds of society. They believed that athletics would help to preserve order and advance the future prosperity of a rapidly changing American culture. Writers were particularly sensitive to the issue of adult men playing children's games, so they stressed the "manliness" of athletics. For example, Porter's Spirit insisted that in cricket, "patience, fortitude, self denial, order, obedience, and good-humor, with an unruffled temper, are indispensable." In countless newspaper and magazine articles and Sunday sermons, journalists and clergymen preached the gospel of athletics that made possible the rise of modern sports during the middle decades of the nineteenth century.

PHYSICAL TRAINING FOR WOMEN AND CHILDREN

Catherine E. Beecher was born on 6 September 1800, the eldest daughter of Rev. Lyman Beecher of East Hampton, Long Island. Her brother, Henry Ward Beecher, became a prominent clergyman, while her sister, Harriet Beecher Stowe, was a leading abolitionist and author of *Uncle Tom's Cabin*. Educated at home and at private schools, as a young woman she founded academies for female students at Hartford, Connecticut and Cincinnati, Ohio. Later in her career she championed the cause of higher education for women and recruited instructors to teach in the frontier communities of the expanding South and West. She also campaigned in favor of introducing domestic science and physical education into the curriculum of the nation's schools and colleges. In her writings she argued in favor of equal educational opportunities for males and females, but she opposed woman suffrage. She died on 12 May 1878.

In the following document she argues for the value of gymnastics for all members of society. This selection includes excerpts from her *Calisthenic Exercises for Schools, Families, and Health Establishments* (New York, 1856), pp. iii-vi, 14-19, 40-47.

CALISTHENIC EXERCISES FOR SCHOOLS, FAMILIES,
AND HEALTH ESTABLISHMENTS
by Catherine E. Beecher

INTRODUCTION
ENCOURAGEMENT TO ADOPT THIS COURSE

The author wishes it were possible to present all that she has learned or observed that would prove the benefits of the method here set forth. But only a few hints can be attempted.

First, then, all allow that *exercise in pure air* promotes health and the perfect development of the body.

Next, in all those countries where physical training has been made a part of school culture, there has been such improvement of health, strength, and beauty, as fully to establish the value of such a course.

Next, it is generally conceded that the children and youth of this country, during the period of school, college, and professional education, have *relatively* too much stimulus of the brain and nerves, and too little training of the physical system. Next, experience in our schools and colleges proves, that unless such training is made *imperative as a school duty,* it will be neglected; especially by those who need it the most. For the more the body is enervated, the more does exercise become irksome.

Next, the author has known cures performed in health establishments and elsewhere, by means of these exercises, in connection with a strict enforcement of the laws of health, very much greater than any thing she has ever known effected by *any* method of medical treatment. Headaches, dyspepsia, all varieties of nervous diseases, lung and liver complaints, local diseases and weakness, and a great variety of deformities, have been remedied by this method. Great changes also have been made by these exercises in the size, figure, and graceful carriage, not only of the young, but of men and women, and some of them over forty years of age.

The following testimony from medical writers is abridged from an introduction to a work containing the system of *Ling,* the author of the celebrated Swedish course of Gymnastics and Calisthenics.

Were these exercises made an *indispensable* part of *school* as well as family education, many diseases consequent on constitutional debility, or neglect, or abuse, would be prevented. And thus, *through our free schools, the number of the infirm and ailing poor would be diminished.*

The art of *preventing* disease is surely superior to the art of curing it. Galen, the celebrated ancient physician, declared him to be the best physician who was the best teacher of gymnastics.

Gymnastics not only give fullness and strength to the muscles, but they increase force, flexibility, and dexterity of movement, and thus contribute to grace of person and skill in the use of the hands and other limbs.

Gymnastics, by opening the chest, and increasing the size and action of the lungs, give a tone and vigor to the whole organism. Debility, scrofula, rickets, and various deformities can thus be remedied.

Obesity, or an excess of fat, is almost certainly removed by such exercises. So a weak digestion, diseases of the liver, tendencies to dropsy, are all remedied by the increased activity of the muscles, and the consequent increased power of digestion.

Gymnastics, by increasing the circulation of the blood in the skin, renders its complicated system more active in carrying off the seeds of disease, while its nerves become less impressible to heat and cold, and other changes in the atmosphere.

Gymnastics, as above remarked, have a most direct influence on the organs of digestion. The equilibrium between food and waste is re-established, sleep becomes regular, the senses are sharpened, and all the faculties invigorated. In the commencement of consumption, in piles, and in other abdominal diseases, the gymnastic exercises are important means of cure. So in nervous debility, hysterics, and the evils of too early puberty.

It is known that scrofula often disappears with the use of gymnastics. Franke, the physician, says, "We daily see many children with large stomachs, and constipation of the intestines, cured as soon as they begin to walk and run about in the open air."

Galen says, "If diseases take hold of particular parts of the body, there is nothing more sure to drive them out than diligent exercise." Herodicus, a celebrated ancient teacher, cured himself and many others of disease by gymnastics. Galen, who, at thirty, was weak, became strong and healthy by devoting several hours a day to gymnastics.

Several other ancient wise men, with Lord Bacon among moderns, are quoted as declaring gymnastics to be almost a universal medicine; "because there is no disease whose further development could not be prevented, or which at its commencement could not have been cured by bodily exercise."

But the effects of gymnastics on the body is not their chief benefit. Says Montaign, "It is the soul, and not the body, alone, which we educate, and we must not train the one without the other."

Plato, that wisest of the ancient philosophers, says, "Exercises of bodily exercise may render us wild and unmanageable, but excess of arts, science, and music makes us faddled and effeminate. Only the *right combination* makes the soul wise and manly." The great Hufeland advises that children, till the seventh year, spend most of their time in bodily exercises in the open air.

"If young children are compelled to sit quietly in a room, and their young minds urged to action, we *take from them the noblest part of their strength, and consume it in the function of* thinking. Thus growth is retarded, the limbs imperfectly developed, the muscles weakened, the digestion becomes bad, scrofula perhaps appears, and then ensues a great predominance of the nervous system. Any *unequal* development of our faculties is injurious, and it is certain that mental exertions weaken the more they are unaccompanied by bodily movements. It is also certain that those who, *between their mental occupations, go through suitable bodily exercises can work mentally much more than those who neglect this exercise of their bodily powers...."*

FIRST COURSE—SCHOOL-ROOM EXERCISES
EXERCISES TO PERFECT THE MUSCLES OF THE
ARMS AND HANDS

A round and perfectly formed hand and arm are deemed some of the most attractive points of womanly beauty. Although by birth some must necessarily be without these attractions, yet multitudes who now are entirely destitute of them might possess them by proper cultivation.

A course of training that shall develop *all* the muscles of the hand and arm *equally* tends to produce roundness of outline, grace of movement, and purity and cleamess of skin. Especially is this the case if all other portions of the muscular system are harmoniously trained....

EXERCISE 8.
Words of command—"First Arm Position: Arms Up!"
Place the arms in the first position *(Fig. 7).* Then, at the word "Arms Up!" throw them upward as at *Fig. 10* opening the hands. This exercises the muscles that shut and open the hand, as the hands are to be open when up and shut when down.
Count *one* when throwing up the arms, and so on to *twelve.*

Fig. 7.   Fig. 10.   Fig. 11.   Fig. 12.

EXERCISE 9.

Word of Command—"Perpendicular Movement!"

Place the arms and hands, as in *Fig. 11* about six inches from the face and body, and then change places, putting the *down arm* up and the *up arm* down.

Thrown the up arm over the head, and *as far back as possible.*

Count *one* at the first movement, and so on to *twelve*.

EXERCISE 10.

Word of Command—"Arms Out: Rolling Movement!"

Both arms are to be extended forward *(Fig. 12)*. Then the two hands, at the word *"Rolling Movement!"* both at once, are to be turned first upward and then downward, as in *Fig. 13*.

The hand must be turned as far as possible both ways. This exercises the muscles that roll the lower part of the arm.

Count *one* in turning the arm up, and so on to *forty*.

In all ordinary uses, when the arm is raised it should be with the palm down, as in *Fig. 13*. When pointing, or presenting an article, the arm should be turned *after it is raised,* with the palm upward. This is indispensable to a graceful use of the hand and arm.

EXERCISE 11.

Word of Command—"Shoulder Whirl!"

Place the right arm as at *Fig. 14,* and swing it forward in a circle. Then change, and swing it backward.

Be careful to stand in the Military Position, and make the arm describe a circle.

Count *one* on completing the first circle, and so on till twelve circles forward and twelve backward are completed. Then perform the same with the left arm. This exercise is very effective in *warming cold hands,* as it sends the blood downward.

EXERCISE 12.

World of Command—"Elbow Whirl!"

Place the elbows on the hips, and hold them there. Then swing the lower arms in a circle, as at *Fig. 15.*

Swing them first outward, and then inward, till *twelve* are counted each way.

EXERCISE 13.

Word of Command—"Wrist Movements!"

Place the wrists on the hips, and hold them there. Then move them around in a circle, as in *Fig. 16,* first outward and then inward, till *twelve* are counted each way.

Up Down and Side Wrist Movement.

Place the wrists firmly on the hips, with the hands open. Then, at the word *"Side!"* move the hands as far as possible to the right and then to the left, keeping the wrists firm on the hips, till *twelve* are counted. Then, at the word *"Up and Down!"* move them upward and downward as far as possible, still holding the wrists on the hips, till *twelve* are counted.

EXERCISE 14.

Word of Command—"Finger Exercise!"

Place the fingers of both hands as at C in *Fig. 17* and then rest them on the points of the shoulders. Then throw *both* arms out, as is seen on the right side of Fig. 17, *spreading the fingers* as far as possible. The fingers are to be brought together on every return to the shoulders.

Count only on throwing out the arms, to *twenty*.

SECOND COURSE—HALL EXERCISES
CONSTRUCTION OF A CALISTHENIC HALL

Fig. 62 represents a Calisthenic Hall on the scale of twenty feet to an inch. Around the outer portion is a walking-path. The dots represents *stations* for the pupils while exercising. They are to be made of bits of black walnut four inches square, inlaid. They are to be five feet distant, and arranged as in the drawing. Every pupil is to have her appointed station, so as to have no confusion in arranging for exercises.

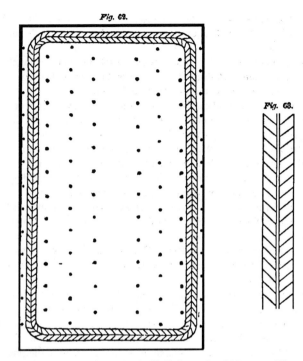

Fig. 62.

Fig. 63.

In a properly constructed Calesthenic Hall there should be a *walking-path* on one or both of the longest sides of the room, or entirely around the room. It should be made of alternate boards of white pine and black oak, forming a path, as illustrated by this drawing *(Fig. 63)*. The obligue boards are to be at angles of thirty degrees with the middle line, so that they form sixty degrees with each other. The middle line should be black oak half an inch wide. The oblique boards should be three inches wide. The path should be two feet wide.

Around the wall of the whole room should be seats. One portion of these seats should have lids in which to place the weights used.

Every pupil should make two oblong bags, six inches wide and from eight to twelve inches long, of unbleached cotton. These should be filled with *corn,* but not stuffed so as to be stiff. At one end of the hall should be two or three sets of perpendicular bars....

EXERCISES FOR THE CALISTHENIC HALL

Let the tops of the windows always be down during exercise, for it is better not to exercise at all than to do it in impure air. All must be *dressed loosely.* Let every pupil have a partner. Let the partners be named *numbers one* and *numbers two.* If there are boys and girls, let the boys be *numbers one* and the girls *numbers two.*

Let these all be arranged in *four* divisions, placing the tallest in the first division and the smallest in the fourth division, and the medium sizes in the second and third divisions.

Let each division have two leaders, one for the *numbers one and* the other for the *numbers two* of that division. These are to be called the *First or Second, Third or Fourth Division Leaders.*

All the numbers *one* are called *First Section* of each division, and numbers two are called the *Second Section.* In each division the partners are called *couples,* and are numbered *first* and *second* and *third couples,* and so on.

Of the second division leaders, the numbers one are to have charge of section one, and numbers two of section two of the divisions which they lead.

Each division is to have its quarter of the hall, and all the members of it are to have one of the stations marked on the floor in that quarter. Thus there are *Divisions, Sections, Couples, Leaders,* and *Partners Number One and Number Two.*

The classes are to form and pass into the Calisthenic Hall in order, the leaders each at the head of their sections. In performing the walking exercise they are to step out to notice the performance of their section. In other exercises the two leaders of each division are to place themselves in front of their sections, to set an example and superintend the exercises.

The teacher having charge of the Health Department will have the care of the training of the Division Leaders. In return, these leaders will train the sections committed to them in like manner.

In commencing the exercises with new pupils the first aim should be to have them perform the movements *exactly right.* The second aim should be to have the exercises performed with great *force* and *energy of will.* The more vigorous the movements the more benefit is secured. But great care must be taken not to proceed too fast, or do too much at first. There will be great diversities in strength among the pupils, and the teachers must take care that the delicate ones are not tempted to go beyond their strength by those more vigorous. Some of the exercises must always be slow.

EXERCISE 51.
Standing and Walking.

The pupils should form in division before entering the hall, as directed above, and then the first should be a walking exercise around the walking-path.

The sections should walk in single file. The leaders should walk on the inside of the path, and notice the walk of each of their section, in order to correct all defects.

Standing Exercise.

There are few things which more agreeably influence the appearance than the manner of *standing* and *walking.* A great majority of both men and women in this nation stand in an unnatural and inelegant posture; while the accomplishment of a light, graceful, and easy walk is as rare as it is beautiful. In some countries of Europe the art of walking with ease and elegance is much cultivated and esteemed, and in such countries the women are celebrated for their grace of person and movement.

The main object in the standing position is to place the body in such a position as that *every muscle and limb is in its natural atitude.* Thus every movement becomes both easy and natural, except when the body is distorted or misformed.

Walking Exercise.

This is the same as the military position, except that the arms are to be allowed to hang easily at the sides. The elbow is to be turned out a little from the sides, so as to give a slight curve to the arm. The fingers are to hang loosely and easily. See *Fig. 64.*

First. Take the *walking position,* throwing the weight of the body on to the front part of the feet.

Second. Extend the left foot, having the knee straight and foot turned out, the same as when standing, and the toe bent down by curving the instep a little, the same as at *Fig. 65.* The body may be steadied by touching the floor slightly with the toes.

Third. Set the foot down gently, keeping the knee straight, throw the weight on to the foot so that the pressure shall come first *on the ball of the little toe.*

Fourth. Set the foot down so that it will be in a straight line with the point from which it is moved.

Set the right foot forward in the same manner, and each pupil say "left" or "right" as the foot is set down.

The distance of the steps apart must be *about that of the length of the foot.*

Here is a drawing representing footsteps on a walking-path. *(Fig. 66).*

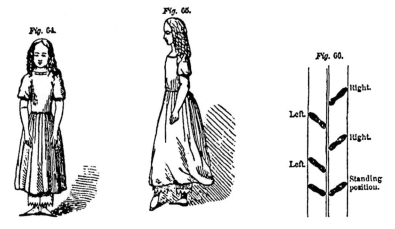

Fig. 64.

Fig. 65.

Fig. 66.

Right.

Left.

Right.

Left.

Standing position.

In a quickened step, the body is to be thrown more forward.

The following are the most common defects in walking:

First. Wrong positions of the body, such as the neck projecting, the back crooked, the arms drawn back or placed close to the sides, the feet turned either too much out or too much in. Any of these positions prevent a natural and graceful walk.

Second. A method of setting the feet too far apart. This makes what is called a *wiggling* gait.

Third. Turning in the toes too much. This makes what is called the *cow* walk.

Fourth. A habit of inclining the body toward the foot that is set down, instead of keeping it in a steady and upright position. This makes a *waddling* gait.

Fifth. A habit of lifting and bending the knee, instead of keeping the limbs straight. This makes what is called the *up-stairs* walk.

Sixth. A method of walking without lifting the feet. This makes a *shuffling* gait.

Seventh. Setting the foot down flat on the heel first. This prevents all grace and elasticity. For this reason no one can walk gracefully with heels on the shoes. Neither can any one walk gracefully who cramps the muscles with tight shoes.

The pupil should be made to imitate these faults till they are understood. They should march to music, singing appropriate tunes and words. This tends to strengthen the lungs.

EXERCISE 52.
Skipping Exercise.

The pupils should next learn to skip on the toes—at first very slowly, afterward to quick music.

EXERCISE 53.
Exercise with Weights.
Word of Command—"Take Weights!"

After the walking and skipping exercise, the boxes should be opened, and the pupils march in order, and take the weights, one in each hand. When all are thus furnished, they should march to music at the discretion of the teacher.

EXERCISE 54.
Word of Command—"Weights Out!"

Let the pupils carry the weights as at *Fig. 68,* marching to music.

EXERCISE 55.
Word of Command"Weights Up!"

Let the weights be carried as at *Fig. 69,* still marching to music.

EXERCISE 56.
Word of Command—"Weights Balancing!"

Let the pupils keep time by changing the weights up and down as the teacher says *"left up! right up!"* This should keep time with the music.

EXERCISE 57.
Word of Command—"Weights on the Head!"

Here both the weights are to be *crossed* on the head, and the military position of the arms and body taken. Thus, they are first to march to music, and when well trained they are to *skip to* music with the weights on the head. In skipping, the arms are to be held in the walking position.

EXERCISE 58.
Word of Command—"Form Lines!"

Here the numbers 1 are to form a line and numbers 2 another, to face, and at the distance of four or five yards.

Fig. 68.

Fig. 69.

Fig. 70.

Fig. 71.

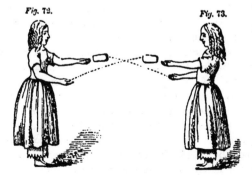

Fig. 72.

Fig. 73.

Then they are each to take one weight and toss it with the right hand, and receive another with the left. Then they are to toss with the left, and receive with the right.

At the close of this they are to march to music and place the weight in the boxes.

MUSCULAR CHRISTIANITY

Thomas Wentworth Higginson was born in Cambridge, Massachusetts on 22 December 1823. A graduate of Harvard College and a minister, he was one of the first of the New England clergymen to endorse athletics openly. During the late 1850s he practiced what he preached as president of the Lincoln Cricket Club of Worcester, Massachusetts. Before the Civil War he became an activist for social reform, especially in the woman suffrage and antislavery movements. During the war he served as colonel of the first black regiment in the Union army, the First South Carolina Volunteers. After the war he served one term in the Massachusetts legislature and wrote numerous magazine articles, one novel, and many volumes of essays, sketches, biography and history. He died on 9 May 1911. This essay attracted a great deal of attention when it was first published because of the author's use of moral and theological arguments to defend athletics. It first appeared in Atlantic Monthly, Vol. I (March, 1858), pp. 82-95.

SAINTS AND THEIR BODIES
by Thomas Wentworth Higginson

Ever since the time of that dyspeptic heathen, Plotinus, the saints have been "ashamed of their bodies." What is worse, they have usually had reason for the shame. Of the four most famous Latin fathers, Jerome describes his own limbs as misshappen, his skin as squalid, his bones as scarcely holding together, while Gregory the Great speaks in his Epistles of his own large size, as contrasted with his own weakness and infirmities. Three of the four Greek Fathers—Chrysostom, Basil, and Gregory of Nazianzen—ruined their health early, and were wretched invalids for the remainder of their days. Three only of the eight were able-bodied men,—Ambrose, Augustine, and Athanasius; and the permanent influence of these three has been far greater, for good or for evil, than that of all the others put together.

Robust military saints there have doubtless been, in the Roman Catholic Church; George, Michael, Sebastian, Eustace, Martin, and Christopher the Christian Hercules. But these have always held a very secondary place in canonization....The mediaeval type of sanctity was a strong soul in a weak body; and it could be intensified by strengthening the one or by further debilitating the other. The glory lay in contrast, not in combination....It was reserved for the Pre-Raphaelites to attempt the combination of a maximum of saintliness with a minimum of pulmonary and digestive capacity.

It is to be reluctantly recorded, in fact, that the Protestant saints have not ordinarily had much to boast of, in physical stamina, as compared with the Roman Catholic. They have not got far beyond Plotinus. We do not think it worth while to quote Calvin on this point, for he, as everybody knows, was an invalid for his whole lifetime. But we do take it hard, that the jovial Luther, in the midst of his ale and skittles, should have deliberately censured Juvenal's mens sana in corpore sano, as a pagan maxim.

If Saint Luther fails us, where are the advocates of the body to look for comfort Nothing this side of Greece, we fear, will afford adequate examples of the union of saintly souls and strong bodies....

It would be tedious to analyze the causes of this modern deterioration of the saints. The fact is clear. There is in the community an impression that physical vigor and spiritual sanctity are incompatible. We knew a young Orthodox divine who lost his parish by swimming the Merrimac River, and another, who was compelled to ask a dismissal in consequence of vanquishing his most influential parishioner in a game of ten-pins; it seemed to the beaten party very unclerical. We further remember a match, in a certain sea-side bowling-alley, in which two brothers, young divines, took part. The sides being made up, with the exception of these two players, it was necessary to find places for them also. The head of one side accordingly picked his man, on the presumption (as he afterwards confessed) that the best preacher would naturally be the worst bowler. The athletic capacity, he thought, would be in inverse ratio to the sanctity. We are happy to add, that in this case his hopes were signally disappointed. But it shows in which way the popular impression lies....

But, happily, times change, and saints with them. Our moral conceptions are expanding to take in that "athletic virtue" of the Greeks....

This is as it should be. One of the most potent causes of the ill concealed alienation between the clergy and the people, in our community, is the supposed deficiency, on the part of the former, of a vigorous, manly life. It must be confessed that our saints suffer greatly from this moral and physical anhoemia, this bloodlessness, which separated them, more effectually than a cloister, from the strong life of the age. What satirists upon religion are those parents who say of their pallid, puny, sedentary, lifeless, joyless little offspring, "He is born for a minister," while the ruddy, the brave, and the strong are as promptly assigned to a secular career....We distrust the achievements of every saint without a body; and really have hopes of the Cambridge Divinity School, since hearing that it has organized a boat-club....

Everybody admires the physical training of the military and naval schools. But these same persons never seem to imagine that the body is worth cultivating for any purpose, except to annihilate the bodies of others. Yet it needs more training to preserve life than to destroy it....Do not waste your gymnastics on the West Point or Annapolis student, whose whole life will be one active exercise, but bring them into the exceptional cases, the stern truth remains, that the great deeds of the world can be more easily done by illiterate men than by sickly ones. Wisely said Horace Mann, "All through the life of a pure-minded but feeble-bodied man, his path is lined with memory's gravestones, which mark the spots where noble enterprises perished, for lack of physical vigor to embody them in deeds.

Physical health is a necessary condition of all permanent success. To the American people it has a stupendous importance, because it is the attribute of power in which they are losing ground. Guaranty us against physical degeneracy, and we can risk all other perils—financial crisis, Slavery, Romanism, Mormonism, Border Ruffians, and

New York assassins, "domestic malice, foreign levy, nothing" can daunt us. Guaranty us health, and Mrs. Stowe cannot frighten us with all the prophecies of Dred; But when her sister Catherine informs us that in all the vast female acquaintance of the Beecher family there are not a dozen healthy women, we confess ourselves a little tempted to despair of the republic.

The one drawback to satisfaction in our Public-School System is the physical weakness which it reveals and helps to perpetuate. One seldom notices a ruddy face in the school-room, without tracing it back to a Transatlantic origin. The teacher of a large school in Canada went so far as to declare to us, that she could recognize the children born this side the line by their invariable appearance of ill-health joined with the intellectual precocity,—stamina wanting, and the place supplied by equations. Look at a class of boys or girls in our Grammar Schools; a glance along the line of their backs affords a study of geometric curves. You almost long to reverse the position of their heads, as Dante has those of the false prophets, and thus improve their figures; the rounded shoulders affording a vigorous chest, and the hollow chest an excellent back.

There are statistics to show that the average length of human life is increasing; but it is probable that this results from the diminution of epidemic diseases, rather than from any general improvement in physique. There are facts also to indicate an increase of size and strength with advancing civilization....It is also known that the strongest American Indians cannot equal the average strength of wrist of Europeans, or rival them in ordinary athletic feats. Indeed, it is generally supposed that any physical deterioration is local, being peculiar to the United States....

No one can visit Canada without being struck with the spectacle of a more athletic race of people than our own. On every side one sees rosy female faces and noble manly figures. In the shopwindows, in the winter weather, hang snow-shoes, "gentlemen's and ladies' sizes." The street-corners inform you that the members of the "Curling Club" are supposed to meet to-day at "Dolly's" and the "Montreal Fox-hounds" at St. Lawrence Hall to-morrow. And next day comes off the annual steeplechase, at the "Mile End Course," ridden by gentlemen of the city with their own horses; a scene, by the way, whose exciting interest can scarcely be conceived by those accustomed only to "trials of speed" at agricultural exhibitions. Everything indicated out-door habits and athletic constitutions....

Who in this community, really takes exercise? Even the mechanic commonly confines himself to one set of muscles; the blacksmith acquires strength in his right arm, and the dancing-master in his left leg. But the professional or business man, what muscles has he at all? The tradition, that Phidippides ran from Athens to Sparta, one hundred and twenty miles in two days, seems to us Americans as mythical as the Golden Fleece. Even to ride sixty miles a day, to walk thirty, to run five, or to swim one, would cost most men among us a fit of illness, and many their lifes. Let any man test his physical condition, we will not say by sawing his own cord of wood, but by an hour in the gymnasium or at cricket, and his enfeebled muscular apparatus will groan with rheumatism for a week. Or let him test the strength of his arms and chest by raising and lowering himself a few times upon a horizontal bar, or hanging by the arms to a rope, and he will probably agree with Galen in pronouncing it robustum validque laborum. Yet so manifestly are these things within the reach of common conditions, that a few weeks or months of judicious practice will renovate his whole system, and the most rigorous exercise will refresh him like a cold bath.

To a well-regulated frame, mere physical exertion...is a great enjoyment, which is, of course, enhanced by the excitement of games and sports. To almost every man there is joy in the memory of these things; they are the happiest associations of his boyhood. It does not occur to him, that he also might be as happy as a boy, if he lived more like one. What do men know of the "wild joys of living," the daily zest and luxury of outdoor existence, in which every healthy boy beside them revels?—skating, while the orange sky of sunset dies away over the delicate tracery of gray branches, and the throbbing feet pause in their tingling motion, and the frosty air is filled with the shrill sound of distant steel, the resounding of the ice, and the echoes up the hillside?—sailing, beating up against a stiff breeze, with the waves thumping under the bow, as if a dozen sea- gods had laid their heads together to resist it?—Climbing tall trees, where the higher foliage, closing around, cures the dizziness which began and, and one feels as if he had left a coward beneath and found a hero above?—the joyous hour of crowded life in football or cricket?—the gallant glories of riding and the jubilee of swimming?

The charm which all have found in Tom Brown's "School Days at Rugby" lies simply in this healthy boy's life which it exhibits, and in the recognition of physical culture, which is so novel to Americans. At present, boys are annually sent across the Atlantic simply for bodily training. But efforts after the same thing begin to creep in among ourselves. A few Normal Schools have gymnasiums (rather neglected, however); the "Mystic Hall Female Seminary" advertises riding-horses; aud we believe the new "Concord School" recognizes boating as incidental;—but these are all exceptional cases, far between....Tradition spoke of Dr. Follen and German gymnastics; but the beneficent exotic was transplanted prematurely, and died. The only direct encouragement of athletic exercises which stands out in our memory of academic life was a certain inestimable shed on the "College Wharf," which was for a brief season the paradise of swimmers, and which, after having been deliberately arranged for their accommodation, was suddenly removed, the next season to make room for coal-bins. Manly sports were not positively discouraged in our day,—but that was all.

We cling still to the belief, that the Persian curriculum of studies—to ride, to shoot, and to speak the truth—is the better part of a boy's education. As the urchin is undoubtedly physically safer for having learned to turn a somerset and fire a gun, perilous though these feats appears to mothers,— so his soul is made healthier, larger, freer, stronger, by hours and days of manly exercise and copious draughts of open air, at whatever risk of idle habits and bad companions. Even if the balance is sometimes lost, and play prevails, what matter?...

The hours the idle schoolboy squandered.
The man would die ere he'd forget.
Only keep in a boy a pure aud generous heart, and, whether he work or play, his time can scarcely be wasted.

Should it prove, however, that the cultivation of active exercises diminishes the proportion of time given by children to study, we can only view it as an added advantage. Every year confirms us in the conviction, that our schools, public and private, systematically overtask the brains of the rising generation. We all complain that Young America grows to mental maturity too soon, and yet we all contribute our share to continue the evil. It is but a few weeks since we saw the warmest praises, in the New York newspapers, of a girl's school, in that city, where the appointed hours of study amounted to nine and a quarter daily, and the hours of exercise to a bare unit. Almost all the Students' Manuals assume that American students need stimulus instead of restraint, and urge them to multiply the hours of study and diminish those of out-door amusements and of sleep, as if the great danger did not lie that way already. When will parents and teachers learn to regard mental precocity as a disaster to be shunned, instead of a glory to be convened? We could count up a dozen of young men who have graduated at Harvard College, during the last twenty years, with high honors, before the age of eighteen; and we suppose that nearly every one of them has lived to regret it....

One invaluable merit of out-door sports is to be found in this, that they afford the best cement for childish friendship. Their associations outlive all others. There is many a man, now perchance hard and wordly, whom we love to pass in the street simply because in meeting him we meet spring flowers and autumn chestnuts, skates and cricket-balls, cherry-birs and pickerel. There is an indescribable fascination in the gradual transference of these childish companionships into maturer relations. We love to encounter in the contests of manhood those whom we first met at football, and to follow the profound thoughts of those who always dived deeper, even in the river, than our efforts could attain....

Luckily, boy-nature is too strong for theory. And we admit, for the sake of truth, that physical education is not so entirely neglected among us as the absence of popular games would indicate. We suppose, that, if the truth were told, this last fact proceeds partly from the greater freedom of field sports in this country. There are few New England boys who do not become familiar with the rod or gun in childhood....

Again the practice of match-playing is opposed to our habits both as a consumer of time and as partaking too much of gambling. Still, it is done in the case of "firemen's musters," which are, we believe a wholly indigenous institution. We have known a very few cases where the young men of neighboring country parishes have challenged each other to games of base-ball, as is common in England; and there was, if we mistake not, a recent match at football between the boys of the Fall River and the New Bedford High Schools. And within a few years regattas and cricket matches have become common events. Still, these public exhibitions are far from being a full exponent of the athletic habits of our people; and there is really more going on among us than this meagre "pentathlon" exhibits.

Again a foreigner is apt to infer, from the more desultory and unsystematized character of our outdoor amusements, that we are less addicted to them than we really are. But this belongs to the habit of our nation, impatient, to a fault, of precedents and conventionalisms. The English-born Frank Forrester complains of the total indifference of our sportsmen to correct phraseology....And yet, careless of these proprieties, Young America goes "gunning" to good purpose. So with all games. A college football-player reads with astonishment Tom Brown's description of the very complicated performance which passes under the name rugby. So cricket is simplified; it is hard to organize an American club into the conventional distribution of prompt and cover-point, long slip and short slip, but the players persist in winning the game by the most heterodox grouping. This constitutional independence has its good and evil results, in sports as elsewhere. It is this which has created the American breed of trotting horses, and which won the Cowes regatta by a mainsail as flat as a board.

But, so far as there is a deficiency in these respects among us, this generation must not shrink from the responsibility. It is unfair to charge it on the Puritans. They are not even answerable for Massachusetts; for there is no doubt that athletic exercises, of some sort, were far more generally practiced in this community before the Revolution than at present. A state of almost constant Indian warfare then created an obvious demand for muscle and agility. At present there is no such immediate necessity. And it has been supposed that a race of shopkeepers, brokers, and lawyers could live without bodies. Now that the terrible records of dyspepsia and paralysis are disproving this, we may hope for a reaction in favor of bodily exercises. And when we once begin the competition, there seems no reason why any other nation should surpass us. The wide area of our country, and its variety of surface and shore, offer a corresponding range of physical training....

We have shown, that, in one way or another, American schoolboys obtain active exercise. The same is true, in a very limited degree, even of girls. They are occasionally, in our larger cities, sent to gymnasiums,—the more the better. Dancing-schools are better then nothing, though all the attendant circumstances are usually unfavorable. A fashionable young lady is estimated to traverse her three hundred miles a season on foot; and this needs training. Bot out-door exercise for girls is terribly restricted, first by her costume, and secondly by the remarks of Mrs. Grundy. All young female animals unquestionably require as much motion as their brothers, and naturally make as much noise, but what mother would not be shocked, in the case of her girl of twelve, by one-tenth the activity and uproar which are recognized as being the breath of life to her twin brother? Still, there is a change going on, which is tantamount to an admission that there is an evil to be remedied. Twenty years ago, if we mistake not, it was by no means considered "proper" for little girls to play with their hoops and balls on Boston Common; and swimming and skating have hardly been recognized as "ladylike" for half that period of time.

...American men, how few carry athletic habits into manhood! The great hindrance, no doubt, is absorption in business; and we observe that this winter's hard times and consequent leisure have given a great stimulus to outdoor sports. But in most places there is the further obstacle, that a certain stigma of boyishness goes with them. So early does this begin, that we remember, in our teens, to have been slightly reproached with juvenility, because, though a Senior Sophister, we still clung to football. Juvenility! We only wish we had the opportunity now. Full-grown men are, of course, intended to take not only as much, but far more active exercise than boys. Some physiologists go so far as to demand six hours of out-door life daily, and it is absurd in us to complain that we have not the healthy animal happiness of children, while we foster their simple sources of pleasure.

Most of the exercise habitually taken by men of sedentary pursuits is in the form of walking. We believe its merits to be greatly overrated. Walking is to real exercise what vegetable food is to animal; it satisfies the appetite, but the nourishment is not sufficiently concentrated to be invigorating. It takes a man out-doors, and it uses his muscles, and therefore of course it is good; but it is not the best kind of good. Walking, for walking's sake, becomes tedious. We must not ignore the play-impulse in human nature, which according to Schiller, is the foundation of all Art. In female boarding schools, teachers uniformly testify to the aversion of pupils to the prescribed walk. Give them a sled, or a pair of skates, or a row-boat, or put them on horseback, and they will protract the period of exercise till the teacher in turn grumbles. Put them into a gymnasium, with an efficient teacher, and they will soon require restraint, instead of urging.

Gymnastic exercises have two disadvantages: one, in being commonly performed under cover...another, in requiring apparatus, and at first a teacher. These apart, perhaps no other form of exercise is so universally invigorating. A teacher is required, less for the sake of stimulus than of precaution. The tendency is almost always to dare too much; and there is also the need of a daily moderation in commencing exercises; for the wise pupil will always prefer to supple his muscles by mild exercises and calisthenics, before proceeding to harsher performances on the bars and ladders....The feats once learned, a private gymnasium can easily be constructed, of the simplest apparatus, and so daily used; though nothing can wholly supply the stimulus afforded by a class in a public institution, with a competant teacher. In summer, the whole thing can partially be dispensed with; but we are really unable to imagine how any person gets through the winter happily without a gymnasium.

For the favorite in-door exercise of dumb-bells we have little to say; they are not an enlivening performance, nor do they task a variety of muscles,—while they are apt to strain and fatigue them, if used with energy. Far better, for a solitary exercise, is the Indian club, a lineal descendant of that antique one in whose handle rare medicaments were fabled to be concealed. The modern one is simply a rounded club, weighing from four pounds upwards, according to the strength of the pupil; grasping a pair of these by the handles, he learns a variety of exercises, having always before him the fears of the marvellous Mr. Harrison, whose praise is in the "Spirit of the Times," and whose portrait adorns the back of Dr. Trall's Gymnastics. By the latest bulletins, that gentleman measured forty-two and a half inches round the chest, and employed clubs weighing no less than forty-seven pounds.

It may seem to our non-resistant friends to be going rather far, if we should indulge our saints in taking boxing lessons; yet it is not long since a New York clergyman saved his life in Broadway by the judicious administration of a "cross-counter" or a "flying crook," and we have not heard of his excommunication from the Church of the Militant. No doubt, a laudable aversion prevails, in this country, to the English practices of pugilism; yet it must be remembered that sparring is, by its very name, a "science of self-defence"; and if a gentleman wishes to know how to hold a rude antagonist at bay, in any emergency, and keep out of an undignified scuffle, the means are most easily afforded him by the art which Pygmalian founded. Apart from this, boxing exercises every muscle in the body, and gives a wonderful quickness to eye and hand. These same remarks apply, though in a minor degree, to fencing also.

Billiards is a graceful game, and affords, in some respects, admirable training, but it is hardly classed among athletic exercises. Tenpins afford, perhaps, the most popular form of exercise, among us, and have become almost a national game, and a good one too, so far as it goes. The English game of bowls is less entertaining, and is, indeed, a rather sluggish sport, though it has the merit of being played in the open air. The severer British sports, as tennis and rackets, are scarcely more than names, to us Americans.

Passing now to out-door exercise (and no one should confine himself to in-door ones,) we hold with, Thalesian school, and rank water first....A square mile even of pond water is worth a year's schooling to any intelligent boy. A boat is a kingdom. We personally own one,—a mere flat-bottomed "float," with a centre-board. It has seen service,—it is eight years old,—has spent two winters under the ice, and been fished in by boys everyday for as many summers. It grew at last so hopelessly leaky, that even the boys disdained it. It cost seven dollars originally, and we would not sell it to-day for seventeen. To own the poorest boat is better than hiring the best. It is a link to Nature; without a boat one is so much less a man.

Sailing is of course delicious; it is as good as flying to steer anything with wings of canvas, whether one stand by the wheel of a clippership, or by the clumsy stem-oar of a "gundalow." But rowing has also its charms; and the Indian noiselessness of the paddle, beneath the fringing branches of the Assabeth or Artichoke, puts one into Fairyland at once, and Hiawatha's cheemaun becomes a possible possession. Rowing is peculiarly graceful and appropriate as a feminine exercise, and any able-bodied girl can learn to handle one light oar at the first lesson, and two at the second; this, at least, we demand of our own pupils.

Swimming has also a birdlike motion. The novel element, the free action, the abated draper, give a sense of personal contact with nature which nothing else so fully bestows. No later triumph of existence is so fascinating, perhaps, as that in which the boy first wins his panting way across the deep gulf that severs one green bank from another, (ten yards, perhaps,) and feels himself thenceforward lord of the watery world. The Athenian phrase for a man who knew nothing was, that he could "neither read nor swim." Yet there is a vast amount of this ignorance; the majority of sailors, it is said, cannot swim a stroke, and in a late lake disaster, many able-bodied men perished by drowning, in calm water, only half a mile from shore. At our watering-places it is rare to see a swimmer venture out more than a rod or two, though this proceeds partly from the fear of sharks,—as if sharks of the dangerous order were not more afraid of the rocks than the swimmers of being eaten. But the fact of the timidity is unquestionable; and we were told by a certain clerical frequenter of a watering-place, himself a robust swimmer, that he had never met but two companions who would venture out with him, both being ministers, and one a distinguished ex-President of Brown University. We place this fact to the credit of the bodies of our saints.

But space forbids us thus to descant on the details of all active exercises. Riding may be left to the eulogies of Mr. N.P. Lilywhite's "Guide." We will only say, in passing, that it is pleasant to see the rapid spread of clubs for the latter game, which a few years since was practiced only by a few transplanted Englishmen and Scotchmen; and it is pleasant also to observe the twin growth of our indigenous American game of base-ball, whose briskness and unceasing activity are perhaps more congenial, after all, to our national character, than the comparative deliberation of cricket. Football, bating its roughness, is the most glorious of all games to those whose animal life is sufficiently vigorous to enjoy it. Skating is just at present the fashion for ladies as well as gentlemen, and needs no apostle; the open weather of the current winter has been unusually favorable for its practice, and it is destined to become a permanent institution....

For, after all, the secret charm of all these sports and studies is simply this,—that they bring us into more familiar intercourse with Nature. They give us that *vitam sub divo* in which the Roman exulted,—those out-door days, which, say the Arabs, are not to be reckoned in the length of life.

We know persons who, after years of abstinence from athletic sports or the pursuits of the naturalist or artist, have resumed them, simply in order to restore to the woods and the sunsets the zest of the old fascination. Go out under pretense of shooting on the marshes or botanizing in the forests; study entomology, that most fascinating, most neglected of all the branches of natural history; go to paint a red maple-leaf in autumn, or watch a pickerel-line in winter, meet Nature on the cricket ground or regatta; swim with her, ride with her, run with her, and she gladly takes you back once more within the horizon of her magic, and your heart of manhood is born again into more than the fresh happiness of the boy.

THE VALUE OF PHYSICAL TRAINING

Oliver Wendell Holmes was born in Cambridge, Massachusetts, on 29 August 1809. A graduate of Harvard College and Harvard Medical School, he combined a career as a physician and professor of anatomy with an avocation as an essayist, poet, novelist, and biographer. He wrote a number of medical papers and was an expert on contagious diseases. Among his best known poems are "Old Ironsides," "The Chambered Nautilus," and "Wonderful One-Hoss Shay." Renowned as a lecturer and writer, he was an active contributor to Atlantic Monthly, beginning with its founding in 1857. His series of articles, "The Autocrat of the Breakfast-Table," blended commentary on a variety of subjects with light and serious verse. It appeared in book form in 1858. He was a prolific writer up to his death on 7 October 1894. His son, Oliver Wendell Holmes Jr., became a prominent jurist and associate justice of the United States Supreme Court. In the following essay Holmes discusses his views on exercise and athletics. A classic statement of the physiological and moral benefits of athletics, it is reprinted from Atlantic Monthly, Vol. I (May, 1858), pp. 877-882.

THE AUTOCRAT OF THE BREAKFAST TABLE
by Oliver Wendell Holmes

As to *giving up* because the almanac or the Family Bible says that it is about time to do it, I have no intention of doing any such thing. I grant you that I burn less carbon than some years ago. I see people of my standing really good for nothing, decrepit, effete, *la levre inferieure deja pendante,* with what little life they have left mainly concentrated in their epigastrium. But as the disease of old age is epidemic, endemic, and sporadic, and everybody that lives long enough is sure to catch it, I am going to say, for the encouragement of such as need it how I treat the malady in my own case.

First. As I feel, that, when I have anything to do, there is less time for it than when I was younger, I find that I give my attention more thoroughly, and use my time more economically than ever before; so that I can learn anything twice as easily as in my earlier days. I am not, therefore, afraid to attack a new study. I took up a difficult language a very few years ago with good success, and think of mathematics and metaphysics by-and-by.

Secondly. I have opened my eyes to a good many neglected privileges and pleasures within my reach, and requiring only a little courage to enjoy them. You may well suppose it pleased me to find that old Cato was thinking of learning to play the fiddle, when I had deliberately taken it up in my old age, and satisfied myself that I could get much comfort, if not much music, out of it.

Thirdly. I have found that some of those active exercises, which are commonly thought to belong to young folks only, may be enjoyed at a much later period.

A young friend has lately written an admirable article in one of the journals, entitled, "Saints and their Bodies." Approving of his general doctrines, and grateful for his records of personal experience, I cannot refuse to add my own experimental confirmation of his eulogy of one particular form of active exercise and amusement, namely, *boating*. For the past nine years, I have rowed about, during a good part of the summer, on fresh or salt water. My present fleet on the river Charles consists of three rowboats. 1. A small flat-bottomed skiff of the shape of a flat-iron, kept mainly to lend to boys. 2. A fancy "dory" for two pairs of sculls, in which I sometimes go out with my young folks. 3. My own particular water-sulky, a "skeleton" or "shell" race-boat, twenty-two feet long, with huge outriggers, which boat I pull with ten-foot sculls—alone, of course, as it holds but one, and tips him out, if he doesn't mind what he is about. In this I glide around the Back Bay, down the stream, up the Charles to Cambridge and Watertown, up the Mystic, round the wharves, in the wake of steamboats, which have a swell after them delightful to rock upon; I linger under the bridges—those "caterpillar bridges," as my brother Professor so happily called them; rub against the black sides of old wood-schooners; cool down under the overhanging stem of some tall India-man; stretch across the Navy Yard where the sentinel warns me off from the Ohio,—just as if I should hurt her by lying in her shadow; then strike out into the harbor, where the water gets clear and the air smells of the ocean,—till all at once I remember, that, if a west wind blows up of a sudden, I shall drift along past the islands, out of sight of the dear old State-house,—plate, tumbler, knife and fork all waiting at home, but no chair drawn up at the table,—all the dear people waiting, waiting, waiting, while the boat is sliding, sliding, sliding into the great desert, where there is no tree and no fountain. As I don't want my wreck to be washed up on one of the beaches in company with devils'-aprons, bladder-weeds, dead horse-shoes, and bleached crab-shells, I turn about and flap my long, narrow wings for home. When the tide is running out swiftly, I have a splendid fight to get through the bridges, but always make it a rule to beat,—although I have been jammed up into pretty tight places at times, and was caught once between a vessel swinging round and the pier, until our bones (the boat's that is) cracked as if we had been in the jaws of the Behemoth. Then back to my moorings at the foot of the Common, off with the rowing dress, dash under the green translucent wave, return to the garb of civilization, walk through my Garden, take a look at my elms on the Common, and, reaching my habitat, in consideration of my advanced period of life, indulge in the Elysian abandonment of a huge recumbent chair.

When I have established a pair of well-pronounced feathering-calluses on my thumbs, when I am training so that I can do my fifteen miles at a stretch without coming to grief in any way, when I can perform my mile in eight minutes or a little less, then I feel as if I had old Time's head in chancery, and could give it to him at my leisure.

I do not deny the attraction of walking. I have bored this ancient city through and through in my daily travels, until I know it as an old inhabitant of a Cheshire knows his cheese. Why, it was I who, in the course of these rambles, discovered that remarkable avenue called Myrtle Street, stretching in one long line from east of the Reservoir to a precipitous and rudely paved cliff which looks down on the grim abode of Science, and beyond it to the far hills; a promenade so delicious in its repose, so cheerfully varied with glimpses down the northern slope into busy Cambridge Street with its iron river of the horse-railroad, and wheeled barges gliding back and forward over it,—so delightfully closing at its western extremity in sunny courts and passages where I know peace, and beauty, and virtue, and serene old age must be perpetual tenants,—so alluring to all who desire to take their daily stroll, in the words of Dr. Watts,—

"Alike unknowing and unknown,"—

that nothing but a sense of duty would have prompted me to reveal the secret of its existence. I concede, therefore, that walking is an immeasurably-fine invention, of which old age ought constantly to avail itself.

Saddle-leather is in some respects even preferable to sole-leather. The principal objection to it is of a financial character. But you may be sure that Bacon and Sydenham did not recommend it for nothing. One's hepar, or, in vulgar language, liver,—a ponderous organ, weighing some three or four pounds,—goes up and down like the dasher of a churn in the midst of the other vital arrangements, at every step of a trotting horse. The brains also are shaken up like coppers in a money-box. Riding is good, for those that are born with a silver-mounted bridle in their hand, and can ride as much and as often as they like, without thinking all the time they hear that steady grinding sound as the horse's jaws triturate with calm lateral movement the bank-bills and promises to pay upon which it is notorious that the profligate animal in question feeds day and night.

Instead, however, of considering these kinds of exercise in this empirical way, I will devote a brief space to an examination of them in a more scientific form.

The pleasure of exercise is due first to a purely physical impression, and secondly to a sense of power in action. The first source of pleasure varies of course with our condition and the state of the surrounding circumstances; the second with the amount and kind of power, and the extent and kind of action. In all forms of active exercise there are three powers simultaneously in action,—the will, the muscles, and the intellect. Each of these predominates in different kinds of exercise. In walking, the will and muscles are so accustomed to work together and perform their task with so little expenditure of force, that the intellect is left comparatively free. The mental pleasure in walking, as such, is in the sense of power over all our moving machinery. But in riding, I have the additional pleasure of governing another will, and my muscles extend to the tips of the animal's ears and to his four hoofs, instead of stopping at my hands and feet. Now in this extension of my volition and my physical frame into another animal, my tyrannical instincts and my desire for heroic strength are at once gratified. When the horse ceases to have a will of his own and his muscles require no special attention on your part, then you may live on horseback as Wesley did, and write sermons or take naps, as you like. But you will observe, that, in riding on horseback, you always have a feeling, that, after all, it is not you that do the work, but the animal, and this prevents the satisfaction from being complete.

Now let us look at the conditions of rowing. I won't suppose you to be disgracing yourself in one of those miserable tubs, tugging in which is to rowing the true boat what riding a cow is to be striding an Arab. You know the Esquimaux kayak, (if that is the name of it.) don't you? Look at that model of one over my door. Sharp, rather?—On the contrary, it is a lubber to the one you and I must have; a Dutch fish-wife to Psyche, contrasted with what I will tell you about.—Our boat, then, is something of the shape of a pickerel, as you look down upon his back, be lying in the sunshine just where the sharp edge of the water cuts in among the lily-pads. It is a kind of a giant pod, as one may say,—tight everywhere, except in a little place in the middle, where you sit. Its length is from seven to ten yards and as it is only from sixteen to thirty inches wide in its widest part, you understand why you want those "outriggers," or projecting iron frames with the rowlocks in which the oars play. My rowlocks are five feet apart: double or more than double the greatest width of the boat.

Here you are, then, afloat with a body a rod and a half long, with arms, or wings, as you may choose to call them, stretching more than twenty feet from tip to tip; every volition of yours extending as perfectly into them as if your spinal cord ran down the centre strip of your boat, and the nerves of your arms tingled as far as the broad blades of your oars,—ringed under your own special direction. This, in sober earnest, is the nearest approach to flying that man has ever made or perhaps ever will make. As the hawk sails without flapping his pinions, so you drift with the tide when you will, in the most luxurious form of locomotion indulged to an embodied spirit. But if your blood wants rousing, turn round that stake in the river, which you see a mile from here: and when you come in in sixteen minutes, (if you do, for we are old boys, and not champion scullers, you remember,) then say if you begin to feel a little warmed up or not! You can row easily and gently all day, and you can row yourself blind and black in the face in ten minutes, just as you like. It has been long agreed that there is no way in which a man can accomplish so much labor with his muscles as in rowing. It is in the boat, then, that man finds the largest extension of his volitional and muscular existence; and yet he may tax both of them so slightly, in that most delicious of exercises, that he shall mentally write his sermon, or his poem, or recall the remarks he has made in company and put them in form for the public, as well as in his easy-chair.

I dare not publicly name the rare joys, the infinite delights, that intoxicate me on some sweet June morning when the river and bay are smooth as a sheet of berylgreen silk, and I run along ripping it up with my knife-edged shell of a boat, the rent closing after me like those wounds of angles which Milton tells of, but the seam still for many a long rood behind me. To lie still over the Flats, where the waters are shallow, and see the crabs crawling and the sculpins gliding busily and silently beneath the boat,—to rustle in through the long harsh grass that leads up some tranquil creek,—to take shelter from the sunbeams under one of the thousand-footed bridges, and look down its interminable colonnades, crusted with green and oozy growths, studded with minute barnacles, and belted with rings of dark muscles, while overhead, streams and thunders that other river whose every wave is a human soul flowing to eternity as the river below flows to the ocean,—lying there moored unseen, in loneliness so profound that the columns of Tadmor in the Desert could not seem more remote from life,—the cool breeze on one's forehead, the stream whispering against the half-sunken pillars,—why should I tell of these things, that I should live to see my beloved haunts invaded and the waves blackened with boats as with a swarm of waterbeetles? What a city of idiots we must be not to have covered this glorious bay with gondolas and wherries, as we have just learned to cover the ice in winter with skaters!

I am satisfied that such a set of black-coated stiff jointed, soft-muscled, paste-complexioned youth as we can boast in our Atlantic cities never before sprang from loins of Anglo-Saxon lineage. Of the females that are the mates of these males I do not here speak. I preached my sermon from the lay pulpit on this matter a good while ago. Of course, if you heard it, you know my belief is that the total climatic influences here are getting up a number of new patterns of humanity, some of which are not an improvement on the old model. Clipper-built sharp in the bows, long in the spars, slender to look at, and fast to go, the ship, which is the great organ of our national life of relation, is but a reproduction of the typical form which the elements impress upon its builder. All this we cannot help; but we can make the best of these influences, such as they are. We have a few good boatmen,—no good horsemen that I hear of,—nothing remarkable, I believe, in cricketing,—and as for any great athletic feat performed by a gentleman in these latitudes, society would drop a man who should run round the Common in five minutes. Some of our amateur fencers, single-stick players, and boxers, we have no reason to be ashamed of. Boxing is rough play, but not too rough for a hearty young fellow. Anything is better than this white-blooded degeneration to which we all tend.

I dropped into a gentlemen's sparring exhibition only last evening. It did my heart good to see that there were a few young and youngish youths left who could take care of their own heads in case of emergency. It is a fine sight, that of a gentleman resolving himself into the primitive constituents of his humanity. Here is a delicate young man now, with an intellectual countance, a slight figure, a sub-pallid complexion, a most unassuming deportment, a mild adolescent in fact, that any Hiram or Jonathan from between the ploughtails would of course expect to handle with perfect ease. Oh, he is taking off his gold-bowed spectacles! Ah, he is divesting himself of his cravat! Why, he is stripping off his coat! Well, here he is, sure enough, in a tight silk shirt, and with two things that look like batter puddings in the place of his fists. Now see that other fellow with another pair of batter puddings,—the big one with the broad shoulders; he will certainly knock the little man's head off, if he strikes him. Feinting, dodging, stopping, hitting, countering,—little man's head not off yet. You might as well try to jump upon your own shadow as to hit the little man's intellectual features. He needn't have taken off the gold-bowed spectacles at all. Quick, cautious, shifty, nimble, cool, he catches all the fierce lunges or gets out of their reach, till his turn comes, and then, whack goes one of the batter puddings against the big one's ribs, and bang goes the other into the big one's face, and, staggering, shuffling, slipping, tripping, collapsing, sprawling, down goes the big one in a miscellaneous bundle.—If my young friend, whose excellent article I have referred to, could only introduce the manly art of self-defence among the clergy, I am satisfied that we should have better sermons and an infinitely less quarrelsome church-militant. A bout with the gloves would let off the ill-nature, and cure the indigestion, which, united, have embroiled their subject in a bitter controversy. We should then often hear that a point of difference between an infallible and a heretic, instead of being vehemently discussed in a series of newspaper articles, had been settled by a friendly contest in several rounds, at the close of which the parties shook hands and appeared cordially reconciled.

But boxing you and I are too old for, I am afraid. I was for a moment tempted, by the contagion of muscular electricity last evening, to try the gloves with the Benicia Boy, who looked in as a friend to the noble art; but remembering that he had twice my weight and half my age, besides the advantage of his training, I sat still and said nothing.

There is one other delicate point I wish to speak of with reference to old age. I refer to the use of dioptric media which correct the diminished retracting power of the humors of the eye,—in other words, spectacles. I don't use them. All I ask is a large, fair type, a strong daylight or gaslight, and one yard of focal distance, and my eyes are as good as ever. But if your eyes fail, I can tell you something encouraging. There is now living in New York State an old gentleman who, perceiving his sight to fail, immediately took to exercising it on the finest print, and in this way fairly bullied Nature out of her foolish habit of taking liberties at five-and-forty, or thereabout. And now this old gentleman performs the most extraordinary feats with his pen, showing that his eyes must be a pair of microscopes. I should be afraid to say to you how much he writes in the compass of a half-dime,—whether the Psalms or the Gospels, or the Psalms and the Gospels, I won't be positive.

But now let me tell you this. If the time comes when you must lay down the fiddle and the bow, because your fingers are too stiff, and drop the ten-foot sculls, because your arms are too weak, and after dallying awhile with eye-glasses, come at last to the undisguised reality of spectacles,—if the time comes when that fire of life we spoke of has burned so low that where its flames reverberated there is only the sombre stain of regret, and where its coals glowed, only the white ashes that cover the embers of memory,—don't let your heart grow cold, and you may carry cheerfulness and love with you into the teens of your second century if you can last so long. As our friend the Poet, once said, in some of those old fashioned heroics of his which he keeps for his private reading,—

Call him not old, whom visionary brain
Holds o'er the past its undivided reign.
For him in vain the envious seasons roll
Who bears eternal summer in his soul.
If yet the minstrel's song, the poet's lay,
Spring with her birds, or children with their play
Or maiden's smile, or heavenly dreams of art
Stir the few life-drops creeping round his heart,—
Turn to the record where his years are told,—
Count his gray hairs,—they cannot make him old!

PHYSICAL FITNESS

As a sports mania swept across North America during the late 1850s editors of major city newspapers began to reflect upon the meaning of the new rage for exercise and athletics. They could ignore no longer the proliferation of baseball, cricket, rowing, gymnastic, and other athletic clubs. While some skeptics remained, more and more of these molders of public opinion praised the new trends as long overdue. These journalists applauded the British for their physical fitness and love of sports, and they urged the Americans to follow their example. The visit of England's famed national cricket eleven in October of 1859 prompted the following editorial, which is reprinted from the New York Times, 11 October 1859.

NATIONAL GYMNASTICS

The cricket match at Hoboken and the interest it has excited seems to have led some people to the conclusion that a new era is about to be inaugurated, that every doctor, lawyer, editor and merchant in the country will hence-forward devote himself to the bat and ball, and present himself to the admiring gaze of his friends with a pair of rosy cheeks and a stomach of leather, that dyspepsia will become an historical disease like the leprosy, and the vendors of bitters be obliged to call meetings of their creditors and wind up their affairs. We share the interest with which everybody has regarded the brilliant introduction of the noble game amongst us by the "Eleven" at Hoboken, and we have no doubt it will henceforth be oftener resorted to as a means of recreation than ever it has been, before; but we are sorry we cannot share the glorious sanitary previsions with which so many people's minds are now filled.

That a good deal of progress towards greater health has been made within the last few years nobody can deny. Active exercise has become a little more fashionable amongst both sexes. Ladies walk more, and wear thicker boots for that purpose. Last Winter they skated a great deal, and this Winter we hope will skate a great deal more; and we do not doubt that these exercises, as well as riding, rowing, and bowling, will henceforward become every year more general. The men, too, have been giving their digestions a slight fillip, by frequenting gymnasiums a little, going to the Adirondack a little, fishing a little, hunting a little, bowling nine pins a little. Some few will now play cricket a little. But we honestly confess we still feel somewhat despondent about the prospects of "exercise," because we feel that to become general, useful, destructive of dyspepsia, consumption and hypochondria, and all the ills that follow in their train, it must be sought and obtained for its own sake, and with a hearty relish and enjoyment of it, not resorted to as part of a course of medicine, and swallowed with wry faces, and fled from at the earliest possible moment. To give it its proper position in the popular estimation of America, our men of sedentary habits must undergo a little moral change. As long as business occupies their minds as intensely and earnestly as it does now, they will never get any lasting good either from cricket or anything else, because they will never take up bat or ball with thorough; as long as we go off to the country, and mount our horses, and seize our rides with doubts, and reluctance, and misgivings, with anxieties innumerable about bills payable and bills receivable, and cases and points weighing us down, and seize the first decent opportunity of hurrying back to town, and "buckling down," we might as well submit to our dyspepsia without a struggle.

Exercise, like everything else which involves effort, to be thoroughly enjoyed, and to be thoroughly profitable, must be cultivated steadily, year after year. As long as we rush about, now and then, when there happens to be "a rage" in cricket, just as there is a rage in chess, and a rage in base ball, and a rage in rope-walking, or in obedience to a doctor's orders, as a last resource, bitters and tonic failing, our exercise will be painful, laborious and a bore. We must take exercise steadily, boldly, and because we like it; take a holiday now and then all the year round, and not be ashamed of it, if we wish to love cricket, or horseback riding, or rowing. At present we skulk and sneak to our out-door amusements. The old lawyer and old merchant sit down under their dyspepsia, and neuralgia, and gout, and gravel, and liver complaint, just as one submits to a wet day. They have had them all their lives, and despair of cure and find distraction in intense devotion to business. The young lawyer and young merchant, who takes them as his patterns, tries to walk in their footsteps. He scorns vacation, sticks to his noonday pie and desk. If he goes out of town for a week in summer, he tries to hide it, and make believe he is only away for a day and will be back to-morrow. Rude health he at last begins to think discreditable, as it indicates laxity of devotion to business, he fears. After a few years, he is no longer to take any exercise, and leisure brings no enjoyment. Flabby muscles and a used-up stomach make motion either on foot or on horseback disagreeable, and long absorbtion in business renders it impossible for the mind to tear itself away from it. A final break down probably sends him to Europe for two years, if he can afford it, when it is too late for thorough restoration, and so the years drag on.

Now, if you want to make outdoor sports racy of the soil, to become good cricketers and bid defiance to British deportations, to become bold riders, ardent hunters, and get through life without being dependent for all our energies on our high strung nerves alone, we must begin by making it reputable to amuse one's self, by exalting health above business in the public estimation, instead of keeping it subordinate to it. A young man must be able to look at his friends in the face and say—"I'm going for a day's cricketing or fishing, and I'm not ashamed of it;" and his friends must learn to feel, on hearing the announcement, that he is a lucky dog, and not that he is a hopeless vagabond,

We are always talking about English health and English devotion to outdoor sports, but we totally forget how the English acquire and keep these habits which we admire so much. In the first place they have a large idle aristocracy who have made manly sports fashionable and customary, and their influence is felt through every class and profession. The English Courts rise in June, and "the long vacation" follows. The lawyers rush out of town, and are not seen again until October. None of them ever thinks of confining himself to a miserable fortnight in August. Every business man who can possibly get away follows their example, and glorifies in it. Nobody is ashamed of going to the moor, and blazing away for two months, or "going on a tramp" for the same period to the Highlands or Switzerland. It is "the thing" which all who can are sure to do, and all who can't would fain do if they could. Health is fashionable; and therefore healthgetting, because it is a habit, is pleasant. Instead of trying to make believe that they are in town all Autumn, they try to make believe that they have been out of town—that instead of working they have been "on the moors," or in Norway. This we admit is "snobbish," but it produces its effect. They get fond of exercise, and rush to it whenever an opening offers.

The Central Park will bring cricket to our doors. Five cents, and a half hour, will bring it, and divers other sports, within reach of every man in New-York. If we do not cultivate them enough to get a love for active exertion, it will be our own fault. But we must not forget that exercise and health, like law, or physics, or dry goods, must be pursued assiduously to be really won and enjoyed. They won't reveal their charms to every brokendown fellow who comes hobbling along and tries to set himself up by two or three days' worship at their shrine. Hard muscles, capacious lungs, and the vigorous digestion which carry a man through the Winter's toil, can only be acquired by steady devotion every week of Summer and Fall to laborious exercise in the open air.

PUBLIC PARKS

During the 1850s New York City took the lead in urban park design in the United States. For decades city officials had resisted calls for the planning of open space on Manhattan island because of the belief that the Hudson and East Rivers provided the population with a healthy natural environment. But the increasing congestion, disease, and disorder persuaded many influential citizens that a park was essential. William Cullen Bryant, a poet and editor of the New York Post, and Walt Whitman, poet and editor of the Brooklyn Eagle, led the campaign. In 1856 the town fathers agreed to hold a competition for the design of an urban park. Frederick Law Olmsted and Calvert Vaux submitted the winning plan. One year later they supervised the beginning of the construction of Central Park. Olmsted hoped that it would serve as the "lungs of the city," and that it would provide a tranquil refuge where the inhabitants could experience nature free from the pressures of the metropolis. He and the park's commissioners wished to reserve the park's fields for passive enjoyment of the picturesque vistas. They restricted adult ball playing and other sports that attracted crowds. As the following document suggests, one of the feature attractions of Central Park during its earliest years was the skating pond. This editorial is reprinted from the Spirit of the Times, 10 March 1860, p. 54.

THE ATHLETIC REVIVAL AND THE CENTRAL PARK

The athletic revival of our time appears to have become so general throughout the country, and to promise so much substantial improvement in our people—physically first, and then, and therefore, intellectually and morally—that it is interesting to examine the circumstances and conditions of its progress.

Cricket we have always had, as an exotic. It has been played for years at Hoboken and other retired localities, but chiefly by Englishmen, and it is still regarded, even by American players, as an English game. Base ball has been a school-boy's game all over the land from immemorial time, but it was, until recently, considered undignified for men to play at it, except on rare holidays, and then they were wont to play on some out-lying common, where they would be unseen of their more staid associates. Within five or six years all this has changed; B. B. clubs outnumber the debating societies almost as much as they surpass them in enthusiasm. The infection seems to have seized all classes of people—intellectual youth, corpulent gentlemen, lawyers, butchers, dry goods clerks, doctors, every one, in short, if possessed of sound limbs and tolerable wind, must play one or two afternoons in each week, or be voted "slow."

Gymnasium succeeds gymnasium in the larger cities. The ladies of Boston and thereabout commenced with skating, at which they excel; then they took up rowing, and at that they hope to give the undergraduates of Cambridge a hard try for the championship; more recently it is rumoured that they are learning the "manly art of self-defence." Ladies in New York go timidly yet the mania is not yet fully upon them, but they evince such premonitory symptoms as balmoral skirts and ankle boots—heavier than some young gentlemen would care to walk Broadway in.

Cambridge has a "chair of gymnastics," and Yale—that venerable, elm-shaded seat of orthodox rigidity—has recently added to its laboratory a bowling alley, whose balls and falling pins may resound through the legislative halls whence issued the "blue law" prohibiting the playing of the wicked game of nine-pins within the puritanic pale of Connecticut....

It is useless to multiply examples, everything indicates the incoming of the new era. Not only here, but in all large towns at the North, the appropriate shops are running over with bats and balls, spiked shoes stare at one from every cordwainer's window, tailors advertise every form of exercising dress, skates are sold as never skates were sold before, everything that athletes require they readily find and as readily buy. More than all this, a something that cannot be bought—which is not found in shops—the dawning of a healthier gleam in the eye and a brawnier pose of the figure, which can be found only in joyous out-of-door exercise, begins to show itself in our streets.

Labor in the open air is very well, but, especially for citizens, it is not sufficient. One might swing the "Indian club" for a week without one-half of the real advantage that would be gained from half a dozen innings in a closely contested and exciting game of base ball or cricket. A brisk ride on a fine horse, with good roads, pleasant scenery, and above all, good company, yes, and a goodly company to admire his horsemanship, will give one such a freshening of body and soul, as twenty mortal hours of dyspepsia chair, in a dull room, with dull company, cannot even imitate.

And herein lies the distinction. We do not want simple "physical exercise," we want "athletic sports." Not only a development of muscle but a development of spirit as well. Heaving coal may be as good *exercise* as pitching quoits, or sawing wood as rowing in a regatta, but they are infinitely less inspiring, and therefore infinitely less healthful. Of two men exercising strictly under the two systems, one will be of clear complexion, ruddy, happy-looking, and full of healthful vigor, the other equally strong perhaps, and as enduring, but the countenance will be heavy and dull—he may look firm and resolute, but it will seem like "resolution from despair." You and I, reader, would not long hesitate as to which of the two conditions we would choose for our own. Indoor exercise with dumb-bells and clubs, or on bars and ladders, is of inestimable value when coupled with real, hilarious, open-air sport, but especially in cities it is impossible to rear or preserve healthy men and women, unless they are provided with a cheerful and beautiful place of recreation, where old and young may pursue their several inclinations under every influence which may tend to enhance their enjoyment. New York is now providing herself with a spot which is to be kept forever sacred to this purpose. Eight hundred and forty odd acres have been rescued from actual desolation and prospective house building and are now being moulded, with consummate skill, into a magnificent park, wherein will be displayed more tasteful adornment and adaptedness to proposed uses than in any other park in the world. European visitors, proud as they are of their parks at home, concede that ours will be the finest metropolitan pleasure ground in the world. We might, with profit, dilate on the details of the work and its artistic merits, but our present purpose, is to show its nice dove-tailing with the growing taste for sports to which we have alluded, and to record our prediction that it is to be the most beneficial of our public charities and our proudest "Public Institution." Its leading features are to be as follows: A drive of about seven and a half miles for the airing of dowagers, and for the temporary or occasional parade of the fashion which will, before long, find its way into the saddle; a ride of five miles, nearly two miles of it a level road, forty feet wide, around the new reservoir, whereon we expect to see a general reduction of obesity, a pounding out of dyspepsia, a development of manly and womanly vigor, and such love-making as can only be done in the saddle; a labyrinth of walks—twenty-five miles of them coiled up within the compass of the park; and such walks!—who has not tried them already? dry, and grass-bordered, with flowers and brooks; what a relief will they be after the eternal flagging of the grown up-town; cricket fields and ball grounds, large and conveniently located in different parts of the park; a mall two hundred feet wide and a quarter of a mile long; a terrace and fountain between its northern end and the lake, and six acres of shaded grass and gravel throughout its length; thirty acres of ponds for boating and skating; and we hope such a gymnasium as only a grand conjunction of a million of people could expect or afford.

Some of these features are only foreshadowed. The lawns and rollicking grounds for children have not yet the consistency of turf which they require; the play-grounds are not fully seeded and they must lie at least another year to become fit for use; the ride is more inviting on the map than on the present broken ground, and much is yet to be done in all of the uncompleted parts of the park. But the ramble is nearly finished and was a blessing to the hot town during the past summer, three miles of the drive are finished, and a capital drive it is, as any citizen who owns or can hire a carriage will testify. The skating pond commenced the season on Christmas day, and it has mattered little since whether the skating has been good or bad—smooth ice or rough slush, it made little difference—the skaters were there pursuing pleasure, sometimes under difficulties we think, but intently pursuing it and doubtless finding it. The scene, in fair weather, cannot be described, it would be as easy to describe the movements of swarming bees, or the jollity of birds on a spring morning; we merely give an abstract furnished by the efficient and obliging officer in charge of the police of the daily return made to the authorities of the park:

From the commencement of skating to the 24th February	63 days
There has been skating on	45 "
And no skating on	18 "
Of visitors to the pond the least number in one day was	100
The largest number (Christmas) estimated at	100,000
Aggregate number during the season	540,000
Average number on skating days	12,000

Think of it! Twelve thousand people a day for a month and a half, making up for the long years since the "collik," and the canal (in Canal-street) were devastated, years during which there was no good skating this side of the Passaic. Old and young, male and female, the grey hairs of sixty and the too supple ankles of eight or ten, with every intermediate of man and matron, youth and maiden, all were incontinently bent on their newly-found sport, and they and the city are immeasurable the better for it. What has all this cost? No matter—not so much as it is worth by a great deal....

Chapter 2

AQUATICS

The water sports of rowing and yachting experienced increased popularity in North America during the mid-1800s, especially in the cities along the eastern coast of the continent. The proximity of the Atlantic Ocean and numerous major and minor rivers made the cities and towns of the Maritime provinces of Canada and the northeastern United States natural centers for these aquatic recreations. Both pastimes originated in utilitarian activities, and both benefited from the enthusiasm for health and athletics that developed during this era. But the two amusements differed in their respective patterns of growth and in the social class of their participants. The great wealth that was required to own and race large boats excluded all but the elite from yachting, while rowing appealed to a wider range of upper class college students and middle and lower class oarsmen.

Students from Harvard and Yale launched rowing clubs in the 1840s and by the next decade scholars at other institutions were following their example. During that era colleges imposed a rigid and demanding curriculum and strictly controlled undergraduate life. There were no physical education requirements, and the schools had few if any athletic facilities. Without adequate playgrounds or gymnasiums, student exercise was limited to walking or pulling boats and shells on nearby rivers and bays. Young men enrolled at Harvard and Yale organized the first college boating clubs for physical training and socializing. "Notes on our Naval History" narrates the story of the formative years of rowing at Harvard. In August 1852 athletes from Harvard and Yale competed in a crew race on the waters of Lake Winnepesaukee, New Hampshire. This event was sponsored by a railroad and a vacation resort. It generated great interest and excitement, and the crowd it attracted demonstrated the commercial possibilities of intercollegiate sport. The New York Herald's report of this race, reprinted below, describes the contest which inaugurated intercollegiate athletics in the United States.

During the next few years boat clubs appeared at Brown, the University of Pennsylvania, Trinity, Dartmouth, Bowdoin, Union, and other colleges. During this period amateur student boats frequently competed against professional and private crews in their home cities. By the end of the decade there were calls for a regularly organized intercollegiate regatta. Representatives from Harvard, Yale, and Brown organized the first one in 1859 on Lake Quinsigamond, near Worcester, Massachusetts. A document below lists the rules for that event and reports its outcome.

These years also witnessed the revival of rowing in the Maritime provinces of Canada and the northeastern cities of the United States. The earliest center of boat racing in North America was St. John, New Brunswick. Builders and oarsmen from that Canadian town taught and competed against boatsmen from New York, Boston, Philadelphia, and other localities in the United States. Professional racing became a major spectator sport in several cities when men who earned their living in the harbors took up the sport. In New York City the Empire City Regatta Club and the New York Club offered prize money for special events, usually $400 per race. In 1856 a St. John's crew defeated a New York squad in a $1,000 per side match on the neutral site of the Charles River in Boston. A newpaper account reprinted here recaptures the excitement of that contest, which was held in a rainstorm in front of nearly 50,000 spectators. The year 1859 brought great interest in championship competition among individual scullers. Joshua Ward of Newburgh won a silver belt and $100 in a race held off Staten Island. Included here is a report of his triumph in a match for the national championship contested in Boston. By 1860 thousands of spectators were turning out for boating challenges that featured carefully defined rules and numerous officials. "Rules for Boats and Boat Racing" lists the regulations that governed competition in many cities in the northeastern United States.

While there were a few yacht clubs and races in the United States in the 1830s, the modern era of the sport began on 30 July 1844. On that date nine men met on board John C. Stevens's *Gimcrack* and founded the New York Yacht Club. The members built a Gothic clubhouse on Stevens's property at the Elysian Fields, Hoboken, New Jersey. They drew up a Constitution and Bylaws, scheduled periodic meetings and regattas, and sponsored cruises along the Atlantic coast. The original members came from prominent, affluent old Knickerbocker families, but by the 1850s the club also included the nouveaux riches and some wealthy non-New York City residents. By the late 1850s the club's squadron numbered about fifty vessels. Included here is the 1857 edition of the club's Constitution and Bylaws. By 1860 the New York Yacht Club had become the most affluent and most exclusive of all of the city's sporting organizations.

Upper class urbanites in other eastern cities in North America followed the example of the New Yorkers. In Canada the first yacht clubs appeared in the 1850s in Toronto and Halifax. Toronto's Royal Canadian Yacht Club launched operations in 1852, while later a group of Bermudian merchants established the Royal Halifax Yacht Club.

During the 1840s Stevens looked for an opportunity to race a boat in English waters. The chance came in 1851, when he decided to enter a yacht in a gala regatta sponsored by Great Britain's Royal Yacht Squadron to celebrate the Great Exhibition of that year. He organized a syndicate that commissioned George Steers to design *America*, which was built by William Brown. On August 22 *America* easily defeated seventeen English schooners and cutters in a race around the Isle of Wight. Stevens carried off the first prize, a one hundred guinea cup, which he and his partners brought back to the United States in triumph. After his death in 1857 the syndicate offered the trophy as a prize for international competition; since then it has been known as The America's Cup. This chapter includes an account of the highlights of *America*'s victory and the terms of the international challenge for the trophy won by Stevens and his partners.

EARLY HARVARD ROWING

During the mid-1840s Yale and Harvard colleges pioneered collegiate rowing in the United States. In 1843 seven members of Yale's junior class purchased a four-oared boat in New York City. The next year several Harvard sophomores bought an eight-oared boat and founded a club. At both institutions the crew clubs provided their members with both social activities and exercise. Charles W. Eliot, a longtime president of Harvard, recalled that back in the early 1850s "it was not a reputable thing" to belong to the Harvard crew. The floors of their strong lapstreak boats were used "as means of bringing home members of the crew who did not propose to return sober from an evening in Boston." The following piece reviews the origins and early development of rowing at Harvard. It includes accounts of Harvard's earliest competition against local clubs and its first challenge match against Yale in 1852. This anonymous essay originally appeared in Harvard Magazine, (July, 1858), pp. 247-255.

NOTES ON OUR NAVAL HISTORY

About the years 1842 and 1843 regattas, held for boats usually pulled by mechanics, were of frequent occurrence in the neighboring town of Chelsea. These regattas, instituted and conducted by individual enterprise, proved very attractive; and it was, perhaps, the success and example of the contesting boats which suggested the introduction of rowing boats in Harvard. Whether this supposition be a true one or not, it is certain that boating, as an institution in this College, dates no farther back than the Fall of 1844. In September of that year a boat called the Star, which had been built by Holbrook for the before-mentioned Chelsea races, was purchased in Boston by thirteen members of the Class of '46, who had formed themselves into a boat-club. This boat, then about three years old, was secured for the moderate sum of eighty-five dollars; but oars and repairs soon swelled the cost to one hundred and twenty dollars. One of the members, happening to have in his possession a set of silk colors which had formerly belonged to a boat called the Oneida, presented them to his club upon the condition that their new boat should henceforth bear this name. It is to a circumstance so trivial as this that the College clubs are indebted for a name which, among our boatingmen at least, will ever be a loved one, and which for long time to come will grace the list of our Harvard boats.

Imagine, then, a low, black, eight-oared boat, thirty-seven feet in length, propelled with plain ashen oars, by a crew whose holday uniform was of simple, blue-striped calico, and we have a good idea of the "old Oneida," as she appeared when first she found a home in Cambridge waters. Bearing the same name, she was handed down from one College Class to another, until her owners in the Class of '58 sold her hulk to other members of the same Class, retaining her colors and her name. For a year she was known as the Minnehaha, and then, in 1857, was sold to Winde and Clinkard, boat-builders of Boston, who subsequently sold her to a club in Springfield, Massachusetts.

Hardly was the Oneida club in full operation, before another originated in the Senior Class of '45. The boat purchased was eight-oared, thirty-eight feet long, and had

acquired considerable renown at the Chelsea races. When first obtained she bore the
eminently national appellation of Red Michael; but, notwithstanding her past celebrity,
that name was quickly discarded, and Iris adopted in its place. This club, however,
graduated the next summer, and sold their boat in Boston. So the Rubescent Hiberian
made but a brief sojourn in Cambridge. Yet, brief as it was, it was sufficiently long to
incur her defeat by the Oneida. The race took place one evening after tea, and called
together numbers from the whole University. The course, which was subsequently often
used for racing, was from a little below the present site of the Winchester House down
to the lower side of the Brighton Bridge, which the boats were consequently obliged
to pass under. It included the two bends of the river above the bridge, and was between
a mile and a half and two miles in length. In this race the Oneida beat the Iris by about
five lengths.

In the Spring of 1845, just previous to the departure of the Iris Club, members of
the Class of '48, then the Freshmen, secured an eight-oared boat about forty feet in
length, which they called the Undine; and in the succeeding Fall, a new boat, forty feet
long, rowing eight oars, and built by the builder of the Oneida, was purchased in the
Class of '47. She was christened the Huron. Thus, in a little more than one year from
the introduction of the first, four boats were owned in the College.

Up to this time, however, none but the Oneida had known the luxury of a shelter-
ing roof. At the first arrival of this boat, her club had been fortunate enough to obtain
an old boat-house, situated upon Willard's wharf, on the farther side of the river, which,
by lengthening and repairing, was barely made to afford her accommodation. With the
co-operation of the Iris men, a detached dressing-room was soon afterwards built upon
the same wharf. The Undine and Huron, and the Iris, during the few months she remained in Cambridge, had ever made their homes upon the water, and moored near the
Brighton Bridge, slept upon the bosom of the Charles. But in the Spring of '46 one Mr.
Wright erected the boat-house now occupied by the Oneida and Sabrina. This building was originally eighty- feet in length, and could accommodate four boats of the
models then popular. It was built as a speculation, probably at the request of the students, and thirty dollars per year was charged each club for the use of a portion of the
building. Beneath this roof the three Harvard boats were now placed, and their number being immediately increased by a fourth, the new boat-house was fully occupied.

The new-comer was a twenty-six foot, six-oared gig, furnished with stern-sheets.
She was much stronger and heavier than the others, and could hardly be considered a
race-boat. The Oneida Club, desiring a boat with which to make excursions down the
harbor, sold their old one to the Freshmen (Class of '49), and built this, their second
one, naming her the Atalanta. With their new boat also they adopted another uniform,
and appeared in all the glory of white shirts with blue stars and trimmings, duck pants,
and sennet hats. Previous to this, however, the Iris crew had donned white pants and
red shirts, and the Hurons had taken the more sailor-like blue.

In the Atalanta, during the few months preceding their graduation, the crew made
frequent excursions down the bay, now stopping for a chowder at Point Shirley, now
resting their wearied keel on the salt shores of Spectacle or Long Island; and once, 't
is said, they invited the maidens of far-famed Hull to an evening pull. Report adds, that
even hereditary horror for "reckless students" could not withstand such an invitation

from so gallant a crew. The damsels blushingly accepted the proffered compliment, and were afterwards safely and regretfully returned to their anxious parents by the gallant rovers, who had not, like jolly freebooters, hurried the precious freight away to their College homes.

About this time, too, the Boston clubs, having been very courteous and friendly, the Cambridge clubs invited them up to an entertainment. One of the boats was taken from the boat-house, boards laid across for flooring, and the room hung with flags and other decorations. A great plenty of punch, cigars, ham and crackers, and the *et ceteras,* was provided, and a very merry and jovial meeting ensued. Rumor whispers that some of the Boston boats returned with mutinous crews, and that nearly all of them brought up on the mud flats.

Here, also, may be mentioned the first boating contest in which Harvard was engaged with foreign boats. The race took place on the Cambridge course before described, the contestants being the Huron of the College, and a Boston boat called the Wave. The latter was a four-oared boat, and the Huron rowed but six oars against her. The Huron beat her adversary very decidedly. O thou glorious old craft! who didst win her first victory for Harvard, how would thy timbers have creaked and groaned hadst known that, half a score of years afterwards, thy namesake was to inaugurate her defeats!

The next new boat which was added to the College fleet did not appear until about two years after the arrival of the Atalanta. In 1848 the Ariel, a new eight-oared boat, was purchased by a club in the Class of '51. But although so long a time intervened between the arrivals of these two boats, although the first, after passing into the possession of the Class of '47, had been sold to persons who sent her to Rio Janeiro, and although about this time the Huron, which had departed from the Class of '47 into the hands of '50, was sold in Boston (at auction, to pay for rent due the boathouse, so slander has intimated), still boating does not appear to have suffered in popularity. The Oneida was still owned by a club in the Class of '49, whose enterprise in purchasing her while they were Freshman had been but a prelude to their subsequent excellence as oarsmen, and the Undine, soon after the graduation of her first owners, in 1848, was bought by a club in the Class of '50, who proved themselves as enthusiastically devoted to boating as any of the predecessors had been. In the spring of 1849, also, another eight-oared boat, about forty feet in length, built by Winde and Clinkard, and called the Halcyon, was added to the number by the Class of '51. So that in the fall of 1849 we find the list of Harvard boats read thus:—the Undine, eight oars ('50); the Ariel, six oars ('51); the Halcyon, eight oars ('51); the Oneida, eight oars ('52); besides these there was a small pair-oared called the Viola. In 1847, too, there was a great race between the Oneida and the Undine, over the Cambridge course, which created quite an excitment, nearly the whole College having assembled upon the bridge to witness the result. The Undine at first led, but one of her crew having unfortunately "caught a crab," the Oneida gained, took from her the inside on the larger bend of the course and won handsomely enough. There was also a race between the Oneida and some other boat, perhaps the Huron; the distance was from Braman's to the College wharf, and the Oneida won. Possibly, as has been asserted, the enthusiasm for boating may have lulled somewhat between 1847 and 1850; but if such is the fact, it must been piping high previously.

During the academical year of 1849-50, the clubs just enumerated were in excellent condition, all being well supported, and much rivalry existing between them. But the principal event of the year, and the occasion upon which the clubs made their most imposing appearance, was the *fete champetre* given by the late Colonel Winchester, at his new residence upon the banks of the river, near Mount Auburn. All the College boat-clubs were among the invited guests. The black Undine, with her crew dressed in neat navy-blue and white, the red Oneida, with a crew in shirts of the same crimson dye, the straw-colored Halcyon and Ariel,—all went together, in procession, to the appointed rendezvous, with chosen men, flaunting banners, and uniforms bright with the laundress's recent labor. Concerning the festivities of the day a participant writes: "The entertainment was most princely. The whole house and grounds were thrown open to guests the whole day, with billiards, bowling, smoking, music, boating upon the inland lake, and every species of amusement for the four or five hundred gentlemen whom the Colonel had invited to partake of his hospitality. A sumptuous table was kept constantly replenished during the whole time. In the afternoon the boats made a brief excursion upon the river, for the amusement of the company. In the evening there was a display of fireworks, and by the light of the last rockets the crews regained their places in the boats, and rowed back to Cambridge."

The Undine Club graduating the following Commencement, they afterwards sold their boat to a Boston club. Towards the close of this season (1850), the Ariel Club, having been guilty of some "irregularities" in the adjacent city, were disbanded by the College government, who refused for quite a long time afterwards to allow any new clubs to be formed. The Ariel was subsequently bought by residents of East Cambridge. The Halcyon Club continued its existence until the next July, when the club graduated, having sold their boat to members of the Class of '54 of Yale College. And now, in the fall of the year 1851, there was but one boat in Harvard, and that was the old Oneida, at this time owned in the Class of '53.

Not long after the completion of the boat-house, which thus far had been the only convenient one used by the College boats, the proprietor died, leaving, it was said, this property to his widow. If, however, she was dependent for support upon the income derived from the rents of this, her life must indeed have been precarious, as the financial departments of the clubs were subject to many fluctuations. The rents were collected by Mr. Royal Morse, the same venerable gentleman who is the author of the pithy notices which still annually appear upon two of our boat-houses. The worthy collector used to make frequent calls upon the treasurers, portraying the necessities of the widow in the most vivid manner; but after all his assiduity, the unfortunate lady was deprived of much of her just due, as through ignorance he charged each club but fifteen dollars per year, exactly one half the rent which had hitherto been paid. But about the time of which we are now speaking, the property, being no longer valuable, was sold by the administrator of the estate, and the purchaser, having divided the building, removed one half to the foot of Linden Street, and sold the other to the Oneida Club.

From 1851 to 1854 the Oneida remained the sole occupant of her boat-house, and the only club-boat in Harvard College. But during this time occurred the first rowing-match with Yale. The race originated in a direct challenge from Yale, inviting Harvard to meet her at such time and place as should be agreed upon, "to test the superiority of the oarsmen of the two Colleges." This challenge was promptly accepted. The trial took place upon the 3d of August, 1852, at Centre Harbor, Lake Winnipiseogee. The day was fine, and the water was scarcely rippled by a breeze. Harvard was represented by the Oneida (Class of '53); Yale, by the Shawmut (Class of '53), Undine (Class of '53), and the Atalanta. There was a preliminary trial in the morning, in which the Oneida came in ahead, followed successively by the Shawmut, the Undine, and the Atalanta. In the afternoon, the match was rowed. The boats started from about three miles out, and pulled up to a flag-boat stationed near the wharf, which they reached in about the same order as in the morning. The Atalanta, however, did not contend in the afternoon. The Oneida won by about four lengths, and obtained as a prize the black-walnut oars which are now, with other trophies, deposited in Harvard Hall. The occasion proved of so much interest to the many spectators, that a second race was appointed at Wolfboro' upon the 5th; but a severe rain falling that day it was abandoned, and the proposed prize, a walnut boat-hook, was given to the Shawmut, as second prize for the race of the 3d. The clubs, with other students, afterwards passed a very pleasant week at the Lake, and returned together to Concord, N. H., where, amid much good feeling and many fraternal adieus, they finally separated.

THE FIRST INTERCOLLEGIATE ATHLETIC CONTEST
THE HARVARD VERSUS YALE REGATTA, 1852

College sports began in the United States with a promotional scheme by a New England railroad and a New Hampshire vacation resort. In the summer of 1852 James Elkins, a railroad superintendant, offered to pay for the transportation and lodging of the Harvard and Yale crews if they would race at Center Harbor on Lake Winnipesaukee, New Hampshire. Forty-one students from the two colleges accepted the proposal as a "jolly lark." The contestants amused themselves with some spirited competition spiced with a good deal of eating, drinking, and socializing. The sleepy town came alive with the excitement of the match, and the local hotel and steamer profited from the undergraduates' visit. The Harvard men carried off the laurels, but all had a good time. Thus the entrepreneurial spirit generated America's first intercollegiate athletic contest. Commercialism and college sports had joined together for the first time. The future would demonstrate the power of their partnership. The following article is reprinted from the New York Herald, 10 August 1852.

HARVARD VS. YALE

It may, perhaps, be agreeable to some of your readers who have been burying themselves in the political correspondence for the last six months, to give a hasty glance at some other scenes that are transpiring in this great country of ours. A notice of regattas upon Lake Winnepiseogee may have been observed in some of the papers, for a week or two back. This scheme was originated by one of the students of Yale, in conjunction with the Boston and Montreal Railroad Company, who offered to pay all expenses of the boat clubs of Harvard and Yale, on the condition of their coming up with their boats and running several regattas on the lake. This fine offer was accepted, and the boat clubs arrived on Saturday.

FROM HARVARD
The Oneida, eight oars. Uniform, red, white, and blue.

FROM YALE
The Undine, eight oars. Uniform, red and white.

The Shawmut, eight oars. Uniform, white and blue.

The Atalanta, four oars. Uniform, blue, drab and white.

They make a very fine appearance upon the water, and have evidently had considerable practice in rowing. The colors of their boats are quite as diversified as their uniforms, one being red, another black, and another a mixture of the two. There was but one boat club at Harvard to enter the lists, which is, however, provided with a crew apparently very strong, and thoroughly disciplined, their facilities for acquiring perfect discipline being somewhat superior to the Yale students.

A fine band from Concord was engaged for the occasion.

On the day of the regatta, the boats came crowded to overflowing with passengers, and these, together with the people from the villages around, lined the wharfs and shore for some distance. The scene was extremely fine, as the boats lay all abreast, waiting for the sound of the bugle. The beautiful lake, with its hundred islands, stretching far off in front—the summits of the Red Hills in the back grounds—the unruffled smoothness of the water, and the perfect silence of the throng around—all added to the beauty of the scene.

At the sound of the bugle, the boats started off at full speed, and with admirable order—each crew apparently straining themselves to the utmost. The Oneida first reached the goal, having ran the distance, about a mile and a half, in seven minutes. The Shawmut came next, a few seconds behind, next the Undine, and then the Atalanta; the distance between the first and last boats being no more than six boat lengths. No prize was awarded in this regatta, which took place at eleven o'clock in the morning, it being intended only to give the boat clubs some idea of each other's speed.

The prize regatta came off at four in the afternoon. The boats were towed off to a starting point upon the lake, two miles distant from the shore, in order to row towards the shore. It was almost precisely a re-enaction of the scene of the morning, save, perhaps, that the oarsmen bent somewhat more lustily to their oars. The result was the same as in the first race, there being nearly the same space between the boats. A pair of fine black walnut oars were presented, as the prize, to the Oneida. The Atalanta was not allowed to compete in the prize regatta, on account of the disparity in size and number of oarsmen. The time occupied in the second race was eleven minutes by the Oneida, the Shawmut and Undine being a few seconds behind. The crowd dispersed highly gratified with the performance, the performers meanwhile adjourning to a very welcome repast at the Senter House.

The second regatta on Lake Winnepiseogee, which was to come off at Wolfborough, on Thursday, did not take place, owing to the inclemency of the weather.

A very handsome boat hook, ornamented with silver, which was originally intended for a second prize in the first regatta, but was subsequently reserved for a first prize in the second regatta, was presented, as a second prize, to the Shawmut, which came out second in the race. The boat hook was presented, with a few appropriate remarks, by Col. Baker, the chairman of the deciding committee.

It having cleared up somewhat in the afternoon, the boat clubs, in full uniform, preceded by the band, marched from the Pavilion to the wharf, and rowed about the lake, for the gratification of the townspeople.

In the evening, the boat clubs met at the Pavilion, at Wolfborough, and passed several resolutions, expressing their gratification at the treatment they had received, and their thanks to the committee of arrangements; after which they received sufficient funds to pay their expenses to their respective colleges. The whole affair has passed off finely, and as far as we can learn, to the entire satisfaction of all parties. An invitation has been extended to the clubs to renew their visit next year, which will doubtless be accepted.

The affair winds up with a ball at the Pavilion, this evening, which bids fair to be a fine one. An invitation to dinner, for tomorrow, has been tendered to the clubs, by the proprietor of the principal hotel at Plymouth, which has been accepted.

COLLEGE REGATTAS

Harvard Magazine of May, 1858 included a call for "a grand regatta for all the colleges of the United States." Harvard's boating enthusiasts then sent a circular letter to several institutions. On May 26 delegates from Harvard, Yale, Brown, and Trinity met at New Haven and founded the College Union Regatta. They agreed on the rules reprinted below, and scheduled the first race for Springfield, Massachusetts on July 23. Unfortunately, an accidental drowning of a Yale rower forced the cancellation of the 1858 event. The following year the colleges chose Lake Quinsigamond as the site of the challenge. One crew each from Brown and Yale competed against two boats from Harvard. Between 15,000 and 20,000 spectators watched Harvard defeat its rivals. Yale finished second, but the men from New Haven took a measure of revenge the next day when they finished first in a meet sponsored by the city of Worcester. The following rules are reprinted from Harvard Magazine, (June, 1858), p. 215. The account of the race given below first appeared in the New York Herald, 27 July 1859.

RULES FOR THE REGATTA, 1858

1. The race shall be between undergraduates of the different Colleges, including the graduating Classes.

2. Each college may enter one or more boats at discretion.

3. Boats may carry coxswains or not, as they choose.

4. The course shall be three statute miles in length, and two courses shall be surveyed before each race, one straight, the other a mile and a half and repeat. It shall be determined on the day of the race which of these courses shall be rowed.

5. The positions of the boats shall be determined by lot.

6. An allowance of twelve seconds per oar shall be made in favor of smaller boats.

7. Any boat crossing another's bow so as to make her alter her course shall thereby be disqualified to take the prize. Each College entering shall appoint an umpire. These umpires shall choose a referee.

8. A set of silk colors, not exceeding twenty-five dollars in value, and bearing a suitable inscription, shall be presented to the winning boat. The expense of the colors shall be apportioned among all boats entering for the regatta, as entrance fees.

WORCESTER, (MASS.) COLLEGE REGATTA

The first annual College Union Boat Club Regatta, which came off yesterday on Lake Quinsigamond, near Worcester, Mass., and which was participated in by students from Yale College and Brown and Harvard Universities, the last named proving the victors, was one of the grandest affairs ever witnessed in the Eastern States, and will no doubt be the initiative for a long series of similarly interesting yearly exhibitions.

The College regatta, it will be remembered, was postponed from last year on account of the death of one of the Yale crew.

Four boats were entered from three colleges, as follows:—

Brown University entered the Atlanta, a six-oared lap streak boat. This is the only club boat belonging to Brown University—is heavily built and was never designed for racing.

Yale College entered the college boat Yale, a six-oared shell, just finished by Makay, of New York, and manned by a picked crew from the Yale navy. The model is beautiful, and the Yale was far the best boat entered.

Harvard University entered the Avon, a six-oared lapped streak, built by Coyle, of St. Johns. She is owned by four gentlemen of the Senior Class, and manned by a crew from the two upper classes.

This college also entered their famous boat, the Harvard, a six-oared shell boat, built by Makay, in 1857. This is the college race boat, and manned by the six best oarsmen in the college.

Mr. Makay has lately built a new shell for this crew, to carry a coxswain, but the old boat was pulled on this occasion.

The waters of the lake were perfectly still, and the shores near the judges stand were crowded with people to the number of four or five thousand, many seats being erected for the occasion.

At four and a half P. M., the boats came in line and presented a very neat appearance, the red handkerchiefs and white shirts of the Harvard crew being particularly striking.

At the start the boats kept close together. The Harvard taking the lead, the Avon kept close behind, and the Atlanta slowly dropped astern.

The Harvard then pulled ahead, leaving a close contest between the Avon and Yale who kept changing places as far as the stake, where the Yale was thirty seconds ahead.

As the boats came down from the stake the red caps of the Harvard appeared far in advance. They were followed at a respectable distance by the Yale and Avon. The Atlanta still kept far behind.

The Harvard crew came in pulling seemingly at great ease, with the quick clean stroke for which they are so noted. As the boats neared the judges stand loud cheers were given for them, particularly for the winners. The course was a mile and half and repeat. The time as follows—

Harvard—Nineteen minutes and eighteen seconds.

Yale—Twenty minutes and twenty seconds.

Avon—Twenty one minutes and thirty one seconds.

Atlanta—Twenty four minutes and forty seconds.

The names of the Harvard are as follows:—C. Crowningshield, stroke, W.H. Forbes, L.G. Abbot, H.B. Russell, J.H. Wales, J.H. Ellison, bow.

In justice to the Atlanta it should be added that the boat was heavy and they had no hopes of competition with the shells.

The Avon, too, is a lap streak boat, and was at a great disadvantage in rowing against the Yale.

The sport ended with a brisk shower, which quickly scattered the spectators, who otherwise greatly enjoyed the afternoon.

The prize consisted of a set of flags, which were given to the Harvard crew amidst great applause.

THE SCENE OF THE REGATTA

The spot selected for this interesting event is one of the most beautiful and appropriate which this section of the country affords. Lake Quinsigamond is a sheet of water about three miles long, and averaging a third of a mile wide, running North and South, and situated about two miles east of Worcester. The northern part, which was the scene of the race, is, as it were, the stage of a vast amphitheatre. The grassy and mossy banks, deliciously shaded by tall trees, rise at an acute angle from the shores, so that thousands of spectators could view the contest advantageously. About the centre of the lake is the floating bridge, on the line of the road to Shrewsbury, and the stationing of the judges' boat near this locality attracted thousands of spectators to the bridge, which was reached by a new route. The scene of the vast concourse of people on the bridge, on the temporary stands and seats erected on the banks, and under the tents, was at once novel and picturesque. The music from the band, which was stationed on the west side of the lake, added much to the pleasure of the occasion.

The vast crowd of spectators was due in a great measure to the ready means of access to the place. The Boston and Worcester Railroad traverses one side of the pond, and extra trains were run for the accommodation of visitors. Omnibuses, stages, carriages, private vehicles, and every conceivable mode of conveyance, were also brought into requisition and used for carrying passengers to the lake. The property owners in the vicinity obligingly removed some of their walls and fences, and cut the grass in their fields, so as to afford ready access to the lake from the roads, and with the extensive acquaintance of the young gentlemen of the various colleges, added to the general public interest in the race, the country was well represented. Nearly every city, town and village in the East sent its delegations, and not a few were present from New York. The number on the ground has been variously estimated at from fifteen to twenty thousand persons, and it is doubtful whether the plentiful whortelberry and blueberry bushes in the vicinity were ever so thoroughly picked and cleaned as they were on this occasion by the delighted refugees from the dust and heat of the city. The place has long been a favorite one for Sabbath school and other excursions, but the demonstration yesterday was the most memorable in its history and will doubtless draw attention to it for future occasions. As an evidence of the attention which this affair enlisted, we will mention the fact that all the banks and most of the places of business in Worcester were closed for the day.

This regatta originated with the College Boat Club Congress, which was, we believe, suggested by Harvard College, in imitation of the annual regattas for the English universities. The Congress assembled at New Haven on Wednesday, May 26, 1858, but the unfortunate death, by drowning, of Mr. George E. Dunham, while practicing for the race, broke up the arrangements for the time, both from respect to his memory and on account of his being the stroke oarsman in the four-oared shell boat Volante. He was considered one of the best oarsman in the Yale Navy.

The delegates again convened on the 23d of February last in Brown University, the same colleges being represented, and Tuesday, the 26th last, was appointed as the time, and Lake Quinsigamond as the place for the next annual regatta. At the same time the following rules were adopted to control the regatta—

The race shall be between the under graduates of the colleges, including the graduating classes —(meaning by the undergraduates the four classes of the academical department)

Each college shall enter as many boats as they wish.

The course shall be three statute miles in length; and two courses shall be previously surveyed—the one straight, the other at 1 1/2 mile and repeat.

The positions of the boats shall be determined by lot.

An allowance of 12 seconds per oar shall be made in favor of smaller boats.

Any boat fouling another, or otherwise interfering with her course, shall be disqualified to take the prize.

Each college entering shall appoint an umpire—these umpires shall choose a referee.

A set of colors, with a suitable inscription, shall be procured by a committee, to be presented to the winning boat, the expenses thereof not exceeding twenty-five dollars, to be paid as an entrance fee by the boats entering the regatta.

THE METROPOLITAN CLUB OF NEW YORK CITY VS. THE UNION CLUB OF ST. JOHN, NEW BRUNSWICK

During the 1850s rowing clubs from the Maritime provinces of Canada and the northeastern cities of the United States carried on a spirited competition. On September 20, 1856 a crew representing New York City's Metropolitan Club competed against a boat sponsored by the Union Club of St. John, New Brunswick, Canada in a four-oared race on Boston's Charles River. The stakes were $1000 per side. The event matched the best squad from the British provinces against the pride of New York. The New York Clipper reported that about 50,000 people congregated along the banks of the river to witness the challenge. That journal estimated that the crowd included about two thousand spectators from New York and nearly double that number from St. John. The Canadian rowers overcame a tremendous thunderstorm and soundly defeated their adversaries from Manhattan. The following account of this celebrated encounter is reprinted from the New York Clipper, 27 September 1856, p. 179.

GREAT BOAT RACE BETWEEN NEW YORK AND ST. JOHN

The boat of the Metropolitan Club, James McKay, which was rowed by the New York crew is forty-two feet long, and constructed entirely of mahogany, and what is most incredible, her weight is less than one hundred pounds. She was rowed by Stephen Roberts, Charles Wetherel, William Sellers, and Thomas Dorr—coxswain, Joseph Elliott Jr. Dress—pink silk shirt, dark pants, and liberty caps.

The New Brunswick boat is named the Neptune, was built in St. John, is 35 feet long, is considerably heavier than the New York boat, and was rowed by Edward Welch, John Morris, Dennis Morris, and John Lambert—no coxswain. Dress—white shirts, dark pants, red caps.

St. John seemed to be the favorite from the time the match was made until the New York boat was seen, when odds on St. John became somewhat scarce, though eventually they rallied, and New York could find plenty of chances for investment, which they were not backward in taking advantage of, an immense number of wagers being made all through the States and British provinces.

THE START

Everything being in readiness, at 3 o'clock the word "Go," was given—"that little cannon" re-echoed the sound, and immediately off started the race boats, propelled by the brawny arms of "eight good men and true." "They're off—they're off" shouted the immense throng—cheer on cheer attested the fact, and the spectators seemed frantic with excitement. The Neptune had the best of the start, and got away a length in advance of the McKay. The crew of the latter soon got settled down to their work, and were fast making up for what they had lost in starting. On they went—the McKay gradually gaining on her opponent—a few more strokes "with a will" and they were side and side—"now comes the tug of war"—a half mile had been rowed over—New York, cheered on by their success in this early stage of the race, seemed to increase their exertions—"pull away boys, now you've got 'em" was shouted by the friends of the New York crew, while the friends of St. John "shrieked for" (Kansas, we were about to say) "the green boat and white shirts." Go it, ye cripples, how they pull—the shoutings of the spectators become louder, as the two boats endeavor respectively to take the lead—New York was gaining—she was a *few inches ahead* —these inches soon became feet, and at last a gap of some yards was opened between the contending parties. The elements now seemed to be taking part in the general excitement, for the storm commenced in earnest—vivid lightening flashed from the dense masses of black clouds overhead; the thunder pealed forth salute on salute, and the rain fell in torrents—yet that immense multitude of anxious spectators remained immovable, their eyes directed toward the outer turning point, endeavoring to follow the movements of those "aquatic racers."

When we lost sight of the boats, New York was ahead, but on reaching the stake boat, one and a half miles from the place of starting, St. John rounded so closely and beautifully that she left New York several lengths in the rear, and although the crew of the McKay strained every nerve they were unable to change the aspect of the race. On passing the head quarters of the St. John men, on the return, one of the latter raised a hand to his friends on shore, as much as to say "we've got em"—it was understood by those for whom it was intended. No material change took place in the position of the boats, until reaching the buoy at the starting point, when the Neptune made another splendid turn—the Mckay made another "bad break" in endeavoring to turn, and we almost fancied she was going to round the judges' yacht, but she didn't. By this time, the Neptune was some 150 yards up with New York, yet the McKay kept nobly to her work, her crew doing all in their power to make a change, but without success. The storm was now at its height, and the thickly falling rain almost hid the boats from sight.

The remainder of the story is soon told—St. John kept the lead, and reached the winning point in 42 minutes 14 secs. from the time the signal was given to start. New York arrived 32 secs. later. How either boat managed to live in such a storm, we are utterly unable to tell—considering the frail stuff of which the McKay is built, it is really astonishing that she was not swamped. As the two boats reached the goal, they were received with rapturous applause. The crews of the opposing boats fraternized in the most cordial and friendly manner, and the losers convinced all present by their manly actions that they well knew how to bear their defeat. The victors received the honors showered upon them in a modest and becoming manner, making no boast, but, on the contrary, endeavored to smooth the "rough edges" of their opponents' defeat. The entire match, from its commencement till its close, was conducted in a friendly manner by all engaged in it; and although New York had the misfortune to be defeated in the race, it is nevertheless a consolation to them to know that they were beaten by *four of the best oarsmen in the world!* That's so. New York, in our opinion, lost the race on the turning point. The time in which the race was pulled is the quickest ever made in those waters, and had it not been for the tremendous storm, we believe the distance would have been made in something under 40 minutes....

It is supposed that some $50,000 changed hands on the result of this great match between New York and St. John, and Boston has no cause to regret the interest she has manifested in aquatic sports.

SCULLERS' CHAMPIONSHIP RACE, 1859

During the late 1850s a number of men competed for the honor of being acclaimed the champion sculler in the United States. Their races excited the sporting fraternity and attracted large crowds of enthusiasts and gamblers. But matches held at Boston, New York, Philadelphia, Worcester, and Albany failed to produce a consistent winner. Disputes over the accuracy of times and the lengths of courses also fanned the controversy. In the fall of 1859 Boston hosted a gala event that was scheduled to resolve the issue. The victory of Newburgh's Joshua Ward recounted below is reprinted from the New York Clipper, 29 October 1859, p. 219.

CHAMPIONSHIP REGATTA

The grand Regatta for the Championship of the United States came off on Monday, October 24th, and was won by Joshua Ward.

The race was appointed for Wednesday, the 19th, but was postponed from day to day, on account of the roughness of the water. On Sunday, however, all was calm, and the morning of Monday dawned bright and clear, so that it was evident a race would come off. At an early hour the Mill Dam was crowded with spectators, and Braman's baths were covered with eager amateurs, all pressing to have a look at the men and the boats. There were judges to start the men, judges to time them, judges to see that they turned the stake properly, and judges to ride and judges to row alongside and see that from first to last all was fair. The care taken to have a clear course and a fair race was well rewarded by the complete success of the arrangements. The river police kept a clear course, the judges saw fair play, and the rival oarsmen seconded the judges, and, from the beginning to the end, the grand race for the championship was conducted with the utmost fairness, order, and good humor.

Joshua Ward, of Newburgh, entered the Major Morton, mahogany shell, 26 feet long, built by T. Donohue.

John Hancon, of Newburgh, entered the Unnamed, mahogany shell, built by T. Donohue.

M.F. Wells, of Boston, entered the J. Reed, built by J. Reed of Charlestown, pine shell, 27 feet long.

Thomas Daw, of New York, entered the Brooklyn Boy, mahogany shell, 27 feet long, built by James Mackay.

A. Whitman, Jr., of Boston, entered the Mignonne, 27 feet long, built by James Mackay, mahogany shell.

Thomas Doyle, of Boston, entered the Friendship, mahogany shell, 26 feet long, built by James Mackay.

Ward's "uniform" was a white shirt—Hanson's red shirt and red handkerchief—Wells', blue shirt and grey cap —Daw's, red shirt—Whitman's, white shirt and blue cap—Doyle's, white shirt and tri-color cap. The prizes were, two silk flags and $200 in gold for the winner, and $100 for the second man—$50 for the third. The judges were Stephen Roberts, Isaac Wood, Jr., R.M. Pratt, C.F. Shimmin, J.J. Storrow.

A little before ten, the men were pulling about, exchanging now and then a good humored defiance, and engaging in brief conversation, in which Doyle was particularly conspicuous. They all looked well, and in high condition, with the exception of

Daw, whose want of condition was evident to a practiced eye. Nevertheless, the re-
doubtable New Yorker looked cheerful and determined. The positions, assigned by lot,
were: Daw, outside, and close to the judges' boat—Wells, second—Doyle, third—
Whitman, fourth—Ward, fifth—Hancon, sixth, having the inside place, close on shore.
While the men come into line, let us pause awhile, and consider the nature of the contest.

The question, "who is the champion oarsman of the United States?" has been frequently asked of late—but no decisive answer could be given, and the reply has hitherto varied according to the different local or personal partialities of those who have
assumed to know. Many oarsmen had won a high reputation in their own immediate
neighborhood, and had zealous friends who were ready to back them at a moment's
notice against all competitors. But even the most redoutable oarsmen could hardly be
said to have a national reputation. There were, in fact, no national oarsmen: rowing was
not encouraged as a national sport. But with this year, things have changed, and rowing is evidently destined to take a high position among our American sports. Hitherto,
the prowess of our oarsmen has not been sufficiently tested to show who our best men
were, and even if we could select the best men, the training they underwent was by no
means what it should be. When the great race came off between New York and St.
John, everybody knew that the four men who rowed in the Mackay were not the best
four that New York could furnish. This was as well known among those who were
conversant with boating matters before the race as after. Now, things look better, and
if we have the champion crew of England here in the season of 1860, we may reason-
ably hope to meet them with a crew that shall fairly represent the United States, and
the chances of victory ought then to be even.

We have had a number of spirited races, to be sure—but the art is comparatively
young with us. Since the old Volant crew of Boston disbanded, there has been no crew
in the country that can row with the University crew of Harvard College. They were
defeated once by the Yale students, on account of an inferior boat and a heavy wind,
which drove them out of their course, while their adversaries' boat, being so much
lower in the water, was not troubled by the wind—and their time has been excelled by
some Western crews, who row a three mile course in time it would be as impossible
to verify as to repeat. But fairly tried, we believe the Harvard crew can beat anything
on the list. Now, anybody can see that this ought not to be so. They have a crew of
eight stout young men, who are carefully trained, and are admirable craftsmen. But if
the New York watermen would train assiduously and practise scientific rowing with the
same care, they could easily beat any crew of the students. They might not be better
trained, and they could not possibly row with more skill and precision, but they might
equal the Students in these respects, and in strength they would have an overwhelming superiority. In short, the professional oarsmen ought to always beat the best amateurs; as matters now stand, the best amateurs regularly beat the professionals. This
cannot long be so....

THE RACE

After a good deal of trouble, the men were got finely into line, and one of the
judges waved his hand, "are you all ready? Go!" Just before the word, Doyle took his
stroke, and then gained a trifle. No one, however, who knows anything of Tom Doyle,

supposes that he meant anything unfair. It is a hard business not to start in the excitement of the moment.

The start was very pretty, Doyle a little ahead, Daw, Wells, Whitman and Hancon well together, while Ward was behind, apparently not caring to hurry himself. When he did start, his stroke was long and slow, and although powerful, it left him far behind the desperate spurt of the others. Daw, as usual, drew ahead, and was nearly clear of the whole in a dozen strokes. Everybody was full of admiration at the excellence of the start, which was effected precisely five minutes and nine seconds after ten o'clock, A.M.

While Daw took the decided lead, and Ward trailed along slowly in the rear, Hancon was creeping up on the inside, and nearer the front than one would at first have thought. Whitman was well up, with a spendid stroke, while Doyle was pulling with a wonderful quickness and impetuosity, throwing his whole force into every effort, and gradually leading all his rivals. Wells now drifted out of his course in a singular manner, and rapidly fell behind the others. Daw, who pulls a quick stroke of great power, with queer twisting of the wrists in finishing his stroke (this peculiarity alone would enable any judge of rowing who had once seen him pull to tell Daw from the others) had now lost his lead, and Whitman took the start, leading magnificently, with Daw second and Doyle third—then Doyle second and Daw third, then Daw again second. After the first quarter of a mile, the "dark horse" had a decided advantage and Ward's backer declared "the race lay between Mr. Ward and Mr. Whitman." Ward was now gaining, hand over hand, on Hancon, who seemed to be slipping back to his adversary.

The race between Doyle and Daw was splendid, but the prodigiously quick stroke of the Boston man told gradually, and he slipped away from the New Yorker, and challenged Whitman for the lead. The two Boston men were now ahead of the whole, and straining every nerve for the victory. Again Doyle's quick stroke told and he took the lead of the field, with Whitman second and Ward third, Daw fourth, on the outside, Hancon behind, and Wells, as all had expected, last of all.

Unfortunately, by a singular turn, Whitman sprained his wrist, and of course fell off instantly in his rowing. Doyle now drew clear ahead, while Ward and Daw both passed Whitman, Daw pulling like a tiger ahead of the champion. Whitman's brilliant prospects were obscured at once, and although he rowed pluckily on, he was fast losing ground.

Doyle, who pulls always as if he were blind, made for the wrong side of the stake, still well ahead, while Daw came next, Ward third. In vain did his friends call to the unlucky Doyle that he was wrong—he tried to turn the wrong way. At last, Doyle heard the warning calls, and backed, and tried to turn the other way. Daw, who was not far behind, and now come up, and as Doyle backed directly athwart Daw's course, Daw backed water, with a fairness and promptitude generally admired, and prevented a foul. But meanwhile up came Joshua Ward, hand over hand, and slipped inside, rounding the stake first, and stretching for home. Doyle rounded next, and Doyle and Daw, although greatly disheartened by their unfortunate delay, pulled after Ward with desperate efforts. But the latter was not to be caught, his advantage was too great, nor in the steady, powerful champion, the man to lose a start he has once gained. Down came the boats beautifully, Doyle leaving Daw far behind and rowing so fiercely after Ward, that he seemed yet a dangerous opponent. Doyle gained, and gained, and gained—but the cool champion evidently had the race in hand, and rowed down well ahead, with the same long, steady stroke as at the first. A few vigorous strokes to close with, and Joshua Ward, still the champion, made his boat fly rapidly along, and crossed the line first, amid ringing cheers! Doyle came in next, ten seconds later. Daw came pulling slowly after that, closely followed by Hancon, who had easily passed the disabled Whitman. Both men were pulling in a heavy, discouraged way. Daw well ahead, and sure of the third prize, Hancon apparently exhausted. Whitman came in at his leisure, and Wells pulled in last, sooner than had been expected.

The time was as follows:

| Joshua Ward | 23:16 | Thomas Daw | 24:11 | A. Whitman | 24:48 |
| Thomas Doyle | 23:26 | John Hancon | 24:14 | M.F. Wells | 25:21 |

Doyle was prompt to congratulate Ward on his victory, and two braver fellows never shook hands than the two winners. The prizes were awarded without any complaint, and Ward modestly disclaimed any superiority over Doyle, who, on the other hand, frankly owned up to a fair defeat. Doyle also thanked Daw for his forbearance at the stake, and the gallant New Yorker returned his kind words with hearty good will. No man in boating circles has been more misrepresented than Mr. Daw, who is entitled to great credit for his whole conduct before and during the race. But for the delay at the stake, Daw would have been a prominent competitor for the championship. It should also be remembered that Daw has not been in good condition this year, having suffered from overtraining.

Ward is entitled to great credit for the gallant manner in which he won his victory, and the modesty and good sense with which he bore it. But he has been taught two things by the race. He has found that he cannot play with such antagonists as he had to day, and he may consider himself a very fortunate man that so steady and powerful a man as Whitman was disabled, and that Tom Doyle, by his inadvertance, threw both his own and Daw's chances away. Doyle is acknowledged by Ward to be the best man he ever tried. A match is now talked of between Ward and Doyle, when the claims of the latter may be satisfactorily adjusted. If it should come to anything, Ward will remain in Boston for the present. The second thing that Ward has learned is, that Boston miles are at least eight furlongs in length, which cannot be said of the miles in many other places. It is much easier to row five miles in New York than on Charles River, and Ward's average of seven minutes two seconds to the mile for *five miles,* may not, after all, be as good time as his average of seven minutes, forty-five seconds to the mile, for *three miles only,* on the 24th. If Ward and Doyle do have another trial, Daw may, perhaps, put in his claim as well. It is probable, however, that, barring all accidents, Ward is the best man, and this year, at all events, is not likely to deprive him of the laurels he has so worthily won.

RULES FOR BOATS AND BOAT RACING

On the eve of the Civil War in the United States boat racing was one of the most popular sports in many eastern cities. The harbors of New York City, Boston, Philadelphia, and many other large and smaller communities teemed with all kinds of crafts. Dozens of clubs sponsored regattas which attracted thousands of spectators. In order to instruct enthusiasts on the proper methods and procedures for establishing and maintaining boat clubs, the New York Clipper published a series of articles on aquatics in 1860. The selection reprinted below presents rules and regulations for races and guidelines for resolving disputes. It suggests that matches were keenly contested and controversies were commonplace. This piece first appeared in the issue of 5 May 1860, p. 20.

BOATS AND BOAT RACING

The rules which are to govern a race, and the course to be rowed over should be rendered as simple and described in as plain language as it is possible to do, and all parties should, before they go upon the course be perfectly conversant with their rights and restrictions, without having to depend upon the judges for instructions or explanations, at the last moment, as is too often the case. We have watched and studied the rules of racing for a long time both in England and in this country, and have finally arrived at the conclusion that the following are about as near the object desired as they could conveniently be brought, always subject of course to such alterations as may be required to suit different localities:

First.—No boat should be allowed to contend for a prize, unless regularly entered on or before some specific time previous to the taking place of this race.

Second.—Entrance fee should be paid at the time of entering as an earnest of the intention to put the boat in the race, and no boat should be allowed to re-claim the entrance fee on any pretence.

Third.—Time should be allowed as follows:—five seconds to the oar per mile; sculls against oars, the former to allow two and a half seconds per oar to the mile—calling the sculls, oars; skeleton single scull boats against barge built four or six oared boats, no time should be allowed; skeleton single scull boats against four, six or eight oared shell race boats, five seconds for each man over one up to the mile.

Fourth.—When a boat is challenged to row for any reasonable amount, she must meet the challenge, if she has no other on hand to be disposed of, as a refusal or silence would be justly taken as an acknowledgement of inferiority. It will not do for her to entrench herself behind the plea that the amount offered to be rowed for is too large, if reasonable, or too small if not absolutely ridiculous, because such an assumption would have very litlle weight in convincing the community that it was not a subterfuge. Neither does it matter how often a challenge is repeated by a defeated party, if offered in a proper spirit and with the intention of following it up, because it is reasonable to presume that the beaten boat will soonest get tired of seeking matches with a superior.

Fifth.—Choice of position should always be decided by lot, and the position of all the other boats in a regatta should be governed by the first—number two taking the place next to that selected by the boat having the first choice, number three next to number two, and so on.

Sixth.—The boats should start from a real or imaginary line, opposite the judges' boat, and return to the same point, or rather to a point on the said line, extending no further out from the boat in which the judges are stationed than the position occupied by the boat farthest away at the time of starting. It has frequently been decided that a boat reaching any point in a direct line with the starting place, without regard to the distance it may be from the judges, before either of her antagonists arrived at the judges' boat, was entitled to the race. We cannot but think that such decisions, when adopted as precedents, are entirely over estimated, because in many cases they would be very unjust. A boat might find it convenient and advantageous to drift or be blown off in an oblique direction a great distance from the place whence she took her departure, and with comparative ease reach a point on a line with it, while her competitor would be struggling against an adverse wind or current towards the stake-boat, and thereby lose the race under such a decision.

Seventh.—When boats foul, they should clear themselves as best they can without prejudice to either; but when a clear violation of justice, propriety, and common understanding in these matters is apparent, such as crossing or attempting to cross another boat's bows to prevent her from passing, designedly running into, interfering with, or impeding a boat when turning a stake or any other palpable annoyance or attempt to check the progress of a rival, should be held as disgraceful, and the guilty party should be immediately ruled out of the race; and equally disgraceful should it be on the part of the judge that if they refuse or neglect to take cognisance of such transgressions, and to punish the offenders.

Eighth.—No decision which judges may make should be binding or have any force, when such decisions are clearly in contravention of previously agreed upon rules; but all doubtful points or matters in dispute should be decided by the majority of the judges, and such decisions should be final.

Ninth.—Not less than three judges should be appointed, but if more are required the number should always be odd.

Tenth.—The judges should designate one of their number to start the boats, and the one so appointed should act in the capacity of chairman at all consultations, clothed with the powers granted by parliamentary usage.

Eleventh.—When the starter announces either by call or a signal gun that the boats must appear and make ready for a start, fifteen minutes may be allowed for preparation, at the end of which time the judges should have the power to rule out any boat which does not answer the signal.

Twelfth.—The coxswain of a boat should be considered her representative, but a boat's crew may appoint one of their number to represent them. On all questions of dispute, a crew should be allowed to be heard by counsel before the judges; and in no case should the judges refuse to take evidence or hear argument, before making their decision. A trial on the rendition of a decision may be postponed to some future day from that on which the race takes place.

Thirteenth.—When a boat is entered and the names of the men composing her crew recorded, neither the boat, her name, nor any member of her crew should be changed, without the consent of all the parties with whom she has to contend, except in cases of removal, sickness or death, or some unforeseen and uncontrollable circumstance which would render a change absolutely necessary.

Fourteenth.—All complaints should be made to the judges within fifteen minutes after the close of the race, and if none are offered at the expiration of that time, the judges should proceed to declare the winners.

STARTING

The best and probably the surest method of starting two boats in a match race, having in view the avoidance of collisions and fouling, would be to place the contestants one on each side of the judges' boat, and allow each to turn its own stake boat in opposite directions, the stakes being placed at such exact and equal distances as to preclude the possibility of any advantage being gained by either. By so doing, the boats would be most likely to keep themselves apart. At regattas where more than two boats are contending for the same prize, we cannot see that any improvement can be made upon the old style of starting, but the boats should be bound by the most stringent rules to keep away from each other as much as possible.

DECISIONS—A CHAPTER FOR JUDGES

Decisions are arbitrary when they do not fall directly under some general acknowledged or established rule, and when not based on a previously agreed upon compact. We can therefore lay down no general rule to be followed, except such as would naturally spring from the honest convictions of disinterested men. It is too often the case that judges are chosen with minds biased in favor of one party or the other and when a nice point presents itself for adjustment which will admit of cavil, they naturally lean to the side which previously elicited their sympathies, and often an unjust judgment is thus rendered. To avoid this feeling, judges might better be chosen from a community of strangers; but by this advice we do not mean that they should be unacquainted with the general rules of racing. They should on all occasions exercise the greatest caution, and bring to bear deep reflection and mature judgement on all cases where they are called upon to render decisions. They should not be actuated by fear nor influenced by favor, for this one reason, if no decision, although, perhaps of very little importance at the time, if wrongly settled, might be the means of producing an act of injustice, on some future occasion, where it might be held up as a precedent.

The rules under which the regatta or a race has been contested should in all cases be first consulted by the judges; and full force given to them. Doubts and differences will sometimes arise in regard to their interpretations on certain points, and questions thus arise for judges to determine. In such cases a liberal construction should be given, and the decisions rendered on the side which is the nearest to justice. Precedent may be taken into consideration, and have its due amount of weight, and facts should always have preference over the opinions of those who are to be affected by the result. If a rule is wantonly violated by a rower, or a boat's crew, it should always be considered sufficient cause to deprive the offender of the benefits which might otherwise accrue to him; and ignorance of the establishment of the rule should not be allowed to plead in extenuation of the offence, because such an excuse may be too easily rendered, and if it were not even so, the result to the party that might suffer by it would be the same. A rule may be unwittingly or unintentionally violated, which act in a moral point of view would be divested of its criminality, but if advantage is attained thereby, one party must suffer in consequence, and the advantage on the one side and the suffering on the other is precisely the same as though the act was committed by design. Therefore we say to judges, when called upon to decide upon palpable violations of rules, the motive should not be taken into consideration, when any degree of advantage has been gained by so doing.

MATCH RACES

Match races should be subject as far as they can be made applicable to the standing rules of some regatta club, but a private understanding should always be had, which should be written plainly and signed by the representatives of both parties, each party retaining a copy. The agreement should cover all points out of which any dispute might arise, and although it may be desirable to avoid the using of unnecessary and superfluous words, it is better to make it as explicit as it is possible to do so.

THE ORIGIN OF THE AMERICA'S CUP

The news of the victory of Commodore Stevens's yacht *America* in England in 1851 at the Royal Yacht Squadron's regatta produced a wave of excitement and nationalistic fervor in the United States. American sportsmen and journalists interpreted the triumph as another sign of the growing power and prestige of the young country. Many gloated over this latest example of Brother Jonathan humbling John Bull. When Stevens, his partners, and his crew returned to New York City they were honored at a special celebration given by the New York Yacht Club. After being introduced by J. Prescott Hall, Stevens recounted the race around the isle of Wight, and also *America*'s defeat of *Titania* in a separate challenge. In 1852 the syndicate that lauched *America* decided to offer the cup won in England as a prize for an international competition. After Stevens died on 10 June 1857 the letter authorizing the gift of the trophy to the New York Yacht Club was found among his papers. The deed to the cup was redated 8 July 1857, and a circular letter was sent to eighteen yacht clubs in seven foreign countries. The first selection below, reprinted from the New York Times, 3 October 1851, presents excerpts from the speeches made at the dinner of the New York Yacht Club that honored Stevens. It is followed by the circular letter announcing the competition for the America's Cup, reprinted from the Times, 25 July 1857.

DINNER OF THE NEW-YORK YACHT CLUB HONORING
JOHN C. STEVENS AND THE YACHT AMERICA

Gentlemen- But for the zeal, the energy, and perseverance of our gallant Commodore, this Club would never have come into existence, for he breathed into it the breath of life. And if there had been no New-York Yacht Club, then there had been no struggle for nautical superiority upon the British waters, and no triumph to bring us together upon this festive occasion. Born, almost upon the sea, Commodore Stevens has, from his youth, sported the waves. By degrees, he imparted his own taste to others- to others he cannot impart his own knowledge and power. That which, to the scientific, is the consummation of a noble art, is to him an amusement, and his pleasure is to struggle with the winds and waves, and overcome them by his skill. By his influence, this Club has been established, and upon it the nation has been pleased to bestow a legal existence. While our models are open to inspection, we are permitted to carry an ensign, which is to be respected, wherever our Eagle flies upon Atlantic or Pacific coasts. By law, we are authorized to carry, as our own, a flag nearly identical with that which has "braved the battle and the breeze," ever since we became a nation; and who will say, that under the charge of our gallant Commodore, one star has been dimmed, or one stripe stained or defaced? (Prolonged cheers.) We welcome you, sir, (turning to Commomdore Stevens) back to your native land. We welcome you and your companions to the fair scenes of your youth, to the fields of your manly years, and to the solace of kindred, friends, and countrymen.

I give you, gentlemen, as a sentiment

"Commodore John C. Stevens, and his distinguished associates, in the last voyage of the yacht America. They are welcome, ever welcome, to their native land."

This sentiment was received with great applause. Commodore Stevens then rose and made the following reply:...

You may perhaps have observed that my hair is somewhat grayer than it was when I last met you. I'll tell you how it happened- but I am trespassing on your good nature.

In coming from Havre, we were obliged by the darkness of the night and a thick fog, to anchor some five or six miles from Cowes. In the morning, early, the tide was against us, and it was a dead calm. At nine o'clock a gentle breeze sprang up, and with it came gliding down the *Laverock*, one of the newest and fastest cutters of her class. The news spread like lightning, that the Yankee clipper had arrived, and that the *Laverock* had gone down to show her the way up. The yachts and vessels in the harbor, the wharves, and windows of all the houses bordering on them, were filled with thousands of spectators, watching with eager eyes, the eventful trial they saw we could not escape; for the laverock stuck to us, evidently showing she had no intention of quitting us. We were loaded with extra sails, with beef and pork and bread enough for an East India voyage, and were some four or five inches too deep in the water. We got up our sails with heavy hearts- the wind had increased to a five or six knot breeze, and after waiting until we were ashamed to wait any longer, we let her go about two hundred yards ahead, and then start in her wake. I have seen and been engaged in many exciting trials at sea and on shore. I made the match with Eclipse against Sir Henry and had heavy sums, both for myself and for my friends, depending on the result. I saw Eclipse lose the first heat and four-fifths of the second, without feeling one-hundredth part of the responsibility and without suffering one-hundredth part of the fear and dread I felt at the thought of being beaten by the *Laverock* in this eventful trial. During the first five minutes not a sound was heard, save, perhaps, the beating of our anxious hearts, or the slight ripple of the water upon her sword-like stem. The captain was crouched down upon the floor of the cockpit, his seemingly unconscious hand upon the tiller, with his stern, unaltering gaze upon the vessel ahead. The men were motionless as statues, with their eager eyes fastened upon the *Laverock* with a fixedness and intensity that seemed almost unnatural. The pencil of an artist might, perhaps, convey the expression, but no words can describe it. It could not, nor did not, last long. We worked quickly and surely to windward of her wake. The crisis was past, and some dozen of deep-drawn sighs proved that the agony was over.

We came to anchor a quarter, or, perhaps, a third of a mile ahead, and twenty minutes after our anchor was down, Earl of Wilton and his family were on board to welcome and introduce us to his friends. To himself and family, to the Marquis of Anglenon and his son, Lord Alfred Paget; to Sir Bellingham Graham, and a host of other noblemen and gentlemen, were we indebted for a reception as hospitable and frank as ever were given to a prince or peasant. From the Queen herself, we received a mark of attention rarely accorded even to the highest among her own subjects: and I was given to understand that it was not only intended as a courtesy extended to myself and friends, but also as a proof of the estimation in which she held our country; thereby giving a significance to the compliment infinitely more acceptable and valuable. Long may the bonds of kindred affection and interest, that bind us together at present, remain unbroken! As a further proof of the feeling of the Government and the people towards us, I will mention the following act of kindness. We had the misfortune , the day of the race with the *Titania*, to knock off a part of our outer shoe. This rendered it necessary that we should haul her out, and we repaired to the government dock, at Portsmouth, for the purpose. On the instant the application was made, an order was issued by the Admiral to repair her in the shortest time possible. If you could have witnessed the vigor and good will exhibited, from the Admiral down to the humblest mechanic in the yard, you would, I am sure, have felt the obligation (rendered so doubly binding by the manner in which it was tendered,) as deeply and sincerely as ourselves, that any cause of quarrel should arise to separate two nations that want but to be better acquainted with each other's good qualities, to become and to remain fast friends. She was docked at 12 and finished by 8 o'clock the same evening. For this important service no remuneration, in any shape or way, would be listened to, the Admiral, in expressing the pleasure it gave him to do us a service, endeavoring to prevail upon us to believe the obligation altogether upon his side. I trust, with confidence, that if occasion should occur, this delicacy and feeling will be as promptly and as delicately reciprocated.

In the race with the *Titania*, I suspect -although I do not know the fact- that too much of her ballast was taken out. It gave her an advantage in going before the wind, but told very much against her returning. There was a steady breeze and a good sea running, and she fell so rapidly to leeward as to be hull down, and nearly out of sight. We beat her, according to the Secretary's report, three or four minutes going down, and some forty-eight or fifty minutes in returning, on a wind. In the race for the Queen's cup, there were I think, seventeen entries, most of which, I believe, started. In addition to them , there were seventy or eighty, or perhaps, one hundred, under weight, in and about the harbor; and such another sight no other country, save England , can furnish. Our directions from the sailing committee were simple and direct; we were to start from the flag ship at Cowes, keep the No Man's buoy on the starboard hand, and from thence make the best of our way round the island to the flag ship from which we started. We got off before the wind, and in the midst of a crowd that we could not get rid of for the first eight or nine miles; a fresh breeze then sprang up that soon cleared us from our hangers on, and sent us rapidly ahead of every yacht in the squadron. At the Needles there was not a yacht that started with us in sight, so that the answer said to have been given to a question from a high personage, of who was first? The *America.* Who was second? There is no *second*—was literally true. After passing the Needles, we were overtaken by the Royal steam yacht *Victoria and Albert*, with her majesty and her family on board, who had to come down to witness the trial of speed between the models adopted by the old world and those of the new. As the steamer slowly passed us, we had the gratification of tendering our homage to the Queen, after the fashion of her own people, by taking off our hats and dipping our flags. At this time the wind had fallen to a light breeze, and we did not arrive at the flag-ship until dark. I could not learn correctly at what time, or in what order the others arrived. The cup before you is the trophy of that day's victory. I promised, half jest and half earnest, when I parted with you, to bring it home to you. The performance of the promise is another exemplification of the truth of an old saw, "that what is oftentimes said in jest is sometimes done in earnest." I am requested, by the gentlemen owning this cup, to beg your acceptation of it as a testimony of their gratitude for the interest you have so keenly felt, and so often and kindly expressed in our welfare and success. I have but to regret that the late hour at which I made up my mind to attempt a reply, has put it out of my power to make it what it ought to be, (and, perhaps, but for that, what it might be,) more worthy of your acceptance. With your permission I will propose, as a toast,

"The health of the Earl of Wilton."

The Commodore's toast and speech were cheered enthusiastically. His admirable description of the intentness of expectation on board the *America*, on her first trial with the *Laverock*, spell-bound all listeners, and almost transformed them into statues to which he likened his crew. Each allusion in the address to the courtesy and manly fairplay of his competitors, during his stay at Cowes, and especially the liberal and prompt conduct of the Admiral of the station, in putting Her Majesty's dock and Workmen in requisition for repairing an accident to the *America*, called forth very marked expression of gratification.

Mr. George Talman, first Vice President, after some complimentary remarks upon the liberal courteous and manly reception given to our yacht in England and to her officers, proposed a toast—

"The Royal Yacht Squadron of England."

Here another explosion of enthusiasm, and the toast was cheered to the echo.

The President, after a few appropriate preliminary remarks proposed the health of "The President of the United States."

This was drank standing, and with all the honors. Commodore Stevens then said, he was sure to have the hearts of the whole company to the toast he was about to propose- that of the Sovereign of England, whose gracious visit to the *America* was not one of the least memorable incidents connected with the affair. He proposed

"Her Majesty the Queen of England."

The audience rose to their feet at once, and drank this toast with prolonged cheers....

Mr. Chas. A. Davis, second Vice-President, after calling attention to the name of the builder of the yacht America, Mr. George Steers, and referring to the remarkable skill and enterprise of our ship builders generally, offered this sentiment:

"The mechanics and artizans employed in the construction and outfit of the yacht America- by their science, skill and taste, they have added honor to this country."

No toast of the evening was more warmly received. When the applause had subsided, on a general call,

Moses H. Grinnell rose to return thanks in behalf of those of whose good qualities and rare skill he knew so much; there were others in the room who could do this better than himself, but being called upon he would not hold back from doing his part; he thought this a just compliment to our shipwrights, who had no superiors either in character, or fidelity, or skill, anywhere. Mr. Grinnell dwelt at considerable length, and with much earnestness, upon the benefits which our city and country had derived, and were always deriving, from this class of our citizens, and concluded his remarks with a toast to one of the most eminent among them,

Wm. H. Webb—Drank with great applause.

LETTER ANNOUNCING THE
COMPETITION FOR THE AMERICA'S CUP

The following circular has been addressed to the secretaries of the different Yacht Clubs:

New-York Yacht Club,

New-York, U.S.A., July 27, 1857.

Sir: I am directed to inform the members of your association, that the One Hundred Guinea Cup, won by the yacht America at Cowes, England, Aug., 22, 1851, at the Regatta of the Royal Yacht Squadron, as a prize offered to yachts of all nations, has been presented to the New-York Yacht Club, subject to the following conditions, viz.:

"Any organized Yacht Club of any foreign country shall be always entitled, through any one or more of its members, to claim the right of sailing a match for this Cup, with any yacht or other vessel, of not less than thirty or more than three hundred tons, measured by the Custom House rule of the country to which the vessel belongs.

The parties desiring to sail for the Cup may make any match with the Yacht Club in possession of the same that may be determined upon by mutual consent; but in the case of disagreement as to terms, the match shall be sailed over the usual course for the Annual Regatta of the Yacht Club in possession of the Cup, and subject to its rules and sailing regulations; the challenging party being bound to give six months notice in writing, fixing the day they wish to start- this notice to embrace the length, Custom House measurement, rig and name of the vessel.

It is to be distinctly understood that the Cup is to be the property of the Club, and not of the members thereof, or owners of the vessel winning the match, and that the condition of keeping it open to be sailed for by Yacht Clubs of all foreign countries, upon the terms above laid down, shall forever attach to it, thus making it perpetually a Challenge Cup for friendly competition between foreign countries."

The New-York Yacht Club, having accepted the gift, with the conditions above expressed, consider this a fitting occasion to present the subject to the Yacht Clubs of all nations, and invoke from them a spirited contest for the Championship, and trust that it may be the source of continued friendly strife between the institutions of this description throughout the world, and therefore request that this communication may be laid before your members at their earliest meeting, and earnestly invite a friendly competition for the possession of the prize, tendering to any gentlemen who may favor us with a visit, and who may enter into the contest, a liberal, hearty welcome, and the strictest fair play.

Respectfully, your obedient servant,

N. Bloodgood,
Secretary, New-York Yacht Club

CONSTITUTION OF THE NEW-YORK YACHT CLUB, 1857

Each year the New-York Yacht club published a pamphlet in which it presented its Constitution, a list of its members, a copy of an act of Congress authorizing the licensing of yacht clubs, and a uniform and dress code. During the decade of the 1850s its membership increased from 157 to about three times that number. The following document outlines the strict rules that governed both the maintenance and the competition of the yachts. The edition of 1857 that appears below incorporates revisions of the club's original laws as they were first drafted in 1844. It is reproduced from the *Rules and Regulations of the New-York Yacht Club* (New York, 1857), pp. 23-39.

CONSTITUTION

I.

The officers of the New-York Yacht Club shall consist of a Commodore, a Vice-Commodore, a Secretary, a Treasurer and a Measurer.

II.

Any person shall be eligible to be elected a Member.

III.

The Secretary of the Navy, the Commodore of the Station and the Commander of the Navy Yard at Brooklyn, shall be *ex officio* Honorary Members. Officers of the Army and Navy, and of the Revenue Service, and Consuls, American or Foreign, and Officers of Foreign Yacht Clubs, and Members of such Clubs who may visit New-York with their Yachts, and shall be approved of at a general or special meeting, shall be eligible as Honorary Members.

IV.

Each candidate for admission must be proposed and seconded in writing; the name and address of the candidate, with the names of the members proposing and seconding him, must be sent to the Secretary. Members shall be elected by ballot. A quorum to consist of representatives from five Yachts, and two black balls shall defeat an election.

V.

Each member, on his election, shall pay the sum of twenty dollars, which will include his dues for the current year. Each subsequent annual payment to be ten dollars, and to become due at the first general meeting in each year. Foreigners, Members of Yacht Clubs in their own country, and not residing in the United States, shall be exempt from all payments, except the first, of twenty dollars. If any member shall allow his dues to remain unpaid for two years in succession, he shall be considered—unless he be absent from the United States—as having tendered his resignation, which may be accepted at any general meeting. Members who are absent from the United States for the whole fiscal year, commencing on the first Wednesday of February, shall be exempt from their dues for such year.

VI.

There shall be four General Meetings in each year. The first on the first Thursday of February, in the City of New-York; the others at the Club House on the first Thursday of May, the second Thursday of July, and the second Thursday of October.

VII.

The Annual election of Officers shall take place at the first general meeting in each year. Vacancies may be filled at any general meeting.

VIII.

Special meetings may be called by the Commodore at his pleasure; and he shall call a special meeting whenever requested to do so by three representatives of Yachts. Notice shall be sent to all representatives of Yachts of such special meetings, and of the purpose for which they are called; and the business of any special meeting shall be strictly confined to the purposes for which it was called.

IX.

All voting to be by representatives of Yachts; each Yacht to be entitled to one vote. A yacht to be represented by its owner, or by any one its owners, (if there be more than one,) or by any member who has a written authority from the owner or owners to represent the same. No yacht shall be represented unless she has been launched and a certificate signed by the Measurer, filed with the Secretary, specifying her tonnage and rig; and no representation shall be admitted upon any Yacht not now represented in the Club, smaller than twenty-five tons, and no other than full decked vessels, reasonable cockpits excepted.

X.

No Yacht shall be represented in the Club, unless by her design and construction she is well suited to accompany the Squadron in a cruise, and the Measurer shall withhold his certificate from any Yacht which may not, in his opinion, be suited to meet this requirement. The owner of the Yacht, however, may appeal from such decision, to the Club, and if the appeal is sustained, the Measurer will then furnish the necessary certificate.

XI.

Yachts shall be divided into three classes:

The first class, to contain those carrying 3,300 square feet of sail and upwards.

The second class, those carrying 2,300 and upwards, but less than 3,300 square feet.

The third class, those carrying less than 2,300 square feet.

For the purpose of this classification, all sails are to be excluded except the mainsail and jib of sloops, and the mainsail, foresail, and jib of schooners.

XII.

The distinguishing signal of the Club shall be a pointed burgee, its width being two-thirds of its length; the device, a white five-pointed star in the centre of two red stripes; they being in width one-fifth of that of the signal, one running lengthwise through it, in the middle, the other running crosswise through it, in the middle, the other running crosswise through it, at one-third of the length of the signal from its head—all on a blue field.

XIII.

The Commodore, when afloat, will wear a broad pendant, with a foul anchor encircled by thirteen five-pointed stars in white, on a blue field; and the Vice-Commodore will wear a broad pendant, with a similar device on a red field.

XIV.

All yachts when in service shall hoist their signal flag and ensign at 8 o'clock A. M. of each day, and haul them down at sunset. When sailing, the ensign may or may not be set, at the option of the Captain; and when a Yacht is away from the harbor of New-York or Long Island Sound, she shall hoist the signal of the Club in lieu of her signal flag.

XV.

Each Yacht is required to have a set of such signals as may be ordered by the Club; also a distinguishing signal flag, and to show it when signalled by another Yacht. The flag of each Yacht to be one inch in length for each foot of length of deck; width, two-thirds of length.

XVI.

Whenever any Yacht shall join the Commodore at an anchorage, the Captain shall report his arrival; and whenever a Captain shall desire to part company with the Commodore, or to leave the Squadron, he shall report his wish to the Commodore or senior officer in command.

XVII.

When the Yachts are upon a cruise, the Commodore shall appoint a flag-officer, whose duty it shall be to communicate in his behalf with the officers and members of the Squadron.

XVIII.

Each Yacht, at the general meeting in July, shall be designated by the Measurer with a number, in the direct order of which she shall, when in Squadron, get under way or enter a port, when so directed by the Commodore or senior officer in command.

XIX.

There shall be an annual Regatta for Prizes to be given by the Club. The Regatta shall commence on the first Thursday in June. There shall be an annual expedition of the Squadron, the time to be decided by a majority of the representatives of Yachts present at the general meeting in July.

XX.

At the first general meeting in each year a Committee of three members, not being owners of Yachts, shall be appointed to make arrangements for and direct the annual Regatta. Vacancies occurring thereafter may be filled at a general or special meeting.

XXI.

Owners of Yachts, proposing to enter for any Regatta, shall give notice in writing to the Measurer, specifying the time and place, when and where their Yacht's sails may be measured; such time to be not less than twenty-four hours after the delivery of said notice, and during the ten days next preceding the limited time for entry, and such place some convenient part of the New-York harbor.

Upon such measurement, the Measurer shall receive such reasonable aid as he may require from the crew of the Yacht measured.

Sails havng been once measured need not be remeasured, except upon the written request of a Yacht-owner or of the Regatta Committee.

XXII.

No member shall be interested in more than one Yacht entered for a Regatta.

XXIII.

Every Yacht entering for a prize, as well as the spars, sails, boats, &c., must be bona fide the property of one or more members of the Club.

XXIV.

No Yacht shall be allowed to start for a prize until the dues for the year, of the member or members representing her, have been paid.

XXV.

A statement containing the name of each Yacht and the name of the owner or owners, (all of whom must be members of the Club,) the rig, dimensions and tonnage, as computed by the Measurer, in accordance with the laws of the United States, shall be filed with the Secretary, before such Yacht can be entered for a Regatta.

XXVI.

Time shall be allowed for sails by their areas.

XXVII.

A true model of each Yacht shall be deposited with the Secretary before she can enter for any Regatta. The model shall be the property of the Club, and retained in its possession, and no person other than a United States Naval Constructor shall be permitted to copy it, except he shall have obtained written authority from the owner or builder of the Yacht.

XXVIII.

On the day prior to a Regatta, the Measurer shall make a return in writing to the Secretary of the Club, specifying the names of the Yachts, the sails of which he has measured, and the square contents, in feet and decimals, of each sail. The return shall be filed with the Secretary, and no Yacht, the sails of which have not been measured and returned, shall be allowed to enter any Regatta.

XXIX.

No change in the dimensions of sails shall be made between the time of measurement and the conclusion of a Regatta, except by reefing; and no sail shall be set during a Regatta which has not been measured and returned by the Measurer.

XXX.

There shall be no restriction on duly measured sails carried by Yachts contending for prizes.

XXXI.

No entry for any Regatta shall be received within forty-eight hours before the hour of starting; all entries to be made in writing, and delivered to the Secretary of the Club.

XXXII.

One second per square foot shall be allowed by Yachts of the first class for difference in the area of sails. One second and a quarter shall be allowed in the second class; and one second and a half in the third class.

This allowance shall be based upon the mainsail and jib of sloops, and the mainsail, forsail and jib of schooners, and upon any other duly measured and returned sails actually set at any time during a race. As between sloops and schooners, this allowance shall be based upon nine-tenths of the areas of the schooners's sails.

XXXIII.

Yachts contending for prizes shall be allowed to carry men as follows:
1st. Class. One for every four tons of her measurement.
2d. Class. One for every three and a half tons of her measurement.
3d. Class. One for every three tons of her measurment.

XXXIV.

Every Yacht under fifty tons shall carry, during a Regatta, a serviceable boat not less than ten feet in length; and Yachts over fifty tons shall carry one not less than twelve feet in length.

XXXV.

If any objection be made with regard to the classification, sailing or sails of any Yacht in a race, such objection must be made in writing to the Regatta Committee before ten o'clock of the next day after the Regatta.

XXXVI.

A competent person shall be placed by the Regatta Committee on board each station vessel, to make observations.

XXXVII.

There shall be a Member of the Club on board each Yacht sailing for a prize.

XXXVIII.

Nothing but a hand lead and line to be used in sounding during a Regatta.

XXXIX.

A Yacht touching any mark, boat, or buoy, used to mark out the course, shall forfeit all claim to the prize, unless as in case specified in the forty-fourth Rule.

XL.

Any Yacht achoring during a race, shall forfeit her claim to the prize, provided it shall be won upon that day.

XLI.

All Yachts, during a Regatta, to keep their floors down and bulkheads standing. No starting or taking in water or ballast permitted within forty-eight hours of the time named for starting, nor any trimming by dead weight allowed.

XLII.

Yachts on the port tack must invariably give way to those on the starborad tack; and in all cases where a doubt of the possibility of the Yacht on the port tack weathering the one of the starboard tack shall exist, the Yacht on the port tack shall give way; or, if the other Yacht keep her course and run into her, the owner of the Yacht on the port tack, not complying with this rule, shall be compelled to pay all the damages that may occur, and forfeit his claim to the prize.

XLIII.

Any Yacht bearing away or altering her course to *leeward*, and thereby compelling another Yacht to bear away to avoid collision, shall forfeit all claim to the prize, and pay all damages that may ensue, unless when two Yachts are approaching the windward shore, a buoy or stake boat together with a free wind, and so close to each other that the weathermost cannot bear away clear of the leewardmost, and by standing further on would be in danger of running on shore, or touching a buoy or stake boat, then such leewardmost Yacht, on being requested to bear away, is immediately to comply, and will forfeit all claim to the prize for not doing so. The weathermost Yacht must, however, bear away as soon as the one she hails, if she can do so, without coming into contact.

XLIV.

When rounding a mark, boat or buoy, the Yacht nearest thereto is to be considered the headmost Yacht; and should any other Yacht in the race compel the Yacht which is nearest to any mark, boat, or buoy, to touch said mark, boat, or buoy, the Yacht so compelling her shall forfeit all claim to the prize, her owner shall pay for all damages that may occur, and the Yacht so compelled to touch a mark, boat, or buoy shall not suffer any penalty for such contact.

XLV.

Yachts going free, must invariably give way for those by the wind, on either tack.

XLVI.

When two Yachts (by the wind) are approaching the shore, a buoy or stake boat together, and so close to each other that the leewardmost cannot tack clear of the weathermost, and by standing further on would be in danger of running onshore, or touching a buoy or stake boat, such weathermost Yacht, on being requested to put about, is immediately to comply, and will forfeit all claim to a prize for not doing so. The leewardmost Yacht must, however, tack at the same time as the one she hails, if she can do so without coming into contact.

XLVII.

In case the distance assigned for the race shall not have been performed in ten hours, the Regatta to be repeated from day to day. If any Yacht shall perform the distance in ten hours, the race shall be considered made, and the prize or prizes awarded.

XLVIII.

The Regatta Committee shall have full power to decide all questions that may arise in the sailing of the Regatta, and also to exclude all Yachts which by their decision have violated any rule of the Club. There shall be no appeal from the decision of this Committee.

XLIX.

It shall be the duty of the Measurer to measure the sails of all Yachts.

L.

The Measurer shall receive from the Treasurer of the Club ten dollars for the first measurement of any Yacht's sails, and five dollars for any re-measurement.

LI.

The sailing ground for prizes shall be from the anchorage at the Elysian Fields, Hoboken, to the buoy at the Southwest Spit and back; also, from Robins' Reef Light, around the light-ship off Sandy Hook and back; subject, however, to the rules and regulations of the Regatta Committee.

LII.

An [sic] Uniform* and Dress shall be adopted by the Club, and worn by the members of the Club and crews of Yachts when cruising.

LIII.

No amendment of the Constitution passed at any general or special meeting shall be valid until approved of at a subsequent general meeting.

*The Club Buttons can be obtained upon application to the Measurer.

Chapter 3

BASEBALL

During the 1840s and 1850s North Americans played a variety of bat and ball games that were earlier versions of modern baseball. In Canada a form of the pastime was popular in Ontario, where it may have been introduced by immigrants from the United States. Below the border the sport was a favorite amusement for youngsters and a few adults, especially in New England and the middle states. These years witnessed a competition among these types of games which resulted in the triumph of the rules and style of play developed in the New York City metropolitan area.

On 30 December 1907 Abraham G. Mills, a former president of professional baseball's National League, issued the final report of the special commission that had been charged with deciding the true origins of America's national pastime. His task was to determine whether baseball derived from the English schoolyard game of rounders or whether it was a purely native product. Henry Chadwick, a prominent sportswriter for fifty years who was known in many quarters as the "father of baseball," argued for the rounders theory, which prevailed before the 1880s. He had played the game as a boy in England before he emigrated to the United States. After a half century of watching and promoting the rise of baseball, he was convinced that rounders and the young American sport were related because they shared essential principles and were close in fundamental structure.

Albert G. Spalding, an American-born baseball star and sporting goods magnate, countered Chadwick's view, declaring that baseball was "of purely American origins and no other game or country has any right to claim its parentage." He recognized that rounders and baseball shared certain features, but he stressed the many differences in rules. Spalding believed that rounders was closer to cricket than to baseball, that it was never played in the United States, and that any similarity between rounders and the American national pastime was simply a coincidence. A patriot at heart, he could not believe that in 1840 "our national prejudices would permit us to look with favor, much less adopt any sport or game of an English flavor."

Spalding was certain that baseball descended from the colonial game of "old cat" in which a player batted a ball and ran to one or more bases. According to him, "old cat" evolved into the townball matches that were popular on village holidays in many early nineteenth-century American communities, and modern baseball was simply a modification of townball. Endorsing the testimony of Abner Graves, who credited Abner Doubleday with the invention of the modern rules of baseball at Cooperstown, New York in 1839, Spalding admitted: "It certainly appeals to an American's pride to have had the great national game of Baseball created and named by a Major General in the United States Army."

The Mills Commission also weighed evidence concerning the founding of New York's Knickerbocker Base Ball Club in 1842 and its first written rules of 1845. John

M. Ward, a star player for the Providence Grays and the New York Giants during the late nineteenth century, informed Spalding that several prominent Manhattan business and professional men had turned to the boys' game of baseball for exercise. Spalding forwarded Ward's letter to the commission, which also considered a statement by Duncan Curry, an original Knickerbocker, who testified that "a diagram, showing the field laid out substantially as it is today, was brought to the field one afternoon by a Mr. Wadsworth."

In the end, Mills himself chose among Chadwick's case for rounders, Spalding's and Graves's argument for Doubleday perfecting townball, and the Knickerbocker claim for their New York City version. Mills endorsed Graves's story, while noting that it was possible to link the Doubleday and Knickerbocker diagrams of 1839 and 1845. He concluded: "First, that 'Base Ball' had its origins in the United States. Second, that the first scheme for playing it, according to the best evidence obtained to date, was devised by Abner Doubleday at Cooperstown, N. Y., in 1839."

Many scholars have debunked the Doubleday-Cooperstown myth, which nonetheless remains powerful in the American imagination due to the efforts of Major League Baseball and the Hall of Fame in Cooperstown. For the record, one must acknowledge that research has proven that Abner Doubleday enrolled as a cadet at West Point in the fall of 1838 and possibly never even visited Cooperstown. Although he may have played ball with Graves during his boyhood, in his published writings he never mentioned anything about his role in the creation of modern baseball. Furthermore, Mills had known Doubleday ever since their service in the Civil War, but his friend apparently had never told him about his notable brainstorm in Cooperstown. Finally, Mills's verdict rested entirely on an old man's recollection of an event that had occurred sixty-eight years earlier. Graves's mental capacity at the time of his testimony is also suspect. A few years after he wrote to Spalding he shot his wife and was committed to an institution.

If Abner Doubldeday did not invent baseball, then who did? The answer is that no single individual created the sport; rather, it evolved in stages from earlier bat and ball games. Historians today believe that Chadwick was correct in linking baseball to English rounders. Townball seems to have been an Americanized variation of rounders, and both probably developed as team versions of the traditional game of "old cat." Strictly speaking, modern baseball is a refined, United States variety of townball and therefore is certainly an indigeneous sport. While its ancestry is English, its essence is clearly American. Thus a distinctly American process of modernization changed a traditional folk game into a mid- and late nineteenth-century sport. This transformation began in Philadelphia, Boston, and New York City during the period 1830-1860, as each of these cities developed a form of baseball. During the 1850s these types competed for dominance throughout the United States, and by the Civil War the New York City variety had established itself in most parts of the nation.

A few young sportsmen began a new era of Philadelphia ball playing in 1831, when they crossed the Delaware River for regular contests of "two old cat" at Camden, New Jersey. Before long they had recruited enough players for Saturday afternoon townball. These ball players competed on public grounds, where neither rent nor permission was required, and made their own bats and balls. After another group of townball enthusiasts joined them in 1833, the two formally merged and organized the Olympic Ball

Club, drawing up a constitution and field rules to govern their play. Townball remained popular through the late 1850s in the Philadelphia area, with several clubs in Camden and Germantown joining the Olympics, Excelsiors, and Athletics of that city. There is some evidence that emigrants from the City of Brotherly Love carried their sport to Cincinnati, Ohio and neighboring towns in northern Kentucky, where townball flourished before the Civil War.

New England varieties of townball were called "base" or "roundball." The pastime that became widely known as the "Massachusetts game" matched sides of eight to fifteen men on a square field with bases or tall stakes (up to five feet high) at each corner. The batter stood midway between first and fourth (home) base and tried to hit a ball consisting of yarn tightly wound round a lump of cork or rubber, and covered with smooth calfskin. The round bat varied from three to three and a half feet in length and was often a portion of a rake or pitchfork handle wielded generally in one hand. The pitcher threw the ball swiftly overhand. The batter could strike the ball in any direction, there being no foul territory. After hitting the ball, the striker ran around the bases until he was put out or remained safely on a base. He could be retired if the catcher caught three missed balls, or if a hit ball was caught on the fly, or if he was struck with a thrown ball while running the bases (called "soaking" or "burning" the runner.) Usually one out ended the inning, and the first team to score a fixed number of runs won the game.

The first modern baseball organization in Massachusetts was the Olympic Club of Boston, whose members began play in 1854, formally established the club in 1856, and published rules and regulations in 1857. That year brought many spirited intraclub games and matches against newly formed clubs on Boston Common. In late June about 2000 spectators attended the informal Massachusetts championship between the Olympics and the Wassapoag Ball Club of Sharon. Each team had twelve men to a side, twenty-five runs were needed to win a game, and three victories decided the match. Wassapaog defeated the Olympics but then lost to the Unions of Medway. A dispute over rules cancelled the return contest and eventually led to the Massachusetts Baseball Convention, called for Dedham in May 1858, which created the Massachusetts Association of Base Ball Players. Its "Constitution, By-Laws, and Rules and Regulations" appear below.

The convention's labors bore fruit, for during the years remaining before the Civil War the "Massachusetts game" flourished. Proof of the baseball fever sweeping New England was evident in a match played in September 1859 for the Massachusetts state championship between the Unions of Medway and the Winthrops of Holliston. Several railroads issued excursion tickets to Boston's Agricultural Fair Grounds, where a large crowd bet heavily on the two-day encounter, won by the Unions, 100-71. In 1860 seventy-five clubs played by the rules of the Massachusetts Association of Base Ball Players, and half of them were members of that organization.

A variation on Massachusetts townball was popular in southwestern Ontario during this period. The "Canadian game" differed from the New England form in two ways. First, there was generally a rule that distinguished fair from foul territory for balls struck by the batter. Secondly, the batsman usually stood at or near the fourth base (home). Both of these features were also central to the New York City version. But the

"Canadian game" shared much in common with the Yankee style of play, including the square layout for the bases and similar rules for retiring batters and ending innings.

While the Massachusetts form of baseball thrived during the late 1850s, it faced a formidable rival in the New York City version, which mushroomed in popularity during these years. Modern baseball derives most immediately from the sport created by the New York Knickerbockers during the mid-1840s. Some baseball historians believe that Alexander J. Cartwright was the man who first suggested that the Knickerbockers try a diamond instead of a square for the bases, with the batter standing at home plate. It is more certain that he was the chief organizer of the club and the man responsible for the codification of its first rules—namely, that the ball had to be pitched underhand, not thrown; that a ball knocked outside the range of first or third base was foul; and that a player was out if a hit ball was caught on the fly or first bounce, or if a fielder held the ball on a base before the runner arrived, or if, between bases, a fielder touched the runner with the ball. "Soaking" the runner was prohibited, three outs retired the side, and twenty-one aces (runs) decided the game, provided each side had an equal number of outs. The Knickerbockers played intraclub games in the Murray Hill section of Manhattan, then moved to the Elysian Fields of Hoboken, New Jersey in 1846. Reprinted below is an 1845 newspaper account of an early match between another New York City club and a Brooklyn team in which at least a few of the Knickerbocker regulations governed play. Following that piece is an 1855 edition of the Knickerbocker rules.

The Knickerbocker version spread very slowly until the late 1850s, when a veritable baseball mania swept across the greater New York City region. More than two hundred junior and senior clubs sprang into action in Brooklyn, Queens, Manhattan, Westchester, and northern New Jersey. The New York game then conquered the Northeast and parts of the South and West because of several factors. These were the personal mobility of players, intercity competition and feature events, newspaper publicity provided by such sporting periodicals as the New York Clipper, Porter's Spirit of the Times, and Wilkes's Spirit of the Times, and the work of the annual New York City baseball conventions.

Individuals, clubs, and the press all gave the New York style of baseball a big boost during the 1850s, but perhaps the key event in the sport's early modernization was the founding in 1857 of its first centralized governing body—the National Association of Base Ball Players (NABBP). Located in New York City, the group's self-designation as a *national* association indicated ambitious designs. Although only clubs from the New York City vicinity were represented, the aim was to rule the continent. Its officers did work to increase membership, and the NABBP grew from 14 clubs in 1857 to 74 as of early 1861. The last two meetings before the Civil War drew delegates from Boston, New Haven, Philadelphia, Baltimore, Washington, D.C., and Detroit. In the long run, the most important work of these annual gatherings involved rule revisions. Included here is the 1858 edition of the NABBP's "Constitution, Bylaws, and Rules and Regulations of Base Ball."

During the late 1850s New Yorkers and Brooklynites taught the rules of their game to friends in neighboring towns and distant cities. All-star contests and championship challenges stirred great excitement. The summer of 1858 brought a showcase presentation of the "New York game" when select nines from Manhattan and Brooklyn met on the diamond. An account of the first contest in this three game series appears below. The next year witnessed another great event for the ball playing fraternity—the visit of the All-England cricket team to North America. The tour of the famed British athletes drew attention to the status of England's national game in the United States and Canada (See Chapter 6). It also highlighted the competition between the two pastimes. "Cricket and Base Ball" presents the New York Herald's description of both sports and its views on their relative prospects for popularity in the United States. In 1860 a series of trips by the Brooklyn Excelsiors promoted the New York version of baseball in upstate New York, Baltimore, and Philadelphia. That year the three-game match between the Excelsiors and the Brooklyn Atlantics became the feature attraction of early baseball. The final document in this chapter presents a summary of the action in the dramatic and controversial final game of this series, along with editorial commentary from the New York Times and the New York Clipper.

By 1860 a few clubs in Canada, New England, the Philadelphia region, and the southern and western United States had switched to the New York rules, but variations of townball or the "Massachusetts game" remained the sportsmen's favorite form of ball play in those areas. But during and after the war the New York style of baseball defeated its rival and became the national pastime. Why did the "New York game" prevail? One answer is simple: both spectators and players favored its rules. To a modern eye, the New York version seems more efficient and appealing, especially considering the symmetry of the diamond compared to the townball square. The containment of play by foul lines permitted spectators to crowd closer to the action and reduced the ground the fielders had to cover. Furthermore, the NABBP game was undoubtedly safer, simpler, and easier for adults to learn and master. Older players may have preferred the force and tag rules for putouts, instead of the townball custom of throwing (or "burning") the ball at the runners. James D'Wolf Lovett was a prominent New England writer who remembered in *Old Boston Boys and the Games they Played* that he preferred the "New York game" because "The pitching, instead of swift throwing, looked easy to hit, and the pitcher stood off so far, and then there was no danger of getting plugged with the ball while running bases; and the ball was so lively and could be batted so far!" Three outs to a side also seemed to be an improvement over the New England custom of "one-out, all-out," permitting more action, more base runners, and hence more tension and drama. Nine innings brought the game to a conclusion within three hours, whereas many Massachusetts matches failed to reach the deciding one hundred runs before nightfall. Yet the latter game had its good points and excitement, such as overhand pitching and the fly rule, later adopted by the NABBP and its successors. Rule differences thus provide only part of the reason why the "New York game" won out over its rivals.

A better explanation may be found in the "urban imperialism" of the great city on the Hudson. During the middle decades of the nineteenth century New York City extended its economic influence throughout the nation via its monumental transportation network of canals, railroads, and steamships. New York traders and bankers were active in attracting business toward their home city, and in doing so they established contacts with many strangers who came under their influence. At the same time the city was becoming a cultural center and a major rival to Boston as a leading literary and communications headquarters. Its sporting weeklies, as previously emphasized, also played a significant role in promoting New York baseball. Wherever New York businessmen and newspapers appeared, they carried with them their local sport. Thus, just as New York was defeating its major trade rivals and strengthening its position as the largest and most powerful city in the United States, it was also exporting and promoting its native sport as the American national pastime — an entertaining product that it marketed extremely well. Even Boston came under New York's influence as it fell further behind in population and commercial clout. The "Masachusetts game" was not as attractive and could not compete with the game from Gotham.

EARLY BASEBALL

Alexander Cartwright and his ball-playing friends formally organized the Knickerbocker Base Ball Club in September 1845. Their first act was to adopt the rules that they had devised earlier that year. The Knickerbockers scheduled intraclub practice games that fall on their old field in the Murray Hill section of the East Side of Manhattan and on their new grounds at the Elysian Fields of Hoboken, New Jersey. At that time there were several other nines that played baseball in New York City and its vicinity, including an outfit known as the New York Club. In October and November the New York Club won two contests against a group of Brooklyn cricketers who were clearly novices at the American pastime. Newspaper accounts of those matches suggest that the participants used at least some of the Knickerbocker regulations. The New York Club trounced the Knickerbockers 23-1 at Hoboken in June 1846 in the latter team's first interclub contest. The following newspaper account of a match between the New York Club and the Brooklyn squad is from the New York Morning News, 22 October 1845. The Knickerbocker rules are reprinted from the Spirit of the Times, 12 May 1855, p. 147.

BASE BALL MATCH, 1845

A friendly match of the time-honored game of Base was played yesterday at the Elysian Fields, Hoboken, between eight members of the New York Ball Club and the same number of players from Brooklyn. A cold wind from the North made the day somewhat unpleasant for the spectators, yet a large number, among whom we noticed several ladies, assembled to witness the sport. Play was called at 3 o'clock, P.M. Umpires — Messrs. Johnson, Wheaton and Chase. The toss was won by the Brooklyn players, who decided in favor of giving their antagonists the first innings, and accordingly Hunt took up the bat, and the game commenced. The match was for the first twenty-one aces — three out, all out. Hunt made a single ace, but before another was added to the score, three of the New Yorkers went out in rapid succession, and the bats were yielded to Brooklyn. Many of the Brooklyn players were eminent cricketers, but the severe tactics of the N. Y. Club proved too effective, and they soon resigned their innings to their opponents, not scoring one.

New York now took her second chance, and the score began slowly to tell. During this innings, four aces were made off a single hit, but by the arbitrary nature of the game, a single mistake sometimes proving fatally irretrievable, they were soon driven to the field again. The second innings of the Brooklyn players proved alike disastrous, and the close of the third still left them, all their tickets blank. On the fourth innings the New York Club made up their score to twenty-four aces. The Brooklyn players then took their fourth, against hopeless odds, but with undiminished spirits. They were, however, forced to yield with a score of four only, and the New Yorkers were declared winners with a spare three and a flush of twenty. The fielding of the Brooklyn players was, for the most part, beautiful, but they were evidently not so well practiced in the game as their opponents.

The following abstract shows the aggregate of the four innings:

NEW YORK BALL CLUB.

	Runs.	Hands out.		Runs.	Hands out.
Davis	5		Case.	2	2
Tucker	2	3	Vail	3	1
Miller	4	1	Kline	2	3
Winslow	4	2		—	—
Murphy	2			24	12

BROOKLYN PLAYERS.

	Runs.	Hands out.		Runs.	Hands out.
Hunt		2	Sharp		1
Gilmore	1	2	Whaley	1	1
Hardy	1	2	Ayres		1
Forman	1	2		—	—
Hine		1		4	12

At the conclusion of the match, both parties sat down to a dinner prepared by McCarty in his best style; and the good feeling and hilarity that prevailed, showed that the Brooklyn players, though defeated, were not disheartened. A return match will be played on Friday next, commencing at 1 o'clock P.M., on the grounds of the Brooklyn Star Club, Myrtle avenue. Those who would witness genuine sport, should improve the opportunity.

THE KNICKERBOCKER RULES

RULE 1. The bases shall be from "Home" to second base 42 paces; and from first to third base 42 paces, equi-distant; and from "Home" to pitcher not less than 15 paces; i. e. 21 paces from the centre of the field to each base.

2. The game to consist of 21 counts or aces, but at the conclusion an equal number of hands must be played.

3. The ball must be pitched, not thrown for the bat.

4. A ball knocked outside the range of the first or third base is foul. (Range from Home, *i. e.,* the ball must be knocked down the field and not sideways. The striker's stand is at the Home Base.)

5. Three balls being struck at and missed, and the last one caught, is a hand out; if not caught, is considered fair, and the striker bound to run. Tips and foul balls do not count.

6. A ball being struck or tipped, and caught either flying or on the first bound, is a hand out.

7. A player must make his first base after striking a fair ball, but should the ball be in the hands of an adversary on the first base before the runner reaches that base, it is a hand out; the ball must be fairly in hand, and the base touched.

8. Players must make the bases in their order of striking, and when a fair ball is struck and striker not put out, the first base must be vacant, as well as the next base or bases, if similarly occupied. Players may be put out under these circumstances in the same manner as when running to the first base.

9. A player shall be out if at any time when off a base he shall be touched by the ball in the hands of an adversary. The ball must be held after the man is touched, if the ball drops it is not a hand out.

10. A player who shall intentionally prevent an adversary from catching or getting a ball is a hand out.

11. If two hands are already out, a player running home at the time a ball is struck cannot make an ace if the striker is caught out.

12. Three hands out, all out.

13. Players must take their strike in regular rotation, and after the first round is played, the turn commences at the player who stands on the list next to the one who lost the third hand.

14. No ace or base can be made on a foul strike.

15. A runner cannot be put out in making one base, when a balk is made by the pitcher.

16. But one base allowed if the ball, when struck, bounds out of the field.

17. The ball shall weigh from 5 1/2 to 6 ounces, and be from 2 3/4 to 3 1/4 inches in diameter.

THE MASSACHUSETTS GAME

On May 18, 1858 delegates from ten prominent Massachusetts baseball clubs met at the Phoenix House in Dedham to draft a constitution, bylaws, and rules and regulations for their favorite pastime. Cities and towns represented included Boston, Charlestown, Dedham, South Walpole, Walpole Center, Sharon, Medway, and Holliston. Although representatives from Boston's Tri-Mountain Club argued for the rules of the "New York game," the majority supported traditional New England townball. They endorsed a square field, overhand pitching, no foul territory, ten to twelve men per side, one out to retire all in each inning, and victory belonging to the club that first scored one hundred runs. The Tri-Mountain contingent withdrew after the convention rejected the New York style of play. A.S. Flye of Boston's Olympic Club called the meeting to order and was chairman of the rules committee. The convention elected the following officers: president, S.H. Hoyt, of the Olympic Club (Boston); vice-President, O.P. Johnson, of the Wassapoag Club (Sharon); secretary, Daniel Mahoney, of the Wassapoag Club (Sharon); treasurer, L.E. Rockwood, of the Winthrop Club (Holliston). After adjourning the men celebrated their achievement with a two hour friendly game of baseball. The following is reprinted from The New York Clipper, 29 May 1858, p. 44.

CONSTITUTION, BY-LAWS, AND RULES AND REGULATIONS
ADOPTED BY THE MASSACHUSETTS BASEBALL CONVENTION, 1858

This Association shall be known by the name of the "Massachusetts Association of Base Ball Players."

ARTICLE I. The object of this Association shall be to improve and foster the Massachusetts game of Base Ball, and the cultivation of kindly feelings among the different members of Base Ball Clubs in this State.

ARTICLE II. — *Members* — *sec. 1*. This Association shall be composed of two delegates from each of the Base Ball Clubs in this State which has been duly admitted to a representation in the Convention forming this Constitution.

Sec. 2. Any Base Ball Club desiring to be represented in this Association, shall present to the Secretary, at least one month before the annual meeting of the Association, a written application, signed by its President and Secretary, setting forth the name of the Club, its officers and delegates. Such Club shall be declared duly entitled to representation in this Association.

Sec. 3. No Club shall be represented in this Association until its delegates have signed this Constitution.

ARTICLE III. — *Officers* — *Sec. 1*. The officers of this Association shall be a President, Vice President, Secretary, and Treasurer.

Sec. 2. The first election of officers shall be held immediately upon the adoption of this Constitution, and the officers then elected shall respectively hold office until the next annual meeting, and thereafter all officers shall be elected by written ballot and general ticket, a plurality of votes electing.

Sec. 3. Each officer shall hold his office or appointment for one year.

Sec. 4. Any vacancy in either of the offices may be filled at any meeting of the Association regularly organized.

ARTICLE IV. — *Duties of Officers* — *Sec. 1*. It shall be the duty of the President to preside at all meetings of the Association, to preserve order, to see that the laws are carried into effect. He shall have no vote except in the election of officers, and except in the case of an equal division of the members of any question, when he shall give the casting vote.

Sec. 2. The President shall have power to call special meetings of the Association whenever he may deem it expedient; and he shall authorize the Secretary to call a special meeting whenever requested to do so, in writing, by five Clubs. He shall appoint all committees, unless otherwise ordered.

Sec. 3. The Vice President, in the absence of the President, shall be invested with the powers of that office, and perform all the duties of the office.

Sec. 4. The Secretary shall be a medium of communication with other Associations and the public. He shall retain copies of all letters written by him, and also preserve all letters received by him. He shall affix his name to all advertisements and notices of the Association, unless otherwise ordered. He shall attend all meetings of the Association; and in the absence of the President and Vice President, he shall call the same to order. He shall accurately record the proceedings of all meetings in the journal of the Association; also notify Clubs of their election, and issue all notices of meetings. He shall deliver to his successor in office all books or other property belonging to the Association in his possession.

Sec. 5. The Treasurer shall receive and hold all the funds of the Association. He shall keep a correct account of all money received and disbursed by him in a book to be provided for that purpose. He shall pay no bills unless approved by the President, or a majority of members; he shall have power to assesss each Club their proportionate part of any sum paid out by him, when authorized to do so by a vote of the Association. He shall be prepared to report the amount of funds in his possession at the annual meeting, and whenever requested by a vote of the Association.

ARTICLE V. — *Meetings* — *Sec. 1.* The annual meeting of the Association shall be held on the first Saturday of April, at such hour and place, in the city of Boston, as the President shall direct.

Sec. 2. All meetings of the Association shall be advertised in one or more of the daily journals of the city of Boston, at least one week previous to that of the meeting, and when a special meeting is called, its nature shall be stated in the announcement of the meeting.

Sec. 3. At all meetings of the Association, thirteen delegates shall constitute a quorum for the transaction of business.

ARTICLE VI. — *Rules* — The Rules and Regulations herewith annexed shall govern all match games of Base Ball played between Clubs belonging to this Association.

ARTICLE VII. — *Amendments* — No alterations, additions, or amendments to the Constitution and By-Laws, or the Rules and Regulations, shall be adopted, unless the same shall be submitted to the annual meeting, nor unless the same shall be adopted by a vote of a majority of all the members present at such meetings.

BY-LAWS.

Sec. 1. The order of business at all meetings shall be as follows: 1. Reading of the report of previous meeting. 2. Election of officers. 3. Reports of committees in order of their appointment. 4. Report of officers. 5. Unfinished business. 6. New business.

Sec. 2. No member shall be allowed to discuss any question under debate without rising and addressing the chair; nor shall he speak more than twice on any question, nor more than five minutes at any time, unless by unanimous consent.

Sec. 3. Every member present shall be required to vote on all questions, unless he is directly or personally interested, or excused by the vote of a majority of members present.

Sec. 4. Any member may, at any time, call for the reading of any article of the Constitution or By-Laws, or minutes of any meeting, or any other paper relating to the question under consideration.

Sec. 5. The yeas and nays shall be taken on any question at the request of five members.

Sec. 6. Any member belonging to this Association behaving in an ungentlemanly manner, or rendering himself obnoxious to the Association, may, by a vote of two-thirds of the members present, be expelled.

Sec. 7. All charges against any member, or Club, must be submitted in writing, and notice of such charges furnished such members or Clubs so charged, who shall be entitled to submit a written defence.

RULES AND REGULATIONS OF THE GAME OF BASE BALL

1. The ball must weigh not less than two, nor more than two and three-quarter ounces avoirdupois. It must measure not less than six and a half, nor more than eight and a half inches in circumference, and must be covered with leather.

2. The bat must be round, and must not exceed two and a half inches in diameter in the thickest part. It must be made out of wood, and may be of any length to suit the striker.

3. Four bases or bounds shall constitute a round; the distance from each base shall be sixty feet.

4. The bases shall be wooden stakes, projecting four feet from the ground.

5. The striker shall stand inside of a space of four feet in diameter between the first and fourth base, twenty-five feet from the first base, and thirty-five from the fourth. The catcher shall not enter within those lines, and must stand in all cases while catching the ball. The thrower shall stand thirty-five feet from the striker, on a parallel line occupied by the striker.

6. Players must take their knocks in the order in which they are numbered; and, after the first innings is played, the turn will commence with the player succeeding the one who lost on the previous innings.

7. The ball being struck at three times and missed, and caught each time by a player on the opposite side, the striker shall be considered out. Or, if the ball be ticked or knocked, and caught on the opposite side, the striker shall be considered out. But if the ball is not caught after being struck at three times, it shall be considered a knock, and the striker obliged to run.

8. If a player, while running the bounds, be hit with the ball thrown by one of the opposite side, before he has touched the goal, while off a base, he shall be considered out.

9. The ball must be thrown (not pitched) to the bat, on the side preferred by the striker, and within reach of the bat.

10. A player having possession of the first base when the ball is struck by the succeeding player, must vacate the base, even at the risk of being put out; and when two players get on one base, either by accident or otherwise, the player who arrived last is entitled to the base.

11. The ball must be caught flying in all cases.

12. A person engaged on either side shall not withdraw during the progress of the game, unless he be disabled, or by the consent of the opposite party.

13. Not less than ten nor more than twelve players from each Club shall constitute a match in all games.

14. In playing all match games, one hundred tallies shall constitute the game, the making of which by either side, that side shall be judged the winner.

15. A player, after running the four bases, on making the home bound, shall be entitled to a score.

16. The referees shall be chosen, one from each Club, who shall agree upon a third man from some Club belonging to this Association, if possible, their decision shall be final and binding upon both parties.

17. The talliesman shall be chosen in the same manner as the referees.

18. In all match games, when one is out, the side shall be considered out.

19. Should a striker stand at the bat without striking at good balls repeatedly thrown at him, for the apparent purpose of delaying the game, or of giving advantage to players, the referees, after warning him, shall call one strike; and, if he persists in such action, two and three strikes; when three strikes are called, he shall be subject to the same rules as if he struck at three fair balls.

THE NEW YORK GAME

The idea of a national baseball convention originated toward the close of the 1856 season in New York and Brooklyn when several clubs considered the advantages of revising the Knickerbockers' rules and regulating interclub competition. As the senior organization, the Knickerbockers issued a call in December for a meeting that would "promote additional interest in ball playing." The first meeting in January 1857 in Manhattan established the National Association of Base Ball Players. The next year the organization decided to perpetuate itself by drawing up a permanent constitution, by-laws, and rules of the game. It permitted junior clubs to attend meetings, but denied them voting privileges. The NABBP's officers in 1858 were: president, William H. Van Cott (Gotham, New York City); first vice president, J.B. Jones (Excelsior, Brooklyn); second vice president, Thomas S. Dakin (Putnam, Brooklyn); recording secretary, J. Ross Postley (Metropolitan, New York City); corresponding secretary, Theodore F. Jackson (Putnam, Brooklyn); treasurer, E.H. Brown (Metropolitan, New York City).

The most important work of these gatherings concerned rule revisions. The 1857 session adopted virtually all of the Knickerbocker regulations but changed the method of deciding the outcome of matches from twenty-one runs (aces) to nine full innings. One year later the delegates approved a rule that permitted the umpire to call a strike if a batter repeatedly refused to swing at "good balls." The most heated debate occurred over the rule that counted a batter out if a fielder caught the ball on the first bounce. Opponents of this rule wished to replace it with the "fly game" rule, which preserved all of the other modes of retiring a runner but mandated that a ball caught on the first bound was fair and in play. Tradition and conservatism prevailed for several years until the "fly game" rule finally was adopted in 1863.

To promote good sportsmanship and friendly competition, the NABBP also legislated on the eligibility of players, gambling, and professionalism. In particular, it required competitors to be regular members of the clubs they represented for at least thirty days prior to a contest. This was done to prevent a club from using talented outsiders to gain an advantage. The ban on gambling by contestants and spectators was designed to elevate the moral respectability of the new sport and curb corruption. The prohibition of professionals in 1859 was an attempt to preserve baseball as a recreation rather than as a vocation. The following is reprinted from the New York Clipper, 8 May 1858, p. 21.

CONSTITUTION, BY-LAWS, AND RULES AND REGULATIONS OF THE NATIONAL ASSOCIATION OF BASE BALL PLAYERS, 1858

CONSTITUTION

ARTICLE I

This Association shall be called "The National Association of Base Ball Players."

ARTICLE II

The objects of this Association shall be to improve, foster and perpetuate the American game of Base Ball, and the cultivation of kindly feelings among the different members of the Base Ball Clubs.

ARTICLE III

Sec. 1. This Asssociation shall be composed of two delegates from each of the Base Ball Clubs which have been duly admitted to a representation in the Convention forming this Constitution and from each of the Clubs which may be admitted to a representation in the manner hereinafter provided.

Sec. 2. Any Base Ball Club desiring to be represented in this Association shall present to the Recording Secretary, at least one month before the annual meeting of the Association, a written application, signed by its President and Secretary, setting forth the name of the Club, date of its organization, days and place of playing, names of its officers and delegates, and the number of members composing it, which shall be immediately submitted to the Committee on Nominations. Said committee shall thereupon ascertain the condition, character and standing of such Club, and report the same to the annual meeting, with the said application, and their opinion thereon; and a ballot shall thereupon be had at such meeting upon the admission of such Club, when, if two thirds of the members present vote in favor thereof, such Club shall be declared duly entitled to representation in this Association.

Sec. 3. No Club shall be represented in this Association by any delegate under twenty-one years of age; nor shall any Club be so represented until its delegates have signed the Constitution and paid the fee hereinafter designated.

ARTICLE IV

Sec. 1. The officers of the Asssociation shall be a President, first Vice-President, Second Vice-President, Recording Secretary, Corresponding Secretary, and Treasurer.

Sec. 2. The first election of Officers shall be held immediately upon the adoption of this Constitution, and the Officers then elected shall respectively hold office until the next annual meeting, or until their successors are respectively elected: and thereafter all officers shall be elected by ballot, on the second Wednesday of March, annually.

Sec. 3. Each officer shall hold his office or appointment for one year or until another is elected to succeed him.

Sec. 4. Any vacancy in either of the offices may be filled at any meeting of the Association regularly organized.

ARTICLE V

Sec. 1. It shall be the duty of the President to preside at all meetings; to preserve order, and to see that the laws are carried into effect; to call extra meetings whenever he shall deem it necessary. He shall have no vote except in the election of officers and new members, and except in equal divisions, when he shall have the casting vote. He shall call special meetings whenever requested to do so, in writing, by five Clubs; and shall also appoint all committees, unless otherwise ordered.

Sec. 2. It shall be the duty of the First Vice President to perform all duties of the President in his absence; and in case of absence of both the aforementioned officers, the Second Vice President shall discharge all the duties appertaining to the President.

Sec. 3. It shall be the duty of the Recording Secretary to keep an accurate record of all the proceedings of the Association in a book, to notify, by certificate, Clubs of their election; and to issue all notices of meetings. He shall deliver to the successor in office all books, papers, or other property of the Association in his possession.

Sec. 4. It shall be the duty of the Corresponding Secretary to take charge of all communications, and reply thereto in accordance with such instructions as he may receive from the Association, and keep and record in a book a copy thereof; and shall deliver to his successor in office all books or other property belonging to the Association in his possession.

Sec. 5. The Treasurer shall receive and hold all the funds of the Association, and disburse the same as he may be authorized to do by any vote of the Association, or by order of the President and Secretary. He shall keep a correct account of all moneys received and disbursed by him in a book to be provided for that purpose, which shall at all times be open to the inspection of any of the officers of the Association, or any committees duly authorized therefor by the Association; and shall report at the annual meeting, or whenever required by a vote of the Association.

ARTICLE VI

Sec. 1. The Annual Meeting of the Association shall be held on the second Wednesday in March each year, at such place in the city of New York as may be designated by the officers of the Association at least one month previous thereto.

Sec. 2. Special Meetings shall be called by the President, at the written request of five Clubs, provided that at least one week's notice of such meeting shall be given, by publication in at least two newspapers published in the city of New York, and by depositing written or printed notices thereof in the post offices of said city, directed to each of the delegates at their respective places of business or residence.

Sec. 3. Any meeting may be adjourned from time to time by vote.

Sec. 4. Twenty-one delegates shall constitute a quorum for the transaction of business; but a smaller number present, at any adjourned or regularly called meeting, may adjourn to any specified day.

ARTICLE VII

No delegate shall be admitted into the Association unless he shall have filed with the Recording Secretary a certificate of his election, signed by the President and Secretary of the Club he may represent.

ARTICLE VIII

Sec. 1. Each Club represented in this Association shall, at or before the Annual Meeting in each year, pay to the Treasurer a sum of Five Dollars, as annual dues; and each Club hereafter admitted shall pay the same sum in addition, as an entrance fee.

Sec. 2. The Association at any meeting may levy an assessment upon each of the Clubs belonging to this Association, of such sums as may be deemed requisite to pay deficiences or anticipated expenses.

Sec. 3. No delegate shall be entitled to vote at any meeting if the Club which he represented shall be in arrears for fees, dues, or assessments: and if such Club shall be in arrear one year, it shall cease to belong to the Association.

ARTICLE IX

The Rules and Regulations hereunto annexed shall govern all match games of Base Ball played between Clubs belonging to this Association.

ARTICLE X

Immediately after the election of officers at the annual election, the President elect shall appoint a committee of the delegates, who shall constitute a standing Committtee on Rules and Regulations: and also a committtee of three delegates, who shall constitute a Committee on Nominations — both of which committtees shall hold offices for one year, or until their successors are appointed.

ARTICLE XI

Sec. 1. All proposed alterations, additions, or amendments to the Constitution or By-Laws, shall be submitted in writing to the Committee on Rules before the annual meeting, and shall be by said committee reported at said annual meeting, with their opinion thereon; and no such alteration, addition, or amendment shall be adopted, unless it shall have been so proposed and reported; nor unless two-thirds of all the members present, at a meeting regularly organized, shall vote in favor thereof.

Sec. 2. No alterations, additions, or amendments to the Rules and Regulations shall be adopted, unless the same shall be submitted at the annual meeting; nor unless the same shall be adopted by a vote of a majority of all the members present at such meeting.

BY-LAWS

Sec. 1. The order of the business at all meetings shall be as follows: 1. Roll call. 2. Reading of minutes of previous meeting. 3. Propositions and ballotings for new members. 4. Election of officers. 5. Dues and fees collected. 6. Reports of Committees, in order of their appointment. 7. Reports of Officers. 8. Unfinished business. 9. New business.

Sec. 2. No member shall be allowed to discuss any question under debate, without arising and addressing the Chair.

Sec. 3. No member shall speak more than twice on any one question, nor more than five minutes at any time, unless by unanimous consent.

Sec. 4. Every member present shall be required to vote on all questions, unless he is directly or personally interested, or excused by the vote of a majority of members present.

Sec. 5. Any member may, at any time, call for the reading of any article of the Constitution or By-Laws, or minutes of any meeting, or any other paper relating to the question then under consideration.

Sec. 6. The yeas and nays shall be taken on any question, at the request of five members.

Sec. 7. Any member belonging to the Association, behaving in an ungentlemanly manner, or rendering himself obnoxious to the Association, may, by a vote of two-thirds of the members present, be expelled.

Sec. 8. All charges against any member, or club, must be submitted in writing, and notice of such charges furnished such member or club so charged, who shall be entitled to submit a written defence.

RULES AND REGULATIONS OF THE GAME OF BASE BALL

1. The ball must weigh not less than six nor more than six and a quarter ounces avoirdupois. It must measure no less than ten nor more than ten and a quarter inches in circumference. It must be composed of Indian rubber and yarn, and covered with leather, and in all match games shall be furnished by the challenging Club, and become the property of the winning Club, as a trophy of victory.

2. The bat must be round, and must not exceed two and a half inches in diameter in the thickest part. It must be made of wood, and may be of any length to suit the striker.

3. The bases must be four in number, placed at equal distances from each other, and securely fastened upon the four corners of a square, whose sides are respectively thirty

yards. They must be so constructed as to be distinctly seen by the umpire, and must cover a space equal to one square foot of surface. The first, second, and third bases shall be canvas bags painted white, and filled with sand or saw dust; the home base and pitcher's point to be each marked by a flat circular iron plate, painted or enameled white.

4. The base from which the ball is struck shall be designated the Home Base, and must be directly opposite to the second base; the first base must always be that upon the right hand, and the third base that upon the left hand side of the striker, when occupying his position at the home base.

5. The pitcher's position shall be designated by a line four yards in length, drawn at right angles to a line from home to the second base, having its centre upon that line at a fixed iron plate placed at a point fifteen yards distant from the home base. The pitcher must deliver the ball as near as possible over the centre of said base, and for the striker.

6. The ball must be pitched, not jerked nor thrown to the bat; and whenever the pitcher draws back his hand, or moves with the apparent purpose or pretension to deliver the ball, he shall so deliver it, and must have neither foot in advance of the line at the time of delivering the ball; and if he fails in either of these particulars, then it shall be declared a baulk.

7. When a baulk is made by the pitcher, every player running the bases is entitled to one base, without being put out.

8. If the ball, from the strike of the bat, is caught behind the range of home and the first base or home and the third base, without having touched the ground, or first touched the ground behind those bases, it shall be termed foul, and must be so declared by the umpire, unasked. If the ball first touches the ground, or is caught without having touched the ground, either upon or in front of the range of those bases, it shall be considered fair.

9. A player making the home base shall be entitled to score one run.

10. If three balls are struck at and missed, and the last one is not caught, either flying or upon the first bound, it shall be considered fair, and the striker must attempt to make his run.

11. The striker is out if a foul ball is caught, either before touching the ground or upon the first bound.

12. Or, if three balls are struck at and missed, and the last is caught either before touching the ground or upon the first bound;

13. Or, if a fair ball is struck, and the ball is caught either without having touched the ground or upon the first bound;

14. Or, if a fair ball is struck, and the ball is held by an adversary on the first base, before the striker touches that base;

15. Or, if at any time he is touched by the ball while in play in the hands of an adversary, without some part of his person being on a base.

16. No ace nor base can be made upon a foul ball, nor when a fair ball has been caught without having touched the ground; and the ball shall, in both instances, be considered dead and not in play, until it shall first have been settled in the hands of the pitcher. In either case the players running the bases shall return to them, and shall not be put out in so returning unless the ball has been first pitched to the striker.

17. The striker must stand on a line drawn through the centre of the home base, not exceeding in length three feet from either side thereof, and parallel with the line occupied by the pitcher. He shall be considered the striker until he has made the first base. Players must strike in regular rotation, and after the first inning is played, the turn commences with the player who stands on the list next to the one who lost the third hand.

18. Players must make their bases in the order of striking; and when a fair ball is struck, and not caught flying nor on the first bound, the first base must be vacated, as also the second and third bases, if they are occupied at the same time. Players must be put out upon any base, under these circumstances, in the same manner as the striker when running to the first base.

19. Players running the bases must, so far as possible, keep upon the direct line between the bases; and should any player run three feet out of this line, for the purpose of avoiding the ball in the hands of an adversary, he shall be declared out.

20. Any player, who shall intentionally prevent an adversary from catching or fielding the ball, shall be declared out.

21. If a player is prevented from making a base, by the intentional obstruction of an adversary, he shall be entitled to that base and not be put out.

22. If an adversary stops the ball with his hat or cap, or takes it from the hands of a party not engaged in the game, no player can be put out unless the ball shall first have been settled in the hands of the pitcher.

23. If a ball from the stroke of the bat is held under any other circumstances than as enumerated in Section 22 and without having touched the ground more than once, the striker is out.

24. If two hands are already out, no player, running home at the time a ball is struck can make an ace, if the striker is out.

25. An inning must be concluded at the time that the third hand is out.

26. The game shall consist of nine innings to each side, when, should the number of runs be equal, the play shall be continued until a majority of runs, upon an equal number of innings, shall be declared, which shall conclude the game.

27. In playing all matches, nine players from each club shall constitute a full field, and they must have been regular members of the club which they represent, and of no other club, for thirty days prior to the match. No changes or substitution shall be made after the game has been commenced, unless for reasons of illness or injury. Positions of players and choice of innings must be determined by captains, previously appointed for that purpose by the respective clubs.

28. The umpire shall take care that the regulations respecting the ball, bats, bases and the pitcher's and striker's position are strictly observed. He shall keep a record of the game in a book prepared for the purpose; he shall be the judge of fair and unfair play, and shall determine all disputes and differences which may occur during the game; he shall take especial care to declare all foul balls and baulks immediately upon their occurrence, unasked, and in a distinct and subtle manner.

29. In all matches the umpire shall be selected by the captains of the respective sides, and shall perform all the duties enumerated in Section 28, except recording the game, which shall be done by two scorers, one of whom shall be appointed by each of the contending clubs.

30. No person engaged in a match, either as umpire, scorer or player, shall be either directly or indirectly interested in any bet upon the game. Neither umpire, scorer, nor player shall be changed during a match, unless with the consent of both parties, except for a violation of the law, and except as provided in Section 27, and then the umpire may dismiss any transgressor.

31. The umpire in any match shall determine which play shall be suspended; and if the game cannot be concluded, it shall be decided by the last even innings, provided five innings have been played, and the party having the greatest number of runs shall be declared the winner.

32. Clubs may adopt such rules respecting balls knocked beyond or outside the bounds of the field, as circumstances of the ground may demand, and these rules shall govern all matches played upon the ground, provided that they are distinctly made known to every player and umpire previous to the commencement of the game.

33. No person shall be permitted to approach or to speak with the umpire, scorers or players, or in any manner to interrupt or interfere during the progress of the game, unless by the special request of the umpire.

34. No person shall be permitted to act as umpire or scorer in any match, unless he shall be a member of a Base Ball Club, governed by these rules.

35. Whenever a match shall have been determined upon between two clubs, play shall be called at the exact hour appointed; and should either party fail to produce their players within fifteen minutes thereafter, the party so failing shall admit a defeat.

36. No person who may be in arrears to any club he may have belonged to previous to the one he is then a member of, shall be competent to play in a match unless such arrears are paid.

37. Should a striker stand at the bat without striking at good balls repeatedly pitched to him, for the apparent purpose of delaying the game, or of giving advantage to a player, the umpire, after warning him, shall call one strike, and if he persists in such action, two, and three strikes, when three strikes are called, he shall be subject to the same rules as if he had struck three fair balls.

THE FIRST ALL STAR GAME

Intercity competition was a major means of popularizing the "New York game" before the Civil War. Perhaps no urban rivalry was more intense than that between New York City and Brooklyn. Since civic pride was keen on both sides of the East River, it was only natural for the leading Brooklyn teams to challenge their Manhattan counterparts to a three-game series between their best players. The following report of the New York victory in the first all-star game in the history of baseball is reprinted from the New York Clipper, 24 July 1858, p. 110. Brooklyn avenged its defeat with an easy 29-8 triumph in the return match in August, which set the stage for a deciding encounter in early September, won by the New Yorkers, 29-18. While the Manhattan men carried off the laurels, the "New York game" in general benefited enormously. Thousands of people witnessed the games, while probably more than a million followed the series in newspapers across North America.

THE GREAT BASE BALL MATCH: ALL NEW YORK VS. ALL BROOKLYN

The great match, which has been in contemplation for several weeks past, has, in connection with Base Ball, had the effect of directing the public mind to the great question of athletic sports for the people, and it has been growing and growing until the excitement has become so intense that it has been made the chief topic of conversation, and every one met with has had opinions to express as to who would be the ultimate victors in this grand contest. Such untoward interest being manfested by the public, caused the Committee of Arrangements to change their original plan of operations, and, instead of having the match played on their usual playing grounds, it was deemed expedient by them to pay more attention to public convenience, consequently the Fashion Race Course, L. I., being neutral ground, and considered the place most suitable to accomodate the thousands that were expected, as well as combining the requisites for play, it was secured, and measures immediately taken to put it in the best possible condition; and we are happy to say their efforts were fully successful, as no better or more suitable place could have been possibly selected.

The match was originally arranged to be decided on the 13th instant, but owing to the storm that prevailed on that day, the play was unavoidably postponed, much to the regret of the thousands then assembled on the ground. The following Tuesday, the 20th, was, therefore, selected for the play.

The selection of the players was no easy task for the committee appointed for that purpose, and it is needless to say that rivalry ran high for the honor of contending in this match, and that in the preparatory matches played, the various players showed off in their best style, to be considered, if possible, available men for the occasion. To this end, and to aid the committee, opposition nines were organized to play the selected nine, which resulted in various changes. . . . it has been finally settled that the following named gentlemen should be the champions of the positions they were to fill:

ALL BROOKLYN NINE			NEW YORK NINE		
Name	Club	Position	Name	Club	Position
M. O'Brien	Atlantic	3d base	T.G. Van Cott	Gotham	Pitcher
P. O'Brien	Atlantic	Field	Wadsworth	Gotham	1st base
J. Price	Atlantic	1st base	DeBost	Knickerbocker	Catcher
J. Leggett	Excelsior	Catcher	Davis	Knickerbocker	Field
J. Holder	Excelsior	2d base	Bixby	Eagle	3d base
A.E. Burr	Putnam	Field	Gelston	Eagle	Short
T.S. Dakin	Putnam	Pitcher	Miller	Empire	2d base
F. Pigeon	Eckford	Short	Benson	Empire	Field
J. Grann	Eckford	Field	Pinckney	Union	Field

This selection appeared to give every satisfaction to the fraternity, and to the clubs which they were to represent; although, in comparing the relative merits of the two nines, opinion was rather in favor of the Brooklyn. In case any accident or untoward circumstance should arise, to prevent any of the players being present, the precaution was taken to choose others, who should be on hand to fall into the vacancies; these were S.D. Gifford, of the Union Club; Tooker, of the Gotham; Welling, of the Knickerbocker; Marsh, of the Harlem; Wandell, of the Eagle; and Thorne, of the Empire, for the New York side; and Messers. Minault, of Eckford; Reynolds, of the Excelsior; Hamilton, of the Atlantic; and Masten, of the Putnam Club, for the Brooklyn party. So far, all the arrangements were every way complete; tents for the accommodation of the ladies were provided, the commisariat well looked after, of which Mr. Welling of the Knickerbocker Club, was to take charge; an efficient police force organized, as well as every means for conveyance of passengers arranged. And now all hands were anxiously awaiting for the day and time for the commencement of the sport.

Tuesday, July 20th, opened beautifully. The sky was not dimmed with a single cloud during the early part of the day, and the air was cool and exhilarating. At an early hour the roads leading to the Fashion Course exhibited unusual signs of animation, vehicles of every conceivable description being called into requisition to convey the thousands of spectators to the scene of contest. Many of the Base Ball Clubs had chartered large omnibuses, which were decorated in various ways, and gave additional zest to the scene. Pedestrians could be seen in hundreds and thousands making their way to the battle ground. Steamboats plying between the New York and Long Island shores were thronged throughout the day with passengers going to, or returning from the sport. In the enclosure, the scene was one of the most brilliant we have witnessed since the great trotting matches, at West Philadelphia, a few years since, when the stands there erected were covered with thousands of spectators. The stands at the Fashion on Tuesday were crowded, the ladies seeming to preponderate; on different parts of the course were gathered immense numbers of spectators, while hundreds of vehicles were arranged at various places about the track. There could not have been less than 10,000 persons present. About 2 o'clock the sky became overcast, thus protecting all from the rays of the sun which otherwise might have somewhat detracted from the pleasure of the players as well as spectators. A more pleasant day could hardly have been selected.

The necessary arrangements having been duly arranged, and everything in readiness for the grand event, the two elevens were called for play, at 2 1/2 o'clock, P.M.

ALL BROOKLYN NINE	H.L.	RUNS	NEW YORK NINE	H.L.	RUNS
J. Leggett, catcher	3	1	Pinckney, 2d base	3	3
J. Holder, 2d base	4	2	Benson, right field	3	3
F. Pigeon, short	3	1	Bixby, 3d base	4	1
J. Grum, middle field	1	4	DeBost, catcher	3	2
P. O' Brien, left field	3	2	Gelston, short	3	1
J. Price, 1st base	3	3	Wadsworth, 1st base	4	3

M. O' Brien, pitcher	3	3	Hoyt, left field	2	4
Masten, 3d base	4	1	T.G. VanCott, pitcher	1	5
A.E. Burr, right field	3	1	Wright, middle field	4	0
Total		18	Total		22

Umpire—Mr. Brown, of the Metropolitan Club

Betting at the start, 100 to 75 on Brooklyn, about the middle of the game even, and towards the finish, odds on New York. It will be seen by the score that various changes were made in the list of players first selected.

A COMPARISON OF BASEBALL AND CRICKET

The visit of an English all-star cricket team to North America in the fall of 1859 excited the ball playing fraternity in both Canada and the United States. When the All-England Eleven defeated select United States squads in Hoboken and Philadelphia, rumours circulated of an impending baseball match between the famed foreign athletes and an American all-star nine. The Englishmen's triumphant tour increased interest in the British national pastime; it also heightened the rivalry between cricket and the New York variety of baseball which had mushroomed in popularity since the mid-1850s. The visitors did not agree to a formal baseball contest, but they did try the new pastime in a few friendly informal games with mixed sides of cricketers and baseball players. Several sporting periodicals and daily newspapers printed commentaries which accompanied their reports of the results of the international cricket matches. These accounts explained and compared both games and reflected on each sport's chances to become the dominant form of ball playing in North America. The following editorial from the New York Herald praises both amusements but also explains why baseball was more appealing to sportsmen of the United States. It is reprinted from the New York Herald, 16 October 1859.

CRICKET AND BASE BALL

For the sake of the uninitiated in cricket and base ball—and they are the greater number as regards both games, but particularly cricket, which is scarcely known at all by Americans—we propose to give some explanation of the two games, and to compare and contrast them in those points in which they are similar and different.

Cricket has been only recently introduced into this country, the first club—the St. George's—having been established here about twenty years ago. From this sprang a few other clubs, both in the United States and Canada. But, on the whole, the game has not extended much, and that for two reasons: first, because base ball—an American national game—was in possession, and was too like cricket to be superceded by it, and secondly, in the points on which it differs from cricket it is more suited to the genius of the people. It is rapid and simple. Even if there were no base ball in existence cricket could never become a national sport in the America—it is too slow, intricate and plodding a game for our go ahead people.

Cricket—which is derived from the old Saxon word *crice,* a stick or bat—is a purely English game, and base ball—although originally imported from England when England was more "merrie" than she is now—is peculiarly American, while in the old country it is not so general as it was formerly.

Base ball has been from time immemorial a favorite and popular recreation in this country; but it is only within the last fifteen years that the game has been systematized and clubs formed for the purpose of playing at stated periods and under a code of written laws. The Knickerbocker Club, of New York, organized in 1845, was the first, and since then numerous clubs have sprung up in this city and Brooklyn, and throughout the country. But the great increase has been within the last three or four years. Till 1854 there were only four clubs organized here, and in that year two more. In 1859 [sic] a convention of the clubs of New York City and its vicinity was held for the purpose of establishing a uniform code of regulations. Sixteen clubs were represented. In the last year a second convention was held when a resolution was adopted declaring the Convention permanent. A constitution and by-laws were adopted and the society was duly organized as "The National Association of Base Ball Players." The first annual meeting [sic] of this association was held at the Cooper Institute on the 9th of March of the present year. Fifty clubs were represented and enrolled—the greatest number being of New York and Brooklyn. We suppose the number since has been nearly doubled. The most distinguished clubs at present are the Knickerbocker, of New York, the Union, of Morrisania, the Excelsior, the Star, and the Putnam, of Brooklyn. Perhaps the Excelsior is the best of all.

The good effect produced on the health and strength and morals of the young men engaged in this outdoor exercise is the theme of all who are conversant with them. It has taken them from the unhealthy haunts of dissipation indoors, and given them a taste for manly sport which cannot fail to have a beneficial effect, not only in the physical development of our citizens, but on the national character. No 'refreshments' are allowed on the occasion of matches, which are visited by thousands of spectators, including a large number of ladies.

Base ball, which is played by nine on each side, is so called from the game being played by a ball struck with a bat, whereupon the striker runs to points called "bases," of which there are four, at the four corners of a square, placed diagonally or diamond wise. The batman or striker standing on one corner called the home or last base, after striking away the ball, runs for the first base, which is to his right hand; if he can get there before the ball is caught, he is so far safe; if it is caught he is put out, but if not, and if he thinks he has time to run for the second base, he runs for that too, and likewise to the third and fourth, or home. If he can get any of these before he is touched with the ball in the hand of his opponent he is safe, and if he makes good the last base, he counts one and retires, and one of his companions on the same side takes the bat and follows his example, till three are put out, and that is called an inning, and the outs then come in and make their inning, and so on alternately, till nine innings are made by each, and that ends the game, the party counting most winning it. Thus in base ball every man gets the bat three times in all to make his runs. In cricket every man only gets the bat twice. In cricket there are two batmen, and base ball only one.

The bases are thirty paces or ninety feet apart, so that a distance of three hundred and sixty feet must be run by each man before he counts one. In cricket the successful running of sixty feet counts one. The first, second and third bases are, or ought to be, canvas bags, painted white and filled with sand or sawdust, covering each a space equal to a square foot. The home base is marked by a flat circular iron plate, painted white. The pitcher's point, that is the spot from which the player pitches the ball to the batman or striker, is likewise designated by a circular iron plate painted white, and is within the square fifteen yards or forty five feet from the home base, and in a direct line with the second or furthest base. There is great art in pitching, and the pitcher's position in base ball corresponds with the bowler's in cricket, though not quite so important. The ball must be pitched, not jerked, nor thrown, that is, the hand is held down to the hip or below it, and it must be aimed for the centre of the home base, or at the batman. It must not touch the ground before it reaches the batman, but the art of pitching consists in throwing it with such force that the batman has not time to wind his bat to hit it hard, or so close to his person that he can only hit it a feeble blow, which enables one of his antagonists to get the ball before he has time to reach the first base. The batman strikes overhand at the ball. In cricket, he strikes underhand, because the ball is thrown low, and must strike the ground before it reaches the batman.

In base ball, on or before the third fair ball, the batman throws down his bat and runs for the first base; otherwise he is put out. In cricket the batman is never compelled to run till he thinks proper, so that he has rarely any risk in making at least one run of sixty feet between the two wickets. We say sixty feet; for though the wickets are 60 feet apart, it is sufficient for the runner to put the tip of his bat inside the popping crease. If he has time he runs back again, and counts another, and so on; but if he is caught out, it does not deprive him of counting the successful runs he had already made, as is the case in base ball. Hence the English game is so slow and tame, and the American so full of life. In the latter the player is compelled to go. If the ball is caught, either flying or or on the first bound from the earth, after being struck with the bat, the batman is put out without counting; or if it is held by the adversary on the first base before the striker touches it, or if at any time he is touched by the ball in the hands of an adversary without some part of his person being on the base. Formerly it was sufficient to strike the adversary with the ball by throwing it at him. This practice is now abolished, as it was dangerous and unnecessary to the game. At each of the bases is stationed one man to watch the runner, and the fielders, who are outside throw the ball to him in order that he may touch the runner with it before he reaches the base. Hence the necessity of the fielders being fleet of feet and accurate throwers, and of the men guarding the bases being good catchers. The ball is often thrown from an astonishing distance and caught. A blow from it hurts severely, though it is not so heavy in proportion to its size as a cricket ball. The weight of a base ball must not be less than five and three-quarter ounces, nor more than six ounces. It must measure not less than nine and three-quarters, nor more than ten inches in circumference. It is made of India rubber and yarn. The weight of a cricket ball must be not less than five and a half ounces, and not more than five and three-quarter ounces. It must measure not less than nine inches, nor more than one and a quarter inches in circumference. There is still greater difference in the two bats. The base ball bat must be round, and must not exceed two and a half inches in diameter in the thickest part. It may be of any length. The cricket bat is flat, and must not exceed four and a quarter inches in the widest part, it must not exceed thirty eight inches in length. In cricket the batman has his legs cased in leather for protection, and so has the wicketkeeper who stands behind him to catch the ball after it glides off his bat or hand. The wicketkeeper has also strong gloves. Behind the batman in base ball stands a catcher, who, if he catches the ball flying or on the first hop puts out the batman. Thus the batmen in both games correspond, also the pitcher corresponds with the bowler, and the catcher with the wicketkeeper and these three are the men who, in both games, do the principal part of the work. In both games each man on each side must take the bat, in turn; in both games a bowler and a pitcher, a wicket keeper and a catcher are selected for their peculiar skill, and they play those parts throughout. It is important also for a player to be a good batman, otherwise he can count but little. In base ball the man who has charge of first base occupies a highly important position, for by his activity there he cuts short his adversary in his run for the first base. Sometimes the whole four bases are made in one run.

In base ball the game centres around the bases; in cricket it centres around the wickets. In base ball the batman, when he runs, is put out by being touched with the ball when he is off his base. In cricket the batman is put out if he is caught outside of an enclosure in front of the wicket by his adversary, who does not touch him with the ball, but knocks down his wicket either by throwing the ball at it or by throwing it to the wicket keeper or any other player, who, with ball in hand, knocks it down. Thus running and throwing and catching are equally important in both games.

In the game of cricket the wicket consists of three round stakes, called stumps, placed upright in a row, twenty-seven inches out of the ground, and on the top is placed a small piece of wood called a bail, eight inches long, which binds them together but in such a way that, with the least touch given to it or the stumps, it comes off, and puts the batman out. There are two of these wickets, pitched opposite to each other, at a distance of twenty-two yards, or sixty-six feet; at each of these stands a batman to defend them with the bat against being knocked down by the ball. These two play against the whole field. In base ball one plays against the whole field. Cricket is played by eleven on each side. The eleven who go in—that is, get first possession of the wickets and bats, which is won by lot or "a toss" of a coin—send two of their number to take those positions, and the remaining nine continue out of play till they are called in succession, as the two batmen are put out and make vacancies for them, until the whole eleven are thus put out. While they are in each makes all he can, and that is called his score, and the time they are thus in is called their "innings," and their united scores therein are known as so much on their first innings. The party out now come and make their first innings. Each side has two innings in which to make their scores. Whoesoever makes most on both innings wins the game. Two batmen of one side are thus continually plaing against the whole eleven of the other side. The object of the batman is to score by runs between the wickets; the object of his adversaries is to prevent him, by knocking down his wicket with the ball. The attack is made on the wicket, which he has both to defend and make the runs as best he can. If his wicket is fairly down he is put out, and another of the same sides takes his place. The bowler from beside one of the wickets bowls at the opposite one to knock it down. The batman stops the ball with his bat or strikes it away. In this consists the greatest art of the game. The ball must be bowled, and not thrown or jerked, and the hand must not be above the shoulder when delivering the ball, otherwise it is foul. Sometimes the bowler bowls it with great force and very low, direct for the wicket. Often the safest way for the batman is to block it—that is, to put the bat on the ground right before it, as it is hard to get a good stroke at it coming in that way, and if missed it goes into the wicket. Sometimes the artful bowler throws the ball, not direct for the wicket, but at an angle, in order to deceive, and gives it a twist when leaving his hand, which makes it come right to the wicket, for which dodge a good batman is also prepared. If the bowler throws the ball too far from the batman to permit him to strike it, it is called "wide," and counts one in favor the batman; or as many runs as he can make. A ball thrown foully from the hand is called "no ball," and also counts one for the batman. If the batman drive the ball out of the bounds it is called a "lost ball," and counts six for him without running—in the matches at Hoboken it only counted three, because the bounds were narrow. If a ball is caught in the air without touching the ground no run is reckoned, but the striker is not put out; if it is caught after a hop or rebound, that does not affect the game one way or the other. The difficulty of the batman is to stand near enough to his wicket to protect it and yet be able to give the ball a good stroke. If he winds his bat he is in danger of knocking down his own wicket and of thus being put out, and if he does not drive the ball sufficiently far away he cannot get a run. A stroke called square leg, by which the batman sends the ball with a powerful blow to his left hand side at right angles with a line between the two wickets, is considered a great feat and generally gives him a successful run, or perhaps several; it is difficult to make, and dangerous to attempt this stroke. If the batman stops the ball with his leg or any part of his body when it is going straight for the wicket he is put out; he cannot stop it except by the bat. The striker is out if the bail on either of the wickets be bowled off, or if a stump is bowled out of the ground, or, if the ball from his bat or hand is caught before it touches the ground, or if in striking at the ball or at any other time both his feet should be outside of "the poppping crease" and his wicket is put down by the adversary, except his bat be grounded within the crease. A batman may therefore either be "bowled out" or "caught out." When a batman makes any number of runs the bowler is said to "bowled" as many for him, and it is contracted to "b.," and when he is "caught" the letter "c." is used and the player by whom he is caught is named.

We must explain to the reader what the popping crease is. It is a sort of enclosure made by a line in the grass around the wicket, and within this the batman must stand. It is a line drawn parallel to the wicket, four feet distant and in front of it, unlimited in length. We should mention the bowling crease is a line six feet eight inches long, running parallel to this line and right through the wicket, which is placed in its centre. It has a return crease or line at each end drawn at right angles to it. Within this square enclosure the bowler must deliver the ball, and with one foot behind the front line, and he can select either the left or right side of the wicket to bowl from. There is only one bowler on the ground at the same time, and of course only one wicket is bowled at, but after every fourth ball the bowler changes over and bowls at the other wicket. The batman who guards that wicket which is not bowled has the privilege of making his run to the other wicket, when the ball is struck, just the same as the striker, and they generally run together, crossing each other. Sometimes they are both successful and sometimes only one, and sometimes both are put out. All who are opposed to them, except the bowler and the wicket keeper, are called the fielders. There are thus always nine fielders out. In base ball there are not so many, for there are three men left to watch first, second, and third bases, who, with the pitcher, and the catcher, and the stop short, who stands nearly in front of the batmen, make six and thus only three fielders. The fourth base is sufficiently protected by the stop short, who looks out for the short balls in front of the bat, and by the catcher behind the bat. In base ball the batman must not send the ball behind the first or third bases, that is the two nearest him on either hand. The exact terms of the rule are—

If the ball from the stroke of the bat is caught behind the range of home and the first base, or behind the range of home and the third base, without having touched the ground, or first touches the ground behind those bases, it shall be termed foul and must be so described by the umpire unasked. If the ball first touches the ground, or is caught without having touched the ground, either upon or in front of the range of those bases, it shall be considered fair.

By this rule the number of fielders required is lessened, the ball being driven for the most part to the front. It is to be observed that three of the nine who are in may be all running together, for instance, the man who first takes the bat gains only the first base in his first attempt. After he runs at all he cannot come back. The next on the list takes the bat, and then both run together; if neither of these get home, but only gain another base each, then when the third batman comes in, and runs, all three will run at once.

The only points in which the base ball men would have any advantage over the cricketers, in a game of ball, are two—first, in the batting, which is overhand, and done with a narrower bat, and secondly, in the fact of the ball being more lively, hopping higher, and requiring a different mode of catching. But the superior activity and practice of the Eleven in fielding would amply make up for this, even if they have not already practiced base ball at home, which is more than can be easily determined.

In cricket a very smooth ground is wanted on account of the bowling as the ball must strike the ground before it reaches the batman or strikes the wicket, and every obstruction on the surface would spoil the bowling. In base ball very smooth ground is not required, but a rather larger space than is necessary for cricket. In both games the players wear a peculiar kind of buckskin shoes with a long spike in the sole, to prevent them from slipping.

In cricket clubs and in base ball clubs the merits of the players are ranked first nine, second nine, third nine, &c., first eleven, second elevem, third eleven, &c. The captain of the club promotes or puts down men according to their performances. In all matches with other clubs only the first nine in base ball and the first eleven in cricket are selected to play. It occupies on an average about two hours to play a game of base ball—two days to play a game of cricket.

From the foregoing description and comparison of the two games, the reader will see that base ball is bettter adapted for popular use than cricket. It is more lively and animated, gives more exercise, and is more rapidly concluded. Cricket seems very tame and dull after looking at a game of base ball. It is suited to the aristocracy, who have leisure and love ease; base ball is suited to the people. Cricket is the better game for warm weather; base ball when it is cold. In cricket, those actually engaged, except three—the bowler, the batman and the wicket-keeper—do little or nothing three-fourths of the time; and for half the day, sometimes longer, nine out of one side are not on the field at all. In the American game the ins and outs alternate by quick rotation, like our officials, and no man can be out of play longer than a few minutes. Still, the game of cricket is one of great merit and skill, and we should be glad to see it cultivated by all who have sufficient time for the purpose. Both games seem suited to the national temperament and character of the people among whom they respectively prevail.

ATLANTICS VS. EXCELSIORS, 1860

A major factor that accelerated the rise of the "New York game" was the excitement generated by the unofficial city championship of Brooklyn in 1860. While other states, cities, and towns held local tournaments, most baseball enthusiasts recognized Brooklyn as the sport's capital and that city's champion as the best in the nation. The three leading contestants in Brooklyn were the Excelsiors, the Atlantics, and the Eckfords. The three-game series that began in July between the Excelsiors and Atlantics attracted throngs estimated at 8000 to 20,000 people, include hundreds of players from nearby New Jersey cities, Washington, D.C., Baltimore, Philadelphia, Boston, and Rochester, Buffalo, Troy, and Newburgh, New York. The Excelsiors won the inaugural match in a romp, 23-4, while the Atlantics triumphed in the second game, a 15-14 thriller. All awaited the deciding game in late August, but that contest ended abruptly when intense crowd heckling forced the Excelsiors' captain to remove his men from the field. The Atlantics retained their crown by default, then successfully defended it in a hard three-game series against the Eckfords later that fall. The first document, reprinted from the New York Times, 24 August 1860, p. 8, presents a play-by-play account of the action along with some sharp criticism of the behavior of the rowdies. The second selection is an editorial published in the New York Clipper on 1 September 1860, p. 154.

GRAND BASE BALL MATCH

About twenty thousand persons assembled on the Putnam ground at Gates and Lafayette avenues, Brooklyn, to witness the deciding contest between the Atlantic and Excelsior Clubs, on Thursday, Aug. 23d. The only cause of regret on this occasion is that any body of men should so far forget themselves as to act in the shameful manner that characterized the conduct of those individuals that were instrumental in breaking up the game. It would not be entirely correct to say that this result was unlooked for, as statements have been openly made within the last few days that the Excelsiors would not be allowed to win in a close contest. That the Atlantic nine were privy to any such plot, we are unwilling to believe, but a little stricter enforcement of order on their own ground would undoubtedly tend to greater quiet and more agreeable results when their hangers-on follow them to other grounds. The following is a detail of the innings as far as played:

EXCELSIOR—FIRST INNINGS— Russell took his place at the bat; after waiting some time sent the ball to short, making his first. Flanley followed and drove the ball to the right field, Russell going to the third, and the ball hitting him and rolling off, Flanley started and made his second, a wild throw by Smith to the second, giving him his third, Russell coming home. Whiting made his first on a low hit muffed by P. O'Brien at short and under protection of Whiting went to the second. Polhemus by a splendid strike to left field sent the other two home and made his first, from which he gained his third on a ball struck by Brainard to the right field. Reynolds, who succeeded Brainard tipped out and was succeeded by Holder, who drove home his two predecessors on a hit to centre field, and went to the second on a wild throw of P. O.'Brien to head off Reynolds. Leggett was out at the first base on a ball passed by Oliver from the second, and Creighton tipped out, leaving Holder on his third.

ATLANTIC—FIRST INNINGS— Pierce led off with a heavy hit to the right field, but got no further than the first on it, a pass ball lettting him go to the third. A strong strike of Smith was intercepted by Russell at the first base so quickly as to stop Pierce's intention of coming home. McMahon stood for some time, and then sent a bomb-shell into the left field, where Flanley smothered it admirably on the fly. Pierce then stole in, and P. O.'Brien followed up this success with a beautiful grounder, caroming on Holder's legs for one base, which was changed to the third by a pitch over the catcher. Price tipped out, leaving P. O'Brien on the third base.

EXCELSIOR—SECOND INNINGS— Russell was again the first striker, but after a much shorter stay than in the first, was caught on the bound by McMahon, at centre-field. Flanley sent up a skyrocket taken on the fly by John Oliver, when Whiting filled his place only to send a favor to Smith, to be returned to the first, ending the innings for *nil*.

ATLANTIC—SECOND INNINGS— John Oliver began operations by an apple of contention given to Reynolds and Whiting, which neither caught, the batter taking the first base. He then got to the second by a brilliant rush, going home on Hamilton, the next batter, who made his second by a left field hit. Jo. Oliver, after striking twice, tipped, and was caught finely on the fly by Leggett. M. O'Brien sent a grounder to Holder, who passed it to Russsell, heading off the striker, Hamilton coming home. Pierce struck a fine ball to the right field, but Brainard took it on the bound, closing the innings for two.

EXCELSIOR—THIRD INNINGS— Polhemus had the first strike, and sent up a foul, which was missed on the fly by Smith—a favor duly aprreciated, for the next hit was a grounder for one base, the second being made on a pass, from whence he came in on a centre-field hit by Brainard, which was missed on the fly by McMahon, Brainard making his first only. Reynolds sent out by a splendid bound catch by M. O'Brien on a staving [sic] hit; the ball being passed to the second, Brainard was also put out. This was deservedly applauded, as was a magnificent fly catch by P. O'Brien from Holder, who had been previously missed on a foul fly by Price at the first.

ATLANTIC—THIRD INNINGS— Smith prefaced his batting with a high tip and a powerful foul, creating a commotion among the ladies. After another heavy foul he sent a grounder through Holder's legs, and the ball being muffed by Brainard he gained the second base. A bad throw by Creighton to the second gave him another base, and he came in on another hard hit of McMahon, which again went to Flanley, taken this time on the bound. P. O.'Brien was caught by Leggett on a high tip, and gave way to Price, who hit a short ball by the pitcher, passed to the first to head him off.

EXCELSIOR—FOURTH INNINGS— Leggett started with two fouls and ended with a high ball caught by M. O'Brien, making room for Creighton who got to his first on a ball over the first base, and to the second on a high pitch. Russell, after another long wait, was caught on bound ball by Hamilton at right field, Creighton gaining the third, and coming home on a hit of Flanley, which was missed on the fly by P. O'Brien, the batter getting to his first, and thence to the third on a pass ball, and home on a ball striking the home base and glancing off. The innings closed by a very fine fly-catch of John Oliver, disposing of J. Whiting.

ATLANTIC—FOURTH INNINGS—John Oliver hit the ball to Whiting at the third base, who passed it quickly to the first in time to put Oliver out. Hamilton after hitting two fouls and striking twice a left-field hit gave him the field base. John Oliver gave place to M. O'Brien on a tip after which Hamilton gained the second and a ball passing the catcher, he gained his third where he was left by a good fly catch of Holder from M. O'Brien. No run for the Atlantic.

EXCELSIOR—FIFTH INNINGS— Polhemus began the innings with a tip out, which ill-success was followed by a ground ball of Brainard to short, which found its way to the first before Brainard. P. O.'Brien passed another ball to the first putting out Reynolds and giving the Excelsiors no runs.

ATLANTICS—FIFTH INNINGS— Pierce struck first and tipped, the chance being missed by Leggett, which was followed by a grounder muffed by Holder, giving him one base. Smith made a splendid strike to the left field, sending home Pierce and making two bases for himself. Smith got home on the strike of McMahon who had a close time at the first overrunning the third, was put out. Price was caught by Reynolds on a fly ball at short.

EXCELSIORS—SIXTH INNINGS— Holder was headed off at the first by a throw from Smith, and Leggett, after a miss on the fly by M. O.'Brien, was forced off the first by a hit; Creighton to short, who passed it to the second, getting rid of Leggett, and Creighton had a narrow escape at the first.

The rowdy element which had been excited by a fancied injustice to McMahon in the preceding innings now became almost insupportable in its violence, and shouts from all parts of the field arose for a new umpire; the hootings against the Excelsior Club were perfectly disgraceful. Mr. Leggett was supported by the Atlantic nine in his endeavors to secure order, and by their united exertions a temporary lull was secure, but, although Mr. Leggett distinctly stated that the Excelsiors would withdraw if the tumult was renewed, the hooting was again started with increased vigor, and the Excelsiors immediately left the field, followed by a crowd of roughs, alternately groaning the Excelsiors and cheering the Atlantics. The game is drawn, and, if ever played out, will take place in comparative privacy, on some inclosed ground. The determination shown by the Excelsior Club on this occasion is worthy of great praise, and meets the approval of the vast majority of the respectable portion of the base ball community.

SCORE

EXCELSIOR	OUTS	RUNS	ATLANTIC	OUTS	RUNS
Russell, 1st b	2	1	Pierce, c	1	2
Flanley, l. f	1	2	Smith, 3d b	1	2
J. Whiting, 3d b	2	1	McMahon, c. f	3	0
Polhemus, c.f	1	2	P. O'Brien, short	2	0
Brainard, r. f	2	1	Price, 1st b	3	0
Reynolds, short	3	0	John Oliver, 2d b	1	1
Holder, 2d b	2	0	Hamilton, r. f	0	1
Leggett, c	3	0	Jo. Oliver, l	2	0
Creighton, p	1	1	M. O'Brien, p	2	0
Total		8	Total		6

RUNS IN EACH INNINGS

	1st.	2d.	3d.	4th.	5th.	Total
EXCELSIOR	5	0	1	2	0	8
ATLANTIC	1	2	1	0	2	6

Umpire—Mr. Henry Thorn, of the Empire Club.
Scorers, Excelsior, Mr. Wm. H. Young.
Atlantic, Mr. George R. Rogers.

THE BASE BALL MATCH BETWEEN THE ATLANTICS AND EXCELSIORS

On the 23d ult....these clubs entered the lists a third time this season to decide the disputed question of the championship; and we regret to state that the result was most unsatisfactory, alike to the members of the two clubs, and to the thousands of admirers of this manly game that were interested spectators on that important occasion.... Many, among the ball playing community, attribute it to the habit of betting heavily on the result of these contests, and doubtless that is a prominent means of giving rise to such disturbance. But there is a something beyond this that exerts its influence in creating such riotous proceedings, and that is the *spirit of faction* that characterizes a large portion of the community, and in which the foreign element of our immense metropolitan population, and their native offspring especially, delights to indulge. This factional spirit is the bane of every community wherein it is once allowed to obtain a foothold. It largely prevails in the politics of our country, giving rise to almost all the bitterness of party spirit and sectional strife. It is the great curse of our noble fire department, and is the sole cause of the evils that have led to the almost total abandonment of the self-sacrificing and manly volunteer force of the department; and it is the great element of discord wherever it uprears its hideous head; and its poisonous breath permeates through the lower strata of our heterogeneous population, with a pernicious effect that destroys every noble instinct of humanity, and imparts rapid growth to those human *fungi* known as "Dead Rabbits" in New York, "Killers" in Philadelphia, and "Plug Uglies" in Baltimore, etc. It even invades the sanctuary of religion, imparting sectarian jealousies where peace and brotherly love should alone prevail. In short, whether it is "our country," "our Party," "our company," "our club," or "our church," the same evil spirit rules the actions and paralyzes the virtuous tendencies of all who succumb to its baneful influence, replacing kindly feelings with bitter hatred, and manly emulation and generous rivalry with revengeful retaliation; thereby turning every source of pleasure with which it comes in contact into a cause of feuds and quarrels that end in disgraceful and riotous conduct. This is the great motive power that gives rise to such occurrences as those that marred the pleasure that would otherwise have been received from the contest of the 23d ultimate. Betting is a mere accessory evil—the chief conspirator is Faction; and while that exists we may fully expect to see just such scenes as that of Thursday, the 23d ult., on all occasions where this cursed spirit is allowed to have control. In the ball match it controlled the "Excelsior crowd" and the "Atlantic Crowd," in the great fight at Farnborough it ruled the "Sayers party" and the "Heenan party," and its effects may be traced throughout all the riotous proceedings that have been recorded for a hundred years past. The remedy of the evil lays in the *self-control* of contending clubs and parties, *and in a strict adherence to the rules that guide the actions of a man of honor and a gentleman,* and those who cannot observe this line of conduct had better leave the manly recreation of Base Ball to others who can and will, or else the sooner the game becomes obsolete the better.

Chapter 4

BLOOD (ANIMAL) SPORTS

Animal sports remained popular throughout North America during the middle decades of the nineteenth century. The premodern pastimes of canine battles and cockfighting were commonplace in rural regions and towns and cities in the United States and Canada. They were patronized by a variety of enthusiasts from a wide range of social classes. Despite opposition from humanitarian reformers and laws prohibiting these exhibitions, blood sports continued to draw crowds throughout the 1850s.

As the Victorian values of discipline, hard work, punctuality, and self-control spread throughout middle class society, a number of elite gentlemen and lower class workers rejected the prevailing ethos. They constituted a "sporting fraternity" which sought camaraderie and excitement in low brow amusements. Young and older aristocrats, bachelors, newly arrived immigrants, and laborers gathered to talk, drink, gamble, and watch commercial spectacles. Their favorite meeting places were billiard rooms, volunteer fire departments, fraternal lodges, labor union halls, gambling dens, theaters, livery stables, street corners, and especially saloons. Barrooms frequently featured brilliantly lighted windows, frescoed ceilings, glittering mirrors, and paintings of famous race horses, prize fighters, and voluptuous semi-nude women. Saloonkeepers often sponsored a variety of amusements in specially constructed rooms that were connected to their establishments by alleys or passageways.

During the 1850s the most popular animal spectacles were cockfights, dogfights, and ratting contests. In the latter amusement, dogs were required to kill a given number of rodents within a specified time. As the documents in this chapter demonstrate, sporting periodicals gave considerable coverage to these entertainments by publishing rules and regulations and descriptions of leading events. Despite the New York state legislature's ban on all blood sports in 1856, the New York Clipper dedicated separate columns to "canine" and "cocking" news and announcements. But although Boston and other cities also prohibited these contests, enforcement was sporadic and penalties were not severe enough to force them underground or out of existence. A more concerted effort to abolish animal sports came during the next decade, especially with the founding of the American Society for the Prevention of Cruelty to Animals in 1866.

CANINE SPORTS

DOGFIGHTING

Whether sportsmen thought of a dog as a man's best friend in the mid-1800s is not certain, but there is no doubt that many raised these favorite domestic pets to be vicious fighters. They established a system of weight classifications and rules to govern the combat. Men pitted their animals against each other for prize money and substantial side bets. As the following extracts from the canine columns recount, the sporting fraternity also enjoyed watching dogs attack raccoons and kill rats. Promoters like New York City's Harry Jennings staged weekly exhibitions and usually provided rats and the use of the pit free. The following accounts of these canine events in New York, Kentucky, New Orleans, and Toronto, Canada are taken from the New York Clipper, 16 December 1854, p. 2; 5 June 1858, p. 51; 14 August 1858, p. 135; 23 January 1859, p. 319; 5 March 1859, p. 363; 12 March 1859, p. 371.

NEW YORK CITY DOGFIGHT

Red Jack vs. Connaught Lad, at McLaughlin's Pit, 155 First Ave.

FOR 200$ A SIDE

The long expected fight between Mr. McLaughlin's dog Red Jack, and Marriott's dog Connaught Lad, took place at McLaughlin's on Wednesday evening, 6th inst. The pit was crowded in every part; men from Boston, Philadelphia, Baltimore, Albany, and other places having come to the city on purpose to witness the contest.

The odds previous to the battle were on Connaught Lad, at 2 to 1, &c. Mr. McLaughlin handled Red Jack, and Mr. Marriott the Connaught Lad. About 10 minutes past 8, the dogs were brought into the pit, both dogs appearing in tip-top condition, showing the handiwork of their trainers. It is the custom for the handlers to ascertain if there is anything poisonous on the dogs before setting them to work. For this purpose Mr. McLaughlin went over to Marriott's dog, Connaught Lad, to taste him on the parts where it was most likely the other dog would fasten. While in the act of tasting Marriott's dog, which was in the hands of Marriott at the time, Connaught Lad slipped from his handler, and immediately fastened on to McLaughlin's left cheek, close to the eye—he had a terrific grip, and the blood flowed profusely—Mr. McLaughlin after 15 or 20 seconds only succeeded in forcing the dog to release his hold on him by choking him. This caused guite an excitement in the pit, and for a short time delayed the fight. At length the preliminaries were settled—the Umpires and Referee appointed, and then commenced.

THE BATTLE

On the word being given both dogs went off like flash, and immediately fasted on to each other. The struggle was of the most intense description, the dogs seizing upon each other in different parts, and tearing away in the most furious manner—now one was down, now the other, in fact it was hard to tell which had the best of it, so well and stoutly did they contend for the superiority.

The dogs continued to fight in the most furious and stubborn manner for the space of about 25 minutes, without much advantage on either side, and bets were even. At this point, however, Red Jack got a grip on the Lad's right ear, getting him down on his back, and bit the Lad so hard that he snapped and showed his teeth for a moment, but he immediately succeeded in regaining his feet again, and commenced business as if nothing had touched him. The fight now raged again as before for about 5 minutes, when Red Jack turned, but was not picked up by his handler, and in another moment were fastened to each other again. It was at this turn of affairs that Red Jack and the Lad stood for a second or two face to face—and the Lad turned partly around but did not seem to move his feet or body. Marriott seeing this, instantly seized his dog, the Lad, for a turn, supposing that it was all right. McLaughlin seeing this, and knowing that the Lad had not turned, according to the rules instantly picked up his dog and claimed the fight on the ground that the Lad did not turn, and Marriott had no right to pick up his dog.

The confusion was now great, every person present seeming to have something to say—the friends of the Lad insisted that the dogs should be put together again, but McLaughlin resisted, claiming that Red Jack had won the fight, according to the rules of the pit. The confusion lasted a few minutes, the friends of one dog claiming that the fight should go on—the others that Jack had won the money. At length order was restored, and silence was obtained in order to hear the decision of the Referee, to whom the Umpires had appealed. The Referee, Mr. Farrell, a well known sporting man, then arose, and stated that, "according to the rules of dog fighting, Mr. Marriott loses the fight by picking his dog up without a turn." This decision admitted of no further appeal, and although some parties refused to give up their bets immediately, we learn that they have since been paid, in consequence of the original stakes having been paid over to Mr. McLaughlin by Mr. Marriott. Therefore, all who bet on the dog Red Jack, of course win the money. A very heavy amount of money was wagered on the result of this battle, the backers of each dog seeming confident of winning. The fight was a most capital one, and occupied in all 32 minutes.

ANNOUNCEMENTS

CANINE ASSOCIATION CLUB—Harry Jennings, of the Sportsman's Hall, 49 Madison Street, through the suggestion of several canine fanciers of New York, Brooklyn, and Williamsburgh, is induced to appoint one day in every month, and which will be the last Wednesday in every month, for the express purpose of gentlemen trying and practising the abilities of their young dogs previous to their being matched for money against their own weight. Every subscriber in the Association will have the privilege of trying his dog out, and will have at least four weeks notice to get his dog into condition; every subscriber has the chance of winning the prize of the handsomest collar and slip that New York can produce, as a trophy for the winning dog for his abilities. Several of the canine fancy had already enrolled their names, at the head of which is Harry Jennings, who has not less than sixty dogs of all weights, and will accomodate all comers at all weights. H.J. invites his friends, acquaintances, and the canine fancy at large to come and enter their names and the weights of their dogs, as three handsome collars and slips will be awarded to three different dogs of three respective weights, on Wednesday, June 30th, 1858. All dogs that contend for the prizes will each take their turn in rotation. It is entirely optional whose dogs contend for the prizes, but they must be equally matched. Any one would do well to give a call and see the collars and slips, which any man would feel it to be a pride and a credit for his dog to win and wear. Entrance for the collars and slips free. Doors open at seven; to commence at half past seven. Admission, 25 cents.

A Great Handicap Rat Match will take place at Harry Jennings's Sportsman's Hall, 49 Madison street, on Wednesday evening, June 9th, 1858, for a handsome London made collar and slip. Open to all dogs not exceeding 21 lbs. weight, and will be handicapped as follows:—Dogs not exceeding 10 lbs. weight to kill 3 rats each; dogs not exceeding 15 lbs. weight to kill 5 rats each, and dogs not exceeding 21 lbs. weight to kill 6 rats each; and the dog that kills his rats in the shortest time will be awarded with the prize. H.J. will also introduce his pet rat, two pounds weight, which will have a friendly shake with anything twice its weight. The prairie wolf and coon will be baited for a handsome collar on this occasion. There will be several interesting set to's during the evening between Bull and Sullivan, Spring and Sambo, Sirus and Hoboken, Crib, Rattier and Boney, Tinker slut Fan and the Patterson slut Clipper, Lilley and Bessey—and the wind up will be between little Beaney and Paul of Patterson. H.J. will also show his Irish dog Waterford Jack, who defeated "Syksey" of Brooklyn for $400, who is acknowledged to be a game and well bred dog. Also H.J.'s ferret will kill a few rats on this occasion. Doors open at seven; to commence killing at half-past seven. Rats and entrance for the collars and slips free. Admission, 25 cents.

RULES OF DOG FIGHTING IN THE WEST

A correspondent at Covington, Kentucky, has forwarded us a copy of some new rules for dog fighting which have just been established out there. Although there is but little difference from the rules which are adopted in New York and Philadelphia, yet as they may prove interesting to some of our readers, we publish them in full:

Rule 1. To be a fair scratch and turn fight.

2. Both dogs to be examined and tasted, and washed, if required by either party before the fight.

3. Both dogs to be shown to the scratch fair in front of his pitter.

4. No throwing or shoving of either dog over the scratch, under forfeiture of the fight.

5. There shall be four bottles of water procured, with some colored ribbons around the neck of each, with two sponges, with the same colored ribbon in each sponge.

6. To prevent any possibility of trickery, the bottles and sponges shall be placed in charge of the referee, and when empty, to be filled by his directions, and handed to the pitters.

7. Half minute time to be allowed between every fair goaway; twenty-five seconds allowed for sponging, and at the expiration of that time, the time-keeper shall call, "Make

ready, let go;" and then the time-keeper, or any person he may appoint, shall count from one to five, as the parties agree upon. The dog refusing to go to his opponent by the expiration of the count, shall be the loser.

8. Should either pitter pick up his dog by mistake, he shall put him down immediately on the request of the referee, or lose the battle.

9. Two umpires and a referee shall be chosen before fighting; in case the umpires should not agree, the decision of the referee to be final.

10. Either dog exceeding the stipulated weight on the day of weighing, to forfeit the money deposited.

11. All deposits to be made punctually according to agreement.

CONTEST BETWEEN A COON AND TERRIER

One of the great features of Christmas Day in New Orleans was a contest between a Kentucky coon and a famous terrier dog, known as "Fighting Bob," which came off in a pit prepared for the purpose in the vicinity of the Varieties theatre, before a refined, fashionable, and aristocratic audience. The following details we gather from the Sunday Delta:

"The judges were two of our most prominent citizens, and necessarily well known to the community, and whom we must acknowledge acted with the dignity and impartiality becoming so important an occasion. At the hour appointed, and when all was expectation, the two animals were brought into the arena and pitted after the most approved style. The first attack was tremendous, the dog going in confident, while the coon backed to his side of the ropes, and stood on the defensive. The terms of the fight were, that the dog should kill the coon, or that the coon should cause the dog to run and throw him out of time, which, in this instance, was two minutes. The betting at the start was two to one on the dog, a large number of which bets were taken. After the fury of the first attack was over, the dog evidently found that he had an enemy to deal with worthy of his steel, and began to scan more closely the vulnerable parts of his country cousin, and came up to scratch with less haste than at the lead. The cousin snapped his eyes, but adhering to the Fabian policy, retreated before the dog, and advanced again in oblique directions, thus worrying his antagonist and keeping him at bay. The cry of foul play was raised just here, as some shrewd observer discovered that the ground had been watered before the fight, which was against the stipulations, the backers of the dog claiming that the coon could play a great deal upon wet ground; but upon the questions being put to the judges, they decided that the point at issue was not of sufficient weight to be considered by them, and ordered that the fun proceed. The ring was again cleared, and the dog, which had apparently gained confidence from the interruption, darted at the coon and seized hold of him, and was seemingly about to finish his mortal career, when his sly old antagonist, by an agile movement, threw his quarters out of reach, and while the dog lay down a moment for wind, seized hold of a paw and led him a three-legged dance around the ring. The backers of the coon shouted, while those of Fighting Bob' looked wise and said that the terrier would soon recover himself. But alas! for the vanity of knowing ones, and the short-sightedness of dog fanciers; the coon continued his advantage, threw his opponent about easily, mauled him most incontinently, and finally threw him down and out of time. The excitement in the crowd at this unexpected denouement was intense, and bats and canes went flying up to the ceiling enthusiastically, as the winners reached out their hands and pocketed the stamped paper which was held to them by the losers. The game old coon was nearly smothered in the anxiety of his friends to get near him, some of whom picked up locks of his hair, which the dog at the outstart had plucked from his hide. He was borne out in the arms of his owner, with testimonial papers of peanuts showered upon him, which he was too much indisposed to accept, acknowledging the honors heaped upon him with a wave of his tail. Fighting Bob is a fine animal, and weighs twenty-four pounds, and we believe he has never before been vanquished. The coon has yet to lose a battle, and his owners challenge the whole light weight dog world to fight, for from $10 to $1,000."

GREAT CANINE EXHIBITION

The monthly canine exhibition at Harry Jennings's Kerrigan's Hall, 22 Waite street, came off on Wednesday evening, 23d ult. There was a very numerous attendance of those interested in canine sports present on the occasion, and gave convincing proof of the increasing estimation in which those amusements are regarded by the general public. The rat killing handicap, for which thirteen dogs were entered, was the principal feature of the evening's sport. The following is the entry, and the time made:

Property	Name of Dog	Weight	Rats	Time
W. McDonald's	Fan	11 lb	3	44s
J. Lister's	Gip	21	5	22
M. Cavanagh's	Jack	16	4	—
Jas. Money's	Snake	17	4	—
E. Wilson's	Topay	11	3	40
J. Hurley's	Cora	14	3	—
M. May's	Fan	12	3	50
Geo. Kensett's	Fan	30	6	—
J. Copper's	Fan	22	6	60
M. Nolan's	Codger	25	6	35
Geo. Nolan's	Grinder	18	5	—
J. Kelly's	Jim	20	5	61
Mr. Taylor's	Fan	10	3	20

The last named proved the winner, owing to the handler of Gip picking her up before the rats were all killed, and thus losing his chances of the prize, which consisted of a handsome collar and slip. The time of many of the dogs was not taken, owing to the specified number of rats not being killed in time to have a chance of success.

On Thursday evening another canine exhibition, for the benefit of Jack Jennings, came off at 49 Madison street, on which occasion his friends rallied around him numerously, and the place was completely filled. The sport shown was of the very highest class, and the entire proceedings conducted in a most orderly and respectable manner. The performance of a young sucking bull terrier pap, by the celebrated dog Waterford Jack, which killed three full grown rats, was highly admired.

FIGHT IN CANADA—CRIB AND BONEY

London, C.W., March 3d, 1859—

DEAR CLIPPER: I am astonished at not seeing ere this, an account of the long-talked of fight between Mike Carroll's dog Crib, and Kelly's celebrated dog Boney, (son of Boney, the conqueror of the Buffalo dog Tinker). It was from first to last as well contested a fight as ever I witnessed. They fought in Toronto, at Mr. Wm. Vines' pit, near his saloon, to whom all honor be for the gentlemanly and straightforward manner in which everything was conducted. There was a very large concourse of people assembled on the occasion, and the betting at the start was brisk, being five to four on Crib, whose well-known gameness made him the favorite, although he had been ill for some days previous to the day of fighting; and, when placed at the scratch, his weakness and utter want of condition was apparent even to the uninitiated; but all the sickness in the world could never get his big game heart out of condition, as it was that and not his strength won him his fight. Crib got the first two falls, and it was very even for the first ten minutes, when his strength failing, Boney had it all his own way, worrying Crib like a rat; but the poor fellow would sometimes get a hold that would make everything "crack again." After fighting thirty minutes, he got Boney by the under jaw, a lip hold, and held on for 23 minutes, when Boney made a turn, and at the call refused to scratch, and the stakes, $100 a side, were handed over to Crib's owner, Mr. Carroll. A gamer dog than Crib it has never been my lot to witness, and had he been in condition the fight would not have lasted twenty minutes; as it was, they fought 57. Mr. Carroll now offers to fight Crib against any 47 lbs. dog in America, give or take one pound, for $100 or $500, a fair scratch fight. A deposit and articles with ED. CLIPPER will meet attention.

Canis

COCKFIGHTING

Cockfighting was the most popular blood sport in Canada and the United States prior to 1860, and was second only to horse racing in recreations that involved animals. While the breeding of chickens for battle had a long history in agricultural areas, sportsmen successfully introduced it in cities across the continent. Spectators wagered sizeable sums on these deadly encounters. The desire to rationalize the pastime and resolve disputes over the outcomes led to the codification of rules to govern the matches. Promoters also arranged intercity challenges to determine which community had the strongest and bravest cocks. They ignored local ordinances which banned these events, but sometimes the police did spoil the fun. The first four selections below present the regulations on cockfighting adopted in Boston, New York, the American South, and San Francisco. They are reprinted from J. M. Cooper, M.D., *Game Fowls.*

Their Origin and History (West Chester, Pa., 1869), and the New York Clipper, 6 March 1858, p. 362. The final document reports on a "main," a challenge between a number of cocks representing New York and Massachusetts, which was broken up by the Boston police. It first appeared in the New York Clipper, 5 February 1859, p. 331.

RULES OF THE PIT
RULES AND REGULATIONS FOR THE BOSTON UNION
CLUB COCK PIT

Art. 1st.	All fowls brought to the pit must be weighed and marked down, for those to see that have fowls to fight.
2d.	Fowls within two ounces are a match.
3d.	A Stag is allowed four ounces when he fights a Cock.
4th.	A Blinker is allowed four ounces when he fights a sound fowl.
5th.	Fowls being ready, brought to the pit.
6th.	Each man takes his station, and sets his fowl to the right or left, as he pleases, there remains till the fowls are in one another, or in the tan, or on his back.
7th.	The handler shall not assist his fowl from where he sits him, if he does, he forfeits the battle.
8th.	In no case shall they handle the fowls, unless they are in one another, or can count ten between fighting.
9th.	The fowls in hand, each man to his station; either counting ten, the fowls must be set, or the delinquent loses the match.
10th.	The fowls, set, either refuses to show fight, the last that showed has the count, which is five times ten, and then they are breasted.
11th.	The fowls are breasted at every five times ten, after once breasted.
12th.	The fowls brought to the breast, the one that had the count counts five times ten more, and then twenty; then he claims the battle, which is his.
13th.	In case the fowls show while counting, it destroys the count, and they commence again.
14th.	In case a fowl is on his back, his handler can turn him over.
15th.	In all cases the parties can select Judges from the company present.
16th.	In case there are no Judges, it will be left to the keeper of the pit.
17th.	In no cases shall any person talk with the handlers while the fowls are fighting.
18th.	All disorderly persons will be requested to leave IMMEDIATELY.
19th.	All weighing will be left to a man selected for the purpose.
20th.	All matches will be fought with round heels, unless otherwise agreed upon.
21st.	A man known to use any other, unless agreed upon, forfeits the battle.
22d.	All cutters, slashers and twisted heels are barred from this pit.
23d.	In all cases the last fowl that shows fight, has the count.
24th.	All fowls brought to the pit that do not show fight, do not lose the battle, unless otherwise agreed upon.

Gentlemen are requested not to Smoke in this Room.

NEW YORK RULES ON COCKING

Art. 1. The pit shall be a circular pit, at least eighteen feet in diameter, and not less than sixteen inches in height—the floor of which shall be covered with carpet, or some other suitable material; there shall be a chalk or other mark made as near as can be to the centre of the pit; there shall also be two marks, which shall be one foot each way from the centre mark.

2. The pitters shall each choose and judge, who shall chose a referee—said judges shall decide all matters in dispute during the pendence of a fight; but in case of their inability to agree, then it shall be the duty of the referees to decide and whose decision shall be final.

3. Chickens shall take their age from the first day of March, and shall be a chicken during the following fighting season, to wit: From the first day of March, 1859, to the first day of June, 1860.

4. It shall be deemed foul for either of the respective pitters to pit a cock with what is termed a foul hackle, that is, any of the shining feathers left whole upon the mane or neck.

5. The pitters shall let each cock bill each other three or more times, but this is not to be so construed that the pitter of a cock has a right to bill with his opponent's cock for the purpose of fatiguing him.

6. No person shall be permitted to handle his cock after he is fairly delivered in the pit, unless he counts ten, clear and distinct, without either cock making fight: or shall be fast in his adversary, or fast in the carpet, or hung in the web of the pit, or in himself.

7. Any cock that may get on his back the pitter thereof shall turn him off it, but not take him off the ground he is lying on.

8. Whenever a cock is fast in his adversary, the pitter of the cock the spurs are fast in shall draw them out; but the pitter of a cock has no right to draw his own spur except when fast in himself, or in the carpet, or in the web of the pit.

9. When either pitter shall have counted ten times successively, without the cock refusing fight making fight, again breasting them fair on their feet, breast to breast and beak to beak on the centre score or mark, on the fifth ten being told, and also on the ninth ten being told, shall have won the fight. The pitters are bound to tell each ten as they count them, as follows: once, twice, etc.

10. No pitter, after the cocks have been delivered in the pit, shall be permitted to clean their beaks or the eyes, by blowing or otherwise, or of squeezing his cock or pressing him against the floor, during the pendency of a fight.

11. When a cock is pounded, and no person take it until the pitter counts twenty twice, and calls three times "who takes it?" and no person does take it, it is a battle to the cock the odds are on; but the pitter of the pounded cock has the right to have the pound put up, that is, twenty dollars against one; should not this demand be complied with, then the pitter shall go on as though there was no poundage.

12. If a cock is pounded and the poundage taken, and if the cock the odds are laid against should get up and knock down his adversary, then if the other cock is pounded and the poundage not taken before the pitter counts twenty twice, and calls out three times "who takes it?" he wins, although there was a poundage before.

13. It shall be the duty of the respective pitters to deliver their cocks fair on their feet on the outer mark, or score, facing each other, and in a standing position, except on the fifth ten being told, and on the ninth ten being told, when they shall be placed on the centre score, breast to breast and beak to beak, in like manner. Any pitter being guilty of shoving his cock across the score, or of pinching him, or using any other unfair means for the purpose of making his cock fight, shall lose the fight.

14. If both cocks fight together, and if then both should refuse until they are counted out, in such cases a fresh cock is to be hoveled and brought into the pit, and the pitters are to toss for which cock is so set-to first; he that wins the toss has the choice; then the one which is to set-to last is to be taken up, but not carried off the pit; then the hoveled cock is to be put down to the other and let fight, whilst the judges or one of them shall count twenty, and the other in like manner; and if one fight and the other refuse, it is a battle to the fighting cock; but if both fight, or both refuse, it is a drawn battle.

15. If both cocks refuse fighting until four, five, or more or less tens are counted, the pitters shall continue their count until one cock has refused ten times, for when a pitter begins to count, he counts for both cocks.

16. If a cock should die before they are counted out, although he fought last, he loses his battle. This, however, is not to apply when his adversary is running away.

17. The crowing, or the raising of the hackle of a cock, is not fight, nor his fighting at the pitter's hands.

18. A breaking cock is a fighting cock, but a cock breaking from his adversary is not fight.

19. If any dispute arise between the pitters on the result of a fight, the cocks are not to be taken off the pit, nor the gaffle taken off until it is decided by the judges or the referee.

20. Each cock within two ounces of each other, shall be a match, except blinkers, when fighting against two-eyed cocks, an allowance of from three to five ounces will be made; when blinkers are matched against each other, the same rule to apply as to two-eyed cocks.

21. Any person fighting a cock heavier than he is represented on the match list, shall lose the fight, although he may have won.

22. In all cases of appeal, fighting ceases until the judges or the referee give their decision, which shall be final, and strictly to the question before them.

23. When a bet is made, it cannot be declared off unless by consent of both parties. All outside bets to go according to the main bet.

24. Any person violating any of the above rules, shall be deemed to have lost the match.

RULES OF COCKPITS IN THE SOUTH

RULES TO BE OBSERVED IN CONDUCTING A SHOW OR A MAIN OF COCKS

ARTICLE 1.—On the morning the main is to commence, the parties decide by lot who shows first. It is to be remembered that the party obtaining the choice generally chooses to weigh first; and consequently obliges the adverse party to show first, as the party showing first weighs last. When the show is made by that party, the door of the cockhouse is to be locked, and the key given to the other party, who immediately repairs to his cockhouse, and prepares for weighing. There ought to be provided a pair of good scales, and weights as low down as half an ounce. One or two judges to be appointed to weigh the cocks. Each party, by weighing the cocks intended for the show a day or two beforehand, and having all of their respective weights, would greatly facilitate the business of the judges. There should be two writers to take down the colors, weights, marks, etc., of each cock. There ought to be no feathers cut or plucked from the cocks before they are brought to the scale, except a few from behind to keep them clean, and their wings and tails clipped a little.

ARTICLE 2. As soon as the cocks are all weighed, the judges, the writers and the principles of each party, and as many besides as the parties may agree on, are to retire for the purpose of matching. They are to make all even matches first, then those within half an ounce, and afterwards those within an ounce; but if more matches can be made by breaking an even or half-ounce match, it is to be done.

ARTICLE 3. On the day of showing, only one battle is to be fought. It is to be remembered, that the party winning the show gains also the choice of fighting the first battle with any particular cock in the match. Afterwards they begin with the lightest pair first, and so on up to the heaviest fighting, then in rotation, as they increase in weight. This first battle, too, will fix the mode of trimming.

RULES TO BE OBSERVED IN THE PIT

ARTICLE 1. When the cocks are in the pit, the judges are to examine whether they answer the description taken in the match bill, and whether, they are fairly trimmed, and have on fair heels. If all be right and fair, the pitters are to deliver their cocks six feet apart (or thereabouts), and retire a step or two back; but if a wrong cock should be produced, the party so offending forfeits that battle.

ARTICLE 2. All heels that are round from the socket to the point are allowed to be fair; any pitter bringing a cock on the pit with any other kind of heels, except by particular agreement, forfeits the battle.

ARTICLE 3. If either cock should be trimmed with a close, unfair back the judge shall direct the other to be cut in the same manner, and at the time shall observe to the pitter, that if he brings another cock in the like situation, unless he shall have been previously trimmed, he shall forfeit the battle.

ARTICLE 4. A pitter, when he delivers his cock, shall retire two paces back, and not advance or walk around his cock until a blow has passed.

ARTICLE 5. An interval of—minutes shall be allowed between the termination of one battle and the commencement of another.

ARTICLE 6. No pitter shall pull a feather out of a cock's mouth, or from over his eyes or head, or pluck him by the breast to make him fight, or pinch him for the like purpose, under penalty of forfeiting the battle.

ARTICLE 7. The pitters are to give their cocks room to fight, and are not to hover or press on them, so as to retard their striking.

ARTICLE 8. The greasing, peppering, muffing, and soaping a cock, or any other external application, are unfair practices, and by no means admissable in this amusement.

ARTICLE 9. The judge, when required, may suffer a pitter to call in some of his friends to assist in catching his cock, who are to retire immediately as soon as the cock is caught, and in no other instance is the judge to suffer the pit to be broken.

ARTICLE 10. All cocks on their backs are to be immediately turned over on their bellies by their respective pitters at all times.

ARTICLE 11. A cock, when down, is to have a wing given him, if he needs it, unless his adversary is on it, but his pitter is to place the wing gently in its proper position, and not to lift the cock; and no wing is to be given unless absolutely necessary.

ARTICLE 12. If either cock should be hanged in himself, in the pit or canvas, he is to be loosed by his pitter; but if in his adversary, both pitters are to immediately lay hold of their respective cocks, and the pitter, whose cock is hung, shall hold him steady whilst the adverse party draws out the heel, and then they shall take their cocks as under a sufficient distance for them fairly to renew the combat.

ARTICLE 13. Should the cocks separate, and the judge be unable to decide when fought last, he shall at his discretion direct the pitters to carry their cocks to the middle of the pit, and deliver them beak to beak, unless either of them is blind—in that case they are to be shouldered, that is delivered with their breasts touching, each pitter taking care to deliver his cock at this, as well as at all other times, with one hand.

ARTICLE 14. When both cocks cease fighting, it is then in the power of the pitter of the last fighting cock, unless they touch each other, to demand a count of the judges, who shall count forty deliberately, which, when counted out, is not to be counted again during the battle. Then the pitters shall catch their cocks and carry them to the middle of the pit, and deliver them beak to beak, but to be shouldered if either is blind, as before. Then if either cock refuses or neglects to fight, the judge shall count ten, and shall direct the pitters to bring their cocks again to the middle of the pit, and pit as before; and if the same cock in like manner refuses, he shall count ten again, and call out, "twice refused," and so proceed until one cock thus refuses six times successively. The judge shall then determine the battle against such cock.

ARTICLE 15. If either cock dies before the judge can finish the counting of the law, the battle is to be given to the living cock, and if both die, the longest liver wins the battle.

ARTICLE 16. The pitters are not to touch their cocks whilst the judge is in the act of counting.

ARTICLE 17. No pitter is ever to lay hold of his adversary's cock, unless to draw out the heel, and then he must take him below the knee. Then there shall be no second delivery—that is, after he is once delivered, he shall not be touched until a blow is struck, unless ordered by the judge.

ARTICLE 18. No pitter shall touch his cock, unless at the times mentioned in the foregoing rules.

ARTICLE 19. If any pitter acts contrary to these rules, the judge, if called on at the time, shall give the battle against him.

RULES OF THE SAN FRANCISCO GAME CLUB

1. When the cocks are brought to the pit, the pitters enter the same, and no other person or persons shall be admitted, within its limits. The pitters then proceed to examine

the cocks, and see that they have on fair heels. Secondly, that neither of the parties have resorted to the unmanly and foul practice of greasing, soaping, peppering, or making any other external application; all of which are foul and inadmissable.

2. All things being right and fair, the pitters shall deliver their cocks fairly on their feet upon the score, and then retire one or two steps, and not move their hands or walk around their cocks until a blow is struck; then they may approach their cocks for the purpose of handling them when they hang; but they are not to hover over the cocks so as to retard or prevent them from making a blow; and if either cock refuses to make fight it shall then be considered no match.

3. When the cocks are hanged the pitters shall lay hold of their respective cocks, and the party whose cock is hanged shall hold him steadily while the reverse party draws the heel; nor shall either party cause in any manner unnecessary injury or punishment while the heel is being extracted, and as soon as the cocks are freed they shall again be delivered on the score.

4. All cocks hanged in the canvas, ground, or in themselves, shall be loosened by their respective pitters at all times.

5. When one or both cocks are hanged, it is necessary to handle them and deliver them at the score so they may renew the combat fairly.

6. When the cocks are put to, if either cock refuses to fight, the other pitter has a right to the count, when he proceeds to count forty deliberately, which when counted is not to be counted again during that battle.

7. Should either or both cocks, after being delivered, not make fight, the pitter whose cock fought last shall be entitled to the count, when he shall count deliberately six times ten, and at every count they shall both handle and deliver their cocks on the score. On the third and sixth count they shall deliver their cocks breast to breast, and if on the sixth count, after being so delivered they do not make fight, the pitter having the count shall have won the fight.

8. If in counting the law the other cock makes fight, that breaks the count, and if he is the last fighter he is entitled to the count; but one must refuse or neglect to make fight six successive times before the battle can be decided against him.

9. If either or both cocks die before the pitters finish counting the law, the fight shall be awarded to the last fighting cock.

10. Neither pitter shall be allowed to touch or handle his cock while counting the law.

11. No pitter shall be allowed to suck or sling blood from his cock's throat or mouth, nor pluck feathers from over his eyes or out of his mouth.

12. All cocks lying on their backs shall be turned on their bellies by their respective pitters, at all times, provided the other cock is not standing on him. If his pitter neglect or refuse to turn him, it is then admissable for the other pitter to turn him gently on his belly.

13. All cocks shall have a wing given them provided the other is not upon it. In giving the wing it is to be placed gently by his side, without raising the cock or helping him on his feet.

14. When both cocks break together, and the pitters and judges are unable to decide which fought last, or when both are hanged in each other, it shall be the duty of the judges to order them to the score; and if both refuse to fight, the pitters shall count

the law, and have them put to as if the count were actually going on; and if neither make fight before the count is finished the fight shall be pronounced drawn.

15. Any pitter acting contrary to the foregoing Rules forfeits the battle.

MAIN BETWEEN NEW YORK AND MASSACHUSETTS
DESCENT OF THE POLICE—CAPTURE OF THE BIRDS AND THEIR OWNERS

The main to be fought in Boston, on the 26th ult., between New York and Massachusetts, was put a stop to by the authorities of Boston, while the fourth battle was in progress. We stated in our last that the main was to show 21 cocks, and fight all that weighed in. The Boston papers are full of the details of the grand onslaught of the police, and the result of the main as far as it had proceeded. It seems that the authorities resolved to make an example of the principal offenders who chose to engage in this pastime, which, although it has its devotees in Spain, France, and among the aristocracy in England, as well as among our people in various parts of America, is altogether unpuritanical and extremely wicked in the eyes of those people who deem it *cruel* to allow these ambitious and pugnacious birds to be put to death in any other way than by *wringing their necks* for the pot, or *torturing* them into capons for *aldermanic stomachs*. Arrangements had been made for the match in Tammany Hall, adjoining the National Theatre, where a pit twenty feet in diameter, and elevated about eighteen inches from the floor, was erected in the middle of the room, and surrounded by seats in amphitheatrical form, where three hundred or more spectators could be comfortably placed in full view of the arena of the combat. Some two hundred persons, consisting of the leading members of the sporting fraternity of Boston, and others, were assembled. About eight o'clock the first pair of fowls were weighed and pitted against each other. The Boston fowls on the "main" were the favorites at from 100 to 60, to 3 to 1, and there was a little business transacted upon the single battles at about the same rates. The first battle resulted in favor of Boston, the New York cock having been fricasseed in the space of 4 1/2 minutes. The victim was game to the last, but an unlucky blow from his antagonist in the commencement of the fight had put him at great disadvantage. The birds were carried off, and in about ten minutes the second pair of combatants was brought out. The New York crower was a most savage creature. While an attempt was being made to weigh him he escaped from his handler and pitched into the front row of spectators with a fury which brought any number of backers on his battle. At it they went, and the New Yorker cooked the Boston bird in four minutes, when the latter, after a spirited fight, was carried off entirely disabled, and victory perched upon the banner of New York. For the third battle, two fine looking cocks were put into the arena. Boston was altogether defiant, and New York was entirely spiteful. The Boston fowl, however, at the first flip inflicted a wound upon the throat of his antagonist, who defended himself with determined pluck four minutes and a quarter, and was then carried off vanquished. The fourth battle promised to be a better one than either of the preceeding ones. Two noble cocks of variegated plumage and most ferocious temperament were brought out, and expectation rose on tiptoe to witness their duel. Expectations, however, suddenly subsided into its boots, for, just as the cocks were whetting their beaks to attack each other's vitals, the "beaks" (cockney for policemen) made their appearance and put an instant stop to the proceedings. The assembly was struck with astonishment, which paralyzed their faculties for a moment, and was succeeded by a panic. They attempted a stampede, but found the doors guarded by the inexorable police, twelve officers of the first station, headed by Deputy Ham, Captain Savage and Bishop Whitecomb. Their egress was prevented until the officers had divested the principals of their cocks, which were locked up in safety, and arrested such as they chose among the company. There were present some gentlemen from New York, from New Bedford, from Providence, from Manchester, N. H., and from various cities in the suburbs of Boston. A portion of the crowd discovered a mode of exit by a rear door, and the way they tumbled over each other down stairs to the street, was a caution to birds of any feather known in ornithology. The principal cock fighters obeyed the summons to stand and deliver, without parley, and were escorted to the 1st station. They were eight in number, and gave the following names:—John Saunders, George Austin, John Morrissey, John Lawrence, William Brown, Samuel Smith, John Doe and Richard Roe. On arriving at the station house, Judge Maine was sent for to receive their bail, and bonds were promptly furnished by their friends. Four of them recognized in $900 each, and the remainder in S400 each. They are held for appearance upon three charges or counts, viz:—Giving an entertainment without license, aiding and abetting in an unlawful game, and cruelty to animals.

The arrested parties appeared before Judge Rogers, on the 27th. They were complained of, first—"For severally setting on foot, maintaining and carrying on a certain public exhibition, to wit, a cock fight." Second—"For using an unlawful game, to wit, the game of cock fighting." Third—"For cruelly torturing two live cocks." The defendants, through their counsel, Hon. B.F. Butler, pleaded not guilty, and after a short discussion relative to bail, the Court ordered that each individual recognize in the sum of $200 for appearance on the 3d inst.

Chapter 5

BOXING

The manly art of prize fighting was the most popular spectator sport throughout most regions of North America during the middle decades of the nineteenth century. Despite the objections of genteel society, the respectable press, and clergymen, bare-knuckle bouts excited the masses in Canada and the United States. Urban politicians, gamblers, and the sporting periodicals promoted these brutal contests, which often matched foreign (usually Irish) and native born antagonists. Workingmen and more than a few from the middle and upper classes eagerly awaited the encounters between such pugilistic heroes as Yankee Sullivan, Tom Hyer, John Morrissey, and John C. Heenan. The challenges attracted great interest because they symbolized ethnic conflicts and presented dramatic and violent displays of manly courage and skill. They also offered participants and spectators an opportunity to collect large sums of money from prizes and winning bets. Although many states banned these battles, they were still the featured commercial spectacles of the era.

During the 1840s North American boxers observed the newly adopted rules of the London prize ring, framed in 1838. They continued the earlier regulations that specified that a round ended when a man was down and that each fighter then had thirty seconds to toe a mark in the middle of the ring (called the "scratch"). The old code also banned hitting below the belt and striking a fallen opponent, and it provided for seconds to assist the contestants, umpires to settle disputes, and a referee to declare a final verdict. The new laws prohibited many of the tactics tolerated under the old system, including pulling hair, butting heads, gouging eyes, kneeing the groin, and choking the neck. Despite these reforms, most leaders of public opinion in the United States condemned prize fighting as barbarous and immoral. They charged that the sport celebrated violence, promoted insubordination, brutalized taste, bred crime, encouraged gambling, demoralized laborers, and corrupted the youth. To them boxing threatened republican ideals and undermined the progress of civilization. As a result of these objections many states banned bare-knuckle fights, although the local authorities did not always strictly enforce these laws. On a few occasions fighters and their followers fled across the border to Canadian towns where the police tolerated the matches.

The opponents of the ring objected to the fights in part because they frequently caused severe injury or even death to one or both of the contestants. The bouts often lasted dozens of rounds and took several hours to complete. Men often bled profusely and refused to yield even if they had suffered broken limbs. "The Horrible Death of McCoy" and "The Slaughter of McCoy" describe the first recorded fatality in American boxing, the death of Thomas McCoy at the hands of Christopher Lilly at Hastings, New York, 13 September 1842.

The outcome of the Lilly-McCoy battle sparked a rage of protests that deflated interest in prize fighting, but by the end of the decade the sport was showing some signs of life. From the late 1840s down to 1860 a series of charismatic champions excited the crowds who flocked to see them batter each other into a pulp. First among this parade of heroes was Yankee Sullivan, an Irish immigrant whose real name was probably James Ambrose. Born in Banden, near Cork, in 1813, he arrived in America in 1840. After defeating a few opponents he became a New York City celebrity, but his role as a promoter of the ill fated Lilly-McCoy match landed him in Ossining prison for a few months. In 1845 he opened a saloon in the Bowery and two years later he decided to renew his pugilistic career. In 1849 he fought Tom Hyer in a battle that went only sixteen rounds and lasted only seventeen minutes and eighteen seconds. A document below describes Hyer's victory, which paved the way for the boxing mania of the 1850s.

The next celebrated boxer to enter the ring was John Morrissey. Also a native of Ireland, he came to the United States with his family at the age of three. Raised in poverty in Troy, New York, he moved to New York City, where he earned a reputation as a brutal street fighter. Nicknamed "Old Smoke," he won a contest for $2000 a side in California when his backers threatened his opponent during the match and forced him to forfeit. Back in New York City in September 1853 Morrissey agreed to terms with Yankee Sullivan for a match that was held at Boston Corners, a small town close to the intersection of the borders of New York, Massachusetts, and Vermont. The matchmakers picked the location to reduce the chances of interference by the police. The fight was the first one in the United States to be governed by the newly revised set of rules drawn up in England earlier that year. The "New Rules of the Ring as Revised by the Pugilistic Association" presents these regulations, which were promulgated by the Pugilistic Benevolent Association as a reform of the code adopted in 1838 for the London prize ring. The following document tells the story of the Morrissey-Sullivan slugfest, which ended in a free-for-all. The referee decided in favor of Morrissey, although Sullivan objected and demanded a rematch. While Morrissey continued his career in New York, Sullivan moved to California to start a new life as a political enforcer and ballot box stuffer. In 1856 San Francisco's authorities jailed him and ordered him deported as an undesirable. Four days after he was sentenced he was found dead in his cell, an apparent suicide or perhaps a victim of murder.

The next champion pugilist to emerge was John C. Heenan. Born in Morrissey's hometown of Troy, New York, Heenan was also from an Irish family. Seventeen years old in 1852, he journeyed to California where he labored in the workshops of the Pacific Mail Steamship Company in Benicia. Nicknamed the "Benecia Boy," he had a few adventures in San Francisco politics before he moved to New York City. There he decided to try the prize ring with the support of Frank Queen, editor of the New York Clipper. The young man challenged Morrissey to a fight, which took place at Long Point, Canada West on October 20, 1858. As with previous championship contests, the pugilists had to evade the law and finally settled on a Canadian site to foil the New York authorities. Old Smoke outlasted the Benecia Boy in eleven rounds. Although Heenan demanded a rematch, Morrissey retired from the ring and devoted the rest of his life to his political career and gambling interests.

Heenan's greatest hour came in the spring of 1860, when he traveled to England to face the British champion, Tom Sayers. This contest matched the bare-knuckle brawlers of two nations, and the press promoted it as a titanic struggle between the two great branches of the Anglo-Saxon race. The Heenan-Sayers fight of April 17, 1860 was the most publicized sporting event in North America during the middle years of the nineteenth century. As the newspaper accounts of this battle reprinted below suggest, the bout generated an enormous amount of excitement and nationalistic fervor on both sides of the Atlantic. Its controversial ending left all the enthusiasts dissatisfied. After weeks of negotiation each fighter was awarded a championship belt. Although Sayers's retirement left Heenan as the new heavyweight champion, most Americans felt that the Benecia Boy had been cheated out of a well deserved clear cut victory by British foul play. Sporting periodicals and genteel newspapers devoted many columns to news reports and editorial commentary about the fight. The final document in this chapter presents the reactions of the London Times and the New York Times.

Bare-knuckle prize fighting enjoyed tremendous popularity in North America during this era because it appealed in many ways to men who were struggling to cope with the pressures of life in their towns and cities. As immigrant and native born workingmen labored long hours under dangerous conditions for low pay, they naturally turned to amusements during their limited leisure time. Bachelors and young men were particularly attracted to boxing matches for a variety of reasons. The fights provided an opportunity for the spectators to vent their feelings of ethnic, occupational, or social class pride. Witnessing a match bound men together and permitted them to express their collective hatred for a despised enemy. In addition, the contests were displays of craftmanship that artisans could admire for the skills exhibited by the pugilists. Prize fighting offered poor men a chance to earn great wealth while their backers reaped the rewards of successful wagers. Fighting provided an alternative model of success, especially to Irish newcomers who stood little chance to rise in the ranks of respectable society.

It was no accident there was a close connection between urban political machines and pugilism since both gave lower class natives and foreigners opportunities for advancement. Most major prize fighters had affiliations with urban gangs such as New York City's Bowery Boys. These gangs in turn usually attached themselves to factions of various clubhouses or parties, who used their recruits as "shoulder hitters" (enforcers) or ballot box stuffers.

Finally, the bare-knuckle bouts celebrated a concept of masculinity that was the opposite of the manly ideal of the middle and upper classes. While the Victorian standard of a gentleman stressed discipline, self-control, sobriety, and the work ethic, the sporting fraternity valued courage, toughness, ferocity, power, and honor. The bloodiness of the battles appealed to men who knew first hand the violence of the streets. For all these reasons many workers and some from the more respectable classes intently followed the progress and champions of the manly art of self defense.

CHRISTOPHER LILLY VS. THOMAS McCOY, 1842

In the late summer of 1842 Yankee Sullivan arranged a prize fight betwen his friend Christopher Lilly and Thomas McCoy. Sullivan had recently won a bout with William Bell and enjoyed great popularity as a saloon keeper and pugilist. The fifteen hundred men who journeyed up the Hudson River to Hastings, New York anticipated a good spectacle, but instead they witnessed a fatal encounter. The battle lasted two hours and forty-three minutes and ended with the death of McCoy, who drowned in his own blood which had drained into his lungs. A Westchester County grand jury indicted eighteen accessories. Most of them escaped with fines, but Sullivan and two other backers of the fight were tried and convicted of fourth-degree manslaughter. The outcome of the contest created a wave of revulsion among New York City journalists. The following document presents the editorial opinion of Horace Greeley of the New York Daily Tribune, reprinted from the issues of 19 and 20 September 1842.

THE HORRIBLE DEATH OF McCOY

...Christopher Lilly, by whose hands McCoy met his death, is a young man of English parentage and 'sporting' habits, about 23 years old. He lately fought a pugilistic battle with one Murphy, and came off victor. He has since been engaged in sparring exhibitions in the Bowery, where he met Thomas McCoy, a Whitehall boatman, only 20 years old, of Irish parentage, and it seems a young man of fine character, marred by a fondness for pugilistic display and for the company and the scenes to which this taste introduced him. These two young men had been old acquaintances, and there was an unsettled grudge between them. They met at one of the flash groggeries [working class saloons] where pugilism is the staple of excitement, soon after Lilly's victory over Murphy, which was the theme of general applause, in which McCoy refused to join. Being challenged for his opinion, he gave it against Lilly's achievement. This nettled the champion, who asked him to put on the gloves and try a round with him; McCoy refused, and instantly Lilly struck him a blow which laid him on the floor. He rose and rushed at the assailant, but they were separated and a regular fight instantly agreed on by their respective friends; $200 being the original stakes, but thousands were afterwards bet upon the result. The day was fixed, and the parties went directly into training.

On Tuesday morning last, being the day agreed on, the pitted boxers, their seconds, doctors, friends, judges, &c., and some thousands eager to be spectators, left in two steamboats for the selected battle-ground, near the little village of Hastings, in Westchester Co., 20 miles from this City. McCoy had been in training at Hoboken, and was taken on board there. He lay down during most of the passage.

And here we approach the horrors of this bloody business. In the first place, McCoy had been sick, and was evidently in an inferior condition for such an affray. Then he was an inch the shorter, four or five pounds the lighter, and three years the younger of the two, rendering him plainly no match for his antagonist. He was also too high on flesh [flabby], showing that he had not been carefully trained for such brutality, if any lad of twenty is hardy enough to be so pitted. He was brave to rashness, (how awful a perversion of courage!) and his backers and those who by their presence and silence encouraged the fight are in the eyes of Justice his destroyers.

Let none say that his death was accidental. He openly avowed, on starting to the battleground, that he went to *"win or die."* He tied a *black* handkerchief to his post in the ring as his colors, to evince the same determination. Not one of the fifteen hundred who quietly looked on could have been ignorant that his life was the fearful stake of the contest.

We shall not of course enter upon the details of this horrid conflict. Its result was never doubtful, except through some accident. Lilly was cool, cautious and husbanded his strength; McCoy rash, eager, probably smarting under a sense of wrong, exposing himself constantly, and wasting his energy in furious, ineffective lunges. His *seconds* and backers had not even sense enough to caution him against his errors until he was virtually beaten. They saw him sweat like rain, and their only expedient was to deluge him repeatedly in cold water! The judges twice decided that Lilly struck 'foul,' giving the battle to McCoy; but his principal backer waived the 'advantage,' as he called it, and suffered the fight to go on! And their beautiful *doctor!* who was there, if for any thing, to save the life of their champion in extremity, saw the murder perfected without a word, only interpolating to *lance the eyes* of the victim, as directed, when they had been entirely closed by the blows of his antagonist!

It is of course understood that McCoy was a willing victim. He probably sought— he certainly did not shun—the conflict. At the opening of the fight, he drew from his pocket two $100 bills, and bet them on the result with his opponent. He evidently fought throughout under the influence of personal feeling. At the 113th round, after he had been thrown or had fallen at least one hundred times, when he could hardly see at all, he called to his seconds. *"Nurse me—nurse me! and I'll whip him yet!"* And this when his face and breast had been beaten to a bloated, pulpy mass of corruption— when his lifeblood was gurgling from his mouth, and choking his breath, and when every minute he was ejecting it upon the body of his antagonist!

Where were his seconds? his doctor? and the fifteen hundred spectators? The first urging on the fight; the second doing nothing; of the last a few murmured and two or three remonstrated aloud, but not one stirred to rescue him from inevitable death! It is but just to say that Lilly twice or thrice called out that he ought to be taken away, and one of his seconds did the same; but at the 19th round Chanfroid, one of McCoy's backers, replied to a remonstrance, *"He a'nt half licked yet!"* And this when there was not probably fifteen minutes' life in him if he had then been taken away!

How shall we speak of the getters up and encouragers of this fight?—the gamblers, the brothelmasters, and keepers of flash groggeries, who were ever the chief patrons of 'the ring,' and who were the choice spirits of this festival of fiends? They were in raptures as the well-aimed, deadly blows descended heavily upon the face and neck of the doomed victim, transforming the image of God into a livid and loathsome ruin; *they* yelled with delight as the combatants went down—often on their heads—with a force that made the earth tremble around them—as the blood spirted in rills from the fated sacrifice, or as his conqueror came down heavily upon him and lay there to beat the breath out of him, until taken off by the seconds! They enlivened the shocking scene, as McCoy's eyes closed beneath the blows of his antagonist, with "Shutters up! There's a death in the family!", "Finish him, Chris!" "Knock out his eye!" &c., and still as the work of death went on rang out at intervals the infernal chorus, "2 to 1 on Lilly!" "100 even on McCoy!"

—But why linger on the dreadful scene? At the o*ne hundred and twentieth* round, McCoy stood up as erect as ever, but with his eyes closed in funeral black, his nose destroyed, his face gone, and clots of blood choking the throat which had no longer power to eject them. He could barely walk, but still sparred with some spirit, though unable to get in a blow at his still vigorous antagonist, though the latter was evidently suffering severely from blows in his body. The fight had now lasted *two hours and forty-three minutes,* McCoy had received not less than *one hundred* square blows, and had been thrown or been knocked down *eighty-one times,* his opponent falling heavily as possible upon him. For the last time was this repeated; and, when Lilly was lifted off, McCoy was found lifeless, and sank inanimate as lead in his second's arms. 'Time' was called, but for him Time was no more! Lilly was declared victor, and, appearing little hurt and less disfigured, jumped with a cry of exhultation and sprang out of the ring! McCoy still gasped for breath, sucking his remnants of lips far back into his mouth by the violence of the effort. A moment more, and his struggles ceased—the widow's darling child had been immolated on the altar of *"Sport!"*—he was dead! And even in that moment of freezing horror—when it would seem that the blood of the hardiest ruffian must have curdled with conscious guilt and remorse, and a shadow darkened the most indurated brow—even then, in reference to the fact that *another* fight had been arranged to come off on this occasion, one voice was raised in the crowd, exclaiming, "Come, *carry off your dead, and produce your next man!"*—thus closed the fight at Hastings and the life of Thomas McCoy!

THE SLAUGHTER OF McCOY, ITS CAUSES, &C.

...Thomas McCoy is dead, from blows inflicted in a gambling fistfight with Christopher Lilly. In the eyes of all law, Lilly is guilty of manslaughter, if not of willful murder. But who will say that he alone is guilty! Who does not know that in the eyes of all law, justice, common sense, the seconds, backers, doctor, &c. are equally so and the seconds of McCoy, if possible, more so?—Lilly and his seconds protested against continuing the fight after McCoy had been mangled beyond hope of victory; but McCoy's seconds insisted that "He aint half licked yet," and continued to place him on his feet to fight. But were these all the guilty? Law and Justice again thunder out their emphatic negative.

The spectators, who crowded to the ground to see two men pound each other out of the likeness of Humanity, and stood by to see it done without resistance, were guilty;

The owners and officers of steamboats, who knowingly and willingly conveyed them to the battle-ground, were guilty;

The Police, who knew that this fight was getting up, yet took no efficient measures to prevent it, were guilty;

The keepers of groggeries and dens of vice, in which pugilism is practiced, encouraged, honored and promoted, are guilty;

And that portion of the Press which has published advertisements of fights to take place, with flash reports of those which have occurred—which sends reporters to the battle-grounds, and dishes up a lively, admiring account of 'Round 1,' '2,' '3,' &c., embellished with the choice terms of 'the fancy'—these are deeply guilty.

We will say nothing of their patrons—will carry the scrutiny no farther at present. We have already culprits enough. Now let us inquire how and by whom these brutalities are got up.

In the first place, we rejoice to know that the originators and fosterers of pugilism in this country are almost entirely foreigners by birth. This species of ruffianism is not native here, nor is our atmosphere congenial to it. To say nothing of the combatants; the seconds, trainers, &c. of this fight, as of former fights, are, with hardly an exception, from abroad. *Yankee* Sullivan is an Irishman; so is McCleeskey, McGhee, Shanfroid, and other parties to this homicide are also from Europe. This is encouraging. This horrid vice—alas that we must more correctly say, this *form* of a horrid vice—has but a sickly hold on our soil, and may be wholly extirpated if proper exertions are made at the proper time. That time, we need not state, is now.

But again: the principal patrons of the pugilistic *science!* among us are the keepers of drinking-houses of the very worst description, professional gamblers, and a few who unite with one or both of these highly reputable and useful callings the keeping or protecting of brothels! To this rule there is hardly an exception. The three seconds who have run away were all keepers or drunkards at least; we believe one or more of them added to this one or both of the other vocations. The principal promoters and backers of the fight were what are called 'king gamblers'—keepers of faro banks, roulette tables, and the like. We believe the world might be safely challenged to produce a single patron of 'the ring' who lives by industry in any useful calling.

We have now a few questions to ask, which we trust will be answered to the public satisfactorily and speedily. They are these: Who licenses foreigners of at best suspicious character to keep houses of public entertainment in our city? If those pugilistic grog shops are kept without licenses, whose duty is it to close them? Why is it not done? We believe some of these were located in the Second and Sixth Wards, and that the one in the former was shut up some days before this tragedy. How was and is it in the Sixth? Let us hear!

We have now a word to say of the organized bands in which pugilism and kindred vices have their main strength in our city. It is already well known that most of the backers of the late fights were members or associates of the far-famed 'Spartan Band,' and that several of them marched at its head in the late Tyler Indignant Procession. It is known that these men were prominent in the Sixth Ward Riots of last spring, and that they were then allowed to break heads and ballot boxes with wide impunity! This band are to a great extent masters of the city, the Police being either afraid of them or instructed to treat them with a most meek and loving kindness.

It is high time that our citizens enquired into this business, and ascertained what terms of mutual consideration and service exist betwen the most lawless and dangerous combination of our City on the one hand, and our highest Executive authorities on the other....

TOM HYER VS. YANKEE SULLIVAN

The fight between Tom Hyer and Yankee Sullivan in 1849 was the first of four spectacular championship bouts that preceded the Civil War. The match became a symbolic clash between the Irish and the Americans, for Hyer was native born and the hero of those who detested the immigrants who had flooded into America's cities during that era. As was frequently the case in early boxing, the contestants had to first elude capture by the police before they squared off in the ring. The following report of Hyer's victory first appeared in the Spirit of the Times, 17 February 1849, pp. 618-19.

THE GREAT PRIZE FIGHT BETWEEN TOM HYER AND YANKEE SULLIVAN

The great prize fight, which has been the standing topic of conversation for the last six months in fighting circles, and which to confess the truth, has occupied a large share of the attention of refined society during the same period of time, came off, according to agreement, on Wednesday, the 7th inst., at Rock Point, mouth of Silk Pond Creek, in Kent county on the Eastern Shore of Maryland, about 40 miles from Baltimore.

The location originally intended for the arena, was Pool's Island, in the upper part of Chesapeake bay, which had been selected by Sullivan three weeks before, as the most eligible spot for the intended meeting as he had heard that its jurisdiction was disputed, or divided by the state of Maryland and the Government of the United States. Moreover, it was thirty miles away, and apart from the light-house stationed on it, it had but two dwellings, and therefore, could not promise much local interference with the invading [illegible], who would pour upon it, as if from the mouth of the everlasting pit, on the indicated day.

But while Pool's Island lay perfectly quiet, showing no signs of disgust or opposition, obstacles were breeding in Baltimore, and by and by that virtuous city, which usually has a man a week killed in its streets, or two or three women ravished in the same period of time, became so indignant at the idea of making a hundred thousand dollars or so, by having a match of fisticuffs within electric distance of its borders, that it organized voluntary patrols to frown down the outrage, and stuffed a broken winded steamboat with crowds of sogers armed to the teeth, to rake the Chesapeake up and down, and in default of capturing the combatants, to sing Watt's hymns in honor of Gov. Thomas the night through.

These preparations on the part of the authorities of the State of Maryland, and the city of Baltimore, commenced on Tuesday morning, and both the steamboats which had been chartered by the several crowds, were paralyzed by the authorities with writs against their captains, and one of them, the Boston, was chartered by the State for the pursuit. While things were in this condition, Hyer apprehending, and correctly as proved, that warrants would be despatched after him and his trainers, slipped away from his training ground and went to Carroll's Island, a little island next to Pool's. Sullivan had anticipated him in this prudent course, having arrived at Carroll's Island on Monday afternoon, and crossed to Pool's before Hyer's arrival. Hyer shortly after crossed to Pool's Island also, and put up at the house attached to the lighthouse, with his two trainers, while Sullivan had secured the only other place for human accommodation, at some distance off. Leaving the principal parties thus bestowed, we will now return to Baltimore, to see how matters progress with those who have charge of the grand preliminaries of the affair, and with those likewise who were endeavoring to get a thimbleful of reputation out of the excitement, by trying to stop it.

Late in the afternoon of Tuesday, the backers, judges, referee, bottle-holders, &c., of both parties, finding that there was to be no steamboating on the following morning, hired two oyster smacks, and embarked, to the number of one hundred each side, and at 10 o'clock, put out upon the Chesapeake, in a bright but tempestuous night, which almost intimidated the captains of the pungees themselves. The name of the boat containing Sullivan's party was the "Whig" and as she swung from the dock, the Boston was "firing up" to carry military cargo to the same place to intercept them. However, the smacks sailed away unmolested. At the same hour, High Constable Gifford, of Baltimore, left with thirteen men, across the land to the nearest point opposite the designated scene of combat. At quarter before 12, the Boston got off on her errand. We have now three expeditions all directed to one spot, two of which were in pursuit, and the third dodging the chase.

THE DESCENT OF THE POLICE.

The pungees arrived at the island first, the "Whig" reaching the shore at half-past one P.M. Joe Beard, of Baltimore, and Country McCleester, were sent ashore to see if Sullivan were on the island, receiving directions, if he were asleep, not to awake him, but to let him have his natural rest till five o'clock, and then to wake him and tell him the steamboat was coming, and to hurry him on board. Following these directions, Joe, finding him asleep, sat down by the fire as a sentry, and went to sleep himself. Hyer's boat had now arrived, and a similar course was pursued in relation to him, the two boats meanwhile swinging to their anchors, and waiting for the daylight and the embarkment of their men.

In the meantime, Captain Gifford and his thirteen arrived upon the beach of the bay, at three o'clock, and seizing a boat in the name of the State, they unmooored, and set out in the biting atmosphere for the island. As they approached it, they perceived the steamer Boston, which had set out after them. They passed under her bows, but, such was the howling of the wind and the coldness of the night, that they were unheard. Gifford then departed, and with his forces proceeded to Hyer's house.

HYER'S ESCAPE.

The friends of Hyer were not keeping a bright look out; but one of them, nevertheless, heard the tramp of the police and ran up stairs and gave Tom notice. Tom jumped up instantly and putting Thompson his trainer in his bed, ran downstairs and crept under the cot of a negress on the ground floor. Dutch Charley conveyed him his clothes, and he then came out and commenced dressing, while the officers were being led up stairs by the owner of the house, who knew nothing of the metamorphosis that had taken place. The owner of the house pointed to Thompson in the bed. Seeing that he was a huge man, and taking him for Hyer, the officers soon desisted from their attempts to pull the cover from this face, and leaving a small detachment in charge, set out with the rest for Sullivan's house. As soon as they had gone, Hyer broke through the sash and commenced running toward the beach, but he was hailed by Winrow from a tree, who joined him in his flight. Arriving at the beach, they found two men with a boat belonging to the steam propeller "Columbia," which had just arrived off the island with about one hundred passengers from Philadelphia, to see the fight. They thus reached their schooner and were safe.

SULLIVAN'S ESCAPE.

When the police arrived at Sullivan's house, after leaving Hyer's, Joe Beard was dozing by the fire, but not so sound as not to hear Gifford ask and the man of the house reply, that Sullivan was up stairs. He gave the alarm in time, and Sullivan sprang out of the window, but being confronted with two men, one of whom levelled a pistol at him, was glad to retire back. He then started Tom O'Donnell from his sleep, and with that cloak over O'Donnell's shoulders, and clapping his hands, exclaimed, "Run, Sullivan, run, as if h-ll had kicked you! The officers completely deceived at this, seized O'Donnell, while the real Simon Pure slipped away. Sullivan then ran to a tree and climbed it for a few moments in case the officers should return, but seeing they did not, he slipped down, and crawling low into the advancing dawn, made for the beach like his opponent. Meantime the officers were lugging O'Donnell along, while Gifford would renew his grip on his collar every minute, like a man who doubted he was in a dream of fortune, and exclaim at intervals in half soliloquy, "Ah Sullivan, you're pretty smart, but you're not smart enough for us!" What he said when he discovered how Sullivan had fooled him, we have not heard. At the beach Sullivan was met by Johnny McGrath, who taking him on this shoulders marched with him through the surf, and placed him in the propeller's boat and had him rowed on board.

THE EMBARCATION.

Soon after this the Cumberland moved towards Sullivan's pungee and put him aboard. The propeller then started up the bay, and the Boston, with the military, mistaking her motions, supposed the two men had been taken on board of her and were going off to fight, and set out in chase, leaving the two pungees, which really contained the objects of their search, behind. Sullivan's boat then hailed Hyer's, and Colton, to guard against surprise in case they should leave the island and Hyer's party remain on the ground and win by being present merely, called put; "Show us Hyer and we'll show you Sullivan." Hyer and Sullivan were then brought up and as soon as they gazed upon each other the eyes of the latter [illegible] and he shook his fist at his tall opponent with a passionate epithet. "Look here my little man," said the captain of the "Whig," "if you allow yourself to get in such a passion on the start, you'll get whipped." "Will you follow us ?" said Becket to the opposite Judge. "Yes," said Hyer, "follow you anywhere." They then bore up the Chesapeake, finishing up the picture of the chase, the propeller being ahead, in the distance, the Boston next, and the two pungees, which were taken for outsiders going to see the fight, coming at last. After Sullivan's schooner had got well away they found they were not followed by the other pungee, when, dreading a ruse of Hyer's party again, they returned. But when they got back they found their suspicions were unjust, and that Hyer's pungee was aground.

Sullivan took this opportunity to send ashore for his fighting shoes which he had left behind, in his flight. Meantime, the Boston had discovered her error and was returning fast. By good luck for the fighters, howvever, Hyer's schooner got afloat just as she came up, and by bad luck for the hungry sogers the Boston got aground at the same time, and the two pungees, free at last, sailed off together, with their fingers to the bowsprits, in derision at the ineffectual attempts of all Baltimore and Maryland to interfere with New York. It was now settled that Hyer's boat should take the lead, and all hands being rather wolfish by their numerous disappointments, agreed to drop upon the first convenient - spot, whether it was in Maryland, or Delaware, or Virginia or hell. At half past one o'clock they espied a creek in which laid four or five small oyster schooners, and judging this to be a proper place, the crowd, to the number some two hundred, debarked.

THE DEBARCATION.

The motley crowd, glad to set foot on shore after the lengthened cramp which they had undergone in their close quarters, hastily debarked and swarmed in little buzzing knots upon the shore. Sullivan was among the first who felt the terra firma which he was to make such familiar acquaintance with before the afternoon was out, and espying a house at the distance of some three quarters of a mile ahead, set out to reach it before the opposing party, in order to secure what advantage there might be in earliest acquaintance with the inmates. Hyer, more prudent, however, preferred to avoid the trudging through the snow, and laid himself to be driven easily to the same place. A mile by a circuit, which might have been shortened by another path, brought them to the dwelling on the beach, and under its roof both the combatants found equal shelter. Each took up his quarters in large rooms on either side of the main hall, and huge fires of crackling hickory, soon streamed up the capacious chimney pieces, either in honor of the unexpected comers, or in deference to their powers of annoyance, should they be treated with any less deference than was due to the actual lords in fee simple and manorial right, to the estate.

The principals, both in good spirits, took their seats by the cheerful fires, while their satellites in reverential silence, grouped themselves around to listen to the least expressions which might fall from those who were to be the heroes of the day.

SETTING THE STAKES.

Meanwhile the more interested of the attaches of the separate side, occupied themselves in making preparations for the ring. The spot selected for the arena by Sullivan's friends, was between the house and the farm, and the location was considered favorable to the former, from the lumpy character of the surface, as it was expected that his wrestling qualities would enable him to throw his heavier antagonist, and punish him the more severely by the sharpness of his falls. The friends of Hyer seemed, however, to have a due appreciation of the policy of this intention, for after the snow was shovelled from the surface they spaded fresh earth and sprinkled the entire platform of the ring, so that it was made as soft and elastic as a carpet. The stakes were then procured from pine-billets found in the neighborhood, and for want of better gear, the top gallant halyards of the "Whig" were taken for the ropes. In the haste of their mechanics, the ring was not set exactly square but had an oblique twist towards the sun, while the southern side presented a slight acclivity which promised, when it was caught by interested and observant eyes, to become the bitterest battle ground. At ten minutes past four everything was set, and notice was given to the parties in the house that all was ready.

IN THE RING.

Sullivan shortly after this summons emerged from the house, being preceded by one of his seconds who carried a pair of hot bricks, which were intended for his feet while waiting for the signal to begin. As he approached the ring his appearance was hailed with cheers, and when he threw in his cap, which was a velvet one of a rich dark green, the most enthusiastic shouts were heard from his friends. He took his seat upon a chair that was provided for him, and with his feet upon the bricks, waited for the entrance of his foe. In two or three minutes more, Hyer came forth, borne on the brawny shoulders of his friend Dutch Charley, and as he neared the ropes, he shyed his castor, a foggy looking piece of felt, into the arena before him. Another burst of clamor then rent the sky, and amid increased enthusiasm, each man tied his colors to the stakes. That of Hyer was the spangled ensign of his country, while Sullivan's was a green fogle with oval spots of white. Both men sat down on their seconds' knees, and confronted each other while the final preliminaries were arranged.

While thus awaiting the summons to the ordeal, the seconds, Joe Winrow, and John Ling, the first for Hyer, and the latter for Sullivan, came forward and made the toss for choice of ground. This was won for Sullivan, who, therefore, reserved the corner where he already sat, giving to his antagonist the bright and dazzling sun directly in his eyes. The seconds now took their corners. Tom Bune taking the place of the captured Thompson, Hyer's regular trainer, and country McCleester supplying the absence of Tom O'Donnell, on the part of Sullivan. Outside the ropes, in waiting on the latter, was Stephen Wilson, acting as a bottle-holder and on the other corner, similarly affixed, was the brother of the lofty champion. At twenty minutes past four exactly, Winrow asked the question, Are you ready? Yes, said Sullivan, rising and beginning to strip off his outer clothes - an operation in which he was immediately followed by Hyer, and which was accomplished by both with the celerity of a stage metamorphosis. In less than a minute they stood stripped to the waist, and attired in their neat fighting clothes. Such was the absorbing interest which held possession of all minds during these proceedings, that but a single bet was offered and made. Indeed $35 was the entire amount that was wagered on the ground.

THE MEN.

As the antagonists stood up, all ready for the strife, there was a marked disparity in the appearance of the men. Hyer stood six feet two and a half inches, and Sullivan but five feet ten and a half. The weight of the former, moreover, was in the close neighborhood of 175, while the avoirdupois of Sullivan was rated no higher than 155, making the difference of thirty pounds in Hyer's favor. As to condition, both seemed equal. They were as finely developed in every muscle as their physical capacity could reach, and the bounding confidence which sparkled fiercely in their eyes, showed that their spirits and courage were at their highest mark. Sullivan with his round compact chest, formidable head, shelving flinty brows, fierce glaring eyes, and clean turned shoulders and arms, looked the very incarnation of the spirit of mischievous genius; while Hyer, with his broad formidable chest, and long muscular limbs, seemed as if he could almost trample him out of life at will.

THE FIGHT.

Before coming to the scratch, the umpire for Sullivan asked the seconds of his side, if they intended to examine Hyer's shoes, but they declined the formality as a matter of but little consequence, when the word was given and the men came up. According to rule they were obliged to shake hands before they began, but they performed this ceremony warily and at extreme arms length. It was the business of the seconds next to do the same, but before they could reach the scratch to go through the idle ceremony, the eager crowd shouted them back, and they gave way at once to the gladiatorial show.

Round 1. Sullivan with his arm well up, and every muscle swelling with preparation, darted towards Hyer, who stood resolutely waiting for him, with his body well forward and in formidable readiness; and coming up to him with a sort of run, let fly with his left at Hyer's head but did not get it in; he then got away from a short attempt of Hyer to counter with his left, but Hyer followed the effort with an instant discharge of his right on Sullivan's forehead, which made a long abrasion of the scalp, but which notwithstanding the power of the blow, showed neither blood nor discoloration at the time. Gathering himself for a return, Sullivan then rushed in at the body, and after two or three ineffective exchanges clinched his antagonist with the under hold and struggled for the throw. This was the great point on which was to depend the result of the fight. Sullivan relied mainly for success upon his superior wrestling, and it was calculated by his friends and backers, that a few of his favorite cross-buttocks would break his antagonist in his lithe and graceful waist, and not only render him limpsey with weakness, but stun him with the falls. The most terrible anxiety therefore existed as to the result of this endeavor. In its fierce agitations the spectators, who stood in an outer ring of plank laid over the snow, some feet distance from the ropes of the arena, involuntarily rushed forward and swarmed against the ropes. Two or three times did Sullivan knot his muscles with an almost superhuman effort, but all served only to postpone his overthrow for when he had spent his power by these terrible impulsions, his iron adversary wrenched him to the ground with the upper hold, and fell heavily proud [?] upon his body. This decided the largest part of the outside betting in favor of the winner, and shouts of the most terrific joy went up for Hyer. The depression of Sullivan's friends was equal in degree, and they began to get an inkling that they had underrated their opponent.

Round 2. As soon as time was called both men hurried to the scratch, Hyer working to the upper slope of the ring, where stood the judges and the referee, and thus slanting the sun between his body and that of his opponent, instead of taking its beams directly in his eyes. As Sullivan came up this time the blood from the scratch upon his forehead make crimson confession of its severity, and elated the friends of the tall one with shrieks of " first blood for Hyer." Sullivan at this hosanna rushed desperately in, and meeting Hyer where he paused to receive his charge, delivered a heavy blow with his right on Hyer's left eye, taking a counter on the opposing ogle in return. Sullivan kept close up, and both kept striking with the rapidity of two clocks as they fly together, rendering it almost impossible to see where, or how, they were discharged. It was evident, however, that the rally had not been attended with serious effect to either side. A feint from Sullivan, and a dodge from Hyer, intervened, when another rally followed, Sullivan taking in return for a couple of body blows two severe discharges on the left eye, by a sort of half-upper cut with his right hand, which brought the blood again. Sullivan then rushed in and clinched; he caught the underhold again, but his efforts were naught, and he was twisted to the ground as if he had been a man of grass, his huge antagonist falling on him as before, with his entire weight. Shouts for Hyer.

Round 3. The hopes of Yankee's friends were now fading fast, and indeed he seemed impressed himself with the idea that he was overmatched. He looked at his opponent with a sort of wild astonishment as he came up, but with a desperate courage, as if conscious that nothing but the most reckless policy alone could help him, he rushed up to the scratch, and gathering cautiously, after a wicked pause, he softened his apparent intention with a feint, but finding Hyer would not be drawn out, he let fly right and left, and catching Hyer with the latter blow upon the body (some say neck,) staggered him backwards a couple of steps and brought him to a sitting position on the ground. The shouts now went up on Sullivan's side and amidst the uproarious glee he went smiling to his corner....

Round 14. Sullivan giving out fast; Hyer perceiving it, entered briskly on the offensive, fought him to the ropes, and fibbed him on them as before. After an exchange of this kind of work, Hyer dragged him from the ropes, and clinching, wrenched him to the ground and fell upon him.

Round 15. Sullivan shaky on his pins, and Hyer apparently as strong as ever. As Sullivan came up and attempted to hit out, he slipped; Hyer rallied him to the ropes, hitting him right and left in the pursuit, and bending him again over the ropes. During this struggle he caught his arm, and bending it backward in its socket, gave it a wrench that must have caused the most agonizing pain; he then clinched and threw him to the ground and fell upon him as before.

Round 16. When time was called, Sullivan was slow in rising from his second's knee, and it was evident that his fighting star had set, for the day at least. He walked in a limpsey manner towards the score, but when he put up his left arm the tremor which shook it showed that it was distressed by pain. Hyer did not wait for him, but advancing beyond the score, let fly both right and left in Sullivan's face, who, though he could not return it, took it without wincing the least. Hyer then rushed him to the ropes again, and after a short struggle there, threw him and fell heavily upon him, in which position Sullivan locked his leg over him again, as if he would hold him in his place. When he was taken off, Sullivan was found to be entirely exhausted, and when lifted up reeled half round and staggered backward towards the ropes. The fight was done. He could not come in again, and one of his seconds took him from the ring, without waiting for time to be called. Hyer's second, as soon as this took place, advanced to take Sullivan's colors as their trophy, but being interfered with and denied by Ling, Hyer rushed forward himself, and seizing Ling by the arm, enabled his friend to take the prize. The shouts then went up for the victor, and the party commenced unthreading the stakes of their halyards for the voyage back.

Thus ended a contest which has excited more interest than any other pugilistic encounter that ever took place in this country; but which, though it engaged thousands of minds for a period of six long months, was done up, when once begun, in seventeen minutes and eighteen seconds.

The boats soon got up sail after the battle was over, and made for Pool's Island again on their return. On arriving at that place, they found the steamer still aground, and as her warlike freight came crowding to the side the pungees gave them three times three as a compensation for the disappointment they had received in neither arresting the principals, nor in getting a peep at the fight.

REMARKS.

The foregoing contest may be aptly termed a "hurricane fight." From the commencement to the close it was bitter, unremitting, and determined. On the part of Sullivan, it consisted of a series of almost superhuman efforts to outfight and stun his antagonist from the start, while Hyer, who seemed to be thoroughly aware of his intent, contented himself with standing at the scratch and forbidding any entrance to his side, by the tremendous counter hits which he delivered in return for Sullivan's rapid visitations. He did not attempt to make parrying a leading feature of his policy, but for the greater portion of the time cheerfully met Sullivan's blows for the chance of countering back. He had evidently settled upon this as his policy for the fight, judging correctly, that if hit and hit was to be the order of the day, the weakest structure must go to pieces in the struggle. In addition to this, Hyer showed excellent skill in fighting, and his method of hitting short with the left, as a preliminary to the paixhan discharge of right, in the style of a half upper cut, could not have been excelled in the use which he made of it, by the best hitters who have shown themselves in the prize ring. To help him still further, he was cool and self-possessed, with the exception of a moment or two at the opening of the fourth round, when he seemed either shaken by his fall, or stung from his control, by the cheers which greeted Sullivan for the handsome blow. Sullivan, on the other hand, fought wild and ever eager. He did not display that shrewdness and care which has characterized all his previous fights, but seemed to consider himself in the ring only to revenge upon Hyer, in the bitterest and most sudden manner, the personal hatred that stood between them. He hurried to the scratch at every round, and commenced leading off right and left, and when obliged to take it more severely than he bargained for, invariably rushed in for a clinch, notwithstanding each succeeding round proved more conclusively than those which had gone before, he could not throw his man, and that those reverses invariably brought upon him the severest punishment of all. He was twisted to the ground invariably by the superior strength of his antagonist, and what in view of this was surprising to his friends, he would resist strongly every time, instead of slipping down as easily as possible to save his strength.

As to Hyer's lying on him to the extent he did, there has been much dispute, and while one party claims it to have been "foul," the other insist that it was a pardonable advantage. Between these two opinions the referee decided "fair." He decided so, properly. There is no rule in "Fistiana" which prescribes the length of time which a man may be allowed to lie upon another between the rounds, but the common law of the ring gives to each side the possession of their man, the instant the round is ended. Sullivan was, therefore, the property of his seconds the instant he touched the ground, and they were entitled to him, though obliged to throw twenty men from his body to get at him. It was natural for Hyer's seconds to let him lie when he had the advantage, but it was the duty of Sullivan's seconds to insist upon their rights and to acquaint the other side that, if they did not take their man off in time, they would throw him off. This they had a right to do, and the result of their not having done it, was, that while Hyer, after the struggle and the throw, would repose at ease on Sullivan's body and draw respirations of fresh atmosphere, Sullivan was crushed with the incumbent weight, and capable of catching only a few muffled breaths. In addition to this, Hyer being lifted first, got to his second's knee in advance, which Sullivan would scarcely reach his corner and have his blanket thrown upon his shoulders, before time would be called, and he would be started to his feet. He would then run at his enemy, and irritated from his balance, would rush upon the punishment which he received. Had he been well treated, he might have preserved his temper and fought a little longer, but no treatment could have make him win. He was overmatched, and the man whom he was fighting against, exceeded all expectations, both for skill and strength. It is due to Hyer to state at this portion of our remarks, that he is not personally chargeable with any impropriety in lying on Sullivan as he did. It was his duty to lie exactly where he fell till lifted by his seconds altogether, and the fault lay heaviest against the seconds of Sullivan himself, for not insisting more promptly and courageously on their rights. Had the other side seen that they were determined to have their man the instant he touched the ground, they would have been glad to have removed Hyer out of their way. The claim of "foul" therefore, for what was the result of their own negligence, could not stand, and Sullivan was the victim of untoward circumstances. From the first to last, however, he had no chance to win. The reception of the first hit staggered him and his friends, while the loss of the fall after the most desperate efforts of his underhold, must have convinced him that he was overmatched. There was nothing left but desperate fighting and an instalment of revenge upon the mutual quarrel. What share he got of this, the reader has already seen, but it is our business to say, that he might have got more personal satisfaction if he had received proper care, and not been stifled out of a large portion of this time. He fought well under the circumstances, and nothing could have exceeded the courage with which he confronted an assured fate. It was a terrific struggle. The motives which governed it were Ambition, Avarice and Revenge, and the combination of such master passions could not but stimulate a bloody climax.

There never was, perhaps, a battle in which there was so much fighting in so short a space of time; none, certainly in which more resolute punishment was given and taken, without flinching on either side. The history of the fight consists in the fact that Sullivan was overmatched; and in the further fact that Hyer showed himself capable of matching any man of his size and weight, doubtless, who exists in Britain or the United States. We will conclude, therefore, with our remarks of last week, that he has earned all the laurels which may be gathered from the brutal soil of the arena, and we trust that while he regards himself as the "Champion of America," he will deserve the title in a double sense, by striving henceforth to be the most peaceable and unoffending man. He has borne that reputation to a large extent heretofore, and he should seek to earn it anew. Under no circumstances, nor on any provocation, should he fight again, and to this resolute example all similar aspirants should conform.

BOXING RULES, 1853

In 1853 England's Puglistic Benevolent Association revised the rules of the London Prize Ring which had been in force since 1838. Although they were formulated in Great Britain, they are included here because they were adopted for the contests between Yankee Sullivan and John Morrissey in 1853, Morrissey and John C. Heenan in 1858, and Heenan and Tom Sayers in England in 1860. The regulations listed below indicate the degree of modernization that prize fighting had attained during this era. Enforcement of these rules proved to be very difficult, as is clear from the riotous endings of so many matches of this period. This document is reprinted from the New York Clipper, 30 May 1857, p. 45.

NEW RULES OF THE RING
AS REVISED BY THE PUGILISTIC ASSOCIATION

In 1853, it having been found that many of the Rules of the Ring, as they then stood, were insufficient to provide for the various contingencies which were continually arising in prize battles, an entire revision was determined on, and a committee of gentlemen, members of the Pugilistic Benevolent Association, undertook the task. When the revision was complete, the laws were submitted to a general meeting of the members of the prize ring (being members of the Association), and were unanimously agreed to. These new rules we now lay before our readers.

1. That the ring shall be made on turf, and shall be four and twenty feet square, formed of eight stakes and ropes, the latter extending in double lines, the uppermost line being four feet from the ground, and the lower two feet from the ground. That in the centre of the ring a mark be formed, to be termed a scratch; and that two opposite corners, as may be selected, spaces be enclosed by other marks sufficiently large for the reception of the seconds and bottle-holders, to be entitled "the corners."

2. That each man shall be attended to the ring by a second and a bottle-holder, the former provided with a sponge, and the latter with a bottle of water. That the combatants, on shaking hands, shall retire until the seconds of each have tossed for choice of position, which adjusted, the winner shall choose his corner according to the state of the wind or the sun, and conduct his man thereto, the loser taking the opposite corner.

3. That each man shall be provided with a handkerchief of a color suitable to his own fancy, and that the seconds proceed to entwine these handkerchiefs at the upper end of one of the centre stakes. That these handkerchiefs shall be called "the colors," and that the winner of the battle at its conclusion shall be entitled to their possession, as the trophy of victory.

4. That two umpires shall be chosen by the seconds or backers to watch the progress of the battle, and take exception to any breach of the rules hereafter stated. That a referee shall be chosen by the umpires, unless otherwise agreed on, to whom all disputes shall be referred; and that the decision of this referee, whatever it may be, shall be final and strictly binding on all parties, whether as to the matter in dispute or the issue of the battle. That the umpires shall be provided with a watch, for the purpose of calling

time; and that they mutually agree upon which this duty shall devolve, the call of that umpire only to be attended to, and no other person whatever to interfere in calling time. That the referee shall withhold all opinion until appealed to by the umpires, and that the umpires strictly abide by his decision without dispute.

5. That on the men being stripped, it shall be the duty of the seconds to examine their drawers, and if any objection arises as to insertion of improper substances therein, they shall appeal to their umpires, who, with the concurrence of the referee, shall direct what alterations shall be made.

6. That in future no spikes be used in fighting boots except those authorized by the Pugilistic Benevolent Association, which shall not exceed three eighths of an inch from the sole of the boot, and shall not be less than one eighth of an inch broad at the point; and it shall be in the power of the referee to alter, or file in any way he pleases, spikes which shall not accord with the above dimensions, even to filing them away altogether.

7. That both men being ready, each man shall be conducted to that side of the scratch next his corner previously chosen; and the seconds on the one side, and the men on the other, having shaken hands, the former shall immediately return to their corners, and there remain within the prescribed marks till the round be finished, on no pretence whatever approaching their principals during the round, under a penalty of 5s. for each offence, at the option of the referee. The penalty, which shall be strictly enforced, to go to the funds of the Association. The principal to be responsible for every fine inflicted on his second.

8. That at the conclusion of the round, when one or both of the men shall be down, the seconds and bottle-holders shall step forward and carry or conduct their principal to his corner, there affording him the necessary assistance, and that no person whatever be permitted to interfere in this duty.

9. That at the expiration of thirty seconds (unless otherwise agreed upon) the umpire appointed shall cry "Time," upon which each man shall rise from the knee of his bottle-holder and walk to his own side of the scratch unaided, the seconds and bottle-holders remaining at their corner; and that either man failing so to be at the scratch within eight seconds, shall be deemed to have lost the battle.

10. That on no consideration whatever shall any person be permitted to enter the ring during the battle, nor till it shall have been concluded; and that in the event of such unfair practice, or the ropes and stakes being disturbed or removed, it shall be in the power of the referee to award the victory to that man who in his honest opinion shall have the best of the contest.

11. That the seconds and bottle-holders shall not interfere, advise, or direct the adversary of their principal, and shall refrain from all offensive and irritating expressions, in all respects conducting themselves with order and decorum, and confine themselves to the diligent and careful discharge of their duties to their principals.

12. That in picking up their men, should the seconds or bottle-holders wilfully injure the antagonist of their principal, the latter shall be deemed to have forfeited the battle on the decision of the referee.

13. That it shall be "a fair stand-up fight," and if either man shall wilfully throw himself down without receiving a blow, whether blows shall have previously been exchanged or not, he shall be deemed to have lost the battle; but that this rule shall

not apply to a man who in a close slips down from the grasp of his opponent to avoid punishment, or from obvious accident or weakness.

14. That butting with the head shall be deemed foul, and the party resorting to this practice shall be deemed to have lost the battle.

15. That a blow struck when a man is thrown or down, shall be deemed foul. That a man with one knee and one hand on the ground, or with both knees on the ground, shall be deemed down; and a blow given in either of those positions shall be considered foul, providing always, that when in such position, the man so down shall not himself strike or attempt to strike.

16. That a blow struck below the waist shall be deemed foul, and that, in a close, seizing an antagonist below the waist, by the thigh, or otherwise, shall be deemed foul.

17. That all attempts to inflict injury by gouging, or tearing the flesh with the fingers or nails, and biting, shall be deemed foul.

18. That kicking or deliberately falling on an antagonist, with the knees or otherwise when down, shall be deemed foul.

19. That all bets shall be paid as the battle money, after a fight, is awarded.

20. That no person on any pretence whatever, shall be permitted to approach nearer the ring than ten feet, with the exception of the umpires and referee, and the persons appointed to take charge of the water or other refreshment for the combatants, who shall take their seats close to the corners selected by the seconds.

21. That due notice shall be given by the stakeholder of the day and place where the battle-money is to be given up, and that he be exonerated from all responsibility upon obeying the direction of the referee, and that all parties be strictly bound by these rules, and that in future all articles of agreement for a contest be entered into with a strict and willing adherence to the letter and spirit of these rules.

22. That in the event of magisterial or other interference, or in case of darkness coming on, the referee shall have the power to name the time and place for the next meeting, if possible, on the same day, or as soon after as may be.

23. That should the fight not be decided on the day, all bets instead of being drawn, shall be put together and divided, unless the fight shall be resumed the same week, between Sunday and Sunday, in which case the bets shall stand and be decided by the event. That where the day named in the articles for a fight to come off is altered to another day in the same week, bets shall stand. The battle-money shall remain in the hands of the stake holder until fairly won or lost by a fight, unless a draw be mutually agreed upon.

24. That any pugilist voluntarily quitting the ring previous to the deliberate judgement of the referee being obtained, shall be deemed to have lost the fight.

25. That on an objection being made by the seconds or umpire, the men shall retire to their corners, and there remain until the decision of the appointed authorities shall be obtained; that if pronounced "foul," the battle shall be at an end, but if "fair," "time" shall be called by the party appointed, and the man absent from the scratch in eight seconds shall be deemed to have lost the fight. The decision in all cases to be given promptly and irrevocably, for which purpose the umpires and referee should be invaribly close together.

26. That if in a rally at the ropes a man steps outside the ring, to avoid his antagonist or to escape punishment, he shall forfeit the battle.

27. That the use of hard substances, such as stones, or sticks, or of resin, in the hand during the battle shall be deemed foul, and that on the requisition of the seconds of either man, the accused shall open his hands for the examination of the referee.

28. That where a man shall have his antagonist across the ropes in such a position as to be helpless, and to endanger his life by strangulation or apoplexy, it shall be in the power of the referee to direct the seconds to take their man away, and thus conclude the round, and that the man or his seconds refusing to obey the direction of the referee, shall be deemed the loser.

29. That all stage fights be as nearly as possible in conformity with the foregoing Rules.

JOHN MORRISSEY VS. JAMES SULLIVAN

In 1853 John Morrissey was the hero of New York City's Irish immigrant community that was battling with nativist factions in politics, on the street corners, and in the saloons of the town. Tom Hyer remained the champion of the Anglo-American party. Morrissey challenged him to a fight, but he lost his one hundred dollar deposit after his backers could not raise the ten thousand dollars demanded by Hyer's friends. Old Smoke then turned to Yankee Sullivan as his next opponent. Even though both were Irishmen, the press portrayed Sullivan as the standard bearer for home grown Americans. The following document narrates the background to the bout and includes the "Articles of Agreement," which is representative of the kind of contract that normally was signed before the major matches of this era. This selection also presents a summary of the preliminaries and an account of the evasion of the police and the chaotic conclusion to the encounter. It is reprinted from the New York Clipper, 15 October 1853, p. 2.

BOSTON CORNERS, OCTOBER 12, 1853

Since the first announcement of this match, much anxiety has been manifested in regard to the ultimate result; and for the last six weeks, the fight has been the talk not only of the sporting circles, but of other classes of the community. The origin of the match was the consequence of a little disturbance between the parties at a saloon in Broadway, the particulars of which were given at the time in the *Clipper*. A challenge was at once given by the one party, and as readily accepted by the other, it being understood, that the parties should meet again and sign the articles of agreement, and make the first deposit on Wednesday evening, the first of September, at the house corner of Whitehall and Bridge-streets. The matter was soon noised about the city, some thinking it was mere "talk," and that it would fall through, while others considered it a money making affair gotten up by the parties themselves. Those however, who were in the secret, knew that a fair and honourable match would be made. It was thought also that Morrissey would not be on hand on the evening in question to make the match. About this time a letter appeared in the *Clipper* from a person in Brooklyn, in which the writer offered to bet heavy odds against Sullivan. The following letter was afterwards received from Sullivan, which it may not be out of place to insert in this report.

Letter from Sullivan

Money to be put up on the 1st September

To the Editor of the *Clipper,*

Sir:—According to the appointment made with the California Champion, (?) I will be ready with my money at the house of Mr. Fays, corner of Whitehall and Bridge streets, on the 1st of next month, and if either party absents himself, the absentee shall be deemed a coward.

In regard to the $5,000 challenge of the Brooklyn man, there is but little dependence to be placed on it. His $5,000 is all moon-shine.

If any of the friends of Morrissey have money to bet, 2 to 1, as boasted of, they can be accomodated by calling on me at 82 1/2 Chatham street. After the 1st of next month, perhaps they can receive a better offer.

Yours,

James Sullivan.

The appearance of this letter from Sullivan, gave a great degree of certainty that the quarrel could not be settled except through the medium of the Prize Ring.

On the first of September, an advertisement from Sullivan, appeared in the Herald, reminding his opponent that he would be on hand that evening to make the match, and deposit the first sum of money.

On Wednesday evening, September 1st, we proceeded to the spot indicated to obtain a report of the proceedings. Quite a number of the fancy were present, anxious for the arrival of the "lions" of the evening.

About 8 o'clock, Sullivan made his appearance, and at once became the grand object of attraction. In about 20 minutes after the arrival of Sullivan, Morrissey made his appearance, and soon found himself pretty well surrounded by a dense mass of humans. Morrissey meaning business, did not remain in the bar-room long, but at once signified his readiness to arrange the matters for which they had assembled. The two opponents with their respective friends, immediately proceeded to a room up stairs, where the match was made and the first installment of money deposited.

In order that our readers may be well posted in the articles of agreement, we obtained a copy from the original document in the possession of one of the parties, which we give below, merely omitting names, which it is entirely unnecessary to publish.

Articles of Agreement for the Fight
BETWEEN
JOHN MORRISSEY AND JAMES SULLIVAN
NEW YORK, September 1, 1853

This is to certify that I, John Morrissey, do agree to fight James Sullivan in a twenty-four foot rope ring, in strict accordance with the new rules of the London Prize Ring, in six weeks from this date, making the fight to come off on the 12th day of October, Wednesday, between the hours of 11 o'clock A.M. and 2 o'clock P.M., for the sum of one Thousand Dollars aside; Two Hundred and Fifty Dollars deposited this date, September 1st; Two Hundred and Fifty Dollars to be deposited September 14th, at the house of George Kensett, between the hours of 8 and 10 P.M.; Two Hundred and Fifty Dollars to be deposited September 28th, at the house No. 4 James Street, between the hours above named; the remaining and final deposit of Two Hundred and Fifty Dollars to be made at the house No. 324 Broadway on the 5th day of October. And we do hereby agree that _____ shall hold the stake money in this engagement, to be given to the party receiving the decision of the referee of having won it, fairly and honorably, according to these agreements. Either party failing in the deposits, shall forfeit the amount in the stakeholder's hands. Each party on the night of the last deposit to select a man, they to choose by toss who shall name the ground of fighting, it to be within one hundred miles of the city of New York, and notice to be left with the loser of the choice, four days previous to the battle day, the 12th of October. Either party failing to be in the ring between the hours of 11 o'clock and 2 o'clock on the 12th of October, forfeits the battle money. In case of magisterial interference, the referee shall decide the next time and place of meeting.

Signed, {JOHN MORRISSEY
{JAMES SULLIVAN

After the first deposit of $250 a side had been made by the above named men, Sullivan offered to bet Morrisey $50 that he would draw the first blood, Sullivan generally having the luck to obtain this advantage in his battles. Morrissey did not seem inclined to accept the wager, but immediately offered to wager Sullivan $1,000 to $800 that he (Morrissey) would win the fight. The wager was not accepted, however, and the parties separated.

The Training.

The men immediately made arrangements for putting themselves through a course of training, although the time allowed was rather short, giving them but six weeks in which to get themselves in good condition for the battle. Sullivan chose his training quarters at a public place a few miles from Brooklyn, on the new Plank Road. Being conversant with all the requisites necessary for training, Sullivan depended upon his own knowledge rather than the services of a regular trainer. He went into training on Saturday, September 1st; although it must be remarked, that from the first agreement to fight until the match was made, he had abstained from everything calculated to weaken or debilitate a man; and on the day that he went to his training quarters he looked well, better in fact than he had looked for a long time previous. His weight at that time was in the neighborhod of 170 lbs., a portion of this, however, being superfluous flesh, which it would be necessary to reduce. He walked and ran from twenty to thirty miles a day, exercised with the "sand bag" and "dumb bells," and when his pugilistic friends were present he had a "bout" with them.

Morrissey also went into active training on the 3d of September, and selected his quarters in the neighborhood of McComb's Dam. Orville Gardener, better known by the name "Awful Gardener" was selected by the friends of Morrissey as his trainer, and from the appearance of Morrissey in the ring, Gardener spared no pains in bringing his man to a high state of perfection as regards strength, and capability to endure severe punishment. Gardener kept a vigilant eye on every movement of his pupil, and we have every reason to believe that he "acted well his part" in the whole matter, although some of the friends of Morrissey seemed a little dissatisfied that a more experienced man had not been chosen. Morrissey took long runs at different periods of the day, tried his strength in hitting the "sand bag," also had set-to's daily with his trainer, who did not at all like some of his "hearty weights."

Interference of the Police.

Whilst things were thus quietly progressing at the respective training quarters of the men, the excitement in the city was on the increase, and some of the "pious papers" called upon the authorities to put an end to the battle *before* it had *begun*. Accordingly warrants were issued for the arrest of Morrissey and Sullivan, with the intention of binding them over to keep the peace towards each other. The warrants were placed in the hands of some of our best officers, who, on the 26th of September, proceeded to the training grounds of the men to serve their warrants, and arrest the men.

It so happened, however, that on that very morning Sullivan had changed his quarters to a more suitable place on Coney Island, so that the officer sent to arrest him had a little difficulty in finding the spot, but toward evening he spied Sullivan taking a walk on the beach, at old Coney; making his business known to Mr. Sullivan, that gentleman begged to be excused for a few moments, and thus took his departure for parts unknown.

Morrissey was visited about the same time at McComb's Dam, but he also succeeded in escaping from the hands of the officer sent to arrest him. Immediately on getting out of the way, he proceeded to Troy, within a few miles of which place he quietly proceeded in his training, unmolested and free from care.

Sullivan finished his exercises on Staten Island after his escape from the New York officers.

Last Deposits, and toss for Choice of Ground.

The first, second and third installments of $250 having been deposited according to agreement, the friends of the parties met on Wednesday evening October 5th, to make the last deposit, and toss for choice of ground. The toss was won by the friends of Morrissey, who seemed highly delighted with this first success. Sullivan's friends of course were rather down in consequence of their ill-luck.

Selection of the Ground.

The whole amount of the stakes having been deposited, and the selection of the ground having been won by Morrissey, a little journey was necessary in order to find a spot where the sport would not be likely to be interfered with by the authorities. This was a delicate piece of business to undertake, but the parties appointed for the purpose succeeded admirably.

The "Spot."

The spot chosen for the battle, was at Boston Corners, about 96 miles distant from this city, and in close proximity to the State lines of Massachusetts and Vermont. Boston Corners, we believe, is in an anti-rent district, where officers are not held in very high estimation by the "settlers," and where "high- rents" are never heard of. Thus it will be seen the parties were not likely to be molested. On Monday evening last, the "word" was given to the sporting community, through the mediums of the different sporting houses about the city, and arrangements were forthwith made to reach the spot. Sullivan and Morrissey arrived within a few miles of the ground on Monday, where they remained until the day of battle.

The Journey Up.

The mode of conveyance was by the Harlem Railroad, the 7 o'clock morning train going within a few hundred yards of the battle-ground. The afternoon train stopping about 7 miles from the spot. A number of persons went up on Monday, but a large number started in the 7 o'clock morning line, on Tuesday. Several hundred got off on Tuesday afternoon. On Wednesday morning, however, was the great rush, and extra cars had to be put on, as that was the last train from this city that could reach the ground in time. Those who started on Tuesday afternoon, had to remain over-night at a little place about 7 miles distant from Boston Corners, and all sorts of ways were adopted in order to pass the night; those who could procure lodgings, were greatly envied by those who could not, and the great majority were content to find shelter of any kind for the night. In the morning, all the means of conveyance in the place, were brought into requisition by those who could pay, but the majority trusted to their own legs to carry them to the "camp meeting." All, however, reached the spot in good season, and added considerably to the already large concourse of spectators present.

The Ring and its Appearance.

The stakes and ropes had been furnished by Mr. Robert Whittaker, and both rings were arranged by that gentleman in first rate style. The spot selected was a beautiful piece of ground situated between two hills.

The Referee.

Much time was occupied in selecting a referee, one person being named, and objections made, and so on, until one hour and a half had elapsed, when a person named O'Aller, as near as we could learn, was chosen for that responsible station, and it was about 15 minutes before 2 ere this was settled.

The Spectators.

Full three thousand persons were present from all parts of the State, and nearly all obtained a good view of the ring and the combatants. A considerable number were in between the outer and inside ring, and the reporters of the press had stations assigned them in the same circle.

Entering the Ring.

About ten minutes before 2 Morrissey made his appearance in the ring, accompanied by Tom O'Donnald and Awful Gardner, his seconds.

Sullivan entered the ring about five minutes after, and at once made preparations for the battle. Sullivan's seconds were Andy Sheehan, and Bill Wilson.

The Colors.

Sullivan had for his flag a black silk handkerchief, having intimated before he entered the ring that if he lost the battle, he would lose his life also. Sullivan's flag was tied to the stakes, and Morrissey's colors, the American flag, was also tied to the stake, amid tremendous cheering from all parts of the ring.

Matters having thus far progressed, and everything being in readiness, time was called, and both men walked up to the scratch, and after shaking hands, during which Sullivan laughed heartily, both men struck an attitude, and at once commenced.

The Fight.

Round First.

Both men looked in beautiful condition, and it was impossible to judge by their appearance, on which superiority had the ascendancy. Sullivan quite anxious to commence business, at once went to work, and with his left sent in a powerful blow, which reached Morrissey's left eye, the blow also taking effect partly on the nose, the blood flowing copiously from both wounds.

First Blood for Sullivan.

Morrissey, in attempting to return, got in a slight blow, and in a rally for the fall, Sullivan down.

Round 2d.

Sullivan up to the scratch as lively as a cricket, and with mischief in his eye. He went to work immediately, and sent in some heavy blows. Morrissey in returing, was rather short, and Sullivan went down....

Round 4th.

This was a tremendous round, and both men seemed determined to make themselves felt. Morrissey went into his man with all the impetuousity of a wild bull.

Sullivan, in the meantime, retreating, and delivering some blows with good effect while doing so. Morrissey was doing good work at the same time. He sent in a terrific cut with his right hand on Sullivan's eye, which at once showed marks of swelling. Sullivan returned right and left, reaching Morrissey's body as well as his frontispiece. Morrissey got in another powerful hit on Sullivan's body, but received in return, a heavy blow on the nose, which began to get completely out of shape. This round was contested fiercely by both men, Morrissey receiving and countering in good style, and Sullivan doing his best to obtain the mastery. Morrissey, we think had the best of this round, as Sullivan began to show a slight sign of weakness. A rally, and Sullivan down. This round lasted between 4 and 5 minutes, and during the time each man was cheered by his friends, until the place fairly rang again with the shouts.

Round 5.

Both men appeared at the scratch, looking rather the worse from the effects of the last round. No time for play. Sullivan took the lead, and after giving Morrissey a good body hit, in which Morrissey was short in his return, Sullivan went down laughing....

Round 17.

Sullivan remarked to his second that he could not see his man from his right eye, which Morrissey in getting in a heavy hit had injured severely with his finger. Sullivan, however, went to work, and after a short rally, went down.

Round 18 to 20.

In favor of Sullivan.

Round 21.

Sullivan came up lively, and Morrissey seemed a little weak, though we may have been mistaken. Sullivan led off, reaching his opponent's blind side, but caught it in return.

Round 22d to 24th.

Sharp rallies, the betting in Sullivan's favor, though Morrissey showed his game qualities. Morrissey bleeding terribly, and losing his strength.

Round 25th.

Morrissey came up spunky not minding the blood which covered his body all over. Sullivan hit Morrissey one, two, three, on the eye and nose, but in return received a body blow from Morrissey.

Round 26th and 27th.

Morrissey, notwithstanding the punishment he received went up to his man boldly, getting in a heavy hit beneath Sullivan's ear, drawing more of the claret from Sullivan, and leaving a mark. Sullivan returned sharply, however, and went down.

Round 28 to 30.

Sullivan the favorite, at 100 to 50. Sharp shooting—hit and hit, though Sullivan having the best of it.

Round 31.

Both men evidently growing weaker and weaker, though considering the great quantity of blood lost by Morrissey, it is astonishing how he was able to stand up as he did. On coming to the scratch, Sullivan hit him, and went down cunningly.

Round 32d.

Morrissey, though very weak, led off, catching Yankee, slightly. Sullivan returned on the old spot, though weak.

Round 33d.

Sullivan was still lively, though there was no denying the fact that his strength would not hold out much longer. Morrissey showed his game by coming up again courageously, but was hit away by Sullivan, though the blows were of no great weight.

Round 34 to 36.

Sullivan as usual led off in these rounds. Morrissey's sight almost gone, though he followed up his man with determination and desperation, and seemed to have made up his mind to win the battle or perish in the attempt. Slight hits from Sullivan, and returns from Morrissey. The blood running from the wounds in Morrissey's face, which was terribly cut in all parts, presenting a most disgusting and shocking appearance. Sullivan's eye was pretty severely marked, and was also badly punished.

Round 37th and last.

Was a strange round in every respect, and deserves particular notice. Morrissey, spunky as a chicken, came up to the scratch at the call of time, he was shaky, and evidently could do little more execution. Sullivan seeing his condition, gained greater confidence that it required but a few more strong and well aimed blows to gain the battle.

Morrissey, owing to his organs of sight being so damaged, could not well see all the movements of his adversary, and received a slight hit on the old spot. Morrissey, nothing daunted, rushed in, caught his adversary, and by main strength drove Sullivan to the ropes. Morrissey got him on the ropes, and had him in this awkward position, when as far as we could see, for the crowd began to be uproarious, Sullivan tried to get down, but couldn't. Sullivan, by a very clever manoeuvere, succeeded in turning Morrissey, and getting him on the ropes, and it seemed to us at the same time, that Sullivan got on his knees in the struggle, but immediately rose and struck Morrissey, when O'Donnal, seeing this and judging it to be a foul blow rushed in and shoved Sullivan back; no sooner had Wilson, the second of Sullivan, observed O'Donnal at Sullivan, then he gave O'Donnal a blow, knocking him down; and Gardner, one of Morrisey's seconds, also got into the row. Sullivan, in the meantime was hitting away at O'Donnal, and Gardner, and the friends of Morrissey, seeing that a general row was inevitable, went into the muss. Morrissey during this time had appealed to the referee, who decided that Morrissey had won the battle, owing to the foul blow, and the friends of Morrissey at once took him out of the ring.

Owing to the great confusion, however, very few of those engaged in the row heard the referee's decision, and "time" was once more called, when Sullivan went up to the scratch, and Morrissey not appearing, the friends of Sullivan claimed the money.

This round was nothing but a general riot, and the ring was broken in upon by the crowd, who seemed determined on taking a hand in the fight themselves.

Sullivan, though past 40 years of age, showed himself equal to his palmiest days, and surprised even his most sanguine friends. He is a splendid hitter, and his superior scientific abilities were never better displayed in his battle yesterday. We cannot speak too well of him, as we were not prepared to witness such splendid hits as he delivered, having sent in sometimes three blows in rapid succession.

Morrissey, with a little more experience, will be a good pugilist.

He always followed his man up well, and done all in his power to win the battle. As to the disposal of the stakes we have not heard to a certainty. It is said this morning, however, that Sullivan has obtained the stakes. This we merely give as reported to us.

According to the articles of the agreement our readers will see who has the word to give in the disposal of the money.

We have nothing at present to say, except that if either man is honorably entitled to it, Sullivan is the man.

JOHN C. HEENAN VS. TOM SAYERS

No sporting event of the middle of the nineteenth century generated more excitement on both sides of the Atlantic Ocean than the prize fight between John C. Heenan and Tom Sayers at Farnborough, England on 17 April 1860. The "Benecia Boy" from Troy, New York and California was five inches taller, twenty-eight pounds heavier, and eight years younger than his adversary. Sayers was a London bricklayer who had defeated a dozen challengers and proudly wore the champion's belt. Despite the disadvantage in height, weight, and age, Sayers was the favorite because of his skill and his opponent's lack of experience in feature events. He also had the backing of Morrissey, the conqueror of Heenan, who was angered by the Benicia Boy's claim to be champion of the

United States. The following excerpts from the New York Clipper and Bell's Life in London recount the excitement building up to the event, the intensity of the bout, the controversial ending, and the resolution of the dispute over the championship belt. The selections are reprinted from the New York Clipper, 5 May 1860, p. 20, 19 May 1860, p. 33, 9 June 1860, p. 64.

THE INTERNATIONAL MATCH
THE GREAT BATTLE

On Saturday morning, April 28, at about 7 o'clock, news was received that the steamship Vanderbilt was on her way up the bay, and as it was known that this vessel would bring the first intelligence regarding the great event for the Championship of the World, the news spread like wildfire, everybody running hither and thither, eagerly questioning his neighbor as to what the result of the battle was. Soon the newspaper bulletins announced the fact that the men had met, the battle been fought, and an unsatisfactory conclusion arrived at. This only served to whet the public appetite for the particulars, and in the hurry of the moment some of our neighbors issued small extras giving false reports of the result. The neighborhood of Ann and Nassau streets, where the *Clipper* office is located, was besieged by the crowds of anxious inquirers at an early hour in the morning. Our special reporter, Mr. Wm. T. Bryant, who witnessed the battle, came passenger in the Vanderbilt, and reached our office at about 7 1/2 o'clock. Then the excitement was increased; everybody being on the out for our extra, but as we had immense orders to fill, we issued a poster announcing that no papers would be delivered until 5 o'clock, P.M. Our compositors were at once set to work in getting up our report of the battle—in a short time the forms were completed—then the stereotyper commenced his operations, and took five sets of plates from the type forms, so that we could have five presses running at once. Everything worked beautifully, and soon after noon we had our presses running like lightning. In the meantime, numbers of papers hurriedly got up in London and in this city were put into the market here, but the great demand was for the *Clipper,* and when our "INTERNATIONAL" appeared; with its beautiful supplemental engraving, all other extras fell flat, and our agents were completely run down by purchasers. We kept our presses running all Saturday night, Sunday, and Sunday night, and part of Monday; in that time printing between 200,000 and 300,000 papers.

The excitement regarding the news eclipsed anything we ever witnessed in the newspaper world. The Tom Hyer and Sullivan affair was nothing to it—the Burdetti murder case was nowhere, and the Charleston Convention was almost entirely forgotten. Scarcely any work outside of the newspaper world was done on that day. On Saturday night, the city was wild with enthusiasm. Our places of amusement felt the pressure. Sporting houses were thronged the entire night. The fight, and the heroic conduct of both Heenan and Sayers was the topic of conversation at the family fireside, in the markets, stores, and everywhere. Go where we might, it was nothing but fight talk. Fight here, fight there, and fight everywhere. Little children became infected, and lunged out in true Benician style. Coy and modest damsels touched upon the prevailing subject, with becoming delicacy, and roundly berated the mob for their treatment of the Boy. Maidens and matrons talked of the cowardice of the Referee, Mr.

Dowling, in running away from his post. Staid and somber "Governors," like the Benicia Boy, went "one eye" on the report of the fight, and spoke in condemnation of the breaking in of the ring by the mob. Even ministers of the gospel had something to say concerning the "fair field," whereon the battle was fought. In fact, nothing could be approached but the subject of pugilism—if the Charleston Convention was broached, some one would intimate that it was a "dead cock on the pit," just now; some of our friends even had an idea that Brother Beecher would deliver discourse upon the text of—"May the Best Man Win," and his tabernacle in Brooklyn was thronged with anxious inquirers after the truth....

...before the ring was really put in order, Tom Sayers made his entree. There was no shying of castors, on either side, and everything was done in the plainest manner. Sayers, on getting inside the ropes, very carelessly divested himself of his cloak. The appearance he presented after this was flashy in the extreme. He was dressed in a suit of plaid, green and red being the predominant colors.

Heenan, who had been standing outside the ring with his friends, now entered it, followed by Cusick and McDonald. He was dressed in a suit of heavy gray clothes, the overcoat being buttoned closely round the neck, and having a thick comforter round his throat to protect it from the wind. Cheers from the Americans went up, on his entrance, and though they were not numerous, no one could doubt their sincerity. When the Boy entered the ring he walked over to Sayers, extending his hand, and said:—"How do you do, Tom- how do you find youself this morning?" Sayers, taking the preferred hand— "Very well, I thank you, how do you find yourself?"
Heenan— "I feel very well, indeed. We have a fine morning for it."
Sayers—"Yes; if a man can't fight such a day as this, he can't at all." [Sayers pulling out a roll of bills]— "Do you want to bet anything?"
Heenan— "No; I've bet all my money."
Heenan then walked towards McDonald, and had some conversation with him. Sayers, who had never seen the Boy before, now took a careful observation of him. It was plain to be seen he was disappointed in his antagonist, but it did not last long, as the determined eye and firmly compressed lips told only too plainly that he would make the best of a bad bargain.

Next in order was the toss for corners, Heenan winning the choice, and choosing that looking towards the west, when just then, a gentleman from New York took an old heel of a shoe or boot from his pocket and handed it to Heenan, saying "this is the heel from one of Yankee Sullivan's boot. He never lost a fight when this was in the ring. Go in, old boy, and win." Heenan good naturedly took it, remarking, "You can bet your life I'll try hard enough. If I don't win, it'll be because they won't let me." The heel was then planted in his corner, where it stopped until the fight was over, when Falkland picked it up, and gave it to your reporter to carry to New York.

The ring, when formed, presented an appearance of grandeur. Long before the day named for the fight, the names of 87 noble-men headed by the Earl of Branfort, were sent to Falkland, all wishing to be posted as to the time and place of the battle. We were glad to see them there, as it added importance to the contest. There was also a minister, from Cambridge, who witnessed the fight, and though we did not see him go down into his pockets to bring forth the necessary, the pleasant smile on his phiz, assured us he was ready and willing to see a fair and manly contest.

We had almost forgotten to mention the appearance of the seconds of the respective men, and their importance to the ring. McDonald, whose name does not appear in Fistiana, has had a number of turn-ups, and come out of them without a scratch. His great forte, though, is training, or bringing a man into good condition. Cusick, the other second of the Boy, once fought Sayers a friendly fight, some 13 years ago, and made a draw of it; but then Sayers had never entered the roped arena, and the fight, like all turn-ups, ended dissatisfactorily.

Mac was dressed in a white flannel suit, wearing a cap, and his neck was enveloped with one of Heenan's colors, the stars appearing at the ends. Cusick had on a dark brown travelling shirt, and his throat was also protected by one of the Boy's colors.

The expression of McDonald's face, on entering the ring, was as pleasant as a schoolboy who had just received a reward of merit. Cusick's compressed lip and protruding chin, on the other hand, told plainly there was a determination in his composition, and no one who examined his features, had need to be disappointed at his work.

Brunton, the principal second of Sayers, wore a white cotton shirt and black pants. He is a good looking man, and his motions are very quick. He is a tavern keeper, and does a good business. He has had three fights in the Prize Ring, two of which he won, only being defeated in his last when he met the celebrated Bill Cain, one of the best men of his time in England. Sayers's other second was the celebrated Jemmy Welsh, who is an old bruiser, and who, according to Fistiana, has entered the Prize Ring six times, but not on all occasions successful. However, he is a game 'un, and his advice in husbanding the strength of a man in the ring receives much attention.

He certainly must have been bought off from honesty, or let his prejudice get the better of his discretion, as he acted like a bloodhound during the close of the fight. Heenan very properly sent him to mother earth on the occasion of his unmanly interference between the Boy and Sayers, and though we regretted it, Welsh deserved all he got.

Both men were now ordered to peel, which they did in short time. They had taken the precaution, before coming on the ground, to put on their fighting habiliments, so that little or no time was lost in getting ready. At 20 minutes to 8 the seconds commenced making the toilet of their men; many and quick were the speculations when Heenan's stalwart frame was exposed to view. "S'elp me G-, he's a fine 'un. If he's as good as he looks, he must win," said Jerry Noon. Exclamations from many gentlemen were heard to the effect that they never recollected to have seen a finer built man.

The Boy, though so much interfered with in his training, had scarcely an ounce of superfluous flesh on his body. In fact, we thought he had been brought down too fine. The muscles of his back, breast, and arms, seemed round as an egg, and hard as iron, and the only fault to find was that his face was too fat, and a very short time justified our opinion.

Sayers never looked better. His skin was brown, and to all appearances as hard as the face of an old weather-beaten salt. His face, bronzed by the wind and sun during his training, looked hard as hickory.

Soon everything was in readiness, and the men, followed by their seconds, came up to the scratch, when the usual formality of shaking hands was gone through with.

The seconds then retired to their respective corners, and left the men ready at precisely __ to 8 for...THE FIGHT....

ROUND 33. Both men up together. Sayers was now very weak, and bleeding freely from the mouth, nose, and a cut over the right temple. Heenan's face was much swollen, and the blood was coming out from the cut on the right cheek and nose. The Boy seemed more punished about the face than the champion, though he had not received half the number of visitations to it, that Tom had to his own. No time was lost in getting to work, Heenan quickly letting go his left, but Sayers was not home at it. Some sparring. The blood was now coming so fast, both men turned to their corners for a wipe of the sponge. At it again, when some light exchanges took place, Sayers getting on the Boy's left eye, and the latter on Tom's nob. A rally and clinch, the Boy trying to get Sayers' head in chancery, but the latter slipped out of his embrace prettily, and ran to the middle of the ring. Another wipe. Heenan now went after his man with determination. He led out his left, catching Tom on the forehead, followed by a light one from the right on the champion's neck. Tom led off his left, planting a good one on Heenan's mouth, The Boy returning with a terrific left hander on Sayers' nob, which knocked him flat to the ground. [Cheers from Heenan's corner, and offers of 5 to 1 on him. Sayers' friends now looked blue, and Heenan was gaining friends among the respectable portion of the English.]

34. Heenan first to the scratch and very fresh. Tom slow and groggy. The Boy quickly opened the ball, sending his left out on Tom's nob, which brought more of the ruby. Sayers getting within distance, got a light one on Heenan's left eye, and was away without a return. A close; in which Heenan threw the champion, falling heavily upon him. [During the whole of this round there were cries of police, and rioting in Sayers's corner, the crowd frequently pushing against the ropes and stakes. The ring keepers seemed unable or unwilling to keep order. A number of the champion's friends now made their way towards his corner, to get a look at him, as he was very weak at the commencement of the last round, and the heavy fall the Boy gave him must have been any thing but strengthening. On the other hand, the friends of Heenan were quiet and confident, only wanting to see the men brought to the scratch as soon as possible after time was called.]

35. Heenan, who seemed to have got all his strength back, met Tom at the scratch, and went to hard work quickly. The Boy led off with his left and got heavily on Tom's mouth, and followed it with another on the champion's ivory box. Some feinting then followed, when Heenan let go his right, catching Sayers just below the throat. A close, when Heenan threw his man, falling on him like a log. ["Good, Johnny," said McDonald, kissing him as he raised him from the ground; "you've got the belt!" The Americans were excited, and cheer and cheer followed for their man. The crowd on Sayers's side now became more unruly, pushing forcibly against the ropes; and it was with greatest difficulty, the ring-keepers could force them back. Cries of "Shame, shame! give the American fair play- he's a good 'un!"- now came from all quarters of the ring; but it was evident the American was not to have fair play.]

36. Heenan first to the scratch, Tom very slow in coming up— [cries of, "Time, time! keep the time."] Tom looked forlorn as he came up, and, at each feint of the Boy, acted like the timid schoolboy who is about to receive the ferule from his master. Heenan

to work immediately, and delivered a paster on Tom's nose, which sent him half way across the ring. The Boy now bored Sayers to the rope, where he got his head in chancery and delivered some soggy right-handers on the nose and mouth. Tom tried to shoot up, but without effect. Heenan now lifted Sayers in his arms and dashed him to the ground. Cusick and McDonald seized their man and brought him to his corner, amid cheers from all quarters of the ring. It was evident, from the repeated attempts at Sayers's corner, to force in the ring, that the Boy's only chance for winning would be by some stroke of good fortune, such as knocking the champion out of time. There was every chance of this, as Sayers was very weak from the last four rounds, and Heenan had got his second wind long before this. This cowardly conduct at the champion's corner was still running riot, when time was called for round.

37. Heenan actually ran to the scratch, and put up his mawleys. Sayers, approached slowly and carefully. As soon as the champion got within reach, the Boy delivered his left on Tom's jaw. It was a hard one, but not enough steam in it to send Sayers to grass. Sayers again came too near, when the Boy dropped old "Broadway" on the champion's ribs, bending him almost double. Heenan, blind as he was, made a quick race for his antagonist, and caught him near the ropes in his left vice, squeezing Tom until he was black in the face (cries now went forth from Sayers' corner, "S' help me G- he's choking poor Tom; cut the ropes, cut the ropes!) Tom managed to drop out of the Boy's grasp, and as he did so, Heenan sent forth his right on Sayers's neck, which sent him to mother earth again. [A scene of confusion now arose, which beggars all description. The din of Kirk Alloway's ruins, on the night when Tom O'Shanter passed it on the back of his favorite Meg, might give you a faint description of it, but only a faint one. The spies and blood hounds were now at their work. "Police—police!" was cried out by the Sayers party. "Shame—shame! keep the ring," by others. Before the end of this round, Referee Dowling, the unmanly and cowardly scrub, left his position without the slightest cause, and without even giving notice for a cessation of hostilities.]

38. Heenan first to the scratch, and spoiling for a fight. Sayers, as usual, slow. The Boy lunged out his left and caught Tom a spanker on the jaw, which staggered him. Heenan immediately followed this with another from his left, on Sayers's nob, which knocked him off his pins and sent him to bed, [cries from the Americans of "go in, John, you've got him now." McDonald- "That's the champion that was going to win in a canter is it- ha, ha!"] [A man was now trying to drive down the stakes, but the rioters were interfering with him. However he effected something in the way of it.]

39. Heenan came up fiercely; and as soon as Tom put in an appearance, dashed out his left at him, but without effect, Sayers ducking and getting away. The Boy now, intending to make hay while the sun shone, commenced a foot race after the bold Tom, whom he caught near the ropes with a terrific right-hander on the ribs. Heenan then closed with him, getting his head in champion's neck, and having him helpless on his hip, reached out with his right and caught hold of the ropes, for a few moments squeezing his antagonist until his face was black. [Cries of "Cut the ropes- cut the ropes." Jack Hamilton, or Shepperd, or *Maquire,* or whatever one might choose to call him but an honest man, now broke through the crowd towards Heenan with a life-preserver, or billy, in his hand, but the quick and determined eye of Jim Hughes, backed up by an injunction, met him, and the coward tried hard to conceal the weapon

behind his back, affecting to explain he meant no harm. Sayers, from the terrific hug of Heenan, was frothing at the mouth. The Boy still had hold of the ropes with his right and no inclination to let go. At this juncture, one of the ring keepers, whose name we could not learn, caught Heenan by the leg, with the intention of tripping him, but he did not succeed. Shortly after this the ropes were cut, when both men fell heavily to the ground. [The rioters had now got into Sayers's corner of the ring.]

40. Heenan rushed to the scratch, "eager for the fray." He waited there some seconds, crying out, "bring him up." Sayers at length came forward very weak, when Heenan dealt out a left- handed poultice, which sent the champion on another kissing visit to the earth. It was now all day with the British Lion, for the American Eagle had pounced upon him too often. All expected to see the Union Jack go up in distress, but no. *Sayers now got through the ropes to the outside of the ring,* where a blanket was put over him. ["There he goes- there he goes," from McDonald and Cusick]. Time being now called for round.

41. Heenan put in an early appearance at the scratch. Sayers, who had been brought back into the ring, approached him after some delay, very groggy. Tom was bewildered at the quick passes of the Boy, but did his best by ducking and running away to avoid them. The Boy now bored him to his [Heenan's] own corner, when Jemmy Welsh got between them, and Heenan let go his left on Welsh's nob, sending him to the ground, and afterwards giving him a kick. Turning quickly round he made a pass at Brunton, but the latter got out of danger. Sayers, who was during this time resting, now received another visitation on the nob from the Boy's left mawley, which prostrated him again. [Sayers' corner was filled with ruffian friends. At this juncture a few of the Boy's friends got in at his corner; and indeed, they were few, though they stood their ground manfully].

42. Heenan was again first to the scratch on time being called Sayers came up slowly amid the din and confusion. Both men eyed each other for a short time, being closely followed by their respective seconds. The Boy sent out his left, catching Tom on the gob. Some sparring. Heenan now got "Broadway" on Tom's breast, knocking him against one of his seconds. The Boy then rushed at Tom like an enraged tiger, catching him near the ropes, where he again got the champion's head in chancery, and delivered some telling blows to it. The crowd closed on them, when Welsh caught hold of the Boy's arm. Heenan now lifted Sayers like a child from the ground, and dashed him to the earth again, falling heavily upon him. [Cheers for Heenan, and cries of "clear the ring- clear the ring."]

[This was no round, but we merely mention it as the men were still in the ring.]

43. Heenan, at the call of time walked up to the scratch, but Sayers was sitting on a chair, not being allowed to come up. The Boy made a rush for his man, Sayers getting up and putting himself in position, but the crowd interfered, and no blow was struck. Heenan went to his corner and took a seat, McDonald advising him not to leave the ring until Sayers had gone. Sayers, with the assistance of his seconds, got over the ropes, and walked slowly away, with a hand on each of their shoulders. Heenan, who was dreadfully excited, called for him to come back to the scratch. The Boy then jumped nimbly over the ropes, and after walking a few steps commenced a run towards the railroad track, 600 yards distance, crossing two fences on his way, and leaving many of his friends behind. [The fight lasted two hours and twenty minutes.]

And thus ended the great fight for the championship of England, establishing that the expression of British "Fair play, and may the best man win," is a humbug. After the fight was over, Mr. McCabe went to John Morrissey and offered to match Heenan against him, to fight in three or four months, for $5,000 or $10,000 a side, but the latter took no notice of it. Another American, at the railway station, offered to double the stakes, should Heenan and Sayers fight again, or would match him against any man in the world for $10,000, but no one answered to it.

An hour and a half was consumed before the "iron horse" was again harnessed for the start home. During this time, many and bitter were the exclamations from the friends of Heenan. Some of them remarked that it was too bad to have come 8,000 miles for a "dead beat." The British, however, thought not so much of it. Seemingly, the only fact to be established to their minds was, whether the American was pluck. For at least nineteen twentieths of them, we must say they owned they had no doubt of it now, nor of his abilities as a fighter. In the journey back, Americans concentrated themselves, as nearly as possible, together.

Though the day was beautiful, and the sun shone brightly, the journey home, to the Americans, was a gloomy one. The train arrived at the Bricklayer's Station at 1:00 P.M., at which place there was at least 15,000 people, all expecting to hear the American had been defeated. No story to the contrary would satisfy them, so great was their confidence on the prowess and generalship of Sayers....

From *Bell's Life in London,* 29 April 1860

His [Heenan's] claim to the belt is simply preposterous. Had the fight progressed we are satsified Sayers would have won, barring an accident; and had we not been prevented seeing the 37th round we should inevitably have decided against Heenan for lifting Sayers off his knees, for that he did this we have now the assurance of several gentlemen whom we had not seen when we penned our last remarks on the subject, and who have no interest whatever in the affair. Heenan seems to have forgotten, too, the 28th rule of the Ring, by which the referee had the power of ordering the men to be separated—a power which he unquestionably would have exercised had he witnessed the latter part of the round. On Friday we received the following letter from Heenan, which as it touches no new point, requires no comment. We have only to repeat, in answer to it, that he never did win the belt; and that had the referee done what in strictness, perhaps, he was bound to do, order Heenan to fight again the same day, all dispute would have been at an end, as Sayers must have won. His not doing this was a piece of favoritism to Heenan, and not to the champion.

TO THE REFEREE AND EDITOR OF *Bell's Life*

London, April 27, 1860.

"Sir: I, John C. Heenan, of the city of West Troy, in the State of New York, Champion of America, having, in pursuance of my challenge to Thomas Sayers, the Champion of England, and in pursuance also of articles of agreement, drawn and executed between him and me on the 16th of December last, conditioned for L200 a side and the Champion's Belt, met the said Thomas Sayers near Farnboro', England, on Tuesday, the 17th inst.; and having then there fought with the said Thomas Sayers, in accordance with the terms of said contract and the rules of the Pugilistic Benevolent Association, until the said Sayers was forcibly extricated from my grasp in a perfectly helpless state; and having failed to obtain a decision therefore, awarding me the said stakes and belt, or to obtain any decision whatever in the premises; and having, after waiting three days for some decision to be made, demanded in writing that the said Sayers should according to the rules and customs for such cases made and provided, meet me again within the week, or resign to me the said stakes and belt according to the terms of said agreement; and no answer having been made to said demand of mine within said week, or down to this date, which is a full week from the date of such demand; therefore, I do hereby demand and claim that the said stakes and belt have been duly won by and are forfeited to me; and I do consequently, hereby further claim and demand the said stakes and belt shall be delivered over to me by you, who are the referee, and also the custodian thereof.—Yours, & c.

JOHN C. HEENAN.

From *Bell's Life*, 20 May 1860

Our readers and the public will hail with delight the announcement we now make, that on Friday last Tom Sayers and his gallant opponent met by appointment in our office, and settled their dispute in a most friendly manner. Sayers was accompanied by Mr. Gideon and two other friends, and Jack Macdonald appeared as the adviser of Heenan.

Several propositions were made on both sides, in the presence of all parties, which, however, ended in smoke. The first proposal on behalf of Heenan was that the old belt should be cut in half, that each should take a moiety, and that each belt should be made complete by subscriptions raised by either side. Sayers at once replied to this, that he would not consent to give up the old belt, or any part thereof, adding he would rather die in the ring than allow any portion of it to go out of the country. We then suggested that Tom should resign the old belt into our hands to be fought for by other aspirants, and that each champion should head a subscription to purchase a *facsimile* to be handed to his adversary. We represented that the feeling of the country was unanimous, especially among the higher classes, that both men had done enough for honor and renown, that by agreeing to this proposition neither would be giving a point to his adversary, and that it would be a method of settling of the affair which would meet with general approbation. Heenan at once assented to this, but Sayers, after conferring with one of his friends, said he would give Heenan a new belt, but would prefer keeping his own, for which he had fought so long. This was another hitch. It was clearly Heenan's object that Tom should not have the original, or, at any rate, the whole of it, as he considered this would be tantamount to a defeat; and at this stage of the proceedings we had fears that after all no amicable arrangement would be made. It then occured to us that if the men were left alone with us, and allowed to state their own individual wishes, unbiased by the opinions of others; in all probability we could put them together. A hint was sufficient; the friends of both instantly left our *sanctum*, and in five minutes the men shook hands in the most friendly way possible, and agreed to our proposal that each should have a new belt, and the old one should be left with us, and that in the event of Heenan's thinking fit to remain in this country and defend it against all comers for three years, it should become his own. Tom undertook not to put in any further claims for it, intimating that he should now retire from the Ring, and leave its fortunes and its vicissitudes for younger men. Heenan, in a few well expressed words, said he had always respected our Champion as a brave man, and one of the wonders of the age; he had come over to try whether he could lick him, and he was bound to acknowledge he found in him an adversary quite as good, or even better, than he expected, and he might add, now that the question of the belt was done away with, what he could not have said publiciy before, viz., that even had he defeated Tom Sayers in the Ring, it was his intention to have given the belt right back to him on the spot, feeling it would have been far from manly on his part to have deprived so good a man of his hard earned trophy, after waiving his rights so far as to allow him a chance of trying for it. Tom replied in suitable terms, that he had always respected Heenan; he looked upon him as a brave man, and the best he had ever met, and he considered him in every way worthy to uphold the position of Champion of England should he feel disposed so to do.

This arrangement, we think, cannot but give satisfaction to every one. All difficulties as to the division of the belt, or its removal from the country, are disposed of, and it still remains to be fought for. Each of the late combatants will receive a trophy which he may wear with pride, and show to future generations as the fruits of his prowess. The public generally, and especially the Corinthian patrons of the Ring, will be pleased that the men will not again meet in a hostile way. All were delighted with the spectacle afforded on the 17th of April, by the indomitable pluck and endurance exhibited on both sides, and however much all must have regretted that the question was not settled one way or the other, still the feeling was, as we have stated, pretty general that a second meeting should not take place. As to whom might have proved the winner in the event of a second meeting was of course a question open to much debate; each man naturally had his partisans, and equally open to dispute was the point as to who would have come off victorious had there been no interference.

EDITORIALS ON THE HEENAN-SAYERS FIGHT

The international match between John C. Heenan and Tom Sayers received a tremendous amount of newspaper coverage in both Great Britain and North America. While sporting periodicals such as Frank Queen's New York Clipper and George Wilkes's Spirit of the Times argued for the positive benefits of pugilism, the daily press generally condemned the sport as brutal and uncivilized. But while their editorials severely condemned prize fighting, their news columns included detailed reports on the major events. The editors of the New York Times explained that the bouts deserved coverage because of their importance as news, but they also hoped that the graphic accounts of these violent contests would vividly illustrate their barbaric nature. The following selections suggest that the London Times was more willing than the New York Times to concede that boxing had some socially redeeming value. These excerpts are reprinted from the New York Times, 2 May 1860, p. 1.

THE LONDON TIMES, APRIL 19, 1860

The prophets of enlightenment and progress must sometimes be a little sore at finding that human nature does not show that steady advance which they would attribute to it. The broad assertion that men are the same in all ages and all the world over is certainly a fallacy which will find acceptance only with cynical minds, but, on the other hand, reformers must not expect to change us too quickly. It may be that to some Darwinian lapse of ages the Ethiopian may change his skin and the leopard his spots, and it may also be that a time will come when men will lose all interest in their own bones and muscles, and value each other solely, according to the power of the brain as tested by competitive examinations. But that time has not yet arrived. The Quakers were much astonished that within three years after the peaceful gathering of 1851 their country men should have rushed into war with the alacrity of Caffres. The philosphers of the last century could not understand how the people who had been penetrated by the gentle teachings of Rousseau should shout with triumph when the *charrettes* passed to the guillotine. So the representatives of respectability, refinement, progress, education, social science, and all the other ameliorating abstractions which are in vogue, will be somewhat disconcerted by the fact that two great divisions of the Anglo-Saxon race have been worked to the highest pitch of excitement by the prospect of two half-naked men punching each other's countenances for some hours in a meadow. The low, the disgusting, the immoral practice of prize-fighting, as we have been accustomed to consider it, has suddenly resumed its interest for, we may truly say, every class of the population. If an Archbishop and a Chief Justice had met on Tuesday evening we will venture to say they would not have talked for ten minutes without some mention of the "Champion" and the "Benicia Boy." The *Times,* which cannot neglect any subject of national interest, is forced, for once, to dedicate its columns to the "P. R." Muscle and bottom, clever hitting and neat stopping, must be recorded like a debate on the Budget or the Swiss demonstrations against France; for the fight of the 17th of April, 1860, is a great national event, and has been accepted as such by inhabitants of two hemispheres. For weeks the general knowledge of society respecting "the noble art of self defence" has been on the increase. But a short time since we were most of us painfully ignorant on this great subject. Living in a state of utter respectability, many of us were unaware that England had a champion, or else thought that the office was hereditary in the family of DYMORE. The public-houses in the region of St. Martin's lane and Leicester-square were then vaguely known as disreputable haunts, instead of being, as now, sources of important information and centres of the deepest interest. The portraits of the two antagonists in every variety of style, from the penny wood-engraving to the nearly-executed photograph, have stared us in the face from shop-windows for the last month. In fact, people have, in spite of their better judgment, been brought to take an interest in a pursuit usually associated with the most offensive characters and the most vicious habits. All this has been brought about by the fact of an American pugilist coming over to fight an Englishman. National rivalry and the curiosity regarding a singular spectacle have overcome in a day all the intellectual and moral teachings of a generation. The fastidious public of the reign of Victoria have for once been carried back to the days of their fathers, when "Corinthians" attended the encounters of CRIBB AND MOLYNEUX....

So we will take men and their nature as we find them, and not preach a homily against the fight for the championship. Whether it be a battle between pugilists on a county border, or a war between empires for the supremacy of Europe, men will interest themselves in the struggles of strength and courage. Nor is poor Tom Sayers standing up against his gigantic antagonist, and coming up round after round to receive "punishment," an unworthy object of admiration. These men display in their miserable trade qualities which on a better field make individuals and nations great. That amid debauchery, and drunkenness, and petty gambling, these virtues of courage, endurance and fair play should be cultivated, and carried to their highest point, shows that there is indeed a soul of goodness in things evil. England and America have many a better arena for rivalry than the boxers' ring, but still nations without great qualities could not have brought together two men willing to pass through such an ordeal as the terrible fight of Tuesday. Nor are there wanting fields of contention which, though more reputable than the prize ring, are not more worthy of our regard. The apostles of progress would bring us to a state in which all worldly success, all distinctions, all influences over mankind, would depend only on shrewdness and quickness, applied principally to the acquisition of wealth. Yet, what is competition but a fight, and a fight in which the laws of fair play are too often disregarded? When we see the manufacturer distancing his rival by the sale of short measures, or the speculator made rich by a bubble which ruins hundreds when it bursts, we cannot think that a world where such men flourish will have any reason to boast even though the prize ring be a forgotten institution.

THE NEW YORK TIMES, MAY 2, 1861

This, then, is the verdict of England on the Prize Ring: that it illustrates the "great qualities" of great nations. The wisest men of heathen antiquity, a Plutarch and a Socrates, looked upon the original pugilism of their times as the least honorable and useful of the gymnastic arts. They saw nothing glorious to the State in the careful feeding and careful training of two vigorous men up to a point at which they make fine sport for a crowd of idle gazers, by inflicting and enduring an extraordinary number of extraordinary quick and savage blows. The London times now complacently informs England and America, the lands of a CROMWELL and a WASHINGTON, of a SHAKESPEARE and a MILTON, the two great nurseries of the boldest seamen, and the most high-spirited adventurers the world has seen, that when they are asked to give mankind assurance of their manhood, they may confidently point to the reciprocal pummeling which SAYRES and HEENAN gave and took on Farnborough common.

If this be not the height of vulgar cant, it is assuredly the height of shameless absurdity. That any man of any nation and calling deserves to a certain extent whatever praise is due to personal courage, self-reliance and strength of will, when he deliberately exposes himself for any object whatever, to the certainty of great suffering and the risk of death, is no doubt perfectly true. His object, however, in this exposure, and his object only, can decide whether the fortitude which he displays in seeking it shall rank him with the higher or the lower classes of his kind. ...As a mere matter of fact, the ordeal of the terrible fight through which SAYERS and HEENAN passed though disgusting and painful enough, was a "gentle and joyous passage of arms" when compared with the English prize-fights of fifty years ago, and, above all, with those prize-fights of the ancients, from which the modern English ring is but a faded plagiarism....

Nay poor black MOLYNEUX himself, that unappreciated American who has apparently been robbed by the *ex post facto* operation of the Dred Scot decision, of his rights in our ring—black MOLYNEUX took a punishment at the hands of CRIBB in his fight for the belt, which ought to prove, on the reasoning of the Times, that the "negro race" is at best equal in its "great qualities" to either branch of the great British family. But granting the severity of the test to which the prowess and the powers of HEENAN and SAYERS were subjected, pray what is there in the motives of their meeting to illustrate the "great qualities" of England and America?

For the young American it may be claimed, indeed, with some show of reason, that he was led across the Atlantic by a kind of "noble rage." He had been robbed, as he believed unfairly deprived, of the "championship" of the American ring. He put himself on the mettle, and determined to show what stuff he was made of by a bold foreign venture. A queer form of ambition this, certainly, but let it pass for what it is worth, to the credit of the boy of Benecia.

What is to be said, however, for Mr. THOMAS SAYERS? With him, the whole matter is a matter of business. He received three years ago a silver belt, value L200, for beating another previous "champion." This belt he holds on the condition of fighting once every six months anybody who may challenge him for three years' time....

There is something worse than contemptible in any attempt to invest such proceedings as those which disgraced the police and the aristocracy of England on the 17th of April with lofty significances and broad national attributes of honor. Why not be honest about the matter? Two well-trained men go into a field to try and batter each other literally out of countenance. As they happen to belong to different nations, a certain kind of national feeling inflames the general curiosity which the wisest philosopher need not attempt to deny that he always feels to know "how the matter ended," without any regard to what the matter may have been. He would be a very dubious patriot who could see an American and English boat stretching their canvas on the Solent; an American and English horse racing on the Epsom turf, or an American and an English boxer squaring off in the ring, without secretly hoping that his own side might win.

The feeling is not very lofty, perhaps, but very natural. Why dress it up in solemnities of meaning which make it criminal by making it hypocritical? The only "great qualities" which the "great fight" proves to exist in England and America, are a great passion for excitement, common to both countries; a great love of gambling, certainly not confined to either country; and a secret delight in the instinct of combativeness, which happily or unhappily belongs to the whole human race. Promise a Dutchman and a Malay the ten or twelve thousand dollars which depended for HEENAN and SAYERS upon the issue of their meeting, and we will guarantee as "terrible an ordeal" as the most zealous of "sporting men" can desire to see. Our Japanese friends, who are now just coming to see us, have a "prize-ring" of their own as remarkable for its "great qualities" in the way of indomitable thumping, kicking and mutual annihilation as the noble arena, to whose history another brilliant chapter has not been added.

Chapter 6

CRICKET

Although a few cricket clubs were organized in the British colonies during the eighteenth century, the sport's modern era in North America did not really begin until the 1830s. In Canada English immigrants, military garrison men, and native-born subjects pioneered the sport. It flourished wherever British influence was strongest, especially in prestigious private schools and urban centers where English officers and political officials resided. Cricket was most popular in Toronto and other settlements in Upper Canada; by 1858 that region held fifty-eight clubs. Prior to the 1860s the English pastime also attracted enthusiasts in Montreal, Halifax, Quebec City, Ottawa, St. John, and Victoria.

In the United States several groups in the Albany, New York vicinity played formal matches during the 1830s, but the St. George Cricket Club of Manhattan claimed to be the first regular outfit governed by rules and regulations. During the fall of 1838 several sides of Englishmen resident in New York and Brooklyn played two matches that led to the founding of the St. George Cricket Club in 1839. In the spring of 1844 the St. George club found itself with a new rival in the field, the New York Cricket Club. John Richards, the English-born publisher of the Spirit of the Times, was the club's founding father and his editor, William T. Porter, served as its first president. They recruited many members from the Spirit's staff and others from New York's literary and artistic communities. Thanks to the generosity of John C. Stevens, the club secured a fine playing ground near Hoboken's Elysian Fields across the Hudson River in New Jersey.

Although New York and its neighboring cities dominated American cricket during the sport's formative years, Philadelphia was destined to become the cricket capital of the United States. Natives of the City of Brotherly Love were treated to cricket demonstrations by groups of affluent and working-class Englishmen. As early as 1831 several members of the Tichnor family played on a ground on the west bank of the Schuylkill River. A few years later a group of mechanics competed on the Kensington common. About 1840 a party of hosiery weavers at Wakefield Mills scheduled matches on Whitmonday, holidays, and Saturday afternoons. The Union Cricket Club was founded in 1843 when Robert Waller of the St. George club moved to Philadelphia and brought together several English importers, a few Kensington men, and a sprinkling of American townball players. The Union cricketers played on their own specially leveled and turfed ground, at Camden, New Jersey.

William Carvill, a gardener, encouraged an interest in cricket among students at Haverford College in Pennsylvania as early as 1834. This club, probably the first composed entirely of Americans, lasted only a few years, but the college fielded two new elevens in 1848. The Union club gave a big boost to the future of the game in the

United States when it sponsored the Junior Cricket Club at the University of Pennsylvania in the mid-1840s. The older Union players recruited William Rotch Wister, then a student at the university, who enlisted about forty fellow scholars.

These bright beginnings for Philadelphia cricket soon dimmed, for the Union club vanished after the 1846 season, a victim of financial problems and dissension among members. When Robert Waller returned to New York, the club lost one of its driving forces. With the loss of its patron and ground, the Junior Cricket Club also disbanded, in Wister's words, "to the sincere rejoicing of the fathers of most of the members, who, while tolerating the game, yet constantly dreaded that their sons might be carried by it into dissipation."

A new era of American cricket dawned in 1854 when a few gentlemen launched the Philadelphia Cricket Club. One of its first constitutions appears below. A Germantown association appeared six months later, composed of young men who were at least sixteen years old. In 1855 members of the Germantown club denied admission to their younger brothers and friends. The upstarts launched the Young America club, which soon grew into a powerhouse of juvenile cricket.

During the two decades that preceded the Civil War cricket enthusiasts promoted their pastime throughout the United States and Canada. To assess their efforts and to survey the status of the sport and its geographical extent as of 1860, it is necessary to focus on five key factors: geographical mobility and the willingness of the English immigrants to teach cricket to younger and older Americans; the New York City sporting journals and the local dailies; intercity competition; the New York City cricket conventions; and special all-star and international matches. As a result of these forces, North American cricket showed considerable strength on the eve of the war, even as it faced some serious internal problems and a powerful rival in the upstart sport of American baseball.

Many of the Englishmen who founded the first North American cricket clubs were merchants, professionals, or representatives of their government. A love of cricket, coupled with a high degree of personal mobility, motivated them to assist in the formation of new clubs and to teach novices. Robert Waller of the St. George club was instrumental in founding Philadelphia's Union club in 1843, while two other Dragon Slayers, Robert Bage and George Wheatcroft, organized a group of skilled craftsmen into the Newark Cricket Club in 1845. George Aitken, the British Consul in San Francisco, founded that city's first modern sporting organization in March 1852 when he launched the San Francisco Cricket Club. During the 1850s several prominent cricketers headed west to seek their fortunes and to play the game of cricket in their spare time in Cincinnati, St. Louis, and San Francisco.

The admirers of cricket realized that the future of the game in North America rested with the younger generation born in Canada and the United States, but they had to contend with the prevailing attitude that exercise and sport did not mix with education. A few British and American schoolteachers boldly introduced the game to their pupils. Some senior cricketers tried to foster a love of the game among boys and young men by admitting them as limited, nonvoting members of their clubs. In general, the New York City region lagged far behind both Philadelphia and New Jersey in popularizing cricket among its youth, partly due to the habit of permitting older, more experienced players to dominate batting practice during club play days. Although this helped the first-eleven cricketers prepare for interclub contests, it limited a novice's chance to learn the sport well enough to become addicted to it.

While English and native-born cricketers spread their gospel across the land, daily and weekly newspapers gave valuable coverage to North America's first modern team sport. Local periodicals provided only limited announcements and results for hometown clubs, but the New York City sporting journals granted extensive space to cricket news. John Richards's Spirit of the Times nurtured North American cricket during its infancy, while he and William Porter led the New York Cricket Club to a prominent position among the city's sporting crowd. During the 1850s the New York Clipper and Richards's, Porter's and George Wilkes's versions of the Spirit published editorials extolling the merits of the game, announcements of upcoming contests, detailed stories and box scores, and names of club officers. These journals also printed the official rules of the prestigious governing institution of English cricket, the Marylebone Cricket Club of London (reprinted below), model constitutions and bylaws, summaries of the proceedings of the annual cricket conventions, and year-end reviews of club records and batsmen's and bowlers' averages. The box scores and year-end statistics published by the various New York papers are especially signficant for two reasons. First, they reveal the high degree of modernization achieved by North American cricket before the Civil War. Second, they indicate the cricketers' interest in comparative performances and improvement of their skills. Thus, before 1861 North American cricketers clearly displayed a fascination with statistics and an urge to set and break records—two key characteristics of modern sport.

The New York City periodicals advertised the benefits of cricket, and they helped to foster the intercity competition that stimulated the founding of new clubs and heightened interest in the sport. The keen rivalry between the St. George and Philadelphia Union clubs, begun in the mid-1840s, intensified during the 1850s. Other teams from New York, Brooklyn, Philadelphia, and Boston traveled throughout the Northeast to engage their respective adversaries. The West also had many intercity cricket matches, which both reflected and intensified that region's traditions of urban rivalry and boosterism. During the 1850s cricketers pitched wickets in the West for clubs representing Cleveland, Pittsburgh, Chicago, Cincinnati, and Milwaukee. Local boosters were enthusiastic about cricket contests that might give some free publicity and perhaps a competitive edge to their hometowns in the struggle for supremacy among frontier communities.

While these intercity challenges demonstrated the potential for the growth of cricket in the United States in the mid-nineteenth century, the game's advocates realized the need for a national association that would nurture and promote the game throughout the nation. From 1857 to 1860 the leaders of American cricket held a series of conventions in New York City that aimed at creating such an organization. It was an ambitious and important undertaking. The account of the 1858 meeting reprinted below suggests some of the difficulties United States cricketers encountered as they tried to promote their sport. The sessions served the needs of cricketers from the Middle Atlantic region but failed to create a truly national organization that could promote the sport in other parts of the country. Participants were most successful in appointing the committee that picked the players for the all-star events of each season. The two most important of these were the match in which eighteen Americans challenged eleven Englishmen, normally scheduled for June or early July, and the international contest betwen Canada and the United States, usually held in August. These events primarily served the cricketers of New York, Philadelphia, and vicinity. During the last few gatherings before the Civil War a bitter feud between the St. George and New York clubs undercut the delegates' efforts to adapt the game to American conditions or to create a truly national association.

These cricket conventions did not achieve all of their goals; yet the special events they arranged attracted players and other enthusiasts and did much to popularize the sport in the United States and Canada before 1860. During the 1850s the premier event of each season was the annual United States versus Canada contest. This series began in 1840 and was the first international competition in the history of cricket. Since virtually all of the United States representatives were English-born, it must be conceded that these contests were not strictly between Americans and Canadians. From 1840 to 1860 members of the St. George club, Philadelphia's Union club, and the Toronto and Montreal clubs competed in several events that generated considerable excitement (and gambling) on both sides of the border. Unfortunately, they also produced a number of misunderstandings and disagreements.

The series began with an embarrassing start in August 1840 when the St. George club accepted an invitation to journey to Upper Canada to play the Toronto club. Upon their arrival the Dragon Slayers discovered that an imposter had issued a bogus challenge. Fortunately the Toronto gentlemen agreed to play a match, which was won by the visitors. In 1843 a Toronto team defeated a St. George eleven, but the 1844 return match in Canada was never played because of a dispute over the composition of the St. George eleven. Instead a new contest was arranged for the St. George grounds in Manhattan. The visitors from north of the border defeated the Dragon Slayers and took home the $1000 prize and much more in side bets. The two games played in 1845 might technically be called the first truly international matches, since both elevens included men from more than one city. The American contingent lost both encounters to a side that included mostly men from the Montreal Cricket Club. The 1846 game ended in an ugly controversy caused by a fight between opposing players. After that incident the series was interrupted for seven years. The resumption of these games in 1853 gave a big boost to North American cricket down to the outbreak of the Civil War in 1861. A report of the results of the match held in 1858 is included here.

The most significant special event in the history of early North American cricket was the tour of the All-England Eleven in 1859. Officers of the St. George, Montreal, and Philadelphia clubs financed and arranged these matches. Proponents of Canadian and United States cricket predicted many positive benefits from this foreign invasion. Excerpts from the extensive newspaper coverage of this series conclude this chapter. But while the Englishmen's display of skill had an immediate and powerful effect on those who were already enamoured of the sport, its long-term effects are more ambiguous. The complete domination by the All-England Eleven and their agents' concern for turning a profit detracted somewhat from the beneficial results of their journey. The showcase demonstration of cricket by the best players of Britain did excite interest among the baseball playing fraternity, but unfortunately the momentum generated by the English tour was halted by the outbreak of civil war in the United States in 1861.

By 1860 England's national game had taken root in North American soil, with several flowerings of enthusiasm in both Canada and the United States. Toronto and its surrounding towns in Upper Canada were strongholds of the sport, while Montreal, Halifax, and other cities also fielded many elevens. South of the border cricketers had founded clubs throughout New England's factory towns and larger cities during the 1850s, including a few in Maine, New Hampshire, and Rhode Island and many more in Massachusetts and Connecticut. The formation of the Boston Cricket Club boded well for the game in that area. The Middle Atlantic states provided the game's greatest concentration of activity. Upstate New Yorkers from Albany, Utica, Rochester, Syracuse, and other cities emulated their downstate rivals from New York City and Brooklyn. Across the Hudson River, New Jerseyans formed at least two dozen clubs between 1845 and 1860. Philadelphia clearly established itself as the cricket capital of the United States, with by far the most clubs and the largest contingent of American-born players.

The English sport also caught on below the Mason-Dixon line and beyond the Appalachians. More than a dozen southern towns produced teams for at least one season, including Richmond, Baltimore, Savannah, and New Orleans. Cricket was far more prevalent in the West than in the South, with at least twenty-five communities fielding elevens in Ohio, Illinois, Michigan, Wisconsin, Minnesota, Iowa, Kentucky, Missouri, and even California. Cricketers from Cleveland, Cincinnati, and Chicago were annoyed when easterners ignored their requests for representation in the major all-star and international matches.

Despite its successful beginnings, North American cricket faced serious problems at the end of the 1850s. First, the meteoric rise of baseball in the United States overshadowed its progress and limited its chances to recruit large numbers of younger Americans. Furthermore, many people still viewed the sport as a disreputable one patronized by gamblers and saloon frequenters. A low standard of play also hurt the sport, especially in fielding, which was one of the most attractive features of baseball for spectators. Poor grounds further detracted from the game's appeal. Lengthy matches and tedious delays alienated many sportsmen, whereas Anglophobes rejected the sport simply because it was a British import. Yet despite these difficulties, in 1860 cricket's adherents still expected great advances in North America over the rest of the century. In fact, the English game would never achieve popularity among the Canadian or American masses.

THE RULES OF CRICKET

In 1787 the Marylebone Cricket Club was founded in London, England. In that year a young Yorkshireman named Thomas Lord arranged for the club to play on an open field. By the end of the eighteenth century the Marylebone club had achieved preeminence as the ruling body of the English sport, and Lord's ground had become the cricketing capital of the nation. The club codified its rules in 1835, and the document below presents the revisions that were approved in 1854. Although several cricketers in the United States lobbied for changes in the game that would make it more attractive to the masses of Americans, the English residents of New York City and Philadelphia respected the authority of the Marylebone rules. In the annual cricket conventions held in New York City prior to 1860 the delegates endorsed the English laws because any variation would create a sport that would be "not cricket." The following is reprinted from the New York Clipper, 25 April 1857, p. 8.

THE LAWS OF CRICKET
AS REVISED BY THE MARY-LE-BONE CRICKET CLUB, MAY 15, 1854

1. The BALL must weigh not less than five ounces and a half, nor more than five ounces and three quarters. It must measure not less than nine inches, nor more than nine inches and one quarter in circumference. At the beginning of each innings, either party may call for a new ball.

2. The BAT must not exceed four inches and one quarter in the widest part; it must not be more than thirty-eight inches in length.

3. The STUMPS must be three in number: twenty-seven inches out of the ground; the Bails eight inches in length: the Stumps of equal and of sufficient thickness to prevent the ball from passing through.

4. The BOWLING CREASE must be in line with the Stumps; six feet eight inches in length; the Stumps in the centre; with a return crease at each end towards the Bowler at right angles.

5. The POPPING CREASE must be four feet from the Wicket, and parallel to it; unlimited in length, but not shorter than the Bowling Crease.

6. The Wickets must be pitched opposite to each other by the Umpires, at the distance of twenty-two yards.

7. It shall not be lawful for either party during a match, without the consent of the other, to alter the ground by rolling, watering, coverage, mowing, or beating, except at the commencement of each innings, when the ground may be swept and rolled at the request of either party; such request so made to one of the Umpires within one minute after the conclusion of the former innings. This rule is not meant to prevent the striker from beating the ground with his bat near to the spot where he stands during the innings, nor to prevent the bowler from filling up holes with sawdust, &c., when the ground is wet.

8. After rain the wickets may be changed with the consent of both parties.

9. The BOWLER shall deliver the ball with one foot on the ground behind the bowling crease, and within the return crease; and shall bowl four balls before he change Wickets, which he shall be permitted to do only once in the same innings.

10. The ball must be bowled, not thrown or jerked, and the hand must not be above the shoulder in delivery; and whenever the bowler shall so closely infringe on this rule in either of the above particulars as to make it difficult for the Umpire at the Bowler's

wicket to judge whether the ball has been delivered within the true intent and meaning of this rule or not, the Umpire shall call "No Ball."

11. He may require the Striker at the wicket from which he is bowling to stand on that side of it which he may direct.

12. If the Bowler shall toss the ball over the Striker's head, or bowl it so wide that in the opinion of the Umpire it shall not be fairly within the reach of of the batsman, he shall adjudge one run to the party receiving the innings, either with or without an appeal, which shall be put down to the score of Wide Balls; such ball shall not be reckoned as one of the four balls; but if the Batsman shall by any means bring himself within the reach of the ball, the run shall not be adjudged.

13. If the Bowler deliver a "No Ball" or a "Wide Ball," the Striker shall be allowed as many runs as he can get, and he shall not be put out except by running out. In the event of no runs being obtained by any other means, then one run shall be added to the score of "No Balls" or "Wide Balls" as the case may be. All runs obtained for "Wide Balls" to be scored as "Wide Balls," the names of the Bowlers who bowl "Wide Balls" or "No Balls" in the future to be placed on the score, to show the parties by whom either score is made. If the ball shall first touch any part of the Striker's dress or person (except his hands) the Umpire shall call "Leg Bye."

14. At the beginning of each innings the Umpire shall call "Play;" from that time to the end of each innings no trial ball shall be allowed to any Bowler.

15. The Striker is out if either of the bails be bowled off, or if a stump be bowled out of the ground;

16. Or, if the ball, from the stroke of the bat, or hand, but not the wrist be held before it touch the ground, although it be hugged to the body of the catcher;

17. Or, if in striking, or at any other time while the ball shall be in play, both his feet shall be over the popping crease, and his wicket put down, except his bat be grounded within it;

18. Or, if in striking at the ball he hit down his wicket;

19. Or, if under pretence of running, or otherwise, either of the Strikers prevent a ball from being caught, the striker of the ball is out;

20. Or, if the ball be struck, and he willfully strike it again;

21. Or, if in running, the wicket be struck down by a throw, or by the hand or arm, (with ball in hand,) before his bat (in hand) or some part of his person be grounded over the popping crease. But if both bails be off, a stump must be struck out of the ground;

22. Or, if any part of the Striker's dress knock down the wicket;

23. Or, if the Striker touch or take up the ball while in play; unless at the request of the opposite party;

24. Or, if with any part of his person he stop the ball, which, in the opinion of the Umpire at the Bowler's wicket, shall have been pitched in a straight line from it to the Striker's wicket, and would have hit it.

25. If the players have crossed each other, he that runs for the wicket which is put down is out.

26. A ball being caught, no run shall be reckoned.

27. A striker being run out, that run which he and his partner attempting shall not be reckoned.

28. If a lost ball be called, the Striker shall be allowed six runs; but if more than six shall have been run before lost ball shall have been called, then the Striker shall have all which have been run.

29. After the ball shall have been finally settled in the Wicket keeper's or Bowler's hand, it shall be pronounced dead; but when the Bowler is about to deliver the ball, if the Striker at his wicket go outside the popping crease before such actual delivery, the said bowler may put him out, unless (with reference to the 21st law) his bat in hand, or some part of his person be within the popping crease.

30. The Striker shall not retire from his wicket and return to it to complete his innings, after another has been in, without the consent of the opposite party.

31. No substitute shall in any case be allowed to stand out or run between wickets for another person, without the consent of the opposite party; and in case any person shall be allowed to run for another, the Striker shall be out if either he or his substitute be off the ground in manner mentioned in Laws 17 and 21, when the ball is in play.

32. In all cases where a substitute shall be allowed, the consent of the opposite party shall also be obtained as to the person to act as substitute, and the place in the field which he shall take.

33. If any Fieldsman stop the ball with his hat, the ball shall be considered dead, and the opposite party shall add five runs to their score; if any be run they shall have five in all.

34. The ball having been hit, the Striker may guard his wicket with his bat or any part of his body except his hands, that the 23d Law may not be disobeyed.

35. The Wicket-keeper shall not take the ball for the purpose of stumping, until it has passed the wicket; he shall not by any noise incommode the Striker; and if any part of his person be over or before the wicket, although the ball hit it, the Striker shall not be out.

36. The Umpires are the sole judges of fair and unfair play; and all disputes shall be determined by them, each at his own wicket; but in case of a catch which the Umpire at the wicket bowled from cannot see sufficiently to decide upon, he may apply to the other Umpire, whose opinion shall be conclusive.

37. The Umpires in all matches shall pitch fair wickets, and the parties shall toss for choice of innings. The Umpires shall change wickets after each party has had one innings.

38. They shall allow two minutes for each Striker to come in, and ten minutes between each innings. When the Umpire shall call "Play," the parties refusing to play shall lose the match.

39. They are not to order a Striker out unless appealed to by the adversaries;

40. But if one of the Bowler's feet be not on the ground behind the bowling crease and within the return crease when he shall deliver the ball, the Umpire at his wicket, unasked, must call "No Ball."

41. If either of the Strikers run a short run, the Umpire must call "One Short."

42. No Umpire shall be allowed to bet.

43. No Umpire is to be changed during a matach, unless with the consent of both parties, except in case of violation of 42nd law; then either party may dismiss the transgressor.

44. After the delivery of four balls the Umpire must call "over," but not until the ball shall be finally settled in the Wicket Keeper's or Bowler's hand; the ball shall then

be considered dead; nevertheless, if an idea be entertained that either of the Strikers is out, a question may be put previously to, but not after, the delivery of the next ball.

45. The Umpire must take especial care to call "No Ball" instantly upon delivery; "Wide Ball" as soon as it shall pass the Striker.

46. The players who go in second shall follow their innings, if they have obtained 80 runs less than their antagonists, except in matches limited to only one day's play, when the number shall be 60 instead of 80.

47. When one of the Strikers shall have been put out, the use of the bat shall not be allowed to any person until the next Striker shall come in.

THE LAWS OF SINGLE WICKET

I. When there shall be less than five Players on a side, Bounds shall be placed twenty-two yards each in a line from the off and leg stump.

II. The ball must be hit before the Bounds to entitle the Striker to a run, which run cannot be obtained unless he touch the bowling stump or crease in a line with his bat, or some part of his person, or go beyond them, returning to the popping crease as at double wicket, according to the 21st law.

III. When the Striker shall hit the ball, one of his feet must be on the ground and behind the popping crease, otherwise the Umpire shall call "No Hit."

IV. When there shall be less than five players on a side, neither Byes nor Overthrows shall be allowed, nor shall the Striker be caught out behind the wicket, nor stumped out.

V. The Fieldsman must return the ball so that it shall cross the play between the wicket and bowling stump, or between the bowling stump and the bounds; the striker may run until the ball be so returned.

VI. After the striker shall have made one run, if he start again he must touch the bowling stump, and turn before the ball cross the play to entitle him to another.

VII. The Striker shall be entitled to three runs for lost ball, and the same number for ball stopped with hat, with reference to 28th and 33d law of Double Wicket.

VIII. When there shall be more than four Players on a side there shall be no bounds. All Hits, Byes, and Ovethrown shall be allowed.

IX. The Bowler is subject to the same laws as at Double Wicket.

X. Not more than one minute shall be allowed between each ball.

BETS

I. No bet upon any match is payable unless it be played out or given up.

II. If the runs of one player be betted against those of another, the bet depends upon the first innings, unless otherwise specified.

III. If the bet be made on both innings, and one party beat the other in one innings, the runs of the first innings shall determine it.

IV. If the other party go in a second time, then the bet must be determined by the number on the score.

THE PHILADELPHIA CRICKET CLUB

In 1854 a few Philadelphia gentlemen, who had been playing Saturday scrub matches, decided that to enjoy their favorite pastime to the fullest they required a more formal structure, including a regular schedule of practice, intrasquad and interclub competition, and a better playing field. To this end they founded the Philadelphia Cricket Club at William Rotch Wister's office. Their club became one of the premier cricket associations in the United States. The following document is reprinted from the New York Clipper, 8 May 1858, p. 20.

CONSTITUTION AND BYLAWS OF THE PHILADELPHIA CRICKET CLUB

ARTICLE I -Name- The Association shall be called "The Philadelphia Cricket Club;" and shall be composed of such persons as shall be elected according to the Constitution and By-Laws.

ARTICLE II -Nominations- No person shall be elected a member unless he shall have been nominated at a meeting held at least one month previous to such selection.

ARTICLE III -Elections- *Sec. 1.* The election of all members shall be by ballot, provided:-that with the unanimous consent of the members present, the votes may be taken viva voce:-two dissenting votes shall prevent any nominee from being elected a member.

Sec. 2. The election of a member shall not be deemed complete, until he shall have signed the Constitution and paid his entrance fee; should he neglect to pay his entrance fee for three months after his election, he cannot become a member under such election.

Sec. 3. Persons may be elected members at any meeting of the Club, by the unanimous vote of those present, who shall not be liable to pay an entrance fee or assessment , and who shall not be entitled to vote or serve in any office.

Sec. 4. A member may be expelled at any annual or special meeting by the vote of two-thirds of the members present; provided that at least ten votes are cast in favor of such expulsion.

ARTICLE IV - Officers.- The officers shall consist of a President, a Vice President, a Secretary, a Treasurer, and a Ground Committee.

ARTICLE V - Ground Committee- *Sec. 1.* The Ground Committee shall consist of five members, of whom the President shall be one.

Sec. 2. In case of a vacancy or vacancies occurring in the Ground Committee during the year for which they shall have been elected, they shall appoint some member or members of the Club, to fill such vacany or vacancies, until the next election of officers takes place.

ARTICLE VI - Meetings- *Sec. 1.* There shall be a stated meeting of the Club held at some suitable place in the city of Philadelphia, on the second Monday in January in every year- at which ten members shall be a quorum: when officers to serve for the ensuing year shall be elected, and all general business to be transacted.

Sec. 2. There shall be a stated meeting held on the first day of playing of every month during the playing season- at which seven members shall be a quorum, for the purpose of electing members.

Sec. 3. Upon a request in writing signed by five members, the President, or in his absence from the city, the Vice President, shall direct the Secretary to call a special meeting of the club, stating in the notice the object for which the meeting is called, at which the same number shall constitute a quorum, and like business may be transacted as at the stated annual meeting.

ARTICLE VII - Entrance fees and Assessments- The amount of the entrance fee and assessment for the current year, shall be determined by the club at its stated annual meeting.

ARTICLE VIII - Expenses of Matches- The expenses of all matches shall be paid by voluntary contribution, and not from the funds of the club.

ARTICLE IX - Amendments- No amendment to the Constitution or By-Laws shall be made, except at the stated annual, or a special meeting of the club:-and any amendment to the Constitution, to be valid, must be approved by the votes of at least two-thirds of the members present.

By-Laws

ARTICLE I. - President- 1. It shall be the duty of the President to preside at all meetings of the club: 2. In the absence of the President, it shall be the duty of the Vice President to preside: 3. In the absence of both the President and Vice President, a chairman from those present shall be chosen pro tempore.

ARTICLE II. - Treasurer- It shall be the duty of the Treasurer to collect and receive all entrance fees, assessments, and dues to the club; and make all necessary disbursements , under the direction of the ground committee.

ARTICLE III. - Secretary- It shall be the duty of the Secretary to attend all meetings of the club, and keep minutes of their proceedings in a book provided for that purpose; to notify members of their election, or expulsion, within eight days thereafter, and give such notices as may be required of him by the ground committee.

ARTICLE IV. - Ground Committee- It shall be the duty of the ground committee: 1. To assume general direction of the grounds: 2. To provide and have control of all necessary implements, for the use of the club: 3. To appoint the time when the playing season shall commence and terminate: 4. To appoint the playing days- which shall be at least one day in every week during the playing season: 5. To direct the disbursements of the funds, and all payments for services rendered to the club during the year for which they shall have been elected: 6. To decide upon and arrange all matches, and appoint the players and umpires- provided, that the captains of sides shall be chosen by those selected to play; and to keep a record of all matches, for the information of the members: and 7. To make general reports from time to time, to the club, of all matters pertaining to their office.

ARTICLE V. - Invitations- The ground committee may extend invitations to any persons, to play with the club, during the playing season.

ARTICLE VI. - Persons Introduced- Any person introduced by a member, may play with the club on the playing days provided:- that the name of such person with the name of the member introducing him, be entered in a book provided by the ground committee.

ARTICLE VII. - Any member who shall not have paid his assessment for any current year, previous to the first day of June of the following year, shall no longer be a member of the club.

ARTICLE VIII. - Playing Laws- The laws of the game of cricket, as adopted by the Marylebone Club, shall be the playing laws of the Philadelphia Cricket Club.

NEW YORK CITY CRICKET CONVENTION

The first New York City cricket convention in 1857 addressed the sensitive subject of adapting the sport to conditions in the United States. Daniel W. Baker, an American-born cricketer and former president of the Newark, New Jersey club, wished to "Americanize it." He hoped for "some plan by which we also might have our Marylebone Club, or supreme power, to devise and arrange laws for the government of the game in America." But his proposal met a cool reception, as several men objected to any alteration of the rules of the Marylebone Club. At the 1858 meeting Baker went along with the majority decision to follow the Marylebone code as the standard for American cricket. Many American cricketers, including Baker, were concerned as well about revising some of the local customs of selecting participants for interclub matches. They did not approve of the use of professionals, but they were more upset about cricketers who joined several clubs in order to play in more matches. Baker pointed out that the practice of permitting multiple-club membership created a monopoly by the few talented players and that "clubs were never certain whom they had to play against." In 1858 the convention delegates agreed to exchange club membership rosters, from which the contending elevens would be chosen one week prior to a match. On a related point, they required that professionals be played as such, not as members of clubs for which they were engaged. The following account of the 1858 convention is reprinted from The New York Clipper, 8 May 1858, p. 19.

GREAT CONVENTION OF CRICKETERS

A highly intelligent and numerous body of cricketers met in convention at the Astor House, N.Y. City, on Monday, May 3d, pursuant to a call made by the committee appointed at a similar convention held in 1857, for the purpose of centralizing and nationalizing the game of Cricket. At about 8 1/2 o'clock, P.M., the meeting was called to order by Mr. R. Waller, Chairman of the last convention, when they at once proceeded to elect a Chairman and secretary for the one in question, when the choice fell upon Mr. H. Sharp, of New York, for the former office, and Mr. Baker, of Newark, for the latter....

The minutes of the last meeting were then read by Mr. Stedwell, and accepted unanimously.

Letters were next read, the first from Mr. Bradshaw, of Cincinnati, encouraging to the good cause, and full of bright hopes for the future; the second, from Jas. J. Cassidy, of the Buckeye Club, of the same city, pledging themselves to support the action of the Convention; the third from J.F. Burgess, of the Clinton, Mass., C.C., containing suggestions for the good of cricket, and avowing allegiance to whatever might be adopted by the Convention. On motion of Mr. Stedwell, these letters were ordered to be placed on file. The Committee appointed at the last convention handed in their report, advising 1st. The arrangements of playing rules. 2nd. That professionals be played as such, and not as members of the clubs. 3rd. That lists of players be exchanged between club and club before the playing of matches.

On motion of Mr. Stedwell, the Chair appointed Messrs. Stedwell, of Yonkers, and Jefferson, of Newark, a committee to report to this meeting a plan for the permanent organization of a National Cricket Association.

Moved by Mr. Maxwell, and seconded by Mr. Baker, that the laws of the Mary-le-bone Club, England, as they now exist , or as they may hereafter be amended, be adopted by this convention as the standard of Cricket for this country. Carried unanimously. On suggestion of Mr. Waller, it was moved by Mr. Maxwell, and seconded by Mr. Jefferson, that each club, through its delegates, have one vote only on all questions before the Convention, which was carried by 15 affirmative , against one negative vote.

The next clause in the Committee's report, viz.; that professionals be played as such, &c., &c., was put on motion by Mr. Maxwell, to which an amendment was offered by Mr. Waller, that professional players be defined to mean all players who were paid for their services in any way or shape. The amendment was lost, the vote standing 13 against, 1 in favor, 2 not voting and 1 divided. The original motion was then put and carried. Ayes 16, Nays 1.

It was also put and carried that lists of memberships of clubs be exchanged, from which elevens are to be selected one week prior to the playing of a match. In second and third eleven matches it was moved by Mr. Baker, and seconded by Mr. Jefferson, that the opponents should have the privilege of naming the eleven or elevens that shall be debarred; to which a counter-motion was made by Mr. Waller, and seconded by Mr. Boyd, to the effect that this subject be laid on the table. Carried by 9 affirmative against 4 negative votes.

The report of the Committee on the organization of the Association was then unanimously adopted.

On motion of Mr. Maxwell, the appointment of a committee of five to make arrangements for the Canada match was given into the hands of the Chair, who made the following selction: Messrs. Walker, of St. George; Castles, of N.Y.; Wheatcroft, of Newark, Facon, of Philadelphia; and French, of the Utica Club. Moved by the same gentleman and carried, that the match, "Eleven English vs. Eighteen Americans," be played in Philadelphia; to carry out the arrangements for which the following committee was appointed by the Chair: English-Messrs. Tilt, Barlow, and Sharp; Americans-Messrs. R.Wister, Bashford, and Baker.

The match "East vs. West," on motion of Mr. Waller, was voted inexpedient.

A committee of one from each of the three city clubs, New York, St. George, and Manhattan, was then appointed by the Chair to wait on the Commissioners of the

Central Park, in reference to the laying out of the cricket ground, for which they understood an appropriation had been made. The committee consist of Messrs. Vaux, Maxwell, and Campbell.

No charge being made for use of the room, &c., a vote of thanks was unanimously tendered to the proprietor of the Astor House, for his liberality, and a committee appointed to convey to him the sentiments of the meeting. An ajournment then took place, until the first Monday in May, 1859, at the same place. Thus closed one of the most effective meetings ever held in America in hopes of the "noble game of cricket," which is fast becoming one of the favorite pastimes of the sons of Columbus.

UNITED STATES VS. CANADA, 1858

The premier event in early American cricket was the annual United States vs. Canada contest. This series began in 1840 and was the first international competition in the history of the sport. Since the American representatives were apparently all English-born, it must be conceded that these contests were not strictly between Americans and Canadians. From 1840 to 1846 members of the St. George club, Philadelphia's Union club, and the Toronto and Montreal clubs competed in several contests that generated considerable excitement (and gambling) on both sides of the border. Unfortunately, these events also produced a number of misunderstandings and disagreements. The two games played in 1845 might technically be called the first truly international contests, since both elevens included men from more than one city. In the following year, the match at New York ended abruptly in a controversy caused by a fight between opposing players. This ugly incident must have soured many on these international matches, for the series was interrupted for seven years.

U. S. - Canadian matches were resumed in 1853, the Americans winning five of seven contests through 1860 (there was no match in 1855). These events produced more publicity and drew larger crowds than any other cricket contest, with the exception of the all-England visit in 1859. Unlike the encounters of the 1840s, they were relatively free of ill will on the part of the contestants, although there was considerable disagreement on both sides over the selection of the respective elevens. In Canada, bad feeling between the Toronto and Montreal clubs led to the exclusion of all of the eastern (Lower Canada) cricketers in 1858 and 1859. In the United States, the feud between the New York and St. George clubs ended in a partial boycott by the Dragon Slayers in those same two years. St. George refused to participate "as a club" but did permit a few members to play as individuals. Also at issue was the composition of the United States eleven, especially the nationality of participants. Only a few American-born cricketers played for the United States in the 1859 contest. The annual convention's selection committee picked five Americans from the Philadelphia vicinity for the 1860 challenge, and their participation gave the United States victory a more native flavor. The following account of the 1858 match is reprinted from the New York Clipper, 7 and 14 August 1858, pp. 126, 133.

THE GRAND CRICKET MATCH AT HOBOKEN. UNITED STATES VS. CANADA

This great contest in this truly "noble" game, between the strongest elevens that either country could muster, has been looked foward to both by the fraternity and the public with more interest than like contests in former years, which may be accounted for, first by the greater publicity given through the medium of the press; in the second place, through the removal of those erroneous impressions formed of them, by a more liberal education of the younger branches of the community on reference to sports; and last, but not least, the general awakening of those who in a measure, mould and control the public mind, whether they be in the pulpit, on the forum, in the school-room, or the sanctum, to the necessity that exists for occasions and places where our young men shall be trained so that their physical may keep pace with their mental capabilities. To show to what extent public interest has grown in reference to sports, we point to the great base-ball match played a few weeks since, at which there was an attendance of 10,000 persons, also the last grand cricket match played here in 1856, between the States and Canada, where not less than 10 or 15,000 persons were present. Compare this with occasions of the kind some five or six years since, when 1000 would be considered a tremendous crowd — and what deduction may we draw? Nothing more or less than that we are less lucre-seeking, and that we are becoming more alive to our mental, physical, and moral wants. This is as it should be, and we glory in the fact that the *Clipper* has been in no small degree, instrumental in bringing about so desirable a state of things. For several weeks past it has been known that this match was to be commenced at Hoboken, on Monday, 2d inst., and in our last issue we gave the names of those who were likely to be sent forth as champions on both sides; since when, however, owing to sickness and business arrangements, some one or two alterations were made, as a reference to the score list will show, but not so as to materially effect their strength. By way of comparison, we here give the names of those who were selected to play in the four former matches:

U. S. ELEVENS

1853	1854	1856	1857
Sharp,	Walter,	S.Wright,	Lang,
Blackburne,	Sams,	Wilby,	Sharp,
Dockery,	Bingham,	Senior,	Wilby,
Barker,	S. Wright,	Barlow,	Barlow,
Walter,	Gibbes,	Gibbes,	Bigham,
Fletcher,	Fletcher,	Waller,	Comery,
Comery,	Barker,	Higham,	Crosley,
Wilson,	Cuyp,	Sharp,	S.Wright,
Barnett,	Comery,	Barker,	Bury,
Cuyp,	Tinson,	Cuyp,	Cuyp.

CANADIAN ELEVENS

1853	1854	1856	1857
Howard,	Philpotts,	Howard,	Howard,
Parsons,	Madison,	Parsons,	Starling,
Napler,	Howard,	Hardinge,	Rykert,
Denne,	Denne,	Gale,	Head,
Bradbury,	Bradbury,	Jones,	Parsons,
Pickering,	Pickering,	Pickering,	Dykes,
Galway,	Galway,	Lousada,	Bradbury,
Farmer,	Parsons,	Dexter,	Hore,
Keane,	Napler,	Boultbee,	Pickering,
Philpotts,	Dexter,	Alexander,	Dexter,
Stanley,	Philpotts,	Draper,	H. Phillips.

The match played in 1853, at the Red House, Harlem, was won by the United States by 44 runs; the one in 1854, in Canada, was won by the Canadians by 10 wickets; that in 1856, at Hoboken, was won by the United States by 9 wickets; and that of 1857, in Canada, was won by the Canadians by 7 wickets. Here we have the strength of the elevens in these four matches, and as it will be observed, each party won on their own dunghill, which has added to the interest of the present one, as it may be considered as the game which gives the winning party the preponderance.

The morning for the commencement of this decisive engagement opened gloomily, although, "Old Sol," in his good natured benevolence, made several unsuccessful attempts to show his face. During the major part of the forenoon the rain continued, and at times it seemed doubtful whether we should have the pleasure of witnessing the play at all on Monday, but a little after one o'clock p.m. it was thought good policy to replenish the inner man, so as to be prepared for any emergency, which turned out to be a good precaution, for at about two, P. M. the sky gradually brightened, the clouds rolled off in majestic grandeur to the westward; the spectators, to the number of about two thousand, emerged from the tents and other hiding places; the wickets were pitched; the champions of the occasion marched into the playing arena; the umpires took their position, and at 2:10 play was called. The Canadians, who had gained the choice of innings, were the first to undertake the defence of the wickets, H. Phillips and Rykert being the first representatives. The United States players took the open field, and were immediately, under Major General Higham, ranged in position....

At the conclusion of the battle, we had the pleasure of drinking the health and prosperity of the players and friends of both parties in a regular bumper, after which the success of the "Clipper," as America's sporting journal, was drank with a rousing three times three. The ceremony of giving up and receiving the trophy of victory came next in order, Mr. Howard making the presentation on the part of the Canadian eleven, accompanied by some of the most appropriate remarks, enjoining on all cricketers to promote friendly and amicable feelings between club and club as well as individuals; also, the necessity that existed for infusing young blood into selected elevens for great matches. He also thanked them for the generous treatment that they had received at the hands of every one, cricketer or no cricketer, assuring them that they would endeavor to pay them off in their own coin on the States' party's next visit to Canada. Mr. Castle replied in his usual jolly strain. The umpires and scorers were next thanked for their correct attention, to which Messrs. Madison and Boultbee responded, in the most humorous strains, when the inside of the tent was sought, and the health of the President of the United States and the Queen of England was drank with nine hearty cheers, and the company dispersed, leaving the great contest of August 2nd, 3d, and 4th, 1858, between the cricketers of the United States and Canada, as a most generous reminiscence of the past—one which will cause them to look foward to future meetings with the most lively anticipation. Annexed is the complete and correct score of the game, with analysis of bowling, &c.

CANADA

First Innings		Second Innings	
H. Phillips b Hallis	1	b Senior	17
Rykart b Hallis	4	run out	11
T. Phillips b March	6	b Hallis	6
Howard not out	31	b Hallis	6
Parsons c H.Wright b Hallis	1	b Hallis	1
Hardinge c Crossley b March	5	b Hallis	10
Head c Bingham b Crossley	10	set out	11
Peerless b Hallis	0	run out	0
Sneath[?] b Marsh	7	b Senior	6
Napier b Marsh	0	c Sharpe b Hallis	7
Fourdrinier b Marsh	0	b Marsh	0
Byes 3, leg byes 4, wides 9		Byes 19, leg byes 3,	
	16	wides 6	26
Total	81	Total	101

STATES

First Innings		Second Innings.	
Sharp c Peerless b Head	24	not out	10
Walter c Peerless b Hardinge	2	b Hardinge	4
Bingham c Peerless b Hardinge	34	1 b w b Hardinge	5
Senior c T. Phillips b Hardinge	9	b Head	2
Wilby b Hardinge	0	b Head	2
Marsh b Head	0	c Parsons b Head	4
H.Wright b Hardinge	0	b Hardinge	0
Bingham c T.Phillips b Hardinge	5		
Jefferson c H.Phillips b Parsons	14		
Crossley not out	16	not out	1
Hallis c Peerless b Hardinge	9		
Byes 14, leg byes 6, wides 14	34	Byes 2, leg bye 1, wides 5	8
Total	147	Total	36

ANALYSIS OF BOWLING
States—First Innings

Names	Balls	Runs	Maidens	Wickets	Wides.
Hallis	101	14	21	4	6
Marsh	115	28	15	5	1
Crossley	36	15	5	1	2

Second Innings

Marsh	87	22	8	1	3
Hallis	128	29	15	5	2
Senior	56	17	4	2	0
Crossley	3	5	0	0	1

Canada—First Innings

Head	80	16	9	2	3
Hardinge	165	52	12	7	6
Parsons	68	32	5	1	0
Napier	12	9	1	0	0
Peerless	3	4	0	0	0

Second Innings

Hardinge	57	17	5	3	2
Head	54	11	7	3	3

THE VISIT OF THE ALL-ENGLAND ELEVEN, 1859

By far the most celebrated episode in antebellum North American cricket was the visit of the All-England Eleven in 1859. During the summer anticipation reached fever pitch in Montreal, New York, and Philadelphia. The British team agreed to play five matches against Canadian and American sides of twenty-two players each, with two contests scheduled in Canada and three in the United States. The celebrated English athletes arrived in Canada in September, led by their captain, George Parr, known as the best batsman in Great Britain. They opened their tour with an easy victory over players from Lower Canada, then journeyed to New York for a match against twenty-two players chosen by the St. George club. Ideal weather and intense interest attracted thousands of spectators to Hoboken's Elysian Fields for the three-day match in early October. While everyone enjoyed a fine spectacle, the United States suffered a crushing defeat, as the Englishmen triumphed by sixty-four runs without even batting in their second innings.

The next stop for the Englishmen was the City of Brotherly Love, where the Philadelphia club selected nine New Yorkers and thirteen local players to compete against them. William R. Wister's side, with ten Americans, made the best showing of any of the opponents of the All-England Eleven, losing by only seven wickets. Although poor weather on the first day held down the crowds, a large turnout for the concluding days made the match a financial success. Despite the loss, it was something of a sporting triumph for the United States' native contingent, who outscored their English teammates. After a week's play, the British continued their circuit of North America with a victory at Hamilton against a western Canadian side. In early November they concluded their sweep with still another lopsided win over a combined United States - Canadian team at Rochester (N. Y.), playing in the cold and snow. The following reflections on the first three of these matches are reprinted from the New York Clipper, 8, 15, and 22 October 1859, pp. 195, 202, 203, 212.

THE GREAT CRICKET MATCH
THE ELEVEN VS. TWENTY-TWO OF CANADA EAST

The cricketing community are fully aware by this time of the fact of the arrangement of the four great cricket matches between an eleven selected from the two best elevens of England, and twenty-twos selected at Montreal, New York, Philadelphia, and Hamilton, Canada West, each place presenting its best players to contest with the eleven. The first match of the series was played at Montreal—the result of which we give below—the second is now pending at Hoboken, the third will commence at Philadelphia on the 10th inst., and the fourth at Hamilton, Canada West, on the 17th. The most important contest is that between the eleven and twenty-two at Hoboken, the strongest players in the country being amongst those selected to represent the States in that match. The result of the four matches will lead to the selection of an eleven of the United States and the Canadas that will give an interest to the future contests between the two localities such as they have not yet possessed; and we have no doubt ultimately that this country will present an eleven for an annual contest between England and America, that will possess attractions far greater than the ones we record. The fact is we, as Americans, do not relish the idea of playing twenty-two of this country against eleven of another. Among cricketers who are cognizant of the weakness of the majority of our cricket players in comparison with the best among those of England, it is well understood to be a tolerably fair contest, all things considered; but among those of the admirers of all out door sports in this country, and those who take an interest in a fair contest, whether in the ring, on the water, in the field or on the course, it seems a very uneven affair, and hence their interest in the match is not as great as it would be were it a contest between two elevens.

The players selected on the part of England in the matches in progress are the best that ever played together in any match previous to these. They have the finest wicket keeper the cricketing world ever saw. They have the fastest bowlers, as well as the very best bowlers in other respects that have ever taken a wicket: and in batting their strength is above everything else, George Parr alone being equal to any half dozen ordinary players in that respect; and in addition they possess the advantages derived from constant practice against the very best players in the community they represent; whereas on the part of America, only a few are professional players, and those not first class, and the gentlemen that have been selected have had comparatively little opportunity of availing themselves of the practice so requisite to keep them in good play. Under these circumstances therefore, it is not surprising that we endeavor to supply our deficiency in the quality of our representatives by excess of numbers. The result of the recent contest at Montreal affords sufficient proof of the correctness of our remarks, for if the eleven, a day or two after a stormy passage across the Atlantic of two weeks duration, with its enerving effects, can go into the field and with apparent ease defeat twenty-two of the best players in a community where cricket flourishes, what may be expected at their hands when they are in perfect health, and by again having their regular practice are enabled to put forth their utmost efforts for success? But without further preface, we will proceed with our account of the first match of the series, which took place at Montreal on the 24th, 26th, and 27th of September, the result being in favor of the eleven with eight wickets to fall.

Saturday, September 24th, 1859, will be a day long to be remembered by the cricketers of Canada East as being the occasion of the first appearance on a cricket field on this contest, of the greatest cricket players England has ever had. The unpropitious state of the weather the previous week, and the consequent uncertainty that existed in relation to the time for commencing the match, led to a somewhat slim attendance of spectators at an early period of the day, but before the close of the innings, a very numerous and highly respectable assemblage were present; and on the following day, every available place on the ground was occupied by a large crowd of visitors, the spectators being encircled by a great number of carriages belonging to the elite of Montreal. Every preparation for the convenience of visitors had been made by the parties to whom the Montreal Club had let the ground, the only failure we noticed, but a rather prominent one, by the by, being the total absence of anything in the way of accommodations for the reporters of the Press, a large number of whom were present from this and other cities of the States and Canadas. For the discourtesy in this respect the members of the press are indebted to Mr. Pickering, who took this means of revenging himself on the New York journals for an alleged slight in not awarding them the lion's share of the credit attached to the matter of bringing out the eleven from England. The ground on Saturday was in anything but fine condition for play, but this was unavoidable, as it was owing to the rain, for everything had been arranged for the pitching of good wickets, and had the weather been at all fine, and the ground dry, the wickets would have been all that could have been desired. At eleven o'clock the players were all assembled on the ground, and after the usual preliminary practice, during which the Umpires—Messrs. Carpenter and Major Campbell—were pitching the wickets, the bell rang to clear the ground, and at 12:20 the "great eleven" took their respective positions on the field. The toss having been won by the English side, and the Canadians having been sent in to the bat, their first representatives, Messrs. Surman and Swain, took their places at the wickets, Jackson and Caffyn bowling, Lockyer being at wicket, Diver at long stop, Parr at point, Lillywhite and Hayward alternately long leg and mid-off, and the others in the slips and covers....

ST. GEORGE VS. ENGLAND

The second match of the series of international contests at cricket was commenced at Hoboken, on Monday, October 3d, and terminated on Wednesday, 5th, in favor of the English Eleven, the result being a signal defeat of the twenty-two English representatives of the States, in one inning! with 64 runs to spare! We should like to account on some satisfactory manner for this very surprising result, but we cannot do so, otherwise than by attributing it to the mediocre play of the leading cricketers of this city, who have so long held sway over the cricketing fraternity, chiefly owing to the supposition of their being first class players, and so they are, as far as the States are concerned, but no further. It is true that they had opposed to them the finest players in the world, but it is also true that there were two players to one to effect this superiority. It is useless trying to explain the matter, when the plain fact reveals itself in the shape of such an overwhelming defeat as they have sustained. In common parlance, the leading players of the New York and St. George clubs have had the starch taken out of them completely, and the best thing they can now do to redeem their lost credit is to go to work in earnest, forget all past differences, build up their clubs on a permanent footing, eschew all old fogyism and its supporters, *encourage Young America*, for to that source will they have to look for a successful future, and liberally and freely open a way for the progress of the noble game in the esteem of the many admirers of out door sports that we are proud to see our city can present when occasion requires. Of the remarkable ability displayed by the eleven in batting, bowling, and fielding, we could fill more space than we can possibly spare in warm praise of it. But we cannot refrain from again selecting Lockyer, Caffyn, and Hayward, for special mention of the great pleasure they have afforded us by their admirable display of every qualification that constitutes a thorough cricketer; their bonhomie at all times being not the least commendable characteristic they possess. Another pleasant feature of their presence here, that in a measure affects annoyance of the defeat we have sustained at their hands, is the courteous and gentlemanly demeanor that has marked their conduct throughout. It has met its just reward in the very gratifying manner in which they gratefully acknowledge they have been received in this city. They have made many warm friends, besides cementing still stronger the ties of friendship that already existed among their many admiring countrymen in this city.

We cannot begin our account of the play of the match without calling special attention to the admirable conduct of the orderly and highly respectable assemblage that were collected together to witness the contest on each of the three days. It was creditable in the highest degree to the good name of our citizens, and we attribute it chiefly to the influence our ball clubs exert in controlling the behavior of the crowds who collect together on the numerous ball grounds of New York and vicinity. The members of this fraternity pride themselves and justly too, on their conduct in this respect, and fully one-third of those present at Hoboken, last week, were members of the many ball clubs that exist in this section of the country. But without further digression, we proceed with the particulars of the game, which was commenced on Monday morning, resumed on Tuesday, and terminated at noon on Wednesday, the stumps being drawn each day at 5 p.m. The weather on Monday, Tuesday, and Wednesday was lovely in the extreme and in consequence the attendance was exceedingly numerous, especially on the two first days, when at least 10,000 people must have visited the grounds each day. The St. George's club, through the sale of tickets at the gate, at 50 cents and one dollar each, and tickets to subscribers at five dollars each, together with the private subscriptions from the merchants and hotel proprietors, and also the proceeds of the sale of the privileges of supplying refreshments, must have realized a very handsome sum, and we presume that the net profits of this speculation will be devoted to the interests of cricket in the form of preparing and sustaining the ground used on this occasion. They have had their full share, and more, of the credit attached to bringing out the eleven; for, after all, Mr. Pickering was the prominent personage through whose services they were brought out here, and we do him the justice to say so, even if he has behaved rude and uncourteous to the press, for the St. George's club did pretty much the same....

THE ELEVEN VS. TWENTY-TWO OF PHILADELPHIA

The third match of the series of international contests, inaugurated at Montreal, took place at Philadelphia last week, commencing on Monday afternoon, the 10th inst., being resumed on Wednesday, and closing on Thursday, the 13th inst., the result being another victory for the English eleven, their score exceeding that of their opponents, with seven wickets to fall. A defeat, of course, was anticipated, but we notice with pleasure that the eleven acknowledge having encountered at the hands of the twenty-two of Philadelphia a more determined and effective opposition than they have yet met with. Another gratifying fact is the very excellent display of cricketing in batting and fielding made by the American portion of the twenty-two. From what we have seen of the play, we think that we could select twenty Americans who, with the assistance of two bowlers , could undoubtedly make a better score against the eleven than any yet made. As far as fielding is concerned they are decidedly in advance of all others on this side of the water, and in many instances there are examples of first class play at the bat. One fact, however, connected with the last contest stands out in bold relief, and that is, that Philadelphia takes the lead in the United States as the fountainhead of cricket. It is a permanent institution there, having taken firm hold at the root, as it were, of popularity, as Base Ball has in New York. Everybody in Philadelphia, who plays ball at all, knows cricket thoroughly, there being over a hundred clubs in and around the city, whereas here we cannot count over a dozen clubs altogether, and half of those are anything but in a flourishing condition, and the large majority of our ball players know as much about cricket as they do about the hieroglyphics of Egypt, and what is worse, care less if anything.

Before we refer to the score we avail ourselves of the only opportunity we have had during these contests of returning our sincere thanks to the committee who had charge of the arrangements in Philadelphia, for their gentlemanly and courteous conduct to the members of the press throughout the match. Their attentions were in such striking contrast to the neglect and indifference that characterised the proceedings of the St. George club in this city, and still more so to the positive discourtesy received at the hands of Pickering and his confreres at Montreal, that we feel specially called upon to notice it in most praiseworthy worthy terms. We also noticed with pleasure that all the ladies who visited the grounds at Philadelphia were amply provided with comfortable seats, and were not permitted—as they were at New York—to either stand or take their seats on the ground, the only exceptions in the latter case being those who held the $5 subscribers tickets. We refer to this particularly, as it is a blot on the escutcheon of St. George that we trust to see effaced on the occasion of the next contest. The following is the score in full:

UNITED STATES

First Innings		Second Innings.	
Lang b Parr	2	c Lockyer b Grundy	8
Sharatt b Jackson	0	b Grundy	1
W R Wister b Wisden	9	b Grundy	3
Barclay b Jackson	0	b Wisdenh	3
Newhall b Parr	3	c and b Wisden	0
Hammond c Grundy b Parr	0	b Wisden	0
Gibbs c Caffyn	20	b Grundy	6
H Wright b Parr	1	c Stephenson b Jackson	7
Hall ht wkt b Caffyn	3	run out	0
Wilby b Caffyn	0	b Jackson	0
Collis b Jackson	0	st Lockyer b Wiseden	0
Senior b Jackson	3	b Wisden	6
Vernou c Cesar b Jackson	5	run out	2
Kephardt b Jackson	0	run out	10
S Wright st Lockyer b Carpenter	3	c and b Wisden	2
Morgan c Lockyer b Carpenter	9	b Jackson	3
Hunt c Caffyn b Jackson	1	l b w b Jackson	0
Bayard c Caffyn b Carpenter	1	c Carpenter b Jackson	0
J Wister run out	19	b Jackson	5
H Fisher b Jackson	4	b Jackson	2
Hallis not out	7	c Jackson b Wisden	0
Waterman c Carpenter b Caffyn	0	not out	0
Byes	4	Leg Byes	2
Total	94	Total	60

ENGLAND

First Innings		Second Innings.	
Heyward c Wilby b H Wright	34	c Lang b Kepkardt	0
Carpenter c Gibbs b Senior	22	c Hammond b Senior	7

THE ELEVEN VS. TWENTY-TWO OF PHILADELPHIA

Diver b H Wright	2		
Caffyn b Senior	4	not out	6
Lockyer not out	31	st Barclay b Lang	9
Grundy c Newhall			
b Senior	5	not out	2
Stephenson b Senior	1		
Lillywhite b Senior	0		
Wisden b Gibbs	3		
Jackson c W Wister			
b Senior	6		
Parr disabled	0		
Byes 4, Leg Byes 3,			
Wides 11	18	Wides 4, no ball 1	5
Total	126	Total	29

ANALYSIS OF BOWLING
England—First Innings

	Balls	Runs	Maidens	Wickets	Wides
Parr	144	18	23	4	0
Jackson	236	37	41	8	0
Wisden	32	2	6	1	0
Caffyn	82	24	11	4	0
Carpenter	44	9	6	3	0

Second Innings

Wisden	157	39	20	8	0
Grundy	92	12	16	4	0
Jackson	64	7	10	6	0

United States—First Innings

Hallis	120	25	16	0	3
Gibbs	100	32	10	1	2
Waterman	68	17	10	0	0
Senior	105	20	12	5	5
H Wright	56	14	7	2	1

Second Innings

Kephardth	16	5	1	1	1
Wilby	24	7	1	0	3
Senior	23	7	2	1	0
Lang	12	5	1	1	0

Umpires—For Philadelphia, Mr. Sharp, of New York Club; for the Eleven, Caesar.

Scorers—For Philadelphia, G. Newall, of Young America Club; for the Eleven, Mr. Baker, of Ottowa, C.E.

The Following are the respective scores of the English and American players of the twenty-two of Philadelphia.

AMERICANS				ENGLISH			
Names	*1st. In.*	*2d In.*	*Total*	*Names*	*1st. In.*	*2d In.*	*Total*
J Wister	19	5	24	Gibbs	20	6	26
W Wister	9	3	12	Lang	2	8	10
Morgan	9	3	12	Senior	3	6	9
Kephardth	0	10	10	Hallis	7	0	7
H Wright	1	7	8	S Wright	3	2	5
Vernou	5	2	7	S Sharratt	1	0	1
H Fisher	4	2	6	Hammond	0	0	0
Newhall	3	0	3	Wilby	0	0	0
Hall	3	0	3	Collis	0	0	0
Barclay	0	3	3	Total			58
Bayard	1	0	1				
Hunt	1	0	1				
Waterman	0	0	0				
Total			90				

Chapter 7

EQUESTRIANISM

Various forms of equestrian sports were extremely popular throughout North America during the middle period of the nineteenth century. Because the horse was of central practical importance in everyday life in both Canada and the United States, it is not surprising that it also figured prominently in the amusements of the people. Both countries were still overwhelmingly agrarian societies prior to 1860, and their populations depended upon horses for farm work and transportation. The upper classes sponsored thoroughbred races, while the middle ranks increasingly supported trotting and pacing. The patrons of the sports of the turf justified their pastime on utilitarian grounds, arguing that competition on the track encouraged improvements in the breeding of horses for endurance and speed. But many clergymen, newspaper editors, and other guardians of public morals condemned horse racing because of its close ties with gambling, corruption, drinking, and crowd disorders. Despite this opposition, the sport attracted a sizeable following among sportsmen. Equestrianism was also one of the very few athletic recreations that featured female participants; a number of women competed in riding exhibitions during the 1850s.

In Canada horse racing borrowed heavily from the English upper class traditions, and it was a favorite amusement at British military garrisons at Halifax, Quebec City, Montreal, Toronto, and other cities. During this era there were no regularly scheduled racing calendars in the British North American provinces. Jockey clubs such as the Toronto Turf Club, the Western Racing Association in Windsor, and the Montreal Trotting Club generally lasted only a few years. Yet certain social trends and early patterns of commercialism appeared before 1860. First, while horse racing was an important part of the leisure activities of the elite, the events also drew spectators from the middle and working classes who bet considerable sums at the tracks. Secondly, merchants, hotel and tavern keepers, jockey clubs, proprietors of courses, and railroads joined together to raise money for purses. These business, sporting, and transportation interests invested in the commercial possibilities of thoroughbred meets. Finally, trotting and pacing were related closely to the breeding industry, and they became increasingly prevalent in both French Quebec and British Ontario. Many small towns organized annual agricultural fairs, which featured races that tested the speed and stamina of local horses. As was the case with thoroughbred races, sportsmen competed for purses and wagered on the results.

In the United States thoroughbred horse racing was a favorite pastime of the upper classes in both the North and the South. Although it was an elite sport, its promoters appealed for broad public support in a number of ways. First, horse breeders and track managers lobbied to overcome the religious and ideological objections to their racing. Secondly, these horsemen had to solve numerous practical and financial problems in order to make their events both entertaining and profitable. Meet organizers such as the New York Jockey Club had to offer substantial prize money to attract quality horses for exciting contests, and they had to construct ample and comfortable facilities for owners, trainers, attendants, horses, and spectators. In addition, they usually had to arrange transportation for their prospective audiences.

As these sporting entrepreneurs struggled to popularize racing during the 1840s and 1850s, they began to modernize it. Owners and breeders increasingly relied upon stud books for authentic information about the performances and pedigrees of their horses. Jockey clubs began to publish their track's rules in national sporting journals such as the Baltimore-based American Turf Register and Sporting Magazine and New York's Spirit of the Times. These and other sporting periodicals helped to coordinate the racing calendar and to standardize practices on fixing the ages of horses and the weights they carried in handicap events. They also provided invaluable news and publicity about regular meets and special events across the nation.

While the regular racing sessions at northern tracks were never consistently profitable during these years, the great intersectional matches generated an enormous amount of excitement and drew tens of thousands of spectators. As the traditional tensions between the North and South intensified during the debates over slavery, the encounter between champion horses from each region took on heightened symbolic meaning. The series that began in 1823 with the triumph of the North's American Eclipse over the South's Sir Henry climaxed in the 1840s. One of the documents below narrates the victory of North's Fashion over the South's Boston at the Union Course on Long Island, New York in 1842. It is followed by one that tells the story of the South's revenge as Peytona defeated Fashion over the same course in 1845.

Despite the widespread interest in these major events, thoroughbred horse racing experienced a significant decline in the United States between 1845 and 1860. A number of factors contributed to the depressed state of the sport, including continued religious and ideological opposition, lack of adequate patronage by affluent members of jockey clubs, poor management by track owners, the high costs of maintaining the horses, low attendance at regular meetings, and the deterioration of the northern breeding industry. The problems were particularly evident in the New York City region, where several attempts to revive racing failed before the Civil War.

Although thoroughbred racing struggled through hard times between 1845 and 1860, these years did witness an international challenge sponsored by a sportsman from the United States. Richard Ten Broeck owned and raced a number of fast horses at tracks throughout the South and the Middle Atlantic states. A heavy gambler, during the 1840s he brought several of his thoroughbreds to Canada and Cuba in search of stakes money and big payoffs on his bets. In 1856 he took on the ultimate challenge when he crossed the Atlantic to compete in England. Although initially his horses fared poorly, in 1857 Ten Broeck won his first major stakes race. "Glorious Victory of Prioress" recounts the victory of the American mare in the Ceasarewitch Stakes at Newmarket.

Whereas the upper classes patronized thoroughbred racing in the United States before 1860, the city-dwellers and rural folk preferred harness racing. Trotting originated at country fairs and on early city streets, but its main development occurred in urban areas where road improvements permitted tests of speed among horses in harness. New

York City became an important early center of this sport, as drivers challenged their rivals to races along Third Avenue. The urban middle classes and farmers favored trotters and pacers over the thoroughbreds for both social and utilitarian reasons. Only a wealthy aristocrat could afford to own a thoroughbred, but any butcher, baker, shopkeeper, or farmer who kept a horse for personal or business reasons could race against his friends on local streets. Furthermore, while there was no longer any real usefulness for thoroughbreds in American society, the breeding of faster and stronger trotters and pacers still had a practical function. This was especially true as stagecoaches and wagons increasingly replaced the saddle horse for transportation in the northeastern and midwestern states.

Harness racing became the first organized modern sport in the United States during this era in part because it was a more democratic amusement than thoroughbred racing. The urban masses enjoyed watching races that featured horses that were part of their everyday experience. In addition, the trotters and pacers were cheaper and more durable than their more refined and aristocratic counterparts. "The Rules and Regulations Adopted for the Union Course, Long Island" presents the code that governed trotting at one of the leading centers of the sport in the country.

During the 1850s harness racing strengthened its position as the most popular spectator sport in North America. In the United States the greatest concentration of acvtivity was in the New York City metropolitan area, which had at least seven tracks. But trotting also thrived nationwide at county fairs and at newly constructed facilities, which numbered about seventy by 1858. During this era Flora Temple succeeded Lady Suffolk as the dominant horse in harness. But the success of trotting also brought increasing suspicion about the integrity of the track managers and owners. Sporting journalists commented on irregularities in certain contests, and they charged that horsemen were rigging contests, to assure profits for all. Critics attacked the practice of "hippodroming"—the making of races for the sole purpose of splitting gate receipts. They argued that patrons who wagered at the tracks were cheated by this practice; they vehemently demanded honest races for stakes and purses only. The final document in this chapter includes reports on the series of races in 1859 between Flora Temple and her California rival, Princess, along with editorials that question the legitimacy of these matches.

Equestrian sports remained popular in the American South during the 1840s and 1850s, although the decline that marked northern racing also was evident below the Mason-Dixon line. New Orleans remained the center of the pastime for southern turfmen, as is clear from the "Rules and Regulations of the Metairie Jockey Club." During the 1850s the South also witnessed a revival of interest in medieval pastimes and chivalry. Jousting tournaments enjoyed a mild vogue, as southern gentry and their belles imitated the lords and ladies of Europe in earlier times. The first document in this chapter presents a few examples of these curious vestiges from a long lost era of ritual combat on horseback.

Women also participated in equestrian sports in the United States during this era. Before the Civil War public opinion generally frowned upon athletic competition for females, although a few health and educational reformers and journalists did advocate more exercise and wholesome recreation for the fair sex. They especially recommended calisthenics, ice skating, and horseback riding for their value as physical training and because these activities featured aesthetically pleasing displays of feminine grace and style. During the 1850s there were several equestrian exhibitions that were restricted to girls and ladies. Usually they were held at agricultural fairs. Accounts of a sample of these contests from the states of Ohio, New York, and California appear below.

JOUSTING TOURNAMENTS IN THE SOUTH

During the antebellum period in the American South a few members of the planter aristocracy indulged in a curious pastime that conjured up memories of medieval times. Tournament jousting appealed to those who thought of the South as a land of plantations, masters, and slaves that resembled the manors, lords, and serfs of earlier times. Romantic chivalry was in vogue; the novels of Walter Scott stirred fantasies of knights in armor fighting heroic battles for their ladies in waiting. Beginning in 1840 young southern gentlemen clad as knights on horseback tilted at suspended small rings as southern belles waved their handkerchiefs. The targets were sometimes only one half inch in diameter. They were placed in a straight or curved line about 25 or 30 yards apart. Generally a course of 125 yards had to be completed in ten seconds. As the following document suggests, the victorious knight won the honor of selecting the Queen of the tournament. The first example below, from the Spirit of the Times, 4 November 1854, p. 449, was reprinted in that journal from the Louisville Courier, 17 October 1854. The second, from the Spirit of the Times, 27 August 1859, p. 344, first appeared in the Alexandria, Virginia Gazette, 13 August 1859.

GRAND TOURNAMENT AT LOUISVILLE KY.

Yesterday was a triumphal occasion. It witnessed the inauguration in our midst of a species of amusement long popular among the brave men and women of the middle ages. The sports of yesterday were of thrilling interest, and have revived a taste for the sports of the olden time that must continue to strengthen as our people becomes more cognizant of the delights of these ennobling and healthful recreations.

The spacious amphitheatre of the Agricultural Association was densely filled at an early hour, and the vast crowd continued to receive accessions until after the noon hour. Never within the history of Kentucky has there been gathered together so great a body of spectators, nor so formidable an array of beauty. Our own city was brilliantly represented, and so likewise the county and those adjoining. There were many also from every section of the State and from our sister States. The novelty of a tournament west of the Alleghanies, on land where not more than a half century ago Indian fights formed the chief species of amusement drew together a vast concourse.

The sports of the day were introduced by the trumpeter, who proclaimed from afar the opening ceremonies, the clear notes of this Instrument ringing through the air with beautiful effect. Then, preceded by the Herald, the procession of Knights entered the arena. Each was clad in costly costume, thus designating the characters intended to be represented. Owing to the limited time in which the arrangements were made, the number engaged in the tournament was not so great as expected. Only ten Knights entered on the first list. In the afternoon trial there were three others. The following list comprises the Knights engaged in the first and second tilts:—

Knight of Virginia, represented by Mr. Edward Crockwell.
Knight of Jefferson, represented by K. Carter.
Knight of Berkely, represented by Mr. Tabb.
Knight of the Plain, represented by Mr. Phillips.
Knight of the Leopard Couchant, represented by Mr. Hardin.
Rhoderic Dhu, represented by Mr. Berry, of Oldham county.
Knight of Beargrass, represented by Mr. John Jones.
Young America, represented by Thomas Y. Brent, Jr.
Knight of Kentucky, represented by ——
Knight of Bourbon, represented by John Brent.

These gallant gentlemen were all handsomely attired, and presented a brilliant spectacle. Having been ranged about the central stand, the President, John B. Tapscott, Esq., delivered the following charge to the Knights.

"*Gallant Sir Knights*—I welcome you here, and tender you in behalf of 'the Beautiful' around us, the warmest and sincerest gratulations.

You appear upon this interesting occasion as the representatives of an age which will ever present the deepest interest to every lover of romance. The Genius of Chivalry has twined the tightest wreaths that grace the poet's lyre, and the muse of history has recorded on her immortal pages the gallant deeds of the Knights of old. They, like you, were worshippers at the altar of beauty. They ever bowed in obedience to her will. The wild enthusiasm and noble daring which characterized their actions in tournament, should animate you upon this occasion. Thousands of joy-lit eyes are beaming upon you, like rays of heavenly light, and morn ne'er painted the orient sky with lovelier blushers than those which mantle the cheeks of "the fair" around you.

In the midst of this magnificent and imposing pageant the Queen of Love and Beauty will be crowned in the name of the victor. This should inspire each of you with the determination to win the honor of choosing the peerless one. The successful champion will be rewarded with her sweetest smiles, and the richest treasure of her heart.

I charge you now, nerve yourselves for action. The path to victory runs not through sunny plains or verdant lawns. No flowery meads, from which the zephyrs waft delicious fragrance, are seen along its course, no beams of radiant light e'er burst from the clouded sky above it; but be not discouraged. Hope will cheer you onward, and a thousand love-wreaths will fall upon the gallant Knight who shall win the prize of glory.

Then on to the contest, and remember that

Faint heart never won fair ladye."

Immediately afterwards the contest commenced. Each Knight made the circuit of the arena at full speed, with lance aimed at the suspended rings. There were three trials, and he who succeeded in taking the largest number of rings was declared victor, having liberty to make choice of the Queen of Love and Beauty. Subjoined is the result of the three tilts, the number of rings taken each time being given: —

	First	Second	Third	Total
Knight of Virginia	5	5	3	13
Knight of Jefferson	4	1	3	8
Knight of Berkely	3	3	2	8
Knight of the Plain	4	4	3	11
Knight of the Leopard	0	0	3	3
Rhoderic Dhu	3	4	4	11
Knight of Beargrass	5	3	2	10
Black Knight	2	3	3	8
Young America	1	1	0	2
Disinherited Knight	1	0	0	1

There being a tie between the Knight of the Plain and Rhoderic Dhu, they engaged in another contest, in which the latter was successful. The Queen of Love and Beauty was then chosen by the Knight of Virginia, who was victor in the lists, and a Maid of Honor by Rhoderic Dhu. These two ladies (Miss Julia Chamberlain as Queen and Miss Molly Brent as Maid,) were introduced into the arena and crowned. Thos. S. Phillips, of this city, then delivered the coronation speech as follows:—

"*Lady*—The pleasing duty devolves upon me to place upon your brow this graceful emblem of love's devotion to beauty. Each bursting bud and blown flower speaks, in silent eloquence, the glowing language of the heart. Beauty has ever reigned supreme. The tones of her lyre echo in every heart, and words of enchanting sweetness ever fall from her lips. The days of chivalry are fraught with evidence of her power, and we have now before us a most brilliant illustration of the homage which is due to her supremacy."

The most touching passages in our histories carry us back to the times and manners of chivalry. Everything connected with that age awakens our sensibility. All the graceful and noble virtues of chivalry are reflected in the Tournament, and the warriors who had displayed them in the list could not but feel their mild and beneficent influence. Even in the battle-field skill and address insensibly softened the ferocity of the mere soldier, and he soon came to consider war itself a great Tournament. Thus the tournying lists were schools of chivalric virtue as well as chivalric prowess while the splendor and joyousness of the show brought society into kind and merry intercourse. In Western Europe the Tournament survived chivalry, whose image it had reflected and brightened, and the world long clung with fondness to those splendid and graceful shows which had thrown light and elegance over the warriors and dames of yore. To-day it has been revived in all its pristine brilliancy, and made brighter by the intelligence and beauty which surrounds you. Love and beauty have ever been the reward of chivalric deeds. The gallant Knight who has so proudly won the honors to-day has selected you as most worthy to wear this beauteous wreath; and now, in the name and by the authority of the Knight of Virginia, I crown you Queen of Love and Beauty."

After a recess for dinner there was a second series of tilts, in which the Knight of Beargrass was declared victor, the palm being strongly contested by the Black Knight. A second maid of honor was then chosen in the person of Miss Emeline Fontaine.

During the progress of the contest the most intense feeling of sympathy for the various knights pervaded the large assemblage. We have never seen such manifestations of enthusiasm by any gathering as on yesterday. All seemed absorbed in the spectacle before them, to the utter exclusion of other thoughts. We but utter the common public sentiment when we express a desire for perseverance on the part of the young gentlemen engaged in this gallant undertaking. A year hence we may expect a contest excelling anything of a similar nature ever seen in the Old Dominion. The daughter State surely has more of genuine chivalry than her mother.

TOURNAMENT IN PRINCE WILLIAM

A large party of ladies and gentlemen participated in the picnic and witnessed the tournament which came off at Bentsville on Thursday. It is needless to say that the affair was pleasant throughout,—the dancing was good, the music excellent, and the riding "at the ring," in many instances, very fine. A place had been prepared in the green for dancing, and before twelve o'clock a number availed themselves of the opportunity to "trip it on the light fantastic toe." That was continued until the provisions provided for the occasion. After which the dancing was recommenced, and continued until the "Sir Knights" were called upon to display their horsemanship in contending for the honor of crowning the queen of love and beauty.

Very soon the gallant knights were mounted and on their way to the scene, if not of knightly valor, at least of generous knightly rivalry. Here all had been prepared for the tournament. The judges, who had been previously selected, took their positions opposite the ring. The knights were then marched in a body, under the direction and command of the herald, Mr. J. T. Leachman, and the marshal, Dr. L. A. Jennings, to a position in front of the judges when they were briefly and appropriately addressed by Mr. Aralland Marsteller. Then, after returning to their proper place, the riding commenced—each knight riding when his knightly name was called—in the following order:

Knight of Alexandria, J. E. Williams; Knight of Montmoreacy, Richard I. Reid; Ivanhoe, J. Taylor Williams; Knight of Lochinvar, Lucien A. Davis; Knight of Brentsville, James B. Pridmore; Knight of Marmion, John W. Fewell; Knight of the Chase, James R. Purrell; Knight of the Wild Horse, Richard T. Meredith; Knight of Greenville, E. Meredith; the Black Knight, P. D. Williams; Knight of the Woods, J. R. Rudd; the Unknown Knight, Edgar Weir.

Some of the riding was excellent, and elicited the applause of the "faire ladyes" who witnessed it. The result of it was the success of the Knight of the Chase, who won the honor of crowning the Queen. Ivanhoe had the honor of designating the First Maid of Honor, Marmion the Second, and the Knight of Brentsville the Third.

The coronation ceremony, which took place at night, was very interesting. Although, as may be supposed, the selection of the Queen was difficult from the number present who would have graced the dignity, the successful knight manifested an appreciative taste when he crowned Miss M. C——, of Prince William, as the Queen of Love and Beauty. The First Maid of Honor was the accomplished Miss T——, of Caroline; the second, the young and amiable Miss W——, and the third, the beautiful Miss —— of Georgetown. The merry throng afterwards joined in the dance, which was continued to a late hour.

FEMALE EQUESTRIANISM

Horseback riding was one of the few athletic sports open to women in the United States prior to the Civil War. Girls and young ladies from all regions enjoyed this pastime, and a few of them competed for prizes in exhibitions. As the following examples suggest, the judges evaluated the equestriennes on the basis of their skill in handling their horses and their displays of form. While women were not supposed to race their animals, it is evident that some of them were also adept at that sport. The first selection below narrates the action at a fairgrounds at Circleville, Ohio in 1854. It is taken from the New York Clipper, 18 November 1854, p. 3, where it was reprinted from the Columbus State Journal, 11 November 1854. The second example is an account of an event held in September 1857 in Stockton, California. A local society offered "the most accomplished equestrian lady" a saddle valued at $75; second and third prizes were a silver plate ($30) and a riding whip ($10). A large crowd of spectators arrived well before the starting time. That story originally appeared in the Stockton, California Republican and was reprinted in the New York Clipper, 14 November 1857, p. 236. The final selection describes a New York City contest on Long Island's Union Course which was disrupted by some rowdy spectators. It is reprinted from the Clipper, 4, 18 September 1858 pp. 159, 170.

EXHIBITION AT OHIO, 1854,
THE OHIO FAT WOMAN (WEIGHT 400 POUNDS) A CONTESTANT

The grand finale of all the Ohio exhibitions for this season came off at Circleville, on Wednesday and Thursday of this week. The exercises were held in the splendid natural amphitheatre of the Pickaway fair grounds, which, for such a display, has no equal in the State, either for the evenness of the track or the convenience of the back grounds, which will allow a perfect view of all that is going on in the arena, to 50,000 spectators.

At ten o'clock on Wednesday, the match confined to ladies of Circleville was called, but for some reason not fully explained, the contestants did not appear. At twelve o'clock same day there was a spirited drive of trotting horses, with five contestants, for a silver pitcher, valued at $20, which was awarded to Miss Elizabeth Baker, of Pickaway. At 2 o'clock P.M. the Pickaway ladies rode for prizes confined to that county; there were seven competitors, and they all rode fully up to the limit of the rules, which forbid racing, and took a few smart jumps over—just because they couldn't help it.

The awards in this class were to Miss Nancy Campbell, gold watch, $50; Miss Hattis Gilbert, bracelets, $30; Miss Polly Engle, locket, $20.

The official exercises for the day being over, just at sunset the ladies from Franklin County, with several others, went in to try their horses, and as there were no rules to be observed, they had a very refreshing time. The horses were willing and the ladies were willing, and the consequence was that some lively steps were taken. Mrs. Julia E. Harris, of Columbus, being upon a fine racer, distanced everything upon the ground, without disturbing her own or the horse's serenity in the least. Mrs. M.J. Stombaugh also executed some pretty spry riding. The party left the ground in high glee, Mrs. Dr. Davis, of Shadeville, singing "O! talk of the promised land!"

At ten o'clock on Thursday the Franklin county prizes were contended for; there were five competitors between whom it was exceedingly difficult to decide. The first prize, a silver service valued at $100, was given to Mrs. Davis, and the second, a gold watch, $50, to Miss Mellhenny. At 12 o'clock there was a driving of matched horses, in which Mrs. Schooley, the "Ohio Fat Woman," participated with four others. The prize, a pitcher worth $20, was awarded to Mrs. Stombaugh, of Columbus. Then there was a drive of single pacing horses—won by Miss Gilbert, of Circleville—prize same as above.

At 2 P.M. the whole party—seventeen in number, rode for the grand sweepstakes premiums....

Here was an array of equestrian talent never before brought together in this country, and to equal which the managers do not hesitate to challenge any district in the Union. As the troupe swept abut the arena, with their fine horses and elegant costumes, and above all, their own graceful and queenly bearing, the display was enough to bewilder any man of weak nerves; and how the judges ever come to a decision, is more than we can imagine; certainly it was not from any marked pre-eminence in either of the fair riders. But as the three prizes must be awarded, the judges gave to Miss Van Pelt the first premium, a horse worth $150, the second, a watch and chain $100, to Miss Custer, and the third, a saddle and bridle $88, to Miss Campbell. The multitude then left the ground, in good order, and thus closed, without accident or ill feeling, the most successful exhibition of ladies' horsemanship ever held in the United States.

CALIFORNIA, 1857

The course and the grounds adjacent presented a most gay and lively scene, while the people were waiting for the announcement that the riders were ready to start. Finally, the entrees, (irregular,) were announced, the order issued to clear the track, the fair contestants were in the saddle, the crowd fell back and away they went. The riders who started were Mrs. Grattan, of San Joaquin, Miss Anna Stephens, of Sacramento, and Miss Lucy Phelps (aged eight years) of San Joaquin. Mrs. Grattan rode Sam Patch; Miss Stephens rode Pat Gallagher; both well known horses of blood and medal; Miss Phelps rode a scrubbish looking colt, evidently a stranger to blankets, curry combs, and shelter, but of superb action and speed of good account. Miss Stephens only arrived in the city in the morning and never saw her horse until she was ready to mount him. Mrs. Grattan, we believe, never before backed the horse she rode. Miss Lucy, we understood, was familiar with her colt; which gave her, perhaps, a slight advantage. That, however, was counteracted by her riding a common vacquero saddle, naked tree, with a clumsy wooden stirrup, covered and obstructed with the uncouth leather shield used by vacqueros.

Mrs. Grattan took the lead and kept it. Miss Stephens and Miss Lucy running well together for half the distance, the latter coming last to the mark. It was one of the finest exhibitions of female grace, skill, and courage ever witnessed. After the grand heat, the ladies performed many extraordinary feats of horsemanship. Miss Lucy, her horse going at high speed, several times changed position, throwing her foot over the horn of the saddle, and riding at pleasure, in the male or female posture. This feat was performed with singular grace and agility, made all the more charming by her petit figure and child-like attire. She also dismounted, took the saddle from her horse, placed it upon another, fastened it and mounted again, in less time than the same thing could be done by a veteran dragoon. Miss Stephens dismounted, unsaddled her horse, and mounted again, on his bare back, and in that position rode at all gaits, with a degree of ease and grace that could not be excelled. After riding about half an hour, the contest was closed, and the judges proceeded to pass upon the merits of the contestants. They unanimously awarded to Miss Stephens the first premium, Mrs. Grattan the second, and Miss Phelps the third. Throughout the exhibition the excitement was intense, and the course more or less obstructed by the crowd forcing in upon it, which the Marshals could not prevent.

ANNOUNCEMENT OF A LADIES NATIONAL EQUESTRIAN CONVENTION UNION COURSE, LONG ISLAND, 1858

Particular notice—The Managers of the Convention respectfully announce that all ladies who desire to participate in the approaching Equestrian Festival, must send in their names to be enregistered, on or before the FIRST DAY OF SEPTEMBER. The Managers are compelled to limit the time to this date, in order that arrangements may be perfected, suitably to carry out the original design, which must be materially affected by the number of ladies participating in the competition for the rich premiums to be awarded.

Ladies will likewise signify to the Managers whether they desire to be furnished with horses by the Committee, so as to be secure against disappointment. It is, however, preferable that they furnish themselves, in case of accident.

An erroneous impression being entertained that the names of the ladies participating in the Festival and competition will be published in the public prints, the management beg to assure those honoring the Convention with their presence, that every precaution will be taken to secure perfect privacy, and not even the names of the successful competitors will be promulgated unless with their express sanction. All communications to be addressed to THOMAS THORP AND PHILIP LEVY, Managers, 19-h no. 131 Bleeker St., New York.

THE CONVENTION

The Ladies National Equestrian Convention, which for some time past has been brought so prominently before the notice of the public, and excited so much interest among those of the fair sex who possessed any equestrian abilities, came off on Wednesday, the 8th inst., on the Union Course, L.I. It was anticipated by many, even among those connected with the management, that, as a pecuniary speculation, it would prove a complete failure. The result, however, has shown that in that respect, at least, it has been most successful. There were upwards of four thousand persons assembled to witness it, as far as we could form an estimate, and the most sanguine of the projectors must have found the result exceed his expectations. The day was remarkably favorable, a fine breeze tempering the sun's rays. The Grand Stands were crowded, and a very large proportion of the fair sex was present; the assemblage, taken altogether, was a most respectable one. The Exercises were announced for 3 p.m., but it was nearly 5 o'clock before the cortege of fair horsewomen made its appearance, the toilettes of the ladies having been made at Snedicor's Hotel....The ladies were all distinguished by large silk badges bearing a number....

As the cavalcade of ladies came riding up the Course, in their picturesque attire, their horses, as if conscious of their burden of beauty and elegance which they carried, proudly caracolling, the scene was beautiful in the extreme, exciting the universal acclamations and admiration of the spectators. It is not for us to describe the varied costumes of the Equestrians, but only the excercises which they exhibited. These commenced with a cavalcade of ladies, eight abreast, riding half way round the course, past the Judge's stand, and returning to the starting place near the south entrance. Afterwards came the *Fete de Manege,* in which the ladies ought to have ridden in turns past the judges, and thus singly and separately exhibited their skill and dexterity in the management of their steeds. This, however, they did not do, as the fair riders were apparently unwilling to submit to any control or obey the instructions of the managers in this respect, but persisted in riding up and down in defiance of all rules. Perhaps this originated from the circumstance of the track not being kept free from the irruptions of the spectators, who crowded the course in front of the judges' stand, and made it a matter of astonishment that no accidents occurred to themselves or the equestriennes. One man, indeed, was knocked down by No. 5, with her horse, who, finding that there were no attempts made to clear the track from the intruders, commenced along with No. 21 to do so with their horses, and in a great measure succeeded, though the latter lady, coming rather too roughly into collision with an irate spectator, had her bridle rein seized by him in a most ungallant manner. The crowd, however, taking the lady's part, released his hold, and he was unceremoniously ejected from the enclosure, for his unmanliness and brutality.

The only exciting proceeding in the affair, in the opinion of the assembage, was the scrub race, (the hurdle race having been prohibited, and properly so, by the proprietors of the track for fear of accidents). For this race about a dozen entered, the prize being a splendid silver mounted saddle, worth $100. This was a magnificent affair. The lead was taken by No. 21, and she gradually increased it till about half way round, when, holding in her horse, No. 2 crept up to her and an excellent struggle ensued. No. 21, however, increased her speed and came past the judges' stand a full distance in advance, her features glowing with excitement, and her hair streaming in the breeze, her hat and plume having fallen from her head in the struggle. She was greeted with the repeated acclamations of the spectators for her excellent display of horsemanship.

The judges who acted on this occasion were John Clancy, William M. Tweed, R.C. Deming, Joseph Russell and E.C. Sedgewick, and the award of prizes was as follows:

The three prizes were, first, a magnificent grand action piano worth $500, which has been for some time on exhibition in this city, and was much admired for its superb tone and excellence of finish.

The second was a silver pitcher, and a pair of goblets of silver richly chased and of the most elegant antique design, valued at $300.

The third was a splendid gold watch, set with diamonds upon dark enamel, worth $200.

An additional fourth prize was also added to the lists, and consisted of a magnificently mounted ladies' saddle, worth $100.

The fortunate winner of the first prize was No. 5—a handsome lady, understood to be a Mrs. Lawrence of New York City.

The second prize was taken by No. 2, a pretty young lady from Red Hook, Dutchess county, named Miss Lydia Shultz.

The third was claimed by No. 13, Miss M.B. Smith, of 128 Christopher Street, New York.

The fourth prize was gallantly won by No. 21, a young lady from Troy, named Miss Elizabeth Morey.

In Conclusion we will only remark that there was a gross failure in the managers of this affair, in neglecting to provide the efficient clearing of the course, and which detracted so much from its success. They announced that they would have an efficient and ample police force in attendence to keep order and enforce regulations, but this they neglected to do, and hence the dissatisfaction caused. Indeed the real managers of the convention appear to have entirely neglected their duties, and the mismanagement which characterized this part will effectually prevent the success of another Ladies Equestrian Convention.

THE NORTH VS. THE SOUTH—FASHION VS. BOSTON, 1842

During the fall of 1841 Fashion, the leading northern thoroughbred, defeated Boston, a southern horse, in a purse race at Camden, New Jersey. Seeking revenge, Boston's owner James Long of Virginia and his turf advisor, Colonel William R. Johnson, proposed a $20,000 match race for the spring of 1842 at the Union Course on Long Island, New York. Many turfmen doubted that Fashion's owner, William H. Gibbons, would accept the challenge, because he did not personally wager on his prize filly. But Gibbons yielded to the request of Henry K. Toler, operator of the Union Course, and loaned Fashion to him and a group of twenty to thirty sponsors.

Over the winter the Spirit of the Times and other newspapers promoted the encounter as one of the greatest matches in the history of thoroughbred racing. Foaled in Virginia in 1833, Boston had won 40 of 45 races and had earned over $50,000 in prize money. Fashion, a chestnut filly born in New Jersey in 1837, had an equally brilliant record. When the great day finally arrived between 50,000 and 70,000 spectators converged on the Union Course. The multitude numbered 40 United States senators and other dignitaries. The large throng caused several incidents that threatened to ruin the day, but in the end the northern champion triumphed over the southern rival in record time. The following accounts of the challenge, the scene at the racetrack, and the race are reprinted from the Spirit of the Times, 6 November, 4 December 1841, pp. 426, 474, 14 May 1842, p. 126.

A CHALLENGE:

To the Friends of the distinguished Race Nag Fashion

In the four mile race recently run over the Camden and Philadelphia Course, Boston was distanced by John Blout and Fashion in the first heat—Blount winning the heat in 7:42. The second heat was won by Fashion in 7:48—Blount breaking Down.

We, the undersigned, now propose to run Boston against Fashion, a match, Four mile heats, over the Union Course, Long Island, agreeably to the rules of said course, in Spring, 1842, or on any day during the month of May, for $20,000 a side—one half or one fourth forfeit, as may be most agreeable to the friends of Fashion. The forfeit to be deposited (in New York money, in any bank of the city), and the day of the race to be named, when the match shall be closed. The challenge shall remain open during the month of November.

WM.R. Johnson
James Long.

New York, *Astor House,* November 5, 1841.

The spirited and liberal challenge above, demonstrates conclusively that Boston's owners still have the most implicit confidence in him, notwithstanding his defeat at Camden. Since that race we have conversed with twenty gentlemen who witnessed it, and they entertain but one opinion as to Boston's performance on that occasion. He not only would not run, but he was so much amiss that he could not: he was 2:10 in running the first mile. Arthur Taylor, his trainer, strenuously desired his owners not to start him, and Mr. Long, instead of backing him at $1,000 to $300, *nineteen times over,* as usual, did not lay out a dollar on him.

The friends of Fashion are exceedingly anxious to close the match, but her owner is not disposed to assume the degree of responsibility to the public, implied by such an engagement, while Mr. Laird is alike unwilling to risk his reputation as a "public trainer" upon an event of so much importance. The owner of Fashion runs only those horses which are bred by himself; he runs them for sweepstakes and purses merely, with no other interest in their success than the amount of public money they may earn—in plainer terms, he does not bet, in any case whatever. The only chance to make up the match, therefore, is for a party of gentlemen to purchase the filly; the sum of $12,000 is demanded for her, but we hope and believe, that under the circumstances, her owner will be induced to part with her on more liberal terms, taking into consideration the express purpose for which she is purchased.

BOSTON'S CHALLENGE TO FASHION ACCEPTED

The following letter containing the acceptance of Boston's challenge to Fashion has been communicated exclusively to the "Spirit of the Times," by the gentleman who made the match on behalf of the friends of Fashion: —

William R. Johnson, Esq.: Dear Sir,-The challenge from yourself and Mr. James Long, to run Boston against Fashion, Four mile heats, over the Union Course, L.I., agreeable to the rules of the Course, in Spring 1842, or any day during the month of May, for $20,000 a side (New York money), one-half, or one-fourth forfeit, as may be agreeable to the friends of Fashion—is accepted by me on their behalf. I name the second Tuesday in May (the 10th), 1842, as the day for the race; and 5,000 (or one-fourth) as the amount of forfeit, which sum has been placed in the hands of J. Prescott Hall, Esq., President of the New York Jockey Club. The same amount being received by him from you, the whole forfeit ($10,000) will be deposited by him in one of the city Banks.

THE SOUTH BEATEN BY THE NORTH IN 7:32 1/2—7:45

The great sectional Match for $20,000 a side, Four mile heats, between THE NORTH and THE SOUTH, came off on Tuesday last, the 10th inst. Since the memorable contest between Eclipse and Henry, on the 27th of May, 1823, no race has excited so much interest and enthusiasm. It attracted hundreds of individuals from the remotest section of the Union, and for months has been the theme of remark and speculation, not only in the Sporting Circles of this country but in England, where the success of the Northern Champion was predicted. It was a most thrilling and exciting race!—one which throws in the shade the most celebrated of those wonderful achievements which have conferred so much distinction upon the High Mettled Racers of America!

At an early hour on Tuesday morning our streets were filled with carriages of all descriptions, wending their way to the Ferries, while thousands upon thousands crossed over to the cars of the Long Island Rail Company. But after eleven o'clock the Company found it impossible to convey to the course the immense crowd which filled and surrounded the cars, though they continued to sell tickets after they were fully sensible of the fact! Indeed, from the first, the arrangements of the Company were an imposition! They charged the most extravagant price for the transportation of passengers, and their preparations were in no way equal to the occasion; above all, they continued to sell tickets after they knew that several thousand more persons had purchased them than they could transport. A train, bearing over two thousand passengers, did not reach the course until after the first heat, and hundreds who had purchased tickets, despairing of reaching the course in the cars, started on foot, and reached it before them. At half past eleven o'clock there were not less than five thousand persons waiting a conveyance by the cars at the Brooklyn terminal, all of whom had purchased tickets! Under these circumstances, it will not be very surprising to any one to hear that upon the return of the cars after the race, the indignant passengers rolled several of them off the track over the hill, and smashed others, while "a perfect mash" was made of the ticket office! The race was a golden harvest to the Hack, cab, and omnibus proprietors. The anxiety to reach the course was so great that ten dollars were offered for a standing—up place in a charcoal cart! Our contemporary of the "Courier and Enquirer" thus pleasantly describes his own "peculiar position:" —

"Finding that our ticket was valueless, we engaged a deck passage on an omnibus; and never have we witnessed so curious an exhibition as the road to the Course presented. We have neither space nor time to describe it; but the reader may form some idea of the anxiety to get ahead, when we state that beside the thousands that were footing it with railroad tickets in their pockets, and the immense number in all sorts of vehicles, we overtook a charcoal cart, from which the cry of ch-a-r-co-al was heard to proceed in full chorus; and on getting alongside some twenty heads were obtruded, presenting faces which we readily imagined had once been white, but which were now of the most perfectly sable hue. They were a set of very clever fellows who deemed themselves fortunate to have procured even this mode of conveyance to the Race Course."

Having engaged a carriage the day previous, we were enabled to reach the Course
at an early hour. The roads from town were thronged almost to reach the entire distance
with a procession of carriages and frequently with several abreast, all crammed. It
would require the pen of the "Troubadour of the Corporation Dirt Carts" to give a
description of them. Flatbush wagons and six- penny bonesetters were jammed in
between four-in-hand landaus, fast crabs in match carts, elegant stanhopes, and the
superb turn outs of out wealthy cits. The Communipaw clam-boxes, stylish cabs, and
every variety of barouche were inextricably mixed up and jostled by great lumbering
omnibuses and thousands of fancy go-carts, wagons, and hackney coaches.

Upon reaching the course, such tableau was presented as we never saw before. The
field inside of the course was thronged with carriages and equestrians, while the fences,
booths, and trees, were densely covered, so much so that several accidents occurred
from their breaking down. It is stated that there were no less than Eight Thousand persons in the stands, and yet there were nearly as many who could obtain but a partial
view of the race, while many could not see at all! The number of spectators in attendance is variously estimated at from FIFTY TO SEVENTY THOUSAND!! Among them
the U.S. Senate and House of Representatives, the British Army and Navy, as well as
our own, the Bench and the Bar, and the Beauty and Fashion of New York were all
represented. The Ladies' Stand was appropriately graced by the presence of a large
number of the most brilliant of our city belles, who, with hardly an exception, gave
suffrage of "their most sweet voices" to the beautiful daughter of Bonnets o'Blue! The
enclosed "privileged space" in front of the stands, reserved for the Members of the
Jockey Club and strangers (who were charged $10 for admission without distinction!)
was thronged with Turfmen, Breeders, and Amateurs! At one o'clock, however, owing
to the want of efficient police, and their inability to see the race, more than a thousand
persons climbed over the pickets, from the field, into the enclosed space, while a mob
on the outside tore down a length of a fence, and stove through a door in the stand, and
swarmed into the cleared space. For a time it seemed impossible for the match to take
place at all! A crowd of loafers made a rush up the stairs leading to the Club Stand, but
they were summarily ejected. At length Yankee SULLIVAN, JEROLOMAN, RYNAS, and
several other distinguished members of The Fancy, undertook to clear the course, which
they did in an incredibly short time, by organizing a party of their friends, who formed
in line, with clasped hands, quite across the space, and marched from one end to the
other, thereby driving outside of the gate every person without a badge. Of course there
were among this mob several ugly customers, but Yankee Sullivan had only to "let fly
with his right," or Jeroloman give any one of them "a teaser on his smeller," to fix his
business! On the whole, the mob conducted themselves very well under the circumstances; the great majority were in perfectly good humor, and had the proprietors taken
the precaution to paint the tops of the pickets with a thick coat of tar, and engage a
strong body of police, no such disgraceful scene would have occurred.

The race commenced about 2 o'clock. For more than a quarter of a mile in front
of the stands, the spectators ranged on the side of the course and of the field presented
one dense mass of thousands, through which the horses ran the gauntlet. The course
itself, owing to the rain of Sunday night, was not deemed quite so well adapted for
speed as upon some other occasions; still it was fine order. The prospect of weather,

in the morning, was unfavorable, but though at ten o'clock there was a slight sprinkling of rain, it soon cleared off. The day was warm and pleasant, but with scarce a glimpse of the sun.

The betting was a shade in Boston's favor. Before the race came off, however, his friends were obliged, in order to get on their money to lay 100 to 60, and in some cases 2 to 1. We never saw so little money bet on a race here of any importance; of heavy betting we did not hear of a solitary transaction, though the backers of each were sanguine....

THE RACE

First Heat.—Boston on the inside went away with the lead at a rattling pace, the mare laying up within two lengths of him down the straight run on the backstretch; the half mile was run in 55 seconds. The same position was maintained at the end of the mile, (run in 1:53) but soon after Fashion made play and the pace improved. Both made strong running down the backstretch, over the hill (opposite the half mile post) and down the slight descent which succeeds, and though this seemed favorable ground for Boston, the mare gained on him, at this place, in this mile, and placed herself well up. Boston threw her off on the turn, and led through clear, running the mile in 1:50.5. The pace seemed too good to last, and Boston's friends, as he led cleverly down the back stretch, were "snatching and eager" to take anything offered. Again Boston led through, this mile (the 3d) being run in 1:54, Fashion keeping him up to the top of his rate. The contest was beautiful and exciting beyond description; there was no clambering, no faltering, no dwelling on the part of either; each ran with a long rating stroke, and at a pace that kills. Soon after commencing the 4th mile Joe Laird shook his whip over her head and gave Fashion an eye opener or two with the spur, and not 100 yard from the ground where Boston took the track from Charles Carter, *she collared and passed him in a half a dozen strokes* at a flight of speed we never saw equalled, except in the desperate brush at the stand between Grey Medoc and Altorf, in their dead heat! When Fashion responded to the call upon her and took the track in such splendid style the cheers sent up from the "rude throats" of thousands might have been heard for miles! Fashion made her challenge after getting through the drawgate and took the lead opposite the quarter mile post. Boston, however, like a trump, as he is, did not give back an inch, and though it was manifest the Northern Phenomenom had the foot of him, he gave her no respite. He lapped her down the back stretch for 300 yards, when Gil. Patrick very sensibly took a strong bracing pull on him and bottled him up for a desperate brush up the hill, where Eclipse passed Henry. Here Gil. again let him out, but unfortunately he pulled him inside so near the fence that Boston struck his hip against a post, and hitting a sharp knot or a nail cut through the skin on his quarter for seven or eight inches! He struck hard enough to jar himself very much, and we observed him to falter; but he soon recovered, and though at this moment Fashion led him nearly three lengths, he gradually closed the gap round the turn to within a few feet. At this moment the excited multitude broke through all restaint in their anxiety to witness the termination of the heat, and the course was nearly blocked up! On coming out through a narrow gauntlet of thousands of spectators excited to the highest pitch, both horses very naturally faltered at the tremendous shouts which made the welkin ring! Up the quarter stretch Gil made another desperate effort to win the race out of the fire. He applied his thong freely, while Joe Laird drew his whip on the mare more than once, and tapped her claret at the same time. Inside of the gate it was "a hollow thing," though Boston nearly closed the gap at the distance stand. Gil. fairly caught Joe by surprise, but the latter, shaking his whip over her head, gave Fashion the spur, and she instantly recovered her stride coming through about a length ahead with apparently something in hand to spare, closing the heat in 7:32.5—the fastest, by all odds ever run in America.

The time was kept on the Jockey Club Stand by Messrs. ROBERT L. and JAMES STEVENS, and in the Judges' stand by Senator BARROW of Louisiana, Hon. Mr. BOTTS, of Virginia, J. HAMILTON WILKES, Esq., and the official Timers. We took the time of each mile from the Messrs. S., between whom we stood. Mr. NEILL, Major RINGGOLD, and other gentlemen of acknowledged accuracy as timers stood in the same circle,and there was but a fraction of difference in the time each declared, "by watches, too, not made in Kentucky!" Messrs. S. made the time 7:33, but as they kept the time on the half, and in some cases, of the quarter, miles, their difference of but half a second from the Timers in the Judges' stand demonstrates the remarkable accuracy of the parties.

The result of the heat, was the more astonishing to a few of Boston's friends as no one ever supposed Fashion could make *this* time, though she might *beat* him. We were prepared to expect the best time on record, not only from the fact that we had been informed of the result of Fashion's *private trial* on the 25th ult., but from a circumstance which we shall be excused, we trust, for alluding to here. After retiring to our room at the Astor House on Monday night, at a late hour, we had the pleasure of a "domicilary visit" from Mr. Long, the owner of Boston, and several mutual friends. The "party" were attired in costumes that would be esteemed somewhat unique out of the circle of the Marquis of Waterford's friends, who ride steeple chases in their shirts and drawers! Nevertheless there was no lack of fun nor spirit; in the course of an interesting "horse talk," Mr. Long gave us several "items," one of which was that Boston would run the 1st heat, "sure," in 7:34! Said Mr. L., "He will run the 1st mile in about 1:53, the 2d in 1:52, the 3d in 1:54 , and the 4th in 1:55." After he retired we made a memorandum of the time as a curiosity after the race. And we refer to it now, to show that though beaten by the Northern Phenomenom, the gallant Boston amply sustained all the expectations formed of him from his trials and previous performances. He not only made vastly better time than he ever did before, but better time than ever had been made!—Time that quite eclipses the most wonderful achievements on the American Turf! The vaunted performance of the Southern "cracks" at New Orleans, are almost thrown in the shade, wonderful as they are! Had anyone offered to beat the time of Eclipse and Henry on the Union Course, 3 to 1 would have been laid against it; or had the friends of Boston been assured that he could run, as Mr. Long told us he could, in 7:34, his friends would have staked a million of dollars upon his winning the match! For the first two miles Boston, in the opinion of many shrewd judges had the foot of the mare, and it is thought that had he trailed her as he did Charles Carter, the result of the first heat might have been different. But what shall be said of the incomparable daughter of Trustee and Bonnets o' Blue! Too much cannot be said of her, or her jockey. She ran as true as steel, as game and honest a race as was ever recorded of a High Mettled Racer!

Both horses cooled out well. Boston always blows tremendously, even after a gallop, but he seemed less distressed. Neither was Fashion; her action is superb, and as she came through on the 4th mile, it was remarked that she was playing her ears as if taking exercise. She recovered sooner than Boston, and though her friends now offered large odds on her, Boston's were no less confident; the seventh mile they thought would "fetch her." We should not have been surprised to have seen both swell over the loins, nor to have found them greatly distressed. We examined them carefully after the heat, and state with great pleasure, that though they "blowed strong," they recovered in a few minutes, and came to the post again comparatively fresh. After the heat was over, the crowd rushed into the enclosed space en masee; an endeavor was made to clear a portion of the track of the multitude who had now taken possession of it, and after great exertions, a lane was formed, through which the horses came up for the

Second Heat: Fashion led off with a moderate stroke, and carried on the running down the back stretch with a lead of about three lengths. After making the ascent of the hill Boston challenged, closed the gap, and lapped her. A tremendous shout arose on all hands at this rally, but as it subdued on the part of Boston's friends, it was again more tumultuously caught up by the friends of the mare, as she outfooted him before reaching the head of the quarter stretch. She came through (in 1:59) three or four lengths ahead, and kept up her rate down the entire straight stretch on the rear of the Course. After getting over the hill, Boston, as before, made a rush, and succeeded in collaring the mare while she, as before, again threw him off, and led through by two or three lengths in 1:57. Gil relieved his horse for the next 600 yards, but instead of waiting for Fashion to ascend the hill at the half mile post alone, he called on Boston just before reaching it, and the two went over it nearly together; no sooner than they commenced the descending ground, than gathering all his energies for a final and desperate effort, Boston made a dash, and this time he succeeded in taking the track! The scene which ensued we have no words to describe. Such cheering, such betting, and so many long faces, was never seen nor heard before. After being compelled to give up the track, Joe Laird, with the utmost prudence and good sense, took his mare in hand, and gave her time to recover her wind. This run *took the shine out of* Boston! Instead of pulling him steadily, and refreshing him with slight respite, Gil. Patrick kept him at his work after he took the track, and run this mile (the 3d) in 1:51.5! The pace was tremendous. Nothing short of limbs of steel and sinews of catgut could stand up under such a press! On the first turn after passing the stand Fashion now fresh again, made a dash, and as Boston had not another run left in him, she cut him down in her stride opposite the quarter mile post, and the thing was out. The race, so far as Boston was concerned, was past praying for! If anything can parallel Fashion's turn of speed it is her invincible game. She now gradually dropped him, and without another effort on his part to retrieve the fortunes of the day, she came home a gallant and easy winner in 7:45! Boston pulled up inside of the distance stand, and walked over the score. As she came under the Judge's cord extended across the course, Boston was exactly sixty yards behind, though he could have placed himself in a better position had

Gil. called upon him. As Joe Laird rode Fashion back to the stand, the shouts were so deafening, that had not the President of the Club and another gentleman held on to her bridle, she would have not only, "enlarged the circle of her acquaintance" very speedily, but "made a mash " of some dozen of the "rank and file" then and there assembled. She looked as if another heat would not "set her back any."

And thus did *The North* settle its account with *The South* for the victory achieved by Bascombe over Post Boy! It was a magnificent race—one that will be remembered by every one who witnessed it "while memory holds her seat!" Though beaten, it is conceded an all hands that Boston has aquired a more "vast renown" by this wonderful race than by this Thirty-five previous victories combined! "All that can be said is, that Boston has beaten himself, and Fashion has beaten Boston!" The spirit of his owners on this as upon like a memorable occasion in May 1823, is worthy of them and of the Old Dominion. Of one of them it has been well said , that, "like another Napoleon, he is never more to be feared than in his reverses!"

In congratulating each other upon the brilliant triumph achieved by a Northern Champion—now the Champion of the American Turf—let no one forget to do honor to those whose admirable skill and judgement the North is mainly indebted for its victory! To Mr. SAMUEL LAIRD, the trainer and manager of Fashion, and to his fine spirited son, who jockeyed her in a style that would have conferred credit upon Jem Robinson, too much credit cannot be given. Nor let us forget that to the gallant Boston we are indebted for maintaining the indomitable game and surprising speed of our Champion! Who else could have displayed it in such bold and beautiful relief? Arthur Taylor brought him to the post in the very finest possible condition, and Gil. Patrick, his jockey, rarely distinguished himself more than upon this occasion. Most of our contemporaries state that he rode with spurs. He wore one only and that only in the second heat.

It is peculiarly gratifying to ourselves, though we have the pleasure of numbering all the parties among our personal friends, that Mr. GIBBONS, the owner of Fashion, is among the oldest, most staunch, and most generous of the numbers. Unfortunately he was prevented from witnessing the race in consequence of an accident which for some reason confined him at home. In his absence, another tried friend, WALTER LIVINGSTON, Esq., the owner of Trustee, (the sire of Fashion) was congratulated on all hands; he has never doubted Fashion's success from the first. Col. W. LARKIN WHITE, of Virginia, who was also in attendance, came in for a liberal portion of the good feeling displayed. Nor should it go unrecorded that Col. JOHNSON, was by no means forgotten in the general outburst of congratulation. He "sold the stick which broke his own head," and no mistake, for after breeding Bonnets o'Blue from his own Sir Charles, and running her with great success, he parted with her to Mr. Gibbons, who bred from her a filly which has beaten the best horse Col. J. has had in his stable, since the days of his favorite Reality, the renown granddam of Fashion herself!

RECAPITULATION

TUESDAY, MAY 10, 1842—Match, **THE NORTH VS. THE SOUTH**, $20,000 a side. $5000 ft. Four mile heats.

Henry K. Toler's (William Gibbons') ch. m. *Fashion,* by Imp. Trustee out of Bonnets o'Blue (Mariner's dam) by Sir Charles, 5 yrs., 111 lbs...*Joseph Laird* 1 1
Col. Wm. R. Johnson's & James Long's ch. h. *Boston,* by Timoleon out of Robin Brown's dam by Ball's Floritzel, 9 yrs., 126 lbs....*Gil. Patrick* 2 2

First Heat		*Second Heat*	
Time of First mile	1:53	Time of First mile	1:59
Time of Second mile	1:50 1/2	Time of Second mile	1:57
Time of Third mile	1:54	Time of Third mile	1:51 1/2
Time of Fourth mile	1:55	Time of Fourth mile	1:57 1/2
Time of First Heat	7:32 1/2	Time of Second Heat	7:45

THE NORTH VS. THE SOUTH—FASHION VS. PEYTONA, 1845

The climax to the series of intersectional challenges came in 1845, when the southern horse Peytona faced Fashion on the Union Course. This time between 70,000 and 100,000 persons turned out to witness the event—the largest crowd ever to watch a contest on the Long Island racetrack. The race was extremely close, but in both heats Peytona outran his northern rival. Although Fashion came back fifteen days later to defeat Peytona in a purse race at Camden, New Jersey, this victory did not redeem northern racing. Peytona's 1845 triumph marked the end of an era. New York City thoroughbred racing already was showing signs of decline, and the last North-South encounter did little or nothing to reverse that trend. The sport remained in depression in New York and elsewhere in the North until after the Civil War. The following document is reprinted from the New York Herald, 5 May 1845.

THE GREAT CONTEST

It was an exciting, but very beautiful morning; exciting because the contest between the North and the South for the dominion of the turf was to be settled, before the shades of evening closed on the well-trodden race ground. It is well understood that the ambiguity of the relative pretensions of the two great sections of the country to this honor, is the natural result of former well balanced successes. The North beat the South twice, and twice the South returned the compliment; their yearnings then for victory were as keen as Damascus sword blades. In addition to the sectional feeling and the strong rivalry of sportsmen, and in one sense partizans—the vast sums of money pending on the race, attached a degree of absorbing interest to the result, quite proportionate to the great demonstration that took place.

More than three thousand persons crossed the South Ferry yesterday morning before 8 o'clock, for the races. As the morning progressed, the crowd increased rapidly, and a scene of tumult, disorder, and confusion ensued. Apple women's stands were overturned, an omnibus upset, fighting, swearing, pushing, screaming and shouting in abundance.—All seemed eager to reach the ground. Long trains of carriages, filled with all sorts of people, reaching to Broadway, lined Whitehall street. Here was the magnificent barouche of millionaire, full of gay, laughing, dark-eyed demoiselles, jammed in between a Bowery stage and a Broadway hack—here were loafers and dandies, on horseback and on foot-sporting gentlemen in green coats and metal buttons- Southerners from Louisiana, Mississippi, and Alabama, with anxious faces, but hearts full of hope, "a pocket full of rocks," and a calm determination to await the result. The whole Union had in fact sent delegates to represent it in the grand contest which this day ushered in—all business seemed laid aside—one spirit animated the vast multitude. Omnibusses of all dimensions, cabriolets, chariots, drays, wagons, and every description of vehicle were put in requisition.

"Bill," said a singular specimen of humanity, whose slouch cap, plaistered soaplocks, and "forty inch" trowsers, denoted him as belonging to that class of our citizens commonly styled the "Boys"—"Bill, I tell yer Petuny's the crack hoss o'the track—she's bound to beat, she is, and if you want to bet, I'll go ye anything from an oyster stew to a new top piece at Tice's, or a hot supper at Sweeney's."

"By the blood and bones of old Gineral Putnam vat rid down the stone steps of the Old Bowery (said Bill) if I hadn't no more patriotism than you've got I'd never call myself von of the Boys again. Talk about Petuny. I tell ye Fashion's a York hoss, and a Souther hoss cant begin to touch her, no how. Go way from me, I vont talk to a boy that vants to bet agin his own counrty; go vay vid you." Here a great rush took place towards the gate, in which several persons were more or less injured, draymen cursing, cabmen roaring—"I say, Jack, tell that ere gentleman with the telegraphic nose to leave my way, or if he doesn't, I'm blowed if I don't drive through both him and the gate, without giving him the trouble of opening it...."

On the arrival of the two earlier trains, there was not a very remakable degree of bustle. The passengers were set down immediately beside the course, to which admittance was procured through narrow entrances, about three or four hundred yards from the railway, on the edge of which are half a dozen of dwelling houses. These were all converted into dram shops and places of refreshment, and if they did not do more than their share of the business, they had the honor of an early call from a large portion of the race-going blades, who, after their dusty and perilous journey, per railway, were ready for a grateful draught of something or other to wash down the dust. From this point to the entrance of the course, and, as far beyond it, equal, perhaps to a fifth of the circumference of the course, was a continuous line of tents on one side of the thoroughfare—the other being bounded by the fence of the Course. This passage was about twenty yards wide, so that, their being a good deal of room to spare, it was occupied by all sorts of irregular forces, and indescribable camp followers, sutlers, loungers, rowdies, gamblers, and twenty other species of the genus loose fish. Here you saw a bucket of water, with two or three little negro boys for an escort; there baskets of oranges as thick as yellow gowans; piles of oysters reared their rough exteriors in huge profusion, and the confectionery peered up in tempting masses, albeit in rather a melting mood on account of the sun's vertical rays, which spared nothing, sweet or sour, that memorable day. Business in the tents—wigwams—the culinary camps and conventicles commenced at an early hour, and was carried on with a briskness that betimes looked like voracity, and fears were occasionally excited that the impetuousity of the hungry crowd might find a melancholy end in the prodigious tubs of lemonade and brandy punch that lay in elegant negligence around the tables, whose extended surfaces supported masses of ham, sandwiches, lobsters, loaves, decanters, glasses, and all the paraphenalia of drinking that could be condensed in the space. The rap of the hammer in erecting these tents mingled incessantly with the popping of corks, for a couple of hours, when the music of mastication reigned triumphant. During all this time, from the very beginning of the arrivals, gamblers of all descriptions swarmed about in every direction. In the space of a hundred yards we counted no less than seventeen ill-looking wretches, using their utmost cunning to cajole the natives with three cups and one ball. Various unfavorable characteristics made them conspicuous; but what was particularly striking, hardly one of these thimble-riggers had a table or stand, but as a substitute carried on their operations on their knees, which were raised to a horizontal direction and supported them on the curved heads of their walkingsticks; the look of these worthies in this attitude was quite in keeping with their appearance, character and habits—all of which are as graceless—to use the word in any sense—as can possibly be imagined. Each of them had his jackall or attendant to raise his game, with whom a continual rhapsody of slang sentences was kept up, something like this:- "I'll bet ten or twenty dollars which ball the pea's under." "I'll bet you I do—it's under the middle one." "What will ye bet." "I'll lay you $50 you don't tell me which it's under." "I'll not bet this time." "Let me try." "I'll bet you or anybody can't tell which cup has the pea under; here's fifty dollars in gold, who'll take me up." "I'll bet you five its under that one." "I'll not bet five, I'll stake fifty no one tells where the pea is; its neither there, nor there, but its here, gentlemen, &c." In every part of the space outside the wall, this jargon kept grating on the ear. Of sweat tables, too, there were no scarcity, presided over by gentlemen of all hues of color, whose invitation to passers by to "come win and lose a dollar," were part of the floating harmony....

On the stand there could not be fewer than thirty thousand persons; every train added countless hosts, for the first race of everybody who obtained admission, was to the grand stand, and the solicitude to secure places increased in the direct ratio of the difficulty of finding them, so that the onset of the last was impetuous in the extreme. A harder day's labor no men performed that day, than those who had charge of the stairs. We saw several altercations with fellows who attempted to get on the stand without tickets, but they were invariably foiled. More fortunate by far, however, was the onset made on its left extremity, at about one o'clock. At that hour it became desirable to remove some of the boards of the back wall to give free admission to the air to those below; the rowdies no sooner got a foothold, than they attacked and carried the outer wall, thirty feet high, by escalade. By a species of affinity their chums above collected in sufficient force to co-operate in the movement, and in about two minutes our reporter counted fifty who either rolled over or were hoisted by the coat collar and inexpressibles, to a place among the 30,000. At last the trick was detected and stopped, but not before a strong posse of boys had profitted by the example set them; and for the ensuing half hour, hordes of irregular troops kept prowling about the wall, like a tribe of Bedouins around a doomed caravan. It was understood that the horses were to start at one o'clock, and from this hour of excitement on the stand became intense, and until two, each individual kept his position, or looked for one that was better; with eye constantly bent to the Judge's stand. We saw several persons from Canada among the crowd, and we understood that every section of the Union was largely represented. The lower portion of the stand was occupied by refreshment tables on one side and faro and roulette , and all sorts of gaming tables on the other. Betting and gambling and guzzling went on at a rapid pate, and the work of Satan here progressed with a celerity and promptitude that must have been greatly pleasing to his infernal highness....

On the course itself there was the utmost difficulty in preserving the track clear from intruders, and to the efficiency of a few may be ascribed the comparative order which was at length established. A young gentleman, mounted on a black horse, was quite conspicuous in the part he took, riding up and down, and most fearlessly charging the intruding multitude with his whip. The indomitable Captain Isaiah Rynders, mounted on his famous white charger, rendered most valuable services, and never have we seen such perfect self-possession and invincible good humor as was displayed on this occasion by the leader of the Empires. He was loudly cheered by the members of the Jockey Club, and by his address to the crowd, appealing to their feelings of pride as northerners, to show the southerners assembled that fair play could be given to their horse, succeeded in obtaining a clear course. Country McClusky also appeared on horseback, and used his hands, feet and legs, most liberally. Yankee Sullivan, and others, including Bill Harrington, who, with the rest, preserved their temper and feelings most admirably midst the hundred provocations so plentifully given them, most ably seconded the efforts of the rest. Justice Matsell, by his appearance, was of most essential service, and, where-ever a notorious character, or suspicious-looking individual, fell under the influence of his eye, their stay was short. The worthy Recorder, by his influence and presence, was most efficient in two or three emergencies....

In the meantime all eyes were turned towards the judges' stand, where it was expected the horses would be led out previous to being saddled, and when we mention this stand, we should say that we were surprised to see it occupied by some sixteen or seventeen individuals, amongst whom was one of very questionable character, shouting and cheering, cap in hand. Last year our reporter was refused accomodation of this stand for the public interest, whilst on this occasion some dozen strangers had free admission, and the reporters had to get their information and obtain a sight as best they could.

About half past two o'clock, the bugle sounded to bring forth the horses. They shortly after showed themselves, and each were received with shouts that might have almost been heard from one end of the isle to the other. We have as often described them that it is almost needless to repeat it; suffice it to say that both looked as fine as silk, in first rate condition. Mr. J. Laird topped the pit-skin across Fashion, dressed in a purple jacket and red and gold cap. The "indomitable Barney" mounted Peytona. Two finer animals and abler jockies it is supposed there is not in the States. Having gone to the scales Mr. Laird made up his weight to 125 lbs.; and Barney his to 118. Many thought that Fashion has "a leetle" too much upon her, but she appeared the same as ever.

After some endeavors on the part of those in authority, the track was well cleared as could be expected under the circumstances, thanks to the indefatigable Capt. Ryders, Bill Harrington, Country McCluskey, Yankee Sullivan, Don Casseau, or some such name, on his blind black mare. At 33 minutes past two o'clock the horses were saddled and mounted, and at the first tap they went forth in gallant style, Peytona having the poll, but a most beautiful start—nose and nose. They kept thus together round the bottom, Peytona gently falling off, but yet keeping her nose close to the tail of her rival, evidently waiting attendance. They kept thus to the first quarter, the same to the half. At the third quarter they were close together, Peytona making up, evidently waiting attendance; at the drawgate she came in front, and led to the judges stand a length and a half in front. For the second mile they appeared to keep this position round the bottom, but owing to the clouds of dust prevailing just then, only an occasional glimpse could be caught of them; but they seemed to maintain a similar position round the top to the drawgate, where Fashion appeared to come in front, but on reaching the judge's chair, Fashion's nose was close up with that of Peytona, on the inside. For the third mile they kept well thus together round, to the nearing of the half mile post, where the heavy patch before alluded to occurs. Fashion appeared to gain somewhat, but shortly after Peytona reached her flank, nipping her hard, but Fashion appeared immediately afterwards to make the gap wider. At the drawgate, Fashion appeared two lengths in front, but on nearing the judge's stand, Peytona had her nose close to the flank of her opponent. It was now pretty evident that Barney had it all his own way, and could do just as he pleased with the affair, and faces became elongated, while others could scarce keep their feet....Round the bottom they kept well together, but owing to dust, &c., there was no seeing further, until they reached the drawgate towards home, where Fashion appeared to have the lead, but it was immediately taken from her, and Peytona came home two lengths in front, making the first heat in 7m.39s., amid the most unbounded cheers.

The betting now took a very different turn—50 to 30 was offered on Peytona, but there was great shyness; 50 to 25 was taken to some extent. The course was kept in the best order possible, previous to the second heat, under all circumstance.— This was owing to the indefatigable exertions of Bill Harrington and others. A few light skirmishes took place previous to the commencement of the next heat, but after a sufficient dose of punishment having been administered, pro, and con, matters were adjusted, and every preparation was made for the succeeding heat.

At the first attempt they did not go forth, and were pulled short up, owing to what appeared a rather premature tap. They returned and commenced again, de novo. At the second attempt they went forth Peytona leading a neck, Laird well up round the bottom to the quarter; on approaching the half Fashion went in front, and led to the three quarter. Here the crowd broke in at the lower drawgate, which caused some confusion for a few moments, but owing to the vigilance of those now engaged, was soon got under. Fashion led to the drawgate, where they came together to the Judge's chair, head and head, no telling who had the lead. For the second mile Fashion appeared to have the lead to the quarter, the other well up; they kept so up the backstretch; at the three-quarter it was just so. Fashion still kept the lead, closely waited upon by Peytona; it was thus round the top, but at the drawgate they were again well together, Fashion having the track, but at the end of the second mile, notwithstanding Fashion's advantage, Peytona led to the Judge's stand a head in front. For the third mile they kept so so to the three-quarters; at the drawgate Fashion led on the inside, but Peytona had got her and led her home a length in advance. "Now comes the tug of war." Peytona maintained her position, both well together; she gained a little on her round the bottom, but apparently with little effect; at the half they were well together, which was maintained to the three-quarters, but here the mob closed in so as to obscure sight from the Club stand.—Fashion appeared to have the lead, but on approaching the drawgate, notwithstanding the mob closing in on the track, Peytona led the way a clear length in advance in 7:45 1/4. We have only time to say that it was a quite a waiting race; "Barney" knew what he had to do, and did it nobly, and doubtless more he would have done if it had been required.

The following is a summary of the whole affair.

Miles	First Heat	Second Heat
First	1:54	1:58
Second	1:53	1:54
Third	1:57	1:55 1/4
Fourth	1:55 3/4	1:58
Total	7:39 3/4	7:45 1/4

SPEED OF PEYTONA, THE WINNER OF THE GREAT RACE

	Distance, miles	Distance, feet	Time, seconds	Distance pr sec'd	Stride pr sec'd
First Heat	4	21,120	459 1/4	46	2
Second Heat	4	21,120	465 1/4	45 2/5	2

SOUTHERN RACING

The center of southern thoroughbred racing in the United States before the Civil War was New Orleans. There the meets drew turfmen from the local aristocracy and across the South. As was the case in the North, the races generally were held at distances of up to four miles, with victory going to the first horse that could win two or three heats. While sportsmen of these years admired speed in a horse, they also placed a premium on endurance, which they called "bottom." The conventions of social class were evident at all tracks in all sections, but the regularly scheduled sessions were public events. The following document lists the rules and regulations that governed the Metairie Jockey Club. The code indicates the sportsmen's concern for fair competition and wagering. It is reprinted from the New York Clipper, 23 May 1857, p. 40.

RULES AND REGULATIONS OF THE METAIRIE JOCKEY CLUB

RULE I. *Name.*—This Association shall be known by the name of the "Metairie Jockey Club of the State of Louisiana."

II. *Officers.*—The officers of the Club shall consist of a President, first and second Vice Presidents, a Secretary, and a Treasurer, who shall be elected annually at a meeting succeeding the April meeting; on his election the President shall appoint five Stewards, three Timers, and a Ladies' Committee of three.

III. *Duties of the President and Vice President.*—The President shall preside at all meetings of the club; shall act as judge in all races of the club, assisted by two Vice Presidents; he shall appoint two Distance Judges; and shall have power to appoint all officers of the day necessary to fill the places of absentees. In the absence of the President, the first Vice Presidents shall preside; and in his absence, the second Vice President shall preside. The presiding Judge, whether the President or one of the Vice Presidents, shall decide which horse wins a heat; but should he be unable to decide, he shall call for the opinion of his assistants, and the majority shall govern. The Judges shall keep their stand clear of any intrusion during the pendency of a heat; see that the riders are dressed in Jockey- style; instruct the riders before starting, and proclaim from the stand the time and result of the race. They shall decide all disputes; and from their decision there shall be no appeal, except to the Club; they shall receive no evidence of foul riding, except from the officers of the day. The President, or either Vice President, shall be authorized to call a meeting of the Club, whenever they may deem it proper or upon the written requisition of fifteen members of the Club.

IV. *Secretary.* The Secretary shall attend the Judges on each day's race; keep a book, in which he shall record the names of the members, the rules of the Club, the proceedings of each meeting, and the entries of horses for each day's race. He shall keep an account of each day's race, and shall publish the result in one newspaper published in New Orleans. He shall see that the riders are weighed before starting in the race, and after each heat. It shall also be his duty to see that the horses start with their appropriate weights.

V. *Treasurer.*—The Treasurer shall collect the subscriptions of members, employing assistance for that purpose when necessary. He shall pay out no money except when ordered by the Club, or in the recess of the Club, by the Executive Committee.

VI. *Stewards.*—The Stewards shall attend on the Course, preserve order, clear the track, keep the crowd from the horses when returning to the stand after the close of each heat, exercise vigilance to prevent disorder and detect foul riding. They may call to their aid such assistance as they may deem necessary on extraordinary occasions; and in the absence of the President and Vice Presidents, shall appoint judges for the day from among the members. On the track during a race, they shall be designated by a red badge. The Police of the Course shall be under their control.

VII. *Ladies' Committee.*—The Ladies' Committee shall receive ladies visiting the Course, at the door of their carriage, and escort them to the Ladies stand; and shall attend to their comfort while on the track. They shall be designated by a white badge.

VIII. *Patrol Judges.*—It shall be the duty of the Patrol Judges, preceding each heat, to repair to the places designated by the president, and see there is no foul riding; and after the heat, immediately to repair to the stand and make their report; before which report, the heat shall not be decided.

IX. *Distance Judges.*—During heats, the Distance Judges shall remain in the distance stand. At the termination of each heat, they shall repair to the Judges' stand, and report the horse or horses that may be distanced, and any foul riding they may detect.

X. *Membership.*—Members of the Club shall pay $50 a year, payable $25 at each race meeting. No badge shall be delivered until paid for. No gentleman shall be admitted in the members' or ladies' stand except as hereinafter provided. Any member of the Club shall have the privilege of introducing, at each race meeting, two non-residents of the State, by procuring a badge of the Treasurer, which badge shall have *printed* on it "invitation," and have *written* the name of the wearer and the name of the introducer. The price of the badge shall be $10. All badges shall be personal, and not transferable under any circumstance. Members of the Club shall be elected by ballot; and three black balls exclude the applicant.

XI. *Resignation of Members.*—Members wishing to resign, shall enclose their resignation to the Treasurer, at least ninety days previous to a race meeting; and the names of the members not resigning and failing to pay their subscription when applied to, shall be posted in the Judges' stand by the Treasurer, at 3 p.m., on the last day's race.

XII. *Postponement.*—The President and Vice Presidents may postpone a race for a purse, but only in case of bad weather or upon some extraordinary occasion.

XIII. *Of Persons Expelled from other Courses.* Any person who has been expelled from a Jockey Club, or ruled off any Course, will not be permitted to enter a horse for a purse or in a stake; nor shall he be permitted to turn, ride, or attend in any capacity, a horse on this Course, in any race under the control of the Club.

XIV. *Riders.*—Two riders from the same stable will not be permitted to ride in the same race, except by consent of the Judges; nor shall two horses from the same stable be allowed to run in the same race, except in a single heat race.

XV. *Colors.*—All riders shall be dressed in jockey costume. Gentlemen who first record their colors with the Secretary, shall be entitled to them, and no one else shall be permitted to ride in them. Gentlemen having recorded their colors, shall continue to ride in them until the record be altered with the Secretary. Jockeys shall not ride in colors not announced in the bills of the day. The Secretary shall post on the Judges' stand all colors that have been recorded.

XVI. *Entries.* All entries of horses to run for a purse, shall be made by a member of the Club, sealed and deposited in a box (kept for the purpose by the Secretary) before 4 o'clock, P.M., of the day previous to the race, unless the race of the day be not finished; and in such case, 15 minutes after the close of the race. Every entry shall describe the age, name, color, sex, sire, and dam of the horse, with the owner's name and colors. Any horse having run under a name, if said name be changed, the entry shall state the fact the first-time of entering after said change; and if sire or dam bear a name, said name must be stated. No entry shall be received after the time specified; and the box shall not be opened unless in the presence of two members of the Association. The place of horses to be determined at starting as they are drawn from the box.

XVII. *Weights.*—The following weights shall be carried, viz.: two-year-olds, 80 pounds; three-year-olds, 86 pounds; four-year- olds, 100 pounds; five-year-olds, 110 pounds; six-year-olds, 118 pounds; seven-year-olds and upwards, 124 pounds—three pounds allowed to mares and geldings. If any horse carry five pounds over his proper weight, it shall be the duty of the judge to announce it from the stand. No horse shall be allowed to start in any race, carrying more than five pounds over weight. In making weight, nothing shall be weighed from which a liquid can be wrung, and nothing shall be weighed off that was not weighed on.

XVIII. *Of Age.*—A horse's age shall be reckoned from the first day of May; that is to say, a colt foaled in the year 1850, shall be considered one-year-old on the first day of May 1851.

XIX. *Of Starting.* The horses shall be started by the tap of the drum, after which there shall be no recall.

XX. *False Starts.*—When a false start is made, no horse making the false start, nor any horse remaining at the stand shall have clothes thrown upon them, nor shall the rider be permitted to dismount, nor shall any delay be permitted, but the horses shall be started as soon as brought to the score. Horses making a false start, shall return to the stand by the nearest way. Any infringement of this rule shall be punished by not allowing the party or parties violating it to start in the race.

XXI. *Accidents.*—If an accident happen to a horse or rider at a start, the judges may grant as much delay as there is time allowed between the heats in the race in which the horses are about to contend.

XXII. *Distanced Horses; Distances.*—All horses whose heads have not reached the distance stand as soon as the leading horse arrives at the winning post, shall be declared distanced. All horses not bringing out their proper weight, or within two pounds of it, shall be declared distanced. If any jockey shall ride foul, his horse shall be declared distanced. Whenever the winner of a heat is distanced by any default in riding, weight, or otherwise, the heat shall be awarded to the next best horse. In heats of one mile, 60 yards shall be a distance. In heats of two miles, 100 yards shall be a distance. In heats of three miles, 130 yards shall be a distance. In heats of four miles, 150 yards shall be a distance. In heats of one mile, best of three in five, 80 yards shall be a distance.

XXIII. *Places of Horses.*—The horse to which the track is allotted shall take his place on the inner or left hand side of the Course; the others shall take their places on his right according to allotment. The winner of a heat shall, at the next start, have the track; the others shall take their positions on his right in the order in which they came out of the previous heat.

XXIV. *Winner of a Race; Dead Heats; Ruling Out.*—In the race best two in three, a horse that wins two heats or distances the field in one heat, wins the race. In the race best three in five, the horse that wins three heats, or distances the field, wins the race. The horse that first gets its head to the winning post, shall be considered the winner of the heat. In heats best two in three, a horse not winning one heat in five shall be ruled out. A dead heat shall be considered a heat, except with the horses that make it.

XXV. *Duties of Riders.*—Riders after a heat is ended, shall repair to the Judges'stand; they must not dismount until ordered by the Judges; nor suffer any person to touch or put cover upon their horses until ordered by the Judges to dismount, on pain of being distanced; and then with their saddles, shall repair to the scales to be weighed. A rider thrown, or taken by force from his horse, after passing the winning post, shall not be considered as having dismounted without permission of the Judges; and if disabled, may be carried to the Judges' stand to be weighed.

XXVI. *Bolting.*—If any horse shall run from the track into the field, he will be declared distanced, although he may come out ahead, unless he turn and again enter the course at the point from which he swerved, unless the Judges believed he lost ground by swerving.

XXVII. *Time Between Heats.*—The time between heats shall be twenty minutes for mile heats, thirty minutes for two mile heats; thirty-five minutes for three mile heats; forty-five minutes for four mile heats; and twenty-five minutes for mile heats, best three in five.

XXVIII. *Rider Falling.*—If a jockey falls from his horse while riding a heat, and another person of sufficient weight ride him in, he shall be considered as though the jockey had not fallen, provided he return to the spot where the jockey fell.

XXIX. *Foul Riding and Track.*—If a horse or rider shall cross, jostle, or strike another horse or rider, or do anything that impedes another horse, accidently or not, it is foul riding, and the horse that impedes the other shall be adjudged distanced. And if the Judges are satisfied that the riding was intentionally foul, or that the rider was instructed so to ride, the party or parties offending, shall not be allowed to ride, enter, or attend a horse over this Course in any race under the control of the Club. Although a leading horse is entitled to any part of the track, if he crosses from the right to the left, or from the inner to the outer side of the track, when a horse is so near him that in changing his position he compels the horse behind him to shorten his stride, or if he causes the rider to pull him out of his stride, it is foul riding. And if in passing a leading horse, the track is taken so soon after getting the lead as to cause the horse passed to shorten his stride, it is foul riding. All complaints of foul riding must be made before the horses start another heat; and if it happens in the last heat, then before the Judges leave the stand.

XXX. *Collusion.*—No compromise or agreement between two or more persons not to oppose each other, or to run jointly against any other person or persons, will be permitted. Upon satisfactory proof of the same being produced before the Judges, they shall declare the horses of such person distanced and the parties so offending shall be ruled off the course.

XXXI. *Of Frauds.*—Every horse started shall run a bona fide race. If any fraud be discovered, and the purse, stakes, or match money, has been paid, the same shall be restored on demand of the Judges, and by them paid over to the owner of the next best horse. If the money be not restored by the illegal owner, he shall be expelled from the Club, and shall ever thereafter be inelligible as a member. If not a member of the Club, he shall be prohibited from ever running a horse over the Course again.

XXXII. *Of Forfeits.*—A person owing a forfeit in any stake or match run over, or agreed to be run over any Course, shall not be allowed to start a horse for a purse or sweepstake, but no charge that such forfeit is due shall be heard unless before starting. No horse owned by a person prevented from starting one under the rules of the Club, shall be allowed to run, though said horse be entered in another name or found in another stable. Whenever the Judges are informed that a person has entered, or caused a horse to be entered or named in a race, in violation of any rule of the Club, they shall immediately make an examination of the evidence, so as to enable them to come to a correct decision upon the case.

XXXIII. *Disqualification as to Age.* Where there is a doubt about the age of a horse, the Judges may call in the assistance of persons in whose knowledge and honesty they have confidence to aid them in deciding the question. When a clear case of disqualification is made out, the entrance money is forfeited and they shall not allow the horse to start in the race; but if they have doubts, they may allow the horse to run, and if he prove a winner, they shall retain the money or purse, and give the parties sixty days to procure testimony touching the case. If the disqualification is made out, they shall pay the money to the owner of the horse that was placed best in the race.

XXXIV. *Of Aids.*—No person shall be permitted to strike a horse with a whip over three feet in length, to get him from the stand in the start, or to assist his speed in the running of a race; nor shall any person stand in the track to point out a path for the rider, under the penalty of expulsion from the Course.

XXXV. *Of Decorum.*—If any owner, trainer, rider, starter, or attendant of a horse use improper language to the Officers On the Course, or be guilty of improper conduct, the person so offending shall never be permitted to start, train, ride, turn or attend a horse over the Course again in any race under the control of the Club.

XXXVI. *Selling and Drawing.*—No person shall be permitted to draw or sell his horse (if by the sale the horse be drawn) during the pedency of a race, except with the permission of the Judges, under the penalty of being expelled from the Club.

XXXVII. *Sweepstakes and Matches; Death.*—In sweepstakes or matches, stakes shall be put up or forfeits paid before the riders are weighed for the race, in the order in which the horses are to be placed in the start; the order of starting to be determined by lot. In sweepstakes and matches, the parties to them may select the Judges for the race. All sweepstakes and matches advertised by the Club, are to be under its control and governed by its Rules; and when a stake has been closed, no nomination shall be changed without the consent of all parties to the stake. If an entered horse die, or a subscriber entering him die before the race, no forfeit shall be required.

XXXVIII. *Handicap.*—Horses only that have run the meeting, shall be permitted to start for a handicap purse. No horse shall be handicapped to carry extra weight, but for the purpose of equalizing the horse, a reduction of the regular weight may be made. The President, or acting President, shall handicap the horses, and the weights shall be announced immediately after the race of the day, previous to the handicap race. Gentlemen designing to start, shall, within one hour after the announcement, deposit their entries in the box.

XXXIX. *Cases Unprovided For.*—In all matters relating to the race or running not provided for in these Rules, the Judges for the day will decide and direct according to the best of their Judgement, and the usages of the turf in such cases.

XL. *Quorum.*—Fifteen members shall constitute a quorum, except for the alteration of Rules, when one-third of the members of the Club shall be present, and the affirmative vote of two-thirds of the members present shall be required to adopt any new rule, or to rescind, or alter any existing rule.

RULES FOR RUNNING AND BETTING

RULE I. *Catch Weights.*—Four inches are a hand. Fourteen pounds are a stone. Catch weights are parties to ride without weighing.

II. *Post Match.*—A post match is to insert the terms of the race in the articles, and to run any horse, without declaring what horse, until they come to the post to start.

III. *Winners.*—Horses that win a heat shall be considered better than those that do not win a heat; and those that win two heats, better than those that win but one, provided they not be distanced in the race. Of the horses that each win a heat, he shall be considered best that is best placed in the final heat of the race. Of the horses that have not won a heat, he shall be considered best that is best placed in the final heat of the race.

IV. *Distanced Horses.*—Distanced Horse are beaten by those that are not distanced. Drawn horses shall be considered distanced; horses ruled out shall be considered distanced. A horse distanced in a subsequent heat beats a horse distanced in a previous heat. Horses distanced in the same heat are equal.

V. *Second Horse.*—If, in the final heat of a race, there be but one horse placed, no horse shall be considered as second in the race.

VI. *Bets on the Field and Between Heats.*—Bets on the field are off unless all the horses advertised to run start, sweepstakes excepted; in them, if one horse is backed against the field, and only one of the field start, the bets must stand. All bets made between heats are off, unless all the horses that have the right, start in the next heat.

VII. *Bets During a Heat.*—Bets made during the running of a heat are not determined until the conclusion of the race, if the heat is not mentioned at the time.

VIII. *Dead Heat.*—In running heats, if it cannot be decided which horse is first, it shall be deemed a dead heat, and shall not be counted, but shall be considered a heat as regards all the rest of the horses in the race; and those only shall start for the next heat which would have been entitled had it been won by either horse making the dead heat.

IX. *Bets Off.*—A confirmed bet cannot be off but by mutual consent except in cases hereinafter mentioned.

X. *Making Stakes.*—Either of the bettors may demand stakes to be made; and on refusal, declare the bet to be void.

XI. *Declaring Off.*—If a bettor be absent on the day of running, public declaration of the bet may be made on the Course to the Judges, and a demand whether any person will make stakes for the absent parties; and if no person consent to do so, the bet may be declared void.

XII. *Bets Not Off.*—Bets agreed to be paid, or received elsewhere than at the place of running, or any other specified place, cannot be declared off on the Course.

XIII. *Bets off by Postponement.*—When a race is postponed from one day to another, all by bets, except they are play or pay, shall be off.

XIV. *The Field.*—The field shall comprise all the horses entered except the one who may be named against the remainder, unless in a stake where one horse is a field. The person who lays the odds, can choose his horse or the field; the withdrawal of a horse, previous to starting in the race, annuls the bet.

XV. *Play or Pay.*—When a bet is made on a horse, play or pay, the horse must start, or the party betting on him loses his bet.

XVI. *Untried and Maiden Horses.*—An untried stallion or mare, is one whose produce has never won. A maiden horse or mare, is one that has never one.

XVII. *Placing Horses.*—Where a bettor undertakes to place the horses in a race, he must give each specific place, as first, second, third, and so on. The word last, shall not be construed to mean fourth and distanced, if four start, but fourth only, and so on. A distanced horse must be placed distanced.

XVIII. *Bets and Placing.*—Horses shall be placed in a race, and be decided as they are placed in the official record.

AMERICAN THOROUGHBREDS IN ENGLAND

Between 1851 and 1860 sportsmen from the United States traveled to England to challenge their British counterparts in yachting, horse racing, and boxing. In 1856 Richard Ten Broeck led the American equestrian invasion of Europe with a group of speedy thoroughbreds. Born into an old Dutch aristocratic family in Albany, New York in 1812, Ten Broeck then moved south to become one of the dominant forces in southern racing by the 1840s. During the late 1850s he made a major bid to humble the proud British horsemen on their own turf. But unlike John C. Stevens, he could achieve only mixed success in England. At first he experienced only disappointments and tragedy; his horses ran poorly in their early tests, and two of his best thoroughbreds died. But his luck then changed for the better as Prioress won the Caesarewitch Stakes in 1857. Over the next few years his horses won the Goodwood Stakes and the Goodwood Cup. The following reports on his first major triumph with Prioress are reprinted from the New York Clipper, 31 October 1857, p. 218, and the New York Times, 14 October 1857.

GLORIOUS VICTORY OF PRIORESS

By the Baltic steamer, which arrived in New York on Sunday afternoon last, we received our files of English newspapers up to the 14th inst., the day on which she sailed from Liverpool. From them we learn the pleasing intelligence that one of the race horses which Mr. Ten Broeck took over to England to represent the American Turf, and on their own soil contest with English thoroughbreds for the supremacy of the Turf, *has proved the victor in the greatest handicap race in the Kingdom, after the finest struggle ever witnessed on any Course in the World!* We are proud to be able to record that PRIORESS has won the Caesarewitch Stakes at Newmarket, beating 33 competitors, and nobly retrieving the laurels which her previous running there, along with that of her stable companions, *Prior, Lecomte* and *Babylon,* had, it was thought, irrecoverably, lost. The race is stated to have been one of the finest on record, and our readers may form some idea of the thrilling excitement which pervaded the assembled thousands, that witnessed it, when we state that 34 horses started for the prize, and so closely was it contested at the finish, that the Judge pronounced it a *dead heat between three,* Prioress, El Hakim, and Queen Bess. The betting against Prioress, previous to the race, was *one hundred to one!* but, after the dead heat, when the betting men had witnessed the game performance of the previously despised American mare, it was only two to one against her winning, as they remembered the well-known endurance of our horses, as evinced in their ability to run heats of four miles in quick succession. We take especial credit to ourselves for the course we have pursued in reference to the American Horses in England, and Mr. Ten Broeck's spirited speculation in taking them there. Previous to the Goodwood Cup, when some of our contemporaries were anticipating their success in that race, loudly proclaiming that "it was all over but shouting," and strongly advising their friends and the public to "put on the pile" and back Prior and Prioress for no end of "almighty dollars," we earnestly advised our readers *not to be led away* by such claptrap counsel, but patiently "bide their time," and see what effect a long sea voyage, change of air, climate, and diet, would have upon their constitutions. With every confidence in the integrity and honor of Mr. Ten Broeck, yet knowing that in the Race for the Goodwood Cup, our horses would encounter some of the best and fleetest of English and French Racers, trained on the same soil, and ridden by the most experienced jockeys in the world, we felt justified in counselling our readers and the public to wait and see how our horses performed on the (to them) strange course, before recklessly investing their money on the American representatives. The result proved the wisdom and prudence of our counsel, and we had the satisfaction of knowing that we had prevented the money of our friends being hopelessly lost. But we have never lost our confidence in the capabilities and merits of our horses....Notwithstanding the many defeats of the American horses, we only regarded them as an earnest of the desire of Mr. Ten Broeck to *run his horses into condition,* and that he was of the same opinion on this subject as two of the ablest and cleverest trainers in England, Messers. Thomas Parr and John Osborn, that "to run your horses into condition it is the cheapest, as well as best to run them in public." Prioress seems to have at length, by this mode of training, to have got "fit," and we think that she would be in still finer condition for the Cambridgeshire Stakes, which would be run for on the 26th inst., over a part of the same Course at Newmarket, and for which she at present holds the proud position of *first favorite.* It is gratifying to learn, as we do from the English papers, that the success of the American mare was received with the heartiest cheering by our trans-atlantic brethren, and that Mr. Ten Broeck was warmly congraulated by the patrons of the turf present, on his maiden victory in England. This we fully expected, as one of the most distinguishing characteristics of John Bull, is, a noble and disinterested lover of fair play to all; and we know in New York this victory is equally as much a matter of congratulations and pleasure to Englishmen here, as it is to Americans themselves.

The Caesarewitch stakes, among the winners of which, the name of the American mare, Prioress, is now enrolled, is a race which was established at Newmarket in 1839, in honor of the present Emperor of Russia, who in that year paid a visit to the "Metropolis of the Turf," along with his brother, the Grand Duke Michael, in whose honor the stake which bears that name was instituted.

...no aged horse has yet been victorious for it. The six-year olds have triumphed twice, the fives thrice, the fours seven times, and the three-year olds seven times.

The value of the stake this year is $8,005, out of which the second horse receives $250 and the judge $150. It was stated a short time since in the *Racing Times,* an English sporting paper, that Mr. Ten Broeck had backed Prioress for L800, and as her price at starting was one hundred to one, it is very probable that he would entrust her with an additional sum at that price, so that we may reasonably suppose his aggregate winnings on this single race will be nearly *half a million dollars!*...Fordham was substituted for Tankesley as the rider of Prioress in the second heat. The judiciousness of this step was apparent, as by the change the prince of English light-weight Jockies was entrusted with the pilotage of the mare, and there is not doubt that if he had ridden her in the dead heat that he would have won with her. The ignorant and ridiculous assertion of Gilpatrick, "that if the American horses were ridden in the same manner as English horses are by their jockies, they would run away with them," was proved to be false, as the tiny jockey was obliged to use his whip pretty freely to rouse the mare to enable her to win. It is exceedingly probable that this fortunate and artistic jockey will ride her for the Cambridgeshire, and it may be "on the cards" for him to achieve the hitherto unperformed feat of winning both these great handicaps on the same horse. Should he succeed in accomplishing this on Prioress, the triumph of the American horses will be complete. Their defeats at Goodwood, Lewes, Warwick, and Chester, will be effectually wiped out, and English sportsmen will have learned to entertain a far higher estimate of American bred horses than their opening career led them to expect.

REPORT OF THE RACE FROM THE LONDON TIMES, 14 OCTOBER 1857

The flag was dropped to a beautiful start. Dusty Miller bore his colors to the front, with Queen Bess, Cerva, M. Dobler, and the Plush Colt following nearly in the order named, Odd Trick, Fright, Emulator, Zigzag, Warlock, Princess and Poodle lying in the middle of the ruck. These positions were unchanged until reaching the ditch, when Cerva rushed to the front, Queen Bess being in close attendance upon her, with Odd Trick third, Emulator, El Hakim, Prioress, Fright, Zigzag, Warlock and the Plush Colt forming the next lot. At the Bushes the pace began to tell, and Warlock, Plush Colt, and Poodle dropped back, and Cerva resigned the lead to Queen Bess. As they descended the hill, Odd Trick, Emulator and Zigzag also disappeared from the front. On approaching the cords Queen Bess, with El Hakim at her neck, still held a slight lead, with Prioress running by herself on the far side third, Fright, Zigzag, Warlock and Emulator showing in front of the ruck. One of the most exciting Caesarewitch finishes ever seen then ensued. Prioress half way up the cords seemed to be about coming in alone, but the tiny jockies of El Hakim and Queen Bess made a determined set to, and the judge unable to separate the first three pronounced a dead heat with Prioress, Queen Bess, and El Hakim; Fright was next about a length and-a-half behin them. Zigzag was fifth, about a length in advance of Warlock, who was sixth, and Martinet seventh; Emulator and Saunterer headed the next lot that straggled in. In the extreme rear, pulled up, were St. Giles, Wild Honey, Poodle, Fisherman, Black Tommy and the Poacher.

DECIDING HEAT

Mr. Ten Broeck's Prioress, by Sovereign (bred in America,) 4 yrs. 6 st. 9 lbs. (Fordham)   1
Captain Smith's El Hakim, 3 yrs., 6 st. 9 lbs. (Bray)   2
Mr. Saxon's Queen Bess, 3 yrs., 4 st. 10 lbs. (Grimshaw) 3
Betting — 5-4 against El Hakim, 2 to 1 against Prioress, 3 to 1 against Queen Bess. The "heat" was run after the last race in a deepening twilight, which rendered it impossible to distinguish the colors of the riders at a distance. El Hakim was first off, but after going about 50 yards Prioress, overpowering Fordham, rushed to the front, and carried on the running to the ditch gap, where she was pulled back, and lay about three lengths in the rear. Queen Bess going on with the lead, closely attended by El Hakim. On coming down the bushes hill Prioress hung to the left, and a shout was raised of "the American's beaten!" But Fordham roused the mare with his whip, and before reaching the foot of the hill she bore her colors in advance, and quitting her opponents half-way up the cords won cleverly by a length-and-a half; El Hakim beating Queen Bess by a head only for second place. A loud and prolonged cheer hailed the triumph of the American colors, and Mr. Ten Broeck was warmly congratulated upon the first victory achieved by him in England. An objection was made by the rider of Queen Bess against the rider of El Hakim, on the ground of a cross.

TROTTING

While thoroughbred racing declined in popularity in the North during the 1840s and 1850s, harness racing enjoyed increasing success among the masses. Trotting and pacing were well suited to commercialization because they were relatively inexpensive and had great appeal to middle class city people and farmers. During these years the sport became a favorite amusement at county fairs, but it remained strongest in urban areas, especially New York City. In 1858 there were approximately seventy tracks in the nation, with at least seven in the New York metropolitan area. Between 6,000 and 8,000 attended leading matches each year, and several thousand more turned out to see races featuring such champions as Lady Suffolk, Flora Temple, Ethan Allen, and Princess. The following rules and regulations for trotting on New York's Union Course, adopted in 1848, are reprinted from the New York Clipper, 9 May 1857, p. 24.

RULES AND REGULATIONS ADOPTED FOR THE UNION COURSE, LONG ISLAND, 1848

At a meeting of the supporters and admirers of Trotting and Pacing held at the house of Messrs. Green and Jessel, in New York, on the first day of March, 1848, the following Rules and Regulations for the government of all Trotting and Pacing matches, to come off on the Union Course, Long Island, were unanimously agreed upon.

Article 1.—*Nature of Rules.*—All Matches of Sweepstakes which shall come off over this Course, will be Governed by these Rules, unless the contrary is mutually agreed upon by the parties making such match or stake.

Art. 2.— *Power of Postponement.*—In case of unfavorable weather, or other unavoidable causes, all Purses, Matches, or Sweepstakes announced to come off, to which the proprietors contribute, they shall have the power to postpone to a future day, upon giving notice of the same.

Art. 3.— *Qualifications of Horses Starting.*—Horses trained in the same stable, or owned in part by the same person, within three days, shall not start for a Purse; and horses so entered shall forfeit their entrance. A horse starting alone shall receive but one half of the Purse. Horses deemed by the Judges not fair trotting horses, shall be ruled off previous to, or distanced at the termination of the heat.

Art. 4.— *Entries*—All entries shall be made under a seal, enclosing the entrance money (ten percent on the purse), and addressed to the proprietor, at such time and place as may have been previously designated by advertisement.

Art. 5.—*Weight to be Carried.*—Every trotting horse starting for Match, Purse, or Stake, shall carry one hundred and forty-five pounds, if in harness; the weight of the sulky and harness not to be considered. Pacing horses liable to same rule.

Art. 6.—*Distances.*—A distance for mile heats, best three in five, shall be one hundred yards; for one mile heats, eighty yards; and for every additional mile, an additional eighty yards.

Art. 7.—*Time between Heats.*—The time between heats shall be, for one mile, twenty minutes; and for every additional mile an additional five minutes.

Art. 8.—*Power of Judges.*—There shall be chosen, by the Proprietor of the Course, or Stewards, three Judges to preside over a race for purses, and by them an additional Judge shall be appointed for the distance stand; they may, also, during or previous to a race, appoint Inspectors at any part of the Course, whose reports, and theirs alone, shall be received of any foul riding or driving.

Art. 9.—*Difference of Opinion between Judges.*—Should a difference of opinion exist between the Judges in the starting stand on any questions, a majority shall govern.

Art. 10.—*Judges' Duties.*—The Judges shall order the horses saddled or harnessed five minutes previous to the time appointed for starting; any rider or driver causing undue detention after being called up, by making false starts or otherwise; the Judges may give the word to start without reference to the situation of the horse so offending, unless convinced such delay is unavoidable on the part of the rider or driver, in which case not more then thirty minutes shall be consumed in attempting to start, and at the expiration of that time, the horse or horses ready to start shall receive word.

Art. 11.—*Starting Horses.*—The pole shall be drawn for by the Judges; the horse winning a heat shall, for the succeeding heats, be entitled to a choice of the track; on coming out on the last stretch, each horse shall retain the track first selected; any horse deviating shall be distanced.

Art. 12.—*Riders or Drivers.*—Riders and drivers shall not be permitted to start unless dressed in jockey style.

Art. 13.—*Weights of Riders and Drivers.*—Riders and drivers shall weigh in the presence of one or more of the Judges previous to starting; and after a heat, are to come up to the starting stand, and not dismount until so ordered by the Judges; any rider or driver disobeying, shall, on weighing, be precluded from the benefit of the weight of his saddle and whip, and if not full weight shall be distanced.

Art. 14.—*Penalty for Foul Riding and Driving.* A rider or driver committing any act which the judges may deem foul riding or driving, shall be distanced.

Art. 15.—*Horse Breaking.*—Should any horse break from his trot or pace, it shall be the duty of the rider or driver to pull his horse to a trot or pace immediately, and in the case of the rider or driver refusing to do so, the penalty shall be, that the next best horse shall have the heat; if the rider or driver should comply with the above, and he should gain by such a break, twice the distance so gained shall be taken away on the coming out; a horse breaking on the score shall not lose the heat by doing so.

Art. 16.—*The Winning Horse.*—A horse must win two heats to be entitled to the purse, unless he distance all other horses in one heat. A distanced horse in a dead heat shall not start again.

Art. 17.—*Relative to Heats.*—A horse not winning one heat in three shall not start for a fourth heat, unless such horse shall have made a dead heat. When a dead heat is made between two horses, that if either had won the heat the race would have been decided, they two only shall start again; in races best three in five, a horse shall win one heat in five to be allowed to start for the sixth heat, unless such horse shall have made a dead heat; such horses as are prevented from starting by this rule, shall be considered drawn and not distanced.

Art. 18.—*On Heats and Distances.*—If two horses each win a heat and neither are distanced in the race, the one coming out ahead on the last heat to be considered the best. The same rule to be applied to horses neither winning a heat and neither distanced. If one horse wins a heat, he is better than one that does not, providing he does not get distanced in the race, then the other, if not distanced shall be best. A horse that wins a heat and is distanced is better than one not winning a heat and being distanced in the same heat. A horse distanced in the second heat is better than one distanced in the first heat.

Art. 19.—*Horses Drawn.*—Horses drawn before the conclusion of a race shall be considered distanced.

Art. 20.—*Outside Bets.*—In all matches made play or pay, outside bets not to be considered P.P. unless so understood by the parties.

Art. 21.—*Of P.P. Matches.*—All moneys bet on P.P. matches by outside bettors, are not considered P.P..

Art. 22.—*Betting—Absent Betters.* A confirmed bet cannot be let off without mutual consent. If either party be absent at the time of trotting, and the money be not staked, the party present may declare the bet void, in the presence of the judges, unless some party will stake the money betted for the absentee.

Art. 23.—*Compromised Matches.*—All bets made by outside betters on compromised matches, are considered drawn.

Art. 24.—*Betters of Odds, &c.,*—The person who bets the odds, has a right to choose the horse or the field. When he has chosen his horse, the field is what starts against him; but there is no field unless one starts with him. If odds are bet without naming the horses before the trot is over, it must be determined as the odds were at the time of making it. Bets made in trotting are not determined till the purse is won, if the best heat is not specified at the time of betting.

Art. 25.—*Horses Excluded from Starting or Distanced.*—All bets made on horses precluded from starting (by rule 19), being distanced in the race, or on such horses against each other, shall be drawn.

Art. 26.—*In Cases of Dispute and Improper Conduct.*—In all cases of dispute, not provided for by the rules, the judges for the day will decide finally. In case of a trot or match being proved to their satisfaction to have been made or conducted improperly, or dishonestly, on the part of the principles, they shall have power to declare all bets void.

Art. 27.—*Size of Whips to be Used.*—No rider or driver shall be allowed any other than a reasonable length of whip, viz.: for middle horses, two feet ten inches; sulky, four feet eight inches; wagon, five feet ten inches.

Art. 28. —*In Case of Accidents.*—In case of accidents, but five minutes shall be allowed over the time specified in Rule No. 10, unless the judges think more time is necessary.

Art. 29.—*Judges' Stand.*—No person shall be allowed in the judges' stand but the judges, reporters, and members, at the time of trotting.

Art. 30.—*In Case of Death.*—All engagements are void upon the decease of either party before being determined.

FLORA TEMPLE AND PRINCESS

The success of harness racing in the United States during the antebellum era depended to a great extent on the famed champion trotters of that era. The most celebrated of all was Lady Suffolk, foaled in 1833, who retired in 1853. The "Old Grey Mare" competed in 162 events and won between $35,000 and $60,000 during her distinguished career. Her successor was Flora Temple, the "Queen of the Turf," who eclipsed all previous harness racing records in her contests against Ethan Allen, Princess, and other challengers. The following account of her series of races against Princess, her California rival, highlights the theme of the East against the West in harness racing. It also reveals the deep doubts among sporting journalists about the integrity of these matches. These reports are reprinted from the New York Clipper, 25 June 1859, pp. 74, 76, 2 July 1859, p. 84, 20 August 1859, p. 144, 27 August 1859, p. 151.

TROTTING MATCH BETWEEN FLORA TEMPLE AND PRINCESS
JUNE 16, 1859

At the lowest estimate, not less than twenty thousand persons assembled to witness a three-mile struggle between these two well known trotters, Flora (of course, "Queen of the Turf,") and Princess, who has achieved such a high reputation in California as to be brought back here and matched against any of the prominent champions of this style of equestrian movement against time. Flora's long catalogue of triumphs, and Princess's big lift of $39,500, when she stepped off her ten mile trot in California, were "things to be considered," and betting ranged from 2 to 1 on Flora away round to going promiscuously blind either way. Many, who now saw Princess for the first time, although she is twelve years old, were delighted to observe her graceful beauty, and, as her color is a dark bay, of a much more pleasing shade than that of Flora, "appearances" were very much in her favor. Time bets of the wildest kind were made by parties who felt their preferences in the pockets, but, as the result showed time which could hardly be called remarkable, even for second class horses, we suspect that a good many people must have "got a jog on the funny bone" when they put their hands in to their pockets on the time betting, probably influenced by a remembrance of Old Dutchman's celebrated performances. Flora's friends mustered strong, and, while glancing at her bob tail, bony shanks, and lazy walk, they tipped the wink to each other as they thought of what has been "fetched out of her," especially when "walking the chalk" with such a "straightener out" as Ethan Allen. By the time the crowd got well consolidated and the track cleared, it was four o'clock, and a good rattling shower began to come down. Those who relished a three-mile race, and those who have "no particular fancy," were all alike now, for retreat was impossible, and the result was the only thing cared for, which finally "came out" as follows: —
THURSDAY, JUNE 16 — Match for $5,000, three mile heats, to wagons.

J. McMann named b m Flora Temple		1 1
J. Eoff named b m Princess		2 2
Time	First Heat	Second Heat
First Mile	2:37	2:37 1/2
Second Mile	2:40 1/2	2:36 1/2
Third Mile	2:36 1/2	2:45 1/2
	7:54	7:59 1/2

At the start, Princess led by about half a length on the inside, and at the quarter pole she had increased the lead to a couple of lengths. On reaching the half mile, Flora had gained a little, but Princess shook her off and doubled the distance. In the home stretch, Flora made intimations of closing up, and when they passed the stand, Princess led by only a length. The second mile followed suit, with variations, and they passed the stand in a similar relation to each other, Princess having kept the lead. The first half of the last mile brought out an intense struggle for a change of lead on the part of Flora, and she did just manage to show her nose ahead at the half-mile pole. Princess then made a tremendous rally, and they stepped into the lower turn head and head. The effort thus made by Princess was fatal for this heat, as Flora swung in on the home stretch with the squarest kind of work, putting the yards behind her like a woman with plenty of breadth in her dress, and won the heat by half a dozen lengths, looking as fresh as a shopping dame after buying out of "a bankrupt's stock." That was the broad and the long of that heat. By this time the weather began to clear up, the air was more refreshing, but the betting was more "abroad" than ever. Much dissatisfaction was expressed when observing that Flora was much below her usual condition, while Princess seemed capable of a much easier gait with more speed. Apart from the usual expressions on such occasions, an intense anxiety was felt to know how the next heat would eventuate. When the mares took the word for the second heat, Flora helped herself to the lead with about half a length on the inside. This was increased to three lengths at the quarter pole, and this relative difference was maintaned all through the first mile and part of the second; but, at the close of the second, Flora led by only a length and a half. They jogged along, as the Californians say, "like the Gouginiron Sisters," on the third mile; at the quarter pole, Flora made the diff three lengths, and although she then cast one of her fore shoes, she kept on propelling as if disinclined to take any "nantangiango" (nonsense) from California. Princess also took everything "koind o' comfortable loike," as if she knew manners better than to beat the "Queen" while playing at cards. On the home stretch, Flora got mighty fidgetty, breaking into a gallop and looking around, as if for a favorite doctor. Before she could be brought to her work, Princess gained slowly on her, and when abreast of the draw gate, the California favorite got a sniff of Flora's nearest wheel. Flora broke again, and again did Princess (never breaking once,) range up alongside to do the friendly. Flora now seemed to feel her "bignitude" as the "Queen of the Turf," and made an immense burst of square trotting which brought her in winner half a length. The cheering for Flora was tremendous, while the dissatisfaction with the driver of Princess, (Mr. Eoff,) had amounted to positive execrations. In fact, duty compels us to state that the "good natured public" seemed to be in a considerable of a huff with Mr. Eoff, many persons expressing their belief that the whole thing was a "throw off" of the most barefaced kind. There need be no doubt that Princess, when fairly recovered from her recent return trip from California, would give any competitor in the trotting line a chance to examine her heels while she sets the winning time herself. Her age is now well mellowed, and the many points she owes to a judicious admixture of high blood, seems to make her more valuable than ever. Both these mares may be considered as "well seasoned," if we may be allowed to apply such an expression in relation to the feminine gender.

EDITORIAL

FLORA TEMPLE AND PRINCESS—We have had another great trotting match, and another one-sided affair it proved to be. When Princess, the California mare, and Flora Temple, of New York, were first matched, it was expected that the race would prove to be one of the best of the season, and from the fact that Princess "talked up" as one of the fastest trotters on the turf, and possessing uncommon staying qualities, it was looked upon by outsiders as rather venturesome in the "little bay mare" to tackle her in a match at three-mile heats; and the result was that betting became pretty lively, and the California mare seemed to have plenty of backers. On the day of the race, however, Flora was the favorite at long odds, longer, in truth, than a good, square match would warrant her friends in laying, in some few instances offers being made of 100 to 5 on Flora, and this, too, it should be borne in mind, when it was reported that the California mare, in a trial a day or two previous on the same race track, had made better time by two or three seconds than was ever made by Flora Temple.

It seems to be the general impression that the match was one of those concocted affairs which so frequently occur in this vicinity, by which the unwary are swindled, or what may be a more filling term, robbed of their money. What are the facts? Why, where two of the fleetest trotters in the world are pitted together, it is but fair to presume that uncommon fast time should have been made, yet the pace was moderate, and Princess, it appears, was purposely held in, when, had she been wanted, she could have gone to the fore like a streak. It was not on the cards for her to win on that day, and the well-prepared "arrangements" entered into on making, or soon after making the match, were faithfully carried out to the letter.

The readers of the CLIPPER well know that we have always taken a decided stand against a number of our Long Island jockies, and owners of certain trotting horses hereaway. We have repeatedly urged our readers to be on their guard against these parties; we have pointed out instances where the people have been sold as well as the races; we have endeavored by every means within our power to protect the people from the shameful impositions in turf matters that have been, and still are, perpetuated on Long Island. Were the entire press to speak out, as we have done, and condemn those engaged in thus defrauding the public, the evil might be corrected, but a little advertising patronage seems sufficient to lock the jaws of the press, while the very patrons of that press are being barefacedly robbed, time and time again. Is it to continue thus? If so, it were better to abolish every race track on Long Island.

If a man picks another's pocket, on evidence of the fact he is sent to prison. What is the difference between professional pickpockets and those who rob by means of dishonest racing and trotting on our race courses? Not a particle. A man who bets on an event which had been arranged beforehand, he knowing the secret of the fraud intended, and he with whom he bets being innocent of all wrong, might just as well put his hand in that man's pocket and rob him of his money. The latter has not the ghost of a chance to win....

Why, the money taken at the gates shoud have been sufficient to repay owners, jockies, and all, for the trouble and expense of getting up the race. Now, the question is, are the owners or the drivers to blame, or do the drivers alone deserve censure? Let us have the facts. If the owners do not exculpate themselves from the suspicion that now attaches to them, the public will not place confidence in them herafter, but will look upon them as conniving at a wrong upon the public. If *they* are innocent, then we can very well understand who are guilty....

Another match between the same horses is set down for the 23d inst., and we again urge our readers to have nothing to do with the affair. Let your absence from the course show that you will not encourage such disgraceful exhibitions. We presume, according to precedents, that Princess may be permitted to win on this occasion.

SECOND MATCH BETWEEN PRINCESS AND FLORA TEMPLE

ECLIPSE COURSE, L. I. — Match $5000. Two mile heats, in harness.

	First Heat	Second Heat
J.E. Eoff b m Princess	1	1
D. Tallman b m Flora Temple	2	2

Time —	First Heat	Second Heat
Half Mile	1:13	1:17
Mile	2:26	2:34
Second Mile	2:36	2:31
Total	5:02	5:05

There were not so many spectators on this as on the previous occasion; probably about 5000, at the utmost, is a fair estimate; this falling off was occasioned, no doubt, by the unpleasant rumors associated with the former event, the idea being quite prevalent that both matches were part and parcel of the same "little arrangement." Some of our leading turfmen stuck by the little bay mare before the race, and invested freely on her at the rate of 100 to 70; those who are admitted behind the scenes occasionally, and who help to pull the wires now and then, very complacently took the odds as long as they were offered, and managed to "get on" a good pile. Those who read the CLIPPER of last week, in which we gave it as our impression that Princess would win on the occasion, seem to have had a joyous time of it, and our pugilistic friends were at peace with all mankind, for they went California up to the hub.

The course was in good trim, and extraordinary time was looked for, Flora was in fine fettle, and Princess was also well up to the mark. They scored several times without avail, but at last they got a good send off, and now commenced the tug of war. Eoff, who had caused so much dissatisfaction, on the previous match, was again entrusted with the pilotage of the California mare, he having stated that if he did not win the first heat, he would give up his place to another driver, an "instance of confidence" rarely exhibited. The pace was fast from the jump, and although Flora was a trifle in the lead, yet Princess flew past her on the first quarter, and kept in front during the remainder of the mile, Flora making a vigorous effort to regain her place, but without effect; the race was intensely exciting during this struggle, and the quick time made, 2:26, was an evidence that both were doing their prettiest. On going on to the second mile, Princess kept on at the same rapid gait, while Flora fell off slightly; in an endeavor to close up the space between them the Temple fell to pieces, and a long stretch of daylight shone in between them. Up to the half mile pole, making a mile and a half in all, Princess was going at terrific speed. On the backstretch, during Flora's effort to overtake her rival, her hind feet came in contact with her fore, and tore off both shoes, and likewise cutting her forequarters, and drawing first blood. This sad mishap gave Princess no further cause for alarm, and she trotted in a winner of the heat at a moderate pace, Flora following a long way in the rear, some sixty or seventy yards. It would have been merciful to have withdrawn the little mare after the accident; but this was not done; and, after the usual intervening time, they were called up for the second heat. The supporters of

Flora had now turned their batteries against the little thing, and pepper was freely administered, Princess being the favorite at big odds, with few or no takers. Flora behaved badly on getting away, and it was apparent that she would have but little chance now, the effects of the accident beginning to tell upon her. Princess led on the home stretch, with Flora pressing very closely on the half-mile; here, however, the Californian made a spurt, and drew away; on the coming in side, Flora made another effort, but the speed had left her, and Princess went past the stand on the first mile a length in advance. During the second mile, Flora made repeated efforts for the lead, but Princess outfooted her whenever her driver deemed it necessary, and in this way they came home, Princess winning the heat and the race, after some of the best "trials of speed" witnessed on that track. The friends of Flora looked considerably down in the mouth, and talked some of having another dash at the Californian at some future time, contending that as they have had a two, and a three-mile go, it is but fair that a race at mile heats should decide the rubber. The easy movement and stride of Princess was much admired. One of our newsboy friends, who had wagered "coffee and cakes" on Princess, exclaimed in the exuberance of his feelings as he witnessed her leadng the little mare: "Isn't she hell?" We did not stop to argue the point with the little devil, but "left him alone in his glory." We noticed a number of our "representatives in Councils assembled," on the track, and of fast boys there was a legion from the Bowery and Broadway. Livery stable keepers were cleared out of vehicles, at four dollars the half-day for a single nag, and teams in proportion. These big trotting matches are placers of gold to all in any way interested in horse flesh, whether to owner, keeper, or hostler. The various stopping places "on the road," where is to be found "entertainment for man and beast," reap abundant harvests on all such occasions, albeit the "entertainment" at some of them is much better suited to the latter than the former. Flora Temple is still "Queen of the Trotting Turf," and until her time is eclipsed by Princess or some other rival, she will continue to "hold the honor."

UNPRECEDENTED TROTTING
THE QUICKEST TIME EVER MADE IN TROTTING

ECLIPSE COURSE, L. I. — Tuesday, August 9. — Purse, $1,000; mile heats, best three in five, in harness.

J. McMann entered b. m. Flora Temple	1 1 1
J. Eoff entered b. m. Princess	2 2 2

Time, 2:23 1/2; 2:22; 2:23 1/2

There were about five thousand spectators on the ground, at one dollar a pop — a considerable falling off from the previous matches, when some 10,000 to 15,000 were in attendance. Now, the Californian was the favorite previous to the start, although mile heats were known to be Flora's race.

THE START

Flora had the inside place, and on getting off she at once made play for the lead, gradually opening a gap which the Princess did not appear able to close, the little

Queen going at such a gait as to surprise the driver of Princess, who was fearful of urging his mare, she being a bad breaker. Flora went in a winner in *two minutes, twenty-three and a half seconds!* being one second quicker than was ever before made. Of course Flora now had the call, the Californians being very shy, and requiring long odds before investing. On getting away for the second heat, Princess was let out, but almost immediately broke into a run, Flora gliding by like a streak, and keeping down to it beautifully; Princess was in a fair way of being distanced, the break sending her a long distance in the rear. On the back-stretch the Californian settled down at a ripping pace, lessening the space between her and the chase, but without being able to get nearer than thirty yards of Flora, who crossed the score in the unparalleled time of *two minutes and twenty two seconds!* the best time on the record. What a shout went up when this extraordinary performance was proclaimed, and how the Yorkers "smiled" over the success of their little Queen. Princess was now looked upon as a dead cock in the pit, and one individual we heard offer to bet the Astor House against a pile of bricks that Flora would win the race, but the bet was not taken. The third and last heat was the most interesting in the match, Princess doing very well on the first half, both going at terrific speed; Flora, however, put on a little more steam, which Princess was unable to carry, and in the effort to keep up with the Queen, the Californian lost her footing, went up, and Flora Temple won the heat (and race) in the still wonderful time of *two minutes, twenty-three and a half seconds!* Whether Princess could have done better, we have no direct means of knowing. When she arrived here we heard marvelous stories of her speed, and it was remarked that Flora would be compelled to show 2:20 before Princess would acknowledge her superiority. They are to go again on the 16th, at two-mile heats, and if former arrangements are adhered to, Princess ought to win.

FOURTH FLURRY BETWEEN FLORA TEMPLE AND PRINCESS
UNPRECEDENTED TWO-MILE TIME, IN HARNESS

That "honesty is the best policy" is a lesson taught in more places than school rooms or copy books. It was illustrated with any amount of "hi! hi! hi!" on the above occasion, when trotting and truth went along more nearly neck and neck than "some people" intended or expected. A lovely day and a delightful breeze made our humanitarian studies pleasant enough, but the recollection of sundry dirty tricks in relation to suburban trots made the contemplation of "man's inhumanity to man" anything but agreeable. "A" purse of $1,000 was on the programme, but "that" purse seemed very much like a pig's — ear. Such was the tone of public opinion while discussing the two mile time heretofore made, beginning with the days when Lady Suffolk, Ripton, and Confidence, ranged along at about 5:10, and the former put down her best foot at 5:08. How Lady Moscow shaved her strop down to 5:04. But Flora Temple was the gal that first got inside of the even 5m., when put in opposition to Hero, for Flo then showed 4:57, and high old gal she, for every since she has been going on "eclipsing" herself. At last, we now have to record that Missy Flo came in winner on the first heat in 4:50 1/2! This is the fastest two-mile time, in harness; and, if Flora let out her leather at that rate merely for a lift of gate money, there is no knowing what the little bay mare may do next. At present, she must be confessed the Queen of the Trotting Turf....

ECLIPSE COURSE, L . I., Aug. 16. — Trot at two-mile heats, in harness, for gate money, twenty per cent. to the track.

James McMann named b m Flora Temple   1 1
James Eoff named b m Princess   2 2

TIME.

	1st Heat.		*2d Heat*
First mile	2:23	First mile	2:24
Second mile	2:27 1/2	Second mile	2:41
Total	4:50 1/2	Total	5:05

Chapter 8

FIELD SPORTS

During the middle years of the nineteenth century North Americans enjoyed a variety of rural pastimes. Since urbanization was still in its early stages, most of the population lived close to woods, fields, and streams. Recreational fishing, hunting, boating, and coursing (hunting game with dogs) remained very popular in Canada and the United States. Sportsmen transformed a few of these traditional activities into the competitive sports of archery and target and pigeon shooting. By the 1850s various kinds of archery and rifle clubs and target and militia companies proliferated in towns and cities, as enthusiasts of the bow and arrow and the gun began to modernize their favorite amusements.

The history of organized archery in the United States dates from 3 September 1828, when a group of gentlemen founded the United Bowmen of Philadelphia. Between 1841 and 1858 these upper class sportsmen gathered at Fountain Green, a rustic spot overlooking the Schuylkill River about six miles from the center of the city. The members called their grounds "Sherwood Forest" and met regularly for practice and prize contests. The first document in this chapter presents excerpts from the *Constitution and Regulations of the United Bowmen of Philadelphia,* published in 1844. They observed strict etiquette and dressed in uniforms for all meetings, with the exception of an informal picnic every July fourth. In 1858 the club accepted the invitation of Dr. William Camac to shoot on his estate of Woodvale in what is now North Philadelphia. The United Bowmen suspended operations after that season, but later generations of Philadelphians resurrected the association and the founders' love of archery.

Those who preferred the rifle to the bow and arrow formed a variety of clubs. In 1848 a few men founded the Central New York Rifle Club, and in 1858 others launched the National Rifle Club, based in Framingham, Massachusetts. The rules and regulations of the latter organization reflect the influence of the code of the former group. Both sets of laws appear below. In the towns and cities many craftsmen and other middle class citizens joined target companies, which sometimes were linked to regular militia units. Local political organizations usually promoted and financed these associations. During the 1850s target companies generally met once a year for shooting contests accompanied by much music, food, and drink. Several ethnic groups founded their own clubs, as Swiss and German marksmen demonstrated their proficiency in shooting festivals. Finally, the 1850s also witnessed the increasing popularity of pigeon shooting tournaments. This chapter concludes with the rules and results of a grand international competition held in 1858 in Jersey City, New Jersey.

ARCHERY

The United Bowmen of Philadelphia was an exclusive club that limited its membership to twenty-five adult males. Their annual prize-meeting days were important social occasions that attracted an elite audience. The bowmen always shot one at a time in squads of four to a target, and they marched down the field in strict formation with military precision. The silver punch bowl that was awarded to their champion each year is now on display at the Historical Society of Pennsylvania. The following excerpts from the *Constitution and Regulations of the United Bowmen of Philadelphia* (Philadelphia, 1844), pp. 1, 9-11, are reprinted with the permission of the Historical Society of Pennsylvania.

CONSTITUTION AND REGULATIONS OF THE UNITED BOWMEN OF PHILADELPHIA, 1844
PREAMBLE

Archery has been exercised from the most remote ages of antiquity, and, in modern times, has always been considered a useful and polite accomplishment, affording in its practice a vigorous and beneficial exercise, conducive to health and recreation. With these impressions, we, the subscribers, have associated ourselves together, under the name and title of THE UNITED BOWMEN OF PHILADELPHIA; and, for the better advancement of our views, mutually pledge ourselves to be governed by the following Constitution and Regulations....

REGULATIONS

I.

The meetings for practice shall be held weekly at the shooting ground of the club, during the shooting season. The hour meeting on the ground shall be at half past three o'clock during the months of May, June, July and August, at three o'clock in September, and at half past two o'clock in October.

II.

On the last Saturday of each month during the season, a field-day prize, not exceeding three dollars in value, shall be shot for (not less than four members contending for the same) at a distance to be determined by a vote thereon. In case of rain, or other sufficient cause, to prevent the shooting on the regular field day, the prize shall be contended for at the next practice meeting, which prize shall be awarded to the member having the highest value.

III.

The first Saturday in May shall be the commencement, and the last Saturday in October the end of the shooting season.

IV.

The members of the club shall serve in rotation, (commencing at the head of the roll,) as captain of the target, at each field-day and practice meeting. The captain shall have charge of the targets, and arrange the divisions. It shall be his duty to decide on all hits, (from which decision there shall be no appeal,) and see the same are properly registered upon the cards, which he must subsequently deliver to the Recorder.

V.

At practice meetings, the distance shall be at the discretion of the captain of the target, not exceeding, however, one hundred and twenty-five yards, not less than sixty yards, and the number of rounds shall be fourteen.

VI.

Any member absenting himself from eight practice meetings, including the field days, shall render himself liable to be stricken from the roll, unless he furnishes, upon two weeks notice being given to him by the Secretary, a sufficient reason for his absence.

VII.

The targets shall consist of five concentric circles. The inner one eight inches diameter, gilded. The second increasing eight inches, painted red. The third increasing eight inches of white. The fourth, eight inches of black. The fifth, eight inches of light blue. The value of hits shall be as follows:—Gold, 9—Red, 7—white, 5—black, 3—and blue, 1.

VIII.

An arrow which, after striking the target, passes through it, or falls to the ground, shall count in the blue, unless the place of striking can be ascertained.

IX.

An arrow striking two circles shall count in the inner one.

X.

On the second Saturday of June of each year four prizes shall be shot for by the members of the club, in fourteen rounds, at the distance of eighty yards, the first prize to be awarded to the member whose hits value highest. The second prize to the hits next in value. The third prize to the hit nearest the centre, unless made by the member entitled to the first or second, in which case it shall be awarded to the persons whose hits shall be next in approach to the centre. And the fourth prize shall be awarded to him whose hits are sixth in value.

The first prize shall be the club bowl, and the club shall, within one month after each and every annual shooting, append a medal to the bowl, on which shall be inscribed the name of the successful competitor, with the date; and the winner of the same shall, within one year from the receipt of it, have added thereto ornamental work, according to the design adopted by the club, the value of which shall not be less than five dollars, and it shall be returned, so ornamented, to the president, on the day preceding the next annual prize-shooting.

The second prize shall be a silver cup, as near as possible to the value of fifteen dollars; and the third prize a silver cup of similar pattern, as near as possible to the value of ten dollars, both of which shall be the absolute property of the winners.

The fourth prize shall be a silver arrow, presented to the club by E.W. Keyser, Esq. to be designated the Dodonian prize, and shall be awarded to the archer whose hits value the sixth, provided he be not entitled to any other prize; in which case it shall pass to the next in value below, and a medal shall be attached by the club, with his mark and the year engraved upon it, and to be returned to the president on the day of the succeeding annual prize-meeting.

XI.

A captain for the annual prize-meeting shall be elected at the preceding meeting of the club, from among the active members, whose duties and authority shall be the same as the captain of field and practice meetings. He shall act as chairman of the committee of arrangmement, which committee he shall appoint from the club, and report the proceedings of the prize-meeting at the next stated meeting.

XII.

At all prize-meetings, in case a tie takes place, the members so tying shall shoot one round, and to those members valuing highest and best, shall be awarded the prizes respectively, as prescribed by these regulations.

XIII.

The pattern-board for arrows adopted by the club shall be the pattern for painting and ormanenting the same, and any deviation therefrom shall be subject to a penalty of ten dollars, without appeal.

XIV.

The uniform of the club shall be comformable to such patterns as shall be from time to time adopted by the club.

RIFLE CLUBS

The following documents present two examples of the rules governing gun associations in the eastern part of the United States between 1848 and 1858. The first selection, reprinted from the Spirit of the Times, 26 February 1848, p. 7, lists the resolutions and regulations of the Central New York Rifle Club. That outfit was founded at the home of John R. Chapman of Oneida Lake, Madison County. The second item, from the New York Clipper, 14 August 1858, p. 134, draws heavily upon the first piece. It gives the resolutions and rules of the National Rifle Club, which was organized at Framingham, Massachusetts on 16 June 1858. Despite the name of the association, it was controlled by New Englanders; two of its first officers were from Massachusetts and one of its regulations required that the annual meeting be held within 100 miles of Springfield.

CENTRAL NEW-YORK RIFLE CLUB
RESOLUTIONS

1.   That a Rifle Club be and is hereby organized under the general name of the "Central New-York Rifle Club."

2.   That the Officers of said Club shall consist of a President, Secretary and Treasurer, whose term of office shall be 3 years, and be chosen by a majority vote of the members at the annual meeting at the time of the expiration of said term.

3.   That the President, Secretary and Treasurer act as a committee for the management of the business and affairs of said Club, and report to the members at each annual meeting upon the transactions and prospects of said Club.

4.   That the object of this society or Club, be the furtherance of the noble art and science of Rifle shooting, both at rest and off hand, by gathering together once every year on New Year's day, the members of said club, for the purpose of competing for such prizes and on such terms as the committee may deem prudent to offer.

5.   Any person being an inhabitant of the State of New York, may become a member of this Club by transmitting his address to the Secretary, together with a subscription of five dollars, which sum shall be applied to the purpose of getting up suitable prizes for the annual shooting match on new year's day.

6.   Any person not an inhabitant of the State of New York, may become an honorary member of this Club by transmission of address and five dollars to the Secretary, but he cannot compete either by himself or proxy for any prize that may be offered by said Club.

7.   The winner of a prize at the annual shooting match shall not be allowed to compete in any other match at that meeting. However, if a marksman win a prize at rest, he shall not be debarred from competing and winning another at off hand, and vice versa.

8.   All the prizes offered by this Club to be shot for shall consist of money of specie paying Banks of the State of New York, so that the prizes will be good for the amount named.

9.   The annual meeting of the Club shall be held at a place not further distant from Syracuse than 100 miles, (unless the members at an annual meeting decide otherwise,)

and the place of meeting for each ensuing year to be put and carried by a majority vote at each annual meeting.

10.   All matches shall be decided by the rules of this Club, and if any case of dispute arise which is not embraced by the rules already in force, then such case shall be decided by a majority vote of the members then present, and such vote shall form the basis and precedent for a new rule, which shall be added to the list of the rules of shooting.

11.   That John R. Chapman of Oneida Lake, Madison Co. be and is hereby elected President, Joel D. Owens, of Syracuse, Secretary, and William Malcolm of Syracuse, Treasurer, of this Club, in compliance with the terms of the second resolution.

12.   That the resolutions, rules, and future proceedings of this Club be published in that prince of sporting papers, the N. Y. "Spirit of the Times."

by order, Joel D. Owens, Secretary

Syracuse, February 8th, '48.

RULES OF THE CENTRAL NEW YORK RIFLE CLUB

Rule 1.   In matches every marksman may use a Rifle of any construction and mode of sighting that he may see fit to employ, for it is not just to cramp the invention and abilities of our mechanics and marksmen by arbitrary rules in these points.

Rule 2.   The term "Rifle Practice at Rest" to mean that the muzzle end of the weapon be rested only, the butt plate being held against the shoulder or top arm muscle.

Rule 3.   The term "Rifle Practice at off hand" to mean that the marksman shall stand up and use nothing except himself and his weapon, having a perfect right to hip or rib his elbow, or off hand clean.

Rule 4.   Every marksman detected in violating any of the rules of this Club, shall be excluded from all chance of winning any prize he may be contending for.

Rule 5.   All matches shall be decided by string shooting of not less than 3 shots, and the shortest to win; and all strings to be measured from the centre of the target to the centre of each shot, and the aggregate of the distances to be the length of the string.

Rule 6.   Before commencing a string, the marksman must cause to be put up clean paper targets, free from bullet holes and imperfections; and then notify in an audible manner one or both of the judges of his intentions; and when a string is once commenced, no intermediate trial shots shall be allowed, unless the rifle fail or give out. In that case, if it cannot be immediately repaired, the marksman may make with another weapon not more than ten trial shots, and then finish his string. But under any circumstances, the string must be shot in the time stated in the conditions of the prize.

Rule 7.   As a general rule, all accidents and blunders which may befall a marksman in shooting a string, which are caused by his own carelessness and inattention, must be borne on his own shoulders; and those which can be fairly attributed to the weapon, must be overlooked.

Rule 8.   If a marksman fire off his weapon at the target, and afterwards discover that there was no bullet in the place, or that the bullet was in the barrel only so far as the starter reaches, then such shot must be counted and measured. Also, if the marksman fire at the target when the loading muzzle is in the barrel, then the shot must be counted and measured. Also a long fire from a snap cap must be counted and measured as a shot.

Rule 9.   If a marksman find something is not right in loading his weapon, and make a suitable declaration to the judge, then he may fire off his weapon into the air and reload, and such shot shall not be counted and measured.

Rule 10.   Wooden targets for shooting at 20 rods distance to be 12 inches square, for 30 rods 18 in., for 40 rods 24 in., for 50 rods 36 in., for 60 rods 48 in., for 70 rods 60 in., for 80 rods 72 in., for 90 rods 84 in., for 100 rods 100 in., and so on in proportion.

Rule 11.   If in shooting a string a marksman miss his target, the shot shall be counted and measured as one half the width of the target. Thus at 20 rods such shot shall be measured as 6 inches, at 30 rods as 9 in., at 40 rods as 12 in., at 50 rods as 18 in., at 60 rods as 24 in., at 70 rods as 30 in., at 80 rods as 36 in., at 90 rods as 42 in., at 100 rods as 50 in., and so on in proportion.

Rule 12.   Before the commencement of any match, a sufficient number of impartial judges shall be chosen to attend at the Rests and the Targets.

Rule 13.   Each marksman shall provide himself with rests, targets, &c., and in such time that no delay may take place on the match day.

Rule 14.   Each marksman shall provide himself with a marker, who is to have charge of the target; and it is the duty of the judges to see that every string shot be numbered, counted, measured and plugged up as soon as made.

Rule 15.   In all Club matches no marksman shall make more than one string for each prize, shooting by proxy being strictly prohibited.

Rule 16.   All matches to be shot on the day and in the times stated in the conditions of the prizes, if the weather be such that the targets can be seen.

NATIONAL RIFLE CLUB
RESOLUTIONS

1.   That a Rifle club be, and is hereby organized under the general name of the "NATIONAL RIFLE CLUB."

2.   That the officers of said Club shall consist of a President, Secretary, and Treasurer, whose term of office shall be three years, and be chosen by a majority vote of the members at the annual meeting at the time of expiration of said term.

3.   That the President, Secretary, and Treasurer, act as a Committee for the management of the business and affairs of said Club, and report to the members at each annual meeting upon the transactions and prospects of said Club.

4.   That the object of this Club be the furtherance of the noble art and science of Rifle Shooting, by gathering together once a year, on the first Tuesday in October, the members of said club, for the purpose of competing for such prizes and on such terms as the Committee may deem prudent.

5.   Any person being an inhabitant of the United States, or Canada, may become a member of this Club by transmitting his address to the Secretary together with a subscription of Five Dollars; which sum shall be applied to the purpose of getting up suitable prizes for the annual match on the first Tuesday In October.

6.   All prizes offered by this club to be shot for, shall consist of money of specie paying banks, so that the prizes will be good for the amount named.

7.   There shall be a Gold Medal got up by the Club, to be presented to the member that makes the best shooting at the Annual Meeting, and to be kept by him to the next Annual Meeting, when it must be surrendered to the President of the Club for competition as before. Said Medal to be the property of said club, and have suitable inscription engraved upon it to denote its object, and the person winning said Medal shall pledge himself to return it at the next Annual Meeting for competition as before.

8.   The Annual Meeting of the Club shall be held at a place not farther distant from Springfield than 100 miles, unless two-thirds of the members decree otherwise; and the place of meeting for each ensuing year to be put and carried by a majority vote at each Annual Meeting.

9.   All matches shall be decided by the Rules of the Club, and if any case of dispute arises, which is not embraced by the Rules already in force, then such case shall be decided by a majority vote of the members then present, and such vote shall form a basis and precedent for new rules, which shall be added to the Rules of Shooting.

10.   That JOHN WILLIAMSON, of New York, be, and is hereby elected President, H.W. SMITH of Boston, Mass., Secretary, and ABNER HAVENS, of South Framingham, of Mass., Treasurer of this Club, and to act as such to the next Annual Meeting in October, when an election will take place for Officers for the next three years.

RULES OF SHOOTING

1.   In matches every marksman may use a rifle of any construction and mode of sighting he may may see fit to employ, and shoot in whatever way he may think best.

2.   Every marksman detected in violating any of the Rules of this Club shall be excluded from all chance of winning any prize he may be contending for.

3.   All matches shall be decided by string shooting of not less than 10 shots and the shortest to win, and all strings to be measured from the center of the target to the center of the each shot, and the aggregate of the distance to be the length of the string.

4.   Before commencing a string the marksman must cause to be put up for 40 rods a clean paste board target, 15 inches square, free from bullet holes and imperfections, and then notify in an audible manner one or both of the judges of his intentions, and when it is once commenced no intermediate trial shots shall be allowed unless the rifle fail or give out; in that case, if it cannot be immediately repaired, the marksman may make with another weapon not more than 10 trial shots, and then finish his string, but under any circumstances the string must be shot in the time stated in the conditions of the prize.

5.   As a general rule all accidents and blunders, which may befall a marksman in shooting a string, which are caused by his own carelessness and inattention, must be borne on his own shoulders, and those which can be fairly attributed to the weapon must be overlooked.

6.   If a marksman fires his weapon at the target and afterwards discovers that there was no bullet in the piece, or that the bullet was in the barrel only so far as the starter reaches, then such shot must be counted and measured. Also, if the marksman fires at

the target when the loading muzzel is in the barrel, then the shot must be counted and measured. Also, a long fire from a snap cap must be counted and measured as a shot.

7. If a marksman finds something wrong in loading his weapon and makes a suitable declaration to the judges, then he may fire off his weapon in the air and reload, and such a shot shall not be counted nor measured.

8. Wooden targets for 40 rods must be 24 inches square, 50 rods 36 inches square, 60 rods 48 inches square, and so on in proportion.

9. If in shooting a string a marksman miss his target, the shot shall be counted and measured as one half the width of the target.

10. Before the commencement of any match a sufficient number of impartial judges shall be chosen to attend at the rests, targets &c.

11. Each marksman shall provide himself with rests, targets, &c., and in such time that no delay may take place on the match day.

12. In all club matches no marksman shall make more than one string for each prize, shooting by proxy being strictly prohibited.

13. All matches to be shot on the day, and in the times stated in the conditions of the prizes, if the weather is such that the targets can be seen.

14. No shooting will be allowed on match days unless by members of the Club.

15. All expenses of the Club must be borne equally by the members, and everything must be settled up at the annual meeting.

John Williamson, President.
H.W. Smith, Secretary.
Abner Havens, Treasurer.

PIGEON SHOOTING

During the early part of 1858 the New York Clipper actively promoted an international pigeon shooting tournament scheduled for Jersey City, New Jersey in March of that year. In its columns its editors and correspondents urged sportsmen from Canada and the eastern and midwestern United States to enter the contest. As the following document suggests, the organizers were concerned with attracting entries from several regions and with guaranteeing fair competition. This account of the event and list of the rules is reprinted from the Clipper, 13 February, 6 and 13 March 1858, pp. 338, 362, 372.

THE PIGEON SHOOTING TOURNAMENT

At this great event, so pregnant with interest to the lovers of the trigger, is rapidly approaching, and the time for the arrangement of the necessary details is consequently limited, we call the attention of those parties desirous of joining it, to this fact, and to request them at once to forward their nomination entries to the different sweepstakes. From our reply to our Toronto correspondent in last week's CLIPPER, our Canada friends will perceive that they are not excluded from entering for competition for the various prizes, but on the contrary their presence will be hailed with cordial pleasure, and they may depend upon receiving a hearty welcome on the occasion. We fully anticipate, also, seeing a numerous muster of our Philadelphia sportsmen present, and we know by experience that they can boast of some first-rate shots among them. From Albany we have received assurances of the attendance of their representatives, and we may safely anticipate having among us the "dead shots" of Pottsville, Reading, Burlington, and Schuylkill County, whose performances have been so often reported in our columns. Indeed we are confident that we shall be honored with the presence of the representatives of nearly every State in the Union, and the promise of sport in addition to the advertised sweepstakes in the form of matches, sweepstakes, (at single and double birds,) is so abundant as to satisfy the most ardent lover of trapshooting.

In consequence of the importance of knowing at once the extent and character of the arrangements to be made, in the way of providing the requisite number of birds, accomodation on the ground, &c., we again call upon those desirous of, and intending to become subscribers, to forward their nominations to us at once, and we shall be obliged to our respective correspondents in each locality to receive and foward immediately to us the names of those in their district who purpose entering, and stating clearly in which sweepstakes they desire to do so. We have already received several nominations in our immediate locality, and it is those at a distance whose attention is called to the above remarks. We also repeat our suggestion of last week, that in small localities, the lovers of pigeon shooting should unite, and forward as their representatives one or two of their best shots.

It has been suggested to us by a gentleman who has taken a deep interest in this project, and whose great experience renders his opinion of great weight, that no person shall be allowed to have more than two nominations to each sweepstake. He argues very plausibly that a good shot might receive as many as a half a dozen nominations from his friends, and shoot for each person respectively, thus giving him a decided advantage over other competitors who only possess one entry. As this opinion has been endorsed by several experienced "professors of the trigger," whom we consulted, we have made this one of the conditions of the entry, and we think it will be unanimously approved of by the subscribers.

As the number of birds required on the occasion will be great, we shall be obliged if those intending to join, who possess birds, will at once inform us what number they themselves can furnish for the shooting, so that there may be ample supply of pigeons for the sport. In the meantime, if those persons at a distance will forward immediately to Mr. John Taylor, Darcy Hotel, Jersey City, any quantity of good birds, up to 600, suitable for the purpose required, at a fair market price, they will receive payment for them by return of post. As the excellence of the sport depends materially on the quality of the birds used, it is particularly requested that good full grown birds only will be fowarded.

In conclusion we again request the prompt co-operation of intending subscribers, by entering immediately, and we shall be glad to receive as usual the suggestions of our friends and correspondents.

Since writing the above remarks, we have received the subjoined communication from a correspondent, and as we are desirous, equally with him, to see the arrangements "fairly and honorably" carried out, he may rely upon his suggestions being acted upon.

The desirability of having a special committee, whose province it shall be to see every man load his gun, as well as to elect judges and umpires on the occasion, has been already urged by gentlemen in this city, who are taking a warm interest in the affair, and it is on this account that we would strenuously urge those intending to join, the importance of at once entering, so that the appointment of such committee can be immediately made:

New York, Feb. 6, 1858.

Friend Queen: Having seen in your valuable Clipper of this date the editorial notice and the advertisement for the Pigeon Shooting Tournament, and expecting to appear as one of the candidates for the prizes, I am desirous for the satisfaction of all, that all the arrangements should be fair and honorable.

To render it perfectly just and fair, I would earnestly desire that a Special Committee be appointed whose duty it will be to see every man load his gun.

You may not be aware that some persons who frequently shoot pigeon matches use, on such occasions, a loaded wad—that is, a wad constructed on the principle of a cartridge. This of course is unfair and dishonest.

Yours respectfully,   Trigger....

THE RULES OF PIGEON SHOOTING

1. The shooter to hold his gun below the elbow until the bird is on the wing.

2. Any shooter neglecting to cock his gun and in consequence a bird gets away, such bird is considered a missed bird.

3. Should a gun miss fire, the shooter is entitled to another bird.

4. All birds to be gathered by the shooter, within the distance of boundary agreed upon, without anything in hand to throw or strike at them: otherwise they are considered lost birds.

5. Should any disputes arise concerning the shooting, the same to be settled by two judges and a referee, duly elected. Should the judges not agree in their decisions, then that of the referee to be final.

6. Should the quantity of shot used be limited, then it must be measured out to the shooters by one of the judges.

7. Should a bird, after being trapped, walk away, the shooter can follow up in proportion to the original distance from the post to the trap fixed upon. The judges to decide upon the proper distance.

8. A time-keeper to be appointed. Should a bird after being trapped, remain stationary, the trapper can then rise the bird up by the means appointed for the space of half a minute; at the expiration of which time the judges can declare the shooter entitled to another bird, in case such attempts to rise it prove ineffectual.

9. Every effort will be used to prevent outside shooting, but in case a bird should be shot inside the boundary, by outside shooters, the judges have the power to decide whether such bird shall be scored to the shooter or not.

10. Every shooter to snap off his gun in the presence of one of the judges, previous to loading.

The management of the ground selected was deputed to Mr. John Taylor, Darcy House, Jersey City, as that gentleman is regarded as one of the oldest and most experienced pigeon shooters in the States. He is also a keen sportsman and first-rate shot, as the result of the first and principal match will prove. The spot chosen was on the flat meadows by the side of the river, between Hoboken and Jersey City, and was admirably adapted for the purpose, as well as being convenient of access—the stages running close past the ground, from the doors of Darcy House, Jersey City, which was the gathering place of the sportsmen.

The entries showed the interest felt in the affair, as among them were three representatives from Canada, and two from Cincinnati, while Philadelphia, Bordentown, Newark, Delaware, Jersey City, and New York, were well represented by the "crack shots" of those places.

The entries for the principal sweepstakes of $10 each were twenty one in number, and the shooting commenced at one o'clock p.m. The attendance of the spectators was very large, and every effort was used to prevent that curse of the sport, vis., outside shooting. In spite, however, of all exertions used, some fellows would persist in firing at birds approaching them; but still there was no case in which there was any necessity of appeal to the judges. The judges appointed were Mssrs. Young of Philadelphia, and J. Eldridge, of Bordentown; Mr. Evans, of Newark, was referee. They discharged their duties in a manner satisfactory to all. The following was the score of shooting for the first day:

1.	Mr. Pilkington, Newark	010	1
2.	Mr. Oscar Sandford, Newark	110	2
3.	Mr. J. Monkhouse, Toronto, Canada	0	0
4.	Mr. H. Ellis do do	1110	3
5.	Mr. George Ward do do	10	1
6.	Mr. J.W. Beesley, Cincinnati	1111111111	10
7.	Mr. Joseph Ferguson do	110	2
8.	Mr. John Taylor, Jersey City	1111111111	10
9.	do do	10	1
10.	Mr. James Turner, New York	1110	3
11.	Mr. Tomlinson do	110	2
12.	Mr. Johnson, Bordentown	0	0
13.	Mr. S.R. Irven, Philadelphia	1111110	6
14.	do do	11111110	7
15.	Mr. Cornell, Delaware	111110	5
16.	Mr. Mount, Philadelphia	110	2
17.	Mr. King, New York	10	1
18.	Mr. Johnson, Bordentown	111110	5
19.	Mr. William Taylor, Jersey City	111111110	8
20.	Mr. James Turner, New York	1111111111	10
21.	Mr. Brown, Red House, Harlem	0	0

It will be perceived from this score that three gentlemen only killed all their birds (10); consequently, they agreed to decide the question of superiority by shooting at 5 birds each. It resulted as under:

Mr. J.W. Beesley, Cincinnati	01111	4 out of 5
Mr. John Taylor, Jersey City	10111	4 out of 5
Mr. James Turner, New York	11111	5 out of 5

The latter gentleman was consequently declared the winner of the principal prize, and entitled to the proud title Champion Pigeon Shooter of America. Messrs. Beesley and Taylor then shot at 5 birds each, to decide which was entitled to the 2nd and 3rd prizes:

Mr. J.W. Beesley, Cincinnati	11110	4
Mr. John Taylor, New York	11110	4

The result being for a third time a tie between those gentlemen, it was mutually agreed to divide the two prizes equally between them.

Chapter 9

FOOTBALL

Young men played various forms of premodern football in North America during the mid-nineteenth century. In general the sport featured a struggle between two teams, each of which attempted to kick or carry a ball across the opposition's goal line. Each side often numbered dozens of players, and the action was usually quite rough. Football was still in a very primitive state in North America prior to 1860. In that era there was very little indication of its immense future popularity.

Football was popular on several college campuses in the United States before the Civil War, including Harvard, Yale, Princeton, Brown, Williams, and West Point. At those and other schools it had not as yet reached the level of organization of rowing, baseball, or cricket. Students held a few spontaneous matches just for fun, but upper-classmen generally used the sport as part of the hazing and initiation rites and rituals that they used to establish their superiority over the lowly freshmen and sophomores. These interclass battles were often violent encounters which featured much pushing and kicking among the contestants as they struggled to propel the ball across their rival's goal. Students typically used a crude home made ball and improvised a ground and goals on a field between buildings. At Princeton in 1844 one of the players purchased a leather cover and beef bladders, which were blown up with quills and laced inside the cover. Dozens on each side competed on the quadrangle between the East and West College, with the injured parties dropping out rapidly. Handling the ball was forbidden, and the side that kicked the ball to one of the walls first won the contest. College football received only minor coverage in the sporting press of the 1850s; yet a few papers occasionally did print brief accounts of contests. "The Annual Foot-ball Game" presents an example of this pastime as it was practiced at Brown University in 1854. The next document gives a short description and the rules of play of one form of the sport.

As bruised bones and bloody noses multiplied, college authorities grew increasingly alarmed over the tendency of the matches to encourage brutality and the excessive consumption of alcohol among the participants. "The Football Game" and "Sixty-One Up!" are two essays from Harvard Magazine that summarize the arguments for and against the annual "Bloody Monday" game at Harvard. The final document in this chapter is an account of the last event that was held before the university banned the ritual in 1860. But that decree proved to be only a temporary setback for the sport, for during the 1870s football became a major institution at Harvard and several other prestigious eastern colleges.

FOOTBALL AT BROWN

The following account of an annual football game at Brown suggests the competition and hilarity that often accompanied these events. Note that in this case Seniors and Sophomores faced off against Freshmen and Juniors. This story first appeared in the Spirit of the Times, 21 October 1854 p. 432.

THE ANNUAL FOOT-BALL GAME

A Correspondnent of the Providence "Tribune" says that the annual foot-ball game at Brown University, between the Freshmen and Juniors on one side, and the Sophomores and Seniors on the other, came off lately. The trial commenced at 10 A. M., and lasted until 12. Good will and harmony prevailed throughout the contest, although great excitement seemed to exist among the competitors. The tide of victory flowed with uncertainty during the first few games, and Freshmen valor, aided by Junior experience, proved successful in several rounds. At length the Sophomores and Seniors became thoroughly warmed up, and plunging into the melee with redoubled energy, came off conquerors in every remaining game. The whole "concluded with a grand 'scrub-race' for candy! Each man, by throwing in a penny, could enter the lists. When the party (about 45 or 50) reached the candy, a truly laughable scene was presented—Sophomores shouting, Juniors howling, Seniors eating, Freshmen yelling with pain, candy flying, hats, shoes, coat-tails, &c., ditto—rear—tear—pell-mell!"

RULES OF FOOTBALL

As football gained in popularity during the 1850s, several sporting periodicals recommended that baseball and other athletic clubs adopt the sport during the winter months for exercise and amusement. The following description of how to make the ball and how to play the game suggests the sport's rudimentary stage of development in the mid-nineteenth century. This account is reprinted from the New York Clipper, 20 December 1856, p. 276.

THE GAME OF FOOTBALL

A few remarks in last week's CLIPPER, in reference to this really invigorating and exciting winter pastime, has had the effect to draw out several communications, by which we learn that in Philadelphia and other places the game has afforded much amusement to a number of young men, but that never having seen any instructions concerning the correct mode of playing, they request some information on this point, &c. Therefore, in order to set the ball properly in motion, we give the following instructions:

1. THE BALL itself is the only thing required by this game, except a large field to play in. The ball is composed of a leather case, about 8 or 9 inches in diameter, composed of sections of stout calf-leather sewn together. At one of the points where these sections meet a single piece is left longer than the others, two of which are pierced with holes, and laced over this long piece with an ordinary leather boot-lace; a large bladder is then introduced into the ball, and afterwards blown up till it nearly fills the case, leaving a small part outside, which, being tied securely, is pushed into the case, and completely fills it up; the case is then securely laced, and the ball is fit for use. The bladder should always be taken out after play, and hung up to dry distended in the usual way.

2. IN PLAYING THE GAME bounds are fixed 50 or 60 yards apart, or sometimes 100, when the numbers are large and the field will allow of it. The bounds are imaginary lines drawn between two sticks fixed in the ground, at the whole breadth of the field, if an ordinary one, and consequently the game is played in a square space, with a stick at each corner, two sides of which are the bounds, and are prolonged *ad infinitum*. Two captains are selected, who toss for the first choice of men, and the whole number of players is divided into two parties by each captain choosing one in his turn. The toss also decides the first kick of the ball. The captain having gained this, takes the ball, followed by his train, and marches with them to the middle of the space betwen the bounds, where the opposite party are mustered in line ready for the struggle; the ball is then placed on the ground, and the captain gives the first kick towards the opposite bounds, where the opposite party are mustered in line ready for the struggle; the ball is then placed on the ground, and the captain gives the first kick towards the opposite bounds; the other party meeting it, and returning it either by a kick, or carrying it, if preferred, while ten are being counted by the other party; but in any case, whether the ball is carried or being kicked at, the opposite party are privileged to throw down the ball-carrier or kicker by any means in their power; and the usual practice is to run rapidly behind, and endeavor to get the foot inside his leg with a circular sweep, which almost always succeeds, unless it is met by a jump into the air of a peculiar kind. The object of each party is to kick the ball over the other's bounds, and when this is effected the game is won. It might be supposed that severe injuries would follow this rough practice, but it seldom is the case; and though the shins suffer severely at the time, they rarely exhibit any dangerous wounds. It is a game much in vogue in some rural districts. Cold weather is the time for its adoption.

HARVARD FOOTBALL

In describing football at Harvard during the 1840s, Thomas Wentworth Higginson recalled "the feeling of exhilaration as one drew near to the 'Delta,' on some autumn evening, while the game was in progress,—the joyous shouts, the thud of the ball, the sweet smell of crushed grass...the magnificent 'rush.' It seemed a game for men and giants." The traditional "Bloody Monday" contest on the first day of the fall term matched the sophomores against the freshmen. Increasing criticism of the violence, rowdiness, and drinking that accompanied the game moved the administration to ban the event in 1860. It also warned the sophomores that the penalty for disobeying this injunction would be expulsion. The students responded with a mock funeral and burial of a coffin containing a leather-covered bladder. The following essays from the Harvard Magazine present opposing views of the dangers and benefits of the interclass battle. They are reprinted from the issues of June and July, 1858, pp. 181-85 and 233-40. They are followed by a report on the contest of September 1859, which was the last one held before the traditional match was banned. It first appeared in the New York Clipper, 17 September 1859, p. 170.

THE FOOTBALL GAME

We have among us a game of annual occurrence between the Sophomores, on the one hand, and the Freshmen, on the other. It took its origin, we make no doubt, in that antagonism of the Classes which the reader of our history will find so apparent in the intercourse of students up to the beginning of the present century, and which is also to be observed in the disabilities and privileges of the various Classes, and in the laws of the government by which these things were regulated and defined. The time of its origin is of little consequence. If the game be beneficial, it deserves to be perpetuated, whether it be the child of to-day or of antiquity. If, on the contrary, it be injurious, it should be at once overthrown; and the longer the evil has existed, the stronger the reason for its immediate removal.

In mentioning the origin of the Football Game, we have also suggested its aim, which was to establish and perpetuate the artifical superiority of the one Class over the other,—of those who gained over those who lost the victory; to insure which, recourse was then had, and is now, to such means as we shall attempt to describe.

In the first place, the whole game is conducted with exceeding unfairness. We see, on the one hand, a numerous body of disciplined men, well known to each other, confident of success, stimulated by their defeat in the former year, and thus in purpose, feeling, and action a unit. On the other hand, a squad of awkward Freshmen, hurried to the field on the third day after their first meeting, distrusting each other, with no bond of sympathy, with no expectations of success, awed by the united phalanx opposite, ignorant of the bounds, of the rules of the game (if there be any),—ignorant even why they are there,—scattered, irresolute, impotent. In the next place, the game is won by the exercise of deliberate brutality; or, rather, it is changed from a match at football to a trial of physical force and pugilistic ability. One may speak slightingly of bloody noses, swelled lips, and black eyes; but we know not what is to prevent the infliction of more serious injuries, especially when many of the combatants are in that state of irresponsibility and uncontrol which has been the parent of so much evil to the world. To us, few things are more deplorable than to see God's image mauled and beaten; particularly when done, as here, without provocation or cause.

We come next to the accessories of the game, which now cling to it, and have become as much a part of it as the antagonism of the Classes,—the unfairness and the brutality. We intend to speak plainly, and we affirm that large numbers—shall we say a majority?—of those who stand as opponents on the Delta, on the night of the Football

Game, go there excited and maddened by the intoxicating cup,—*drunk!* Students of
Harvard! does not the mention, even, of your disgraceful condition cause the blood to
glow and tingle in your veins with shame? Have you so little self-respect, that you can
dare to appear before many witnesses, perhaps not drunk yourself, but at least banded
together with those who are?—so little regard for that institution whose foster-children
you are, that you thus wantonly expose her to obloquy and contempt? Are there not
dramshops enough everywhere, that you must make Harvard College another? If no con-
siderations of this nature move you, yet think to what you are liable, when, filled with
the poison, you enter upon the contest, with your passions freed from every restraint. You
may by drinking be rendered silly and harmless; you may—for different constitutions
are affected differently—be made infuriate and dangerous. God help you, if, in this latter
state, you do some harm you cannot mend when sober! But the preparation is only a part.
After the game is over, it is customary for the victors to waste the night in debauch, and
not unfrequently for the vanquished, as well. God help you, again, if you sow then a seed
whose fruit you shall reap hereafter in bitterness and anguish!

For the evils, then, engendered by this Football Game; for the perpetuation of a
barbarous relic of the past; for this unworthy barrier to the harmony of the classes; for
the unfairness and brutality exercised in the game; for the attendant vices and dissipation,—for all these, what is the remedy? The immediate abolition of the game.

Members of the present Freshman Class, we appeal to you! In your own hands you
hold the balance,—see to it that the wrong kicks the beam! When the honor of putting
away this evil is within your reach, see to it that you stretch out your hand and grasp
it! Fear not that you are abolishing a time-honored custom;—never grant that evil *can*
be time-honored. Think you to incur reproach in acting thus? What reproach can there
be in upholding the right? You will be accused of cowardice, perhaps. They alone will
dare to make the charge who fear a disgraceful defeat when they are unsupported by
your presence. "But the 'honor of the Class' is in danger." Who is not ashamed to avow
that the honor of a Class is sullied, because it attempts to reform abuses? Some one of
you may say, "What good will be effected by my absence?" We answer, In the first
place, you remove your support from wickedness. "Ah, but I intend to commit no such
excesses as you have mentioned." You cannot countenance anything, without at the
same time giving sanction to all its adjuncts and accessories. There is no such thing as
a support by halves. You must support the whole or nothing. Your absence, then, will
wash your hands of all complicity with the evil. Your example, too, may cause others
to imitate you,—such, for instance, as are naturally timid, and, for fear of being iso-
lated and singular, are induced to join the mass, when their consciences would bid them
stand aloof. You will show your appreciation of fair play. You will show your abhor-
rence of that feeling which leads men who have felt oppression themselves to become
the oppressors, when the occasion offers. Can you affirm that any one of these is not
a positive good, and a sufficient reason for your abstinence? "But my withdrawal will
render those who remain more desperate." What then? Is your duty any the less clear?
Remember, that he who commits a wrong has always to answer for the consequences;
whereas he who does right, as we all are bound to do at all times, leaves the consequences to his Maker, whose law he has obeyed. "We shall render our opponents boast-
ful and vainglorious, and, when they are in our places, they will become the greater
bullies from our refusal to meet them the year before." Once more answer, Whose is
the responsibility?

Consider the conduct of Yale, not because you are unwilling to be distanced by her, but because her conduct was right; she abolished this game, although it was much less objectionable than our own. There, for example, at least a month was allowed to elapse before the match came off. In '56, the Freshmen challenged the Sophomores, but the challenge was refused, and no game took place. Last year, the next class of Freshmen repeated the challenge. But here the Government interposed, and threatened expulsion to all who should engage. Thus was the game abolished. Its abolition has been attended with the happiest results; no substitute has been sought, none needed. Shall we not "go and do likewise"? Whether or not the students of Harvard wish to have it said that they are obliged to made reforms which their own manliness should spontaneously dictate, is a question that is to be settled, in at least one shape, by the Class of '61.

In conclusion, we express the opinion that the time has come for this game to have an end; it has performed its part, has annually received the plaudits of a gaping crowd, but now ceases to delight, and is about to shuffle off the stage. Its death, we think, will be attended with no commotion, but will be eminently easy and peaceful. A decent burial will be provided, though we cannot expect that the mourners will be many. And as for the obituary, we anticipate the pleasure of penning that for the October number of the Harvard Magazine.

SIXTY-ONE UP!

On Thursday, the 24th ultimo, while the world was wagging in the good old-fashioned way, and men were enjoying that ease and indifference which a hot June day naturally engenders, there appeared, in publications widely different in their objects and character, two articles of a most inflammatory nature and of a dangerously revolutionary tendency. I refer, of course, to a piece in the Boston Journal upon College Societies, and an article in the Harvard Magazine against the Football Game. As if delighting in the havoc they expected to make, their learned authors hurled them at their unsuspecting victims without the slightest warning. The ancient gods of Greece and Rome, touched with pity for their miserable children, were accustomed, at the approach of calamity, to warn men of danger by divers freaks of nature and portentous dreams. But no such prodigies, if we except the cut of the Juniors in Latin, ushered in these threatening visitors. No swarm of bees settled upon the belfry of Harvard; no bust in the Library gave signs of animation; not even a crow flew over the College Yard, nor did any Freshman give proof of extraordinary infantile wisdom. As unexpected as unwelcome did they come upon us....

The article in the last number of the Harvard displays the same revolutionary spirit, the same ignorance of College life, and even a still smaller show of argument, which last feature, however, is perhaps in the present case excusable. It is clearly the result of inexperience, which time will undoubtedly remove. The worst effect of such articles is, that they give outsiders a false impression of our College life. I will mention a few of the worst cases of this unintentional perversion of facts....

Any disinterested person, who should receive his first impression of the Football Game from the perusal of the article in question, must involuntarily shrink from the manifest brutality said to be there displayed. He would picture to his excited fancy, on the one hand, a set of fiends thirsting for their opponents' blood, dragging their unsuspecting victims from calm repose to the gory field, and deliberately proceeding to butcher them after the most approved and scientific method; on the other hand, a band of modest and virtuous youth, just torn for the first time from the bosoms of their families, intent upon the acquisition of knowledge, never in their lives having heard of the game before, suddenly made the victims of a brutal and murderous assault. All the terrible accessories of Indian warfare would seem to be here employed, and the bloody tomahawk and scalping-knife of the savage sink into insignificance in comparison with the ponderous fist of the Sophomore. Instead of this accumulation of horrors, the facts of the case are simply these. The two Classes meet at an appointed time and place. Attendance is entirely optional. The Freshmen are sufficiently acquainted with the rules and customs of the game before they enter. Violent blows are somtimes dealt, it is true, but they only are ever beaten, or, to use his own expression, mauled, who their own accord rush into danger. If any one is willing to attend to the ball alone, he is pretty sure to escape without injury. I am inclined to think that the author saw the horror of the fight through the magnifying lens of his own excited fancy.

Next follows the unpleasant and somewhat astounding assertion, that "large numbers, perhaps a majority, of the opponents on the Delta, go there excited and maddened by the intoxicating cup,—*drunk!*" If the author here intends to indulge in a fanciful and perfectly allowable imagery, if he simply desires to adorn his style with the flowers of rhetoric, too much praise could not be awarded him for the beauty of the simile. If he refers to the intoxicating cup of excitement and youthful activity, and that figurative and eminently praiseworthy state of drunkenness produced by an exuberance of health and spirits, the charge is not only true, but should be regarded as a virtue. But if, as the succeeding remarks would seem to suggest, he wished to be understood literally, the utter absurdity of the statement is such as only to provoke a smile. But this is not all. Not content with sending abroad the assertion, having only a slight foundation in fact, that a majority of Harvard students are common drunkards, he goes on to say that both victors and vanquished often spend the night in debauch. As far as my experience goes, all parties concerned, with here and there perhaps a solitary exception, retire to their virtuous couches, and sink to calm repose, on the night of the first Monday of the college year, with minds as tranquil, and consciences, if not limbs, as free from pain as the new-born babe. Even supposing the facts alleged to be true, how it necessarily follows that Harvard College is thereby converted into an enormous depot for the dispensation of alcoholic drinks, is more than, with my unaided vision, I am able to see. I will take the liberty to assure our friends outside, that this venerable institution is at present neither a lager-bier nor a low dram-shop, but still retains its honorable position as the chief seat of learning in our beloved Commonwealth, noted alike for the exemplary conduct of its students and the excellence of its literary reputation.

Having, then, called the much-abused Football Game a barbarous relic of the past, he adjures all well-meaning Freshmen to unite, for the reasons above quoted, in the abolition of this inhuman practice. When the gentleman shall have become somewhat better versed in the subtilties of logic, he will find that from two false premises few conclusions can be satisfactorily proved, especially where the train of reasoning is utterly invalid. He makes the assertion, entirely unsupported by facts, that drunkenness and brutality are the necessary accessories of the game, coupled with the equally false and somewhat astounding principle of morality: "You cannot countenance anything without at the same time giving sanction to all its adjuncts and accessories." Let us enquire a little into the practical application of this doctrine.

...It is undoubtedly a fact, that ten times more liquor is drank every Exhibition-day than on the night of the Football Game, although even on Exhibition-day Harvard College is not precisely a dram-shop, nor would it probably be mistaken for such by a careless observer. Do the Corporation, Faculty, students, nay, more, the large number of lady visitors, countenance this adjunct and accessory of Exhibition by favoring us with their presence? Most assuredly, if the gentleman's doctrine is correct....

In zeal for the cause of temperance and true reform I will not yield him the palm; but we make nothing by putting a stop to these harmless, though boisterous recreations, which are worse in appearance than in reality. What is especially to be feared is that quiet dissipation which is taken in secret, and never dares to obtrude itself upon the public gaze. When all legitimate sources of active amusement are removed, the desire of excitement, ever present in the youthful mind, seeks gratification in other and more dangerous channels. A College community is no better for being free from those slight violations of decorum which were once so common. Furniture and window-glass, Freshman's doors and loose horses, may suffer the less, but the gain is more than compensated by the secret and observed dissipation substituted in their place....

If there is any one thing more than another particularly desirable at the present time for our College training, it is more of this same and barbarous and immoral sport. We need more games, more cricket-clubs, more gymnasiums, more exercise of every kind. One after another of the old institutions of College life is disappearing. Cling with greater tenacity to the rest. Depend upon it, they will be among the pleasantest recollections of after years. The Class of '61 is particularly called upon, by the gentleman whose remarks have been considered, to do away with one of the most beneficial and interesting of these time-honored customs. Upon them rests the responsibility of its continuance or abandonment. Let them banish whatever of its accessories are worthy of rebuke, conduct the game with sobriety and all due care, and thus prove that drunkenness and brutality are not its necessary attendants.

Of one thing, however, I can assure them. In case they are the first to suffer it to fall into disuse, few can be found sufficiently credulous to assign to their conduct the charitable motives so forcibly urged upon them. If they neglect to take their place next fall on the expected night, too little courage, rather than excessive virtue, will be undoubtedly the cause of their non-appearance. But I will not insult the Class by such vain suppositions. I have too much faith in their spirit to fear an instant for the result. When the cry of "Sixty-one up!" shall fill the Delta, I trust they will promptly respond; and may the gentleman himself lay down his eulogistic pen, and pause a moment in the midst of his obituary to give the ball the first kick.

1859 MATCH

Like the celebrated Rugby School, England, the students of Harvard University, Cambridge, Mass., have an annual match at the somewhat rough but hearty game of foot-ball. It is Sophomores vs. Freshmen, nominally, but really enlists every available muscle of all classes; the Juniors sympathising with the Freshmen, the Seniors with the Sophs. The present match was witnessed by an unprecedented number of spectators, and the *Advertiser* gives the following graphic report:

"Fair ladies did not disdain to show by their inspiring presence their sympathy with the tough sport of the students. The sophomores first made their appearance on the classic field, but as there were no freshmen, they disappeared for a while, and at length returned in a long procession, passing by the Library, and of course profoundly impressing the freshmen by their numbers and ferocious appearance. They formed in a well-ordered phalanx at the upper end of the Delta, and the freshmen at the lower end. But the freshmen this year were evidently bent on mischief. They looked slight, but were wiry, tough-looking fellows, and were singularly well organized, numbering in their ranks many experienced players.

"The naming, the kick-off, and the rush followed as usual; but the sophomore charge was met with a fierceness and determination that surprised everybody. One zealous sophomore ran through the freshmen's line and back again, but the head of the sophomore column was effectually stayed, and a most obstinate fight ensued. One way and another the game swayed, but the superiority of the sophomores gradually prevailed, and they beat their gallant adversaries back; until one active freshman sent the ball flying over the heads of all, just in time, and a well directed charge swept away the few sophomores who happened to be near the ball, and it was carried home triumphantly, amid cheers from all sides of the Delta, for the 'best freshmen class that ever entered Harvard!'

"The sophomores entered the second game, eager to retrieve their reputation, and the freshmen, exulting over their incredible success, spared no effort to gain a second victory. They had the ball for this game, and the fight was really desperate. Now one side, now the other, had the advantage, and the general opinion was that the freshmen would win; but the sophomores beat them back, foot by foot, until at length the ball was driven home, and the freshmen were defeated.

"The third game was short. One dangerous shock—a storm of blows—and a fortunate kick and skillful rush decided the game for the sophomores without much of a fight.

"A detachment of sturdy juniors now joined the freshmen, while the sophomores were reinforced by a large body of seniors—'the fighting class of '60.' The juniors and freshmen made a good fight, buth they were entirely outnumbered and in every way overmatched, so that the seniors and sophomores put the ball home three times with comparative ease.

"At the close of the sixth game, the different classes formed in a mass, and joined in cheers and a discordant chorus, and then slowly breaking up, retired to discuss their victories or bind their wounds as they might think proper."

Chapter 10

GYMNASIUM SPORTS

During the mid-nineteenth century several North American cities had gymnasiums where men fenced, wrestled, and performed a variety of physical exercises. Some were open to the public, while others were privately subscribed. A small number of native born men and German immigrants patronized fencing classes in Boston, New York, and a few other cities in the United States. The first document in this chapter presents the *Constitution and By-laws of the Boston Fencing Club* (Boston, 1858).

German immigrants introduced and popularized the sport of gymnastics in the United States and Canada. Beginning in 1848 they founded a number of turnvereins, or gymnastic clubs, in Cincinnati, Louisville, Philadelphia, Baltimore, Brooklyn, New York City, Boston, Utica, Newark, and other towns. By 1860 there were 157 of these societies in the United States. They played an important social and political role for the German community as the newcomers debated such issues as social reform and antislavery. Associations of these clubs, called *Turnerbunds,* sponsored gymnastic festivals in Philadelphia in 1851, in Baltimore and Cincinnati in 1852, and in Louisville and New York in 1853. Over the remainder of the decade political issues threatened the Turner movement, as the German clubs suffered from nativist attacks and internal divisions over the question of the extension of slavery into the American west.

During the mid-nineteenth century there was increasing support in North America for physical training for men and women of all ages. By the late 1850s the trend toward encouraging calesthenics for school children was gaining momentum, as is evident in the essay by Catherine Beecher included in Chapter 1. "Gymnastics in the Kentucky Military Institute," from the New York Clipper, 4 July 1857, p. 84, presents a testimonial for the sport by a cadet in a midwestern academy. As the turnvereins fought among themselves and against outsiders who resented their growing power, they influenced other groups who admired their dedication and skill at gymnastics. Many public gymnasiums adopted the Turners' exercises and apparatus. "Great Gymnastic Performances," from the New York Clipper, 19 June 1858, p. 66, describes the Herculean efforts by a San Franciscan to prove that he was the strongest man in town. The final document below reviews an exhibition held in January 1859 at John Wood's gymnasium on East Twentieth-Eighth Street in New York City, an establishment patronized by many prominent gentlemen and military officers. It is reprinted from the New York Clipper, 5 February 1859, p. 330.

THE BOSTON FENCING CLUB CONSTITUTION

ARTICLE I.
DESIGN OF THE CLUB.

The "BOSTON FENCING CLUB" is organized in the city of Boston, to afford its members, at a small annual assessment, a convenient *"Salle d' armes,"* with a competent instructor, or instructors, free from the objections and inconvenience which apply to Fencing Schools open to the Public, and shall consist of not more than ONE HUNDRED AND FIFTY MEMBERS.

ARTICLE II.
GOVERNMENT OF THE CLUB.

The government of the Club shall consist of a President, a Treasurer, and a Secretary. They shall be elected by a majority of ballots, at the annual meeting of the Club, and shall hold their offices for one year, or until their successors are appointed.

ARTICLE III.
DUTIES OF THE PRESIDENT.

It shall be the duty of the President to make arrangements for suitable rooms for the use of the Club, and to engage the services of an Instructor, or Instructors, in Fencing, or other exercises, on such terms as may have the approval of a majority of the Board of Government, and, through the Secretary, to notify the members of the Club of such arrangements as are from time to time made; Provided, however, that the President shall not lease any room, or rooms, for a longer time than one year from the first day of October, in any year, or cause any debts or obligations to be incurred by the Club, to exceed the amount of the annual assessment for the current year.

ARTICLE IV.
DUTIES OF THE TREASURER.

The Treasurer shall take charge of all the current funds of the Club; shall collect all admission fees and assessments, and all other dues of the Club. He shall make all disbursements, shall render a statement of the accounts of the Club at the annual meeting, or whenever else required so to do by the President, or at any special meeting of the Club; and he shall report at the annual meeting of the Club the number of members, the names of delinquents, and the amounts due from them.

ARTICLE V.
DUTIES OF THE SECRETARY.

The Secretary shall have charge of the Records of the Club, shall issue all notices, except such as come within the department of the Treasurer, and preside at the meetings of the Club in the absence of both the President and Treasurer.

ARTICLE VI.
TIME OF THE ANNUAL MEETING, AND ALTERATION OF THE CONSTITUTION AND BY-LAWS.

The annual meeting of the Club shall be holden on the second Tuesday in March, in each year, and notice thereof in writing shall be sent by the Secretary to each member, ten days before the date thereof.

The Constitution and By-laws of the Club may be altered or amended at the annual meeting, or at any special meeting, notified ten days in advance, for that purpose; provided not less than twenty-five members of the Club shall be present at said annual or special meeting, and that the proposed alterations or amendments to the Constitution or By-Laws, shall receive a vote of not less than three fourths of the number of members present, in favor of amending or altering the said Constitution and By-Laws.

ARTICLE VII.
ELECTION OF MEMBERS.

Members may be admitted to the Club with the consent of the government of the Club, provided the name of the candidate for admission shall have been placed on the Notice-board of the Club-room for a time not less than ten days without receiving ten marks against it. Said number of marks shall be considered as excluding said candidate from membership. No candidate who shall have been rejected shall be again proposed for six months, or shall be admitted to the Club-room as a pupil.

ARTICLE VIII.
ADMISSION OF PUPILS.

Persons desirous of taking lessons of the club Instructor, or Instructors, without being members of the Club, or in case the numbers of members shall be full, may be admitted to the use of the Club-rooms, without the consent and under the direction of the officers of the Club, or two of them, and on such terms as may be established by the government of the Club; Provided, that in all cases payment for instruction shall be made in advance. A list of the names of all such persons shall be kept by the Secretary, with the date of their admission, and the number of lessons they are entitled to receive. Each pupil shall furnish his own equipments.

ARTICLE IX.
ENTRANCE FEE.

The entrance fee, on the admission of any member, shall be three dollars; and no member shall be admitted to the privileges of the Club until he shall have paid his entrance fee. The receipt of the Teasurer shall be evidence of the payment of the entrance fee by the member elect, and of his right to all the privileges of the Club, and assent to the rules of the club, as well as submission to the restrictions they enjoin.

ARTICLE X.
ANNUAL ASSESSMENT.

Each member of the Club shall pay an annual assessement of ten dollars, which shall be due the Treasurer on the first day of October in each year, and no other assessment shall be laid. Any member neglecting or refusing to pay his assessment for thirty days after the same shall have been demanded by the Treasurer in person, or by a written notice sent through the Post-office, shall be deemed to have withdrawn from the Club, and shall not again be admitted to the Club, except on the footing of other candidates for admission, and the payment of his arrears.

ARTICLE XI.
RESIGNATIONS.

Any member may withdraw from the Club, on giving notice in writing, to the Secretary, of his intention so to do, provided he has paid his assessment for the current year. Any member so retiring shall be deemed to give up all claim to any share in the personal property of the Club.

ARTICLE XII.
EXPULSION OF MEMBERS.

In case of persistence in the infraction of any rule by any member, or of any conduct on the part of any member which in the opinion of the government of the Club may tend to endanger the good order, welfare, or character of the Club, it shall be their duty to call a meeting of the Club, specifying the object of the same; and if at such meeting it shall be so decided by a majoirty of votes given, he shall be expelled from the Club.

ARTICLE XIII.
GENERAL POWERS OF THE GOVERNMENT.

The officers of the Club shall have the right to decide all differences between the members while in the Club-rooms, or between the Instructor or Instructors and the members or the pupils, and their decision shall be final, and without appeal. They shall also have the right to regulate the exercises, and assign the hours in which the Club-rooms shall be opened or shut, and to delegate the care of the rooms, and the preservation of good order, to the Instructor or Instructors, or to any member or members of the Club.

BY-LAWS.
I.

The Club-rooms shall be open for the use of members from the first day of October till the first day of June next following, on which conditions and at such hours as the government may direct, excepting that the rooms shall be closed on Sunday, and on every other day at ten o'clock, P.M.

II.

No stranger, or persons residing within twenty miles of Boston, shall be admitted to the Club-rooms, except by invitation of a member of the government, and for such time as the government may see fit.

III.

Each member shall provide his own foils and other equipments at his own expense; the club being responsible only for keeping them ready for use, in the condition they may be left in by the owner.

IV.

No refreshments shall be brought into the Club-rooms, except by permission of the President, in writing.

V.

No dogs shall be kept in the Club-rooms, and any member bringing a dog into the Club-rooms may be fined fifty cents, to the use of the Club.

VI.

No females shall be admitted to the Club-rooms, under any pretext whatever, except by permission of a member of the government of the Club.

VII.

The uniform of the Club shall be a shell jacket, of navy blue, with leather facings, or plastron. The officers of the club, and the Instructor or Instructors, shall wear a distinctive badge thereon.

GYMNASTICS IN THE KENTUCKY MILITARY INSTITUTE

TO FRANK QUEEN, ESQ., *Editor, N. Y. Clipper.*

SIR: Knowing the interest you take in physical exercise, you will be pleased to learn that YOUR DOCTRINES OF AIR AND EXERCISE are being carried out in this *out of the way section* of country.

As a cadet of the Kentucky Military Institute, I take pleasure in informing you that owing to the liberality of our superintendent, Col. E. W. Morgan, A Gymnasium (arranged and constructed by our instructor on Physical Science, Capt. HAMMERSLEY, at a cost of about $2000) has been offered for our use *without extra charge*. We number about 145 cadets, and subdividing us into two or three smaller classes, with a leader of each, whilst he superintends the whole, gives to us all an equal chance of benefit. Our Gymnasium is 70 by 30 feet, and from 16 to 20 feet high, with every modern appliance for *active* and *passive* exercise, culled from the best Gymnasia of Europe, by our Professor, with many adaptations and improvements of his own.

But five months since, and most of us had never *even seen* a Gymnasium; but, at our Commencement exercise, on the 17th of June, some of our gymnasts won golden opinions for their skill and daring. The speaking took place on a platform adjoining the Gymnasium, at the base of a natural amphitheatre, before a large assemblage of people from many miles around, who were comfortably seated beneath the umbrageous shade of a grove of catalpa trees—after which, at the sound of the Captain's bugle, they were summoned to the Gymnasium, which was crowded to every part; every projection and all the beams were scaled by those who dared to climb so high; and as you have given a programme of other Gymnasic Exhibitions, I now presume a brief summary will not be unacceptable.

The Exhibition commenced with *Sabre Play,* by Cadet J.S. Kendall, of N.C., and Captain H.; *Boxing*—W.K. Walker, Texas, and J.H. Leacock; *Fencing*—the Adjutant, D.P. January, being sick, his place was supplied by J.S. Kendall, who had a bout with his teacher. After which the Gymnasts, led by their instructor, went through a series of exercises—on single horizontal bar, double ditto—flying squirrel leaps from swinging trapeze to fixed bar *(clearing 8 feet from bar to bar)* perpendicular poles—parallel bars—grasshopper spring on step bars, &c., &c....

Space will not permit me to enter into further details, but I might mention that your *doctrines* are completed by the construction of the building, which has large folding doors on either sides, independent of windows, so that *air* as well as *exercise* is obtained; a door opens into a spring house, where cool and refreshing draughts of the purest element refresh the gymnast during his labors.

In conclusion, allow me to say that our Superintendant has presented the Cadets with a double set of cricketing apparatus, so that, with our drill and parades, there is no want of occupation for the physique as a relief from the mental employment—and this during all weathers, *wet or dry, hot or cold....*

A CADET

of the Kentucky Military Institute, near Frankfort, Ky.

GREAT GYMNASTIC PERFORMANCES

Some time since, Mr. John H. Moody, of Binney's gymnasium, San Francisco, pulled up two weights, of 14 pounds each, 27,727 times, without stopping to rest. The task occupied him five hours and a quarter. Whereupon Mr. Frank Wheeler, of the Pioneer Gymnasium, same place, offered a wager of $500 that he could beat Mr. Moody's performance. This latter gentleman being about to leave the state, was unable to accept the wager. Mr. Wheeler, however, determined to convince his friends that his banter was no idle boast, and on the 12th of May, he commenced, at 7 o'clock in the morning, to pull at two fourteen and a half pound weights, one with each hand, by means of ropes rove over pullies; the operator remaining in a sitting posture until 5 o'clock in the afternoon, without intermission, making ten hours of intensely hard work. When Mr. Wheeler commenced the performance of this feat, he weighed 175 1/2 pounds, and at its close weighed 171 1/2 pounds, having lost four pounds in the space of ten hours.

As he is in constant practice, and therefore has not a pound of fat on his frame, this enormous loss will give a better idea of the extreme severity of the performance. The following figures will show the performance of each hour: 1st hour, 6250; 2d, 5850; 3d, 6660, 4th, 6400, 5th, 5612, 6th, 5370, 7th, 5790, 8th, 4975; 9th, 5475; 10th, 6536—Total, 58,617. The distance to which each weight was raised was about 4 feet, which by computation will amount to a little more than 44 miles in 10 hours, and equal to raising 851,946 pounds, in separate burdens of 14 1/2 pounds each, in the same time. At the conclusion of this feat Mr. Wheeler thanked those present for their attendance, and stated that it was performed by him not for a wager, but solely to show, by actual experiment, the amount of endurance a man could suffer, who took gymnastic exercises.

During the performance of the feat, Mr. W. partook sparingly of broiled beef, and his thirst was quenched with sparing sips of champagne. He executed the feat sitting down, stripped to the waist in order to give full play to the muscles of the arms and chest, ordinary gymnastic tights, slipers and silk cap. During the period of labor he was frequently rubbed down with coarse towels by attendants. It is said that Mr. Moody intended to attempt to excel this feat.

GRAND GYMNASTIC EXHIBITION

Consonant with their military character, the invited, independent of the citizen broadcloth, were punctual in attendance, and at eight o'clock precisely the band struck up a favorite march, and in stepped a score of gymnasts—led on by Mr. Wood—who promenaded through the large room, in single file, in very rich gymnastic-costume. It really was a pretty sight, twenty young men perfect models of strength—with few exceptions—fully developed in body, with health and happiness beaming in their countenances. They were pupils of Wood, and assuredly a credit to his training, and their own good judgment in preferring the invigorating exercises, to following the unprofitable consumption of time too frequently indulged in by the youths of our city in unnamable things and places....

THE EXERCISES

1. Parallel Bars,	6. Slack Rope,	10. Peg Pole,
2. Ladders,	7. Vaulting Horse,	11. Rack Bars,
3. Inclined Pole,	8. Jumping,	12. Single Bar,
4. Dumb Bells,	9. Double Trapeze,	13. Posturing,
5. Swinging Rings,		14. Somersetting

The room of the Gymnasium, in which the above exercises took place, is 50 by 100 feet, and 25 feet high; by day well lighted and ventilated through 30 large windows high up the walls, and two large ventilators on the roof; at night the gas burners illuminate the building. A space of about five feet from the wall all round is reserved for a race course, the "ground" travelled being covered with a thick coating of saw dust, and covered again with strong sheeting. Over this course, all round the building, a temporary gallery was erected for the invited guests. With this description of the place, the reader can form his idea of the luxurious space of a Gymnasium, where nobody need touch the corns of his neighbor.

THE PARALLEL BARS are forty feet long, about five feet high, and twenty inches apart, made of any hard wood, and fixed to the floor by iron braces. For juveniles, the bars are not so high; in fact, we saw bars of three different sizes in the room, evidently intended for Johnny, Master John, and Mr. John, in every stage of his development and increase in years. The exercises on the bars seem to pass along under the general term of the grasshopper motion. Grassy, like all other living "things," has unquestionably a variety of styles in his locomotion, which would thereby justify the variety of ups and downs, forwards and backwards, outs and ins, and side evolutions that we witnessed under this generic term of grasshopper motion. It is ever invidious to make comparisons of talent; we will, therfore, say that the gentlemen all showed considerable ability and endurance in swinging and jumping—not from the hands, but from the armpits—from post to post, a distance of eight feet; and then in succession from one end of the bars to the other. The gymnasts themselves seem to honor particularly the performances of Mr. Gus. A. Ratz and Mr. Weir, while the spectators applauded everybody, as everything was well done.

THE LADDERS—from the floor to the roof, were placed at an angle of 30 degrees. Up the gymnasts climbed, or rather leaped —for all that pulling and dragging was absent—from round to round. The younger in experience were prudently not so venturesome; but the others sprang with grace, and evidently as easily as if it were "the nature of the animal." Down they came with the same ease, leaping from round to round, both hands off at once, and one gentleman appeared to me—we were some distance from him—to always skip over a bar and take the second all the way down. Another went up to the top of the ladder, swung himself head downwards, and sustained himself by his toes, and went up again and suspended himself in the air with the back of his hand resting on the upper round of the ladder. Mr. Bogart surpassed the ordinary feats by ascending the ladder with one arm: whoever thinks that nothing, had better try it. All this, we are again pleased to record, was warmly applauded.

From the description of the first two exercises, the reader can form a good idea of the Gymnasts, their performances, and the pleasure enjoyed by the Seventh Regiment that witnessed the rational entertainment during the evening, without our giving the remainder of the exercises in detail.

Judge Halstead put up the 35lb. dumb-bell three times, straightly from his shoulder to the extent of his reach, and Mr. Grower put up the 100lb. weight six consecutive times, which was a feat warmly applauded.

Among the most distinguised on the Swinging Ring may be mentioned Mr. S.O. Ryder, who knocked the rings against the ceiling, to the horror of many, as it was at first supposed to be his cranium.

Mr. Ratz was immense on the Slack Rope, and also in the Jumping; and Mr. Verplanck Weir, in the latter exercise was excellent.

The Perche Equipoise, by Messrs. S.O. Ryder, and O. Woodruff, surpassed in the opinion of the Gymnasts even the performances of the celebrated Sengrist brothers, of Hippodrome notoriety.

The DOUBLE TRAPEZE, by Judge Halsted and Mr. Grower, was considered by judges, to be the best performance every witnessed in this country of the kind.

Messrs. Bogart and Ryder, in Giant Swinging on the Single Bar, were very graceful, passing round and round more like a mechanical fixture than the encasement of bones, flesh, sinews, and all the flexible *etceteras* of the human frame.

Mr. Abner S. Brady was greatly cheered on his ascending the Peg Pole, pulling himself up in fixing the peg regularly from hole to hole.

One gentleman, whose name we did not learn, in the ring exercise sustained the whole weight of his body by one arm and drew himself up from the floor three times in succession till his chin touched the ring, which is a feat seldom accomplished.

The Posturing and Somersetting were very entertaining. During the evening Mr. Burnham was very humorous, and frequenlty "brought down the house" with his antics. In fact, a more sociable evening could not have been spent by the one sex of society. It is not at all impossible that some professional Gymnasts could surpass what we have here so highly spoken of, but the operations of the professor and the amateurs are vastly different. The efforts of the former are confined to the creation of momentary sensation, and much is risked by him, and more is feared by the spectators; but in the exercises of the latter it was simply an exhibition of school exercises, which few know, and all should learn, for their advantage in mind and body, and these exercises were so performed without ostentation, and as work well understood and pleasantly accomplished. We don't know that we ever passed a more agreeable evening as a spectator, and the continued applause of such an intelligent company spoke volumes in favor of Gymnastics and their interpretors.

Before the evening terminated, a letter was read from the Hon. Joseph Mayo, mayor of Richmond, Va., expressing his regret that official business prevented him from being present on the occasion, but in his absence begged the following sentiment to be read:

The Seventh Regiment—National by name—National in feeling and character. Wherever the Star Spangled Banner waves, there their hearts are: whenever and wherever peril, there will their arms be in defence of the Union.

This was received with three hearty cheers and a tiger, and three Richmond cheers. The company separated shortly after ten o'clock, satisfied that bodily development and rational exercise were at least something in the order of this progressive age, and the death blow to pills and nostrums.

Chapter 11

LACROSSE

The sport of lacrosse provides an excellent example of the adaptation and modernization of a traditional pastime of North American Indians by Canadians. The game was an integral part of the culture of the Creeks, Cherokees, Choctaws, and other tribes at the time of European exploration and early colonization. It remained popular among natives during the mid-1800s. Explorers and settlers had observed and admired the game of "baggatawa" in the British and French colonies since the early 1700s. Canadians called the game "lacrosse," naming it after the French word for the stick used by the players. By the late 1850s it had established itself as one of the favorite recreations of Montreal.

Indian ball games were similar to premodern European and American amusements in a number of ways, but they differed in their striking display of religious ritual. Like early versions of cricket, baseball, or football, native stickball featured a loosely defined field of play, a lack of standardized equipment, an indeterminate number of players, and restrictions on who was allowed to participate. But what distinguished the native amusement from its Canadian or American counterparts was the ceremonial, sacred element. When tribes, villages, or smaller groups competed, the participants engaged in elaborate rituals. The men observed strict dietary rules and abstained from sexual intercourse for a period before the contest. They spent the night before the event sequestered in a sacred place under the supervision of medicine men. The players danced and chanted prayers to the Great Spirit as their religious leaders smoked pipes. Usually the contestants had their bodies painted and they wore costumes suitable for the occasion. During the all-night vigil the men left the dance at intervals to engage in elaborate ceremonies with beads. Anthropologists have suggested that all of these activities were designed to cure sickness, increase fertility of plants and animals, and produce rain. The ball was apparently a sacred object that could not be touched with the hand and perhaps symbolized the earth, sun, or moon.

The match itself was played on a field that lacked set boundaries. The two goals were two sets of posts, which could be one hundred feet or several miles apart. The object of the sport was to throw a ball between the two posts that marked the opposing side's goal. The beating of drums and frenzied betting accompanied the action, and sometimes female spectators exhorted their men by whipping their legs. At some encounters rival medicine men used mirrors to reflect sunlight onto their team. Games could last a few hours or even a few days. The Cherokee and Choctaw versions generally ended when one side achieved twelve points, or goals. "Indian Ball Games" presents a description of several North American pastimes by the painter and ethnographer George Catlin.

Between the 1830s and 1860s several white citizens of Montreal transformed Indian stickball into the earliest version of modern lacrosse. In 1834 an Indian exhibition sparked interest among residents of that town, who organized the city's first club a few years later. In 1843 and 1844 local athletic festivals featured matches contested among both native and white teams. In 1856 several gentlemen organized the Montreal Lacrosse Club, which was followed by the Beaver club and at least four others by 1860. During this period the driving force behind the modernization of lacrosse was William George Beers, who is known as the "father" of the sport. Beers was an early enthusiast and promoter, and in 1860 he published the first rule book and instructional manual for the game. Excerpts from that volume appear below. A highlight of the game's formative years was an exhibition played for the Prince of Wales on the grounds of the Montreal Cricket Club, 27 August 1860.

Lacrosse occupies a critically important place in the history of Canadian sport because it was developed by a young, native-born, upper class group of men who shared nationalistic sentiments. Although they were products of British schools and colleges and were nurtured in the English love of athletics, these sportsmen sought an indigeneous pastime which they could develop as the national game of Canada. Indian stickball provided them with the foundation for a form of athletics which they modernized through a process of rationalization of rules and the bureaucratic creation of clubs.

INDIAN BALL GAMES

George Catlin was an American traveler, artist, and early ethnographer. Born in Wilkes-Barre, Pennsylvania in 1796, he practiced law for two years in Philadelphia before he turned to a career as an artist and portrait painter in New York City. During the 1830s he traveled throughout the West, visiting, observing, and painting sketches of Indian tribal life. He then journeyed to London, where he published his descriptions and drawings of these natives. The following selection includes three sections from his *Letters and Notes on the Manners, Customs, and Conditions of the North American Indians* (London, 1844), Vol. I, pp. 149-150, Vol. II, pp. 140-45, 165-166. The first piece is a brief description of a Mandan game that involved a ring and stick; the second is an account of a Choctaw stickball match; the third relates how Sioux men laughed and drank themselves into a stupor as they watched their women play a ball game.

THE MANDANS

The games and amusement of these people are in most respects like those of the other tribes, consisting of ball plays—game of the moccasin, of the platter—feats of archery —horseracing, etc.; and they have yet another, which may be said to be their favorite amusement and unknown to the other tribes about them. The game of Tchung-kee, a beautiful athletic exercise, which they seem to be almost unceasingly practising whilst the weather is fair, and they have nothing else of moment to demand their attention. This game is decidedly their favorite amusement, and is played near to the village on a pavement of clay , which has been used for that purpose until it has become as smooth and hard as a floor. For this game, two champions form their respective parties, by choosing alternately the most famous players, until their requisite numbers are made up. Their bettings are then made, and their stakes are held by some of the chiefs or others present. The play commences with two who start off upon a trot, abreast of each other, and one of them rolls in advance of them, on the pavement, a little ring of two or three inches in diameter, cut out of a stone; and each one follows it up with his "tchung-kee" (a stick of six feet in length, with little bits of leather projecting from its side of an inch or more in length), which he throws before him as he runs, sliding it along upon the ground after the ring endeavoring to place it in such a position when it stops, that the ring may fall upon it, and receive one of the little projections of leather through it, which counts for game, one, or two, or four, according to the position of the leather on which the ring is lodged. The last winner always has the rolling of the ring, and both start and throw the tchung-kee together; if either fails to receive the ring or to lie in a certain position, it is a forfeiture of the amount of the number he was nearest to, and he loses his throw; when another steps into his place. This game is a very difficult one to describe, so as to give an exact idea of it, unless one can see it played—it is a game of great beauty and fine bodily exercise, and these people become excessively fascinated with it; often gambling away everything they possess, and even sometimes, when everything else was gone, have been known to stake their liberty upon the issue of these games, offering themselves as slaves to their opponents in case they get beaten....

THE CHOCTAWS

Of fifteen thousand, are another tribe, removed from the Northern parts of Alabama, and Mississippi, within the few years past, and now occupying a large and rich tract of country, south of the Arkansas and the Canadian rivers; adjoining to the country of the Creeks and the Cherokees, equally civilised, and living much in the same manner....

These people seem, even in their troubles, to be happy; and have, like all the other remnants of tribes, preserved with great tenacity their different games, which it would seem they are everlastingly practising for want of other occupations or amusements in life. Whilst I was staying at the Choctaw agency in the midst of their nation, it seemed to be a sort of season of amusements, a kind of holiday; when the whole tribe almost, were assembled around the establishment, and from day to day we were entertained with some games or feats that were exceedingly amusing; horse-racing, dancing, wrestling, foot-racing, and ball-playing, were amongst the most exciting; and of all the catalogue, the most beautiful was decidedly that of ball-playing. This wonderful game, which is the favorite one amongst all the tribes, and with these Southern tribes played exactly the same, can never be appreciated by those who are not happy enough to see it.

It is no uncommon occurence for six or eight hundred or a thousand of these young men to engage in a game of ball with five or six times that number of spectators, of men, women, and children, surrounding the ground, and looking on. And I pronounce such a scene, with its hundreds of Nature's most beautiful models, denuded, and painted of various colours, running and leaping into the air, in all the most extravagant and varied forms, in the desperate struggles for the ball, a school for the painter or sculptor, equal to any of those which ever inspired the hand of the artist in the Olympian games or the Roman forum.

I have made it a uniform rule, whilst in the Indian country, to attend every ball-play I could hear of, if I could do it by riding a distance of twenty or thirty miles; and my usual custom has been on such occasions, to straddle the back of my horse, and look on to the best advantage. In this way I have sat, and oftentimes reclined, and almost dropped from my horse's back, with irresistable laughter at the succession of droll tricks, and kicks and scuffles which ensue, in the almost superhuman struggles for the ball. These plays generally commence at nine o'clock, or near it, in the morning; and I have more then once balanced myself on my pony, from that time till near sundown, without more than one minute of intermission at a time, before the game has been decided....

While at the Choctaw agency it was announced, that there was to be a great play on a certain day, within a few miles, on which occasion I attended, and made the following entry into my notebook, which I literally copy out:—

Monday afternoon at three o'clock, I rode out with Lieutenants S. and M., to a very pretty prairie, about six miles distant, to the ball playground of the Choctaws, where we found several thousand Indians encamped. There were two points of timber about half a mile apart, in which the two parties for the play, with their respective families and friends, were encamped; and lying between them, the prairie on which the game was to be played. My companions and myself, although we had been apprised, that to see the whole of a ball-play, we must remain on the ground all the night previous, had brought nothing to sleep upon, resolving to keep our eyes open, and see what transpired through the night. During the afternoon, we loitered about amongst the different tents and shantees of the two encampments, and afterwards, at sundown, witnessed the ceremony of measuring out the ground, and erecting the "byes" or goals which were to guide the play. Each party had their goal made with two upright posts, about 25 feet high and six feet apart, set firm in the ground, with a pole across at the top. These goals were about forty or fifty rods apart; and at a point just half way between them, was another small stake, driven down, where the ball was to be thrown up at the firing of a gun, to be struggled for by the players. All this preparation was made by some old men, who were, it seems, selected to be the judges of the play, who drew a line from one bye to the other; to which directly came from the woods, on both sides, a great concourse of women and old men, boys and girls, and dogs, and horses, where bets were to be made on the play. The betting was all done across this line, and seemed to be chiefly left to the women, who seemed to have martialled out a little of everything that their houses and their fields possessed, goods and chattel—knives—dresses—blankets—pots and kettels—dogs and horses, and guns; and all were placed in the possession of stake-holders, who sat by them, and watched them on the ground all night, preparatory to the play.

The sticks with which this tribe play, are bent into an oblong hoop at the end, with a sort of slight web of small thongs tied across, to prevent the ball from passing through. The players hold one of these in each hand, and by leaping into the air, they catch the ball between the two nettings and throw it, without being allowed to strike it, or catch it in their hands....

In every ball-play of these people, it is a rule of the play, that no man shall wear moccasins on his feet, or any other dress than his breech-cloth around his waist, with a beautiful bead belt, and a "tail" made of white horsehair or quills, and a "mane" on the neck, of horsehair dyed of various colours.

This game had been arranged and "made up" three or four months before the parties met to play it, and in the following manner:—The two champions who led the two parties, and had the alternate choosing of the players through the whole tribe, sent runners, with the ball-sticks most fantastically ornamented with ribbons and red paint, to be touched by each one of the chosen players; who thereby agreed to be on the spot at the appointed time and ready for the play. The ground having been all prepared and preliminaries of the game all settled, and the bettings all made, and goods all "staked," night came on without the appearance of any players on the ground. But soon after dark, a procession of lighted flambeaux was seen coming from each encampment, to the ground where the players assembled around their respective byes; and at the beat of the drums and chants of the women, each party of platers commenced the "ball-play dance." Each party danced for a quarter of an hour around their respective byes, in their ball-play dress; rattling their ball —sticks together in the most violent manner, and all singing as loud as they could raise their voices; whilst the women in each party, who had their goods at stake, formed into two rows on the line between the two parties of players, and danced also, in a uniform step, and all their voices joined in chants to the Great Spirit; in which they were soliciting his favour in deciding the game to their advantage; and also encouraging the players to exert every power they possessed, in the struggle that was to ensue. In the meantime, four old *medicine-men,* who were to have the starting of the ball, and who were to be judges of the play, were seated at the point where the ball was to be started; and busily smoking to the Great Spirit for their success in judging rightly, and impartially, between the parties in so important an affair.

This dance was one of the most picturesque scenes imaginable, and was repeated at intervals of every half hour during the night, and exactly in the same manner; so that the players were certainly awake all the night, and arranged in their appropriate dress, prepared for the play which was to commence at nine o'clock the next morning. In the morning, at the hour, the two parties and all their friends, were drawn out and over the ground; when at length the game commenced, by the judges throwing up the ball at the firing of a gun; when an instant struggled ensued between the players, who were some six or seven hundred in numbers, and were mutually endeavoring to catch the ball in their sticks, and throw home and between their respective stakes; which whenever successfully done, counts one for game. In this game every player was dressed alike, that is divested of all dress, except the girdle and the tail, which I have before described; and in these desperate struggles for the ball, when it is up (where hundreds are running together and leaping, actually over each other's heads, and darting between their adversaries legs, tripping and throwing, and foiling each other in every possible manner, and every voice raised to the highest key, in shrill yelps and barks)! there are rapid successions of feats, and of incidents, that astonish and amuse far beyond the conception of any one who has not had the singular good luck to witness them. In these struggles, every mode is used that can be devised, to oppose the progress of the foremost, who is likely to get the ball; and these obstructions often meet desperate individual resistance, which terminates in a vioent scuffle, and sometimes in fistcuffs; when their sticks are dropped, and the parties are unmolested, whilst they are settling it between themselves; unless it be by a general stampedo, to which they are subject who are down, if the ball happens to pass in their direction. Every weapon, by a rule of all ball-plays, is laid by in their respective encampments, and no man allowed to go for one; so that the sudden broils that take place on the ground, are presumed to be as suddenly settled without any probability of much personal injury, and no one is allowed to interfere in any way with the contentious individuals.

There are times, when the ball gets to the ground, and such a confused mass rushing together around it, and knocking their sticks together, without the possibility of any one getting or seeing it, for the dust that they raise, that the spectator loses his strength, and everything else but his senses; when the condensed mass of ball-sticks, and shins, and bloody noses, is carried around the different parts of the ground, for a quarter of an hour at a time, without any one of the mass being able to see the ball; and which they are often thus scuffing for, several minutes after it has been thrown off, and played over another part of the ground.

For each time that the ball was passed between the stakes of either party, one was counted for their game, and a halt of about one minute; when it was again started by the judges of the play, and a similar struggle ensued; and so on until the successful party arrived to 100, which was the limit of the game, and accomplished at an hour's sun, when they took the stakes; and then, by a previous agreement, produced a number of jugs of whiskey, which gave all a wholesome drink, and sent them all off merry and in good humor, but not drunk.

After this exciting day, the concourse was assembled in the vicinty of the agency house, where we had a great variety of dances and other amusements; the most of which I have described on former occasions. One, however, was new to me, and I must say a few words of it: this was the *Eagle Dance,* a very pretty scene, which is got up by their young men, in honour of that bird, for which they seem to have a religious regard. This picturesque dance was given by twelve or sixteen men, whose bodies were chiefly naked and painted white, with white clay, and each one holding in his hand the tail of the eagle, while his head was also decorated with an eagle's quill. Spears were stuck in the ground, around which the dance was performed by four men at a time, who had simultaneously, at the beat of the drum, jumped up from the ground where they had all sat in rows of four, one row immediately behind the other, and ready to take the place of the first four when they left the ground fatigued, which they did by hopping or jumping around behind the rest, and taking their seats, ready to come up again in their turn, after each of the other sets had been through the same forms.

In this dance, the steps or rather jumps, were different from anything I had ever witnessed before, as the dancers were squat down, with their bodies almost to the ground, in a severe and most difficult posture....

THE SIOUX

When I was there, Wa-be-sha's band of the Sioux came there, and remained several weeks to get their annuities, which, when they received them fell (as they always will do), far short of paying off the account, which the traders take good care to have standing against them for goods furnished them on a year's credit. However, whether they pay off or not, they can always get whiskey enough for a grand carouse and a brawl, which lasts for a week or two, and almost sure to terminate the lives of some of their numbers.

At the end of one of these a few days since, after the men had enjoyed their surfeit of whiskey, and wanted a little more amusement, and felt disposed to indulge the weaker sex in a little recreation also; it was announced amongst them, and through the village, that the women were going to have a ball-play!

For this purpose the men, in their very liberal trades they were making, and filling their canoes with goods delivered to them on a year's credit, laid out a great quantity of ribbons and calicoes, with other presents well adapted to the wants and desires of the women; which were hung on a pole resting on crotches, and guarded by an old man, who was to be judge and umpire of the play which was to take place amongst the women, who were divided into two equal parties, and were to play a desperate game of ball, for the valuable stakes that were hanging before them.

In the ball-play of the women, they have two balls attached to the ends of a string, about a foot and a half long; and each woman has a short stick in each hand, on which she catched the string with the two balls, and throws them, endeavoring to force them over the goal of her own party. The men are more than half drunk, when they feel liberal enough to indulge the women in such an amusement; and take infinite pleasure in rolling about on the ground and laughing to excess, whilst the women are tumbling about in all attitudes, and scuffing for the ball. The game of *"hunt the slipper,"* even, loses its zest after witnessing one of these, which sometimes last for hours together; and often exhibits the hottest contest for the balls, exactly over the heads of the men; who, half from whiskey, and half from inclination, are lying in groups and flat upon the ground.

LACROSSE IN MONTREAL

William George Beers, the "father" of lacrosse, was educated at Lower Canada College. In 1859 he first conceived the idea of systematizing and organizing the Indian game for his friends and fellow sportsmen of Montreal. A member of that city's Beaver Club, he was goal-keeper in the exhibition that was played for the Prince of Wales in August 1860. The following document presents excerpts from his pamphlet of rules and instructions for play, *The Game of Lacrosse, containing the Construction of the Crosse, Various Methods of Throwing and Catching the Ball, "Dodging," "Checking,"*

Goal-keeping, &c. (Montreal, 1860), pp. 3-5, 8-10, 12-38. It is reprinted with permission of the Municipal Library of the City of Montreal.

THE GAME OF LACROSSE
GENERAL REMARKS

The game of Lacrosse originated with the Aborigines of America, and is their favorite Field Game. How and when it had its origins cannot be traced. The first game known to have been played in Canada was by the Algonquins, and seen by Charlevoix and his party when they were ascending the St. Lawrence, at some point between Quebec and Three Rivers. It is stated in Major Richardson's Novel, *Wacousta,* that a game of Lacrosse was played before Fort Detroit, at the time that three Indian tribes—the Ottawa, Delawares, and Shawnees,—attempted to surprise it. The Ottawas played on one side, and the Delaware and Shawneees on the other. American history will doubtless furnish further accounts of where Lacrosse was seen played.

The game has not existed for over four years among the "Pale-faces" of Montreal, many of whom are now a match for the Red brothers. Montreal has the honor of first introducing the game and forming Clubs among the whites, it being introduced to them by the Iroquois of Caughnawaga.

This game, being now purely Canadian, is likely to become the *National Game of Canada.* Long, long after the romantic "sons of the forest" have passed away, long, long after their sun sinks in the west to rise no more, Lacrosse will remind the pale-faces of Canada of the noble Indians that once lorded it over this continent.

There is a strange and wild beauty about this game that excites the admiration of the spectator, and being very simple and easily understood, is the more interesting to him on that account. The innumerable and fantastic shapes the player is obliged to put himself in while "dodging," &c., is a source of much amusement both to the looker on and player, and as a lady has said in a poem addressed to a club of this city, the spectator will

"Wonder at the players' gait,
For crooked legs predominate."

The game of Lacrosse is highly conducive to muscular strength and activity, conferring beauty and elasticity of form on the player, and developing his muscles, and is in every respect an *invigorating* game. But, if too much *running* is practiced, the player will find it do him more harm than good, for more danger is incurred in taking *too much* exercise than from *too little.*

In Lacrosse every member and muscle of the body is brought into operation at the same time, thus equalizing the exercise over the entire system, and lessening the fatigue of any one particular member. With most other field games this is not the case, and where a single member or muscle of the body is allowed to remain in a state of repose, while its fellows are exercised, that single member receives none of the benefit, and becomes fatigued on the slightest exertion. *The mind* has also an active part to perform in many departments of Lacrosse, such as throwing the ball, goal-keeping, &c.

Lacrosse would be a good game for *girls,* as they want some such active exercise to develop their forms, making them active and strong, "the future mothers of a manly race." *Exercise* would then perform greatly the part of milliners and dressmakers, and artificial and padded forms (!) would be known no more.

This would be a very invigorating game for winter, if a field could be procured where the snow is not deep, but hard. The cold air combined with the excitement and exercise would prove very beneficial to the players.

The Dress of the Players should consist of fine flannel shirt, pants and cap; moccassins of light shoes, and a belt.

Moccassins or light shoes facilitate speed in running, and agility in "dodging," &c., besides being easier to the feet than boots.

The Belt shouold be worn on the loins, so as to pass over the navel, and must not be too tight or too loose. A belt is intended to support the abdomen, liver, &c., and greatly assists the player in running. The Greeks invariably put their belts on before they commenced to wrestle. A light *sash,* such as are worn in Canada in winter, would be preferable to a belt, as it is much easier to the loins. A gentleman has proposed the general use of sashes for clubs in Canada, as being more Canadian-like, and also looking better. This is a very good idea, and deserves notice.

Cooling too quick must be carefully avoided, as also drinking any fluids while the body is in a state of perspiration, laying down on the ground, &c. When a player is in this state he should keep moving till he cools, or sit down in some dry place....

MATERIALS FOR THE GAME
THE CROSSE

This is either a *Hickory* or *Ash* stick, well seasoned and bent, by steaming...*Ash is* the most comonly used, on account of its capability of being bent with more ease than hickory; although the latter is by far to be preferred, as it is much stronger. The weight of the Crosse should be proportioned to the age and strength of the player. A long crosse is to be preferred to a short one; as enabling the player to throw the ball to a greater distance, and *check* with more facility.

THE FLAGS

Four flags of two different colors are required; two flags constitute a "goal." They should not be over 6 1/2 feet in height, and about the same distance apart. The length from one goal to the other should not exceed half a mile, but they may be placed at any distance chosen less than this. The two goals should face each other, if possible.

THE BALL

Should be either solid India Rubber, or a sponge ball. One that *bounces* should be preferred to a ball too hard. Many prefer the solid India Rubber on account of the distance it can be flung, and as it is harder to stop than the sponge ball.

THE GROUND

The larger the field is the better, and where grass is short and no stones on the ground, it is always found the best. An even field would be much better than one otherwise, but this is not necessary; though, often when the ball is flung along the ground, and going straight to the player it was thrown to, a slight rise or defect of the ground will cause it to bound off to one side, and often it bounds to an opposing player.

CONSTRUCTION OF THE CROSSE

The materials used in weaving the Cross are as follows:

1. *Cat-gut, pure, thick and strong.* This is the material most generally used, both by the Indians and "Pale Faces," and is almost superior to anything else, when it is good.

2. *Moose-Skin.* This is rapidly being substituted for cat-gut, among the Lacrosse Clubs of Montreal, on account of its combined softness and strength. It is not, however, equal in strength to the former material. If beauty is desirable in the weaving of a Cross, moose-skin should be preferred to cat-gut. Snow-shoe strings are generally the best of moose-skin, and are preferable to the skin otherwise. It should be left to soak in salt and water over night, and in the morning dried and cut into stripes of the requisite size.

3. *Eel skin.* This is remarkable for its strength, but is little used, as it remains soft on account of the oil it contains.

Leather-thongs, Clock gut, strong cord, and numerous other substances have been used, but cat-gut and moose-skin still reign supreme....

Bagging the Crosse.—This is not allowable by some clubs as it is not used by the Indians, but as it facilitates "dodging" to a great extent by keeping the ball on the Crosse better when an opponent strikes it, it is thought proper to mention it here. It is made either by slackening the material used, or if *gut,* by soaking it near the handle in water, and placing a round weight on it so as to cause it to sink. Allow the two ends of the Crosse to rest on something, so as to cause the gut to be weighed down. Remove the weight when the gut is perfectly dry, and the Crosse is "ready for action."

LAWS OF LACROSSE

The Game of Lacrosse cannot yet boast of any established Laws, but there are generally understood Rules to which most Clubs conform, and which may be enumerated as follows:

1. No *swiping* is allowed.

2. No *tripping, holding,* or any such unfair play is allowed.

3. *Throwing the ball with the hand* is prohibited, though if in a struggle, and opponents around, it may sometimes be kicked with the foot.

4. *Picking up the ball with the hand* is not allowed, except in extreme cases, where the Crosse cannot get it, such as in a hole, &c.

5. After every game the players change *sides,* unless the players who tossed up agree otherwise.

6. If a ball flung at the goal is caught by the "goal-keeper" but breaks through his Crosse and enters the goal, it is *in*. Or, if a player of either side puts the ball in by any accident, it is game for the party who were attacking that goal.

7. In facing, neither of the "facers" shall attempt to gain the ball till "three" is counted.

8. When a player is posted in a certain position, he must remain there, unless a favorable chance presents itself for him to leave it, and then he should return to his former position.

There are others, but not worth mentioning. Standard laws are very much required, and till some of the principal Clubs form such, there will never be an end to disputes.

THE GAME

Choosing Sides.—Two of the best players toss up for the first pick, and after sides have been chosen, each man should be allotted a position either by the players who tossed up, or by the captain of the field. The object of the "two best players" tossing up is to prevent the possibility of their being taken on the same side, as an equal strength of sides makes the game more difficult and interesting.

Posting the men.—A considerable amount of knowledge, both of the game and the qualifications of each player, is absolutely necessary to post each man in his proper position *where he will be of use*. Some players are fit for one place and useless in another, and where a man has been placed in a position that he knows he is of little use in, he should request the player that posted him to give him another. A great dissimilarity exists between the opinions of different players on the manner of posting the men: some station them in a straight line opposite the goal; others cluster half of the players around the goal, and leave a few out on the field. By this latter method, it is a difficult matter to get the ball in the goal, but very little headway can be made on the field, by the few who have double their number to encounter. This plan might answer

1.—Goal Keeper.	A.—Goal Keeper.
2.—Point.	B.—Point.
3.—Cover Point.	C.—Cover Point.
4.—Field Man.	D.—Field Man.
5.—Facing Man.	E.—Facing Man.
6.—Field Man.	F.—Field Man.
7.—Centre Man.	G.—Centre Man.
8.—Field Man.	H.—Field Man.
9.— Do	I.— Do
10. —Do	J.— Do
11.—Do	K.— Do
12.—Home Man	L.—Home Man
	U. U.—Umpires

well in case of a match between two clubs, and where one have the advantage in throwing, etc. Some do not post their men, but leave every one to look out for himself.

The Diagram on page 266 will show something like the plan most generally adopted by the best clubs. There are twenty-four players and two umpires represented:—

When the men are properly posted, there is far more chance of their winning the game, than if they were placed in a useless manner. Every man should remain in his place, always keeping a good look out for the ball.

DUTIES OF EACH PLAYER

1. The Goal Keeper stands near the goal or flags to prevent the ball from entering.

2. *Point* covers the goal-keeper at a distance of not less than 12 feet. He should never leave his place, unless there is no opposing player near. Point should be a skillful checker.

3. *Cover Point's* duties are signified in his name. He should also seldom leave his position except under very favorable circumstances. He should be a good checker, and altogether a good player. *Point and Cover Point should be the best checkers on the field.*

4. *Facing Men* are two of opposite sides, who commence the game by struggling for the ball between their Crosses.

5. *Centre Man* stands on the side, and a little behind his facing man, so as to receive the ball if his side succeeds in getting it. He should be a good runner and an expert dodger.

6. *Field Men* are spread out on the field as shown in the diagram, and ever on the alert for the ball. They require to be good "catchers" as well as "throwers." Practice is necessary to enable them to throw the ball to a certain distance and no further, so that the man they fling it to may be sure to catch it without leaving his position.

7. *Home Men* stand to one side of opponent's goal to put the ball in when thrown to them. They should not stand immediately in front of the goal-keeper, but more to one side.

Fig. 4.

Facing requires considerable practice before any skill can be attained in it. It is performed by a player of each side placing the ball on the ground at an equal distance from each goal, then crossing his Crosse with that of his opponent in the manner shown in Fig. 4, having the ball fairly between them, and after counting "three" tugging to get it away; or the ball is thrown high up in the air *with the hand,* and as it descends is struck at *by the facing men only.* There are numerous ways of "getting the best of it" in facing, but we only mention a few of the methods practiced, and we think the following will be found sufficient in all cases:—

1. *The most common method* practiced of taking the ball is by pressing your opponent's Crosse away till it allows the ball to pass. Strength of arm is the principal

thing requisite for the proper performance of this style. (To succeed at this method the facer must, at the moment "three" is called, give his opponent no time to take the ball, but press his Crosse away, at the same time dragging his own and the ball with it.)

2. *A good plan*, but one which requires some practice to do perfectly, is to half-kneel with the body bent slightly forward, and legs open, and when "time" is called giving your Crosse a sudden twist and passing the ball through your legs to your "Centre man."

3. *Another method* is to stand as is customary in facing, and as "time is called" turn your back to your opponent—hiding the ball from his view—and then giving your Crosse a steady twist and sending the ball to your "Centre man."

The uniformity of position assumed, previous to the game commencing, by the facing men, the players of both sides all standing steady, every man erect in his place with his eyes towards the facing men, and all remaining in this position for a few minutes, presents a very interesting spectacle. At the signal from the captain the game begins, the ball is sent flying through the air, and every man is "up and doing," which sudden change from the inanimate and statue-like players to full life presents a very fine sight.

THROWING THE BALL.

Of all the different parts in the game of Lacrosse, there is none so difficult to acquire as a perfectness in throwing the ball straight, and to a certain required distance. A steady arm, an accurate eye, and considerable mental calculation are positive requirements that cannot be dispensed with if the player would learn to throw the ball with surety. *Practice* will do a great deal for the player, but it must be constant and as long at a time as possible. A few mornings' practice at *throwing alone* at the goal, and from different positions of the field, would be very advantageous to he who desires to be skilled in this particular part of the game. One at a time of these methods should be practised until accurateness and skill is attained, and by this plan the player will soon master the whole. The following constitute even more than are practiced:

1. *Throwing sideways with back to the goal.*—This is a sure method of throwing straight, and being very simple, and requiring but little practice to perform perfectly, the player will find it an excellent mode; you turn your back to the goal with the side you throw past a little around—enough to allow your eye to get a glipse of the goal without turning the head quite around—you then bring your Crosse up by your side and a little out, and the ball is then thrown off with a steady jerk, keeping the Crosse as close by the legs as possible. The Crosse is held with the left hand about the middle of the stick, and the back put up, while the right hand is held with the back part, or knuckels, facing the ground, but the player himself will soon find out the manner of holding it which suits him best.

Fig. 5.

2. *Throwing straight and facing the goal.*—This is the manner in which the player has most frequently to throw the ball. It is held in the bag, if your Crosse has one, or on about the middle. You then throw straight out, holding the

Crosse in the manner described in Sec. 1. By turning your side a little to the goal you will be more able to throw straight and strong. In this manner you may throw the ball along the ground the entire way, or throw it as far as it will go straight out about twelve feet from the ground.

3. *Throwing out from the body.*—This method is much practiced by skilful players, and is very difficult to attain, but by constant practice it can be overcome, and when that is done the player will prefer it to almost any other as it both looks neat and is generally a straight throw. In practicing this your back is turned to the goal, with the side you throw past a little towards it; you hold the Crosse in both hands, and, when about to throw, straight out from the body. The ball is then thrown with a half jerk, keeping the Crosse well out. See Fig. 5....

CATCHING THE BALL.

This *sometimes* requires more practice to perform perfectly, and often even *imperfectly,* than anything else in the game of Lacrosse. Its great difficulty consists in the perplexity experienced by the young player in catching the ball so that it will *remain on his Crosse.* Nothing, however, is simpler when understood and learnt. The Crosse should be held in one hand, and as the ball is thrown in the air the player should watch it, and holding his Crosse out, or half perpendicular, the ball is received on it, while the Crosse is let *sink* and raised again when the ball is safely on. This sinking and rising movement should be practised a great deal if the player would attain any skill in catching. It is something similar to the falling and rising of a wave. A Crosse slightly bagged is preferable for catching. The following are the methods commonly practised, although there are others, but those are used when the player is in some very unusual position; when such is the case he must use his own judgment in the matter, and think for himself. In all these "catches," allow the ball to descend, or be caught in the *front of the body,* and not behind.

1. *Catching the ball as it descends.*—This method is resorted to as the best way of securing the ball before it touches the ground. The perpendicular position of the Crosse, and the sinking and rising movement must be strictly adhered to if the player would perform this neatly, combining beauty with skill. This is a very graceful style of catching, and always looks well when properly done.

2. *After the ball touches the ground.*—This is a much easier and simpler manner of catching than the previous one, and requires far less practice to do well. It may be used when there is no opponent near; as the ball is liable to bounce off on an uneven ground, and perchance it might bound to an opponent. It is a good introduction to the above method.

3. *When the ball is flung along the ground.*—As the ball comes along place your Crosse before its course, and as it touches it sink the handle near the ground, raising it the moment the ball rolls on. When the ball is thrown swift, and is *strong when it reaches you,* instead of catching it you must *stop it* by placing your Crosse before its course, with the handle well advanced so as to keep the ball from rising and striking you in the face. These "grounders" are often very cunning balls, and the player must beware of this lest the ball passes him unawares....

DODGING.

Dodging is a very interesting and exciting part of the game of Lacrosse; and is the more exciting on account of the danger often incurred in its performance. An unskilful player in dodging will often at his first attempt find the ball knocked off his crosse, and his head or fingers a little the worse for sundry cuts, bruises, &c. If the player fears these "undesirables" he can wear gloves.

Dodging in Lacrosse is a good place to train the head and body for a city election, or an Irish wake. It would be rather a difficult matter for the Phrenologist to distinguish the *natural* from the *accidental* bumps on the craniums of some unlucky players of Lacrosse. Dodging is little practised by the Indians, they *throw* the ball more than *carry* it.

The following are the methods most required by the player: —

1. *By bringing the Crosse across the body.*—this is the most frequently practiced manner of dodging, and is very useful when a not very skilled checker is opposed to the dodger. Watch the eye of the checker as he attempts to stop you, and as you see his Crosse descending on yours, bend your arm quickly, and bring your Crosse across your body to your other side, and if the checker attempts to strike there also, bring it back again to its former position, taking care to keep it close to your body. Beware of the checks described in section 1 and 2 on "Checking."

2. *Keeping your back to the checker.*—This is a style of dodging which is very good, and practised to a great extent by the Indians. It has the advantage of placing the checker in rather an awkward position to knock the ball off, and of placing the dodger in the position to throw the ball over his head, if he should find it necessary; and therefore when you attempt to dodge past a skilful checker and find your attempts unavailing, it is a good plan to turn to this position and throw over your head.... By this method some players can tire a checker out, by keeping him running from side to side, and darting from one point to another, always keeping the back to the checker, and never, if possible, letting him get near enough to strike your Crosse.

3. *By balancing the ball on the Crosse.*—You run with your Crosse extended a little from your body, holding it either straight out, or dodging as described in section 1; while you keep your Crosse on a continual waving and rocking motion, when approaching an opponent. Often when the Crosse is struck by the checker, this waving and rocking motion prevents the ball from falling off. It confuses the checker a good deal. The Indians use this balancing movement, and seem to substitute it a good deal for dodging in the styles generally practiced by the "palefaces."

4. *Falling down in dodging.*—Where you have a skilful checker to contend with this is a good defence, though requiring a great deal of practice to perform it with success. Great suppleness of limb and body, quick eyes, and the art of preserving the equilibrium are essential for the proper performance of this dexterous form of dodging. Your back is turned to the checker, and your Crosse lowered almost even with the ground, your entire body is bent forward and often one knee is on the ground; you must watch both your Crosse and every movement of the checker. When you see a favorable opportunity—when, for instance, he has made a blow at your Crosse and missed it—by

a quick dart to one side, spring up and run with the ball or throw it. This falling movement also gives a rest to the dodger, which he often requires....

CHECKING.

Checking is the art of depriving the dodger, or any opponent of the ball, by knocking it off his crosse, or otherwise obtaining it from him. Any player who attempts to
stop an opponent who bears the ball is a checker. He requires to be very quick with his
arms and legs, and the possessor of a quick eye. When a checker becomes skilful in
taking a ball from his opponent, and in all respects a *good* checker, he is the most
useful man on the field where much dodging is carried on. One good checker is worth
half a dozen bad ones, and if the player will consider this fact he will perceive it is a
place worthy of striving to excel in. A skilful checker will seldom let the dodger pass
him with the ball, but will compel him to throw it if he cannot take it from him. The
checker must watch every motion of the dodger, and not allow him time to throw the
ball. He must also be as careful as possible of striking him *on the head,* but a knock
now and then on the fingers *must* be expected. The following comprise the methods
most generally used and required:—

1. *Common Method.*—As the dodger advances with the ball on his Crosse, he will
probably attempt to dodge past you in the manner described in section 1, on dodging;
you then strike at his Crosse on the side he holds it, and before he brings it across his
body, and if you fail in striking it there, and he brings it across, you follow his with
yours, and try to strike it thus. The checker will often succeed by this method, and
though it is more used than any other it is not the best in the world.

2. *Improvement on the above.*—When you strike at your opponent's crosse in the
manner described above, he will often succeed in bringing it across his body and passing you, before you can recover from your first position in time to check him. To prevent this, the following method has been tried and found very useful. As the dodger
advances with the ball, you stand straight before him, with your legs a little apart, and
one foot a little behind the line of the other, to enable you to spring from side to side,
your crosse in front anf held in both hands. When the dodger nears you he will probably expect you to check in the manner described above, but instead of doing this,
watch the moment he attempts to bring his Crosse across his body, and bring yours
down on the side he brought his body to, at the same time and with almost the same
movement. A *feint* may be made at the side he first holds it on, which will perhaps
better enable you to perform this check. Beware of the dodger throwing between your
legs.... this is a very fine check, and seldom fails when quickly performed and at the
exact time to calculate which you must watch every motion of your opponent, and try
to *read his thoughts.* When the checker attains skill in this method it will prove as satisfactory to him, as surprising to the dodger.

3. *The Circular Check.*—This is performed by swinging the crosse in a circle around
the front of your opponent, so that no matter where his crosse is in front of his body you
will be certain to strike it. The only chance of this method failing is in case the dodger
draws his arm and crosse back in time to escape your check. The checker must practice

this method slowly at first, and before he attempts to arrest the progress of a dodger by it, as he might not swing his crosse fairly in front, but might strike the dodger's head....

GOAL KEEPING.

Goal keeping is a post of particular care, as the safety of the game greatly and untimately depends upon its defender. Great self-control and coolness under all circumstances of danger to the goal, a very quick eye and a suplebody [sic] are absolutely essential to become a *perfect* goal-keeper. An excitable or unsteady player should never be placed at the goal, as it is a post of danger to such, especially when a swift thrower flings the ball from a short distance with full force. If the goal-keeper is unable to stop it, he is liable to receive it on his face or body, or let it enter the goal. A constant watch should be kept *on the ball* wherever it is thrown. In contesting with superior players, *two* goal-keepers are generally placed at each goal; but some goal-keepers can manage better by themselves, as an assistant only confuses them. A short-handed crosse is better for minding the goal than a long one.

Fig. 6.

The Position of the Goal Keeper.—He should stand three or four feet from the Goal, and should remain there perfectly steady and watchful, with one foot a little before the other, and crosse in the position shown in fig. 6. He should never leave his goal undefended for a moment, unless under circumstances where he runs out to meet an advancing bearer of the ball, . . . or when the ball is near the goal and there is a favorable chance to throw it. The goal keeper should frequently go out on the field to acquire activity and procure proper exercise, which he does not get sufficiently while guarding the goal. The ground around the goal, for at least five feet, should be created the goal keeper's *"santum sanctorum,"* and no player allowed to come within the bounds unless the ball comes near the goal, or when a struggle ensues near it. The "home man" of the oppositie side, who remains near the goal to put the ball in, should not stand immediately in front of the goal-keper and behind point, but he should remain a little to one side, and which is almost invariably the situation appointed him. If the ball should be flung towards the goal, and does not reach it, and a struggle happens quite near, the goal-keeper should bend slightly forward, and *watch the ball, and nothing else,* so that should a sudden tip send it towards him, he may *see it coming,* which he is not likely to do if he stands erect and does not watch it.

When stopping the ball thrown at the goal, always strike it away to one side, never to the front of the goal, as a slight knock from the crosse of any opponent might send it back again to the goal, and the goal-keeper, perhaps off his guard at the moment, it would enter. Never be too thoughtful where you strike the ball to, as long as you do not send it in front of the goal. If a player of the same side is near, and you think it safe, strike the ball to him. The methods of stopping the ball, when thrown to the goal in the different styles of "throwing," would require more space for their proper explanation than can be spared here. In this matter of stopping the ball, the judgment of the goal-keeper alone can properly determine the best methods of acting, and therefore, no rules can be specified upon this subject from which it will not sometimes he necessary to deviate. We will, however, endeavor to give a few of the most important, and which the goal-keeper has most frequently to contend with: —

1. *When the ball is thrown straight out,* and about four or five feet or more from the ground, the proper way to stop it is to bring your Crosse up to meet it, and strike it away to one side; or if you are skilful enough, strike it with the *wood part* of your Crosse, which sends it much further than when struck by the gut. If there happens to be no opponent near when it is thrown at the goal, instead of striking it away, . . . strike the ball to the ground in front of you, and catch it as it bounces.

2. *When the ball is thrown in the air,* and is *dropping* into the goal,—you stand looking upwards with the face of your Crosse fronting the ball's line of descent, and as it nears you strike it away. The goal-keeper must be cautious in stopping this throw, as it is sometimes very perplexing when it appears very easy.

3. *When the ball is flung along the ground* place your Crosse before you with the handle well advanced to prevent the ball rising, and probably giving your nasal organ an admonitory tap, and as it nears your Crosse give the latter a *twist* and *jerk* that will send the ball to one side, or *tip* it away. Sometimes a goal-keeper is skilful enough to strike the ball with his *toe,* which, when properly done, causes the ball to rise straight up, and is then caught again by the goal-keeper.

4. *When the dodger passes "corner point,"* "point," and any other player, and runs for the goal, the goal-keper should *advance to meet him, watching the ball and nothing else,* while "point" runs up to protect or assist him, and if the dodger throws, the goal-keeper must watch the ball and try to stop it. If the dodger throws before he passes "point," the same watchfulness and care is necessary on the part of the goal-keeper. The necessity of "point" and "cover point" being the best checkers on the field is here obvious. This is a very difficult ball to stop, and nothing but continual practice will ever enable the goal-keeper to perform it even indifferently. Great *self-confidence* is necessary in such a predicament. The goal-keeper must beware of the dodger throwing between his legs....

5. *When the ball is flung at the goal and passes over it.*—When the ball is thrown towards the goal in this manner, and is "too high," it is advisable in some cases to *let it pass,* and not stop it; as in cases where a number of opponents are near, and where it would be dangerous to strike it to the front or side of the goal. In other cases it should not be let pass, as an opponent might get it, and his side close around your goals, and it being then thrown to them, might be struck in.

The goal-keeper must not scorn all *slow* balls, as they are often as cunning and puzzling as those thrown swift. It would be an excellent plan for him to get some of the best throwers to fling the ball towards the goal in all the different styles, from all positions on the field, and with every degree of force. A few mornings' practice of this would soon make skilful players, and would do more for the goal-keepr and throwers than two or three weeks general practice, where they will not, perhaps, get over a half-a-dozen balls each to throw or stop.

The goal-keeper will readily perceive the advantage to be derived from standing three or four feet or more from the flags—as advised in the beginning of this part—when he attempts to stop a few balls while *between* them. For instance a ball is thrown *along the ground,* and is partially stopped by the goal-keeper, but by some accident passes him, if he is standing *between* the flags, he cannot stop it again in time to save the game; but if standing three or four feet from them, he has time to stop it *behind* before it reaches the flags.

CONCLUSION.

In concluding this attempt at instruction in a beautiful and interesting game, the author begs to state that it was commenced with the desire of elevating *Lacrosse* to the same standard among field games as *Cricket*. It is mainly intended as a help to the formation of Lacrosse clubs, and for the purpose of explaining the different modes of playing in every department of the game. This being the first account of the game ever published, there will, doubtless, be found room for criticism, and as opinions differ in Lacrosse as well as in anything else, many may have cause to find fault with the sentiments and ideas here expressed. The author would beg such to pass over the *defects* and *imperfections,* and read it for its *intentions*.

Chapter 12

PUB SPORTS

Throughout North America during the mid-nineteenth century taverns were important centers for a variety of sports, games, and pastimes. The owners of these public houses realized that these amusements and contests attracted crowds of participants and spectators who would spend freely on food and drink. Some of these facilities were located on country roads or in small villages, but most were situated in working-class residential neighborhoods of cities. Open space for outdoor play was in short supply in these districts, so people gathered in these indoor establishments for socializing and recreation. The "sporting fraternity" patronized these saloons—generally young men from the bachelor subculture along with a few from the middle and upper ranks who enjoyed an occasional night out with the lower classes. There they amused themselves with eating, drinking, and gambling at their favorite games, especially billiards, bowling, and quoits.

During the 1840s and 1850s there were two styles of billiards in Canada and the United States. The first featured upper class gentlemen who patronized the game; the second involved the masses who competed in poolrooms that were usually located in saloons. These years witnessed the growing popularity of the latter type and also the emergence of the pastime as a commercialized sport. Criticism of the gambling, drinking, and other vices associated with the game drove many of the elite out of the taverns, but they continued to play at home or in private clubs.

The 1850s witnessed a significant increase in billiards as both a recreational activity and also a competitive, professional sport. Defenders of the game countered the moral condemnation directed at billiards by pointing out that gambling was not inherent in the pastime. They also stressed its patronage by the elite and its many positive attributes. In particular they portrayed it as a wholesome activity that could be enjoyed by both sexes. Moreover, they maintained that it was ideally suited for urban dwellers who could play during all seasons and at day or night. Despite these rationalizations, the real reasons for the rapid advance of billiards at this time have more to do with its simplicity, its low cost, its individualistic nature, and especially its suitability to the environment of the saloon. In fact gambling was one of its main attractions, and the sport fit well with the values of the all-male sporting crowd who enjoyed the betting, drinking, camaraderie, and overall atmosphere of the saloon.

The leading figure in the rise of billiards during the 1850s was Michael Phelan, a New Yorker who promoted the sport through his publications of rules, manufacturing of tables, and challenge matches. In 1850 he produced *Billiards Without Masters,* the first book of its kind to appear in the United States. Excerpts from the revised 1857 edition appear below. In 1854 he developed an india rubber cushion which permitted sharp edges on tables. He then joined with Hugh Collender to form a company that dominated the market in billiard tables until 1884. During the last years of the decade he won a series of contests which established himself as the champion of the United States prior to the Civil War. The newspaper accounts of victories over Ralph Benjamin of Philadelphia in 1858 and John Seereiter of Detroit in 1859 that are reprinted below suggest the extensive excitement and publicity generated by these matches.

Tenpin bowling and a ninepin version called skittles were popular games in many Canadian and American cities prior to 1840, but both were in decline after that date, in part because of the competition with billiards. Yet there were still numerous alleys in taverns in many towns, especially in New York City, where one newspaper counted 400 in 1850. But even there the old Dutch game struggled to retain its former hold on the masses. The pastime remained a premodern amusement with rules varying from city to city, as is clear from "The Baltimore Game of Ten Pins."

Finally, quoits was a time-honored amusement of the British Isles, especially Scotland, which enjoyed a substantial following in both Canada and the United States during these years. The sport originated in the middle ages, when peasants heated and bent old horseshoes into rings, which they threw at an iron peg driven into the ground. It resembles horseshoe-pitching, which was popular among American frontiersman and which actually represents an earlier form of the sport. The editorials and newspaper accounts of quoits that appear below suggest the rural origins of the sport as well as its adaptability to tavern life and club organization.

THE GAME OF BILLIARDS
by Michael Phelan

When Michael Phelan published his *Billiards Without Masters* in 1850 the sport had no uniform set of regulations recognized across North America. His book was an effort to standardize and promote the game. It summarized the history of billiards, outlined the rules of its variant forms, provided instructions with diagrams on how to play, and defended the game against its detractors. Despite its relatively high price of three dollars, the volume went through ten editions over the next twenty-five years. The following selection is reprinted from Phelan's *The Game of Billiards* (New York, 1857).

RULES OF BILLIARDS
THE AMERICAN, OR FOUR-BALL GAME

RULE I.

On Stringing for the Lead.—Whoever, playing from within the string against the lower cushion, can bring his ball nearest to the cushion at which he stands, is entitled to the choice of lead of balls. Provided,

1st. That the player's ball, in stringing, has not touched any other ball upon the table;

2d. Nor fallen into any of the pockets; in either case he loses the choice.

RULE II.

On Leading.—1st. In leading, the player's ball must be played with sufficient strength to pass below the deep red ball, or he loses his choice.

2d. It must not be played with so much strength as to repass the deep-red ball a second time, after having rebounded from the foot of the table. In this latter case, it is optional with the adversary to make the player spot his ball on the pool *spot,* play it over again, or take the lead himself.

RULE III.

On the Opening of the Game.—Once the lead is made, the game is considered as commenced, and neither player can draw except under the circumstances hereafter specified. But no count or forfeiture can be made until each player has played one stroke.

RULE IV.

On Foul Strokes.—The penalty for a foul stroke is this: that the player cannot count any points he may have made by such stroke, and that his adversary is entitled to the next play. The following are among the strokes called foul:

1st. If either player use his opponent's ball to play with, the stroke is foul: and if successful, he cannot count, provided the error is found out before a second shot is made.

2d. Should two or more strokes have been made previous to the discovery, the reckoning cannot be disturbed, and the player may continue his game with the same ball. And

3d. If it be found that the players have changed balls during the game, and if the change can be brought home to neither in particular, each must keep the balls he has, and let the game proceed.

4th. Should both the white balls be off the table together, and should either player, by mistake, pick up the wrong one and play with it, the stroke must stand, and he can count whatever he has made. [The reason of this is obvious; for both balls being in hand and having alike to play from any point within the string, no possible advantage could arise from using the other's ball. Whereas, when the balls are on the table, the case is totally different, for your opponent's ball might be advantageously placed, while your own was directly the reverse.]

5th. If the striker aim at a ball before it is fully at rest, or while any other ball is rolling on the table, the stroke is foul and no count can be effected.

6th. If when in the act of taking aim, a player should touch the ball more than once with his cue, the stroke is considered foul.

7th. If the player, when pushing his own ball foward with the butt of his cue, does not withdraw the butt before the cue touches the object ball, the stroke is foul.

8th. If, when a red ball is holed, or forced off the table, the striker, before playing, does not see that said red ball is replaced, upon its proper spot-supposing such spot to be unoccupied- the stroke he may make while the red is not in its proper place, is foul. But should the spot be covered by any other ball, when the red is pocketed or forced off, the red must remain off the table until its proper position is vacant, and all the balls cease rolling.

9th. If, when the player's ball is in hand, he does not cause it to pass outside the string, before touching any object balls or cushion (except in a case mentioned in the following rule) the stroke is foul, and his opponent may choose whether he will play with the balls as they are, have them replaced in their original positions, or cause the stroke to be played over a second time; or, should the player make a losing hazard under such circumstances, the penalty may be enforced,

10th. Playing at a ball whose base, or point of contact with the table, is outside of the string, is considered playing out of the string; and the stroke is a fair one, even though the side which the cue ball strikes is hanging over, and therefore within the string.

11th. If, after making a successful stroke, the player obstructs the free course of the balls upon the table, he becomes subject to the penalties of a foul stoke, and cannot score his points.

12th. If the player, with his ball in hand, play at an object ball that is exactly on the string, the stoke is foul; for a ball on the string must be treated as if within it.

13th. If the striker, through stretching forward or otherwise, has not at least one foot on the floor while striking, the shot is foul, and no points can be scored.

14th. If a player shall alter the stroke he is about to make, at the suggestion of any party in the room—even if it be at the suggestion of his partner in a double match, except where a special agreement is made that partners may advise—the altered stroke which he plays is foul, and he cannot count any points that may be won thereby.

RULE V.

On Forfeitures.—1st. If the player fails to hit any of the balls upon the table with his own ball, he forfeits one, which must be added to his adversary's count.

2d. The player forfeits two when his own ball is pocketed, after first having touched a white one.

3d. He forfeits two to his opponent, also, when he causes his ball to jump off the table or lodge on the top of the cushion, after having first touched his opponent's ball.

4th. When his own ball is pocketed, or jumps off the table, or lodges on the cushion, as before described, without either having touched any ball at all, or having only touched one or more red ones, the player forfeits three.

[In and around New York, three is the highest number that a player can be mulcted in for any single stroke; but in some other parts of the Union, they add to this forfeiture any number of points which he may otherwise have made by the stroke. Surely the penalty of three, and to lose his count and hand, ought to be enough to satisfy Shylock.]

5th. If the player cause any ball to jump off the table, and should it, by striking against any of the bystanders, be flung back upon the board, it must still be looked upon and treated as if it had fallen to the floor. If a red ball, it must be spotted; if a white one, held in hand; and if it be the cue ball, the player shall forfeit two or three to his opponent, comformably to the terms laid down in the two preceeding paragraphs.

6th. Though the striker, when playing with the wrong ball cannot count what points he may make, except in those cases mentioned in the second, third and fourth paragraphs of Rule IV; nevertheless, whatever forfeitures he may incur while playing with the wrong ball, he is bound to pay, as if he had been playing with his own.

7th. Any player who has commenced a game, as specified in Rule II, must either finish or forfeit it, except under the circumstances particularly set forth in Rule VII.

RULE VI.

On Cases Where the Balls are in Contact.—1st. If the cue ball be in actual contact with any other, no count can be made by the player.

2d. Nevertheless, he must strike and separate the balls, at least one inch, and will lose, as in common cases, should he either pocket his own ball, cause it to jump off the table, or lodge on the cushion.

3d. The player must separate the balls as above stated; but should his ball retrograde to its old position, the onus of separating them will then rest upon his opponent. He cannot be called upon to do it twice.

[This rule, though imperative here, is not recognized in some other parts of the Union. In many places the player can count by first playing on another ball away from his own. We mention this to avoid disputes, which frequently arise on this point, between players from different sections.]

RULE VII.

On Withdrawing From, without finishing a Game.—1st. The player may protest against his adversary's standing in front of him, or in such close proximity as to disarrange his aim.

2d. Also against loud talking, or any other annoyance by his opponent, while he is making a play.

3d. Also against being refused the use of the bridge, or any other of the instruments used in that room in playing, except where a special stipulation to the contrary was made before commencing the game.

4th. Or in the case his adversary shall refuse to abide by the marker's or company's decision; on a disputed point, which it was agreed between them to submit to the marker, or company, for arbitration; in any one, or all of the foregoing cases, if the discourtesy be persisted in, the party aggrieved is at liberty to withdraw, and the game shall be considered as drawn, and any stakes which may have been depending on such, must be returned.

5th. Should the interruption or annoyance have been accidental, the marker, if so requested by the player, who is entitled to repeat his stroke, must replace the balls as near as possible in the position they occupied before the player made the stroke in which he was interrupted.

RULE VIII.

On Cases in which the Marker must replace the Balls, if called on, as nearly as possible in their former Position.—1st. In the case mentioned in the 5th paragraph of the preceding rule.

2d. Where any of the balls when at rest are moved by accident.

3d. Where any of the balls while rolling are suddenly obstructed either by accident or design. In this case the marker, if so requested, by the players, shall place the interrupted ball as nearly as possible in the situation which it would apparently have occupied had it not been stopped.

4th. Where the cue ball, resting on the edge of a pocket, drops into it, before the striker has time to play.

5th. Where the object ball, in a similar position, is rolled back into the pocket by any of the ordinary vibrations of the table or atmosphere.

6th. In all cases aforementioned, where it is specified that in consequence of a foul stroke, the player's opponent shall have the option, either of playing at balls as they are, or causing them to be replaced by the marker.

7th. When either or both of the red balls are pocketed, or forced off the table, it is the marker's duty to spot them before another stroke is played-except the spot appropriate to either be occupied by one of the playing balls, in which case the red one must be kept in hand until its position is uncovered.

8th. If, after playing a ball, the player should attempt to obstruct or accelerate the progress by striking it again, blowing at it, or any other means, his opponent may either play at the balls as they stand, or call upon the marker to replace them in the position they would otherwise have occupied.

9th. If the striker, in the act of taking aim, or otherwise, move his ball ever so little, it is a stroke; and should he strike the ball again, his opponent has the same option as in the preceeding paragraph.

RULE IX.

On the Duty of Players to Each Other.—1st. Each player must look after his own interest, and exercise his own discretion. His opponent cannot be called on to answer such questions as "Is the ball outside or inside the string?" "Are the balls in contact?" and so forth. These are questions for the player's own judgement to decide.

2d. Each player should attend strictly to his own game, and never interfere with his adversary's, except when a foul stroke or some other violation of these rules may call for forfeiture.

RULE X.

On the Duty of the Marker, and the Spectators, to the Players.—1st. In a single game, no one, not even the marker, has a right to interfere with the play, or point out an error which either has been or is about to be committed. The player to whose prejudice the foul stroke is made, must find that out for himself.

2d. Even after a stroke has been made, no one in the room has any right to comment on it, either for praise or blame; for the same stroke may occur again in the course of the game, and the player's play be materially altered by the criticism to which he has just been listening.

3d. Let marker and spectators keep their places as much as possible, for if they crowd or move around the table, they are liable to interfere with the players and certain to distract their attention.

4th. When the spectators are appealed to by the marker, for their opinion on a point which he has been asked, but finds himself unable to decide, such of them as are well acquainted with the game should answer according to the best of their knowledge and belief. Those who know little or nothing of the game would oblige themselves and others by at once confessing their incompetence. Either they may not have seen the disputed stroke, or seeing it, they may not have been familiar with its merits.

RULE XI.

On the Marker's Duties in Particular.—The marker's duties may be thus summed up:

1st. To proclaim each count in a voice that can be heard by the player at his own table.

2d. To post the total run made by each player before the next begins to strike.

3d. To spot the balls when necessary.

4th. To furnish the bridge and other implements of the game, when called for.

5th. To see that the player be not obstructed in his stroke by being crowded by spectators.

6th. To decide without fear or favor all questions of order and fairness which shall be officially laid before him for his opinion. But,

7th. Let him never volunteer a remark upon any portion of the game.

8th. Let him never touch a ball himself, nor allow any other person except the players to touch one, except when officially called upon to replace the balls, as specified in Rule VII., or when asked to decide as to which is the ball that properly belongs to the player. In this case, should the spot be turned down on the table, he may lift the ball to ascertain the fact—but never let him touch them voluntarily.

9th. Finally, when called upon to decide a disputed point, of which he has no personal knowledge—the fairness of a shot which was made when he was looking elsewhere, for instance—let him proclaim silence, and take the opinion of such company as avow themselves competent to judge. The voice of the majority should be allowed to settle all debate; but should their decision be flagrantly in conflict with any of the well-known and admitted rules hereinbefore laid down, the party who fancies himself aggrieved may give notice of appeal to lay the question before what the lawyers would call "a jury of experts" —the marker, meanwhile, or some other responsible party holding the bets, if any, which depend on the decision. This appeal is final; and must be made before another stroke is played.

FURTHER RULES FOR THE FOREGOING GAME,
WHEN PLAYED AS A FOUR-HANDED MATCH.

In a four-handed match—two playing in partnership against two—the foregoing rules of the single game must be substantially observed, with the following additions:

1st. Each winning hazard made by the player puts the opponent who preceded him out of play. Consequently, the partner of the party so put out, steps in and takes his place.

2d. But if the player makes a losing hazard (pockets his own ball,) or makes two misses in succession, or causes his ball to jump off the table, or lodge on the cushion, he loses his hand, and must resign it to his partner.

3d. In this double match the player's partner is at liberty to warn him against playing with the wrong ball or playing, when his ball is in hand, at an object-ball within the string; but he must not give him any advice as to the most advantageous mode of play, &c, &c, except it has been otherwise agreed before the opening of the game.

FURTHER RULES FOR THE SAME GAME,
WHEN PLAYED BY THREE INDEPENDENT PLAYERS.

The rules of the single American game are substantially binding on the three-handed game, with the following additions, to meet the increase of players:

1st. The players commence by stringing for the lead, and he who brings his ball nearest to the cushion (as in the single game) wins the choice of lead, balls and play; and he who brings his next ball nearest to the cushion has the next choice of play. The third player cannot enter into the game until the first hazard is made, or until one of the players pockets his own ball, or makes two misses in succession, or causes his own ball to jump off the table or lodge on the cushion.

2d. All forfeitures in this game count for both of the opponents, at the same rate as in the single-handed match.

3d. If a player makes two misses in succession, or pockets his own ball, or causes his ball to jump from the table, his hand is out.

4th. He who can first make sixty-six points is out; the other two continue until one reaches one hundred.

5th. When he who has first made sixty-six retires from the game, the player whose hand is out adopts his ball; as that ball is entitled to its run, and also to the next play.

6th. If the player should cause both his opponents to become sixty-six by forfeiture, neither of the parties can claim game thereon, but must win it by their next count. But if only one of the opponents be in a position to become sixty-six by a forfeiture, then the forfeiture reckons as usual, and that opponent wins the game when such forfeiture is made.

So much for the American, or four-ball game.

CHAMPIONSHIP BILLIARD MATCHES

By the mid-1850s Michael Phelan had established himself as an authority on the rules of billiards and as a successful manufacturer of tables. He then sought to win recognition as the best player in the United States. When his call for a grand tournament went unanswered in 1855, he set out to challenge the nation's best players. In 1858 he defeated Ralph Benjamin of Philadelphia for a prize of $1,000 in the first recorded billiard match in America. His match against John Seereiter of Detroit the following year generated intense interest in the sporting press and even in the New York Times, which had practically ignored the sport previously. Due to the excitement the original stakes of $5,000 rose to $15,000. A full house of five hundred spectators (paying five dollars each) packed Detroit's Fireman Hall to witness Phelan's triumph over the hometown favorite. The following reports on these matches first appeared in the New York Clipper, 19 December 1857, p. 276, 9 January 1858, p. 298, 19 February 1859, p. 346, 23 April 1859, p. 5.

BILLIARDS AS A WINTER AMUSEMENT

As the season for outdoor sports and pastimes may be considered, to a certain extent, at an end, and as we have before observed that amusements of some kind or other, moderately indulged in, are necessary, inasmuch as they conduce to the public weal, it becomes our duty as a promotor of sports in America, to call the attention of the people to those in-door pastimes which, in our opinion, are best suited to their wants, or in other words, those which are best adapted for the time of the year, or are most seasonable. Our first selection, then, for winter amusements, is the beautiful game of Billiards. Our reason for such a choice is, that in its practice the physical as well as mental faculties are simultaneously brought into operation, that the intellectual powers are not exhausted in undue proportion to those of the body, but that both being occupied at once, both are proportionately strengthened; hence its adaptation as a favorite winter amusement, and hence our recommendation of it as such. A ready appreciation of mathematical precision and geometric truth is its chief attribute, teaching as it does, a correct judgement of distance, and calculation of forces, as well as the most delicate execution, by the body, of diagrams formed and matured in the mind. In a sanitary point of view it is also well adapted—an expansion of the chest, and an easy and graceful movement of the limbs being promoted by practice. "Exercise to be efficacious for good even in the healthy," says Mr. Phelan, in his excellent work on billiards, "must be excited, sustained, and directed by that nervous stimulant or odic force, as it is called, which gives the muscles the chief part of their strength, and contributed to the sustenance of the parts in a state of activity. In short, to obtain the full advantage of the nervous stimulus in exercise, we must be interested in what we are doing. Billiards supplied this excitement, and therefore it is that exercise taken at the game that is so particularly healthy."

Its adaptability as an exercise for both sexes, is also a great point in its favor, and examples are not wanting in which ladies, embracing many in the highest walks of life, have taken delight in the favorite pastime.

With all the intrinsic equalities, it is not to be wondered at that the game is finding so much favor in the public mind at the present day. That such is the case, can easily be proved by visiting some of our billiard palaces, so beautifully furnished and fitted up, and witnessing the interest taken in this favorite recreation by the great number of persons in search of some healthy exercise, after a hard day's work at the desk or in the library....

While upon this subject, it may not be considered out of place, perhaps, to again call the attention of our readers to the great match to take place at Philadelphia on the 30th of the present month, between Messrs. Phelan and Benjamin, for $2000. The Billiard world is looking forward with intense interest to the time when it shall have been decided as a great deal of money has been risked on the issue. The odds which Mr. Phelan gives his opponent, three points out of sixteen at the French three-ball Carom Game, and which is equal to about twenty-five points in a hundred at the American four-ball game, keeps the betting at about even. Both gentlemen are equally confident of winning, and the privileged few who will enjoy a rich treat, as the game to be played is in itelf the most scientific, and the capabilities of the contestants being also of the most scientific character, the beauty of the game will be illustrated in all its perfection on the occasion. The balls to be used will be two and five-sixteenth inches in diameter, much smaller than those generally used, which will also render the carom game much more difficult. The table selected is one of Mr. Phelan's Model Combination, which will of course be put in the most perfect order on the day of play. As the match is to be conducted in as private a manner as the cirumstances will admit, the precise hour and rooms in which it is to come off will not be made public, we presume, until a later date. The readers of the Clipper will be sure, however, to be kept posted in all that transpires and the result and particulars of the match will be published by us as soon after as possible. For the edification of those who have not seen, or may have forgotten, the terms of the match as made, and published by us as this time, (about eight monthes since,) we again present them:

We, the undersigned, Michael Phelan and Ralph Benjamin, agree to play a match of Billiards for $1000 a side, $200 forfeit, play or pay.

Said match to be played in Philadelphia, between the date of this agreement and the 1st of January, 1858, the day to be designated by said Benjamin, who shall give said Phelan at least 30 days personal notice thereof at his place of business.

Said match to be played on one of Michael Phelan's pocket tables with marble or slate bed and combination cushions, and with round balls of two and five-sixteenths inches in diameter; the table to be in good order at the time of playing the match. Said table to be selected by said Benjamin.

Said match to be played in a private room, each party to be at liberty to invite an equal number only of spectators, such number to be previously agreed upon.

Said match to consist of the best out of seventeen of one of the two following games, viz: said Phelan to discount said Benjamin either around the table, or at the four ball carom game; or to give said Benjamin three points out of sixteen at the French three-ball carom game, each carom counting one point; nothing but fair shots to count at either of the above games.

The choice of the game to be made by said Phelan at the time of depositing the forfeit.

Said match to be governed by the strict rules which regulate the playing of billiard matches in New York.

Each party will name an umpire on the day of the playing match, and the umpires shall appoint a referee from whose decision there shall be no appeal.

The full amount of $1000 a side to be deposited in the hands of a stakeholder to be agreed upon by the principals, on the day of and previous to the playing of the match.

In case of the death of either of the above parties, previous playing said match, such match to be considered off.

Michael Phelan
Ralph Benjamin

witness-H.W. Collender
   Mr. C. Sterling
New York, May 25, 1857.

MICHAEL PHELAN VS. RALPH BENJAMIN, 1857

The encounter between these two champions of the cue came off as previously announced in the CLIPPER on Wednesday, 30th ult., at Philadelphia, at the rooms of Mr. Wm. Otter, Twelfth street below Chestnut. As part of the condition of the match, it was understood that there should be no showing of balls, every shot to be made by the point of the cue; also that no part of the body should be outside of the line of the table when playing from the string, and that a ball touched should be a ball played. The referees for the occasion were the "Albany Pony," of New York, for Benjamin, and Chris. Bird, of Philadephia, for Phelan, who, with the umpire, were to decide all disputes. At 6 p.m., all preliminaries being arranged, they "pulled off their coats and rolled up their sleeves" and went at it, each one seeming determined to do their best "by Jingo or die." Caution was the word for the first game or two, when in the third Benjamin redoubled his exertions and won his first game by 9 points. The fourth, the most severely contested game of the match, occupying over 30 minutes, was won by Phelan by 4 points. This gave Mr. Phelan fresh courage, and the way in which he managed the cue amounted almost to a miracle, caroms of the most indescribable description being made apparently with the greatest ease. He came out victor in all the subsequent games except the 9th, which was won by his opponent by 8 points. The most counts made in a run were 6 by Phelan in the 6th game, which for brilliancy of play was the most remarkable of any. He also made a run of 6 and another of 5 in the 11th and conquering game, a feat seldom accomplished in the kind of game played, (French carom,) and but for the proper though stringent regulations, would no doubt have brought down the thunder. At the conclusion of the match, a grand time all around was indulged in, and a merry hour spent in discussing the quality of the viands, provided by Mr. Phelan's friends for all who chose to partake. The feelings of the company were of the most amicable nature, and the whole affair was carried through in such a manner, as will render this beautiful game far more popular than it already is. The table used was one of O'Connor and Collender's manufacture, six pockets, with Phelan's combination cushions attached, and proved itself to be very correct in every particular, a great desideratum when matches so important are to be played.

MICHAEL PHELAN VS. JOHN SEERIETER, 1859

The conditions of this match have been amicably arranged, and the match is to be played at Detroit, Mich., on Tuesday, April 12th. The adjustment took place on Friday evening, 11th instant, two gentlemen from Detroit appearing as Mr. Seerieter's representatives, while Mr. Phelan found an able advocate in the person of Mr. Colton. The terms which Mr. Seerieter's friends are prepared to make the match on, were none too liberal, so that urged on by his friends, and to avoid the appearance of backing down, Mr. Phelan was compelled to concede many points, which in justice he was not bound to do. Be this as it may, however, the match is made, and we are now in a fair way of learning how far the above-named knights of the cue are entitled to the laurels awarded them by their respective friends. That the game will be beyond precedent in the annals of billiards, whether in this country or any other, both in a pecuniary and scientific point of view, is beyond a doubt, and as a consequence, it will create a more intense interest, not only in New York and Detroit, but throughout the world, than any previous match at this scientific game, as both gentlemen have a world-wide fame, which we feel confident will not be tarnished in this encoutner; for whichever suffers defeat, no diminution of an honorable reputation can possibly accrue to him, being defeated by so powerful and skillful an opponent. With the desire that the victory may rest on the one who shall exhibit the most skillful and scientific management of the cue, and that the best results may follow the playing of the match that the most ardent admirers of this delightful parlor pastime could wish, we submit the following articles of agreement under which it is to be played:

"We, the subscribers, agree to play a match of the American 4-ball carom game of Billiards, consisting of 2,000 points up, for $5,000 a side (half forfeit) $1,000 of which to be now deposited in the hands of Henry Colton, to bind the match; $1,500 more to be deposited with the above stakeholder, on or before March 23d; and the final deposit of $2,500, twenty-four hours before the playing of the match, to be played on the 12th of April, 1859, in the city of Detroit, in the State of Michigan, with two umpires, chosen by the parties, who shall choose a referee whose decision shall be final. The game to comence at 7 o'clock, P.M., on one of Michael Phelan's tables (patent of 1858) with round balls of the usual size, 2 3/8: Mr. Phelan to have the selection of any of the said tables now in Detroit, which table is to be put up in some proper place, for this match, in private, with proper lights, at least four burners over the table, upon which there is to be a proper cloth. The expenses incurred from all the above, to be paid equally by both parties. Should they not agree on what is proper in any of the above particulars, then it shall be determined by referees, each party choosing one who may choose a third. Should the parties disagree as to any of the rules of Billiards, which shall govern the above match, such disagreement shall be adjusted by referees as above, who shall also adjust any other disagreement not provided for, which decision shall be final."

Michael Phelan
for John Seerieter,

City of New York, February 11, 1859.   "J.F."

THE MATCH

Mr. Phelan took his departure from New York on Monday, March 28, arriving at the scene of action on Saturday, 2d inst., when all unsettled preliminaries were at once arranged, and both parties allotted their time for practice on the table which had been set up in Fireman's Hall, and on which the match was to be played. Matters continued without any notable event until Saturday, 9th inst., when Mr. Phelan having issued cards of invitation to the elite of Detroit, gave an exhibition of his skill, with which they seemed much delighted, as well as surprised at the command which the champion had over the spherical ivories, the ladies especially expressing their admiration in most complimentary terms. Stereoscopic views of the scene were taken, some of which Mr. Phelan has brought with him to New York. Speculation in the mean time had not been quite so brisk as had been expected, although quite a large sum in the aggregate had been staked in small quantities, the odds being slightly in favor of Phelan. On Monday, however, business improved, but although many bets were made averaging from $100 to $500, still this was not sufficient to allay the anxiety of speculators, who were beginning to fear that they should be unable to risk the amount of "filthy lucre" which they desired.

The eventful day, however, brought the enthusiasm of the respective parties up to fever heat, and bets of a medium standard were frequently made during the day, although there was still a marked hesitancy to risk large amounts, until evening, when Firemen's Hall became the centre of attraction, strangers and citizens, all in one vast concourse marching thitherward, and where at about 7 o'clock P.M., the principals arranged the minor details, and in a short time it was announced that Mr. Ralph Benjamin, of New York, had been appointed Umpire for Phelan, and that Mr. John R. Gillet, of Detroit, would act in the same capacity for Seerieter; the Umpires choosing Judge Strong, of Detroit, for referee. For Markers, Peter D. Braisted, Jr. of New York, and Thomas Gallagher, of Detroit. At 7:25 o'clock they banked for lead and choice of balls, which Seerieter won, when on the instant a gentleman offered to stake $900 or $1000 on Seerieter. This liberal offer was accepted by Phelan, he at the same time placing $1000 on a table, when as if desiring to make a bluff game of it, the same party proposed doubling it, to which Mr. P. acquiesced; "make it $2500 if you choose," again remarked the Detroit man. "That suits me,~ said Phelan, when the bargain was closed, and handed to the stakeholder. This was the signal for one vast murmur of excitement, and every one appeared to be betting with his neighbor; "shiners" and "flimseys" were drawn from their hiding places, and thus within a few minutes some $30,000 or $40,000 were invested. Order being soon restored, all eyes were directed anxiously toward the table. That our friends may have a report of the play as it progressed we take the following remarks from the *Detroit Press*:—

The game was commenced by Seereiter laying off in the jaw of the lower corner pocket. Phelan made no carom, thus giving his competitor the first count, who ran 25. Phelan played with the utmost caution when he got the balls, preferring a safe game to long runs, taking great care to leave no count. The first hundred was run with no remarkable incident, the game standing 99 for Seereiter against 54 for Phelan. On the second hundred, Seereiter continued to gain, making runs varying from 15 to 20 points, while Phelan made three misses and some small counts. On the 20th run, however, Phelan got the balls together and made a run of 40. Seereiter followed with a run of 63, in the progress of which he turned the corner, and scored up to 232, his antagonist standing at 108. Phelan followed with a handsome run of 96, with a fair chance for a continuation, when he missed the carom by the mere breadth of a hair. The play went forward with frequent misses and small counts on both sides, Phelan making one run of 45, until Seereiter turned his third hundred, the game then standing Seereiter 301 to Phelan's 369. The peculiarities of the players manifested themselves in this hundred. Phelan nursed the balls with consummate skill, and displayed a perfect cntrol of them, driving them into whatever position he desired; while, on the contrary, Seereiter seemed incapable of getting them together at all, compelled to make all his counts by long and difficult caroms. This, however, gave him abundant opportunituy of displaying his skill, and many of his shots were of wonderful beauty. The close play of Phelan began to tell on the odds, and, after one or two bad shots, he made runs of 53, 41, and 33, which, with a very poor run of luck on the part of Seereiter, changed the order of the game, and Phelan passed 400 with a lead of 77 points. Soon after Seereiter rallied, and the play ran about even for a short time, when Phelan again went ahead, and at 500 was points ahead, all of which was not counterbalanced on the part of Seereiter. Phelan continued to gain on small runs, scoring another hundred, while Seereiter ran only 25. The luck seemed to be very decidedly against the Detroit player, while his adversary had no trouble in making small runs, invariably pocketing Seereiter's ball and leaving the other balls all in the string. He turned his seventh hundred when Seereiter stood at 486. The play at this point was remarkably devoid of interest, neither party making any extraordinary counts, until, on his 65th count, Mr. Phelan made a brilliant run of 101, turning his string into the eighth hundred and distancing his competitor by 320 points. As usual the white ball was left in the pocket and the others within the string. Seereiter banked and missed; Phelan made 5 and run himself into a pocket for safety, when Seereiter got the red balls together and made a run of 60 off them, scarcely moving them during the greater part of the count. He turned his fifth hundred in this run, and stood 558 to Phelan's 839. His play improved somewhat as he progressed, and although all his counts were made by hard knocks, as it were, the balls spreading badly and rendering it necessary for him to display all the proficiency that he was master of to count, yet he gradually gained upon Phelan, who made very poor playing for several runs. When Seereiter scored 700 he had reduced the odds to 177 points. Immediately after, Phelan made a splendid run, counting 91, and placing him again at a safe distance. Both players remained cool and collected, and there was no appearance of nervousness on part of either. There was far more excitement among the audience than was manifested by the players. As the noon of night approached, the company began to feel the effects of the long sitting, and sandwiches and flasks made their appearance and contributed to the comfort of the inner man. Seereiter began an earnest play, seemingly determined to reduce the odds created by his adversary's last run. He missed a few shots, and when he got the balls, invariably made them tell to this advantage. On his eighty-sixth shot he made a run of 95, placing him 761 to Phelan's 1,068. Phelan made a small run of 26, and both followed with two or three inferior runs, when, on his eighty-ninth play, Seereiter made the most brilliant run that had yet been scored, counting 157. This placed the game in a more favorable sphere for the Detroit player, who now stood 952 to Phelan's 1,099, having reduced the gap to 147 points. Seereiter had evidently become more accustomed to his position, and handled his cue more lightly, touching the balls in the gentlest manner possible and carefully nursing his game. He played a most beautiful game, that elicited universal admiration, so much so, that at times it was almost impossible to restrain the audience from bursting out in rapturous applause. The game from this point moved steadily along, Seereiter gaining by a succession of small runs until he scored his first thousand, which he rounded in a run of 30, putting him 1,020 to Phelan's 1,147.

At this point the game was discontinued, in accordance with previous agreement, for an intermission of half an hour. Some excitement prevailed, and bets were offered on both sides at different odds, some of which were taken. The Detroit men were quite confident that Seereiter was just waking up to his work, in which they seemed to be rightly judging, as he continued to gain on his opponent, and, by a series of very clever runs, gradually narrowed the gap, until, on turning his eleventh hundred, it was reduced to 93. In the meantime, Phelan was doing little in the way of counting, his luck seemed to have abandoned him, while Seereiter was really beginning to lay in earnest. As the gap between them steadily but surely narrowed, the audience manifested the deepest interest, watching every stroke of each player as though their lives were at stake. As the balls rolled across the table, the heads, arms and legs of the spectators moved with them, as if to push them on to count; and, at each run was announced, a hum of whispered praise filled the room, and a manifestation of relief from over excitement was visible on every countenance. Seereiter turned his twelfth hundred in making a run of forty, putting him 1,239 to Phelan's 1,261, a difference of only twenty-two, which was more than overcome when he entered upon his thirteenth hundred. The game then stood, Phelan 1,303 to Seereiter 1,312, making the latter nine points ahead. The odds of 300 against Seereiter were thus overcome by him, while his antagonist made 200. He then lost by degrees, until the odds were about 40 against him, when he again brushed up, and, at the 120th run, the odds being 7 against him, he made a splendid run of 150, being the second brilliant offer that he had made during the evening. The effect was perceptible in the countenances of his friends, who felt their confidence in him renewed. The great advantage gained by this was not permanent, however, for Phelan made a strong effort, and ran 129 on the next count.

Thenceforward the game ran very evenly, the players scoring about alike for a time, when Phelan took a start and ran ahead about sixty. Both players were doing their best to gain a permanent advantage, and Phelan in a short time made a gap of 77. He reached 1,700 with an advantage of 72 points. The game became interesting as this point was reached, as the probabilities were that any decisive advantage gained afterwards would control the issue. Both men played carefully and skillfully, and few bad shots were made, the player preferring, in several instances, to pocket the ball, and leave chances of a difficult shot to his antagonist. When Seereiter reached 1,700 he was but 35 behind, but he gradually fell from this figure, being unable to get the balls under his control, while Phelan made runs of 15, 16, 17, 20, and 45, increasing the gap steadily and surely until it reached 114 points. The game then stood: Phelan 1,899, Seereiter 1,785; Seereiter here picked up again, and made a run of 59, awakening the most intense excitement among his friends, who had begun to look upon his game as hopeless. But the restoration of confidence was but momentary; Phelan took the balls, and by a series of small runs, fully recovered his vantage. Seereiter again rallied a little, and turned his nineteenth hundred with a run of 18, which, however, was his last shot, as he left the balls in a position to give his competitor an easy count and a run of 24, which made him the victor of the match, beating Seereiter by 96 points, which is, perhaps, one of the most remarkable, if not the most remarkable game ever played.

BOWLING

Although billiards eclipsed bowling as the most popular tavern pastime in North America during the middle years of the nineteenth century, the latter game was still enjoyed by many sportsmen. Upper class gentlemen bowled at private alleys, while lower and middle class enthusiasts played at neighborhood saloons. Before 1850 there were local variations in the length of the bowling lanes, the sizes of balls and pins, and the method of keeping score. But even at this time some alleys featured polished wooden boards, side gutters for the ball return, and young pinsetters. The following piece begins with editorial commentary on the hostility towards sport during that era and then refers to different forms of bowling in New York City, Philadelphia, and Baltimore. It is reprinted from the Spirit of the Times, 3 May 1845, p. 106.

THE BALTIMORE GAME OF TEN PINS

[Below we give the report of a match at Ten Pins in Philadelphia, in which the "Baltimore Game," so called, was played, in which each bowler played nine balls. In this city the same game is played differently; here we roll thirty balls, not having a frame of pins set up until *all* are knocked down. In Philadelphia, they roll nine balls, but after rolling three, the pins are again set up, whether all were knocked down or not.]

PHILADELPHIA, Pa., April 6, 1845

Dear Sir—The lamentable proscription of rational amusements, and the consequent increase of vicious habits, has so filled the world with the details, that anything of a contrary tendency is soothing, and deserves to be praised, or at least noticed in the newspapers. Instead of the Onderdonk, the Judd, the Fairchild, and the various murder and crim. con. cases, it is pleasant occasionally to cast the eye upon a Horse-race, a Boat-race, a *race of bi-peds,* a polka, or any of the exciting amusements that contribute to the health and strength of the body. It is pleasant, also to know that the reign of sectarianism is about closing its career. Like the Kilkenny cats, the leaders are devouring each other; and from the complexion of things in this city, it is very probable a new era will suddenly burst upon us. Instead of the former amusements, which gave so much offence to those who pretend to be the engineers of our morals, we have Billiards, Cricket matches, Town-ball, Bowling alleys, &c., for those who can spare the time to partake of the amusement—and for those who are deprived of the means and time, we have Firemen riots, drinking, and such like innocent amusements—but every thing, and every dog, has its day, and as a new sport is springing up among us, I propose giving you the details of a match at Bowling, which came off last evening. Six gentlemen, including the owner of one of the alleys in Chestnut street, gave a challenge to the owner of an alley in the Northern Liberties, which was accepted, on condition that the parties meet, and play eleven "Baltimore" games on the Up-town alley, and the next evening play ten on the Chestnut street alley. The other preliminaries being settled, the first meeting took place on Thursday, and resulted as follows: —

FIRST MATCH—ON THE UP-TOWN ALLEY

	1	2	3	4	5	6	7	8	9	10	11
T.	28	33	41	26	27	25	34	47	21	27	41
B.	36	28	33	45	32	37	29	45	47	34	37
P.	28	38	38	36	29	26	35	34	28	25	39
B.	27	26	31	25	41	32	35	37	38	25	35
D.	28	35	45	25	33	37	36	27	28	26	46
H.	26	35	22	28	28	28	34	28	27	27	45
	173	193	210	185	200	185	203	218	192	164	243
W.	28	26	36	27	25	32	26	43	27	24	27
V.	34	35	39	37	48	59	27	35	39	39	26
K.	43	43	32	36	36	29	40	24	43	25	33
A.	24	49	37	45	24	24	35	32	36	26	41
Vi.	27	37	38	34	41	54	33	35	43	43	29
L.	38	32	33	27	29	31	47	43	36	27	30
	194	222	215	206	203	229	208	212	234	189	186

SECOND MATCH—ON CHESTNUT-STREET ALLEY

	1	2	3	4	5	6	7	8	9	10	Tot.	Aver.
T.	53	34	42	49	47	35	35	37	29	30	744	35.9
B.	27	43	60	36	37	28	40	41	44	48	807	38.9
P.	31	34	36	44	28	40	29	31	48	43	728	34.14
B.	44	34	47	35	37	30	26	43	39	35	722	34.18
D.	38	37	29	26	26	43	33	34	34	63	729	34.15
H.	32	38	30	34	32	26	45	38	33	36	672	32.20
	225	230	244	224	207	202	208	224	227	2554	402	209.13
W.	31	23	28	33	30	33	28	31	32	28	638	30.8
V.	34	40	37	38	36	36	29	27	39	45	769	36.18
K.	28	23	46	42	28	50	32	36	42	28	739	35.4
A.	47	48	30	43	46	40	45	36	26	53	787	37.10
Vi.	36	37	25	34	32	69	43	29	56	43	818	38.2
L.	34	35	35	35	32	38	47	42	34	30	735	34.16
	210	206	201	204	225	266	224	201	229	227	4486	213.13

Thus it appears that the gentlemen of the Up-town alley gained thirteen out of the twenty-one games, and out of 8,888 pins knocked down, they had a majority of 84; 4,459 pins were knocked down on the Uptown alley, of which that party had a majority of 127. On the Chestnut alley, the whole number was 4,429, of which the Chestnut street party had 13 majority. The *total* shows the number of pins knocked down by each person, and the *average* is the result of nine balls at three entire frames. Your ignorance of gaming in New York renders this explanation necessary, and brings the "Baltimore" and the "string game" within the comprehension of your readers. The result, however, is not presented as extraordinary playing, but reported in the hope of producing a competition, and of bringing out some of our best players. So beat it if you can, and let us have the result.

Respectfully yours,
A LOOKER ON

QUOITS

The game of quoits had its roots in the rural pastime of pitching iron rings at a peg in the ground. It continued to be popular in agricultural villages, but it also had a small but devoted following in Canadian towns and several cities in the United States. During the 1850s there were clubs in Montreal, Toronto, and at least four in New York City: the St. Andrew, Thistle, New York, and Caledonian. In Manhattan Scottish immigrants took the lead in forming clubs and promoting their traditional game. The following description of the sport, account of a contest, and list of rules are reprinted from the New York Clipper, 26 July 1856, p. 105, 11 December 1858, p. 268, and the Spirit of the Times, 7 July 1860, p. 268.

THE GAME OF QUOITS COMMENDED

We are glad to see that the taste for athletic exercises is becoming more popular than it was wont to be among our young men, and that the increasing partiality for them includes, progressively, the more innocent and healthful of their number. We refer more particularly to out-door sports and pastimes, which, with the scanty privileges afforded for their full enjoyment, are joined by a large number of our young men who, throughout days, are confined to sedentary occupations. As many more would, no doubt, feel inclined to participate in them, were it not that what is called the "boisterous nature" of the amusements is too much for them—too severe to be regularly indulged in. Base ball and cricket are among these; also rowing. But there are many other amusements which tend to the gradual efficient production of muscular power, and to the restoration of injured health, which might be adopted in lieu of the more robust exercises. Among them is quoiting—or throwing the dise—a sport of the ancient athltea, and one which is now very common in European countries, and can be adapted to any stage of physical strength. We have seen a five pound quoit thrown steadily a distance of 21 yards, and seldom striking more than half its breadth, or about 4 inches, from the mark at which it was aimed during games continuing for several hours. The same accuracy can be associated with the throwing of a quoit only a pound and a half or two pounds weight. Commencing with the smaller weight, and gradually becoming able to use the larger ones, by practice at once easy and healthful in its operation on the muscles, the player, almost before he dares realize the fact, will heave one of the largest quoits three times the distance the mere tyro could do, and do it for hour after hour with ease. It is considered one of the most invigorating of exercises, and taxes the muscular powers of the body alike—lending vigor to the whole. We wish much to see this game become popular; and it only wants a little spirit among our young men who are inclined to enter on the more severe exercises to give it an initiation.

The best quoits are made of malleable iron, and edged with steel. Some players have the upper surface steeled also. The size and weight, as we have intimated, is various. As to both, it may be well here to be somewhat particular, that such of our young readers as may fancy the game may understand how to prepare for it. The diameter of the quoit should be—say for one 2-1/2 lbs. weight—5 inches—the diameter of the centre of the ring one half that of the whole. For a quoit 3 1/2 lbs. weight, (and this is the best size to use in general,) the diameter ought to be 7 inches, and that of the centre 4 inches. Intermediate and large sizes ought to be calculated in accordance with these sizes. The outer circumference of the ring of the quoit—or flange, as it may be called—be hammered to an edge, and the inside should not be thicker than three-fourths of an inch, for the 2 1/2 lbs. size, or an inch and an eighth in the 3 1/2 lbs. size. Whatever size the player may choose, of that he must furnish himself with a pair, and these precisely of one weight and make in all respects. Some have a small notch cut in the edge, in which to put the forefinger when they make a throw; but the surest quoit-players take the ring of the quoit in their hand in the same manner as they would throw a club horizontally at a mark.

The usual distance played is 21 yards, from goal to goal. A piece of smooth, green turf-land, a little wet where the quoits are to fall to the mark does very well; but trenches ought to be made at least a yard square at each of the ends, and filled each a couple of feet deep with tenacious clay, which being kept moist, furnishes a fine bed for the quoits to fall into. The 21 yards being accurately measured off, an iron rod, about 10 inches long should be thrust into the clay at the spot to be considered the goal, at an angle of 45 degrees—the angle receding from the player at the other end of the ground. A white feather, a card, or a slip of paper is set up at the top of the rod, and to strike that, and, if possible, cover the end of the rod, and remain in its nearest vicinity until all the quoits are played from the opposing side, is the object of the player. Thus prepared, the game commences by the players on each side —(two and two make the best game,) playing alternately—the last pair to play remaining at the opposite end to direct the movements of the first two, who in turn take their places and functions until they have also played. That party who have the most of their quoits nearest the hob, or mark, or goal, are the winners. Twenty-one is generally the number of the game; and with good players, may take a couple of hours to win—*dead heats* being not at all unfrequent.

It may seem strange to some that any direction is required in such a game as the one described; but, when it is considered that such accuracy has been attained by some as to enable them to so pitch their quoit as to hoist that of an opponent from the soil, and send it flying yards off, there will be no wonder that such direction as might tend to that accomplishment, or to prevent it, may be necessary. Moreover, sometimes there may be one of the quoits stuck just over the *hob,* and another just inside of it—in a position precisely like a half open oyster shell, with the hob inside the oyster. A grand, and not unfrequent feat, is to "open the oyster," as it is called, and cover the mark, and direction and advice is necessary in such case to a person standing twenty-one yards distant who is expected to accomplish it.

The best quoit players stand straight—place their eye upon the goal—raise the right hand, grasping the quoit, supported by the left, to a level with the right elbow—and throw, inclining the body a little to the right as they swing back the quoit to heave it forth. Others stand crooked, with the dise up to their eyes, and directly in front of their body. These have to swing the quoit round their right hip before its delivery, which is rarely in a straight line, and therefore, they seldom make good players. The most graceful players are always the best and steadiest.

Now, we do not know that anybody may deem it worth while to experiment on our descriptions, but if they do not, they lose the pleasure, and the physical advantages of one of the finest games extant. Our young friends in the country, who have better facilities than those in the city, might try quoiting if they choose. They'll like it.

RETURN MATCH BETWEEN
THE NEW YORK AND CALEDONIAN QUOITING CLUBS

The return match between these two celebrated clubs came off on Wednesday, the 1st inst., on the ground of the New York Quoit club, at Waterman's College Hotel, 76 Varick street. The first game of the match (which was a home and home one,) was played at Brooklyn a short time ago, when the Caledonian Club obtained a decisive victory. On this occasion the New York Club played a much stronger team, and in consequence they were enabled to turn the tables upon their opponents. The ground was in good condition for playing, and the weather fine, though exceedingly cold. The New York Quiot Club was represented by Messrs Dodsworth, S. Southard, S. Wright, Dunning, Heyward, and Ludlow, while Messrs. Cavan, Gibson, Patterson, and two others, maintain the honor and interests of the Caledonian Club. The match consisted of two games at 21 yards distance, and two at 18 yards distance. The first game at 21 yards was won in splendid style by the New York players, Messrs. Wright and Southard; they scoring 31 shots to the Caledonian's 20. the second, at the same distance was won in hollow style by the Caledonian's, who scored 31 shots while their opponents only marked 6.

The two games at 18 yards distance were both won by the New York Club players, they scoring 31 shots in the first game to the Caledonian's 21; and in the second game 31 to their opponents 11. As the subjoined summary shows, the New York Club were conquerors in this match by 21 shots.

	21 yards.		18 yards		Total.
New York Quoit Club	31	31	31	6	99
Caledonian Quoit Club	16	11	20	31	78
			Majority		21

The match did not terminate until the approach of darkness. There was a very large attendance of the members of the two clubs, and of the admirers of this healthy recreation present, to witness the play. The precision and steadiness of play displayed by the veteran, Mr. Dodsworth, one of the New York players, elicited general admiration, he being upwards of 75 years of age, yet possessing unimpaired strength and judgment of play. On the termination of the match, the members of the Caledonian club and their friends were entertained by the New York Club, with an elegant cold collation, provided by Mr. Waterman, the proprietor of the College Hotel, in his best style. Complimentary speeches were exchanged between the presidents, J. Walters, Esq., of the New York, and Cavan of the Caledonian clubs, and the healths of various members and players were proposed and drank amid loud acclamations. Among them the health of Mr. Dodsworth was received with tremendous cheering, and the gentleman in returning thanks in very appropriate terms, expressed his great gratification in seeing his favorite game, which he had played for above sixty years, increasing in popularity and favor throughout the United States. "I, myself," he continued, "furnish a most convincing proof of the beneficial effects of quoiting in producing health and longevity, and I am convinced that with the extension of this and other manly exercises, the idea of the gradual deterioration of the physical organization of the American people would be proved false and untenable." The remainder of the evening was passed in the pleasantest and most convivial manner, and all parted highly gratified with the day's enjoyment.

RULES OF THE NEW YORK QUOIT CLUB

1. The distance shall be eighteen yards and twenty-one yards measuring in a direct line from mot to mot.

2. The mots shall project not more than two and a half inches above the level, and shall incline towards each other at an angle of about forty-five degrees, and shall not be moved in any way during the game, without its being mutually agreed upon.

3. The shots shall measure from the mearest visible iron of the mot to the nearest visible iron of the quoit, without disturbing the clay or quoits in any manner.

4. In case two opposing quoits touching the mot, they shall not be counted; but the next nearest quoit or quoits of the player making a toucher (or his partner or partners), shall be counted, and none others.

5. The points of the dividers in all mesurements must be strictly visible.

6. Any party disturbing the clay or quoits, pending the decision of a shot, shall lose the shot in controversy.

7. The delivery of quoits shall be not more than one pace from the mot—that is, the mot from which the delivery is made.

8. All disputes must be left to a disinterested party present, whose decision shall be final.

9. No quoit measuring over thirty inches from the mot shall be counted.

10. In a case a player is directed by his partner or the judge at the opposite end not to play, he shall lose that shot, only having the right to play his remaining quoit, if he have one.

11. Any player leaving the end from which the shots are made, to inspect those already made at the opposite end, shall not count on that end; but a non playing partner shall have the right to go to the end in which the quoits are played and inform his partner, and set marks for his said partner.

12. The player making the cast shall always play first at the next.

Chapter 13

RACKETS

The sport of rackets (or racquets in the modern spelling) was a favorite pastime of elite North Americans during the middle years of the nineteenth century, especially in Montreal and New York. In the latter city the Allen Street Court was built in 1802, and for the next half century aristocratic Knickerbockers enjoyed this indoor sport, which was an ancestor of squash. During the 1830s a group of Manhattan butchers established their own club at the corner of the Bowery and Broome streets. There are a few accounts of matches between the artisan and upper class clubs who competed against each other despite the difference in their social rank. The butchers' association was defunct by the 1840s, when the Allen Street club also was experiencing problems. A sizeable number of its most influential members seceded to organize the Racket Court Club on Broadway in 1845. The excerpts from its Constitution and By-Laws which appear below suggest that its founders did not wish to mingle with gamblers or other undesirables who had frequented the Allen Street Court. During the 1850s its members were mostly merchants and bankers. The club broke up around 1855, when its property was sold by its owner.

The sporting press paid very little attention to rackets during this period, with the notable exception of an international challenge in 1847 between the Canadian Edward Lamontaigne (also spelled Lamontagne) and the New Yorker Robert Knox II. The second document in this chapter summarizes the action in this three match series. After he moved to New York City, Lamontaigne built a new court in 1854 and formed the Gymnasium Club on Thirteenth Street near Sixth Avenue. That facility was the scene of many feature matches during the late 1850s, and it became a public court when Lamontaigne sold it in 1858 or 1859. Rackets continued to be primarily an upper class sport on the eve of the Civil War. This chapter concludes with a list of the rules published in 1860.

THE RACKET COURT CLUB, 1845

The Racket Court Club was founded in 1845 by a group of New York gentlemen led by Robert Emmet. Instead of following the usual practice of a joint stock ownership, the organizers elected to contract with Richard T. Carman, who operated the club as a business venture. As the document below indicates, the club's bylaws imposed strict limits on gambling and permitted minors to use the facilities with certain restrictions.

The Racket Court soon became one of New York's most prominent social clubs. The aristocrat diarist Philip Hone described its gala opening in 1846 as "a grand entertainment of music, dancing, eating and drinking at which were members of the Club with those belonging to the Union and other kindred associations, each gentleman being provided with four ladies tickets." He wrote: "Soon after twelve o'clock every part of this beautiful edifice—the dining salon, reception, reading and billiard rooms, was crowded with the most genteel people in town. The immense racquet court appeared from the upper galleries like a garden of moving flowers and a band of thirty musicians left no room to doubt that the place was the racquet court." The club remained exclusive into the 1850s, when it banned tradesmen from membership, including the department store tycoon A.T. Stewart. The following are excerpts from the *Constitution and By-Laws of the Racket Court; Adopted 7th May, 1845* (New York, 1845), reprinted with the permission of the Racquet & Tennis Club of New York City.

CONSTITUTION AND BY-LAWS
REPORT OF COMMITTEE

Keeping in view that the main object of most of the signers to the agreement with Mr. Carman is, to provide a place where they and their friends can have the benefit of taking athletic exercise, and enjoying judicious recreation and relaxation of both body and mind, without being compelled to mix with uncongenial associates; and aware that the permanent existence of such an establishment can only be secured by a strict adherence to the restrictions upon gambling, and rules governing the admission of members, and strangers to be introduced by them, most strongly urge upon all the members, not only to assent to the laws which they propose for their government, but to exert individually their own personal influence, in checking any disposition that may be manifested by others to evade them.

It is hoped that should there be any among those who have already joined the association, who think that members should be left unrestricted as to the amount which they may be disposed to stake on any game, they will yield their own wishes on being made aware that past experience in this city clearly proves that no club can continue in existence without the most rigid adherence to strict rules upon this subject, and therefore the only question to be considered is, what the limitation shall be. In recommending the adoption of Article 12th, as it now stands, the committee would not have it supposed that they approve of betting to the extent which it allows, but in view of the necessity of fixing a limit, the evasion or infringement of which, involves *the forfeiture of membership without appeal,* they unanimously agreed to that clause in the article referred to, trusting that the members, individually, will set an example of moderation in this respect, for which it is hoped this Club will be distinguished. In its present form, the committee believe that this by-law meets the views of the large majority of the members, and they trust, that the minority will cheerfully acquiesce in sustaining it. In this way the main objection, that with a show of reason has been urged against clubs in general, will be removed in this one, and the evidence be afforded that instead of encouraging gambling, a club may be organized whose tendency will be exactly the reverse.

Besides the game of Racket, requiring a court of 40 by 120 feet, and a Bowling Saloon in the rear, the premises on Broadway, covering a space of about 55 feet square, will contain a Reading Room, well supplied with newspapers and periodicals, a Billiard Room, two Whist and Chess Rooms, a Refectory, and if approved of by the members, a Gymnasium. The whole under the care of Mr. Benj. R. Theall, subject to such regulations and control as the club may from time to time impose. It may be well to remark here, that the terms of the contract made with Mr. Carman expressly secures to us for twenty-one years all the rights and privileges which we would have under a jont stock ownership, without the trouble and inconvenience of having to manage the financial department, and run the risk of becoming involved in difficulties arising from so large an investment. An arrangement similar to this forms the basis of several of the best clubs in London. The interests of the whole of the parties concerned, members, owner and manager, being identical, and requiring the greatest liberality of the part of the latter in carrying out their obligations, leave no ground to apprehend any cause of dissatisfaction at any time; and considering that no one of the subscribers, should the offer of embarking in the enterprize have been made to him, would have availed himself of it, the profit that is likely to result to Mr. Carman ought not to excite any envy.

With one more remark the committee submit the By-Laws for the consideration of the meeting. Some misunderstanding existing as to the design of the committee in reference to minors, they have framed a By-Law to meet that subject, which they conceive does away with any objection that may be urged against allowing them access to the Racket court and Bowling Saloon, the entrance to which is separate and distinct from the Club Rooms; and as the game of Racket requires time to become skilful at it, the committee secured in anticipation the privilege under certain restrictions, which they believe it for the interest of the Club to avail themselves of.

As the success and continued prosperity of such an establishment rests entirely with the members of the Club themselves, it may be well to recommend to them the utmost caution in using their privileges as to the introduction of strangers and the admission of new members. The commencement of the enterprise is very auspicious; it has the good will and countenance of our most respectable citizens, and bids fair to fulfil the wishes and anticipations of its projectors.

Le them not be disappointed!

E. BOONEN GRAVES,
FRANCES GRIFFIN,
ISAAC TOWNSEND, Committee
ROBT. S. HONE,
PROSPERE M. WETMORE,
ROBERT EMMET,

New York, 7th May, 1845

BY-LAWS

ARTICLE 1.

The Club shall be called the RACKET COURT.

ARTICLE 2.

No person shall become a member of the Club unless he shall have attained the age of twenty-one years; and the number of members shall not exceed *two hundred and fifty,* unless determined otherwise by a vote of two-thirds of any meeting of members called expressly for that purpose.

ARTICLE 3.

Should the Club at any meeting called for that purpose determine to extend the number of members beyond two hundred and fifty, the initiation fee shall then be increased to $50, and $20 a year for three years thereafter, payable in all cases in advance, on the 1st January in each year. Persons joining at any intermediate time, will pay on subscribing, the initiation fee, and their annual dues pro rata up to the ensuing 1st January.

ARTICLE 4.

All resignations shall be made in writing to the President or Secretary, and any member in arrears for annual dues, more than six months, unless caused by absence from the city, will be considered as forfeiting the rights and privileges of a member, and the vacancy thus occasioned, shall be filled the same as if he had resigned....

ARTICLE 6.

Persons wishing the privilege of membership, will apply to either of the members, who jointly with another member, shall communicate the same by note to the Secretary. Not more than ten names can be admitted at one time, and the Secretary shall see that as many ballot boxes, under lock and key, shall be provided as the number to be balloted for requires. These boxes shall have two apartments, one for the balls and the other for slips of paper with the names of the voters, to be deposited by them simultaneously; they shall be placed in a conspicous part of the Club rooms, with the name of the applicant, and the two members recommending him, attached thereto.

Thirty votes are necessary for a constitutional election, and should that number not be deposited within a fortnight from the opening of the poll, the candidate will be considered withdrawn, and can only be again proposed for admission, after the lapse of six months. When thirty votes shall have been deposited for any candidate, and a fortnight shall have expired from the date of his proposal, the ballot box shall be opened in the presence of three members of the "General Executive committee," who on finding the number of ballots correspond with the number of voters, shall certify the candidate to be elected, provided that, nine-tenths of the balls, excluding fractions, are white, or that five black balls in all do not appear among them.

A new election to be called, should the number of ballots not correspond with the number of the voters' names. After payment of the initiation fee, and first year's dues, and signing the constitution, the candidate shall be entitled to all the privileges, and be subject to the obligations of a member....

ARTICLE 10.

Members of the Club alone have the privilege of admission for their sons to the Racket Court and Bowling Saloon, under the following restrictions:—they must be at least eighteen years of age, and not over twenty-one. Shall in no case occupy either place, to the exclusion of the members, and shall be limited to such hours, and be governed by such regulations, as the Committee may designate.

ARTICLE 11.

The establishment shall be open every day for the use of its members at seven o'clock, A.M., in summer, and at eight in winter, and shall be closed on Saturday night at twelve o'clock. No games of any kind shall be permitted between Saturday at midnight and Monday morning.

ARTICLE 12.

No round game of cards shall be allowed to be played in the Club, under any pretence whatever, and no bet shall be made upon any game, in any part of the establishment exceeding five dollars. The stake at short whist, to be not more than half this amount.

Any member discovered to have infringed this By-Law, *shall forfeit his right of membership without appeal....*

INTERNATIONAL RACKET SERIES, 1847

Feature matches between prominent players excited as much interest in rackets as they did in other sports. In 1847 the New York City sporting community witnessed a series between Edward Lamontaigne and Robert Knox II. Lamontaigne was a wine merchant from Montreal who claimed the championship of Canada and was a distinguished performer in several annual athletic games held in his home city. Knox was a celebrated local sportsman and the son and grandson of the proprietors of the Allen Street Court. As the following selection demonstrates, the men played for cash stakes and their competition stimulated some play among gamblers. Lamontaigne won two out of the three contests. A few years later he moved to New York City and became a prominent promoter of rackets in Manhattan. These accounts are reprinted from the Spirit of the Times, 22 May, 5 and 19 June 1847, pp. 147, 171, 194.

RACKET MATCH FOR $500 A SIDE
AT THE ALLEN STREET COURT, NEW YORK

This match came off, according to agreement, on the 17th inst. Mr. L. of Canada, sent a challenge, in April last, to Mr. K. of New York (one of the proprietors of the Court), to play a rub at Racket, 15 aces to each game (eleven being the set game for single matches), for $500 a side, $200 forfeit.

At about a quarter before five o'clock, P.M., the parties appeared in the Court, and were warmly greeted by all present. Mr. K. had the call in the betting at 50 to 40. They tossed for the hand, and Canada won the first inning, but was put out without an ace. Mr. K. being out, Mr. L. made the first ace. L. made seven before K. scored one., which changed the "state of the odds" to 100 to 75 on L. To all who were acquainted with Mr. K's usual style of play, it was very evident that he was amiss, either from over excitement or physical inability; while Mr. L. displayed great strength and activity, and a degree of science seldom before equalled in this Court; his services, in particular, were spoken of with admiration by every player present. The first game L. seemed to have it pretty much his own way, marking fifteen aces, while K. marked only five. No betting.

Second Game.—L. in, and with hands in and out, scored seven before K. got one; $100 to $7 was offered on Mr. L. and taken. Mr. K. here seemed to rally a little, and after several in and out hands, and some fine displays of science, the game stood 8 to 9, K.'s hand in. This was the most exciting stage of the match, and 20 to 25 was on K.'s winning the game. The play continued fine and the excitement increased, as the game drew to a close; many hearty shouts of applause went up from the numerous audience, at the remarkable science displayed throughout the latter part of this game. L. won the game, the score being 15 to 11. Recapitulation: —

FIRST GAME		SECOND GAME	
Mr. L	15 aces.	Mr. L	15 aces.
Mr. K	5 aces	Mr. K	11 aces

After the match, Mr. K. appeared to be decidedly the freshest man, and notwithstanding his apparently being "off" in the first game, it was generally conceded that if it had been game and game, K. would have won the rub. But this of course is problematical. The assemblage was large and highly respectable, the Club having given out about one hundred and thirty invitations; every thing went off in the best possible manner.

The Men.—Mr. L. is about five feet ten and a half inches in height, with a fine form, well adapted for all athletic exercises; he is very active, and a fast runner; he weighs one hundred and sixty pounds, and is twenty five years old. He is the Champion of all Canada as a Racket player.—Mr. K. is five feet six—light frame, but straight and well formed—weighs one hundred and seventeen pounds, and is twenty-four years old.

This Court was built in 1802 by a Scotch gentleman named Knox, and has ever been supported by some of our best citizens. Several were present on the above occasion, that have been members for thirty-five years.

Dimensions of the Court.—Floor 120 feet in length, and 40 in breadth,—Court 52 1/2 feet high at the back.

RACKET MATCH FOR $100 A SIDE

Another match at Racket came off at the Allen street Court on the 27th ult., between the same parties that played the $500 match on the 17th of last month, (Mr. R. Knox of this city, and Mr. E. L. of Canada). This match was offered by Mr. K. to play 31 aces out, for $100 a side.

At five o'clock the parties appeared in the Court, and received a hearty greeting from the audience, which was very large and highly respectable; both men looked well, and appeared confident of winning. They tossed for the hand, and Mr. L. had the first inning (L. had the call about five to four, but very little betting). Mr. L. went off at a killing pace with his tremendous services, and scored five before K. put his hand out. Here some small bets was made on K.'s scoring the next five aces first. K. made one ace, and out; L. one and out; and K. in, and marked four, winning the bets on the five aces. The game now stood six, five, and K. stock began to look up a little. Both men appeared perfectly collected and at their game, but L. continued sending his Capt. May (beg pardon, Col. May) like shots in the way of services, and making some of the most tremendous strides and displays of Racket playing, that fairly electrified the spectators; while K. kept on the even tenor of his way, his countenance as serene as the zephyr, and his confidence not for a moment forsaking him.

After many well contested in and out hands, the game was at 15 to 7, and L. in. Here there were nine hands in and out without scoring an ace on either side. Mr. K. here appeared a little flushed, by the fact of being able to bring his formidable competitor to bay, and took up the play with renewed vigor, putting in some of his usual straight-forward shots that told well; and the game soon stood 17 to 15, L.'s hand in. It was evident here, after the many severe rounds, that K. was the freshest man, but the betting, which was very light, did not change materially. At 17 aces they were even, and some few bets were offered on K. and taken. The play had now settled down to a well contested, scientific display of this manly exercise, Mr. L. not for a moment losing himself or his game; but not, as in the commencement, making such terrific exertions, while Mr. K. (as we say in horse-race parlance) was under a snug pull, holding on the turns and making play on the straight sides. Mr. L. was never even with Mr. K. after 17 aces, but when K. was 25, L. had scored 24. After a few more bouts, L. marked one more ace, and K. won the match.

Every thing went off in the best possible manner. Pretty much all of the old members (who know and can appreciate the game) were present, while some of the young members, and many of the invited guests, that had never seen a game at Racket before, expressed a determination to become members and Racket players. Recapitulation: —

Mr. Knox   31 aces.

Mr. E. Lamontayne 25 aces.

THE RETURN RACKET MATCH.
BY AN EYE WITNESS.

On Saturday, the 5th inst., we had again the pleasure of witnessing the great return Match at Rackets, between Mr. E. Lamontagne, of Canada, and Mr. R. Knox, of this City, for L500 aside, forty-one aces up. Mr. L. having won the first match, and Mr. K.

the second, each, on this occasion, had his particular friends and backers, and the betting before the play commenced was therefore very brisk. The weather was extremely favorable, and both gentlemen appeared very sanguine and in excellent condition. Nothing could surpass the excitement which was felt by the spectators in anticipation of the result.

"Canada" won the "hand-in," but was soon put out by the "New Yorker," without an ace. The New Yorker made several pretty hits, but Mr. L. kept time with him in that respect, and scored four aces before Mr. K. scored a single ace. "Five to two" was now freely offered on Mr. L., but not taken. After about twenty minutes it was quite evident which would win; Mr. L. was twenty to eleven, having made some of the most astonishing reaches. His powerful hits just above the white board were unreservedly admired and applauded, and he could not be beaten at the pace he was going; his antagonist, however, kept cool, and showed all through great confidence in himself; but Mr. L. was too much for him in a long match. In a rubber of 11 aces, Mr. K. would yet have many backers.

After two hours play Mr. L. won by 18 aces. The good humor and feeling which prevailed all through the match, reflect great credit on all parties that were present. The prompt decision given by the gentleman who kept the game, gave unusual satisfaction, and does honor to the Club.

State of the game at its conclusion: —

   Mr. Lamontagne 41 aces.
   Mr. Knox   23 aces
  Mr. Knox being thus beaten by 18 aces.

RACKETS—RULES OF THE GAME

There were several private and public rackets clubs in New York City during the 1850s. As support for exercise and athletics increased, the sporting press recommended wholesome indoor recreation during the winter months. The document below suggests that there was considerable demand for playing time on the city's courts. It also appears that regulations differed depending on the type of facility available for the sport's enthusiasts. These rules were printed in the New York Clipper, 7 January 1860, p. 301.

RULES FOR THE GAME IN A CLOSE COURT

1. Subscribers who agree to Play together must subscribe their names on a Slate placed near the Marker, they can then take the Court in the order their names are inscribed.

2. Three or four players (a double match) may play five Games, two players may play three Games without reference to their rubber.

3. To secure the Court for a Double Match, it is requisite that three of the persons who are to play should have their names inscribed; two for a single match.

4. The name of any one actually playing, cannot as one of a party engage the Court.

5. If a Court is engaged by two parties, that which has a prior engagement cannot waive its claim in favor of a third party.

6. Should the Court be disengaged at the conclusion of a Match, the party playing may re-commence their Match and play it out.

7. If a suspension of play for three minutes takes place during or between Games, or six minutes between rubbers; the Court is to be considered vacant.

8. A subscriber may bring any casual friend not entitled to become a subscriber into Court, and his friend may play and make one of three names necessary to be inscribed on the Slate, to secure the Court for A Double Match, or one of the names for a Single; under no other circumstances can a non-subscriber play to the exclusion of subscribers.

9. The Marker cannot play in a Single Match when other matches are made, and there are subscribers desirous of playing; but if a Match is begun in which he is playing when subscribers are not waiting, the Match may be played out.

10. Persons playing Matches of general interest, may play FIVE Games, whether there are *two, three, or four* players, and secure the Court by giving notice to the Marker three days before the Match is intended to be played, the names of the parties, and the hour the Court is required.

1. The game to consist of 15 aces at 13 all; the players may set the Game to 5 at 14 all; the out players may set the Game to 3, if the Game be not set immediately on its amounting to 13 or 14 all; it cannot be set afterwards.

2. The party of parties, whether giving odds or not, to go in first, to be determined by lot.

3. The party or parties going in first can only take one hand, although they may have odds.

4. In serving, the server must stand with one foot within the compartment allotted for the server, the out player into whose Court the ball is to be served, may stand where he pleases; but his partner, until the ball is served, must stand behind the server and inside the short line; the server's partner must stand behind the server, but outside the short line.

5. The ball must be served above and not touching the cut line on the front wall, and it must strike the ground (before it bounds) within, and not touching the line enclosing the Court opposite to where the server stands.

6. If in serving, the ball hit anywhere before it hits the front wall, it is a hand out.

7. The ball to be served alternately throughout the game to right and left sides, the Marker calling play, right or left.

8. If a ball, whether falsely served or not, be intercepted by an in player, it is a hand out.

9. The out player may take a ball falsely if he pleases, but if he misses it, he loses the ace. If he objects, three false services is a hand out.

10. An out player may take a ball served to his partner, provided, when doing so, he does not put both feet behind the short line.

11. The out players may change their Courts only once during the game.

12. If a ball be prevented from going up by hitting the striker's adversary's racket, it is a hand out, or an ace. If hit below the knee, it is also an ace or hand out against the striker; but if he hits above the knee, it is a lett ball.

13. If a player designedly intercept a ball, it is an ace, or a hand out against him.

14. If a ball, after being struck by a player, touch his partner, they lose the ace or hand out.

15. Each player must give as much room to the party who is to strike as possible.

16. If a player strikes at and misses a ball, his partner may play it.

17. Doubtful aces and letts to be played over again.

18. If a ball lodge in the Gallery during the play, it is a lett; in serving it is a false ball.

19. In serving, if the ball strike the roof blinds or lines, after the front wall, it is a false ball.

20. The Marker is to decide all disputes, if he is doubtful, appeal to the Gallery.

21. In Matches of general interest, the parties may appoint an Umpire instead of the Marker.

22. No one to speak to the Marker while the game is playing, as it is impossible for him to mark correctly if his attention is taken off.

23. Partners can change Courts once only during a game.

24. Every ball served or struck from the service, and not placed above the wood line, is a hand out, or an ace.

RULES FOR THE GAME IN AN OPEN COURT

1. Toss for innings. The party serving must serve from the centre of the court, and shall serve over the "cut" line on the wall and the service line in the court. All such services must be played.

2. A ball served under the line on the wall is termed a "cut ball," and pitching short of the line on the court, is a "short ball." Three short balls is a hand out. Cut balls do not count, but either can be accepted at the option of the retriever, but no player can stop his own service.

3. An opponent getting in the striker's way, and depriving him of a chance of hitting the ball, shall be termed a "lett ball," and be served over again. The ball falling on the server is a hand out. If it falls on the striker, who is the "outer" player, it is an ace against him.

4. A ball, after being hit by the striker, and hitting his opponent above the hip, is also a "lett ball," but if he hits his opponent's racket, the striker can claim an ace.

5. In a four handed match the party winning the toss is only allowed one hand— the first service. The party serving ought to serve alternately into each court, and the parties accepting the service may receive it alternately.

6. As in a two handed match, the striker hitting his opponent above the hip, shall be considered a "lett ball," but providing he hits his own partner, he loses an ace or a hand.

7. A ball being served on the outside line of the court or wall, the striker is out; he is also out if he hit on under the "play board."

8. A player can use either hand.

9. The ball must be played from the first hop or "volley."

10. The positions in a four handed match are: the server must have one foot in the "service ring," his partner taking the right hand corner of the quarter of the "inner" court.

11. When the server has struck the ball, he shall immediately fall back to half way (close to the line) to left hand "outer" court.

12. The striker of the first service shall take the outer play, during which time the "non outer" striker shall take the cross position of two thirds up the court.

13. Players pitted against one another by the marker to be abided by, and considered a fair match.

14. All points of the game to be decided by the marker.

15. The game to consist of the first eleven aces.

Chapter 14

TRACK AND FIELD

Foot races and various kinds of athletic games and feats of strength were part of the sporting culture of North Americans during the middle years of the nineteenth century. Canadians and Americans enjoyed two distinct types of amusements which eventually evolved into modern track and field. The first included athletic festivals and exhibitions sponsored by sporting clubs such as the Scottish Caledonian societies of Montreal, Boston, and New York. Scottish immigrants successfully introduced many of their traditional games into Canada and the United States, and they used these exercises as a means of preserving their national heritage. The second category was pedestrianism, which featured professional running and walking contests. Participants competed for prize money put up by entrepreneurs, who earned a profit on admission fees. Spectators and competitors both wagered on the outcome of the matches.

English and Scottish military officers, diplomats, merchants, and professionals organized sports clubs in North America which sponsored track and field festivals. In 1842 two hundred and forty-one prominent citizens of Montreal founded that city's Olympic Athletic Club. The membership included officers from the local military garrison, Scottish merchants, and both French and British political and professional leaders. An account of the games sponsored by that organization in 1843 appears below. That exhibition and another one the following year were open to all races and nationalities, with medals or cash payments as prizes.

During the late 1850s Scottish societies organized Caledonian games that greatly influenced the development of modern track and field in North America. During these years communities of Scottish immigrants to North America organized Caledonian clubs, which eventually numbered more than one hundred by the later years of the century. These associations helped the members to preserve at least a part of their cultural heritage. Scottish residents of Boston founded a society in 1853, and one of its founders stated that its purpose was to perpetuate "the manners and customs, literature, the Highland costume and the athletic games of Scotland, as practiced by our forefathers." In addition to sponsoring athletics, these organizations also scheduled dinners, dances, and concerts that featured bagpipes.

The year 1856 witnessed the birth of the New York Caledonian Club. That organization began sponsoring annual games in 1857, charging an admission fee of twenty-five cents and awarding prizes to the victors of each event. These sessions marked a significant change in the development of commercialized sports in America because previously individual promoters arranged events and sought profit from gate receipts. The only major exception had been horse racing, where jockey clubs sometimes organized meetings. The new Caledonian model soon was followed by baseball and other athletic clubs. These games also differed from pedestrian contests in that they featured a variety of field events, including leaping, vaulting, and feats of strength such as putting the heavy stone or tossing the caber. The festivities included traditional songs and dances of the old country, as well as such comical competitions as wheel barrow and sack races. "A Day With the New York Caledonian Club" summarizes the results of the second annual games sponsored by that Manhattan organization in 1858. Thus by 1860 sportsmen in Montreal, Boston, New York, and other cities had laid the foundation for the future development of North American track and field.

Pedestrianism enjoyed great popularity as a spectator sport in the United States during the 1840s and early 1850s. Tens of thousands flocked to the Beacon Course in Hoboken, New Jersey and other sites around the country to witness the long distance races. Promoters capitalized on the elements of nationality and race as they matched Americans against Englishmen and Indians. A peak year for this sport was 1844, when the Beacon Course was the site of four spectacles. About 30,000 people watched Henry Stannard win the $1,000 prize, as the Connecticut farmer repeated his victorious performance in a feature race in 1835. The promoter then advertised another race for $1,000 in newspapers in several countries. "The Great Foot Race" describes the outcome of this attraction, which drew thirty-seven entries and seventeen starters from the United States, England, Ireland and one Indian tribe. The surprise winner was John Gildersleeve, a New York chair maker, who passed Englishmen John Barlow and John Greenhalgh in the tenth and final mile. "Great Ten Mile Foot Race" narrates the third contest, which was won by Barlow in front of a huge throng in the record time of 54 minutes and 21 seconds. Greenhalgh barely defeated Gildersleeve in the twelve-mile final event, held in freezing weather in mid-December before a small audience.

Over the next decade a mania for foot racing swept across many communities, men racing against each other and against time. As in horse racing, most events were long distance challenges that tested the competitors' endurance, but there were also some sprints and hurdle contests. The leading professional pedestrians were generally manual workers who toured the country in search of prize money that sometimes amounted to as much as $1,000, divided among the leading finishers. Winners could expect to earn more from side bets. Some runners also issued challenges for match races, with backers putting up the money. The fourth document in this chapter recounts the exploits of William Jackson, "the American Deer," who journeyed to England during the early 1850s in search of fame and fortune.

Walking contests also were popular during these years. Some matches were held at distances of twenty miles or more. There were numerous novelty events which featured women or men walking on planks for extended time periods. This chapter concludes with several accounts of female and male pedestrians who walked continuously for days at a time.

Pedestrianism declined in the United States after 1855 for several reasons. The closing of the Beacon Course in 1845 hurt the long-term prospects of the sport because many of the events of the late 1840s were match races not as popular as purse events that attracted entrants from a variety of regions, races, and nationalities. There were fewer first class runners in the 1850s, and only William Jackson could boast a top notch reputation among Americans. Furthermore, hints of fixed races and opposition to gambling probably damaged long-distance running. Finally, the increasing popularity of harness racing and baseball drew spectators away from pedestrianism on the eve of the Civil War.

TRACK AND FIELD IN CANADA

British sporting traditions had a significant impact on the growth of athletics in Montreal during the 1840s. English and Scottish gentlemen founded the Montreal Olympic Athletic Club in 1842. The following year that association sponsored a festival of amusements. The organizers welcomed participation by French and Indian competitors; many spectators particularly admired the display of skill by Indians in their favorite game of lacrosse. On 20 August 1844 the Montreal Transcript praised the group's efforts to keep alive the sporting heritage of the old country. It stated: "It is very gratifying to see a taste for the old English sports springing up in this country, and to find that the spirit which animated our forefathers, and gave strength and vigor to their arms, is not extinct." The following summary and commentary on the initial games in 1843 is reprinted from the Spirit of the Times, 7 October 1843, p. 384.

MONTREAL ATHLETIC GAMES, 1843

The Montreal Athletic Games commenced yesterday, and with very fair promise, for a commencement. The attendance was very fair in numbers, and most respectable and orderly. The day, though cold and with a rather biting wind, was, on the whole, favourable, at least for the *Athleta* themselves, though somewhat chilly for the spectators.

The "sports," as they say "i' the North," commenced with Rifle shooting, a not very exciting spectacle to the disinterested; but assumed a livelier aspect when the Vaulting commenced, and with the Leaping, the sympathies of all classes seemed to be awakened. There were many plebian competitors for saltatory honours, but the Messers. La Montagne and Burroughs were *"facile-principes."*

In that truly British sport, "putting the hammer," both heavy and light, there were many competitors, and the struggle was very animated.

The long foot-race was well contested. The distance, 400 yards, was run in 49 seconds, and Indian litheness was preeminent. Not the least part of the fun was the climbing the soapy pole, in which Indian agility seemed to have the only chance, and easily carried off the prize.

Altogether, the spirit of the day was well kept up, and it was gratifying to witness the good feeling which prevailed, and the fairness and good humour with which competitors, whose paths of life, and even race and language, are so diverse, met in amicable contest. To-day, we understand, even better sport is anticipated.

Rifle shooting, 100 yards, 8 competitors won by Jas. Spence.

Ditto, 180 yards, 7 competitors, J. M'Nider.

Standing high vault, 6 competitors, A. La Montagne; 2nd, C. Burroughs.

Running high leap, 8 ditto, E. La Montage, 4 feet 10 inches; 2nd., C. Burroughs.

Standing high leap, 4 ditto, C. Burroughs, 4 feet 3 inches; 2nd, E. La Montagne, 4 feet 1 1/2 inch.

Throwing heavy hammer (15 lbs.) 14 ditto, M. Ryan, 77 feet 6 inches.

Ditto light hammer (10 lbs.) 11 ditto, James Curley, 114 feet, 7 inches; 2nd., C. Burroughs, 112 feet, 7 inches.

Long foot race (400 yards), 9 ditto, Tur Onmeatckha, 49 seconds; 2nd., Taiorvricote.

Throwing cricket ball, 12 ditto, E. La Montagne, 94 yards; 2nd., F. Pole, 43d. Regt, 93 yards, 8 inches.

Climbing the pole, 6 ditto, Ositakee.

Grinning through horse-collar, James Fulham.

SECOND DAY

The weather was still more favorable this day than on yesterday, and the sports commenced with—

Steeple race, over 4 feet hurdles, 200 yards—Won by Ed. La Montagne, second, Aug. La Montagne. Six competitors started.

Quoiting.—Won by J. M'Nider; second E. Hagan. 10 competitors.

Short foot race, 120 yards.—Won by E. La Montagne; second, A. La Montagne; third, W. Courselle. 15 competitors.

Putting heavy ball (24 lbs.)—Won by Captain Young; distance thrown, 25 feet, 9 inches. Second Mr. Casey. 10 competitors.

Running hop, step, and leap,—Won by M. Ryan. Distance 38 feet 2 inches. Six competitors.

Standing hop, step, and leap.—Won by Mr. Ryan. 28 feet. Eleven competitors.

Long foot-race (one mile.) Won by Osetakee, (Indian f) second, Tatieshensere (do); third, Areratenhoe (do). Eleven competitors.

Wrestling, collar and elbow—taken by Eascol, (without a contest.)

The running in the short foot race was very fine, and the short hurdle race was won by Mr. La Montagne, in a manner that would do credit to any sporting district, even in the old country. In the long foot race, the Indians left all competitors far behind; but probably the chief sport of the day was the playing of the Indian national game of Lacrosse, by a number of young Indians, and some young gentlemen who joined them. It is, undoubtedly, the most beautiful game of the kind we have ever seen; and the activity, grace, swiftness, and strength displayed by the players, equally delighted and astonished us. Besides the games mentioned above, there was a pig-race, in which a soldier was the winner; and the victor in the wrestling prize having walked off so easily with his booty, a private match was got up, in which the champion, a big man, was beaten, with all the ease in the world, by a little Dutch-Irishman, of the name of O'Connor. There was another wrestling match between two soldiers, but it created little sport. With this last, the amusement of the day ended. We may as well mention here, that Captain Young, the winner of the prize for the heavy ball, handsomely gave it up to the Committee.

We regret that, notwithstanding the fineness of the weather, the attendance was not so great as might have been expected. We trust, however, that the gentlemen who so strenuously exerted themselves to get up the present games will not be disconcerted, but persevere in their praiseworthy undertaking of introducing these good old healthy amusements of our fathers among us. That they will both continue their exertion and meet with final success we feel persuaded. We cannot close these few remarks without mentioning the Secretary, Mr. Myers Solomons, whose activity, good humour, firmness, and love of fair play were so conspicuous throughout the continuance of the games; and whose zeal and attention were so instrumental in getting them up.

THE CALEDONIAN GAMES

The New York Caledonian Club, founded in 1856, enlisted middle and upper class Scotsmen residing in the city. Many were prominent and affluent merchants and professional gentlemen. Its annual games, begun in 1857, soon became a successful vehicle for publicity and a source of increasing revenue for the club. During the early years the events were open only to club members, but visitors from other societies were allowed to compete as honorary participants. Most of the spectators were Scottish residents of New York City and its environs, but the festivities also attracted guests from other Caledonian societies in distant cities in the United States and Canada. The events of the day included dancing and singing contests to complement the athletics. As was the case with cricket and baseball matches, these games concluded with an elaborate dinner. The account below of the festival held in 1858 concludes with a table comparing performances in several cities. It demonstrates an early interest in keeping statistics and records for track and field. John Goldie, winner of four events at this meet, later became a prominent athletic instructor at Princeton University. This document is reprinted from the New York Clipper, 2 October 1858, pp. 186-87.

THE SCOTTISH GAME
A DAY WITH THE NEW YORK CALEDONIAN CLUB

The second annual celebration of the games of the "New York Caledonian Club" came off on Thursday, the 23d ult., at Jones' Wood. This club was only organized last year, on which occasion the games were held in Hoboken. So rapid, however, has been the progress of the club, and the accession of members; (who must be natives of "stern Caledonia," and resident in New York,) so numerous, that this year it was determined to hold the festival on a larger scale, and more in accordance with the importance and high condition of the society. The grounds attached to Jones' Wood were engaged for the purpose, and the members of the club assembled at their head quarters at the Mercer House, and at 8 o'clock a.m. proceeded to the place appointed. The day was remarkably fine, and although in the early part of the day there was a slight tinge of frost in the air, yet the sun's rays soon dissipated it, leaving the weather all that could be desired for the enjoyment of the sports.

The proceedings commenced shortly after 10 o'clock, a portion of the level ground having been enclosed thus forming a ring for the performance of the exercises. The sports opened with a Highland fling, reel and strathspey, in which both members and guests joined with the greatest spirit. The programme of the games, and the rules for the government of the competitors, were as follows:

1. The Heavy Hammer is to be thrown *without turning;* each competitor to throw once before any one makes a second throw. Three throws to each competitor.

2. Putting the Light Stone—same arrangement as above; toe the mark, without a race, neither foot to cross the mark before the stone strikes. Three trials each.

3. Throwing the Light Hammer—same arrangements as heavy hammer—three throws to each competitor.

4. Putting the Heavy Stone—arrangement same as for light stone—three trials each.

5. Tossing the Caber, each competitor to make one trial after it is turned once.

6. The Standing Jump—without weights—three trials to each.

7. The Running Jump—without weights—three trials to each.

8. The Running High Leap—without weights—three trials to each.

9. The Short Race—100 yards.

10. The Highland Fling, one dance each.

11. The Scottish Song or Ballad, optional.

12. The Long Race, say 600 yards.

13. Ghillie Caltum, or Broad Sword Dance, over two broadswords, crossed—one dance each.

14. Running Hop, Step, and Jump (omitted).

15. Wheeling the Barrow Blindfolded. The competitors to be blindfolded with back to Barrow, then turned around and placed before it, starting at the third call.

16. The Scotch Reel, one dance each.

17. The Sack Race—the first at the winning post, by any means without assistance, to win the race.

18. The Shinty—omitted.

The rules provide that no one shall be eligible to a prize without being a member of the club in good standing at the time of competing.

The following are the results of the different sports, and the awards of the judges, Messrs. Gibson, Innes, Shillinglaw, Mason, and Lines, were in every sense most just and impartial.

THROWING THE HEAVY HAMMER

1. Goldie   58 feet   2. Stevens   56 feet.

PUTTING THE LIGHT STONE

1. William Lyons   28 feet 5 inch   2. M. Lyons   25 feet 2 inch.

THROWING THE LIGHT HAMMER

1. Stevens   69 feet 9 inch   2. Goldie   68 feet 4 inch.

PUTTING THE HEAVY STONE

1. William Jones   23 feet 1 inch   2. Matthew Lyons   22 feet 8 inch

STANDING JUMP
1. Mr. Goldie   8 feet 4.5 inch   2. Mr. Montgomery 9 feet 1 inch

RUNNING JUMP
1. Montgomery 15 feet 1.5 inch   2. Goldie   14 feet 2 3/4 inch

HIGH LEAP
1. Mr. Goldie   4 feet 8 inch   2. Mr. Lyons   4 feet 3 inch

TOSSING THE CABER   SHORT FOOT RACE
1. Stevens   2. J. Cummings   1. Goldie   2. Bowman.

HIGHLAND FLING   SCOTTISH SONG OR BALLAD
1. McPherson   2. A. Frazer   1. Cummings   2. A. Frazer.

LONG RACE   BROAD-SWORD DANCE
1. Bowman   2. Montgomery   1. A. Frazer   2. McPherson.

WHEELING BARROW BLINDFOLDED   SACK RACE
1. M. Lyons   2. Sanderson   1. M. Lyons   2. Sanderson.

The winner of the 1st, 4th, and 8th games, Mr. John Goldie, is a young man, only about 22 years old, but possessed of remarkable activity and muscular power. In putting the heavy and light hammers, however, a Canadian visitor, named Alexander Innes, although not a competitor, completely surpassed the feats shown. He threw the former, weighing 17 lbs., sixty feet, and the latter 78 feet. The performance with the heavy hammer has, however, been beaten at Boston, where Mr. J. O. Cameron, a member of the Scottish Club in that city, threw a sledge hammer 18 lbs. weight, seventy-two feet eight inches. "Throwing the Caber" excited considerable interest and as many of our readers are probably ignorant of the *modus operandi*, we will briefly describe it. The "caber" is a heavy pole or log of wood, 19 feet long, and about 12 inches in circumference at the thicker end. Each competitor raises it as high as he possibly can in his arms and then casts it in a direct line from him, so that it may turn completely over in its progress, and the end he held in his arms be the farthest from him after it has fallen. Thr great weight and unwieldy size of the "caber" makes it a most difficult matter to throw it, and on the present occasion, after repeated failures to cast it, its length and weight are obliged to be reduced by sawing off a portion, before it could be accomplished. It was then thrown three times succesively by Messrs. Stevens, Cummings, and Montgomery, in capital style, the former securing the prize for the best cast, and Mr. Cummings the second.

The foot races were run around the enclosed spaces, and were well contested; the long race was won by one of the Highland pipers, Mr. Bowman, in first rate style. The high leap, which was won by Mr. Goldie, clearing 4 feet 8 inches, was over a horizontal rod placed upon two pegs in two perpendicular posts fixed in the ground. The length of run allowed was, of course, unlimited. In the trial of skill in the Highland

Broadstreet Dance, there were three competitors, but one of them, Mr. Singer, from Canada West (who last year won the prize given by George Victoria for the best broadstreet dancer at the Highland festival), only was admitted to honorary competition. The other two, McPherson and Frazer, are remarkably fine looking men, and dressed in the Highland costume, the most picturesque of dresses, looked exceedingly well in the execution of the dance, and were heartily applauded by the assemblage.

Following the dancing contest came that for the singers. There were four competitors, vis: Mr. Cummings who sang the old Jacobite song of "Bonnie Price Charlie," Mr. J. P. Fraser, who gave "O'er the Muir Among the Heather," Mr. R. Post, "My Heather Hills," and Chieftan Alexander Fraser, who sang that inspiring beautiful song, "March of the Cameron Men." We certainly thought the latter the best rendered song of the four, but the judges were of different opinion and awarded the prize of superiority to Mr. Cummings, whose "Bonnie Prince Charlie" was admirably sung.

Wheeling the Barrow blindfolded, and the sack race, were productive of much amusement, and as these sports are not generally known among us we will briefly describe them. In the former the barrows are placed side by side with a short space between them. The contestants are then blindfolded and at a given signal they start at full speed to the winning post at the other extremity of the enclosure. The fun and amusement arises from witnessing the collisions which take place among those who wheel the barrows, and the consequent tumblings and upsettings which ensue. The winner was Mr. Matthew Lyons, who did not obtain the prize without sustaining a heavy fall over his barrow and the ropes.

The sack races are thus managed. Half a dozen men are placed in large sacks, which are tied about their necks and thus confining their arms and hands, their heads only being "above board." At a given signal they make efforts to advance to the other side of the enclosure and back, in the best way they can. Some jump forward, and overbalancing themselves, fall headlong on their faces amid the laughter and cheering of the crowd. Hardly any fail to meet with some contretemps, which bring them to collision with mother Earth, and afford a degree of hearty laughter to the lookers on.

The dinner which took place about 8 o'clock, at the hotel on the grounds, was an excellent one. Captain William Manson, the Chief of the Club, presided, and was supported by Mr. Gibson (the Chief of the Scottish Club of Boston), Mr. Finley editor of the Scottish "American," and other well known gentlemen, about 150 sitting down to dinner. Time would not allow of the regular list of toasts being given, but Chief Manson, after a few brief but appropriate observations, gave, "the United States of America, the country we live in." The health of Chief Gibson, of the Boston Scottish Club, of the Canada and other societies, in cities of the United States, the Press, and Scottish men and Scottish games, and other toasts, were drank, and respectively responded to. An adjournment to the ground for the further continuance of the games was then effected.

The number of visitors was about one thousand, and there is no doubt had the affair been more extensively advertised, it would have been much better attended. Most of the members of the Club were in the ancient garb of the Gael, with kilt and plaid, bonnet and broadsword, while the greater portion of the fair sex who graced the meeting by their presence, showed by the prevalence of the tartan in their dresses, that they also belonged to the "Land of the Mountain and the Flood." Altogether, it was the most pleasant re-union we have witnessed for many a day, and we hope to be able to participate next year in the festivities of the third annual celebration of the Scottish Games of the Caledonian Club of New York.

As it may prove a source of interest to many of our gymnastic friends, we append a comparative table of the distances thrown with the light and heavy hammers, the height and distance leaped, &c., at Boston, Montreal, New York, and Kelso, Scotland.

	Kelso ft in	Boston ft in	Montreal ft in	N. York ft in
Standing Hop, Step, and Jump	30 11	26 6	23 4	———
Running Hop, Step, and Jump	43 7	———	35 10	———
Standing High Leap	4 4	———	4 1	———
Running High Leap	5 4	———	5 5	4 8
Running Long Leap	19 2	17 2	18 8	15 1 1/2
Standing Long Leap	———	9 7	11 2	9 4 1/2
Pole Leap, Height	10 0	———	7 6	———
Throwing Heavy Hammer	35-21lbs	72 8-18lbs	60 2	58-17lbs
Throwing Light Hammer	82-6lbs	———	90 6	69 7
Tossing Heavy Caber	———	———	28 10	———
Tossing Light Caber	———	———	35 0	———
Tossing Light Stone	———	———	42 9	28 5
Tossing Heavy Stone	———	———	33 6	23 1

This table would have been more complete, had we known the exact weight of the heavy and light hammers, cabers, and stones, used in each case, so that an approximate estimate of the relative abilities of the contestants might be made.

PEDESTRIANISM IN 1844

On 16 October 1844 a crowd of between 25,000 and 30,000 spectators turned out to watch a footrace at the Beacon Course, a horse racing track in Hoboken, New Jersey. The total purse of $1,000 was divided four ways, with $600 going to the winner. The contest was to determine who could run the farthest distance in one hour, with the prize money distributed only if the leader completed ten miles in under an hour, and if the second, third, and fourth place finishers covered nine and a half miles in that time. The officials rang a bell every three minutes to help the men maintain the proper pace. The event generated great interest among the sporting fraternity and gamblers, who bet heavily on the three Englishmen who entered. The promoters advertised the competition as a "Footrace between England and America," and racial rivalry between the white runners and the Indian John Steeprock joined with nationalism to heighten interest. The following account is reprinted from the Spirit of the Times, 19 October and 2 November 1844, pp. 402, 426.

THE GREAT FOOT RACE

On Wednesday last an immense throng of spectators assembled on the Beacon Course, opposite this city, to witness the Pedestrian March for $1,000. No sporting event of the kind within our knowledge has excited more general interest, and the keenest anxiety was felt as to the result on all hands. The race was advertised in England, Canada, and throughout the United States, and the fact that three crack pedestrians came across the Atlantic expressly to run for the prizes, greatly contributed to the excitement. Stannard, Gilder, Steeprock, the Indian (alias John Ross,) Carles, and McCabe—each more or less renown for speed and stamina, in their immediate circles—had each a strong party to back them. Consequently we were not surprised to see on the Course a concourse of from 25,000 to 35,000 spectators.

The original entries for the purse were

John Barlow, England	Jonathan W. Plats, N.Y.
John Greenhalgh, "	David Myers, Poughkeepsie
Ambrose Jackson, "	L.S. Lathrop, Vermont
Henry Stannard, Connecticut	Joseph L.P. Smith, N.Y.
John Gilder, New York City	C. Cutling, North Brunswick, N. J.
Wm. Boulton, "	W. Price, Birmingham, England
John Smith, "	P. Hutchinson, Scotchman, Brooklyn.
Samuel Clemens, "	G. Berger.
John S. Van Wert, "	John Lightfoot.
James Byrne, "	John Navils, Irishman
Ralph Meyers, Albany	John Meech, Connecticut
Thomas Ryan, Irishman	J.P. Taylor, "
Thomas Hawler, Philadelphia	John Ross, Indian, Buffalo
Geo. Wood, Third Avenue	Thomas McCabe, Ireland
Wm. Wood, New York	George Jones, Chester, Pa.
Edward Brown, "	David Peabody, Boston
Wm. Carles, Yorkville, N.Y.	Lewis Brown, Maryland
Garet Beck, Ulster Co., N.Y.	Wm. Fowle, Englishman
Charles Wall, American	

The betting was unusually heavy on the three Englishmen —Barlow, Greenhalgh, and Jackson—against the field; 100 to 75 was offered on Gilder vs. Stannard—100 to 75 that Stannard did not do 10 miles within the hour—Even, that two did it—Even on Stannard and the Indian vs. Gilder. The above was the current odds among heavy betting men, and thousands of dollars were laid out at these prices. Of course there were cliques and parties who bet "every which way;" we only pretend to give the "state of the odds" among those who control the general betting, after having "got the points" and "set their own bets."

The race was advertised to commence at 3 o'clock, but after the stands were crammed full—and they will contain some 10,000 persons—a dense multitude of Oliver Twist's broke through two or three lengths of the palings and filled up not only the open space in front of the stands, but encircled the entire course! Nearly 10,000 of these specimens of the tag-rag and bob-tail denizens of New York got admission to the course this way, and more than an hour passed before the track could be cleared. These people were perfectly good humored, however, and merely wanted a chance to see the race. Before the entries were called to start Mr. Browning, the proprietor of the course, announced to them, as he did to the public, from the Judge's Stand, that in case of any pedestrian's being interfered with during the race, he should have an opportunity of running the race over in private with his successful competitors, before the purses were awarded. The judges then begged the crowd in front of the stand—and it extended nearly a quarter of a mile, while the men and boys were not less than fifty deep—to give the pedestrians every facility, by falling back. These appeals to their good feeling coupled with the exertions of a dozen gentlemen on horseback, at length succeeded, and we are happy to state that no accident occurred during the performance of the match, which went off most brilliantly, giving the utmost satisfaction to all parties.

The ringing of a large bell put up in the judge's stand was the signal for the entries to come to the post, when the following regulations, previously agreed upon, were again announced to them:—

"The bell will be struck once at the first three minutes after the start, when the pedestrians should be at the first half mile, and struck again three times at six minutes, and so on until the hour is up, so that each person that wishes to go a mile every six minutes may know that at the tap of the bell once they should be at the half mile, and opposite the Judge's stand at the tap three times. Each person will be required to wear a number on his breast and the same number on his shoulder, so that the Judges will be enabled plainly to see and distinguish each as they pass the stand."

Having previously drawn for positions, seventeen entries of the original thirty-seven came to the post in order annexed:—

No. 1. John Gildersleeve
     2. John Barlow
     3. Thos. Greenhalgh
     4. Ambrose Jackson
     6. George Jones
     7. Thomas McCabe
     9. John Navils
     10. J.P. Taylor
     11. John Steeprock, Indian

     14. Henry Stannard
     16. Thomas Ryan
     18. George Wood
     21. William Carles
     23. L.S. Lathrop
     24. Joseph L.P. Smith
     27. P. Hutchinson
     30. Wm. Fowle

GILDERSLEEVE is a chair-gilder by trade, and resides at 159 Allan street, in this city; he is the son of a Suffolk County (Long Island) farmer. He is very handsomely formed, with well developed muscles, and runs with his chest thrown out and his head back; he has a very easy style of going. He stands 5 feet 5 inches, is 32 years of age, and his running weight is 130 lbs. He lately made a most extraordinary private trial by moonlight on the Union Course. He was dressed to-day in a blue silk shirt and cap, with flesh colored silk drawers. He was trained and admirably managed by Mr. Smith, of this city, who held a timing watch in his hand and ran with him a quarter in each mile.

GREENHALGH, just from England, is 24 years old, 5 feet 6 inches high, and weighs, in running condition, 128 lbs. His action was deemed the finest of any of the pedestrians who started. Our contemporaries call him John Greenhalgh, but his Christian name is Thomas. He has a brother John who was sent for, but having engagements at home Thomas was sent out to this country in his place. He was quite naked with the exception of a pair of lined drawers from which the legs and waist were cut off! He wore "high lows," or "ankle jacks"as they are termed in England, being nothing more or less than a pair of high pumps laced up to the instep from near the point of the toe.

BARLOW, the fellow passenger of Greenhalgh, is 5 feet 6 3/4 inches in height, 140 lbs in weight, and 24 years of age. He was dressed precisely like Greenhalgh, as was Jackson, also. All three Englishmen ran with their hands clinched and elevated, and with their elbows close into their side. Barlow is a pedestrian by profession, as is Jackson, who has been in this country, where he has run short races, for above two years. Greenhalgh never run before, we understand; his brother John is a professed pedestrian and favorably known as such.

STEEPROCK or *"John Ross,"* (as we entered him, not knowing his name,) was one of the tallest and heaviest men who started. He runs on a lope and as if he was going through under-brush, frequently bouncing sideways as if jumping a fallen tree. He is 25 years of age, and weighs, we should think, 150 pounds at least. We have forgotten the name of his tribe, but it is one of those located near Buffalo, in this State.

McCABE, the Irishman, was trained at West Hoboken, with Fowle. He is below the medium height, and rather thick set; his age is not far from 24 years. His action and "pluck" are worthy of "old Ireland."

STANNARD, so well known to the Sporting World, as the first man in the United States who ran ten miles within the hour (In 1835, on the Union Course, L.I.) is now 33 years old; his weight is about what it was then, 165 pounds. He keeps a hotel at Killingworth, Connecticut.

TAYLOR is 5 feet 8 inches high, weighs 150 pounds, and is 28 years of age. He had neither the advantages of training, nor management during the race. (Had he been aware of the precise time he could have easily completed his 10 miles within the hour; he lost by two seconds only.)

As the other ten did not particularly distinguish themselves, owing more to want of training, perhaps, than anything else, we have not deemed it necessary to notice them in detail.

THE RACE

First mile: Gildersleeve bounded off with the lead, with Barlow, Greenhalgh, and Jackson well up to him, Steeprock the Indian 4th, and Stannard in the ruck behind. The immense crowd which lined each side of the track prevented the Judges from seeing distinctly each change of position, though all were immediately aware that the

Englishmen's speed had made a spread-eagle of the field. It was evident that their pace was too good to last, and their backers began to be alarmed lest they should overmark themselves. Before reaching the head of the quarter stretch Steeprock made a tremendous burst, and came in front; he led through with Barlow 2d, Greenhalgh 3d, and Fowle 4th, having changed places with Jackson, who laid back just behind Stannard, Gildersleeve, and McCabe. Lathrop, Navils, and Smith were already tailed off a long way, while Hutchinson and Wood were nearly out of their distance. Time of the 1st mile 5:16.

Second mile: Steeprock's trainer having ordered him to fall back, he gave up the track to Barlow and Greenhalgh, who ran within a yard of each other throughout the entire ten miles! They led through this mile, Steeprock being 3d, and McCabe, 30 yards behind, 4th, the latter having, with Gildersleeve, injudiciously forced the pace. Wood gave in soon after commencing this mile, and Hutchinson also stopped at the close, having a pain in his side. Time of the second mile 5:29.

Third mile: Barlow again led in with Greenhalgh within three feet, and Steeprock only 20 yards behind; McCabe was about the same distance in his rear; Gildersleeve, Jones (who overmarked himself in changing his position from 15th to 6th, and stopt after running another mile) Fowle, Jackson, and Stannard, came in next in a cluster, some 50 yards ahead of Ryan, who led Carles some distance; Lathrop and Smith were tailed off a long way, and Navil's chance was considered out. Time of the 3d mile 5:33.

Fourth mile: Barlow led throughout again, with Greenhalgh sticking to him like a brick. Steeprock was only about 35 yds. in the rear, but he came on jumping and cavorting "like he hadn't run a yard;" the poor fellow cannot speak a word of English, but he looked so confident, and as fresh as paint. Gildersleeve and McCabe came through within reach of each other, Jones and Fowle being well up. Stannard and Taylor came next, and as all these named were inside of their time—10 miles in the hour—the backers of Time looked somewhat grave. Time of the 4th mile 5:41....

Sixth mile: Barlow and Greenhalgh led in 1st and 2d, and nearly 250 yds ahead; Gildersleeve's game now began to tell; he came through 3d, as Steeprock's trainer insisted on his moderating his pace. All were cheered as they came through, and the backers of the American vs. the Englishmen thought they now had "a good look for the money." "Hurray for Gilder!" exclaimed his little wife, waving her handkerchief from a carriage full of ladies, while the immense concourse sent back the cheer with ten thousand added echoes! McCabe, the Irishman—and right gallant fellow—came next, and as he, too, was inside of his time, every Patlander on the ground gave him a hearty shout. Fowle and Stannard came through together, pretty well up to McCabe, while Taylor and Jackson were but a few yards behind him. The others were tailed off a long way, while fears were expressed lest the leading men should catch up with Navills. Time of the sixth mile 5:49.

Seventh mile: Barlow and Greenhalgh, close together as ever, came through 1st and 2d, about 150 yds ahead of Gildersleeve. "Go it, my Gilder!" from one side, was answered by "Hurrah for the Englishmen!" from the other. About 75 yds. behind Gildersleeve —who looked as fine as a star—came Steeprock, bounding like a buck every two or three rods to the infinite amusement of the thousands of boys on the course, with whom he was a prodigious favorite. "Look at him now!"—"There he goes again!"—"go it, my wild Ingine!" they were shouting whenever he came into the quarter stretch. McCabe came next, with Fowle, Stannard, Taylor, and Jackson, in a ruck behind him, but all within their time. J.P.L. Smith stopt in this mile, as Lathrop, Ryan, and Navills should have done, for neither, under the circumstance, had the ghost of a chance. Time of the 7th mile 5:54.

Eighth mile: Barlow came in first, and Greenhalgh 2d again, with Gildersleeve well up, and going like a tramp. Steeprock's trainer kept him at a more moderate pace, thinking the field would come back to him. Fowle amd Stannard rallied a little in the course of the mile, and when they came through, one of the official timers remarked to us they were 15 seconds inside of their time. Taylor and Jackson came in next, but with a fair chance of yet making ten miles in the hour. Ryan was already tailed off some distance, and 200 yds behind him came Lathrop, while Navills was nearly a mile behind, and appeared to be doing no better very fast. Time of the 8th mile 5:58.

Ninth mile: Barlow came in 1st and Greenhalgh 2d, again, amidst tremendous cheers, which were increased, if possible, by Gilder's coming in 3d, and well up. The three had passed several who had not yet completed their eighth mile! Steeprock was 4th, with McCabe but a short distance behind him Stannard and Fowle, still inside of their time were 6th and 7th, while Taylor was only a few seconds behind it. Carles, Lathrop and Navills had not finished their 8th mile when the 9th mile was run by the others, and accordingly gave in. Time of the 9th mile 5:57.

Tenth mile: Greenhalgh for the first time led in this mile, having passed Barlow within three or four yards of the Judge's stand. They were cheered with the utmost enthusiasm on coming through, as was Gildersleeve also, who ran past the stand not more than forty yards behind, like a scared dog; indeed the pace throughout the mile was tremendous! Steeprock came in next, leading McCabe, and close to him was Stannard, with Taylor within two yards of him. The bell announced the completion of the hour just as Stannard passed the judge's stand for the tenth time; he was two seconds within his time, while Taylor was not quite two seconds behind time. Of the seven who started on the 10th mile, he was the only one who failed to accomplish it, Stannard having done so "by the skin of his teeth!" The excitement near the close of the 10th mile, was raised to the highest pitch. Every one seemed to shout with the phrenzy of Bedlamites, whether they had lost or won. We do not remember to have ever witnessed a scene in which the spectators generally were filled with such delirious enthusiasm. Time of the tenth mile 5:45 1/2.

Eleventh mile: By great exertions a gauntlett was made below the stands through which the men could run on, beyond the 10th mile, the crowd not being aware, seemingly, that the race was yet unconcluded. Gildersleeve being informed by his trainer, who managed him capitally, that he had won all his bets —for he merely backed himself to do the 10 miles within the hour, and on this point had put up "every picayune he could raise or scrape"—said in answer to a question how he felt, "I'm pretty good yet," and was told to make play for one of the purses. He accordingly broke off again like a quarter bomb and on reaching the straight stretch on the backside caught up with Barlow who was already so nearly done for, that upon being passed he "pulled up into a jog trot, until the bell rung. Stannard gave up soon after the completing his tenth mile, as did McCabe; Steeprock, however, "the real no mistake Native American Bellgine," as the boys called, continued to "go it like bricks" after all had stopped and the race was over! But the event of most interest in the whole race was the last desperate struggle between Greenhalgh and Gildersleeve. About half down the back stretch the latter over-took the gallant Englishman, but Grenhalgh had yet another brush in him and the thing was not to be done. We could not see the parties from the judge's stand but the shout-ing and motions of the people was sufficiently indicative of what was going on.

One of the Judges was on the spot and from him we learn that when Gildersleeve got up to Greenhalgh the latter made a rush and went away from him. Gildersleeve, however, cheered on by thousands, took heart and bided his time until he reached descending ground between the training stable and the half mile post. Here he made his last effort and it was a desperate one. Collecting all his energies he made a dash at his competitor, reached him, hung an instant, and as twenty thousand people were shouting like devils, away he went past him, some ten or fifteen feet, and the thing was out! Greenhalgh now fell off into a walk while Gildersleeve kept up his rate beyond the half mile post, until the instant when Mr. Browning, who was close to him on horseback, stopt him when the bell announced that the hour was up! Gildersleeve in One Hour, therefore, ran Ten Miles and a Half, and Seventy-five yards! while Greenhalgh ran Ten Miles in Fifty-seven minutes, one and a half seconds! Barlow was not above a second behind Greenhalgh at the close of the 10th mile.

Steeprock kept up his run most gallantly throughout the 11th mile, but hurt his ankle slightly on coming in having run over a boy who could not get out of his way. Immedi-ately upon the ringing of the bell, Gildersleeve stopt and jumped up behind Mr. Brown-ing, and they galloped round to the Judges' stand amidst a scene which baffles all de-scription. Greenhalgh came across the course we presume, as he reached the stand first. On his arrival he was covered by the gentlemen in the stand with overcoats and dressed. The crowd cheered himself vociferously, he was very exhausted, being affected much as poor old Argyle was after his tremendous race of four heats of three miles at Balti-more with Master Henry and Wonder, in 1839. Gildersleeve came forward in the front of the stand and bowed his acknowledgements, for as every man, woman, and child on the course was shouting "like mad," a 42 pounder could not have been heard. He sub-sequently got into a carriage with his wife and a party of friends, rode quite around the course, and finally drove off in the highest spirits. The next morning he was "as fine as silk," while Stannard offered to run 10 miles within the hour on the following day. Up to this time all those engaged in the race are doing well while most of them have quite recovered.

PHILOSOPHY OF THE LATE FOOT RACE

One of the first bankers, and most influential men of the city was on horseback upon the course yesterday, watching the foot-race with keen interest, one of our first lawyers was the Judge of the Stand; at least a thousand citizens were present whose equal thousand, for wealth and standing, was not left behind in the city; most of the strangers in town were there, and the crowd was estimated at from thirty to fifty thou-sand. The event of the day was the talk of the week—paramount over the whirlwind of politics even. It is an important event—a trifle made so by its effect. "What water does it draw!" What is the keel of it, and how much depth of human interest and motive lies under the water-line?

There was "submerged utility" in horseracing, before the invention of the steam and telegraphs—the safety of the state by the transmission of news, and the safety of individuals by speed in the saddle, depending on the qualities of the horse. We think it will not be denied that, since this utility is superseded there has been sensible falling off of interest in the sports of the turf....

The interest on the race yesterday was not abstractly to see the running. Foot races would, it is true, draw a little while as a novelty, but ten as swift men might be advertised to run there every day for the next month, after this, and have few spectators. There is no utility in speed of foot, no dignity in it, and no improvement of the race in the improvement of its unaided locomotion. *The interest arose from the accidental contact of several of the circumstances of the race along with strong undercurrents of natural interest.* It was a trial of the Indian against the white man, on the point in which the red man most boasts his superiority. It was the trial of the peculiar American *physique* against the long held supremacy of English muscular endurance. It was a trial of middle age (in Major Stannard) against his own youthful achievements. *The White Man beat the Indian—the American beat the English,* and, with much better training, and much more mental stimulus, *the limbs of forty years failed to do the achievement of thirty!*

GREAT TEN MILE FOOT RACE

The surprising victory of John Gildersleeve over his English and Indian competition in the October race stirred great excitement in the rematch in November. But this time the British runners turned the tables on their upstart American challenger. John Barlow carried off the laurels in the astonishing time of 54 minutes 21 seconds for ten miles. Following him were Steeprock and Greenhalgh, with Gildersleeve a distant fourth. The report that appears below is reprinted from a "Sporting Reminiscence" column of the New York Clipper, 26 June 1858, p. 73.

THE MATCH.

The match had long been projected in New York, and it accordingly came off on Tuesday, November 19, 1844, before the largest assemblage of spectators ever gathered upon an American race course, the arena being the Beacon Course, Hoboken. A single steamboat from Albany brought down four hundred; New Jersey, Long Island, and the river towns on the Hudson, furnished immense crowds, while New York sent over materials for an army three times larger than that with which Napoleon made his Italian campaign. From the head of the quarter stretch quite around to the draw gate, the enclosed space was so densely crammed as to render it nearly impossible to clear a space wide enough for the pedestrians to run through, though they were preceded by a dozen men on horseback. Thousands filled the stands, but it would have required the Amphitheatre of Titus to have accommodated all.

The runners were two New Yorkers, two Americans, one Connecticut man, one Indian, one Irishman, and two Englishmen—Barlow at the head of the ten-milers, and a trainer of pedestrians; and Greenhalgh among the best English runners at short distances. The names of all, however, will be found in the recapitulation below.

BETTING

The following bets were actually made by a keen speculator, and may be fairly taken as the current prices among heavy betting men in town; $200 even on Gildersleeve and Barlow vs. the field; $250 to $200 on Barlow vs. Gildersleeve; $200 to $80 against Steeprock; &300 to $200 that Gildersleeve ran the ten miles in 57 minutes. Among the outside barbarians, $50 to $30 was laid that neither Englishman won.

THE RACE

After a false start, in which Barlow went off with a bulge like a quarter horse, Mr. Barker (who stood on the course nearly in a line with the men) gave the word "go." The two Englishmen jumped off with the lead, and in a few moments the whole nine were out of sight; the railing on both sides of the course being densely thronged, so that even at the start the pedestrians had to "run the gauntlet." The Judge could only note the position of the leading man by watching that of several horses abreast. The three or four leading men kept pretty well together during the first mile, but their pace was tremendous as to make a spread eagle of the field, before the close of the mile, Barlow finished in 5:10; Steeprock second; Gildersleeve and Greenhalgh, third and fourth, close together; behind them came McCabe and Taylor; Underhill was some distance behind, and "Towhead," as the boys called Smith, was "nowhere"—i.e.—he was not within a four-mile distance. What "possessed" him to start at all is a mystery, for he could not run fast enough to tire himself. Barlow had closed his seventh mile before Smith finished his sixth. We over heard a little ragged Oliver Twist suggest to another incipient soap-lock the feasibility of improving his pace by "setting a dog on him!"

SECOND MILE—Barlow led in, closing the mile in 5:15 with Steeprock well up. Gildersleeve and Greenhalgh next and the rest some distance behind.

THIRD MILE—At the close of this mile, which he ran in 5:22, Barlow had opened a gap on Steeprock of nearly fifty yards. Gildersleeve seemed to have got his pores open and to be going easier than ever; though Greenhalgh was near enough to him to touch him with his hands, and looked as fresh as paint, it was evident how the Englishmen had determined to win this race; which was after this manner: Barlow was to cut out the work at a slashing rate, so as to knock up Steeprock if he kept pace with him, while Greenhalgh waited upon Gildersleeve, he and the Indian being considered the only dangerous competitors. Had Barlow given back, Greenhalgh was ready at any time to take his place. As Gildersleeve changed his rate of speed, so did Greenhalgh, keeping always witin two feet of him, Barlow was satisfied he could beat Steeprock, and his only object in forcing the pace was to over work him; and this he would have done but for the thews of steel, and sinews of catgut of the gallant Indian. Had the latter declined then Greenhalgh would have laid with Gildersleeve until the last mile; and then have run in first or second, and the two Englishmen would have divided the stakes between them. Taylor, at the close of this mile, was two hundred and fifty yards behind, while Jackson gave up the contest.

FOURTH MILE—Barlow led in, doing the mile in 5:25, with Steeprock at least sixty yards in his rear. Gildersleeve and Greenhalgh, the Siamese Twins, came next with McCabe a little closer to him than on the other mile; Taylor a long way behind, and Smith "no where;" Underhill gave in.

FIFTH MILE—Barlow led in, runing the mile in 5:28, having increased his gap on Steeprock. The two G's were pretty well up with Steeprock, though they got on nearer Barlow. McCabe was a long way inside of his time (ten miles an hour), while Taylor might yet "fetch it," though nearly a quarter a mile behind.

SIXTH MILE—This was run by Barlow in 5:31 - he had widened the gap between himself and Steeprock at least 100 yards; the latter having been kept back by his trainer. The two G's were now within about twenty yards of the Indian, but they were exactly forty seconds behind Barlow. The pace now began to tell on McCabe; Taylor too was a long way off, but Stannard ran along by his side encouraging him to pull through and win his bets, which were set on his running the ten miles within the hour. Smith "give in," much to the regret of the boys, though no betting man would match him against a tree.

SEVENTH MILE—It was a "go along" every inch of this mile—run in 5:31. Barlow came through 200 yards ahead of Steeprock, and each was enthusiastically cheered. Steeprock made a run down the bacstretch, but Barlow outfooted him. Gildersleeve increased his rate, but Greenhalgh kept up with him as easy as man walks to his dinner. McCabe was 100 yards behind Greenhalgh and Taylor still further behind.

EIGHTH MILE—Barlow did not widen the gap betwen Steeprock and himself this mile, which was run in 5:36. The game and speed of the Indian amazed Barlow as much as it did the spectators. Greenhalgh was on velvet as far as he was concerned; he knew he had the other G as "safe as a Bank," and was only wide awake for the critical moment when the Indian should falter. The two G's were now exactly a minute behind Barlow, while McCabe was tailed off a long way, and Taylor was at least a quarter of a mile behind him.

NINTH MILE—After a tremendous burst down the quarter stretch, cheered on as he was by thousands, Barlow led in this time by more than 250 yards, running the mile in 5:35; Steeprock covered it by a rush he made in the rear of the course. Gildersleeve and Greenhalgh were now over a minute behind Barlow, nothwithstanding the spectators expected to see them beat both the others. It seemed impossible for Barlow to keep up his rate and Steeprock was apparently already in difficulty and "getting no better very fast." At this point, McCabe was hardly in the quarter stretch at all, while Taylor was still "peggling away" on the rear of the course "somewhere." Still every man as he came through was enthusiastically cheered, as the time of the slowest man in the race was nearly equal to the best Stannard every made.

TENTH MILE—It was apparent that Barlow, barring accidents, had the race safe, upon the commencing this mile. Upon commencing the second quarter of this mile it was evident that Barlow was increasing his pace; but Greenhalgh, who had not yet run a yard at his best, was now going like a scared dog. Gildersleeve, by a tremendous effort, "hurried the mourners" around the first quarter of a mile, where Greenhalgh ran up his side, turned full upon him, exclaiming, "Good by, Gilder!" and left him as if he was standing still. The next three quarters of a mile were run by Greenhalgh faster, probably, than the same distance was ever previously performed in this country. He gained forty seconds upon Barlow, though the latter ran this mile ten seconds quicker than he did the ninth, that is in 5:25. Greenhalgh must have run this mile in 4:48! Barlow beat Steeprock exactly 173 yards while Greenhalgh was less than 90 yards behind him. Gildersleeve was a bad fourth, being about 212 yards behind Greenhalgh. McCabe was a long way behind, and Taylor had not reached the head of the quarter stretch, when Barlow came through. He won his bets that he would do the ten miles within the hour "by the skin of his teeth" only, having only two seconds to spare.

Thus terminated, amidst the most tremendous cheers from all parts of the Course, one of the most extraordinary pedestrian performances on record.

RECAPITULATION—OFFICIAL

BEACON COURSE, N.J., opposite New York City, Nov. 19, 1844—Purse $1,200 for running ten miles, to be divided as follows: $700 to the first; $250 to the second; $150 to the third; $75 to the fourth; and $25 to the fifth in the race. Free for all pedestrians. Entrance $5 each.

					MILES					
NAMES	1st	2d	3d	4th	5th	6th	7th	8th	9th	10th
John Barlow, Englishman	1	1	1	1	1	1	1	1	1	1
John Steeprock, Indian	2	2	2	2	2	2	2	2	2	2
Thos Greenhalgh, Englishman	4	4	4	4	4	4	4	4	4	3
Jn Gildersleeve, New Yorker	3	3	3	3	3	3	3	3	3	4
Thomas McCabe, Irishman	5	6	5	5	5	5	5	5	5	5
J. P. Taylor, Connecticut	6	5	6	7	6	6	6	6	6	6
Joseph Smith, New Yorker	8	8	9	8	7	7	*			
John Underhill, American	7	7	7	6	*					
Thomas Jackson, American	9	9	8	*			* stopped			

Time of 1st	mile	5:10	Aggregate of Time			5:10
" 2d	mile	5:15	"	"	2 miles	10:25
" 3d	mile	5:22	"	"	3 miles	15:47
" 4th	mile	5:25	"	"	4 miles	21:12
" 5th	mile	5:28	"	"	5 miles	26:40
" 6th	mile	5:31	"	"	6 miles	32:11
" 7th	mile	5:34	"	"	7 miles	37:45
" 8th	mile	5:36	"	"	8 miles	43:21
" 9th	mile	5:35	"	"	9 miles	48:56
" 10th	mile	5:25	"	"	10 miles	54:21
Barlow's time		54:21	Gildersleeve's time			55:51
Steeprock's time		54:53	McCabe's time			56:52
Greenhalgh's time		55:10	Taylor's time			59:52

PEDESTRIANISM IN ENGLAND

England was the birthplace of modern sport, and during the 1840s and 1850s the British exerted a powerful influence on the development of North American athletics in many ways. The wave of nationalism that swept across the United States after the Mexican War spurred a number of sportsmen to challenge English rivals in a variety of pastimes. John C. Stevens's glorious triumph off the coast of England with his yacht *America* in 1851 provided a model for his countrymen to emulate. Shortly thereafter William Jackson, a prominent American pedestrian, journeyed across the Atlantic to challenge his Old World rivals in long-distance foot racing. Later in the decade American boxers, horsemen, and chess champions competed in the British Isles. This description of the trials and tribulations of "the American Deer" on foreign soil is reprinted from the New York Clipper, 30 July 1853, p. 1.

WILLIAM JACKSON VS. GEORGE FROST, 1853

Monday, 4th of July

The match of 10 miles, between George Frost (the Suffolk Stag) and William Jackson (better known as the American Deer), for £50 a side, and the Champion's Belt, came off today. The belt had been previously in the possession of the Stag; but the right of retention being challenged by the Deer, gave rise to the present contest. Before we enter into a description of the race, it may prove interesting to give the antecedental contests that have taken place for the possession of this belt; but previously we may observe that, on Thursday, the first of January, 1852, Jackson and Frost had tested their relative celerity, in a five mile race, on the cricket ground, at Leicester, on which occasion Frost proved the winner by between 20 and 30 yards, doing the five miles in 26 1/2 minutes. On the 12th of the same month (January 1852) Mr. John Garratt, the proprietor of the then existing Copenhagen Grounds, offered for competition among all the pedestrian "notabilities" of the day, a very elegant belt, of the value of 25*l*; the winner to be designated Champion (of the runners), but always subject to be challenged, on certain terms, and at certain intervals, the distance to be run being ten miles. On this exciting occasion (which, being the first, was a handicap race) 18 of the crack velocipedes extant started; and among the competitors were the aforesaid Jackson and Frost, and here again the "Stag" proved successful, outstripping all his opponents, and bearing away the prize, Jackson having given in in the fourth mile. Frost that time completed his ten miles in *fifty four minutes and nine seconds*. Frost, however, was not permitted long to wear his laurels unmolested, for shortly after this he was challenged to run 10 miles for the belt, and 50*l* a side, by John Levett of Battersea, to come off at the "Cope" on Monday, the 22nd of the following March. This match, having been accepted, we find the men "toeing the scratch" on the appointed day, when nearly 20,000 spectators assembled to witness the performance. After one of the swiftest and best contested races on record, Frost was defeated, and the proud appellation of "Champion" transferred to the victorious Levett, who went over the ground in the astonishing short space of *fifty-two minutes and thirty-five seconds* (on the following Monday, March 20, Levett defeated Jackson and several others in a twenty mile race). Levett in his turn was next challenged by the "Deer," and on the 31st of the following May we find them struggling for the "premiership" at the "Cope." This time, though the odds starting were 2 to 1 in Levett's favor, Jackson nearly overlapped his adversary in the last round, and ran in a winner by upwards of 500 yards, completing his ten miles in the unprecedentedly short period of *some seconds under fifty-two minutes.* Matters now remained, with regard to the belt, in *status quo* for some time; but all was not to be *coleur de rose* with Jackson for the remainder of the year, for, some time after his victory, Levett again threw down the gauntlet, which the "Deer," as in duty bound, took up (but not till considerable delay, and some epistolary correspondence had taken place) and at length an arrangement was entered into by both men for the match to come of at the "Cope" on the 20th of the following September, same distance, and for same sums as above, and the belt. Some disagreement, however, arising, the match was postponed until the 11th of October, when we once more saw them start away from the scratch, on the old ground, and run a most beautiful race. On this occasion Jackson was doomed to be defeated, despite his every exertion, as Levett was declared the winner, but not by more than two or three yards, Jackson, before leaving the course, challenged the victor to another contest. The 10 miles on this occasion were run by Levett in *fifty-one minutes and forty-five seconds.* It would appear that Levett having gone into business in Sheffield, proved "deaf" to the challenge now given by Jackson, but his old antagonist, George Frost, once more appeared in the field, and a match was made between them (Frost and Jackson), to come off on the 7th of last December. When the day appointed came, however, there was no race, Jackson having been bound in a heavy penalty to Mr. Boswick, of the Royal Oak, to run nowhere within 10 miles of London, for a certain time, without his permission, which he withheld, on this occasion. This oft-contended-for belt was at length again run for by Levett and Frost on the 25th of last March, at the Royal Oak, Barking-road, (the once celebrated "Cope" being defunct), and Levett was once more obliged to resign the prize to Frost, who, at the termination of the race, was about 400 yards ahead of his opponent, having run the 10 miles on this occasion in *fifty-four and a half minutes.* Such is a brief history of this Champion belt, and now to return to our subject, namely, the race of last Monday. It was nearly six o'clock before the men appeared in the field. The appearance of Jackson was everything that could be desired, but Frost looked altogether "out-o-sorts," pale and haggard, with a "lack lustre in his eye," and most dispirited appearance. Even Boswick's brass band, playing up "Cheer Boys! Cheer!" seemed to have lost all influence over him. He has suffered much after his rheumatics. Westhall and Newman waited on Jackson, while Conway and Patterson did "the amiable" for Frost. Jackson at starting was the favorite at 7 to 4, and at 13 minutes past six the men got away with a fair start. Jackson in the first lap took a slight lead, which at the end of the first mile had increased to about 150 yards, and long odds were now freely offered on him. Jackson, as lively as a grig, kept gradually increasing his advantage, and in the eighth lap any odds might have been obtained, but there were not any takers. In the middle of the tenth lap, Jackson being within 50 yards of overlapping his adversary, Frost gave in, to the amazement and disappointment of all beholders. In our opinion, however, he acted wisely, for he had not the "Shadow of a shade" of success. He assured us that he had been for some time past in very indifferent health, and at the time he started from the post was acutely attacked with rheumatic pains. Jackson, despite the retirement of his adversary, pursued his course with almost undiminished speed, and accomplished his ten miles in fifty-four minutes one second.

Jackson to the World —I will run Manks any distance, from 100 yards to 20 miles, for 50*l.* or 100*l.* a side; I will accept Syddal's challenge to run four miles, for 50*l.* or 100*l.* a side, or any man in the world from eight to twenty miles, or I will take 200*l* to 100*l* to 100*l* that I run 11 1/2 miles in one hour or 21 miles in two hours. All these matches to be on a turnpike road within 25 miles of London—Yours &c., W. Jackson, (the American Deer).—July 8, 1853.

Jackson (the American Deer), the present holder of the champion running belt— with the consent of Mr. Boswick of the Royal Oak—to make a sweepstake, open to the world, of 25*l.* each; the first man to receive 10*l.* out of the stakes and the belt permanently, the second and third men to be rewarded proportionally out of the balance of the stakes and the gate money; to be run for at the Royal Oak, Barking-road, on a day hereafter to be agreed upon.

PLANK WALKING

During the 1850s a number of pedestrians of both sexes attempted to set endurance records by spending dozens of hours walking back and forth on platforms constructed out of planks of wood. Although public opinion still frowned upon the participation of women in athletic contests, a sizeable number of them enjoyed archery, calesthenics, horseback riding, skating, sledding, swimming, and other forms of recreation that required physical activity. A few ladies with theatrical experience performed walking feats on raised planks or platforms. Two of these women competed under the nicknames of "Flora Temple" and "Prioress," after the celebrated race horses of that era. Two others called themselves "Highland Maid." The following documents suggest the spirited rivalry and impressive athletic achievements of the females who engaged in the unusual pastime of plank walking. They are reprinted from the New York Clipper, 2 and 9 May 1857, pp. 10, 18, and 23 and 30 October and 20 and 27 November 1858, pp. 211, 218, 242, 250.

MRS. BENTLEY'S THIRTY HOUR MATCH

In our last we stated that Mrs. Bentley has arrived in town, and would perform a pedestrian feat in a few days, but her agent not furnishing the information, we were unable to say where. It was announced in one or two of the morning papers, at the close of last week, that the female pedestrian would perform the laborious feat of walking *thirty consecutive hours,* without rest, at the Broadway Tabernacle, commencing at 4 o'clock, Monday evening, April 27th, and closing at 10 o'clock Tuesday evening, the

28th. She commenced the feat at the appointed time, under the care of Mr. and Mrs. Post, of Ohio, her attendants, and walked through the night, and up to our present writing—late Tuesday afternoon. She is, however, greatly fatigued, and illustrates the peculiar and manifest effect upon exhausted nature, by outward circumstances, such as the enlivening music of the band, the cheerful conversation of friends, and other seductive influences. We have but little doubt but that she will succeed in completing the thirty hours, as she is a woman of proverbial fortitude and untiring energy.

This is the *twentieth* time that Mrs. Bentley has performed this feat, seventeen of which have been performed in the last year. She is now, however, in an advanced stage of consumption, and has manifested distressing signs of physical weakness and depression. Mrs. Bentley was originally a vocalist, well known on the Western "boards," but in consequence of a serious throat infection was compelled to resign that profession, and, for the maintenance of herself and three children, adopted that of the pedestrian. While we regret that her sanguine feelings have prompted her to undertake so severe a task in her present prostrate condition, yet the promptings of a mother's heart are above censure, and we wish her success for the nonce, though we should be sorry to hear of another effort, unless she should be resuscitated from her present illness. We regret, for the sake of the cause, that she is not better patronized, the attendance on Tuesday being rather small and discouraging, probably from the fact of the affair being little known. It is a species of amusement for a knowledge of which the people only look to the sporting journals, and these were comparatively left in the dark.

...THE THIRTY-HOUR FEAT.—Mrs. Bentley, the female pedestrian alluded to in our last, succeeded in finishing the thirty-hour walking feat, on Tuesday evening, April the 28th, at ten o'clock P.M. Through the mismanagement of those having the arrangements in hand, we are sorry to say that the speculation proved a decided failure, the money taken for the tickets falling far short of the expenses incurred.

FEMALE PEDESTRIAN MATCH

The long talked of pedestrian match, between Mr. Lambert's pupil, better known as Flora Temple, and Mrs. Buckley (Prioress of Lynn.) will commence at Montgomery Hall, 76 Prince street, on Wednesday, Oct. 20, at 12 o'clock. Mr. John Grindall will act as referee. Flora Temple's costume bears closely upon the English jockey, over which will be worn the Native American regalia. Prioress sports the French, with tricolored sash. We trust they will be well received, as this is their first appearance in this city. The match is to determine which of the two can walk the greater length of time....

The walking match between Mrs. Jas. Lambert, better known as "Flora Temple," and Mrs. Buckley—"Prioress"—which we briefly referred to in our last, was brought to a termination on Saturday morning, about 3 o'clock. The terms of the match were, that the pedestrians were to walk on a plank, three feet wide, and thirty feet long, and the first to give up, sit down, or fall off the plank, to be considered the loser. They commenced their monotonous march about 12 o'clock, M., on Wednesday, 20th inst., the day of the "big fight." They had but few visitors on that day, but on the following, when the event began to obtain greater publicity, the attendance was quite numerous, and so continued throughout the following day and evening, when the room was crowded. During the earlier part of the performances, Prioress seemed to suffer somewhat from the effects of a cold, but this she managed to work off, and then began to improve, while her competitor, who had been the favorite all along, began to exhibit symptoms of fatigue on Friday. On Saturday morning, quite a number of persons were present to witness the finish, when it was announced that the parties had agreed to make a draw of it, after walking 63 hours. Being the first match of the kind ever walked here, its novelty created quite a lively interest among our Broadway agents, who patronized the exhibition quite extensively. The pedestrians presented quite a fascinating appearance, dressed as they were in short skirts, and "lively colored" tights, which exposed to view the well developed "extenuations" of the lovely twain. It is probable another match will shortly take place here. The saloon in which the walking took place was at Montgomery Hall, 76 Prince street, of which Mr. Martin is the obliging host.

CHALLENGE TO FEMALE PEDESTRIANS

Newburgh, Nov. 15, 1858.—FRANK QUEEN—Among my acquaintances there is a young lady (who in every sense of the word is one) that has figured somewhat extensively as a "female pedestrian" and who in the course of her "pedestrian tours" chanced to perform one of her feats in Brattleboro, Vt. (under the title that she always had borne, and always will bear, and one which she is as much entitled to as any woman living, that of the Highland Maid), where, by the resolution she manifested, and determination of character she possessed, won the golden opinions of all who saw her, and also a small article from some unknown gentleman, which was published at the time in your columns. That article, it seems, produced in the minds of the fair pedestrians around the city of Boston a feeling of jealousy, which found vent in your next week's issue, in the shape of two challenges, one from a woman who styled herself the "Original Highland Maid," and who seemed indignant at the thought of there being another, the other from Flora Temple, both of which were quickly answered, but nothing more from the challengers was ever received. Since then the "Maid" has pursued the even tenor of her way, winning fresh laurels and the good opinion of all. Flora, it seems, now styles herself the Champion, but in order to become so she must first out walk the so called "Brattleboro Highland Maid." In bringing my article to a close I would say that the Brattleboro Highland Maid will walk any woman living, in any city in the United States except Boston, for from $200 to $500. Any notice from you through your paper, stating the reception by you of $50 as a deposit, will meet with prompt attention by the

BRATTLEBORO HIGHLAND MAID

"THE PEN IS MIGHTIER THAN THE SWORD"

In looking over last week's CLIPPER, I noticed an article proceeding from the pen of an unknown plank struck youth, hailing from Newburg, who has mounted his Roseteante [?], and sallied forth, Quixote-like, to right the fancied wrongs of his fair Dulcinea; and to that individual I shall reply, and *not the lady* in question, who, from her looks, appears to be better able to attend to her own business than the youth who has raised the pen in her behalf. Highland Maid, No. 1, made her appearance in Boston the first of March, 1857. Now if Highland Maid, No. 2, can furnish evidence of any of her plank feats *prior* to that date, we are satisfied that she alone should bear the name. With regard to my challenges, as accepted by Highland Maid, the terms were, to use the Maid's own words, "that a match could be made at the termination of her walk with Highland Maid, No. 1. at Springfield," whch trial never came off. As for styling myself champion of the plank, I *deny* the charge, but think, if any woman is entitled to wear the honor, it belongs to Mrs. Jackson, wife of the American Deer, who has walked 110 consecutive hours. Having two plank trial assignments ahead, I shall not be at liberty to walk the Brattleboro Highland Maid until the first of January, when I shall be most happy to accommodate her for the sum mentioned, and will place it in Mr. QUEEN'S hands prior to that date, and beg leave to state to all female pedestrians, that win or lose, I will never mount the plank again, leaving the boards to such aspirants as may choose to battle for the honors (?)

                                                                FLORA TEMPLE

THE OTHER HIGHLAND MAID—Boston, Nov. 22d.—Mr. QUEEN:—Seeing my name handled in last week's CLIPPER, in a very flippant manner, by the 'Brattleboro' Highland Maid, I think proper to take some notice of it.

I am not dependent upon making a show of myself upon a plank for a livelihood, having to earn my living by hard labor. I have no backers, but will make up the amount myself by the middle of December, place it in Mr. QUEEN'S hands, with articles of agreement, and walk the Highland Maid for $50 and the *name*, or as she herself said in reply to my challenge, I will walk her for *fun* at any time. In either case I will name the place as soon as I hear from her.

                                                                HIGHLAND MAID

MALE PLANK WALKING

Not to be outdone by the ladies, the men of New England also took to the boards to see who could stay awake and upright for the longest period of time. The following stories indicate the extraordinary efforts made by the pedestrians as they attempted to extend the endurance record for walking on a wooden platform. These accounts are taken from the New York Clipper, 30 January and 20 February 1858, pp. 323, 347.

A HUNDRED HOURS' WALK

The feat of walking continuously during one hundred hours, which has been accomplished in other cities, has been performed in Springfield, at Smith's bowling alley, ending at 12 o'clock Friday night, Jan. 22d. The *Springfield Republican* says the pedestrian was Alfred Elson, known as the "London Antelope," from his fleetness on the foot as well as his powers of endurance. His fourth and last day was decidedly the hardest. He began to lag at midnight, Thursday night, when within twenty-four hours of the goal, and his attendants had considerable difficulty in keeping him on the plank. Finally, however, by chafing his hands, he was sufficiently revived to use the dumb bells for an hour, after which he felt better. He also seemed to be encouraged by the presence of visitors, during yesterday, although at times he looked as though he was almost ready to "gin eout."

During the last evening there was a large number of visitors, and the interest manifested in the result was not a little enhanced by the unmistakable evidence of failing strength. His diet during the day had been stale bread and water, but he now took considerable brandy, and although at first revived by it he soon began to reel, and had nearly fallen two or three times when he was caught by those attending upon him. The last half hour was one of great difficulty, and required the constant watching and assistance of his friends, who did not hold him up but endeavored, by walking beside him, to keep him awake and renew his courage. The clock struck twelve—he had completed his hundred hours, and the very senseless exhibition was ended.

The feat being accomplished, Elson's method is to first take a warm bath, get his skin a healthy glow, and afterwards sleep for an hour and a half. He is then waked up and walked about the room for half an hour, when he again sleeps for three hours. After another waking and walk, he goes to bed a third time and wakes up fresh.

Elson walked on a raised platform fifty feet long, and was not required to make any particular distance or speed, but only to keep constantly in motion. He therefore ate his food as he walked, having it cut up for him and taking if from a shelf at one end of the platform. When he used dumb bells, which he often did in order to draw the circulation of blood from his legs by giving sufficient exercise to other parts of the body,—he still used his feet, going, however, very slowly.

GREAT WALKING FEAT IN LOWELL

One of the most extraordinary feats of walking took place at Appleton Hall, in Lowell, commencing Tuesday, Feb. 9th, at 12 o'clock M., and was performed by P.J. Buckley, better known as the Lynn buck," for a wager of $500 a side; the "Buck" agreeing to walk 105 hours on a plank three feet wide, and forty feet long, without sleep. The agreement was that the walker should have for rest ten minutes in every twelve hours, and had he taken the time thus allowed him, would have accomplished the feat at 9 o'clock, Saturday evening.

The amount of time taken by him for rest during the walk was as follows:

On Wednesday	3 minutes	On Friday	12 minutes
On Thursday	3 "	On Saturday	11 "
	Making a total of	29 minutes	

The whole time allowed for rest was eighty-seven and one-half minutes. The consequence was, that, taking into consideration the time not taken by the walker, the feat was performed at one and half minutes past eight P.M. Saturday. But in order to convince the Lowelites that he could hold out still longer if necessary, he continued to walk till fourteen minutes to nine o'clock, at which time he left the plank quite fresh, and accompanied by his friends (which were numerous) walked to the hotel some half mile from the hall.

Some of our most respectable citizens, doubting the ability of Buckley to perform the task which he had undertaken, engaged the services of competent persons who kept watch both day and night, thereby affording no chance to the walker to leave, or to sleep, and one and all acknowledged that the feat was honestly and fairly performed. Buckley, on Sunday morning, looked hale and hearty, and felt confident that he could perform the same feat over again with ease.

During the walking, the Hall was visited by large numbers of people, and on Friday evening some 300 persons were in attendance, and remained throughout the entire night. On Saturday evening the excitement was immense, the Hall was completely thronged, and the street was crowded by the people anxious to obtain admittance to the Hall, but who were destined to be disappointed.

It will be seen that in reality Buckley walked on the plank 105 hours 44 minutes and 30 seconds, exclusive of walking one half a mile to the hotel.

Buckley now is willing to perform the same feat for from $100 to $500; the walking to take place in Lowell in four weeks or more from date; the terms to be similar to those of the last walk. Men and money may be found at the Exchange Coffee House, Lowell, Mass.

Lowell, Feb. 15, 1858.   JAMES FOLEY.

Chapter 15

WINTER SPORTS

During the middle years of the nineteenth century North Americans enjoyed numerous winter pastimes on snow and ice. Curling was a favorite Scottish game that immigrants introduced into Canada and the United States. Most of the participants in ice skating and snowshoeing sought simple outdoor recreation, but a few guided the transformation of these activities into organized sports. Most of athletes who braved the frigid conditions were upper or middle class men, yet many women joined in the fun, especially in ice skating. Snowshoeing brought interracial competition when Canadian Indians raced against the English and French citizens of Montreal.

By the 1840s curling had become the dominant winter sport in Nova Scotia and Upper and Lower Canada, especially in Halifax, Quebec City, Montreal, and Toronto. Its Scottish supporters were mostly prominent professionals and businessmen, and the game's enthusiasts were generally fairly affluent. In 1852 Canadian curlers affiliated themselves with the Royal Caledonian Curling Club of Scotland by establishing branch associations in Montreal and Nova Scotia. That action reflected their colonial status, and the Scottish connection remained the leading factor in their sport until well into the twentieth century. In the United States Scottish immigrants organized clubs in Boston and New York City before 1860. The first document in this chapter presents the results of an intrasquad match of the Toronto Curling Club played in 1844, along with a list of regulations and terminology used in the sport during the 1850s.

During the 1850s a skating mania swept through many North American cities, especially in the northeastern United States. Sporting and daily newspapers reported tens of thousands of men and women, young and old, gliding across ponds and frozen flooded fields. In 1850 enthusiasts for the winter pastime in the City of Brotherly Love founded one of the pioneer clubs in the sport; excerpts from the revised 1859 edition of its "Constitution and By-Laws of the Skaters' Club of the City of Philadelphia" appear below. The opening of the Central Park skating pond in New York City in the winter of 1858-59 gave a tremendous boost to the sport. The regulations and instructions for its use are reprinted here. In 1859 the New York Times estimated that New Yorkers had purchased 60,000 skates. Although its estimates of attendance and equipment sold were probably exaggerated, it is entirely possible that skating was the most popular participatory sport among the masses for any season of the year. The large numbers of women who skated is especially significant because during these years public opinion frowned upon the participation of females in athletics, with the exceptions of calesthenics and horseback riding. The increasing acceptance of ice skating by girls, young ladies, and married women provided a model and a foundation for greater future involvement for females in Canadian and American sport. Included here are several descriptions of both recreational skating and several matches held in Madison, Wisconsin and Boston.

Snowshoeing originated as an activity of North American Indians which was adopted by white men as a recreational pastime during the mid-nineteenth century. Twelve citizens of Montreal founded the Montreal Snow Shoe Club during the winter of 1840 when they met to tramp through the outskirts of their city. Later in that decade these hardy souls journeyed out regularly on Tuesday evenings and Saturday afternoons, winding up at a restaurant for good food and drink. During its early years the club also staged a few races (including a steeplechase event over hurdles) at a local horse racing course. Although the organization was a prestigious outfit with an elite membership, its races were open to all, including local Indians. Thus white and red men competed in snowshoe races in addition to their contests in lacrosse and pedestrianism. Quebec City also hosted snow shoe tramps in 1842 and the Quebec Snow Shoe Club sponsored races in 1847.

The Montreal Snow Shoe Club was reorganized formally at "Dolly's Chop House" in 1850. During the following decade two other snow shoe clubs appeared in Montreal, the Aurora (1858) and the St. Georges (1859). The members of these associations combined tramping with racing to create a new form of the sport—cross-country snowshoeing over rugged terrain. The final document in this chapter describes the action in several races held during the late 1850s, and concludes with the By-laws of the Montreal Snow Shoe Club.

CURLING

Scottish sportsmen introduced curling to the Canadian provinces and several cities of the United States during the early decades of the nineteenth century. The following document begins with an account of the results of an intrasquad contest between the married and single members of the Toronto Curling Club. The event also included an individual competition for a medal. The selection concludes with a description of the regulations and terminology of the sport that suggests that curling was growing in popularity in several American cities during the late 1850s. These pieces are reprinted from the Spirit of the Times, 6 April 1844, p. 63, and the New York Clipper, 20 December 1856, p. 276, and 14 February, 1857, p. 340.

TORONTO CURLING CLUB—MARRIED VS. SINGLE

The annual match for *"Beef and Greens,"* between the married and unmarried members of the Totonto Curling Club, came off on Saturday last. The playing commenced at two o'clock, P.M., and continued until half-past five, at which time the bachelors were declared the winners by 25 shots, being a much greater number than upon any previous occasion, although we believe, that for the last five years the *"old ones"* have been obliged to *"foot the bill."*

The players were opposed to each other in the following order:—

RINK—No. 1.

Married—Dr. Telfer, Mr. J. Ewatt, senior, Mr. G. Urqchart, Dr. Primrose, *Skip*— 14 Shots.

Unmarried—Messers. T. Ewatt, S.B. Campbell, J. Leys, A. Morrison, *Skip*—22 Shots.
 Unmarried winning on this rink by 8 shots.

RINK—No. 2.

Married—Messrs. G. Leslie, C. Daly, J. Kennedy, T. Aitkin, *Skip*—12 Shots.

Unmarried—Messrs. R. Cumming, J. Helliwell, R. Mitchell, G. Philpotts, *Skip*—17 Shots.

 Unmarried winning on this rink by 5 Shots.

RINK—No. 3.

Married—Messrs. Herschfelder, A. Badenach, G. Murray, J. McMurrich, *Skip*—11 Shots

Unmarried—Messrs. G. Ewart, W. Ross, R. G. Anderson, G. Denholm, *Skip*—23 Shots.

 Unmarried winning on this Rink by 12 Shots, and winning on the three Rinks collectively by 25 Shots.

 The following detail will show the different *Heads, &c.*

RINK—No. 1

	Heads	Single	Double	Treble	Quad	Total Shots
Married	8	4	3	0	1	14
Unmarried	14	8	3	1	1	22
Total	22	12	6	1	2	36

RINK No. 2

	Heads	Single	Double	Treble	Quad	Total Shots
Married	10	9	0	1	0	12
Unmarried	13	10	2	1	0	17
Total	23	19	2	2	0	29

RINK—No. 3

	Heads	Single	Double	Treble	Quad	Total Shots
Married	7	4	2	1	0	11
Unmarried	15	10	3	1	1	23
Total	22	14	5	2	1	34

 The Medal was played for on Thursday, 29th February, and after a keen contest was won by Samuel Lorimer, from Pinpoint, Dumfrieshire, Scotland. Merrs. Torrance and Gibson, of the Scarboro Club, kindly acted as umpires to the entire satisfaction of every one.

Nearly thirty members of the Club entered for competition; and at the termination of the play it was ascertained that Messrs. Lorimer and Wyllie had gained the greatest number of shots, namely, 10 each. The umpires then, in conformity with the rules of the Grand Caledonian Curling Club, in order to decide which of the gentlemen should wear the Medal, gave them four shots each at "out-wicking"—*at which they were even.*

The umpires then named three shots, the first a draw, the second *"chap-and-lie"* (which is to strike a stone placed upon the "tee" out of the circle and lie), the third *"raising"* (which is to drive a stone placed seven feet from the "tee" with the circle), which shots were also *each* played in beautiful style by both competitors. It was then agreed to give them two shots each, at *"in-wicking,"* at which they were *again equally successful.* Darkness was now fast approaching, and great as the knowledge of Messrs. Torrance and Gibson is universally admitted to be, in the mysteries of Curling, their ingenuity was a good deal taxed to devise how this keen contest should be decided. At last Mr. T. said they would try them at *"chipping the winner"* (which is to strike a stone placed upon the tee, half guarded by another seven feet from it), this shot was prettily played by Mr. Lorimer; but Mr. Wyllie failed, his stone "wicking the guard." Mr. L. was therefore declared the winner of this most closely contested and scientifically played game.

The weather was unfavorable, as it rained in the early part of the day; and the ice at the time the game commenced, at two o'clock, was found to be indifferent; but notwithstanding there were a great many spectators, and the game throughout, but particularly during the last contest, created much interest.

REGULATIONS AND TERMINOLOGY

1. CURLING is always practiced upon the ice, and is, like golfing, a national game peculiar to Scotland. It requires several large stones, one for each player, of from 50 to 70 lb. weight, with an iron handle in the top; and a place of level and strong ice, upon which a "rink" or course, 10 feet wide, and in length varying from 30 to 50 yards, according to the ice, is cleared of snow. At each end of this a small hole is made, called a "tee," round which two circles are drawn, called "broughs," one larger than the other. These are merely intended for the more ready measurement of the distance of each stone from the tow, and must also be cleared of snow. A line, called the "hogscore," is drawn across the rink at each end, at a distance from the tee equal to one-sixth of the rink, whatever that may be.

2. THE PLAY is tolerably simple in principle, but requiring great strength and practice. The first player's object is to slide his stone as near the tee as possible, and in front of it. The next endeavors to beat the first, either by the greater proximity of his stone in the first instance, or by driving that of the first player away. A stone gliding by the tee is almost sure to be out of the game. Those of the same side either guard their partner's stone, if it is in a very likely place, or attempt to obtain a better position for themselves. When all have been played the stone nearest the tee counts one, and all those of the same side which are not beaten by one of the other also score one "shot," as it is called. The whole of the game being 31....

Curling Stones.—These are made of various kinds of stone (usually granite in Scotland,) as they are also various in size, shape, weight, or color, according to local by-laws and the taste of the owner. Some have brass and ivory handles at top, and some have ebony swan-necked handles, inlaid and ornamented more or less according to circumstances. The weights range from 30 lbs to 50 lbs. each. Those in ordinary use usually cost in Scotland about L2 10s. Those intended for presentation or as prizes are quite costly.

Rink.—This term is generally applied to the course of ice used by the players. A "full rink" signifies eight players, with all the implements of the game complete.

Tee.—This is a piece of wood placed in a small hole made in the ice, and around this hoe are marked various concentric circles as if by a pair of compasses, and the largest circle has a radius of seven feet. Another tee is placed on the line of the rink, at distances ranging from 28 to 38 yards, according to the "glibness" of the ice and the state of the weather. Four yards behind this last distance a piece of roughly punched sheet iron is laid down for the player to stand upon, and this would make his total distance 42 yards, which is frequently the case, but the distance may vary to ten yards less or twenty yards more, according to agreement and the weather at the time.

Hogscore.—This is invariably one-sixth of the distance at which the tee is placed, whatever that may be. It is a line drawn across the rink. When a stone does not reach this scratch, the opponents cry out "A hog!" and the player must remove the stone as well as lose his throw.

Raising, or Promoting.—Both of these terms are in use to signify that a previous stone played is now driven by the last player's stone giving it a shove nearer the tee.

Chap and Lie.—This is the expression when the last player's stone shoves forward a previous one and takes its place.

Drawing.—This is said of a player whose skill can make his stone take up a desired position, and not touch any other.

Guarding.—This is a still more difficult style of play, and consists of taking up a position partly or wholly in front of an adversary's stone; or to guard one's own previously played.

Inwicking.—A player who can make use of the rebound from striking some unimportant stone so as to hit an important one out of the way, is said to inwick.

Outwicking.—This operation requires similar skill, but has a different result, for the played stone must hit its object on the outside, and drive it towards the tee, although perhaps flying off itself. The outside of a stone which has been played means that which is the farthest from the player.

Chipping.—This means a brisk tap at one corner or some side of an adversary's stone, so as to drive it away and still proceed onward towards the tee.

Skip.—This is the captain on each side, usually four players on each but the skips play last. Which side may commence is usually decided by the toss of a "bawbee" or copper. After that the players must obey the directions of their respective skips, for they have the responsibility. Of course the skip likes to know that he has three good players as partners.

With our previous descriptions the ambitious curler may now be able to make out some idea of this spirit-stirring sport. The rink must be carefully swept by good users of the broom, not afraid of work. The player's party have the right to sweep from the middle of the rink to the tee played for; but, in case the stone has passed the tee then the adverse party may do the sweeping.

These are the principal rules now in use in the neighborhood of Boston, and which we understand have long since been approved of by "The Montreal Thistle" and "The Caledonian" among our Canadian friends.

SKATING

Tens of thousands of Canadian and American boys, girls, men, and women enjoyed ice skating on ponds, lakes, and streams. Most pursued this pastime purely for recreational purposes; a few competed in races for prizes. The New York Clipper recognized the Skaters' Club of Philadelphia as the pioneer organization in the United States. Excerpts from its Constitution and a description of the equipment its members used for saving lives appear below, reprinted from the New York Clipper, 26 February 1859, p. 360. This document is particularly interesting for what it reveals about the concern for safety in an amusement that could be extremely dangerous. The skating mania was nowhere more evident that on New York City's Central Park pond. Its regulations, directions, and instructions presented here are taken from the New York Clipper, 31 December 1859 and 14 January 1860, pp. 292 and 307. The next three brief articles suggest the varieties of the skating experience. The first story recounts a race held in Madison, Wisconsin; it is reprinted from the Spirit of the Times, 30 December 1854, p. 546. The second piece describes some displays of skill at figure skating on Jamaica Pond near Boston. It first appeared in the Boston Journal and was included in the Spirit of the Times, 17 February 1855, p. 2. The final selection, from Wilkes' Spirit of the Times, 18 February 1860, p. 381, lists the results of separate races for ladies and gentlemen at Boston's Skating Park.

CONSTITUTION AND BY-LAWS OF THE SKATERS' CLUB
OF THE CITY OF PHILADELPHIA, 1859

ARTICLE I

The name of the association shall be the SKATERS' CLUB OF THE CITY OF PHILADELPHIA, and its officers shall consist of a President, Vice President, Secretary, Corresponding Secretary, Treasurer, and an Executive Committee of five members, all of whom shall be elected by separate ballots at the stated meeting in December of each year. The Physicians connected with the Club shall constitute a Board of Surgeons.

ARTICLE II

The object of the Association shall be instruction and improvement in the art of Skating, the cultivation of a friendly feeling in all who participate in the amusement, and the efficient use of proper apparatus for the rescue of persons breaking through the ice....

ARTICLE X

The Club shall provide and maintain in proper order, such apparatus as may be deemed necessary for saving life; and each member of the Club shall provide himself with a *Badge, Cord,* and *Reel.*

DESCRIPTION OF THE APPARATUS
USED BY THE CLUB FOR SAVING LIFE

BADGE

1. The Badge is a small silver SKATE, about one inch and a quarter long, and is worn on the left breast of the coat, for the purpose of desginating members of the Club when skating.

CORD AND REEL

2. The Cord and Reel, carried by each member when skating, is the most simple and important device used by the Club. It consists of a reel about five inches in length, made of hard wood, with a strong cord carefully wrapped thereon, about three-sixteenths of an inch thick, and fifty feet long, with a noose on the end for the wrist. In case of accident, two or three members are sufficient to go to the rescue; and the others should act as a reserve guard to prevent persons from approaching too near the rescuers. The rescuer first securely fastens the cord around his wrist, and then throws his reel to the person in the water, using care not to strike him with it. After the person in the water receives the cord and secures it around his wrist, the first effort of the rescuer should be to calm him, and instruct him to hold to the cord, and strike out with his feet as if swimming; and when in that position, a gentle pull will bring him safely on the ice.

SAFETY LADDERS

3. The ladders are constructed lightly, and of light wood, about fifteen feet long, with eyes or rings near the end, having a grass line about half an inch thick and one hundred feet long attached thereto.

SAFETY HOOKS

4. The hooks are made similar to the ordinary ice hook, without a point, with a pole about fifteen feet in length, to which is attached a line about twenty five feet long.

SAFETY AXE

5. The axe is made similar to the ordinary ice-axe, and is of great importance in case of persons getting under the ice.

SAFETY FLOATS

6. The life floats are made of gum, near the shape of a large life preserver, and have a buoyancy of over seven hundred pounds; they can be thrown to persons in the water, or placed upon any one who is going to the rescue; and in case several persons are in the water at the same time, they will be found very useful.

STATION FLAGS

7. Station flags are to designate the places on the ice where the apparatus is stationed. The pole is twelve feet high, with steel points, and the flag about six feet by four feet, with the word "Station" thereon.

SAFETY FLAGS

8. Safety flags are small flags, the poles about six feet high, and on the flags the word *"Caution."* These flag poles have sharp steel points, and are forced in the ice at all places which are considered dangerous.

SAFETY LINES

9. These lines are one hundred feet long, made of cotton, and are about half an inch thick, with eyes and spring hooks in the ends, so as to be readily attached to anything in time of danger.

AIR HOLE GUARDS

10. Air hole guards are constructed of maple posts four feet long and one inch and a half thick, with sharp steel points to pierce the ice. These posts are forced in the ice around the *air hole,* which is then encircled with a small grass line, about half an inch thick, which passed through a hole near the top of the posts.

BOAT

11. The Boat is small and light, made of cedar, and is about sixteen feet long, with runners attached thereto.

BLANKETS

12. A blanket will be found useful to place around persons when taken out of the water; and if the weather is very cold, and the person has to be removed any distance, it might be the means of saving life.

SKATING REGULATIONS, CENTRAL PARK POND, NEW YORK CITY, 1859

1st. BALL SIGNALS—In approaching the Park, first look for the signals. A Red Ball at the bell tower, just south of the Reservoir, when up at the mast-head, will be visible, in ordinary weather, at a considerable distance from the Park, and, by the use of a glass, from most of the elevated parts of the city. When the ball is up it indicates that "the ice is in condition for skating," or for games, or is safe for those who choose to go upon it.

When the ball is down it indicates that "the ice is not in good condtion for skating," or games, or, that it is unsafe, or is occupied by laborers engaged in removing snow, cleaning or flushing with water to renew the surface.

2d. On entering the Park, observe the notices posted at the gates, stating the condition of the ice from time to time, whether it is in desirable condition to visitors, or whether they are prohibited for the day from going on the pond or any part of it, on account of the cleaning of the ice, &c. By these means visitors will frequently save themselves the trouble of coming to the pond when it is not in condition to afford them amusement; besides, if the laborers are left undisturbed at such times by spectators, they will the more rapidly prepare the ice for use.

3d. On reaching the pond, if the ball at the bell-tower is down, visitors are not to go upon the ice.

4th. Observe all special notices and regulations posted around the pond.

Visitors will go on and off the ice by the regular walks and approaches prepared for them, and by none other, except in case of danger. Persons will be strictly prohibited going upon the pond except at the regular approaches.

Visitors will use the foot-scrapers provided at the approaches, and avoid carrying mud or dirt on the ice.

When notices of "Danger" are put up on the ice, they indicate that the ice is unsafe in that especial vicinity.

When the United States flag at the central station on the pond is down, or when required by any park-keeper, all persons on the ice should rapidly disperse to the nearest points of the shore, avoiding confusion and getting into crowds. If one or more persons have broken through the ice, it is directed as an imperative necessity that all— spectators or companions, on giving the alarm, immediately withdraw to a safe distance, without attempts at rescue, not only to ensure the safety of persons in the water, but for their own. Park-keepers and other aid will always be very near the spot, on the lookout, and provided with ample means for speedy rescue, if not impeded by spectators.

There are but few places where the water is over four feet deep—any person therefore, of ordinary stature when called on by a park keeper, should jump in the water without hesitation to extricate a child or woman.

Each park-keeper's station is provided with a number of cork bathing floats and a coil of strong rope in case of need, and all the gang planks at the approaches to the pond are so constructed that they can be rapidly removed to any break in the ice.

Any person detecting an insecure place in the ice, or a seemingly insecure place, is requested to immediately inform the nearest park-keeper.

Any person observing any act of indecorum, or any violation of the Pond regulations or ordinances of the Park, or if wanting the aid of a park keeper in haste, for any urgent purpose, may signalize a park-keeper by holding aloft, or waving a handkerchief, hat, or cap, or by throwing up a hat or cap in the air, or by calling aloud. These signals must not be used triflingly.

Let all remember that these regulations are necessary, alike for their security, convenienece, and enjoyment, and that a cheerful compliance with them will promote these objects.

By order of the Comptroller of the Park....

There are ten different gravel or plank walks leading to the shore, with gang-planks carried from them on to the ice. No one should approach the pond in any other way than by these. There are foot-scrapers on each gang plank, which should be used before stepping on the ice.

No tobacco, cigar stumps, paper, nutshells, or other article, should be dropped and left on the ice.

Dense crowds should be avoided. Even thick ice is liable to crack so that blocks are formed which may suddenly tip, if a number of persons happen to crowd on one side of them, submerging them all.

The Park-keepers are provided with abundant means of rescue in case of accidents. Cautions or directions form a Park-keeper should in any case be immediately complied with.

The vicinity of laborers engaged in cleaning the ice, &c., should be avoided.

A WHITE PENNANT will be kept hoisted over the Round House in the middle of the main pond whenever the ice may be walked upon with safety by several persons together, or skating can be attempted without serious detriment to the ice, whatever way be its condition in other respects. No one can remain upon the ice with perfect safety, or with proper regard to the general interest in maintaining the ice in good order for skating, when the White Pennant is not flying.

A RED PENNANT over the Round House indicates either that the ice is very dangerous, or that it is being flooded for the purpose of forming a new surface. In the latter case it will be kept flying until new ice is finally formed. The Red Pennant will not be displayed unless there is an absolute necessity that the pond should be cleared.

The above instructions are formed with a design to place no more check upon the inclinations of individuals than is quite necessary to preserve the ice in a condition for the general enjoyment, and it is hoped that they may be so willingly observed by all, that occasion to resort to force for this purpose shall never occur.

SKATING MATCH AT MADISON, WISCONSIN

A skating match for a purse of $10, lately came off at Madison, and produced much sport, of which we give the following account from the "Democrat" of that city: —

The weather was beautiful, the sky serene and cloudless, and ice in the best possible condition. The distance of one half mile, and back, making a course of one mile, was measured with a chain, and was accurate. The track down and back was divided by bushes stuck in the ice. The purse was suspended on a pole at the starting point, to be seized by the skater who came out ahead. The wind was partially in their backs going out and quarterly in their face on their return, but was light, not sufficient to materially aid or impede their progress. The following were the entries:—Wm. Pyncheon, D.M. Glashen, Geo. Storer, Ader Hendricks, S.F. McHugh, J. Campbell, A. Glascott, Bill Clark, and C.H. Billings.

The start was a fair one, made at the tap of the drum. The skaters got off in good style. They were all graceful and easy goers, but it was soon evident that some lacked wind and bottom. On the first quarter two wheeled off, and took the back track and one went down. Another soon after dropped off, so that but four turned the half mile post, and in the act of turning one more, and as good a skater as was on the ice, "went under," leaving the home stretch to the best of three. It soon narrowed down to two, Bill Clark and Geo. Stoner, who came down in fine style within ten feet of each other. The drum sounded, cheers ascended from the vast crowd, the purse hung in reach, the skaters in heat and panting, but making each curve and step with perfect ease—the scene was exciting beyond description. Clark wheeled in ahead, passed under the pole, and took the purse, falling as he turned.

The distance was made in 1:56 which we believe is the best time on record. We remember no match of the New York Club, in which better time was made than 2:06.

A shake purse of $5 was afterwards put up and asked for, Hendricks raking down the pile in about the same time.

A large number of our citizens, in number not less than 1000 or 1200, including a large number of ladies, were spectators of the match, which was on all hands, conceded to be the finest piece of sport witnessed in many a day. We trust for a frequent repetition of the affair.

PHILADELPHIA AGAINST BOSTON

At five o'clock on Saturday afternoon, about one thousand skaters were assembled upon the ice of Jamaica Pond, enjoying the pleasures of healthful exercise in the pure bracing air of winter. Many ladies were present, although doubtless the cold westerly wind prevented a large number from joining in the exciting sport. There was a great number of excellent skaters upon the ice, and the merry laugh and wild halloo of the revellers did not die away until a late hour in the night. But when the stroke of twelve announced the close of the week and the commencement of the Sabbath day, the bright moon looked down upon a scene of peace and stillness—so different from the noise and bustle and gaiety of a few hours before.

There are almost always one or more "lions" among the skaters on Jamaica Pond— one or more gentlemen who skate more gracefully and perform more wonderful feats upon their iron runners than any others. The "lion" upon Saturday afternoon was a Philadelphia gentleman whose remarkable performances excited the admiration of all beholders.

He was continually surrounded by a group of hundreds of skaters, who, forming a ring, would induce him to exhibit within their circle. He was generally regarded as the most skillful skater seen in this vicinity for years, and we think he must be a limb of the legal profession; for we have serious doubts if any person but a "Philadelphia lawyer" could ever become familiar with so many "quirks and quiddities."

One amusing scene is said to have occurred during one of his performances. As he was going through some of his most intricate evolutions, a gentleman skater in the surrounding crowd, thinking he could surpass the Philadelphian in one thing at least, pushed boldly into the charmed ring, amid cries of "clear the circle," "put him hout," and standing upon one foot, proceeded to skate or rather to wriggle, round and round the ring, without touching his other foot to the ground. The Philadelphia gentleman was fairly non-plussed, and acknowledged that there was one thing at least which he could not do.

The skating on Saturday afternooon was not so good as it has been, the ice being dotted with patches of snow. Probably the snow of last night and this morning will oblige skaters to discontinue their favorite amusement for a few days.

P. S. Since writing the above, we find a communication in the "Transcript," stating that "some of the gentlemen resident in Jamaica Plain have taken pains to have the pond freed from snow, so that the lovers of skating can still find some rare sport there. The town authorities, it is said, will cause some protection to be placed around the holes made by cutting ice, so as to indicate those spots to skaters."

THE SKATING RACES AT THE SKATING PARK, BOSTON

Several exciting races came off at the Skating Park, Boston, on Saturday, the 4th inst. The first was for ladies, with prizes of a silver goblet, valued at $25, and a pair of skates valued at $10, for the best time; distance, half-mile. The second race was for gentlemen, consisting of a goblet valued at $35, and a pair of skates valued at $10.

For the ladies' race there were entered, the Misses Lucy Crocker, Addis M. Fogg, Carrie St. Clair, M.B. Lunt, Eliza Yenehki, Alice Twombly, M.D. Lamb, and Mrs. John L. Brown and Mrs. Carrie Ashley of Boston; Mrs. Anna Walker, of Roxbury; Mrs. George Farnum, of Lowell; Miss W. A. Roberts, of Andover. These were divided into two parties, Miss Alice Twombly, Miss M.D. Lamb, Miss Anna Walker, and Miss Addie M. Fogg first. After a pleasant contest, the latter won, making the half-mile in 3:11, and Miss Lamb in 3:35. The others were distanced. The next party consisted of Mrs. George Farnum, Mrs. John L. Brown, and Mrs. Carrie Ashley. The former won in 2:59, her companions being distanced. The prize was awarded to Mrs. Farnum, and the second to Miss Fogg.

Next in order was the gentleman's race, a distance of five miles, for which appeared Wm. F. Smith, F.G. Lawrence, Emory Lawrence, Gabriel F. Worden, Edward Spencer, and George E. Lawrence. The first mile was made well together in 4:24. On the fifth mile an exciting contest took place between the two Lawrences, which was decided in favor of George. Time, 22:46; his borther was two seconds later. The prizes were presented to the winners by the judges, Messers. Wheildon, Fuller, and Cumston. The affair passed off pleasantly, and gave great satisfaction to the large crowd present.

SNOW SHOE RACES IN MONTREAL

The Montreal Snow Shoe Club scheduled races at a course in the city and also at picturesque locations at nearby mountains. By the late 1850s it boasted a membership of one hundred and fifty included a number of Montreal's most prominent citizens. Its annual contests were open to all classes, nationalities, and races and were important social events that drew large crowds. During its early years the association offered cash prizes to the winners, but by 1860 awards to white competitors included silk sashes,

belts, medals and small cups. The following document includes accounts of several
matches and a list of the organization's by-laws. These pieces are reprinted from the
New York Clipper, 13 March 1858, p. 372, 12 March 1859, p. 372, and the Spirit of
the Times, 4 February 1860, p. 620.

MARCH, 1858

On Tuesday afternoon, the annual races of the Montreal Snoe-Shoe Club took place
at Ouimet's race course, near Mile End. The day was rather cold, yet notwithstanding
this, at least a thousand persons were present, to witness the feats of speed in this
manly and exhilarating exercise. The grand stand was filled with ladies, and on the
Steward's stand we noticed Sir William Eyre, Commander of the Forces, with his staff.
The first race was a distance of four miles, and nine Indians from Caughnawaga, entered it. The start was good, and for a considerable distance the same position was
maintained. The first mile was accomplished in six minutes twenty seconds; the second in eight minutes twenty-two seconds; and the third in nine minutes thirty seconds;
the forth was exciting, the contest being very close. The Indian who came in victor
during the three previous miles, and for a long distance on the fourth, was the third;
but when within half a mile of the stand, he made a dash and took the lead, which he
kept and came in some ten yards ahead of the second Indian, and fifteen ahead of the
third. The last mile occupied but seven minutes and ten seconds, and the four miles
were accomplished in thirty-one minutes twenty-two seconds. The winner of this race
seemed to feel himself a very important personage, for he immediately donned a fantastic head-dress, and strutted about his discomfited compeers with a very bombastic
air. The prize for this race was forty dollars.

The next was a hurdle race over four three feet hurdles; the prize being ten dollars.
Preparations for this race were made by six whites and three indians; it was a most
exciting struggle —the first hurdle was leapt almost simultaneously by all the competitors, but between the first hurdle and the second, distances were changed, Mr. Brown
keeping first, followed closely by Mr. Murray, who fell while clearing the third hurdle,
an Indian who was following having trodden on his snow-shoe. He was up in an instant, however, But Mr. Murray's efforts came in first. They all arrived at the Steward's
stand in the following order—Mr. Brown, first—Mr. Murray, second, and an Indian
third.

A race of a half a mile by boys under 14 years of age, for a prize of $5, was eas-
ily won by Master Edward Whitehead.

The next race was a mile; prize ten dollars. A beautiful start was made, and for a
half a mile it was a neck-and-neck race; here an Indian took the lead, followed by another Indian, and Mr. Murray third. Mr. Murray made several vain attempts to take the
lead; and the race was won by the Indian who came in first in the four mile race.

A race of 100 yards for a prize of five dollars then came off. The struggle was a
severe one, and was hardly contested. Mr. William Whitehead came in first. Time,
fourteen seconds.

The most exciting race of the day then took place. It was for the Club Cup. For this
race there entered Messrs. Coffin, Barnston, Brown, and Rintoul. The start was good,

and Indian file was kept for the first half mile, when Mr. Barnston took the lead, followed closely by Mr. Coffin. On passing the stand, (completing the first mile,) Mr. Barnston still had the lead, followed by Mr. Coffin, then Mr. Brown, Mr. Rintoul being last. Just after passing Mr. Brown gave up. The same distance was kept during three-quarters of the second mile, when Mr. Coffin made a dash and came up with Mr. Barnston. A desperate struggle for the supremacy then took place, but when within twenty yards of the winning post, Mr. Barnston gave up exhausted, and Mr. Coffin came in first, and was presented with the cup.

The last race, for two miles across the country, was contested for by four Indians, and was won by one named Mosse.

FEBRUARY, 1859

A large number of members from the Montreal, St. George, and Aurora Clubs of Montreal, repaired, on the 5th ult., to the picturesque mountain of Beloeil, on the invitation of Mr. Compte, of the Mount St. Hilaire Hotel, to compete for a silver medal, to be presented by that gentleman to the winner of a race from the St. Hilaire Station to his hotel on the mountain, a distance of three miles. There was a large gathering of the *habitans* of the surrounding villages to witness the sport of the day, and the greatest excitement prevailed when Messrs. A. Lamothe and Phillip Duchesnay, the stewards, drew up the competitors, twelve in number, on the hill overlooking the station. The appearance of the start was truly picturesque. The by-standers gazed upon the line of smart, athletic fellows, with a feeling of admiration. Some were clothed in Indian costumes, others in light blankets; and in the countenances of all could be seen an animated expression of hope the Dame Fortune would favor each of them. At a given signal, off they go, some running, some walking, and each choosing the direction which he thinks the most likely to reach the goal. Immediately in the rear of the main body could be seen a young man, with his coat thrown off and in a white shirt, quietly following the track of his fellow competitors, till he reached the brink of the first hill above the station. With the greatest ease he took the lead, and dashed into the forest, closely followed by Messrs. Hughes, Rintoul, Coffin, Macauley, and Morris. From that moment the race was blank to the spectators, and the hundred sleighs drove off to the hotel to await the arrival of the winner. Exactly two and a half minutes from the time of starting, while all were standing with anxiety on the gallery of Comte's hotel, a voice cried out, "Here comes the man in the white shirt." And, sure enough, in the distance, Frank Dowd was coming, and, in a short time, touched the winning flag, having accomplished the three miles, uphill and through the forest, in twenty-five minutes. Seven minutes afterwards, the next competitor arrived, and the rest arrived one by one, at intervals of three and four minutes.

A walking match of five miles, for the Champion Medal of the Montreal Snoe Show Club, came off on the 9th ult., over the Mile-End Race Course, Montreal. By the rules of the Club no member is entitled to keep this medal except he wins the annual walking race for two successive seasons; last year it was won by Mr. N. Hughes, after a hard tug with Mr. H.W. Rintoul. On the 9th the following gentlemen were entered for the race: Messrs. Nicholas Hughes, W.H. Rintoul, and Andrew McCulloch. At the word "go" from the Stewards, they all started off in a fine style and kept together for the first half mile, when, unfortunately, one of Mr. Rintoul's snow-shoes came off, and before he could get it properly adjusted the others were so very far ahead that he saw it would be useless to attempt to catch up with them; he, therefore, retired from the contest, to the great disappointment of the spectators, who expected to see a well contested race between him and Mr. Hughes. The tug of war was now between Messrs. McCulloch and Hughes, and for the first four miles they kept close together, Mr. Hughes leading; but at the last mile Hughes, "put on steam," and came in about fifty yards ahead of McCulloch: the five miles were walked in sixty minutes, and considering the very heavy state of the track, this was pretty "tall walking" *a la Raquette*. Mr. McCulloch who had never before attempted a walking race, showed great spirit in the manner in which he kept up the pace through deep snow against such a veteran walker as Mr. Hughes.

JANUARY, 1860

A walk of five miles, for the champion medal of the Montreal Snow Shoe Club, came off last Saturday afternoon, over the Mile End Course. The grand stand was crowded with lookers on, who seemed to take a deep interest in the match; At precisely half-past 3 o'clock, the President of the Club, R.H. Stephens, Esq., gave orders or the start, when five competitors, rigged in fancy costume, made their appearance on the race track. Two of them, however, were obliged to retire from the contest after walking the first two miles. The race was now between Messrs. F.H. Fisher, T.W. Taylor, and W.H. Rintoul. Away all went at a tearing pace, coming in as they passed the winning stand, in the following order:

1st mile—Fisher 1st, Taylor 2nd, Rintoul 3rd. Time 11-1/2 minutes.
2nd mile—Fisher 1st, Taylor 2nd, Rintoul 3rd. Time 11-1/2 minutes.
3rd mile—Fisher 1st, Taylor 2nd, Rintoul 3rd. Time 11 minutes.
4th mile—Fisher 1st, Rintoul 2nd, Taylor 3rd. Time 11-1/2 minutes.
5th mile—Fisher 1st, Taylor 2nd, Rintoul 3rd. Time 10-1/2 minutes.

The total time for this five miles was 56 minutes. During the whole race the greatest excitement prevailed among the spectators, as the men were so well matched, and kept so close together all through, that it was impossible to say who would be the winner. They passed the winning post on the last mile —loudly cheered—Fisher about four years ahead of Taylor, and eight ahead of Rintoul. Owing to the thaw the track was in a very heavy condition. Had it been otherwise, no doubt even faster time would have been made. Nevertheless, this was pronounced by all present one of the best that has ever taken place in this city.

Immediately after the race, the Club walked to Cote des Neiges, to partake of an excellent dinner at Moore's Hotel, to which about sixty gentlemen sat down. The necks of all the turkeys, geese and chickens in the village had been twisted for the occasion, and a sirloin of beef weighing 100 lbs lay smoking on the table, to which the hungry snowshoers did ample justice. The usual toasts, speeches, jokes, etc., were gone through. Several original songs were sung by Messrs. Murray, Hughes and Parys, and about ten o'clock the company returned to town, highly delighted with the evening's entertainment.

Challenge to Snow-Shoers. The Montreal Snow-Shoe Club offer a Silver Cup (value $40), as a prize to be competed for by members of the Club against all comers, for a five mile walk. Entries to be made within ten days of this date, with the Secretary of this Club, Mr. Geo. Parys, by whom conditions of the race will be made known. Montreal, Jan. 17, 1860.

BY-LAWS OF THE MONTREAL SNOW SHOE CLUB

ARTICLE 1. The name of this Association shall be the "Montreal Snow-Shoe Club," and is established with a view to encourage a taste for the exercise of Snow Shoeing.

2. The number of its members shall not exceed One Hundred and Fifty.

3. Its Officers shall consist of a President, Two Vice-Presidents, and a Secretary and Treasurer, to be elected annually by the Club, at a meeting to be held in the month of December.

The Office of Secretary and Treasurer shall be filled by one and the same person.

A Committee of Management, of three Members, shall also be elected at the same time, who with the above Officers shall constitute a Committee to manage all the business of the club. This Committee of Management shall act as councillors to the President.

4. It shall be the duty of the President to preside at all Meetings, to see that the Rules of the Club are strictly enforced, to order Special Meetings of the Club upon the request of the Committee of Management, or of any ten Members, the request of the latter to be given in writing, to declare the votes, and to have a general supervision over the affairs of the Club.

In the absence of the President, one of the Vice-Presidents shall perform his duties.

5. The Secretary and Treasurer shall collect all annual subscriptions, and keep a regular account thereof, which must be submitted to the Committee of Management whenever required, and he can make no disbursements without the President's order in writing, countersigned by the Chairman of the Committee of Management, which Chairman shall be elected by and from among themselves, at their first annual meeting, to hold office during the year.

As Secretary he shall keep a record of the transactions at all meetings, notify members of their election, and conduct all the correspondence of the Club.

6. The Committee of Management shall have charge of, and with the President control all matters affecting the welfare of the Club, subject to this constitution, and decide all questions or differences that may arise affecting the interest of the Club. They shall hold meetings as often as the business of the club requires, and whenever summoned by the President. At any meeting of this Committee, three shall form a quorum for the transaction of business.

They shall have power also to fill any vacancies which may occur among themselves, or other offices of the Club, until the next annual meeting.

This Committee, or any member of it, or any Officer of the Club, can be removed from office, by a vote of two-thirds of the members present, at a meeting called for that special purpose.

7. Every Candidate shall be proposed in writing, by one member and seconded by another; and such proposition handed to the Secretary, at one meeting, to be laid before the next meeting for approval, the election to be by ballot; *one black ball* or *no* in five *yeas*, to exclude. Every member on being elected shall sign the Constitution, and shall pay his dues within ten days. The proposer and seconder to be held responsible to the Club for the annual subscription.

8. The Club shall walk twice in each week during the winter season, the days to be selected at the annual meeting, but they may by changed by a majority of votes, at a meeting called for that purpose. The election of members can take place at these meetings according to the above forms.

9. Annual Races or Games, shall take place in February, in each year, the programme, time and prizes to be decided upon by the Officers of the Club, at a meeting to be held in January.

In determining upon which, they shall adopt those exercises which are most conducive to health and strength, such as Walking, Running, and Leaping.

10. The Annual Subscription shall be two Dollars, payable annually, in advance. The annual meeting shall be held in December, for election of Officers, reception of Secretary-Treasurer's Report, and other matters relating to the welfare of the Club.

11. A member who may have been guilty of ungentlemanly conduct shall be liable and may be expelled by a majority of a meeting of the Club, specially called for that purpose, with six day's previous notice.

12. One month's previous notice being given, this Constitution may be altered or amended at any meeting specially called for that purpose, by a vote of two-thirds of the members present.

Chapter 16

WORK SPORTS

The middle decades of the nineteenth century witnessed new forms of sport in North America which combined work and play. Premodern society featured such pastimes as corn-huskings, barn-raisings, and wood chopping and plough-pulling contests. The advent of modernization introduced several machines which influenced the development of sport and recreation in many ways. Two types of contests which merged work with amusement during this period were fire engine competitions and steamboat racing.

Volunteer fire companies were an important social institution in cities in the United States prior to the Civil War. Before the advent of professional fire departments communities depended on groups of men who met for fraternal purposes and who fought fires as an exciting hobby. The clubs generally enrolled working class members and often had close ties to local political organizations. They sometimes sponsored sporting associations such as the earliest baseball clubs. Intense ethnic and political rivalries among the fire companies frequently led to pitched battles at the sites of conflagrations, as two or more groups fought each other while the building burned away.

Fire engine competition provided a more peaceful if not a more entertaining method of evaluating the talent of fire fighters and the quality of their engines. The contests were designed to test the speed of the companies in reaching a fire and also the power of their machines and their skill in pumping and directing a stream of water. The accounts included below illustrate fire engine playing as it was practiced in Milwaukee and Boston during the late 1850s.

Steamboats were one of the first inventions of the Industrial Revolution to influence the rise of modern sport. Their greatest importance lay in providing easier transportation to athletic contests; yet they constituted a form of competition in their own right as their captains raced their vessels on rivers, lakes, and sounds. Steamboat racing was a very exciting but also an extremely risky and dangerous activity. During the years before reliable telegraph communication or extensive railroad lines steam powered ships were the most important means of carrying news and people across the land. Since the people of the United States were both time-conscious and appreciative of speed in any form, it is not surprising that steamboat racing captured their imagination. Even a series of catastrophes on the lower Mississippi during the 1830s did not stem the enthusiasm for these contests in all regions. Most of these events resulted from spontaneous challenges; only a few were scheduled in advance. Local newspapers and weekly sporting periodicals reported challenges and terms of the most notable races and provided detailed accounts of the results. "Dreadful Calamity on the Hudson River" reports the results of a race between two steamships in 1852 which ended in disaster when one of the boats caught fire. It is followed by two documents which recapture the excitement of steamboat racing on the upper Mississippi during the late 1850s. The first one is from the memoirs of a former pilot; the second is an excerpt from the reminiscences of a Republican politician.

FIRE COMPANY COMPETITION

Improvements in the design and construction of fire equipment during the 1850s combined with traditional rivalries among fire companies to produce the new sport of fire engine playing. Some of the trials matched local groups, others brought together associations from several cities. The selections printed here suggest that the participants were evaluated on both their appearance and performance. The first document describes a contest held in Milwaukee and is reprinted from the New York Clipper, 20 June 1857, p. 68. The second recounts an exhibition that featured groups from Boston, Lawrence, Massachusetts, and Philadelphia. It first appeared in the New York Clipper, 11 September 1858, p. 164.

FIREMEN "OUT WEST."
TRIAL OF MASHEENS

The semi-annual inspection came off on the 1st inst., and was a creditable affair to the city as well as to the Department. At the foot of Martin street, on an island well adapted for the trial, the companies took suction and played, at first through 100 feet of hose, a perpendicular stream, one minute and a half. On this trial No. 1 was awarded the broom. On the second trial each engine played through two lengths of hose 100 feet each; No. 3 was awarded the broom. The hose of No. 1 burst on this trial, and as they did not seem disposed to try again, the companies proceeded to the final and last trial of playing, into a tank arranged for the purpose, through 400 feet of hose, commencing with No. 1., with the following result:

Engine	Depth of Water in Tank	Amount
No. 1	3 feet 6 1/2 inches	839 gallons
2	filled tank in 3 min. 25 sec.	
3	3 feet 5 3/4 inches	817 "
4	3 feet 4 1/2 inches	799 "
5	filled tank in 3 min. 28 sec.	
6	3 feet 3 1/2 inches	779 "
1 (second trial) filled tank in 3 min. 40 sec.		

No. 1 turned out strong, and looked well, as they always do, in their grey coats and red hats.

No. 2 looked well in their red coats and black hats, and is a company of which any city may well feel proud.

No. 3 looked well, and turned in good numbers. Oregon boys are hard to beat, and never say die.

No. 4 presented a fine appearance in their new rig. New York fire hats and red jackets, and always more "Ready than Rough" except when taken hold of.

No. 5 appeared in glased caps and white shirts, and looked finely.

No. 6 looked well in their red jackets. They are having a new engine built for them by Mr. Button, of Waterford. It is to cost $2,500, and will be a splendid machine. This company is a credit to the city.

Hook and Ladder No. 1 appeared well in their red jackets, and are an efficient arm of the service. They turned out with full drag rope.

After the trial the companies marched to Market Square, where they were dismissed, and after giving three cheers for their Chief Engineer and associates, proceeded to their respective houses.

GRAND TRIAL OF STEAM FIRE ENGINES
ON BOSTON COMMON

A PUBLIC trial of steam fire engines, under the auspices of a committee of the Boston City Council, took place on Tuesday, 31st ultimo. The weather was highly favorable, and there were some thousands of spectators present to witness the work of competition. The prizes offered were for the best engine, $500; second best, $300; third best, $200.

The conditions of the trial required that every engine should be provided with Aldcroft's steam guage and water pressure guage; also that the engines shall, under 60 pounds pressure of steam, draft water through suction hose, and deliver it through 200 feet of hose into a guaged tank—the time to be correctly taken; that each engine shall then play five minutes with the same pressure of steam, horizontally, through 200 feet of hose; that each in turn, with the same head of steam, shall play *vertically* through 200 feet of hose; that all the engines shall simultaneously, under 60 pounds of steam, proceed to draft and play for two hours through a pipe 1 1/4 inches in diameter, that at no time shall the pressure on any of the engine boilers be more than 120 pounds to the square inch; that no engine shall be allowed to play through open hose, or through a pipe nozzle of less than 1 1/4 inches in diameter at the mouth; that, in case of an accident to any engine, it shall have another trial, but no more; that the leading hose be of the usual size, and provided by the city.

The principles on which judgment will be founded by the committee of Judges, are to be simplicity of construction, weight as compared with efficiency; time of generating steam from cold water to 60 pounds pressure upon the inch of the boiler; the amount of pressure gained when delivering the greatest quantity of water and at the greatest distance and height; the greatest amount of water delivered into a tank in a given time; the greatest vertical height and longest horizontal distance of stream; the best workmanship with regard to service and durability, and cheapness in price.

STEAM FIRE ENGINES ENTERED

No. 1—The "Lawrence," built by Scott & Bean, of Lawrence, Mass., in June last.

No. 2—The "Elisha Smith," built by Geo. M. Bird and Co., East Boston, Mass., this year.

No. 3—The "New Era," built at the Boston Locomotive Works, Harrison Avenue, Boston, Mass., this year.

No. 4—The "Philadelphia, No. 1," built by Rancy, Neafie, and Co., Philadelphia, Penn., this year.

The Philadelphia commenced the proceedings about 9 o'clock, A.M. She is a beautifully constructed and compact machine, as neat as a new pin, and manned by a crew of as smart-looking men as could be scared up. They were dressed in red shirts, with black neck-ties, black pants, shielded to the knee with patent leather, and black glazed caps. They were 25 in number, and commanded by Captain John Neil. She has a perpendicular boiler; and, at a distance, looks like a miniature locomotive. She was succeeded by the Elisha Smith, the New Era and the Lawrence in the order named. The following shows the time required to get up the steam to the mark of 60 lbs. pressure on the boiler:

Philadelphia	11m	58s	New Era	18m	21s
Elisha Smith	13	51	Lawrence (2d trial)	10	29 1/2
Lawrence	14	10 1/2			

TIME SPENT IN FILLING THE TANK (2,500 GALLS.)

Philadelphia	8	28	New Era	7	32 1/2
Elisha Smith	8	25	Lawrence	8	35

DISTANCE PLAYED HORIZONTALLY

Philadelphia	163 feet	New Era	135 feet
Elisha Smith	140 feet	Lawrence	154 1/2 feet

PERPENDICULAR HEIGHT PLAYED

Philadelphia	110 feet	New Era	95 feet
Elisha Smith	125 feet	Lawrence	110 feet

On the following day the Common was again crowded with the citizens of Boston, to witness the closing feature of the trial of the competing steam fire engines. The programme provided that the engines should start from the centre gate of Charles street mall—each drawn by two horses, and proceed by Charles street, Brighton street, Tremont and Beacon streets, (round the Common) back to Charles street gate, at which they should enter the Common, and proceed to the Frog Pond, where they are to draw their own water and play. The engines were restricted as to the time they should fire up after the start—the furnace to be kindled when about a fourth of the distance from home.

TRIAL OF THE PHILADELPHIA

At 11 hours 6 minutes and 20 seconds the Philadelphia started—arrived at the firing point at 11 hours 15 minutes 0 seconds—and arrived at 11 hours 19 minutes 45 seconds—making the whole distance in 13 minutes and 25 seconds.

The time spent by the Philadelphia from the start until she began to play, was *twenty-one minutes and six seconds*. The distance round the Common is a mile and an eighth.

TRIAL OF THE ELISHA SMITH

This engine started at 11 hours 11 minutes and 39 seconds—passed the firing point 11 hours 25 minutes and 30 1/2 seconds—arrived at the pond at 11 hours 29 minutes 43 seconds—making the whole distance in 18 minutes 4 seconds.

The Elisha Smith was driven round at a steady pace, and made all the turnings at a slow trot. She was in full play in *twenty-six minutes and forty seconds from the start*.

TRIAL OF THE LAWRENCE

The Lawrence started at 11 hours 15 minutes and 23 seconds—passed the firing point at 11 hours 29 minutes 11 seconds—and reached the pond at 11 hours 32 minutes 47 1/2 seconds. She thus made the round of the Common in 17 minutes and 24 1/2 seconds. At 11 hours 45 minutes 58 seconds the Lawrence began to throw her stream—thus requiring, between the start and that consummation, *thirty minutes and thirty-five seconds*.

The result of the trial was, that the Philadelphia received the first prize of $500, the Lawrence the second prize of $300, and the Elisha Smith the third prize of $200.

STEAMBOAT RACING

Steamboat racing continued to be popular on both the Hudson and Mississippi rivers prior to 1860. At 7 a.m. on 28 July 1852 the *Henry Clay* and *Armenia* left Albany for a fateful journey down the Hudson River. A rate war between the two competing lines contributed to the rivalry between the two ships. Although the owners of each boat disavowed any intention of racing, it soon became clear from the action of the boilers and the speed of the boats that both captains and crews intended to beat their rivals to New York City. But even though *Henry Clay* attained a comfortable lead over *Armenia,* it maintained full steam until a fire engulfed the boat near Riverdale, the last community on the Hudson north of Manhattan. The ship reached the shore, but eighty passengers (including many women and children) drowned after they jumped to save themselves from the fire. The catastrophe led to the passage of the Steamboat Inspection Act by the New York state legislature in 1852. That law ended steamboat racing on the Hudson. The following report and editorial on the disaster are reprinted from the New-York Daily Times, 29 and 30 July, 1852. The second and third concluding documents describe races on the upper Mississippi which had happier outcomes. They are reprinted from George B. Merrick, *Old Times on the Upper Mississippi. The Recollections of a Steamboat Pilot from 1854 to 1853* (Cleveland, Ohio, 1909), pp.143-151 and *The Reminiscences of Carl Schurz* (New York, 1907), Vol. II, pp. 152-157.

DREADFUL CALAMITY ON THE HUDSON RIVER
THE FINALE OF A RACE

We are called upon this morning to record another heartrending catastrophe, which has filled our City with gloom, and made vacant places at many a household hearth. Our noble Hudson River was yesterday the scene of a calamity which it is feared, when all its dread horrors are known, will be found to almost equal in disaster the memorable catastrophe which befel the steamer *Swallow* some years since.

About 4 o'clock, yesterday afternoon, intelligence was received that the steamer *Henry Clay*, Capt. TALLMAN, had been burned on the passage from Albany, and that a number of lives were lost....

The steamers *Henry Clay* and *Armenia* left Albany at 7 o'clock yesterday morning for New-York, the latter a little ahead, each crowded with passengers,—the former having between four and five hundred on board. It is stated that the boats commenced racing from the start—the boats belonging, of course, to rival lines. All the landings were missed, in the eagerness of the race, until Hudson was reached. Here the *Armenia* made the landing first, and the *Henry Clay* was obliged to wait until her rival's departure, before she could get to the dock. The *Armenia*, of course, again got the start, taking the west channel of the river. Her competitor followed on the east side of the river—the channels being separated for some distance by a grassy flat. When the boats reached the lower end of this flat, they were about abreast of each other, each striving to make the next landing (Kingston, we should suppose it to be from the description) ahead of the other. The *Armenia*, it will be seen, was nearest the shore on which Kingston is situated. The *Clay*, however, crowded her so hard that they came in collision, and ran side by side for some distance, the wheel-house of the *Armenia* sustaining, meantime, considerable damage.

The passengers, with the exception of a reckless few, had exhibited much alarm during the entire passage thus far, apprehending some fatal result to the hazardous race. When the boats came in collision their alarm increased so much that several ladies fainted, and many others gave expression to their fears in loud outcries and tears. It is proper to state here, that Capt. TALLMAN was confined to his room by sickness, and did not assume command at all. Also, that THOMAS COLLYER, one of the owners of the boat, was on board. We are told that, after the collision, four gentlemen went to the persons who were in command, stating the consternation of the ladies, and remonstrating against the fearful risk to which the passengers were being subjected, and begging that the race should cease. At this time, the heat in the vicinity of the engine and boiler rooms was so great that it had become almost impossible to pass from one end of the vessel to the other. This fact was mentioned as an evidence of the hazardous efforts which were being made to secure a fruitless victory, at the expense of the comfort, if not the lives, of all on board. The remonstrances were unavailing. The reply was, that the boat was getting along very well, and that there was no danger to be apprehended. The race accordingly continued,—the *Henry Clay* succeeding, finally, in crowding her competitor so near the shore, that she was compelled to drop astern, in order to keep from running aground. The *Clay* made the landing, took on board the few passengers in waiting, and secured the few dollars charged for their fare. At what price the paltry sum was obtained, the melancholy sequel will show.

As may be supposed, the feelings of those on board—a large majority of them ladies, many of whom were without protectors—had by this time become so excited that few were prepared to act with presence of mind in the dread emergency in which they were soon to be plunged. The *Henry Clay* maintained her vantage, and came through the Highlands a short distance ahead of the *Armenia*. Emerging from the narrow passage, the latter fell rapidly astern of the *Clay*, which passed Sing Sing some four miles ahead. In the meantime dinner had been served, and the passengers were grouped on the main and promenade decks, somewhat reassured, now that the boats were so far separated. At about a quarter before 3 o'clock, just after passing the village of Yonkers, the thrilling cry of "Fire!" resounded from the centre of the vessel. A glance towards the engine-room showed a column of smoke pouring up from one of the hatches. Almost simultaenously, the flames leaped from the hold near the boiler rooms; and in less than one minute the entire vicinity of the machinery enveloped in flames, cutting off all communication between forward and aft. A western steamboat Captain, who was on board, expresses his conviction that tar, resin, or some other highly inflammable matter must have been in use in the boiler room for fuel, as wood—even heated as was every part of the vessel, near the machinery, by the unusual fires of the day,—could not, by any possibility, have ignited and raised a dense wall of flame, in the few seconds which elapsed after the first alarm, and before communication fore and aft was cut off. This testimony is confirmed by other gentlemen with whom we conversed.

Panic and confusion now assumed the reins. The realization of the gloomy forebodings of the morning seemed to be at hand. Men, women and children, were thrown into an alarming state of confusion. Ladies were calling upon their husbands for succor; mothers clapsed their children to their bosoms, with the energy of despair, as they retreated from the rapidly-spreading destruction. Husbands who were on the forward deck strove in vain to reach their partners left but a moment before in the after-saloon. Groans, cries, shrieks, imprecations, and prayers, were mingled in mournful chorus. From the instant that the fire was discovered despair seemed to settle upon the hearts of a large portion of the passengers, and shut out from view altogether the hope calculated to induce self-possession and effectual efforts for safety.

A cry for "the boats" was raised; but no boats could be found. We cannot ascertain that a single yawl or life-boat was on board the steamer. If there was one such, we are assured that none was brought in use. Nor can we learn that there was any effective apparatus on board with which to extinguish a fire. At all events, every effort to save the vessel became so utterly hopeless, within five minutes after the flames broke out, that it was abandoned, and the steamer's head was turned toward the east bank of the River in order to run her ashore. The necessity for this movement at the earliest moment was fully apparent. Already were the wheel-houses wrapped in flames, the engineers had been driven from their posts, and the devastating element, fanned by a stiff South wind, was sweeping rapidly towards the after saloon, where the greater number of the passengers were located. The dense volume of smoke, too, was blown directly aft, laden with burning cinders, and subjecting them to imminent danger of suffocation. In the meantime, the despairing shrieks for help seemed to be redoubled. It was instinctively seen that, as the steamer would strike the shore bow on, there being no communication from aft to forward, even the approach to the river's bank gave but little hope to the helpless women and children who were astern. And there they stood—the young and the old—battling, inch by inch, with the flame, suffering a thousand deaths in the terrible struggle for life, until the vesel struck, leaving those who were aft some 250 or 300 feet from the shore. At this time it is estimated there were nearly 300 persons huddled together on the after guards, hesitating in agony or terror whether to meet death by the flame or the flood—these dread alternatives, apparently, being the only bitter choice.

The place where the steamer struck is on the river bank, two and a half miles below Yonkers. No boats were to be had there, of any description. The *Armenia* bore rapidly down, and sent our her boats, as also did a number of sailing vesels which were near; but at least a quarter of an hour elapsed after the *Clay* struck, ere any assistance came. In the meantime, the panic stricken unfortunates had nearly all been forced over the stern into the water, where many of them sustained themselves by swimming, or by the aid of a few floating boards, until rescued from their perilous condition. Others clung to the guards of the vessel, with the energy of desperation. The rudder and steering gear furnished temporary safety to others. A number succeeded in getting hold of the braces on the under side of the guards. Several ladies threw the end of a stern line overboard, let themselves down into the water, and sustained themselves by it until aid reached them, fortunately before the line, which was on fire, had become too weak to support them. But many others jumped frantically into the water, and sank to rise no more. A gentleman who was forward, and who got on shore soon after the vessel struck, says that not one of a number of ladies—some with children in their arms—whom he saw jump from the larboard side, were saved. He expresses the conviction that some fifty or sixty lives, at least, were lost....

THE CALAMITY ON THE RIVER

We have before us now a pretty fair amount of testimony in reference to the accident on board the *Henry Clay*. There is undeniably conflict among the statements. A large number of passengers declare that the steamboat had been racing from the time it left the wharf at Albany; and that the fire was due to excessive heat, engendered by the effort to create a large volume of steam. They ascribe the fearful calamity to this fact, and therefore cast the responsibility upon those having charge of the boat. Others, embracing the officers of the boat, and of the *Armenia*, which was supposed to be the other party in the race, deny entirely that the vessels had been trying their speed. A few of the passengers say that there had been racing for some distance down the river, but that their impression is that for the hour previous to the fire, the competition had ceased. As the crime charged upon the officers of the *Henry Clay* is one of terrible atrocity, amounting, indeed, to the sacrifice of scores of lives to the passion of a moment, it is due to them to weigh the evidence carefully. If it be true that the burning of the boat was caused by their recklessness, they should be visited with the most exemplary vengeance of the law, and their names consigned to infamy. If the event was one they could not anticipate or prevent, they should be most distinctly exonerated, for the odium of the crime is too weighty for the innocent to bear. Let us look for a moment at the evidence.

To the assertion that the boats were not racing, we have the testimony of the officers themselves; and of the pilot of the rival boat. But as these are interested parties, whose fame, and means of livelihood, and social positions are at stake in the business, their testimony is deserving of little weight. The pilot of the *Armenia* may be right in saying that that boat was not racing, for it is quite possible that a fast vessel may be moving at its ordinary speed, and an ambitious but less active rival is exerting itself to the uttermost. But he has no right to pronounce upon any fact in reference to the *Henry Clay*. There are others, who concede that there had been racing, but suppose it to have ceased at the time of the catastrophe. Upon examining the testimony of these gentlemen, it appears that the distance of three or four miles intervening between the boats at the moment is the foundation of their belief. They assume that the *Armenia* had abandoned the race, because it had fallen so far behind. They do not conceal the fact that they were surprised at the continued efforts on board the *Clay* to make time, and that they expostulated with the engineer about it. They admit the high speed, but are unprepared to ascribe it to competition with the *Armenia*. As these witnesses give us opinions instead of facts, they are not the best that can be had; and as it was quite as much of an object with the officers of the *Clay* to make a wide difference in the time of the arival of the two boats at New-York as to get one boat's length ahead, the opinions do not amount to much. The vessels might have been ten miles apart, and still be racing. The evidence to the contrary of that fact, amounts, we conceive, to precisely nothing at all.

That the boats were racing, there is an overwhelming amount of evidence. It can be proved that the officers of the *Clay* left Albany with the avowed purpose of "beating" the *Armenia;* that the competition was anticipated and watched for all along the river; that in his eagerness to win, the pilot of the *Clay* ran his boat into the wheelhouse of his competitor; that tar, or some other pitchy substance, was employed to inflame the fires; that the boat amidships was so hot as to render it almost impassable at the point; and that the obvious effort to triumph induced a large number of passengers to leave the boat at various points, through apprehension of some fatality. It is proved that passengers remonstrated with the officers, even after the *Armenia* was left far behind, against the unnecessary speed at which the vessel was moving. It is said that the safety-valve was fastened down. A variety of statements are before us of similar kind; and we cannot hesitate to say that the whole case tends strongly to convict the officers of utterly unprincipled recklessness. Allowance must, of course, be made for the excitement under which the testimony we have is given. It is not impossible that the individual suspicions of passsengers only gather the consistency of facts from apposition and comparison. But when all allowance is made, there is an awful cloud of guilt resting upon the reputations of those in control of the ill-fated steamboat.

The charge that lies against them is, that upon the wish to eclipse a rival boat, and to secure way passengers by arriving earlier at the landing-places, they staked the lives of a throng of people, estimable men, lovely and beloved women, and children, whom parents would have died for, and lost the stake. They are accused of causing sorrow and desolation in a hundred hearts. They stand indicted before public opinion for burning to death, fearfully, painfully, suddenly, a host of human beings. They are answerable for the despair, and heart-rending struggle for life, and the eventual death of the women and children which the waves are still flinging upon the shore. The calamity, and grief, and suffering, which the casualty has caused, cannot be stated in exaggerated terms; and if the evidence before us be correct, the officers of the boat are responsible for every particle of it.

It is hardly necessary to speak of public duty in such a case. Obviously, prompt and examplary treatment is required. Proofs should be gathered carefully and dispassionately; and if, when they are summed up, they sustain the various charges, the prosecution should be urged at once and the heaviest penalty attached to homicide, be inflicted on the offenders. Any leniency must be, in the highest degreee, criminal. It would only tend to encourage a practice that should be terminated forever. All weak, collusion with the guilty, and every unmeritorious acquittal, will have their fruit in further homicides of the kind hereafter. Exemplary severity is imperatively required, and our laws must be miserably defective, if they fail to afford an equivalent remedy for the evil.

OLD TIMES ON THE UPPER MISSISSIPPI

It is popularly supposed that there was a great deal of racing on Western rivers in the olden time—in fact, that it was the main business of steamboat captains and owners, and that the more prosaic object, that of earning dividends, was secondary. There is a deal of error in such a supposition. At the risk of detracting somewhat from the picturesqueness of life on the upper Mississippi as it is sometimes delineated, it must in truth be said that little trial racing was indulged in, as compared with the lower river, or even with the preconceived notion of what transpired on the upper reaches. While there were many so-called steamboat races, these were, for the most part, desultory and unpremeditated. On the upper river, there never was such a race as that between the "Robert E. Lee" and the "Natchez," where both boats were stripped and tuned for the trial, and where neither passengers nor freight were taken on board to hinder or encumber in the long twelve hundred miles between New Orleans and St. Louis, which constituted the running track.

It is true, however, that whenever two boats happened to come together, going in the same direction, there was always a spurt that developed the best speed of both boats, with the result that the speediest boat quickly passed her slower rival, and outfooted her so rapidly as soon to leave her out of sight behind some point, not to be seen again, unless a long delay at some landing or woodyard enabled her to catch up.

These little spurts were in no sense races, such as the historic runs on the lower waters. They were in most cases a business venture, rather than a sporting event, as the first boat at a landing usually secured the passengers and freight in waiting. Another boat, following so soon after, would find nothing to add to the profits of the voyage.

Racing, as racing, was an expensive if not a risky business. Unless the boats were owned by their commanders, and thus absolutely under their control, there was little chance that permission would be obtained for racing on such a magnificent and spectacular scale as that usually depicted in fiction.

The one contest that has been cited by every writer on upper river topics, that has ever come under my observation, was the one between the "Grey Eagle" (Captain D. Smith Harris), and the "Itasca" (Captain David Whitten); and that was not a race at all. It is manifestly unfair to so denominate it, when one of the captains did not know that he was supposed to be racing with another boat until he saw the other steamer round a point just behind him. Recognizing the rival as following him far ahead of her regular time, he realized that she was doing something out of the ordinary. He came to the conclusion that Captain Harris was attempting to beat him into St. Paul, in order to be the first to deliver certain important news of which he also was the bearer. When this revelation was made, both boats were within a few miles of their destination, St. Paul.

Here are the details. In 1856, the first telegraphic message was flashed under the sea by the Atlantic cable—a greeting from Queen Victoria to President Buchanan. Captain D. Smith Harris had, the year before, brought out the "Grey Eagle," which had been built at Cincinnati at a cost of $60,000. He had built this boat with his own money, or at least a controlling interest was in his name. He had intended her to be the fastest boat on the upper river, and she was easily that. As her captain and practically her owner, he was at liberty to gratify any whim that might come into his head. In this case it occurred to him that he would like to deliver in St. Paul the Queen's message to the President ahead of any one else.

There was at that time no telegraph line into St. Paul. Lines ran to Dunleith, where the "Grey Eagle" was taking in cargo for St. Paul, and also to Prairie du Chien, where the "Itasca" was loading. Both boats were to leave at six o'clock in the evening. Captain Harris had sixty-one miles farther to run than had Captain Whitten. But Harris knew that he was racing, and Whitten did not, which made all the difference in the world.

Whitten soldiered along at his usual gait, stopping at every landing, putting off all cargo at each place, and taking on all that offered, and probably delayed to pass the compliments of the day with agents and other friends, as well as discuss the great message that he was bearing. The "Grey Eagle," on the contrary, stopped at only a few of the principal landings, and took on no freight after leaving Dunleith. She did not even put off freight that she was carrying, but took it through to St. Paul and delivered it on her return trip. She carried the mail, but in delivering it a man stood on the end of one of the long stages run out from the bow, from which he threw the sacks ashore, the boat in the meantime running along parallel with the levee, and not stopping completely at any landing. Running far ahead of her time, there were no mail sacks ready for her, and there was no reason for stopping. The "Grey Eagle" had the best of soft coal, reinforced by sundry barrels of pitch, from which the fires were fed whenever they showed any signs of failing. With all these points in her favor, in addition to the prime fact that she was by far the swiftest steamboat that every turned a wheel on the upper river, it was possible for her to overtake the slower and totally unconcerned "Itasca," when only a few miles from St. Paul.

The race proper began when Whitten sighted the "Grey Eagle" and realized that Harris was trying to beat him into St. Paul in order to be the first boat to deliver the Queen's message. Then the "Itasca" did all that she was in her to do, and was beaten by less than a length. Harris throwing the message ashore from the roof, attached to a piece of coal, and thus winning the race by a handbreadth.

The time of the "Grey Eagle" from Dunleith, was eighteen hours; the distance, two hundred and ninety miles; speed per hour, 16 1/9 miles.

The "Itasca," run from Prairie du Chien to St. Paul in eighteen hours; distance, two hundred and twenty-nine miles; speed, 12 2/3 miles per hour.

The "Itasca" was far from being a slow boat, and had Whitten known that Harris was "racing" with him, the "Grey Eagle" would not have come within several hours of catching her.

As a race against time, however, the run of the "Grey Eagle" was really something remarkable. A sustained speed of over sixteen miles an hour for a distance of three hundred miles, upstream, is a wonderful record for an inland steamboat anywhere, upper river or lower river; and the pride which Captain Harris had in his beautiful boat was fully justified. A few years later, she struck the Rock Island Bridge and sank in less than five minutes, a total loss. It was pitiful to see the old Captain leaving the wreck, a broken-hearted man, weeping over the loss of his darling, and returning to his Galena home, never again to command a steamboat. He had, during his eventful life on the upper river, built, owned, or commanded scores of steamboats; and this was the end.

The "Northerner," of the St. Louis Line, was a fast boat, and an active contestant for the "broom." The boat that could, and did run away from, or pass under way, all other boats, signalized her championship by carrying a big broom on her pilot house. When a better boat passed her under way, the ethics of the river demanded that she pull the broom down and retire into seclusion until she in turn should pass the champion and thus regain her title. The struggle on the upper river lay between the "Northerner" and the "Key City." The "Grey Eagle" was in a class by herself, and none other disputed her claim, while actively disputing those of all others of the Minnesota Packet Company, of which the "Key City" was the champion and defender.

The two rivals got together at Hudson, twenty miles up Lake St. Croix—whether by accident or agreement it is impossible to say, but probably by agreement. They had twenty miles of deep water, two miles wide, with only four close places to run. It was a fair field for a race, and they ran a fair and a fine one. For miles they were side by side. Sometimes a spurt would put one a little ahead; and again the other would get a trifle the most steam and the deepest water, and so creep ahead a little. When they came into Prescott, at the foot of the lake, the "Key City" was a clear length ahead, her engineers having saved a barrel or two of resin for the home stretch. With this lead she had the right of way to turn the point and head up the river. Ned West was at the wheel, with an assistant to "pull her down" for him, and he made a beautiful turn with his long and narrow craft; while the "Northerner" had to slow down and wait a minute or two before making the turn. In the meantime the "Key City's" whistles were blowing, her bell ringing, and her passengers and crew cheering, while a man climbed to the roof of the pilot house and lashed the broom to the finial at the top, the crown of laurels for the victor.

The lower river stern-wheel steamer "Messenger" was also a very fast boat. On one occasion she came very near wresting the broom from the "Key City," in a race through Lake Pepin, where also there was plenty of water and sea room. The "Key City" had a barge in tow and thus was handicapped. The "Messenger" seemed, therefore, likely to win the race, as she had passed the former under way. Within four miles of the head of the lake, Captain Worden of the "Key City" ordered the barge cast adrift, having placed a few men on board of it, with an anchor and cable to use in case of necessity. Thus freed from the encumbrance, he put on steam and passed his rival before reaching Wacouta, in spite of the most strenuous efforts on the part of the latter to retain her lead. Running far enough ahead of the "Messenger" to render the maneuver safe, Worden crossed her bow, and circling around her ran back and picked up his barge.

In this race, it was said by passengers who were on board the two boats, the flames actually blazed from the tops of the tall chimneys on both crafts; and on both, men were stationed on the roof playing streams of water from lines of hose on the chimney breechings, to prevent the decks from igniting. Under such conditions it is easy to see how a boat might catch fire and burn. And yet the passengers liked it. Had they been the owners of casks of ham, as legend relates of a passenger on a lower river boat under like circumstances, there is no doubt they would have made an oblation of them to the gods of heat and steam, rather than have the other boat win.

The earliest recorded race run on the upper river was that between the "Nominee," owned and commanded by Captain Orren Smith, and the "West Newton" (Captain Daniel Smith Harris), in 1852. In this event but one boat actually ran, for Harris had no confidence in the ability of his boat to win, and not possessing the temper that would brook defeat, he declined to start. The "Nominee" completed the run from Galena to St. Paul and return, a distance of seven hundred miles, making all landings and handling all freight and passengers, in fifty-five hours and forty-nine minutes, an average rate of speed of 12 1/2 miles an hour, half of it against and half with the current. This was good running, for the boats of that time. As there was no other boat to compete for the honor, the "Nominee" carried the broom until she sank at Britt's Landing, below La Crosse, in 1854.

Bunnell, in his very interesting *History of Winona*, says:

"Captain Orren Smith was a very devout man, and while he might indulge in racing, for the honor of his boat, he believed in keeping the Sabbath, and as long as he owned the boats which he commanded, he would not run a minute after twelve o'clock Saturday night, but would tie his boat to the bank, wherever it might be, and remain at rest until the night following at twelve o'clock, when he would resume the onward course of his trip. If a landing could be made near a village or settlement where religious services could be held, the people were invited on board on Sunday, and if no minister of the gospel was at hand, the zealous Captain would lead in such service as suited his ideas of duty. But the Captain's reverence and caution did not save his boat, and she sank below La Crosse in the autumn of 1854.

Two of the boats on which I served, the "Kate Cassell" and the "Fanny Harris," while not of the slow class, yet were not ranked among the fast ones; consequently we had many opportunities to pass opposition boats under way, and to run away from boats that attempted to humiliate us.

There was a great difference in boats. Some were built for towing, and these were fitted with engines powerful enough, if driven to their full capacity, to run the boat under, when the boat had on barges in tow. Other boats had not enough power to pull a shad off a gridiron. It was the power that cost money. A boat intended solely for freighting, and which consequently could take all the time there was, in which to make the trip, did not require the boilers and engines of a passenger packet in which speed was a prime factor in gaining patronage.

There is great satisfaction in knowing that the boat you are steering is just a little faster than the one ahead or behind you. There is still more satisfaction in feeling, if you honestly can, that you are just a little faster as a pilot than the man who is running the other boat. The two combined guarantee, absolutely, a proper ending to any trial of speed in which you may be engaged. Either one of them alone may decide the race, as a fast pilot is able to take his boat over a long course at a better rate of speed than a man not so well up in his business. If both men are equally qualified, then it is certain that the speediest boat will win.

What conditions determine the speed of two boats, all observable terms being equal? Nobody knows. The "Key City" and the "Itasca" were built for twins. Their lines, length, breadth, and depth of hold were the same; they had the same number and size boilers, and the parts of their engines were interchangeable; yet the "Key City" was from one to three miles an hour the faster boat, with the same pilots at the wheel. It was a fruitful topic for discussion on the river; but experts never reached a more enlightening conclusion than, "Well, I don't know." They didn't.

The boats of the old Minnesota Packet Company averaged better than those of a later era. In the run from Prairie du Chien to St. Paul, as noted above, the "Itasca" averaged twelve miles an hour, upstream, handling all her freight and passengers. The schedule for the Diamond Jo Line boats, in 1904, allowed eight miles an hour upstream, and eleven downstream, handling freight and passengers.

REMINISCENCES OF CARL SCHURZ

My return home from Minnesota was no less characteristic of the western country than the campaign had been. I took passage on a Mississippi steamboat down to La Crosse. Steamboat travel on the Western rivers, which was soon to be affected by the competition of railroads, was then still in full bloom. Most of the passenger boats were large and filled out in a style which at that period was thought to be gorgeous. Many of them served breakfasts, dinners, and suppers that appeared excellent to an unsophisticated taste, and there prevailed ordinarily a tone of hilarious animation among the passengers. On the river south of St. Louis and on the Missouri the clatter of the poker chip and, occasionally, also the crack of a pistol formed part of the entertainment. On the upper Mississippi such things were not so customary and the passengers indulged themselves in more harmless amusements, although, it must be admitted, betting sometimes was lively. I have forgotten the name of the fine boat on which I traveled, but will call her the "Flying Cloud." It so happened that a boat of different ownership, but of about the same size, started at the same time down the river. Let us call her the "Ocean Wave." It was one of those bright, sunny, autumn mornings, which, in the Northwest, are pecuilarly beautiful—an atmosphere so delightfully strong as to fill one with a sense of jubilation. It was my first journey on one of those great steamboats and I enjoyed it beyond measure. When we passed the majestic bluffs of Lake Pepin the "Ocean Way" seemed to be gaining on our "Flying Cloud," and my fellow passengers began to yield forthwith to an irrepresible feeling that this must not be. At first this feeling seemed to be confined to the men, but soon the women, too, began to show an interest in the matter that constantly grew more lively. They crowded around the captain, a short, broad-shouldered, and somewhat grumpy looking man, who paced the "hurricane deck" with an air of indifference. Would he permit the "Ocean Wave" to get ahead? he was asked. "Would you like to be blown up?" he asked in return. "No," was the answer, "we would not like to be blown up, but we don't want the "Ocean Wave" to beat us either." The captain looked up with a grim smile, said nothing, and walked away.

After a while the thumping of the engine grew louder, the guttural, raucous breath-ing of the smokestacks heavier and more feverish, the clouds of smoke rolling up from them blacker and more impetuous, and the quiver of the big vessel, as it rushed through the water, more shuddering. At the same time we noticed that the "Ocean Wave," which was almost abreast of us, showed the same symptoms of extraordinary commotion. She even seemed to have anticipated us somewhat in her preparations for the contest and forged ahead most vigorously. Indeed, a cheer went up from her decks, her passengers evidently thinking that the "Ocean Wage" would soon leave us behind. Our people cheered back defiantly, and the "Flying Cloud" again put in an extra throb.

So we "were in" for a regular Mississippi steamboat race, and I knew from report that such races were sometimes won not by the swiftest boat, but by the one whose boilers could keep longest from bursting. I had often heard the story told of an old lady who before taking passage on a Mississippi steamboat exacted a solemn vow from the captain that he would not race, but who, when another steamboat tried to run ahead, asked the captain not to permit it, and, when the captain told her he had not fuel enough to make more speed, informed him that she had some barrels of pork among the cargo, and would he not have them put in the fire to make better steam? I must confess, when I saw the "Ocean Wave" trying hard to pass us, I keenly appreciated the psychologi-cal truth of that anecdote. I see our captain now before me, as he stood on the upper deck, with his left foot on its low railing, his elbow resting on his knee and his chin on his fist, his cheek full of tobacco, which he was chewing nervously, and his glitter-ing eye fixed upon some spot ahead. From time to time he would turn his head and shout a hoarse order up to the pilot house. The passengers crowding around him, men and women, were almost wild with excitement, which vented itself in all sorts of ex-clamations, some of which, I regret to say, were quite profane. Suddenly the captain looked up and with so much of a smile as the tobacco quid in his mouth permitted, he muttered, "Now, I've got that "Ocean Wave," d—her!" Then we noticed that the "Ocean Wave" suddenly "slowed up" and fell behind, and our "Flying Cloud" shot forward, far ahead. Our passengers sent up a triumphant shout and seemed besides themselves with joy. It turned out that the channel had considerably narrowed so as not to be wide enough for two boats, and made at the same time a pretty sharp turn, and that our boat, having the inside of the curve, had succeeded in rushing into the narrow pass before the "Ocean Wave" could reach it, thus forcing our rival to drop behind, lest she run into us or aground.

But this victorious maneuver did not altogether relieve us of our anxieties. After a while, our fuel being much reduced, we had to land near a big pile of cordwood to take in a new supply. Our passengers were dismayed. "Never mind," said the captain," the "Ocean Wave" will have to take in wood, too." No sooner had the "Flying Cloud" made fast near the woodpile than a large number of my fellow travelers jumped ashore to help the "roustabouts" take in the fuel and thus to shorten our delay. Everybody worked with the utmost ardor. While this was going on the "Ocean Wave" steamed majestically by, her people rending the air with their cheers. When we started again we saw her a formidable distance ahead. But our captain was right. Soon we beheld the "Ocean Wave" lying still to take in a fresh supply of firewood, and we expected to run by and leave her far in the rear. But we had reckoned without our host. Before we had reached her stoppingplace she hastily pulled in her gangplanks and started again. And now came the real tug-of-war. The whistles of both boats blew fierce notes of challenge. For a long stretch the channel seemed to be wide, and the boats ran side by side, neck and neck. The paddle-boxes sometimes almost touched each other. The passengers crowding the two decks were within speaking distance and jeered from one side to the other half good naturedly, half defiantly. Meanwhile the smokestacks heaved and puffed, and snorted, and the engines thumped and thundered, and the lightly built decks shook and quaked and creaked as if engaged in a desperate struggle for life. The captain now seemed to divide his time between the engine room and the pilot house, moving up and down with nervous quickness. Once, when he crossed the deck, I saw a delicate-looking woman stop him with something like anxiety in her eyes, and ask him whether it was "all safe." "Well," he grumbled, "I can slow down and drop behind if you say so!" The poor woman did not say so. She looked abashed as if she had been trying to do something very mean and contemptible, and the passengers cheered.

Both steamboats stopped at one or two places, to discharge and take on passengers and cargo. But they both did this with such marvelous rapidity that neither of them got an advantage. They had also occasion again for sharp maneuvering to get in one another's way where narrow places in the channel were reached. But luck was now on one side and then on the other, and the spirits of the passengers rose and fell accordingly, now to boisterously triumphant assurance, and then to gloomy wrath and even despondency. The two boats were evidently so well matched in quality and handled with skill and boldness so equal, that nobody could fortell the result of the race. The "Flying Cloud" people could not refrain from respecting the "Ocean Wave" very much.

At last La Crosse hove in sight. The end was near, and many hearts beat with anxious expectancy. The crowd on the deck grew still. Hardly anybody dared to say anything or to make any demonstration of his feelings. But now fortune favored us again. The boats were still side by side, doing their utmost with fearful energy. But they had to made a curve in order to swing to the landing place, and the "Flying Cloud"—was it owing to good luck or to the foresight of the captain?—had the advantage of the inside. Running full speed as long as it was possible, and stopping the engine only when it was absolutely necessary, the "Flying Cloud" touched the dock with a crash and had the lines fastened and the gangplanks thrown out with the utmost rapidity, while the "Ocean Wave" was just coming in. The victory was ours, and a tremendous shout of jubilation went up. I wonder whether there were not many of my fellow passengers who were not, like myself, when the excitement of that glorious day had subsided, glad to be on firm ground again, safe and sound, and thankful to the boilers of the "Flying Cloud" for having endured the dreadful strain without bursting!

Chapter 17

WRESTLING

The ancient sport of wrestling was still in its premodern form in North America during the mid-nineteenth century. At gymnasiums instructors taught the fundamentals of the sport along with the basic skills of sparring and fencing. As the following examples demonstrate, the sporting fraternity also patronized rough and tumble matches for prize money and side bets. These encounters were modeled after the bare knuckle boxing events of that era. They usually originated with a challenge which then led to formal articles of agreement that stipulated the rules, the legal holds, and the financial arrangements of the contest. Wrestling was far less popular then prize fighting during this era, but there were a few events which were reported in the sporting press. Among them are the following two accounts from the New York Clipper, 14 January, 1854 (no page), and 28 November, 1857, p. 251.

WRESTLING MATCH BETWEEN MINGO AND COIT
ARTICLES OF AGREEMENT

This is to certify that Caesar Coit and John Mingo do mutually agree to Wrestle on Tuesday afternoon, January 17, 1854, at 2 o'clock P.M. A Square Side Hold, best three falls out of five, according to the rules of Wrestling, for one hundred dollars aside. Parties are to toss for choice of first hold, viz. the odd hold. Each man is to stand fair, no dropping on hands or knees to avoid locks. Any man caught in the act of slipping his hold, and catching [and?] shall forfeit the money, providing he throw his man. A deposit of fifty dollars a side, put up the evening of January 9th, 1854, and the second deposit of fifty dollars, to be put up Monday evening, January 16th, 1854, at Molineaux's house, Metropolitan Shades, 1444 Second Street, Brooklyn, between the hours of seven and nine o'clock. Either party in failing to put up the second deposit on the evening stated, forfeits the first. Two files shall constitute a fall. There shall be two Judges and a referee chosen on the ground.

Signed }   Caesar Coit
}   John Mingo

MATCH BETWEEN COIT AND MINGO

Since the great wrestling match in Brooklyn, between Molineaux and Coit, which was won by the latter, there has been an extraordinary degree of excitement manifested by the friends of the respective men, as to their capabilities when matched in a fair and perfectly honest manner, according to the rules of wrestling, there having been some misunderstanding in regard to the former match. Challenges have passed between Coit and Molineaux, but there always appeared to be some obstacle in the way to frustrate the efforts making for a match. Coit having offered to wrestle Molineaux, for $500 a a side, the latter agreed to accept the challenge, but offered to make the stakes $1000. This was readily agreed to by the backers of Coit, and they repaired to the house of Molineaux to draw up articles of agreement, but Molineaux wishing the match to be made for three square back falls, out of five, which was not according to the challenge offered by Coit, the latter did not feel bound to accept it, and the match was for the time put off.

Molineaux, however, offered to match a man against Coit for the sum of $100 a side, which was accepted by the backers of Coit, and after Molineaux named his man, Mingo, and produced him, the match was made to take place on Tuesday last, Jan. 17th, at the Three Mile House, Fulton Avenue, Brooklyn. As soon as the match was made, each man went into training for the encounter, and the liveliest interest was soon shown by the citizens of Brooklyn and this city in the sport.

According to the articles of agreement as published in the Clipper last week, the men appeared on the ground at half past 3, Coit, accompanied by his second, whose name we could not learn, and Mingo, accompanied by Molineaux. Two gentlemen were appointed Judges, and Mr. J. C—y, an old sporter, was chosen Referee. The spot where the match took place was a large yard in the rear of the house capable of accommodating nearly two thousand individuals. Not only was this enclosure filled by anxious spectators, but the roofs of the adjoining buildings and fences were likewise covered. The ground was muddy and disagreeable, not withstanding the ring had been covered with tan.

As soon as all necessary arrangements had been made, the Judges, Referee, and backers of the men were each presented with a copy of the New York Clipper of Jan. 14, containing the articles of agreement, by which articles the match was to be governed. Coit, who is a man of short stature, being but little over five feet in height, though very muscular and powerful, and weighing about 150 lbs., was dressed in a striped shirt, plaid pants and belt. Mingo a tall man, though we should judge about the same weight as his adversary, was attired in red shirt, canvass drawers and without belt.

Previous to the men entering the ring, Molineaux, the backer of Mingo, appeared, and read the articles of agreement. He then stated that if "Coit won the money, he was perfectly welcome to it, and if we win it, we want it." He then retired to the corner of the ring, and a toss was made by the seconds for choice of hold, which was won by Coit, and the men were then brought to the scratch, betting 15 to 10 on Coit.

1st. Tussle.—Coit having taken his favorite hold, a severe struggle took place for the mastery, which lasted several minutes, when Coit succeeded in beautifully throwing his man, thus winning the first fall. Coit was now the favorite at 2 to 1.

2d Tussle.—Both men appeared at the scratch, when Mingo immediately took his favorite hold upon Coit, and at once the wrestlers went into hard work. With his hold, it was apparent that Mingo had the advantage, and in a short time Coit was thrown on two joints, which was declared a file for Mingo.

3d Tussle.—In this round there was much excitement and quarreling by the friends of the wrestlers. The men having appeared at the scratch, took their hold upon each other, and after some sharp work, both men went down, when Coit, it appeared, slipped his hold, and the Second of Mingo, in consequence thereof, claimed the fall for his man. Trouble immediately commenced; the ring was broken into, and there was a fair prospect of a general row. The judges, in the meantime, were appealed to, who declared no decision would be given until the ring was cleared. Order was soon after, partially restored, when the Judge appealed to the Referee for his decision. This gentleman, a good man for the office, by the way, then announced it as his decision that it was a file for Mingo, thus placing the combatants on an equality, one fall for each man. The backers of Coit objected to Mingo's pants being greased, and his not wearing a belt, which he should have noticed before the match began, and thus prevented unnecessary delay. The referee decided that Mingo must wear a belt, and after considerable delay, a belt was procured.

4th Tussle.—Mingo, notwithstanding the great majority of those present were opposed to him, came up perfectly game and signified his willingness to submit to anything decided by the referree. The men having frozen on to each other, Coit immediately gave Mingo a fair fall, with apparently but little trouble. Coit's friends in high spirits, carrying their man round the ring on their shoulders. Two falls for Coit—one fall for Mingo.

5th Tussle.—This round was looked upon as the deciding point in the match, and consequently there was great anxiety depicted upon the countenances of the "boys." The friends of Coit were sanguine of success, and offered almost any odds, but there were no takers. On coming up both men looked cheerful and "eager for the fray." A freeze took place, and almost instantly a *thaw* succeeded. Mingo being thrown in handsome style by his little opponent, Coit, who thus won the match and the money. The stakes were immediately handed over to the successful party.

REMARKS

We look upon the above wrestling match as merely a tussle —there was no science displayed, and no strict rules of wrestling observed. Too much time was wasted between rounds, which, while it benefitted one man, was injurious to the other. One of the bottle holders should have looked more to the welfare of his man than to have allowed him so many pulls at the bottle, which certainly did not benefit him in the least. As other matches will most certainly grow out of this, we would advise those interested to procure a more suitable place for the exhibition of their muscular powers. In this city, there are several appropriate public buildings, capable of seating a large number of spectators, which can be had at very little expense.

We hope in making rules hereafter for wrestling matches, a clause will be inserted specifying the time allowed between the rounds and the man not appearing at the scratch at the time, to forfeit.

WRESTLING MATCH

A wrestling match came off last evening at Marmory Hall, State street, for $250. the contestants were the well-known Mike Kirk, of Boston, and Lewis Ainsworth, a mechanic from New Britain. The sporting fraternity were willing to bet large odds, in favor of the Boston champion, who would, they claimed, throw his man in eight seconds. But Ainsworth soon satisfied the crowd that he was at least a match for Kirk in "science," spryness, strength, or anything else. Kirk, discovering this, avoided giving fair play to Ainsworth for fear of being floored, but kept up a series of *dodges* for about an hour. Both men being on their guard, neither was thrown, and finally by mutual consent the parties withdrew. The match began at half-past seven and closed at nine; time of holds and wrestling, 1h. 38m. 27s. The men happen to be equally matched in weight—each weighing 149 1/2 pounds; and they are about of the same size. Kirk is a powerful wrestler, and "travels on his muscle." Ainsworth, however, can evidently floor him in two minutes, with straight-along "fair play."

SELECTED BIBLIOGRAPHY

PRIMARY SOURCES

MANUSCRIPT COLLECTIONS
New York Knickerbocker Base Ball Club, Correspondence books, Game books, and Score books, New York Public Library.

Philadelphia Cricket Club, Minute Books and Scrapbooks, Historical Society of Pennsylvania.

Pythian Base Ball Club, Philadelphia, Correspondence and Minutes, American Negro Historical Society Papers, Leon Gardner Collection, Historical Society of Pennsylvania.

NEWSPAPERS AND MAGAZINES
American Turf Register and Sporting Magazine, 1841-44.

The New York Clipper (1853-1860)

Porter's Spirit of the Times (1856-1860)

The Spirit of the Times (1841-1860)

Wilkes' Spirit of the Times (1859-1860)

BOOKS AND PAMPHLETS
GENERAL WORKS
Francis Brinley, *Life of William T. Porter* (New York, 1860).

William Clarke, *The Boy's Own Book Extended* (New York, 1857).

Elisha Noyce, *The Boy's Own Book of Sports, Birds and Animals* (New York, 1848)

AQUATICS
Edward F. Blake, "Shall I Join a College Boat Club?" *University Quarterly*, III (July 1860), 105-106.

BASEBALL
Constitution and By-Laws of the Beaman Base Ball Club, of West Boylston (Worcester, Mass., 1858).

Constitution and By-Laws of the Brooklyn Base Ball Club (New York, 1860).

Constitution and By-Laws of the Hudson River Base Ball Club of Newburgh (New York, 1859).

Eagle Base Ball Club Constitution, By-Laws, and Rules (New York, 1858).

BOXING
American Fistiana, Containing All the Fights in the United States from 1816 to 1860 (New York, 1860).

Life and Battles of Tom Sayers and the Life of John C. Heenan (New York, 1860).

Life and Battles of Yankee Sullivan, Embracing Full and Accurate Reports of His Fights with Hammer Lane, Bob Caunt, Tom Secor, Tom Hyer, Harry Bell, John Morrissey. Together with a Synopsis of His Minor Battles from His First Appearance in the Prize Ring Until His Retirement (Philadelphia, 1854).

CRICKET

Henry Chadwick, *Beadle's Dime Book of Cricket. A Desirable Cricketer's Companion, Containing Complete Instructions* (New York, 1860).

Constitution and By-Laws of the Philadelphia Cricket Club, 1858 (Philadelphia, 1858).

John B. Irving, *The International Cricket Match Played October 1859 in the Elysian Fields at Hoboken* (New York, 1859).

Fred Lillywhite, *The English Cricketers' Trip to Canada and the United States* (London, 1860).

Alexander D. Paterson, *The Manual of Cricket* (New York, 1847).

EQUESTRIANISM

Henry William Herbert, *Frank Forester's Horse and Horsemanship of the United States and the British Provinces of North America*, 2 vols. (New York, 1857).

John B. Irving, *The South Carolina Jockey Club* (Charleston, 1857).

FIELD SPORTS

Henry W. Herbert, *Field Sports of the United States and the British Provinces* (New York, 1849) and by the same author, *Frank Forester's Sporting Scenes and Characters* (Philadelphia, 1857).

PUB SPORTS

Constitution and By-laws of the Providence Bowling Club (Providence, R.I., 1846).

SECONDARY SOURCES

GENERAL WORKS

Melvin L. Adelman, *A Sporting Time. New York City and the Rise of Modern Athletics, 1820-70* (Urbana, Illinois, 1986).

John R. Betts, *America's Sporting Heritage, 1850-1950* (Reading, Massachusetts, 1974), and by the same author, "Sporting Journalism in Nineteenth Century America," *American Quarterly*, 5 (1953), 39-56; "The Technological Revolution and the Rise of Sports, 1850-1900," *Mississippi Valley Historical Review*, 40 (1953), 231-256; "Mind and Body in Early American Thought," *Journal of American History* 54 (March 1968), 787-805; "American Medical Thought on Exercise as the Road to Health, 1820-1860," *Bulletin of the History of Medicine*, 45 (1971), 138-145; "Public Recreation, Public Parks and Public Health Before the Civil War," in Bruce L. Bennett ed., *The History of Physical Education and Sport* (Chicago, 1972).

John A. Blanchard, '91, *The H Book of Harvard Athletics, 1852-1922* (Cambridge, Mass., 1923).

"College Beginnings," *The American College* I (December 1909), 36, 221-224.

R. Day, "The British Army and Sport in Canada. Case Studies of the Garrison at Halifax, Montreal and Kingston to 1871," (Unpublished Ph.D. dissertation, Unversity of Alberta, 1981).

John Dizikes, *Sportsmen and Gamesmen* (Boston, 1981).

Foster Rhea Dulles, *A History of Recreation. America Learns to Play,* rev. ed. (New York, 1965).

Allen Guttmann, *From Ritual to Record. The Nature of Modern Sports* (New York, 1978), and by the same author, *Sports Spectators* (New York, 1986).

Stephen Hardy, "The City and the Rise of American Sport, 1820-1920," *Exercise and Sport Science Review,* 9 (1981), 183-219.

Robert Henderson, *Ball, Bat, and Bishop* (New York, 1947) and by the same author, *Early American Sport. A Chronological Checklist of Books Published Prior to 1860 Based on an Exhibition Held at the Grolier Club* (New York, 1937).

Nancy Howell and Maxwell Howell, *Sports and Games in Canadian Life. 1700 to the Present* (Toronto, 1969).

Richard M. Hurd, *A History of Yale Athletics. 1840-1888* (New Haven, Conn., 1888).

George B. Kirsch, "New Jersey and the Rise of Modern Sports, 1820-1870," *Journal of Regional Cultures,* 4 & 5, (1984-85), 41-57.

John A. Krout, *Annals of American Sport* (New Haven, Conn., 1929).

Peter Levine, "The Promise of Sport in Antebellum America," *Journal of American Culture* 2 (Winter 1980), 623-34.

Guy Lewis, "The Muscular Christianity Movement," *Journal of Health, Physical Education and Recreation,* 37 (May 1966), 27-42.

Peter Lindsay, "A History of Sport in Canada, 1807-1867," (Unpublished Ph.D. dissertation, University of Alberta, 1969), and by the same author, "The Impact of the Military Garrisons on the Development of Sport in British North America," *Canadian Journal of History of Sport and Physical Education,* I (May 1970), 33-44.

John A. Lucas and Ronald A. Smith, *Saga of American Sport* (Philadelphia, 1978).

John A. Lucas, "A Prelude to the Rise of Sport. Antebellum America, 1850-1860," *Quest* 11, (December 1968), 50-57 and by the same author, "Thomas Wentworth Higginson. Early Apostle of Health and Fitness," *Journal of Health, Physical Education and Recreation* 42 (February 1971), 30-33.

Herbert Manchester, *Four Centuries of American Sport, 1490-1890* (New York, 1931).

Alan Metcalfe, *Canada Learns to Play. The Emergence of Organized Sport, 1807-1914* (Toronto, 1987) and by the same author, "Tentative Hypotheses Related to the Form and Function of Physical Activity in Canada During the Nineteenth Century," in *Proceedings of the First Canadian Symposium on the History of Sport and Physcial Education* (Ottawa, Ontario, 1971); "Organized Sport and Social Stratification in Montreal. 1840-1902," in Richard S. Gruneau and John G. Albinson, eds., *Canadian Sport. Sociological Perspectives* (Don Mills, Ontario, 1976); "The Evolution of Organized Physical Recration in Montreal, 1840-1895," *Historie Sociale—Social History,* 11 (May 1978), 144-166.

Roberta Park, "The Attitudes of Leading New England Transcendentalists toward Healthful Exercise, Active Recreations and Proper Care of the Body: 1830-1860, *Journal of Sport History* 4 (Spring 1977), 34-50, and by the same author, 'Embodied Selves': The Rise and Development of Concern for Physical Education, Active Games and Recreation among American Women, 1776-1865," *Journal of Sport History*, 5 (Summer 1978), 5-41; "British Sports and Pastimes in San Francisco, 1848-1900," *British Journal of Sports History* 1 (December 1984), 304.

Frederick L. Paxson, "The Rise of Sport," *Mississippi Valley Historical Review*, 4 (1917), 143-168.

Charles A. Peverelly, *The Book of American Pastimes* (New York, 1866).

Frank Presbrey, *Athletics at Princeton. A History* (New York, 1901).

Benjamin G. Rader, *American Sports*, second edition (Englewood Cliffs, N.J., 1990), and by the same author, "The Quest for Subcommunities and the Rise of American Sport," *American Quarterly*, 29 (Fall 1977), 355-369.

Gerald Redmond, *The Sporting Scots of Nineteenth Century Canada* (Rutherford, N.J., 1982).

Steven A. Riess, *City Games. The Evolution of American Urban Society and the Rise of Sports* (Urbana, Illinois, 1989).

Henry Roxborough, *One Hunded—Not Out—The Story of Nineteenth Century Canadian Sport* (Toronto, 1966).

Ronald A. Smith, *Sports and Freedom. The Rise of Big-Time College Athletics* (New York, 1988).

Dale A. Somers, *The Rise of Sports in New Orleans, 1850-1900* (Baton Rouge, La., 1972), and by the same author, "The Leisure Revolution. Recreation in the American City, 1820-1920," *Journal of Popular Culture* 5 (Summer 1971), 125-147.

Robert B. Weaver, *Amusements and Sports in American Life* (Chicago, 1939).

Luke White, *Henry William Herbert and the American Publishing Scene, 1831-1858* (Newark, N.J., 1943).

James C. Whorton, *Crusaders for Fitness. The History of American Health Reformers* (Princeton, N.J., 1982).

T. Williams, "Cheap Rates, Special Trains and Canadian Sport in the 1850s," *Canadian Journal of History of Sport*, XII (December 1981), 84-95.

S.F. Wise, "Sport and Class Values in Old Ontario and Quebec," in W. Heick and R. Graham, eds., *His Own Man. Essays in Honour of A.R.M. Lower* (Montreal, 1974).

Norris W. Yates, *William T. Porter and the Spirit of the Times. A Study of the Big Bear School of Humor* (Baton Rouge, La., 1957).

AQUATICS

Charles Boswell, *The America. The Story of the World's Most Famous Yacht* (New York, 1967).

Jerome E. Brooks, *The $30,000,000 Cup. The Stormy History of the Defense of the America's Cup* (New York, 1958).

Roland F. Coffin, *The America's Cup. How It Was Won by the Yacht America in 1851 and Has Been since Defended* (New York, 1885).

"The College Regatta," *Yale Literary Magazine* XXX (October 1864), 11.

E. Merton Coulter, "Boating as a Sport in the Old South," *Georgia Historical Society,* 27 (1943), 231-247.

Samuel Crowther and Arthur Ruhl, eds., *Rowing and Track Athletics* (New York, 1905).

Richard A. Glendon and Richard J. Glendon, *Rowing* (Philadelphia, 1923).

Robert F. Kelley, *American Rowing. Its Background and Traditions* (New York, 1932).

Guy M. Lewis, "America's First Intercollegiate Sport. The Regattas from 1852 to 1875," *Research Quarterly,* 38 (1967), 637-648.

Charles F. Livermore, "The First Harvard-Yale Boat Race," *Harvard Graduates' Magazine* II (Dec. 1893), 226.

New York Yacht Club, *Centennial, 1844-1944* (New York, 1944).

Irene W. Norsen, *Ward Brothers. Champions of the World* (New York, 1958).

John Parkinson, Jr., *The History of the New York Yacht Club from Its Founding Through 1973* (New York, 1975).

Douglas Phillips-Birt, *The History of Yachting* (New York, 1974).

W. S. Quigley, *The America's Cup* (New York, 1903).

William P. Stephens, *American Yachting* (New York, 1904).

James Wellman and W.B. Peet, *The Story of the Harvard-Yale Race, 1852-1912* (New York, 1912).

James M. Whiton, "The First Harvard-Yale Regatta (1852)," *Outing* LXVII (June 1901), 286-289 and by the same author, *A History of American College Regattas* (Boston, 1875).

BASEBALL

Melvin L. Adelman, "The First Baseball Game, the First Newspaper References to Baseball, and the New York Club. A Note on the Early History of Baseball," *Journal of Sport History,* 7 (Winter 1980), 132-135.

Robert Knight Barney, "Diamond Rituals. Baseball in Canadian Culture," *Baseball History 2* (1989), 1-18.

"Baseball! The Story of Iowa's Early Innings," *Annals of Iowa,* 22 (January 1941), 625-654.

Warren Goldstein, *Playing for Keeps. A History of Early Baseball* (Ithaca, N.Y., 1989).

Robert W. Henderson, "How Baseball Began," *New York Public Library Bulletin,* 41 (April 1937), 287-291, and by the same author, "Baseball and Rounders," *New York Public Library Bulletin,* 43 (April 1939), 303-314.

George B. Kirsch, *The Creation of American Team Sports. Baseball and Cricket, 1838-72* (Urbana, Illinois, 1989), and by the same author, "Baseball Spectators, 1855-1870," *Baseball History, 1 (Fall 1987), 4-20.*

Fred W. Lange, *History of Baseball in California and the Pacific Coast Leagues, 1847-1938* (Oakland, California, 1938).

Cecil O. Monroe, "The Rise of Baseball in Minnesota," *Minnesota History,* 19 (1938), 62-81.

Harold Peterson, *The Man Who Invented Baeball* (New York, 1969).

Francis C. Richter, *The History and Records of Base Ball* (Philadelphia, 1914).

Harold Seymour, *Baseball. The Early Years* (New York, 1960), and by the same author, "How Baseball Began," *New-York Historical Society Quarterly* 40 (October 1956), 369-385.

Albert Spalding, *America's National Game,* (New York, 1911).

Ian Tyrrell, "The Emergence of Modern American Baseball c. 1850-1880," in Richard Cashman and Michael McKernan, eds., *Sport in History. The Making of Modern Sport History* (Queensland, Australia, 1979), 205-226.

David Q. Voigt, American Baseball, 1 (Norman, Oklahoma, 1966).

Carl Wittke, "Baseball in its Adolescence," *The Ohio State Archeological and Historical Quarterly,* 61 (April 1952), 111-127.

BLOOD (ANIMAL) SPORTS

George P. Burnham, *The Game Fowl* (Melrose, Mass., 1877).

Gerald Carson, *Men, Beast, and Gods. A History of Cruelty and Kindness to Animals* (New York, 1972).

J.W. Cooper, M.D., *Game Fowls. Their Origins and History* (West Chester, Pa., 1869).

F. H. Gray, *Cocker's Manual* (No place of publication, 1878).

BOXING

Nat Fleischer, *Heavyweight Championship. An Informal History of Heavyweight Boxing from 1719 to the Present Day* (New York, 1961).

Elliot J. Gorn, *The Manly Art. Bare-Knuckle Prize Fighting in America* (Ithaca, N.Y., 1986), and by the same author, 'Gouge and Bite, Pull Hair and Scratch,' The Social Significance of Fighting in the Southern Backcountry," *American Historical Review,* 90 (1985), 18-43.

William Edgar Harding, *John C. Heenan* (New York, 1881).

Edwin James, *The Life and Battles of John Morrissey* (New York, 1879), and by the same author, *The Life and Battles of Tom Hyer* (New York, 1879).

Alexander Johnston, *Ten and Out! The Complete Story of the Prize Ring in America* (New York, 1927).

Alan Lloyd, *The Great Prize Fight* (New York, 1978).

Frederick Locker-Lampson, *My Confidences* (London, 1896).

Andrew S. Young, *John C. Heenan, Of Troy, N.Y.. Champion Pugilist of America* (New York, 1882).

CRICKET

George B. Kirsch, "American Cricket. Players and Clubs Before the Civil War," *Journal of Sport History,* 11 (1984), 28-50, and by the same author, "The Rise of Modern Sports. New Jersey Cricketers, Baseball Players, and Clubs, 1845-60," in *New Jersey History,* 101 (1983), 53-84.

John A. Lester, ed., *A Century of Philadelphia Cricket* (Philadelphia, 1951).

John I. Marder, *The International Series. The Story of the United States versus Canada at Cricket* (London, 1968).

Jones Wister's Reminiscences (Philadelphia, 1920).

William R. Wister, *Some Reminiscences of Cricket in Philadelphia Before 1861* (Philadelphia, 1904).

EQUESTRIANISM
Dwight Akers, *Drivers Up. The Story of American Harness Racing* (New York, 1938).

John Hervey, *Racing in America, 1666-1866*, 2 vols. (New York, 1944), and by the same author, *Lady Suffolk, The Old Grey Mare of Long Island* (New York, 1936); *The American Trotter* (New York, 1947).

Charles B. Parmer, *For Gold and Glory. The Story of Thoroughbred Racing In America* (New York, 1939).

William H.P. Robertson, *The History of Thoroughbred Racing in America* (Englewood Cliffs, N.J., 1964).

Nancy Struna, "The North-South Races. American Thoroughbred Racing in Transition, 1823-1850," *Journal of Sport History* 8 (Summer 1981), 28-57.

Charles E. Trevathan, *The American Thoroughbred* (New York, 1905).

John H. Wallace, *The Horse of America, in His Derivation, History and Development* (New York, 1897).

Peter G. Welsh, *Track and Road. The American Trotting Horse. A visual Record 1820 to 1900 from Harry T. Peters "American on Stone" Lithography Collection* (Washington, D.C., 1967).

Hiram Woodruff, *The Trotting Horse of America* (New York, 1868).

Frank A. Wrench, *Harness Horse Racing in the United States and Canada* (New York, 1948).

FIELD SPORTS
Robert Davidson, *History of the United Bowmen of Philadelphia* (Philadelphia, 1888).

Robert P. Elmer, *Target Archery. With a History of the Sport in America* (New York, 1946) and by the same author, *Archery* (Philadelphia, 1933).

GYMNASTICS
Erich Geldbach, "The Beginnings of German Gymnastics in America," *Journal of Sport History* 3 (Winter 1976), 237-272.

Thomas Wentworth Higginson, "The Gymnasium, and Gymnastics in Harvard College," in F.O. Vaille and H.A. Clark, *The Harvard Book* (Cambridge, Mass., 1875), II, 187.

Henry Metzner, *A Brief History of the American Turnerbund*, rev. ed., (Pittsburgh, 1924).

LACROSSE
William K. McNaught, *Lacrosse, and How to Play It* (Toronto, 1880).

Alan Metcalfe, "Sport and Athletics. A Case Study of Lacrosse in Canada," 1840-1889," *Journal of Sport History,* 3 (Spring 1976), 1-19.

PUB SPORTS
Ned Polsky, *Hustlers, Beats, and Others* (Garden City, N.Y., 1969).

TRACK AND FIELD
John Cumming, *Runners and Walkers* (Chicago, 1981).

Don Morrow, "The Powerhouse of Canadian Sport. The Montreal Amateur Athletic Association, Inception to 1909," *Journal of Sport History,* 8 (Winter 1981), 20-39.

George Moss, "The Long Distance Runners in Ante-Bellum America," *Journal of Popular Culture,* 8 (1974), 370-382.

Gerald Redmond, *The Caledonian Games in Nineteenth-Century America* (Rutherford, N.J., 1971).

WINTER SPORTS
Hugh W. Becket, *The Montreal Snow Shoe Club. Its History and Record* (Montreal, 1882).

Sylvie Dufresne, "The Winter Carnival of Montreal, 1803-1889," *Urban History Review,* 11 (February 1983), 25-45.

Don Morrow, "The Knights of the Snowshoe. A Study of the Evolution of Sport in Nineteenth Century Montreal," *Journal of Sport History,* 15 (Spring 1988), 5-40.

WORK SPORTS
Herbert Asbury, *Ye Old Fire Laddies* (New York, 1930).

David Lear Buckman, *Old Steamboat Days on the Hudson River* (New York, 1907).

Frank Donovan, *River Boats of America* (New York, 1966).

Louis C. Hunter, *Steamboats on the Western Rivers. An Economic and Technological History* (Cambridge, Mass., 1949).

J. Frank Kernan, *Reminiscences of the Old Fire Laddies and Volunteer Fire Departments of New York and Brooklyn* (New York, 1885).

Jerry MacMullen, *Paddle-Wheel Days in California* (Palo Alto, California, 1945).

George B. Merrick, *Old Times on the Upper Mississippi* (Cleveland, 1909).

William Petersen, *Steamboating—on the Upper Mississippi* (Iowa City, 1937).

INDEXES

INDEX OF NAMES

INDEX OF SUBJECTS

INDEX OF INSTITUTIONS

INDEX OF GEOGRAPHIC AND PLACE NAMES